LORD GEORGE GERMAIN

Lord George Germain

ALAN VALENTINE

OXFORD
AT THE CLARENDON PRESS
1962

Oxford University Press, Amen House, London E.C.4

GLASGOW NEW YORK TORONTO MELBOURNE WELLINGTON
BOMBAY CALCUTTA MADRAS KARACHI LAHORE DACCA
CAPE TOWN SALISBURY NAIROBI IBADAN ACCRA
KUALA LUMPUR HONG KONG

PRINTED IN GREAT BRITAIN

PREFACE

HISTORY becomes what historians say it is, for the past as we know it is largely the product of their talents and their limitations. 'That certain kings reigned, and certain battles were fought, we can depend on as true, but all the colouring . . . is conjecture', pronounced Samuel Johnson, and, like some other seekers for truth, did not pause for an answer.

The chief characters of the American Revolution have thus become amalgams of actual facts and congealed interpretations. Legend has simplified reality and turned subtle shades of personality into black and white. In America, Washington has become pure hero and Lord North pure villain, though happily both are being restored to a little of their original complexity, as young historians with reputations to make try to prove older historians wrong.

The central figure of this study has been a victim of that kind of encrusted myth, and has been more often pictured black than white, since emotions around him were high, his endeavours failed, and his career was baffling. He was a man of whose true motivations and nuances of character history, as Carlyle put it, 'will say nothing where you most desire her to speak'. Repetitions have elaborated but have not given depth to his portrait, and research only sharpens the contradictions, until one suspects it is not the facts that are contradictory but the character itself. If the men of his own time could not understand him, how can we?

The Lord George of Minden and the American Revolution cannot even be held to a consistent name, for he had three legal identities. To many of his contemporaries Lord George Germain was as stupid as Lord George Sackville had been brilliant, and Viscount Sackville's reputed mellowness consistent with neither. To others, all three characters were uniform; some said in their integrity; others in their devious malignity. History has tended to accept the harsher verdicts, since his critics were more eloquent than his defenders. The difficulty of penetrating these emotional verdicts to the real man beneath is enhanced by the fact that the material offering clues to his private thoughts, so often disguised, is now as sparse as his public documents are numerous. Of no figure in history can it more truthfully be said that his outward career fails to reveal his inner motivations. One is forced to guess at the three-dimensional man behind the flat public façade.

Political animosity unquestionably played a part in turning the real Lord George into a villain that never was. The question is, how great a part? Our own century, schooled to recognize that the extreme judgement is seldom the truest one, not only deflates old heroes but looks behind old villains for extenuating virtues. Some modern biographers try to explain the inexplicable by flights into psychology not always expert—a dangerous indulgence but at least an effort toward more sympathetic understanding. One is tempted to emulate them, and to suggest that the contradictions in the character of Lord George were due to inner conflicts and to his flair for self-dramatization; that his apparent inconsistencies were the varied but valid expressions of a powerful but ill-balanced ego. Where I have hinted such explanations, the reader must judge their worth.

This is not the first preface in which an author has tried to anticipate his critics and to disarm them in advance. To carry that endeavour further, I confess my emotional handicap as a biographer of Lord George. To write about a man one cannot bring oneself to like is to court disaster, yet I could not resist his compulsive fascination. In the effort to avoid doing him injustice, I have searched for every episode and interpretation that could be turned in his favour, but though I have found enough to temper my distaste I have not found enough to remove it. If my portrait of Lord George seems harsh, I believe it is his features and not my prejudices that have made it so.

In dealing with so controversial a character, one's judgements would be vulnerable if one did not meticulously cite one's sources. I have done so at alarming length, and have been troubled how to prevent the paraphernalia of scholarship from overwhelming the reader. The solutions I have attempted do not satisfy me, but they seem less objectionable than any others. Before the reader condemns them I hope he will consider the disadvantages of the alternatives.

Another problem was how to evaluate evidence and testimony often so contradictory. Arbitrarily to discount one authority and accept another is unscholarly, but to present all praise and condemnation at its face value is equally so, and would leave the reader without benefit of the labours of the writer. I have tried to offer judgements only when reasonably confident of them, and with more humility than may appear.

Where I have quoted directly, I have used the spelling and punctuation of the source quoted, except on those few occasions when to do so would confuse the reader more than enlighten him. This method has produced some apparent inconsistencies, especially in the spelling of proper names, in which Hanoverians were casually eclectic. Horace Walpole, for example, usually, but not always, spelled Germain as Germaine, and I have followed his text. But in the case of General Sir John Irwin, whose name even his friends spelled indiscriminately as Irvin, Irvine, and Irwine as well, I have smoothed the variations to ease the reader. Lord George himself often wrote words like HONOUR without the u, and I have followed him, with some amusement at his descent to a spelling adopted by the Americans he so disliked. Material within curved brackets is part of the original quotation; that inside square brackets is my own insertion.

With so many borrowings from so many sources, it is impossible to acknowledge the appreciation I feel toward individual authors, publishers, and libraries that have helped me. I owe great debts to the Bodleian Library at Oxford, the Widener Library of Harvard, the National Library in Dublin, the British Museum, and the Public Record Office and Kenneth Timings of its staff. One of my happiest memories is of work at the William L. Clements Library of the University of Michigan, not only because of the wealth of its material and the almost perfect arrangement of the documents, but because of its tirelessly helpful and hospitable hosts, Director Howard H. Peckham and Curator William S. Ewing. In the latter stages of my work, I have profited immeasurably (and so will the reader) by the gracious advice of a distinguished historian of the period —Steven Watson, Senior Censor, Christ Church, Oxford— though he is not to be blamed for my infelicities. But there were other generous helpers, and if I have offended anyone by failing to give proper acknowledgement, the mistake was inadvertent and I am sorry.

A. V.

Oxford, 1962

ACKNOWLEDGEMENTS

UNPUBLISHED Crown Copywright material in the Public Record Office is published by permission of the Controller of Her Majesty's Stationery Office.

Material from manuscripts in the North Collection is reproduced with the kind permission of the Bodleian Library.

Material from the various collections of the William L. Clements Library is reproduced with the kind permission of its Director.

The frontispiece of Lord George Germain while Secretary of State, from the portrait by Romney now at Drayton, is reproduced by kind permission of Colonel Stopford-Sackville and the Department of Prints and Drawings of the British Museum.

CONTENTS

LORD GEORGE GERMAIN. From an engraving by John Jacobs after the painting by George Romney   *Frontispiece*

I.	THE BOAST OF HERALDRY	1
II.	MANNERS MAKYTH MAN	8
III.	THE POMP OF POWER	16
IV.	PATHS OF GLORY	30
V.	MINDEN	49
VI.	COURT MARTIAL	60
VII.	PURGATORY	71
VIII.	THIS SIDE OF PARADISE	87
IX.	SECRETARY FOR AMERICA	101
X.	DIRECTING A WAR	117
XI.	MEN AT ODDS	136
XII.	PLANS AND MOTIVES	159
XIII.	FRUITS OF ENMITY	182
XIV.	THE CONQUERING HERO	195
XV.	CONTRETEMPS	206
XVI.	THE PLOT THICKENS	224
XVII.	SARATOGA	242
XVIII.	RECRIMINATIONS	253
XIX.	EXPLANATIONS	270
XX.	SCAPEGOAT	290
XXI.	DIGRESSION ON PEACE	305

XXII. OLD SCORES AND NEW HAZARDS 327

XXIII. THIRD BATTLE OF SARATOGA 343

XXIV. ROADS TO NOWHERE 363

XXV. THE INNER CIRCLE 376

XXVI. REBELLION AT HOME 399

XXVII. CLIMAX OF STRATEGY 414

XXVIII. STRATEGY RECONSIDERED 426

XXIX. THE INEVITABLE HOUR 439

XXX. PRIVATE LIVES 461

XXXI. TWILIGHT OF WARRIORS 482

NOTES 497

APPENDIXES 502

BIBLIOGRAPHY 506

INDEX OF PERSONS AND PLACES 517

I

THE BOAST OF HERALDRY*

THE story of a Sackville can well begin at Oxford, where the past is more esteemed than the present, where revolution is more studied than practised, and where change seems an impertinence. Like Oxford, Sackvilles pursued causes as often lost as won, but sometimes enhanced their fortunes from adversity. Oxford and the Sackvilles were natural allies in defence of King against Commonwealth, and of established privilege against the vulgar intrusions of ordinary men.

Sackvilles were more often patrons than sharers of Oxford learning, and their patronage was sporadic and has left few memorials. But over the foot of the entrance stair of the Bodleian Library hangs a portrait of Oxford's Chancellor at the time of the first Elizabeth, and the painted gold letters beneath the red-clothed table on which his left hand rests announce that he was Thomas Sackville, 'Earl of Dorset, Baron of Buckhurst, Knight of ye noble Order of ye Garter'. It is only a copy of the original by Marcus Gheeraerts, but it reveals a personality. The earl stands with an air of slightly world-weary command, his slight figure made august by the black gown and gold-embroidered sleeves of his university office, and amplified by the white pleats of an Elizabethan ruff beneath a tippet of brown fur. Under the high-crowned black hat with its narrow brim, the eyes are close together and look shrewd; the lips are firm above the pointed beard. Around his neck hangs the broad blue ribbon and gold seal of the Lesser George, the undress badge of the Order of the Garter. This is not the face of a scholar but of a man of mundane authority, and the long staff on which his right hand rests is that of the Lord High Treasurer of England. It was he who presented to the university the bust of Thomas Bodley which still presides over the ancient folios in the library that bears his name.

---

* Much of the material of this chapter, and quotations not otherwise identified, are derived from *A History of the Sackville Family*, by Charles J. Phillips, and from *Knole and the Sackvilles*, by Victoria Sackville-West.

An Oxford chancellorship was only an episode in the long history of the Sackvilles, who were powerful two hundred years before Oxford was founded. Herbrand de Sackville had come into England with William the Conqueror, and his descendants had flourished in their big house at Buckhurst, adding to their lands and fortunes by astute politics and shrewd marriages. But it was with Thomas that their earldom and their long residence at Knole began—both the gifts of a grateful Queen Elizabeth.

The Sackville genius took different forms through the centuries that followed, but always colourful forms, for whatever a Sackville did he did in full measure. Some had literary inclinations: Thomas wrote *Gorboduc*, the first English dramatic tragedy, and the third earl is said to have supplied many a flagon and bird to his friends Drayton, Jonson, Beaumont, and Fletcher. Others had been High Stewards of England, Knights of the Garter, ambassadors, warriors, wastrels.

Whether they conformed to the ways of the world or, occasionally, moved by pride or principle, defied convention, Sackvilles did nothing half-way. Of Edward, the fourth earl, whom Van Dyck made 'beautiful, graceful and vigorous', a Sackville descendant wrote: '. . . the vices he had were of his age, which he was not stubborn enough to resist'. But roused to angry dissidence, he not only resisted the Roundheads, who captured his elder son at Mile End Green and killed his younger son at Abingdon,[1] but defied the very king for whom he was fighting. For at Edgehill, having recovered the king's captured standard (as the later James II told the story), '. . . when commanded by the King my father to carry the Prince and myself up a hill out of the battle, refused to do it, and said he was not to be thought a coward for ever a King's son in Christendom'. He was too stubborn, after the execution of Charles I, ever again to leave his own domain of Knole.

Even Sackville entertainment and self-indulgence were on the grand scale. John Aubrey, whose accounts of England's notables enliven history, wrote that the third earl 'lived in the greatest splendour of any nobleman in England', though he left debts equivalent to half a million pounds today. The sixth earl was one of England's most magnificent wasters, and was saved from a charge of murder only by the personal intercession of his

[1] *HMC, Fifth Report*, part i, p. 46.

friend the king. But he was also, in the verdict of Macaulay, '. . . such a patron of letters [as] England had never seen. His bounty was bestowed with equal judgment and liberality'. His liberality extended to the ladies, but not always his judgement. If we are to believe a later Sackville, he was 'During the whole of his life the patron of men of genius and the dupe of women, and bountiful beyond measure to both'. He maintained Mistress Nell Gwynn 'until he tired of her' and let an envious king take his place: he ran through the Middlesex fortune as well as that of the Dorsets, and died, as Knole standards went, poor but impenitent. And of the seventh earl it was recorded: 'On Sundays the front of his house was so crowded with horsemen and carriages as to give it the appearance of a princely levee.'

To the small third son of that seventh Earl and first Duke of Dorset,[1] born on 26 June 1716 in his father's town house in Haymarket, the family history and the family home must both have seemed assurances of Sackville superiority to ordinary men. For Knole was even more magnificent than the family tradition. Of all the great houses of England none was more famous. Built, it was said, on Roman foundations, it was for a while the home of the Pembrokes and of the Saye and Seles, and then the private retreat of Canterbury's archbishops. Cranmer gave it, reluctantly and under pressure, but with new lands and privileges in return, to an acquisitively admiring Henry VIII; Edward VI presented it to the Earl of Warwick; Queen Mary to Reginald Pole, and Queen Elizabeth to her Lord High Treasurer. Since then it has stood massive and dominant, symbolizing the durability of tradition and sheltering generations of Sackvilles from revolutions and realities.

Only in England would so magnificent a mansion be called a family seat. In Scotland or the Rhineland it would be a castle; in France or Italy a palace or a monastery. Knole has been something of all of these, but only incidentally. It once harboured in not unworldly comfort England's greatest prelates; it once engulfed in its huge four-poster a king who envied its owners their home and their silver; it surveyed the leas and coppices around it with feudal scorn of royal usurpers and Roundheads alike. Yet, with English paradox, it has no moats or battlements, and its great oak doors have for centuries stood

[1] Lord George's father, Lionel, was made a duke in 1720 (*HMC, Stop. Sack.* i. 35).

open to its deer park, its pleached orchards, its acres of rect-
angular gardens, and the more well-born of its county neighbours. Kings, archbishops, and rebels have been only intrusions
into its biography.

From the north its castellated stone towers, more solid than
aspiring, still frown against the Kentish skies with Norman
hauteur, yet from the south it is mellow with mullioned windows,
Tudor gables, and warm brown roofs—almost merry with
heraldic leopards leering down on the bright gardens and green
turf. Under leaden skies, Knole's northern aspect is as un-
approachable as a Dorset when crossed, but under a summer
sun its south façade is as cordial and courtly as a Sackville could
be, when he was of a mind.

At home in this fortress of aristocratic security, young Lord
George Sackville could race with two older brothers and three
sisters down the long corridors over dark polished floors made
of solid oak tree-trunks cut in half, the curved side down; and
up and down the great staircase, with its square turns and broad
balustrades, his face taking the colours of the stained glass
windows through which the sun sometimes filtered. He could
stand and stare at the richly ornate plasterwork of the ribbed
ceilings, the coloured Italian marble of the huge Renaissance
fireplaces, the fruits and garlands of carved woodwork, the walls
panelled with oak or hung with velvet and coats of arms, and
that today holds family portraits by Van Dyck, Kneller, Lely,
Hoppner, Reynolds, Romney, and Gainsborough. He could ride
the ungainly white rocking-horse bestridden by four generations
before him since the childhood of its first owner the fourth earl.
Or, coming suddenly into the great hall whose wide doors stood
open to the park, he might surprise, like another Sackville two
centuries later, a puzzled but dignified stag wandered in from
the green lawns.

He could explore the King's Room, over-splendid with its
ostrich feathers, its hangings stiff with gold and silver thread,
and its heavy furniture made entirely in silver. Or the Venetian
Ambassador's Room, handsome in green and gold, Burgundy
tapestries, rosy Persian carpet, and a bed wide enough for a
whole family. Or the Chapel of the Archbishop, small but
bejewelled, with its oak panels and stained glass. Or step out
into one of Knole's six quadrangles, including the paved Stone

Court and the turfed Green Court. He might count the stair-
cases and find them to be, as reputed, fifty-two in number like
the weeks of the year; or verify that its rooms, like the days of the
year, were just 365. But it would take him as long as it took
young Victoria Sackville-West of the twentieth century to learn
the shortest way from one room to another, since 'Four acres of
building is no mean matter'.

Young George, whose godfather George I had attended his
christening, may have liked the outdoors best, especially in the
summer months. In company with his older brothers Charles
and John he could explore the park and walled gardens,
indifferent to gardeners, labourers, and stable boys 'of whom
nobody took any notice'. In the boyhood of George, the indoor
staff of Knole numbered forty-two, not including the chaplain,
the steward, the comptroller, and the master of the household.
He could watch the white pigeons flutter over the serried roofs,
and the deer graze sedately. He could listen to the bees in the
lime-trees and the drum of rising pheasants, or pilfer fruits from
the little square orchards and espaliered walls. He could walk
quietly through the large formal garden that showed earlier
Sackvilles had brought back continental tastes from the Grand
Tours, or he could run more freely across the large, sprawling
pleasance under beech and chestnut, called then as now The
Wilderness.

Sackvilles, or rather their gardeners, planted many flowers at
Knole, but they planted trees still more grandly. Trees stood for
what Sackvilles valued: stature and permanence. The year that
Lord George was seven, Knole records show that among additions to the grounds were stocks of 200 pear, 300 crab apple,
200 cherry, 500 holly, and 700 hazel, as well as '1000 holly for
ye kitchen garden . . . 2000 small beeches in ye Park . . . 10,000
seedling beeches for my Lady Betty'.

The Lady Betty of the 10,000 beeches was Lady Betty Germain,
who had begun life as Lady Elizabeth Berkeley. A close friend
of the duke and duchess, she had her own apartment at Knole,
and it was she who made its great rooms redolent with the
odour of potpourri concocted according to her own receipt; it
was she who had carried on a lively correspondence with unorthodox friends like Pope and Swift. Her portrait, still hanging
in what was once her little private parlour at Knole, shows her

'sitting very stiff in a blue brocaded dress; she looks as though she had been a martinet, in a tight narrow way'. But there is an earlier portrait that pictures a young woman of vivacity and not without beauty. George Selwyn, who could recognize charm and wit as well as any man, wrote of her half a century later: 'Her whole life was distinguished by acts of goodness and generosity; while her wit, her good-humour, and unvarying cheerfulness rendered her one of the most charming companions of the time.'[1]

Knole did not always breed ambition and superiority, but as a young man Lord George proved possessed of both. There were special reasons why he might expect to become as notable a Sackville as the greatest of his ancestors, and to have his portrait hung as prominently as theirs on the walls of Knole. There were reasons, too, why Lady Betty should take a special interest in the youngest son of the Duke of Dorset, and he in her.

The first of those reasons was his own promise. In a family not notably stable or brilliant of mind, he seemed the most talented and steady of the duke's three sons. He had personal charm, a worldly common sense, a capacity for hard work when the mood struck him, and an ability to win the confidence of heads much older than his own. He was the special favourite of his father, of Lady Betty Germain, and of his mother's father, old Marshal Colyear, who had served with distinction under William III in the Lowlands and who thought the boy cut out to be a soldier. What was more, no young man in all England had wider and more useful family connexions, for in his veins ran the blood of Tudors, Howards, Spensers, and Cliffords, and through his mother he could claim powerful Scottish connexions. Though the godfather who had honoured the great four-poster at Knole with his royal corpulence might not live long enough to sponsor a grown Lord George, his successor on the throne might recognize the claim. All things considered, the Duke of Dorset, Knight of the Garter and Lord High Steward of England, 'worthy, honest and good-natured', more genial than brilliant, more handsome than forceful, more ceremonious than original, was justified in seeing in this youngest son a Sackville who would rise above his own limitations and his own worthy but not scintillating career.

[1] Jesse, Selwyn, i. 253.

One ingredient was still needed to ensure a great future in the court and politics of Hanoverian England. That was wealth —the one asset the Duke of Dorset could not adequately provide for a third son unlikely to inherit the title, Knole, and its revenues. Yet fortune seemed to have provided a fairy godmother for Lord George in the person of Lady Betty Germain, 'the mistress of a very great income; which she well deserves; as she distributes great part of it in charities, and other good works'.[1] There was reason to hope that she would leave the greater part of her riches to Lord George, the favourite son of her great and good friend the duke. Thus the final essential to fame and power was almost assured him. No young man seemed more certain of a distinguished and successful career.

Letters of Horace Walpole, Yale edition, ed. Lewis, x, vol. ii, app. 4, p. 341.

II

MANNERS MAKYTH MAN

EIGHTEENTH-CENTURY aristocrats adapted education to their personal ends. Freed from concern about earning a living, they instructed their sons how to make a name, whether in letters, politics, war, or pleasure. Only a few were concerned with ideas and ideals. The rest were realists, and in practice their realism was a devotion to the expedient. Lord Chesterfield's letters to his son were no more worldly than the accepted credo of his class.

To an English nobleman of the time of the Georges, education was a tool with which to increase or maintain family power. In that aim he was no different from upper classes in later and more democratic corners of the world. Henry Adams wrote, a century later, that his Harvard contemporaries all sought power in some form. The Boston system, based on commerce, puritanism, and John Locke, offered few roads to power other than by way of riches and politics, but in the circle Lord George Sackville would enter there were other routes, and the functions of his society were more readily interchangeable. A successful general could become First Minister; a Lord of the Bedchamber could be translated overnight into admiral, ambassador, or bishop. In courts where men prized their 'honour' more than their ethics, education provided a knowledge of worldly ways and polite corruptions. In such circles manners, next to high birth, could make a young man's career, for by manners he could ingratiate men of substance, command inferiors, and please princesses.

Consequently tutors in country houses taught their young charges sophistications and sophistries as well as classics and cricket. They sometimes advised how a young man could lose his virtue without losing his reputation, or how he could win high place without troubling to win high esteem. The public schools instructed future statesmen, generals, and masters of the hunt how to command men as well as Latin phrases; how to be discreet sycophants until they could become domineering masters; how to bully as well as how to survive bullying. Oxford and Cambridge in their turn added the final touches to worldly as well as academic lore: they provided milieux where well-born scions could learn to drink, gamble, and swear like proper lords. Oxford's statutes forbade its undergraduates, sometimes no more than fourteen years of age, to roll hoops down High Street, but stated no penalties for such educational peccadilloes as hilarious roistering or the judicious corruption of a landlady's daughter.

It is only just, therefore, to judge the education of young Lord George Sackville, and its results, in the light of those methods and aims. If he seemed arrogant, arrogance toward nine-tenths of humanity was a proper attitude for a duke's son with a promising future. If deviousness and genteel corruption were in the air, a young man was not to be blamed if he adopted those social and political virtues. The values of our own society are too elastic to entitle us to disapprobation.

Westminster School was then, even more than Eton, the proper place for the education of a Sackville, and it gave Lord George whatever formal schooling he received in England. He appears to have been neither an ardent student nor a dull one. He took from books and masters what he later took from other sources—just enough to serve his immediate personal ends. Certainly he did not develop a love of learning for its own sake, or any inclination to pursue truth beyond its expedient uses. A few eighteenth-century noblemen elected to acquire and wear learning as a personal decoration, but there were other decorations Lord George valued more.

His Westminster schooling was interrupted in 1731 when, at little more than fourteen, he went with his father, the new Lord Lieutenant, to Ireland. The duke was admirably qualified to serve a Hanoverian king: his character was pliable and his ideas unoriginal, so he had few enemies among men and many admirers among women. Lord Shelburne's verdict was reasonably just when he wrote that the duke was '. . . in all respects a perfect English courtier, and nothing else. . . . He never had an opinion about public matters, which together with his qualifications as a Courtier and his being of an old Sussex family . . . kept him during his whole life in a continual succession of great places.'[1] It was a characterization the duke might have accepted with an apologetic laugh.

Lord George may have returned to Westminster for further exposures to its classics and *mores*, but he spent most of his time in Ireland with his father. When the duke came briefly to England in 1732, Lord George remained in Dublin, and Lady Betty Germain wrote to her old friend Dean Jonathan Swift that the duke and duchess 'will take it as a favour, if you will bestow any of your time that you can spare upon Lord George'.[2] It seems unlikely that the elderly Dr. Swift and the youthful Lord George found much in common except a conviction of superiority to other men, and there is no evidence that the Dean pursued Lady Betty's request beyond a dutiful minimum. A few years later the two men would view each other, in both politics and society, a little askance.

The boy grew up rapidly. Mrs. Delany, a niece of Lord Lansdowne, soon pronounced him 'a comical spark'.[3] He entered Trinity College, Dublin, at the age of sixteen, and there, like most of its more prosperous students, sought book-learning only incidentally to broader knowledge. At that time Trinity was, according to the father of Sheridan the playwright, 'half beer garden and half brothel'. Students drank, fought, and flirted with all the fervour of young men rushing toward their idea of maturity. Against coming years of honourable duelling, they practised pistol fire in the rooms and corridors of the college, and discipline was as sketchy as in Oxford and Cambridge. In 1747, a decade after Lord George was at Trinity, Oliver Goldsmith was knocked down and beaten by his tutor, the erudite Dr. Wilder, and the year that Lord George took his Master's degree, at the ripe age of eighteen, he may have witnessed or even shared in an episode so tragic that its memory has survived.

The Junior Dean, Edward Ford, having made himself very un-popular with the undergraduates, received warning that the windows of his room would be broken. The students, duly arriving one evening, commenced to throw stones, whereupon Ford, who had deliberately laid in a stock of ammunition, began to fire down upon them. The infuriated young men ran away, but returned with a gun,

---

[1] Fitzmaurice, *Shelburne*, i. 341.   [2] Ball, *Corresp. of Swift*, iv. 297.
[3] Ibid. 297, note.

and the Junior Dean was wounded and died. Popular opinion sympathized with the students and condemned Ford. The punishment awarded therefore was light, especially as some of the offenders belonged to families of consequence.[1]

Yet life at Trinity College was not all pleasure and riot. 'The entrance examination at Dublin was much more stringent than at Oxford and Cambridge', and Lord Chesterfield, in a letter to the Bishop of Waterford just at that time, wrote that: 'The Irish schools and universities are indisputably better than ours.'[2] Lord George's education may not have suffered from crossing the Irish Sea.

Lord George became his father's private secretary and made use of that position and his own self-confidence at least as far as their proper limits. Dublin was a fine school for politics and Lord George an apt pupil. The Lord Lieutenant probably disliked dispensing bribes and peerages in return for votes, and gladly left such matters to his less narrow-minded son. Irish politics were fortunately quieter than usual, so the duke was popular and Lord George escaped serious criticism. He proved so competent and ubiquitous a politician that his reputation reached Whitehall and Westminster.

Political activity did not distract Lord George from forwarding the military career he had envisaged ever since old Lieutenant-General Colyear's tales of soldiering. He soon became a junior officer in a regiment of the Irish establishment and began to move upward. But then came an interruption. In 1736 the duke ended his term as Lord Lieutenant, and Lord George accompanied his father on a diplomatic assignment to Paris, where French culture must have added a patina to the manners of Westminster, Trinity College, and the Dublin barracks. The following year, however, Lord George was back in Dublin,[3] as an official aide to the new Lord Lieutenant the Duke of Devonshire, a Captain in his regiment, and a member of the Privy Council of Ireland.[4] As for social life, he wrote to his father that

---

[1] Maxwell, *Dublin*, p. 183; also Marlowe, *Sackville of Drayton*, p. 47.

[2] Lecky, i. 321, note.

[3] He returned to Dublin in early October 1737 and was sworn a member of the Irish Privy Council on 10 Nov. 1737 (Sackville to Dorset, 6 Oct. 1737; *HMC, Stop. Sack*. i. 166, 168).

[4] He may well have been the youngest man ever to be a member of the Irish Privy Council.

Dean Swift 'has shown himself more mad and absent than ever',[1]
and that the new Lord Lieutenant had come away from dinner
at Howth 'as drunk as any of his predecessors have been at that
place'[2]—apparently a considerable achievement for a viceregal
neophyte.

At twenty-five Lord George, already recognized as a society
buck and a statesman of promise, turned again to his military
career. In 1741 he was made a Lieutenant-Colonel and in 1743
saw his first war duty. He accompanied George II, the last royal
warrior in British history, on an expedition against the French
and was reported to have 'distinguished himself at Dettingen'.[3]
His immediate reward was to be made, at the age of twenty-
seven, aide-de-camp to George II at the king's own command.
He wrote long letters to his father in a style that shows them to
have been on the best of terms.[4] The duke must also have read
with pleasure a letter from the Bishop of Kildare: 'Lord George's
success ... gives me more joy than I am able to express, for there
is nothing I can have so much at heart as his happiness and I am
sure he will make the best use of every advantage that is given
him. ... No person in the world, not even your Grace, knows
him as well as I do, and it is impossible without that knowledge
to think so well of him as he deserves.'[5] Irish bishops were not
always above expedient flattery, and no eighteenth-century
compliment was a compliment unless in breathless superlatives,
but such praise cannot be wholly discounted.

A year later Lord George's military conduct was even more
impressive. He was seriously wounded at the battle of Fontenoy,
where he was said to have led his attacking regiment so far into
the enemy's camp that when he fell he was carried into the tent
of the King of France—a circumstance Lord George doubtless
regarded as no more than due his flowing Sackville blood.[6] The
day after the battle he was sufficiently recovered to write to his
father that he had been shot in the breast; that he could not tell

---

[1] Sackville to Dorset, 6 Oct. 1737; *HMC, Stop. Sack.* i. 166.
[2] Sackville to Dorset, 20 Oct. 1737; *HMC, Stop. Sack.* i. 167.
[3] Coventry, pp. 257 ff.
[4] He wrote from Biebrich on 2 Aug. 1743, from Worms on 2 and 16 Sept. 1743,
from Spire on 1 Oct. 1743, from Ostend on 19 May 1744, from Bruges on 22 May
1744, and from Beslinghen on 17 June 1744 (Clements, *Germain Papers*, vol. i).
[5] Kildare to Dorset, 14 July 1743; *HMC, Stop. Sack.* i. 37.
[6] Marlowe, *Sackville of Drayton*, p. 86.

the exact location of the bullet but had no fever and was not in great pain.[1] But he recovered only slowly, and years later his political enemies would suggest that the bullet left a deeper scar upon his courage than his chest. He preserved his Fontenoy uniform, with the bullet-hole in the tunic, for the rest of his life.[2]

Lord George saw no further fighting until the Stuart uprising of the Forty-Five, when he served in Scotland under the Duke of Cumberland, 'who combined leonine personal courage with a total ignorance of the art of war',[3] and was regarded as a great soldier. After Culloden, Lord George pursued the scattered Scots through the Highlands with ardour and success.[4] The military capacities of this officer of thirty, so energetic and so well born, impressed the seldom enthusiastic Cumberland. He appointed Lord George acting commander of his forces at Perth, and when the campaign ended he wrote to the Duke of Dorset that he was 'exceedingly sorry to lose Lord George, as he has not only shown his courage, but a disposition to his trade which I do not always find in those of higher rank'.[5] Had Cumberland been an abler commander, his praise would have meant more.

It was surely to the credit of a young man reared in such ease that he proved a durable campaigner amid the discomforts of the Highlands. Lord George sustained those relative hardships with a rather self-conscious philosophy voiced in a letter from Perth to his friend Thomas Younge:

. . . I must confess, that although I should not receive with the least reluctance an order to repair to London, yet I am not fashionable enough to be miserable in my present situation, remote as it is from those I am used to live with. . . . I do not pretend to much philosophy, but the maxim I have laid down, and have hitherto constantly pursued, is to compare my situation with what it might have been, and myself with those who have much greater reason to complain than I have; not envying those who are more fortunate and ought to be more happy. All I pray is that I may never again

[1] Sackville to Dorset, 12 May 1745; *HMC, Fourth Report* (1874), p. 280.

[2] Marlowe, *Sackville of Drayton*, p. 86.

[3] Fitzmaurice, *Charles William Ferdinand*, p. 3. Lord George joined the troops in Scotland on 10 Feb. 1746.

[4] 'The detachments of Lord George Sackville etc. are not yet returned from their expedition, but they have ranged pretty thoroughly through the boasted inaccessible country of Lochaber' (Yorke, *Life of Hardwicke*, i. 544).

[5] Cumberland to Dorset, 20 Sept. 1746; *HMC, Fourth Report* (1874), p. 280.

have occasion any more to visit these Northern Hills, for I think
nothing but a Rebellion can ever call me there again.[1]

Whether he followed his maxim of stoicism in later life its
events will disclose, but his experience in the Highlands did not
enable him to envisage, thirty years later, the difficulties of
winter campaigning in the foot-hills of the Adirondacks.

The pleasures of London were soon his again, for after a short
term as commander at Dover Castle Lord George was living in
the town house of the Dorsets and taking his place in the House
of Commons as member for Dover—not surprisingly, since his
father was Warden of the Cinque Ports. Had the electors of
Dover not proved amenable to his candidacy, Lord George's
place in Parliament would not have been long delayed, since
for generations the Sackvilles had controlled the two seats
assigned to East Grinstead, not far from Knole.

But politics still remained secondary to Lord George's military
advancement. In 1747 and 1748 he was again on active service
on the Continent under the Duke of Cumberland. Though he
won no laurels in battle, he was appointed by the duke to
negotiate an armistice with the French.[2] His orders from the
duke ended in complimentary style: '. . . in the case that [a
capitulation] cannot be obtained, I need proscribe no rule of
conduct to an officer who has already shewn so much gallantry
and conduct.'[3]

In a long letter to his father, Lord George described his
trepidation at the responsibility of that assignment, and his
meeting with the great Marshal Saxe: '. . . You may imagine
that I thought myself greatly honour'd in being thus distinguished by the Duke, but I own I was frightened when I
found so many unexpected difficulties. . . . However, I had the
good fortune to do nothing the H.R.H. disapproved of, and
indeed he was pleased to say much more than I deserved.'[4]
Lord George also won the regard of a young officer of future
fame. Major James Wolfe wrote of the vacancy Lord George
created when he left the regiment: 'Unless Mr. Conway fall to

[1] Sackville to Younge, 6 Oct. 1746; also Coventry, pp. 270 ff.; also Marlowe,
p. 91.
[2] HMC, Stop. Sack. i. 290; 2 May 1748.
[3] Cumberland to Sackville, 2 May 1748; Clements, Germain Papers, i. 17.
[4] Sackville to Dorset, 6 May 1748; HMC, Stop. Sack. i. 290 ff.

our lot, no possible successor can in any measure make amends for his loss.'[1] Lord George was promoted to full Colonel on 1 November 1749, and the first chapter of his military career came to an end.

The world of politics seemed equally appreciative of this most talented of the Sackvilles. In 1750 Lord George was again active in Parliament, and spoke so well that before the year was out the political prophets were predicting as fine a future for him in Parliament as the generals were foreseeing in military affairs. Horace Walpole, not always the kindest of critics, commented that: 'He was now rising to a principal figure.' But Lord George had no sooner gained high esteem in Westminster than he left London again, not to new fields but to a far more powerful post in familiar ones. The Duke of Dorset was again appointed Lord Lieutenant of Ireland, and this time Lord George served not only as his *alter ego* but as Secretary for War for Ireland, with the added prestige of being thought to be 'the Duke of Cumberland's military man of confidence in Ireland'.[2]

Lord George Sackville was then thirty-four. His education in its broadest sense was complete. Precept had given way to practice, and if the precepts had been somewhat worldly the practice had made the most of them. It had been a lengthy education, but learning by doing takes time, and at thirty-four Lord George was judged, and doubtless judged himself, ready to assume with confidence any exalted task that King, Ministry, or Parliament might assign him. He had established claims to the friendship of all three, and made conquests in battlefield and boudoir. He was a man of the world, and his world expected further news of him. Presumably he had little more to learn.

[1] Marlowe, p. 124.
[2] Dobree, *Letters of Chesterfield*, iv. 1777.

III

THE POMP OF POWER

DUBLIN in 1751 was second only to London in the British Isles in size, and second to no city in the extravagant gaiety of its limited but energetic society. Its population of some 120,000 was dominated by an Anglo-Irish upper class whose members thought it better to go into debt than to fail in its round of parties, and better to be a little too drunk than a little too sober. It was a handsome city and Georgian architecture was making it more handsome. Its tall, plain-fronted, well-proportioned buildings along the river Liffey rivalled those of Amsterdam, and Georgian façades were making Merriam Square and St. Stephen's Green two of the finest residential squares in Europe. Its new Parliament House 'was justly regarded as far superior in beauty to the Parliament House in Westminster'.[1]

Dublin's social life was even more exuberant than Lord George had known it twenty years earlier. 'It is said that as many as 300 carriages filled with gentlemen sometimes assembled to meet the Lord Lieutenant on his arrival from England',[2] and Mrs. Delany wrote back to London in 1752: 'High living is too much the fashion here. You are not invited to dinner to any private gentleman of 1000 Pounds a year or less, that does not give you seven dishes at one course, and Burgundy and Champagne; and these dinners they give once or twice a week.'[3]

Even eminent prelates indulged an active interest in the amenities of Mammon. Dr. George Stone, Primate of the Church of England in Ireland, Archbishop of Armagh, and one of the Lords Justices, collaborated with Lord George over a private cellar for the returning Lord Lieutenant, and wrote him in considerable concern after a thorough sampling:

The wines sent out for the Lord Lieutenant are not what could be expected, I have tasted all the different wines and find to my great

---

[1] Lecky, i. 319, 320.   [2] Lecky, i. 324.   [3] Maxwell, *Dublin*, p. 102.

concern that there is nothing but the claret which can be made to answer any purpose. Of the two sorts of champagne, that sealed with yellow wax might go off at balls, if there were a better kind for select meetings. The red wax is too bad for an election dinner at Dover. The four parcels of Burgundy are almost equally bad. If there is any difference, that sealed with black wax and impudently called Vin de Beaune is the worst, and is indeed as bad as the worst tavern could afford; but I am sure that no person will ever drink a second glass of either. I know how unhappy his Grace and you will be to see the tables so provided.[1]

The extravagances of Dublin society were not confined to food and drink. 'The love of the sexes is much indulged in this winter. . . . Horns sprouting abundantly', the *Dublin Spy* announced in 1753.[2] Lord George did not shrink from the varied challenges of this colourful life, and was reported to Lord Holdernesse of the Ministry as 'the gayest man not only in that Kingdom but in all his Majesty's Dominions, except the Lord Lieutenant'. This was friendly banter from Holdernesse to the Duke of Dorset,[3] but not without foundation, for Horace Walpole wrote that Lord George was supposed to have a seraglio, 'which is not at all in the style of a country that is famous for supplying rich widows with second husbands'.[4] But Walpole was never so inaccurate as when inventing or retailing scandalous gossip, and if Lord George had been more precocious in his amours than his companions, others would have recorded it. In a city where gossip was part of the pursuit of pleasure, the loves of the Secretary of the Government of Ireland would have been juicy bits.

How could a son of the Lord Lieutenant, with a record of military bravery, fail to cut a wide swathe in Dublin clubs and drawing-rooms? In those easy Dublin days Lord George was at his most attractive. A portrait painted only a little later pictures an impressive figure: tall, large-framed, and rather dark; not corpulent 'though rather womanly'; long-faced, somewhat heavy-featured and a little saturnine in expression, with a high but backward-sloping forehead, rather full lips, and a nose that

---

[1] Stone to Sackville, 18 May 1751; *HMC, Stop. Sack.* i. 170, 171.
[2] Marlowe, *Sackville of Drayton*, p. 27.
[3] Holdernesse to Dorset, 21 Nov. 1751; *HMC, Stop. Sack.* i. 178.
[4] Walpole to Mann, 13 May 1752; Toynbee, *Walpole Letters*, iii. 93, 94.

could not be ignored and would become the delight of carica-
turists. The firmness of the features could be strength or in-
tolerance, force or conceit, but with them was a disarming
charm of easy confidence that comes so naturally to men
accustomed to deference and success.

No contemporary word-picture of Lord George's personality
is wholly dependable, for few men, even in his youth, aroused
stronger asperities and admirations. But on one point friends
and enemies agreed. Lord George often wore an aloof reserve
that some called dignity and others arrogance. The easy assumption of conscious superiority can be very irritating, and Lord
George seems to have made enemies almost as often as he made
friends, and more permanently. 'Lord George never had the art
of conciliating affection', wrote Walpole—but that was after
later events had given Walpole the advantage of hindsight.[1] In
the Dublin years Lord George was at his easiest and most genial.
He had casual intimacies with young men in his social and
military circles, and one or two of them wrote him badinage
and ribaldry without apparent fear of giving offence. But such
letters are typical of bachelor exchanges in any set and century
and do not signify deep friendships, or that Lord George was
warmly gregarious.

Even Lord George's admiring intimates hinted that a dark
side of his nature sometimes revealed itself to baffle or repel
them—a disturbing shadow of moodiness more manifest in his
two brothers. Lord Shelburne, not a friendly critic but a perceptive one, wrote of the 'mixture of quickness and a sort of
melancholy in his look which runs through all the Sackville
family, such as is seen in the antique statues often accompanying
great beauty'.[2] Percival Stockdale, who served under Lord
George's military command in 1756 and later became 'a kindly
and sensible clergyman', tempered his praises by the codicil:
'But there was, likewise, a reserve, and haughtiness in his
manner, which depressed, and darkened all that was agreeable,
and engaging in him; it shaded those talents which were worthy
to be admired; it naturally and very fairly, hurt the reasonable
self-love of his acquaintance, and friends. His integrity commanded esteem, his abilities praise; but to attract the heart,

[1] Walpole, *Last Ten Years of George II*, ii. 362.
[2] Fitzmaurice, *Shelburne*, i. 362, 363.

was not one of those abilities.'[1] But this too was written in the
retrospect of Lord George's later career.

If this inner coldness was noticeable in the gay Dublin days,
it was no more than a trivial flaw when, his wild oats conventionally sown, Lord George thought it proper to achieve the
stabilizing propriety of marriage. Or perhaps, like some more
ordinary men, he simply fell in love. The object of his attentions
was adequately well-born and well-to-do, but she was not the
marital alliance one might have expected from an ambitious
duke's son of thirty-eight. Diana Sambrooke, second daughter
of John Sambrooke, was descended from an Earl of Salisbury
and her uncle Sir Jeremy Sambrooke was a man of some substance, but from a career point of view Lord George could have
done better. Some of his friends and relations hinted as much.
If Lord George overlooked the financial considerations of the
alliance his intimate associate Thomas Waite did not, and wrote
to him: 'I hope Miss Sambrooke has forty thousand pounds
at least. Indeed, my Lord, you cannot afford to take less.'[2] And
Captain Cunningham, a recent Benedict, offered Lord George
only reserved congratulations, spiced with intimate bedroom
advice.

The courtship began in 1753 and ran for a year along strictly
conventional lines. Lord George's advances were deliberate and
impeccable. His favourite sister, who had become Lady Milton,
took it upon herself to survey the intended bride and her family,
and reported favourably though without striking enthusiasm to
Lord George that: '. . . her mother is pleased with the frankness
and wisdom of your behaviour. . . . [Diana] is certainly very
sensible and clever, and indeed I believe very good tempered.'[3]
From that point Lady Milton seems to have supervised the
courtship. A year later matters had come to a satisfactory head,
and Lady Milton wrote to Lord George: '. . . let me know as
soon as you can guess when the wedding will be', and advised
her brother to get 'more than one new coat . . . two or three at
least new suits of clothes . . . new linnen . . . and certainly some
new laced ruffles'.[4] Lady Milton's guiding hand was again

---

[1] Stockdale, *Memoirs*, i. 436.
[2] Waite to Sackville, 1 June 1754; *HMC, Stop. Sack*. i. 211.
[3] Lady Milton to Sackville, 25 July 1753; *HMC, Stop. Sack*. i. 41.
[4] Idem, 26 July 1754; *HMC, Stop. Sack*. i. 42.

apparent in her note to Lord George the following day: 'You are to be married in town, so far I know, and I suppose go to Knole directly.'[1] Thus abetted, Lord George was wed on 3 August 1754.[2]

Four letters, their careful preservation in itself significant, indicate that the bride of twenty-three began her marriage deeply devoted to the imposing statesman and soldier of thirty-eight. They seem to have been written by a gay, sensitive young woman confident of her brilliant new husband's affection. Two years after the wedding she was still calling him the 'dearest everlasting object of all her cares and kindnesses' and saying how miserable she would be if her 'dearest man' were called abroad.[3] Nothing in Diana's letters show unusual character or originality; she was not reputed for great beauty or distinction of mind, but she had courage and loyalty and people liked her. Until her death at the age of forty-seven in 1778, Diana appears to have been a devoted wife and, with five children, a busy mother.

Thirty-eight years is a long time for a man to live without having encountered any serious disappointment or reversal. It was only after his marriage that the tests of life began to catch up with Lord George. When a man's troubles come they seem to him wholly fortuitous, but his critics can always trace them back to his faults. Only after later events did Lord George's contemporaries recall little weaknesses in his character that they had hardly mentioned in his earlier years. Half-ignored episodes, bits of gossip, and critical whispers were then remembered, perhaps inflated and possibly invented. He had always been an egotist; he was cold and calculating; he was devious when pretending to be open. 'I have often heard the officers of the regiment affirm that he was frequently found in Scotland listening at the officers' tents to hear what was said of him.'[4] 'Haughty, obstinate and overbearing', Horace Walpole ended his tribute to Lord George's courage and eloquence in Parliament in 1752.[5] 'Lord George's pride which was naturally very great, grew into a most intolerable insolence', was another retrospective dictum

---

[1] Lady Milton to Sackville, 27 July 1754; *HMC, Stop. Sack*. i. 42.
[2] Coventry, p. 43.   [3] Lady Sackville to Sackville; *HMC, Stop. Sack*. i. 43 ff.
[4] Fitzmaurice, *Shelburne*, i. 345.
[5] Walpole to Mann, 13 May 1752; Toynbee, iii. 93, 94.

of Lord Shelburne.[1] Others noted or hinted that he had never taken frustration amenably; that he did not wear his laurels with becoming modesty, or put discreet curbs on his ambition, or suffer gladly the many men he thought fools.

It was still too early for even observant men to notice that though Lord George won powerful friends he did not always hold them. But he had not been long in Dublin the second time before the sponsorship of the Duke of Cumberland turned to enmity. The duke's political opinions were often more emphatic than wise, and a rising statesman like Lord George could not risk being too closely identified with the duke's political faction. When in 1751 the duke supported the Mutiny Bill and Lord George spoke against it, relations became strained, and though outward friendship continued a little longer, the polite world soon knew it had ended in bitterness.[2]

But in the 1750's Lord George's career was so clearly still in the ascendant that a number of young men tried to hitch their own ambitions to his star. It was to him that James Murray owed the crucial promotion that led to his distinguished military career.[3] It was to him that young Major Irwin was directed by the Earl of Chesterfield: 'If Lord George Sackville is sincerely in your interest, your affair will certainly do',[4] and in time Major Irwin would become General Sir John Irwin, Commander of Gibraltar, holder of one of the Sackville seats in Parliament, and Lord George's most intimate correspondent. In the same month of 1751 Sir John Cope wrote from Bath to Lieutenant-Colonel Charles Whitefoord: '. . . Your obligation for this small favour . . . is entirely owing to Lord George, whose protection and freindship is worth cultivating. He is able, and the most likely to be very considerable help to any young man in the army.'[5]

During his first tour of duty in Ireland the Duke of Dorset had been as popular there as an English overlord could reasonably hope to be: '. . . a man of dignity, caution and plausibility, and who had formerly ruled Ireland to their universal satisfaction', and Sackville Street commemorated his cordial rule. On

[1] Fitzmaurice, *Shelburne*, i. 350. [2] Coventry, p. 66.

[3] Mahon, *Life of Murray*, p. 52.

[4] Dobree, *Chesterfield*, iv. 1777; Oct. 1751.

[5] Cope to Whitefoord, 5 Oct. 1751; Hewins, *Whitefoord Papers*, p. 103.

his return to Dublin in 1751 the duke was unchanged but his son
was not. Lord George was ready not only to advise his father
but to direct the government of Ireland.

The amiable duke's pride in this precocious son perhaps
blinded him to the dangers, for he left much of the formulation
as well as the execution of State policies to Lord George. The
son's influence on the father was so obvious that Henry Pelham,
then Lord President of the Privy Council, began a letter to Lord
George: 'Rejoicing heartily at the success of the King's affairs
in Ireland under the Duke of Dorset's government and Lord
George Sackville's ministry.'[1] The Earl of Shelburne was less
pleased at the situation: 'Lord George . . . had by these means
a great road open to his father's favour, on which he imposed by
many circumstances so as to gain the entire and exclusive direction of him.'[2] With a determination only half concealed by a
casual manner, and with methods more arrogant than tactful,
Lord George began to ride rough-shod over the susceptibilities
of his Irish 'subjects'.

In driving through his ideas of how to govern Ireland, Lord
George selected as his chief ally another man of high ambition
and dubious judgement, an old friend of Westminster School
days who had selected the Church as the means of his own self-
advancement. As Primate of Ireland Dr. George Stone did not
confine his activities to the religious duties of an archbishop and
to critical researches into the duke's wine-cellar. By virtue of his
office Dr. Stone was technically one of the three top officials of
Ireland, and he made the most of it. His partnership with Lord
George did not seem to many Irishmen a Holy Alliance.

Dr. Stone's qualifications for political, and even for religious,
leadership were curious ones. 'If the qualities which he most
exhibited in his high office were those to which he owed his rise,
he was lifted forward thus rapidly for his fashionable manners,
the profound absence of moral scruple, and a singular dexterity
in handling the political elements of a corrupt or corrupting
time.'[3] Those who believed Lord George to be 'hot, haughty,
ambitious, obstinate' also believed that the archbishop did not
curb those qualities, but encouraged him to indulge them against
Irish statesmen.

---

[1] Pelham to Sackville, 19 Jan. 1752; *HMC, Stop. Sack.* i. 178.
[2] Fitzmaurice, *Shelburne*, i. 344.   [3] Froude, *The English in Ireland*, i. 682.

Together the two men set out to govern Ireland and 'reform' its vestiges of self-government. The Duke of Dorset, whether from lack of acuteness or excess of paternal pride, let them have their head, and '. . . was by 1753 in the hands of two men most unlike himself. One was his youngest son . . . and the other Dr. George Stone, the primate of Ireland.'[1] An Irish historian called the pair '. . . the virtual rulers of Ireland',[2] and for once an English historian agreed. 'Lord George & the Primate ruled Ireland with the help of the Pension list . . . by the free use of these funds among the political leaders.'[3] The duke had avoided corruption beyond the accepted tradition, but his son had no such impractical scruples. 'The poor Duke of Dorset was made by his son and the Primate to commence politician and man of business at sixty.'[4]

In their efforts to force their measures upon a reluctant Irish Parliament Lord George and the Primate won the applause of English oligarchs like themselves, but the outraged hatred of the Irish. Dr. Stone might write to Henry Pelham that Lord George was 'allowed' the ablest Secretary Ireland had ever known, but it was more significant that the Irish statesman Malone was telling the Irish Parliament that loyalty to Ireland was '. . . more laudable than threats, bribes, and promises, which the noble Lord had used to procure a majority', and he named the noble lord as Lord George Sackville. Walpole, who reported the phrase, added on his own account that Malone's accusation 'was not groundless', and gave examples of Lord George's efforts to corrupt.[5]

With patience, tact, and reasonable probity Lord George could probably have induced the Irish House of Commons to accept almost any measure not too offensive to Irish sensibilities. Instead he elected to make an open fight upon an issue certain to raise Irish patriotism to a white heat. He must have felt so sure of winning that he need not trouble to be discreet, and his methods probably offended Irish self-respect as much as his measures.

Urged on by the Primate and uncomfortably supported by his father, Lord George advanced the claim that the Crown was

[1] Walpole, *Last Ten Years*, i. 244.   [2] Sullivan, *Irish History*, pp. 75, 76.
[3] Froude, *The English in Ireland*, i. 683.
[4] Fitzmaurice, *Shelburne*, i. 347, 348.   [5] Walpole, *Last Ten Years*, i. 319.

entitled to dispose as it saw fit, without consulting the Irish Parliament, of any unassigned surplus Irish revenue. It was an issue like that which brought the American colonists to revolution twenty years later, and the Irish reaction was similar. Lord George was vehemently opposed by all those whose birth or sympathies were Irish.

In forcing the issue Lord George attacked where the enemy was strongest. He challenged Irishmen at the very point most certain to bring all their discordant factions into unity—their sentiment for a leader who represented Irish self-respect. By attacking a popular Irish politician Lord George turned him into a hero. Henry Boyle had been for twenty years the Speaker of the Irish House, and was widely regarded as honest, able, and just. During his long tenure he had built up certain privileges for the Chair that had become symbols of that moiety of self-government left the Irish people by their English conquerors. To attack Boyle was to attack Irishmen of all parties, and they rushed to defend him. Lord George would surely have foreseen this had he not been blinded to human reactions by over-confidence or disdain.

In March 1752 Lord George's proposals '. . . raised outrageous clamour; Boyle, the speaker, has headed the reaction against the Castle, and beat them on several occasions. He has affronted Lord George . . . nobody thinks it will be possible to send him [the Duke of Dorset] Lord Lieutenant again. Epigrams, ballads, pasquinades swarm.'[1] An Irish doctor reported the controversy as engaging 'the attention of the whole kingdom', and made it clear that it was Lord George, and not the duke, who had brought about this furore: '. . . The D. of Dorset expresses the highest Regard for the Speaker, and I believe is uneasy that such Dicisions in Parlt. attend his Administration.'[2]

The national sense of outrage would probably have died down had Lord George not compounded his blunder. To win over

[1] Walpole to Mann, 15 May 1752; Toynbee, iii. 93, 94.

[2] 'There has been an open quarrel since the beginning of the Sessions between the Speaker and the Primate, and a Coldness—to give it a mild expression—between him and the Castle. . . . Lord George has exerted all his force. . . . It has grown to such a Height that it has engaged the attention of the whole Kingdom, and every one now considers it as the final Question, whether the Speaker is to stand or fall. . . . It is impossible in this compass of a Letter to describe the Spirit that prevails. . . . This affair already begins to make a noise in England' (Barry to the Earl of Orrery, 4 Mar. 1752; *Orrery Papers*, ii. 101, 102).

Mr. Boyle, Lord George, '. . . whose measures were apt to be abrupt, directly offered the Speaker a peerage and a pension of 1500 pounds a year', to abandon his opposition. He could not have given Boyle a finer opportunity to consolidate the support of every Irishman, and Boyle made the most of it. 'The Speaker replied: "If I had a peerage, I should not think myself greater than now that I am Mr. Boyle; for tother thing, I despise it as much as the person who offers it." '[1] Lord George should have seen that he had lost the battle and retired with the best grace possible. Instead he continued to force the issue and destroyed his father's future as a statesman.

After one of the bitterest sessions ever known in the Irish Parliament, 'Lord George went that night after the affair was over out of the House by the back way. I suppose he apprehended some insult by the mob.'[2] '. . . the Government party became so unpopular that the Duke and his son were glad to get away to London, while Primate Stone durst not venture to leave his house, through fear of the mobs of Dublin.'[3] English court reactions had at first been favourable to Lord George's efforts to bring the recalcitrant Irish to proper recognition of the complete suzerainty of England. In mid-March, before the worst of the outcry was raised, Pelham had written to Lord George from Whitehall congratulating him on his achievements in Ireland and adding: 'Whatever trouble you have had, it has only served to set off your character of ability and integrity. May you be as useful to your King and your friends as you have proved to your father and his servants in Ireland.'[4] But when the affair grew so turbulent that the duke and Lord George thought it expedient to retire to London,[5] not even Pelham could pretend that Lord George's latest demonstration of 'ability and integrity' had been useful to his father and the king. It was far more significant to the welfare of the empire that Dr. Carter, Master of the Rolls in Dublin, was pronouncing before the Irish House of Commons that Lord George was 'the known enemy of this country'. Even countesses diverted their pens from accounts of London balls and gossip to retail breathless

---

[1] Walpole, *Last Ten Years*, i. 246. [2] *HMC, Charlemont*, i (1891), 189.
[3] Sullivan, p. 77.
[4] Pelham to Sackville, 16 Mar. 1752; *HMC, Stop. Sack.* i. 182.
[5] *HMC, Stop. Sack.* i. 209.

inaccuracies about Lord George and Ireland, and credit him with having given Speaker Boyle 'a box on the ear'.[1]

Lord George's attempt to bribe the Speaker brought out tales that he had bribed more successfully in other cases,[2] and before the year 1754 began it was widely thought in London that Lord George Sackville had made necessary the dismissal and almost the disgrace of his father. According to the Earl of Chesterfield, who had once himself been Lord Lieutenant of Ireland: 'It is believed that the House of Commons will proceed to give some personal votes against the Primate and Lord George Sackville, who are the capital objects of their aversion. . . . This only is certain, that the Duke of Dorset is making what haste he can to come over here, and will not, or cannot, go back again.'[3]

The controversy had been brought directly home to the king by the action of Lord Kildare, eldest son of the Duke of Leinster, who presented to George II a memorial against the Duke of Dorset's administration.[4] The king was faced with openly supporting or discrediting his Lord Lieutenant, and he took the former course. The Ministry's reply to Lord Kildare was a reproof which affirmed '. . . the King's entire confidence in the Lord Lieutenant'.[5] But that was in 1753, and a few months later the affair reached a point where British face could be saved only by having the duke serve out his term but remain in England, and thus cover up what amounted to dismissal.

In London the duke and Lord George did what they could to mend their fences. Lord George wrote a defence full of rationalizations and probably sent it to Lord Holdernesse. When the duke had returned to Ireland as Lord Lieutenant some three years earlier he had received a warm welcome, but now Lord George saw fit to report that 'At our first landing my Lord Lieutenant did not find the principal people here in that

---

[1] 'Discontents have rose very high in Ireland, and the whole people are greatly exasperated against the Lord Lieutenant; disputes ran so high between the son and the Speaker, that Lord George, as some say, gave him a box on the ear, and others that he only threatened it, however, 'tis certain great indecencies passed, it seems the Duke wanted the Speaker to resign the chair to his son; which neither he nor the House approved of; they offered him a good place and a seat in the House of Lords, which was not accepted' (Countess of Westminster to the Countess of Denbigh, 12 June 1752; *HMC, Denbigh* (1911), p. 279).

[2] Adderly to Charlemont, 29 Dec. 1753; *HMC, Charlemont*, i (1891), 189.

[3] Chesterfield to Dayrolles, 1 Jan. 1754; Dobree, v. 2070.

[4] Ibid.   [5] Yorke, *Life of Hardwicke*, ii. 50.

disposition as promised any ease to his administration. The
Speaker's friends were setting him up as the protector of the
liberties of Ireland, and declaring that the Ministry in England,
in conjunction with the Lord Lieutenant, were endeavoring to
place all power in the hands of the Primate, who, as an Englishman, could not have their interest at heart.'

The Irish party, Lord George wrote, had planned to show
their support of Lord Kildare's protest by refusing, in their
Address to the King, to include thanks to his Majesty for continuing the Duke of Dorset as Lord Lieutenant. To omit such
thanks, Lord George claimed, would have been a calculated
insult to the Crown as well as to the duke, and he had consequently worked hard to win a majority to support the duke in
that crisis. At the eleventh hour Speaker Boyle had come to the
castle to tell the duke he '. . . had prevailed upon his friends to
do him all possible honour, and that there should be in the
Address to the King the proper thanks to his Majesty for continuing him in the Government'.[1] Lord George tried to interpret
this as an end to the controversy, though everyone knew it was
not. He also reported that he had told Boyle: '. . . that I will
behave with such moderation that if we are obliged hereafter to
disagree you may be convinced that it was not owing to lack of
prudence'. If he made Boyle such a promise, he failed to keep it.

It was becoming increasingly clear to the Ministry that its
policy of delay was not soothing the ire of the Irish, and that the
duke and his son were steadily losing ground in London as well
as in Ireland. The confidential reports that Lord George received
were far from encouraging. Captain Cunningham, whom he had
installed as an aide to the Primate, and who had offered him
bawdy advice before his wedding, now wrote in less jocular
vein: 'The spirit of patriotism is higher than ever and Government more abused. The hopes of your ennemies seem to be
founded upon the supposition of his Grace's being out of favour
with his Majestie.'[2] A week later another of Lord George's
satellites, Thomas Waite, reported: 'The patriots likewise give
out that the King has rumped the Duke of Dorset lately two or
three times and did not speak to his Grace at the levee.'[3] The

---

[1] Sackville to (?) Holdernesse, Oct. 1753; *HMC, Stop. Sack.* i. 198–200.
[2] Cunningham to Sackville, 19 Aug. 1754; *HMC, Stop. Sack.* i. 224.
[3] Waite to Sackville, 27 Aug. 1754; *HMC, Stop. Sack.* i. 226.

Primate, uncomfortably keeping within his ecclesiastical fortress in Ireland, did his best to help avert the inevitable by writing to the Duke of Newcastle explaining away the dissensions in Ireland and denying that they had been caused by the haughtiness or ambition of Lord George Sackville or himself.[1]

But all to no avail. Public opinion in England as well as in Ireland left King and Ministry no option. On 27 February 1755 the Duke of Dorset was officially informed that '. . . he was to return no more to Ireland. . . . He bore the notification ill',[2] and was not consoled by being made Master of the King's Horse.[3] 'Lord George Sackville, who was present, had more command of himself.'[4] As Lord Shelburne put it: 'The Primate was protected by his Primacy; Lord George Sackville escaped with difficulty from the fury of the populace. Another Lord Lieutenant was sent over to quiet things.'[5] The Primate's primacy did not save him from being dismissed for a time from the Privy Council, and the British Government did not escape the painful necessity of making concessions to the Irish Parliament.[6] Within the year Henry Boyle was made Earl of Shannon, but it was several decades before Irish politics became as quiet as they had been before Lord George had set out to improve them. Forty years later Walpole concluded that Lord George '. . . gave rise, by his haughty behaviour, to the factions that have ever since disturbed that country'.[7]

Lord George could take his father's political demise philosophically, since it was clearly not his own. Though his part in the affair was notorious, it did not seriously impair his future. Criticisms of his hauteur and bad judgement were apparently offset by respect for his initiative and forcefulness. Many an Englishman would have liked to bully the Irish, and admired Lord George for his attempt more than condemned him for his failure. As for bribery, few Londoners took their highest ethics to Dublin, and Lord George was not the first or the last English statesman to buy votes in an Irish Parliament. Nor had Lord George's firm line in Ireland incurred the disapproval of Britain's military leaders. The military mind liked firmness,

---

[1] Stone to Newcastle, 25 Oct. 1754; *HMC, Stop. Sack.* i. 282.
[2] Walpole, *Last Ten Years,* i. 374.   [3] Yorke, *Hardwicke,* ii. 51.
[4] Walpole, *Last Ten Years,* i. 374.   [5] Fitzmaurice, *Shelburne,* i. 347, 348.
[6] Froude, i. 684.   [7] *Walpole Letters,* Toynbee, xiii. 314, note.

especially against subalterns and Irishmen, and drew no fine line between firmness and hectoring. Lord George was still a soldier with an excellent record for a man of his years, and the system of military promotions paid little or no attention to defeat in purely political skirmishes. He could afford to show 'more command of himself' than his father did, for only five days before the duke was dismissed, Lord George had been promoted to Major-General.[1] In the same breath in which he condemned Lord George's 'haughty behaviour' in Ireland, Walpole said of his position in English politics: 'Nobody stands higher, nobody has more ambition and common sense.'

Major-General Lord George Sackville, outwardly undismayed and inwardly unrepentant, was ready to take his next step forward. 'His mistakes in Ireland were little attended and less understood. . . . In the military line he had no rival, at least no one who could cope with him in regard to family, fortune, connection, or talents for imposition and intrigue.' But, as often when men praised Lord George, Shelburne ended with a reservation. 'Enough was known of his character for everybody to fear him, as he was generally understood to be of a vindictive, implacable disposition.'[2]

[1] Coventry, p. 278; 22 Feb. 1755.   [2] Fitzmaurice, *Shelburne*, i. 348.

IV

PATHS OF GLORY

As a man who could marshal and direct power, Lord George was regarded with respect in Westminster. Since 1751 he had come to England and spoken on occasion in the House of Commons. He had addressed its members four times in February 1751; and his speeches on 31 March 1752 and 9 February 1753 had been widely praised. After his address in November 1754 Horace Walpole had compared him favourably with the great Pitt himself.[1] By 1755 he had become not only a man with a political future but one to be taken into present account in the House of Commons.

After the Irish denouement, Lord George leapt immediately into the political cockpit. Within two weeks after his promotion to Major-General he spoke so well on the Scotch Bill that Walpole made a special note of it,[2] and three times in the month of December he won the praise of that critical observer. On 5 December he gave 'a manly sensible speech'; on 8 December when the Ministry brought forward the new Militia Bill '. . . the Speaker gave great assistance; so did Lord George Sackville'; and on 10 December he spoke on the French war '. . . with much spirit, and with sense as compact as the other's [Mr. Beckford's] was incoherent'. But Walpole felt compelled to add that Lord George had '. . . a mystery in his conduct, which was far from inviting'.[3]

Leaders in both parties sought the support of this rising statesman. The powerful Duke of Newcastle, with whom the Dorsets had a family alliance, had already solicited Lord George's goodwill with a view to advancing the interests of both. The duke had invited him to second the motion for Parliament's grateful reply to the king's speech in late 1755, and hinted at the possi-

---

[1] 'Pitt spoke after him, but gently, and not well; Lord George Sackville well' (Walpole, *Last Ten Years*, i. 21, 26, 35, 93, 258).

[2] 'Lord George Sackville replied well, and ridiculed the importance with which Mr. Townshend had treated so immaterial a business' (ibid. i. 371).

[3] Ibid. i. 445, 451, 474, 486.

bility of thus securing a claim to a post in the Ministry. To second such a motion would establish Lord George in closer affinity with Newcastle's junto than he cared at the time to proclaim, and he worked carefully over the phrasing of his reply to Newcastle. There is a draft letter in Lord George's hand, greatly altered and emended, in which he informed the duke of his desire 'to remain free from any particular connection'.[1]

In rejecting so flattering an overture and thus risking the duke's enmity, Lord George showed great confidence in his own independent powers. The wording of his reply was polite and implied a strong desire for 'marks of his Majesty's favour', but it also carried the hint of a threat if they were not forthcoming. Lord George implied that if the duke misrepresented the position by making Lord George appear one of his satellites, he might feel forced to join the Opposition, and suggested that the best way the duke could keep him in support of the Ministry would be to get him further military advancement.

That draft illuminated the workings of Lord George's mind. He was determined to play a lone hand and make only temporary political alliances. He was also busily currying favour in another camp, since it did not seem likely that the king would have many more years on the throne. George II was at odds with his son and grandson, who had set up a rival junior court to which the politically rejected and the politically ambitious might repair. Any enemy of the present king was likely to be regarded as a friend by the next one. Lord George had no intention of alienating George II, but it was as well to stand in the good graces of the future George III—a slight risk of the present to insure the future. It was a delicate business to keep a foot in each camp without losing one's balance, but Lord George attempted it. Through the families of his mother and his brother-in-law Lord Milton he had useful Scottish connexions and easy access to the Marquis of Bute, upon whom the future George III depended with something close to schoolboy adulation.[2]

Whether from principle or expediency, Lord George did not

---

[1] Clements, *Germain Papers*, i; also *HMC*, *Stop. Sack*. i. 49, 50.

[2] Lord George may also have been influenced by personal pique. The Duke of Newcastle had not given whole-hearted support to the Duke of Dorset in the Irish finale. That may also have been Lord George's motive, or part of it, when in the following May he joined Pitt in attacking the Ministry, and especially Newcastle,

hesitate to oppose the Ministry on occasion. In January 1756 he spoke 'very sensibly of the situation of affairs, with some reproof on ministers', and when Pitt rose to differ he challenged that venerated figure 'with great spirit and good sense'.[1] In April he joined Pitt in an attack on the Ministry over the loss of Minorca,[2] and no matter what men might think of his principles they were impressed with his talents. 'Then Lord G. Sackville spoke as he always does, well', Henry Digby wrote in December of that year.[3]

Lord George never let the House or the Ministry forget that he was a soldier. The issues he debated most frequently and vigorously had to do with military matters, and in foreign affairs he was always on the side of a strong and aggressive England. He discussed the Militia Bill, the Mutiny Bill, the hiring of German soldiers in the war against the French, the recruiting of Scottish regiments even if their leaders had been rebellious in 1745, and the firm hand that should be taken with the recalcitrant American colonists. After all, he was a Major-General, a hero of Dettingen and Fontenoy and of the Scottish man-hunts, and presently commander of the military camp at Chatham, one of the largest of the five camps in England. In the role of bluff, honest soldier concerned only with the welfare of his country, he could act the independent in politics while always ready to serve the king on the field of battle.[4]

In February 1757 Lord George at last chose the leader he would for the moment openly support and follow. He began to make advances to Pitt, just returned to the Ministry and certain to be its leading spirit. Lord George could be confident that Pitt would urge a more active part in the war with France and thus open the door to some high military assignment to a Major-General who supported him. Lord George wanted further military service and fame, and he much preferred that service on the Continent to its unpalatable alternative in America. It was on the Continent that military reputations were won; in

over the loss of Minorca. The duke wrote then to the Lord Chancellor that 'Lord George Sackville's part is abominable' (Yorke, *Hardwicke Corresp.* ii. 290; 8 May 1756).

[1] Walpole, *Last Ten Years*, ii. 8.
[2] Ibid.
[3] 7 Dec. 1756; *HMC*, viii, part i, no. 223.
[4] Walpole, *Last Ten Years*, ii. 35, 84, 116, 131, 132.

America they were easily lost. Horace Walpole thought he saw another reason for Lord George's sudden alliance with Pitt. Lord George's only military rival was Walpole's favourite, General Conway. Conway was just moving into the political camp of Henry Fox; that was enough, Walpole thought, to send Lord George scurrying into the arms of Pitt. The alliance was declared when Lord George supported Pitt's request for funds to carry on the war more actively, and the significance of his compliments to Pitt in the House was not missed by the observant.[1]

Pitt was grateful for Lord George's timely aid and knew that repayment in kind was expected. He wrote to Lord Bute that Lord George 'deserves every return in our power',[2] and watchers like Walpole waited to see what form the return would take. They did not have to wait long, but before the answer was disclosed Lord George had put Pitt further in his debt by a skilful bit of delicate brokerage. In March he negotiated a partial reconciliation between Pitt and Newcastle, thus bringing together Britain's ablest statesman and its most vote-controlling politician.[3] By May the political soothsayers were predicting that Pitt would soon make Lord George Secretary at War.[4]

But a Ministry appointment required the acquiescence of the king, and Lord George had become known as the chief military politician of the Prince of Wales. George II must also have remembered his part in starting the Irish fracas. When the new Ministry was made up in June, Lord George was not included.[5]

---

[1] On 17 Feb. 1757 Pitt presented to the Commons the king's request for £200,000 to support the Hanoverian forces against the French. 'He was seconded by Lord George Sackville, who affected to speak only for form; yet talked forcibly on his now seeing a prospect of carrying on the war with success', a compliment to Pitt's recent participation in the Ministry. Lord George 'declared himself for Pitt; he had seemed before to attach himself to Fox', but 'of nothing was he so jealous as Conway' (ibid. ii. 141).

[2] 'Let me not omit to do a word of justice to Lord G. Sackville. His part was most friendly and handsome and his weight decided the success of the day. . . . He deserves every return in our power' (Pitt to Bute, 19 Feb. 1757; in *Essays Presented to Sir Lewis Namier*, ed. Pares and Taylor, 1956, p. 120).

[3] Walpole, *Last Ten Years*, ii. 198, 217.

[4] 'Lord George Sackville had been designed for Pitt's Secretary at War' (ibid. ii. 218). '. . . the King would not absolutely give the Secretary at War to Lord George Sackville; Lord Barrington remains' (Walpole to Mann, 3 July 1757; Toynbee, iv. 68). 'In 1757 an administration was attempted to be formed, including Lord G. Sackville as secretary at war' (Coventry, p. 65).

[5] 'On Lord George Sackville the King put a flat negative' (Walpole, *Last Ten Years*, ii. 225).

It was a serious rebuff, and probably the sharpest political disappointment Lord George had yet suffered. From that time he risked his future under the old king in order to assure it under the new. He still courted Pitt, but never forgave the king.

In October Pitt wrote to Lord George: 'I hope it will not be long before I have the succour and consolation of a full consultation with your Lordship. . . . Nothing can be indifferent to me about which you can form a wish.'[1] It seems highly likely that Lord George promptly suggested a payment on account, for only two days later Pitt wrote to Bute: 'Ld. George Sackville should be Lieutenant General of the Ordnance.'[2] In that particular post Lord George could be especially useful to Pitt in several ways. He could strengthen Pitt's position in military matters with the prince and the Leicester House junto; he could bring something of a bipartisan savour to military affairs, and his speaking ability could strengthen Pitt's hand in the House of Commons.

That particular post also had special attractions to Lord George. He would succeed and work with Marshal Ligonier, who was to be Commander-in-Chief of all his Majesty's armed forces; and the Marshal was an old friend from the early Dublin days. It would also save him from the imminent danger of being sent to America to replace Lord Loudon in command there—and America was often the graveyard of British military reputations.[3] Lord George had been lucky to escape assignment to replace General Braddock in America in 1754 'as the most senior and capable officer'. The Duke of Newcastle had saved him from that unpalatable banishment by protesting that 'It would be cruel to send Lord George Sackville', and Loudon had been sent instead.

Now, in late 1757, Lord George became Lieutenant-General of Ordnance and General Abercrombie replaced Loudon in America.[4] Everything about the new prospect pleased. The

---

[1] Pitt to Sackville, 15 Oct. 1757; *HMC, Stop. Sack.* i. 51; also Clements, *Germain Papers, Home Affairs*, i. 36–40.

[2] Pitt to Bute, 17 Oct. 1757; Pares and Taylor, *Essays for Namier*, p. 134.

[3] Lord George 'by that employment escaped an unwelcome command in America, which he could not with any grace have otherwise avoided' (Walpole, *Last Ten Years*, ii. 267).

[4] Von Ruille, *Pitt*, ii. 173. The king's order replacing the Earl of Loudon with Major-General James Abercrombie was issued on 27 Dec. 1757 (PRO, SP 41/43).

ordnance post was a highly influential one; Lord Ligonier was very friendly and often invited Lord George to be his guest at Cobham, and seemed on the whole very susceptible to the opinions and wishes of this forceful younger man. In fact Walpole was soon asserting that the old Marshal was dominated by Lord George—but there were occasions when Ligonier overruled him in appointments.

Lord George's new military post had been gained through political services, and was therefore a political as well as a military gain, for success in any field breeds further success in politics. When Lord Temple, a Grenville power, sent as Lord Privy Seal the new commission to Lord George, he went beyond the call of duty in adding that he rejoiced at '. . . every step your Lordship takes towards the head of your profession, because it affords me the flattering prospect that I may live to see the military glory of this country once again restored'.[1] That flattery was political in significance, and to those who watched the rapid rise of the Duke of Dorset's youngest son it seemed only a question of months before he would be a member of the Cabinet, and of only a few years before a new king might ask him to form a Ministry of his own.

Lord George's relative independence of any of the contemporary political juntos or 'factions' was not the handicap in 1757 that lack of party regularity would be in Britain or America today. Late Georgian Ministries were usually no more than temporary affiliations of politically powerful individuals with only immediately similar ends, each of whom brought to the Ministry the votes of his own personal following. The Opposition was a still looser alliance of disparate groups, held together chiefly by disagreement with the group in power. Men took precedence over measures, and expediency over consistent policies. Principles were eloquently proclaimed in parliamentary speeches, but in ministerial practice the only principle devotedly followed was expediency.

The Old Whig party, which had dominated British politics and George II for many years, was still in control and still maintained the façade of a unified party, but it had lost the impetus and unity of its original principles. By 1757 its strength lay chiefly in its ability to reward its supporters with power,

[1] Temple to Sackville, 31 Dec. 1757; HMC, Stop. Sack. i. 52.

place, contract, or sinecure. In earlier days the Whigs had stood for support of the principles of the Glorious Revolution against the royal power, and of the Hanoverian kings against the Stuart line, in clear-cut distinction from the Tory party's nostalgic reservations in both matters. But by 1757 there were few men still calling themselves Tories who did not accept the Revolution and the Hanoverians, and the issues that had clearly distinguished Whigs from Tories were no longer issues. The names remained, but the lines of demarcation became vague and confused.

Long prosperity in power had undermined Whig solidarity in several ways. It had robbed Whigs of an Opposition sufficiently effective and specific in challenge to keep them alert and unified. They had changed from a party based on specific principles to a mixed horde of place-seekers competing with one another. Their mission accomplished, politicians, like thieves and military allies, tend to fall out. A changing England was bringing new issues into its politics, and in time those new issues would bring new party alignments, but the old party names and loyalties remained to confuse a changing political scene. Men who considered themselves Whigs by tradition might think and act like, and sometimes with, Tories. Men from the old Tory tradition might support certain Whig leaders or join forces with them, yet still keep the old names. Whig factions, each bearing the name of a leader or a family of leaders, competed against each other, and the unsuccessful ones joined the Tories in the Opposition. In Lord George's time the name of Whig had little meaning until a man was identified as a Bedford Whig, a Rockingham Whig, or a supporter of Pitt, Grafton, Shelburne, or the Grenvilles.

There is always corruption in politics, for to those out of power some of the devices used by their successful opponents are invariably corrupt. Long tenure of power by a single party almost invariably breeds ethical decay, and the Old Whigs had been long in power. They had stayed supreme partly by improving on the traditionally accepted corruptions of their predecessors. It was only when the Whig leaders were in the Opposition that they became defenders of political virtue, and charged against the North Ministry 'corruptions' they themselves had practised, and would practise again.

When George III became king in 1760, it was with the avowed intention of ending the factionalism and corruption that he thought were destroying the strengths and virtues of the British system of government. He believed that to end those vices he must break the hold the Whig party had so long held on government, and restore the just balance between royal prerogative and Parliament—strengthening both against the wicked underminings of factions. He was determined to achieve a government not only worthy of the British people but itself an elevating ethical example to them. Such a government would consist of the ablest men without regard to party or factional levels, and all good Englishmen would flock to its support. Those who failed to support it would of course be wicked or unworthy men; George III had no concept of the value of His Majesty's Loyal Opposition, and no place for it in his 'system'. But all that was yet to come when Lord George, a high military official in a Whig government under George II, manœuvred for personal power amid the confused cross-currents of the old and new political forces.

The rival court of the prince at Leicester House had already begun to look upon Lord George as one of its present adherents and future statesmen. As early as January 1757 the Duke of Newcastle, whose ears heard every whisper of political gossip, wrote to Lord Chancellor Yorke: 'Lord Bute had been with Lord George Sackville and had told him that the Prince of Wales had his eye upon him.'[1] Three months later Bubb Dodington, later Lord Melville, an angler for social and political influence through charming little services to the right lords and ladies, recorded in his diary: 'The Duke of Devonshire to be at the head of the Treasury, Lord George Sackville to be Secretary', in the new revision of the Ministry.[2]

No other man had the favour of both a leading Minister and an Opposition leader. The Earl of Shelburne wrote rather enviously in a later year: 'Mr. Pitt and Mr. Fox both bid for him; his Westminster connection secured him instant access to the Duke of Newcastle, and let him into every secret of that house, while he assiduously cultivated and promoted his mother's country people, the Scotch, which made a form of

---

[1] Newcastle to Yorke, 9 Jan. 1757; Yorke, *Hardwicke Corresp.* ii. 384.
[2] Wyndham, 9 Mar. 1757, p. 392.

union between him and the Earl of Bute. . . . He naturally
excelled in that species of dexterity and address which enabled
him to turn all these circumstances to his consideration.'[1]

Pitt's energy in pressing the lagging war against the French in
the Rhineland and Westphalia offered Lord George a rare opportunity to select the setting for his further pursuit of military
glory. There were good reasons for that pursuit. His political
success had bred envious critics and they were beginning to be
heard. The more Lord George demonstrated his superior talents
the more he inspired detraction from his rivals. So long as all
his undertakings succeeded, his critics could only whisper
cautiously, but one mis-step could turn the whispers into mutterings; one failure could raise them into shouts. Had Lord George
possessed no weaknesses, his critics would have had to invent
them: as events developed they were spared that necessity.

Lacking the manpower for large-scale battles with the French
Army, Pitt determined on raids on French seaports. He offered
Major-General Lord George Sackville the leadership of the land
forces in the first of these, a proposed raid on Rochefort. Lord
George declined, presumably dubious of the strategy proposed.
Walpole gave another reason; he said Lord George did not
want to risk his reputation, and used the enmity of the Duke of
Cumberland as his excuse; the duke would use his influence to
see that the expedition got weak support. It was a flimsy reason,
but, true or not, Lord George was criticized for declining, and
also for talking loosely about an undertaking supposed to be
a State secret.[2]

Sir John Mordaunt was made commander instead. The attack
on Rochefort began on 8 September 1757 and, partly because
of bad intelligence and planning, failed miserably.[3] Mordaunt
was blamed, and Lord George was appointed with Major-
General Waldegrave and the Duke of Marlborough (not the
great first duke but the less able and more good-natured third)
to inquire into his conduct. They began their inquiry on 15
November, and reported unfavourably, but the court martial

---

[1] Fitzmaurice, *Shelburne*, i. 349.

[2] 'The persons who offered him the command, would have supported him the
more for his disfavour with the Duke. Lord George was still more blameable in
talking of the design to several persons after he had refused to undertake it'
(Walpole, *Last Ten Years*, ii. 236).

[3] Fortescue, *HBA*, 2, ii. 213.

that followed reversed their judgement and exonerated Sir John.
It was not the last time that Lord George would disagree with a
court martial.

Once convinced of the merit of an idea, Pitt was not easily
discouraged. He planned another raid on the Channel port of
St. Malo. It was to be led by the Duke of Marlborough, and
this time Lord George agreed to go as second in command. The
duke was 'an easy, good-natured, gallant man . . . without any
military experience or the common habits of a man of business,
or indeed capacity for either, and no force of character whatever'.[1] Excessive deference to a superior officer was never one
of Lord George's failings, and Horace Walpole wrote to Sir
Horace Mann that: 'The Duke of Marlborough commands, and
is, in reality, commanded by Lord George Sackville.'[2]

St. Malo brought Lord George into contact with two brothers
with whom he would later have many dealings, and the first
meetings did not promise well for the future. William Howe,
who, it was said, never made friends but at the mouth of a
cannon, was an officer under Lord George, and 'conceived and
expressed a strong aversion to him'.[3] His brother, Viscount
Captain Richard Howe, a man of greater mental capacity
than William, commanded the squadron to carry the troops to
St. Malo and support them by sea. He and Lord George also
developed a mutual dislike. Just after the expedition Walpole
wrote: 'Howe and Lord George are upon the worst terms.'[4]

When Lord George disliked a man he rarely troubled to
conceal it. Of the naval captain's management before landing
the troops at St. Malo Lord George wrote to his father:

. . . the wind being fair westward the Commodore made no use of
it . . . we landsmen could not account for the Commodore's conduct
in doing now what he might have done on the Wednesday before;
it was giving the enemy four days warning. . . . The Commodore
shou'd have stood into the Bay earlier. . . . If the Commodore
expected to raise his reputation . . . the disappointment must have

[1] Walpole, *Last Ten Years*, ii. 305.
[2] Walpole to Mann, 10 Feb. 1758; Toynbee, iv. 123.
[3] 'They agreed so ill that one day Lord George putting several questions to
Howe, and receiving no answer, said, "Mr. Howe, don't you hear me? I have
asked you several questions." Howe replied, "I don't love questions" ' (Walpole,
Last Ten Years, ii. 305).
[4] Walpole to Conway, 8 July 1758; Toynbee, iv. 156.

chagrinned him . . . he might have made a puff in the newspapers
and he might have raised the admiration of our ale drinking politicians, but in the eyes of the judicious he cou'd have got no additional
credit.[1]

Lord George did not let his complete inexperience of naval
matters temper his judgements.

The raid, which took place in June 1758, was another failure,[2]
and for the first time Lord George emerged from a military
venture with diminished reputation. 'If they send a patch-box
to Lord George Sackville, it will hold all his laurels', Walpole
wrote to Lord George's rival General Conway after the raid.[3]
Since he had assumed much of the planning and direction of
the land operations, it was reasonable to give him much of the
blame. That was bad enough, but the rumours were also personal. It was said that he had not shown that aggressiveness
that he had often urged on other military leaders; that his own
conduct was more vulnerable than that of Sir John Mordaunt,
whom he had found guilty of military misconduct only six
months before. It was reported that he had not encouraged his
troops by either word or example to attack vigorously the
French forces, and that he had retreated too promptly before
approaching enemy reinforcements. It was even whispered that
Lord George had been most energetic in leading his troops in
the wrong direction.

How much of this was true it is impossible to be certain.
Perhaps much was made of very little, but it is significant that
the amiable and uncritical Duke of Marlborough did nothing
to denounce these tales about his second in command. Walpole
was one of those who accepted them enough to pass them on to
history: 'It was said that Lord George Sackville was not among
the first to court danger.' Perhaps the most important aspect of
the affair was its creation of a suspicion that Lord George no
longer cared to risk his own skin to enemy fire.

Given their first good opportunity to attack Lord George as
a soldier, his enemies made the most of it. His wound at Fontenoy was said to have made Lord George singularly reluctant to
risk another. One London newspaper printed an uncomplimen-

---

[1] Sackville to Dorset; HMC, Stop. Sack. i. 293-5.
[2] Fortescue, HBA, 2, ii. 346.
[3] Walpole to Conway, 16 June 1758; Toynbee, iv. 146.

tary verse, in which the 'Brig' referred to was the engagingly
uncomplicated and hard-fighting Brigadier-General 'Jack'
Mostyn:

> All pale and trembling on the Gallic shore,
> His Lordship gave the word, but could no more;
> Too small the corps, too few the numbers were,
> Of such a general, to demand the care.
> To some mean chief, some Major or a Brig,
> He left his charge that night, nor cared a fig:
> 'Twixt life and scandal, 'twixt honor and the grave,
> Quickly deciding which was best to save,
> Back to the ships he ploughed the swelling wave.[1]

No questions were asked in Parliament, and no military
committee was appointed to inquire into the conduct of Lord
George. 'It was not the business of any party to attack Lord
George':[2] not that of the Opposition, for Lord George was not
closely identified with the Ministry; not the Ministry, for
criticism of Lord George or the management of the raid would
reflect criticism on itself. The military heads ignored the gossip,
or else remembered that Lord George was, after all, one of
themselves. He was, however, believed to have given some
offence to the king and his great and good friend Pitt by
remarking that he would go buccaneering no more. The
criticism died away (though in time it would be recalled), and
Lord George remained as confident as ever.

In Parliament his confidence sometimes led him to over-shoot
the mark. In some way he offended a powerful friend, for Lord
Mansfield wrote to him on New Year's Day 1758: 'I will be
ingenious to find colours to deceive myself; but the contrast of
yr. Behaviour hurts me to the Soul & almost distracts my Mind.'[3]
Lord George also crossed swords, unsuccessfully, with that
competent old soldier Lord Tyrawly, who while Governor of
Gibraltar spent more on its fortifications than, Lord George
told Parliament, was justified. Tyrawley demanded a chance
to answer these charges before the House of Commons, and did
so with such vehemence, reason, and humour that he disarmed
his hearers. He also attacked Lord George for devious methods

---

[1] Fonblanque, p. 496.   [2] Fitzmaurice, *Shelburne*, i. 351.
[3] Mansfield to Sackville, 1 Jan. 1758; Clements, *Germain Papers*, i.

of bringing his charges, and for avoiding foreign command. Lord George found himself very much on the defensive and hurriedly withdrew his charges.[1]

If Lord George hoped for further military advancement it was time to renovate his military reputation. He must not let some junior officer overhaul him in rank, accomplishments, or reputation. There was, for example, the challenge implicit in the career of Jeff Amherst, his father's protégé since boyhood, who was commanding the successful taking of Louisburg; there was young James Wolfe, who had been a subordinate in Lord George's own regiment in Germany, and now was headed for an important command in America. Wolfe admired Lord George and wrote him occasional long letters,[2] but such admiration would not stop Wolfe from forwarding his own career merely in deference to that of any other man. It was not in America or in tricky coastal raids like that at St. Malo, but in the large-scale and orthodox operations against the French in Germany, that honours were most likely to be won. There one could fight by the book and expect the French commanders to do predictably likewise. Such service would be especially attractive to Lord George if he were second, for a time, to the Duke of Marlborough, whom he had found amenable to his own superior military knowledge and forcefulness. What was more, the Prince of Wales and his mentor the Marquis of Bute had selected Lord George to be groomed as the top military man for the new régime, and it would be wise to demonstrate his capacity to lead large armies.[3] Lieutenant-General Lord George Sackville[4] therefore addressed himself on 3 July 1758 to his political friend William Pitt, and asked for a top assignment to the war in Germany.

His request was granted, and he was appointed second in command to the Duke of Marlborough, who was to head the British Army serving under Prince Ferdinand of Brunswick as Commander-in-Chief of the allied forces on the Continent. Immediately under Lord George would be the Marquis of

[1] See note A, p. 497.

[2] Wolfe to Sackville, from Portsmouth, 11 Feb. 1758, from Halifax, 12 May 1758, from Halifax, 24 May 1758, from Halifax, July 1758; Clements, *Germain Papers*, i.

[3] Yorke, *Hardwicke Corresp.* iii. 119.

[4] He was promoted to Lieutenant-General on 12 June 1758 (Ligonier to Sackville, 12 June 1758; Clements, *Germain Papers*, i).

Granby, son of the Duke of Rutland and already regarded as one of the finest cavalry officers in Europe.[1] It was a promising appointment, especially if anything untoward should happen to the Duke of Marlborough.

There were a few times in Lord George's life when he rashly shook the ladder up which he was so carefully climbing. It was as if, in the moments of his greatest success, something compelled him to defy the fates or to test his power and his friends to the breaking-point. At the peak of his influence in Dublin he had quite unnecessarily alienated the Irish, and had let a valuable friendship with the Duke of Cumberland turn into animosity. In London he had risked alienating the support of the Duke of Newcastle, Lord Mansfield, and the even more powerful Pitt. By too indiscreet a flirtation with Leicester House he had offended the king and lost appointment as Secretary at War. As a landsman who did not hesitate to criticize naval strategy and operations, he had made an enemy of Richard Howe, destined to become a leading Admiral and Sea Lord. Now, once again, on the eve of his departure for Germany, he flouted tradition and courtesy by failing to pay his respects to his royal Commander-in-Chief. George II was not a man to overlook disregard of established military convention or of deference to his royal person. He threatened to recall Lord George, and was only with difficulty persuaded not to do so by the harried Pitt, who pleaded that officers of such ability were extremely scarce.

From that point in early 1758 until the events of late 1759, much of Lord George's conduct can be explained only by the assumption that his self-confidence was outweighing his judgement. Pitt had paid his debt in full, and would be unlikely to react favourably to further immediate complaints and solicitations. Lord George was a soldier, and a good soldier performs his assignment, whether or not it prove a pleasant one. Lord George's new command was one he had ardently solicited. Yet almost before he had entered upon it he wrote to Pitt threatening to resign. The reason he gave was a trivial one: he had expected that the reinforcements sent to Germany would immediately be

---

[1] Lord Granby 'had all the good qualities of the Duke of Marlborough, but with more force of character, more activity, and a natural turn to the army . . . without the least spirit of intrigue' (Fitzmaurice, *Shelburne*, i. 354).

placed under his command; he was angry that they were put temporarily under General Bligh.[1]

The affair was adjusted somehow and Lord George did not resign. But he had not been long in Germany before he began to step on other toes. According to the Earl of Shelburne, he 'took every advantage of the Duke of Marlborough's goodness and weakness of character, and in point of manner trespassed upon him without measure. . . . Everything that was well done, every one that was served, it was all Lord George's doing. Everything that was neglected or ill done, every fault that was committed, every person that was disobliged, it was all the poor Duke of Marlborough.'[2]

In spite of all he owed to Pitt, Lord George continued to court Lord Bute and the Prince of Wales by letter, and in that correspondence did his best to undermine confidence in his commanding officer Prince Ferdinand. This was a dangerous game, since Pitt and the king were almost certain to learn of this correspondence criticizing a Commander-in-Chief whom the king thought magnificent and Pitt was deeply committed to support. Ferdinand was at thirty-eight one of the most trusted of Frederick the Great's former pupils, and had held one of the highest commands in the superb Prussian Army. He was closely related to the King of Prussia and a distant cousin of the King of England. He was a proud and experienced soldier who did not welcome unsolicited instruction or criticism from a subordinate.[3] Yet Lord George had not been three months in Germany before it was generally believed that he was on bad terms with his commanding officer. '. . . Between him and Prince Ferdinand there was by no means any cordiality. Both liked to govern, and neither was disposed to be governed. Prince Ferdinand had gained an ascendant over the Duke of Marlborough and Lord George had lost it; sufficient groundwork for their enmity.'[4]

The Duke of Marlborough died suddenly at Münster on

---

[1] 'I hope I shall meet with your approbation in desiring to withdraw from the active part of my profession, since I can no longer continue in it with any degree of credit or satisfaction to myself' (Sackville to Pitt, 3 July 1758; Taylor and Pringle, *Pitt Corresp.* i. 326, 327).

[2] Fitzmaurice, *Shelburne*, i. 349, 350.

[3] Ibid., i. 352, 353; also Fitzmaurice, *Charles William Ferdinand*, p. 6.

[4] Walpole, *Last Ten Years*, ii. 323.

28 October 1758. A successor had to be appointed at once, and in that choice no men would be more influential than Pitt and Lord Ligonier. As second in command, already on the ground, Lord George was the logical first candidate, and may even have been given assurances of the succession before he went to Germany. He received the king's commission as 'Commander in Chief of all his Majesty's forces, horse and foot, serving on the lower Rhine or to be there assigned with the Allied Army under the command of Prince Ferdinand of Brunswick', and entered upon this high command with the prospect of strong support from high places. Lord Ligonier wrote: 'I am extremely and sincerely concerned for the death of the Duke of Marlborough and could have felt it more as a publick loss had you not been there to supply his place.'[1] Lord Bute wrote that Lord George's appointment pleased the Prince of Wales, and added: 'I hope you won't think it flattery in me to say that your accounts are so clearly and ably drawn that I fancy few like them come over to this countrey. I rejoice extremely at your having the command, it was your due in every way.'[2] And the Duke of Newcastle, adequately reconciled, wrote some months later: 'We repose an entire confidence in you.'[3] Prince Ferdinand rose generously to the occasion: 'Talent and zeal will do much, and he knows of no one so capable as his Lordship of vanquishing even greater difficulties.'[4] After such rapid advancement and exalted praise, any but the most balanced man might reach the conclusion that he could do no wrong.

At the age of forty-three the ambitious son of Knole had attained the highest post of active command in the British Army. But not to his unadulterated satisfaction. He was subordinate to Prince Ferdinand, who seemed to lack a proper appreciation of his talents. And his commission allowed him considerably less power than Marlborough had been given—reflecting perhaps the king's remembrance of an earlier slight, and of Lord George's connexion with Leicester House. Lord George complained to Bute and Ligonier, and wrote to Pitt protesting '. . . the alterations made in the instructions, especially

[1] Ligonier to Sackville, 31 Oct. 1758; HMC, Stop. Sack. i. 53, 54.
[2] Bute to Sackville, 17 Nov. 1758; HMC, Stop. Sack. i. 54.
[3] Newcastle to Sackville, 3 July 1759; HMC, Stop. Sack. i. 57.
[4] Ferdinand to Sackville, 31 Dec. 1758; Clements, Germain Papers, i. 29; also HMC, Stop. Sack. i. 302.

as I know it was expected here, by some who have the best
private court intelligence, that something marking personal disapprobation would happen upon this occasion'. Lord George
went on to assure Pitt, quite untruthfully, that his relations with
Prince Ferdinand were excellent: 'His attention and goodness
to me . . . has been so particular, that I shall always look upon
it as an honour to me and his expressions upon my receiving the
commission were most flattering, so that, upon the whole, I may
compound for a little ill-humour at home.'[1] Pitt must have
known that Lord George was writing disingenuously about his
relations with his commanding officer, for the truth was common
knowledge in London. 'He had thwarted Prince Ferdinand, and
disgusted him, in the preceding campaign; and now was in the
army against the Prince's inclination', according to Walpole.[2]
There were also reports of bickerings, and even of violent
animosities, between Lord George and his next in command
Lord Granby,[3] whom everyone else found easy to get along with.
William Howe, again serving under Lord George, did not conceal his distaste. In fact, Lord George was said to be 'upon the
worst terms' with the whole military staff, and Walpole hinted
at a special reason 'too curious' to confide even in a private letter
to his friend General Conway.[4]

In December 1758, when all was quiet with the armies, Lord
George returned to England, perhaps to mend his fences, but he
was back in Germany on 16 March for the opening of the spring
campaign.[5] Soon after that his resentments against his Commander-in-Chief flared up so strongly that Lord George did not
attempt to conceal them even from Pitt. He wrote that Prince
Ferdinand was permitting 'shameful' waste of the military
goods supplied from British funds, and by loose handling of

[1] Sackville to Pitt, 11 Nov. 1758; Taylor and Pringle, *Pitt Corresp.* i. 367.
[2] Walpole, *Last Ten Years*, ii. 262, 263.
[3] 'You have heard, I suppose of the violent animosities that have reigned for the
whole campaign between himself and Lord Granby' (Walpole to Conway, 8 July
1759; Toynbee, iv. 156). Manners, Granby's biographer, denies that there was
at this point any ill feeling between Granby and Lord George (Manners, *Granby*,
pp. 83, 84), but Granby had certainly resented sarcasms from Lord George in
Parliament in 1758.
[4] 'Howe and Lord George are upon the worst terms, as the latter is with the
military too. I will tell you some very curious anecdotes when I see you, but that
I do not choose, for particular reasons, to write' (Walpole to Conway, 8 July 1759;
Toynbee, iv. 156).   [5] Manners, *Granby*, p. 73.

contracts for forage and provisions. 'I have taken the liberty of saying a good deal upon this subject to his Grace [the Duke of Newcastle]. . . . You cannot conceive how much the discipline of the army in general has suffered by this management.'

Lord George was probably right about the waste, but his method of correcting his commanding officer ultimately did the British cause more harm than whatever peculations the prince had indulged in or overlooked. Lord George's continuous criticisms of Prince Ferdinand's strategy, tactics, and financial management doubtless reached the prince's ears, and would have annoyed a commander more serene than His Serene Highness. According to Lord Shelburne: 'Lord George at once began the same tactics which he had adopted previously against the Duke of Marlborough in the St. Malo expedition, of endeavoring to assume personal credit for all that went well, and to create a popularity for himself at the expense of his chief, Prince Ferdinand.'[1]

No German commanding officer who had served and conquered with Frederick the Great would have taken kindly to so much advice and veiled criticism from an English subordinate. 'I should strongly advise your abandoning the Weser, and confining yourself to keeping those countries which would best enable us to carry on the war. . . . I do not hesitate to declare it as my opinion that it is most for the King's service and the good of the common cause to attempt the saving of our magazines at Neinburgh. . . . I should hope that your Serene Highness, in consequence of a victory, will remain master in Westphalia likewise . . . what I have said in regard to Munster must weigh down all other considerations.'[2] No general struggling against French forces larger than his own would be pleased at the knowledge that Lord George was writing to the Secretary at War: 'I believe the Prince marched with that intention', implying that Prince Ferdinand had not confided in the head of his British forces; or describing a minor reverse as 'a blow so unexpected and so fatal to the Prince's plan of operations', or hinting again at being kept in ignorance by such remarks as '. . . the Prince, I dare say for the best of reasons . . . '.[3]

[1] Fitzmaurice, *Shelburne*, p. 72.
[2] Sackville to Ferdinand, 11 July 1759; *HMC, Stop. Sack*. i. 309.
[3] Sackville to Holdernesse, 18 July 1759; *HMC, Stop. Sack*. i. 309, 310.

To Bute Lord George's letters were more openly critical, and were, of course, intended for the ear of the Prince of Wales: 'The Prince, who seldom asks opinions . . .'; 'It is not easy to form opinions without hearing all that the person knows who puts the questions to you . . . however, I will never make difficulties . . .'; 'However, the other part was taken against [my] opinion, and by it we have given up vast magazines . . .'; and 'It would be a presumption in me to think we could have done better, but . . .'.[1] Nor could it have pleased Pitt to know that Lord George was playing him off against Bute and the Prince of Wales. 'Indeed, a very few days before the battle [of Minden], the refusal to grant him [Lord George] full military patronage, which had been much pressed by Leicester House . . . drew upon Pitt, who had hitherto basked in the favour and under the protection of that power, some extremely improper menaces from Lord Bute.'[2]

So dangerous a game could not go on long without disaster, but Lord George ignored the warning implicit in a letter from Lord Holdernesse only a month before the final débâcle: 'The King, whose confidence in Prince Ferdinand increases every day, has sent him the fullest powers to act as he in his own judgment shall think the best, & most conducive to the cause.'[3]

The trail Lord George was blazing across the skies of Whitehall and Westminster still seemed brilliant, but the esteem he was winning was remote and fickle, while the resentments he was creating were immediate and enduring. In 1759 men were beginning to wonder whether Lord George's egoism might not undermine his talents and his career. But no one could have foreseen how soon and how painfully misfortune, or retribution, would strike down this promising scion of the Sackvilles.

[1] Sackville to Bute, 18 July 1759; HMC, Stop. Sack. i. 310, 311.
[2] Yorke, Hardwicke Corresp. 7 Aug. 1759, iii. 139, 140.
[3] Holdernesse to Sackville, 3 July 1759; Clements, Germain Papers, ii. 44; also HMC, Stop. Sack. i. 56, 57.

V

MINDEN

O N 1 August 1759 the allied army was drawn up on slightly wooded slopes near Minden, which had been occupied by the French Army under Marshal Contades. Early in the morning the French attacked. The British and German infantry, with magnificent discipline and firmness, repulsed unaided four charges by the French cavalry and an infantry brigade; then marched forward in close formation and threw the entire French Army into confusion. At that point an immediate attack by the British cavalry, which had stood inactive behind a nearby ridge on the allied right wing, could almost certainly have turned an allied success into a devastating victory.

At that juncture Prince Ferdinand sent orders by several separate aides to Lord George Sackville, in command of the British and German cavalry, to attack immediately. But something went wrong. There was a delay of more than half an hour, and when some of the cavalry finally moved forward they were too late to take part, for the French had retreated behind their fortifications at Minden. The likelihood of the greatest French defeat since Blenheim was lost.

Sismondi in his *History of the French People* wrote that: 'Contades' army should have been destroyed.'[1] Archenholz in his *History of the Seven Years War* declared that: '. . . the greatest defeat of this century seemed certain, when the faithlessness of an English General saved the French from complete destruction'.[2] Sir John Fortescue wrote in his *History of the British Army* of '. . . a day at once a pride and a disgrace to the British'.[3] Lord Edward Fitzmaurice in his monograph on the Duke of Brunswick stated flatly: 'The refusal of Lord George Sackville to carry out the orders of the Duke alone saved the French army from complete destruction.'[4]

Immediately after the battle there were bitter words against Lord George throughout the allied army. Yet that evening he

[1] Manners, *Granby*, p. 77. [2] Ibid.
[3] Fortescue, *HBA*, 2, ii. 503. [4] Fitzmaurice, *Charles William Ferdinand*, p. 8.

took his place among the officers that dined with Duke Ferdinand
with such outward composure that the duke exclaimed: 'Voilà
cet homme autant à son aise s'il avoit fait des merveilles!'[1]

In his orders of the following day the duke praised certain
British officers but pointedly omitted any direct reference to the
British commander:

His Serene Highness further orders it to be declared to General
the Marquis of Granby that he is persuaded that, if he had had the
good fortune to have had him at the Head of the Cavalry of the
Right Wing, his presence would have greatly contributed to make
the decision of the day more complete, and more brilliant. . . . And
his Serene Highness Desires and Orders the Generals of the Army,
that upon all occasions when orders are brought to them by His
Aides-de-camp, that they be Obeyed Punctually and without Delay.[2]

There could be but one interpretation of the prince's words.
Lord George promptly protested, and was told flatly that he
had disobeyed orders and was responsible for the failure to win
a great victory.

Duke Ferdinand commissioned the Duke of Richmond, then
twenty-four years old, and Colonel Fitzroy, then twenty-two,
grandson of the first Duke of Grafton, to take his report of the
battle to the king and government in London. The next day,
before he left for England, Fitzroy received a letter from Lord
George. That letter and Fitzroy's reply to it were later printed
and circulated in England.

Lord George wrote that Fitzroy had first brought him orders
'to advance with the British cavalry'; that Captain Edward
Ligonier had almost immediately arrived with orders from the
duke that 'the whole cavalry was to advance. I was puzzled
what to do.' Lord George had ridden to the duke for clarification, 'but I am sure the Service would not suffer, as no Delay
was occasioned by it. The Duke then ordered me to leave some
Squadrons upon the Right, which I did, and to advance the
rest to support the Infantry. This I declare I did, as fast as I
imagined it was right in Cavalry to march in Line. I once
halted by Lord Granby to compleat my forming the whole.'
Lord George ended to Fitzroy: 'All I insist upon is, that I
obeyed the Orders I received, as punctually as I was able; and

---

[1] Walpole, *Last Ten Years*, ii. 367.   [2] Manners, *Granby*, p. 78.

if I were to do it over again, I do not think I would have executed them Ten minutes sooner than I did, now I know the
ground, and what was expected. For God's sake let me see you,
before you go for England.'[1]

Colonel Fitzroy's reply was dated the following day:

His Serene Highness, upon some Report made to him by the
Duke of Richmond, of the Situation of the Enemy, sent Captain
Ligonier and myself with Orders for the British Cavalry to advance,
—His Serene Highness was, at this Instant, one or two Brigades
beyond the British Infantry, towards the Left.—Upon my arrival on
the Right of the Cavalry, I found Captain Ligonier with your Lordship.—Notwithstanding, I declared His Serene Highness's Orders to
you; Upon which you desired I would not be in an Hurry,—I made
Answer, that Galloping had put me out of Breath, which made me
speak very quick,—I then repeated the Orders for the British Cavalry
to advance towards the Left, and, at the same Time, mentioning the
Circumstances that occasioned the Orders, added, 'That it was a
glorious Opportunity for the English to distinguish themselves, and
that your Lordship, by leading them on, would gain immortal
Honour'.

You yet expressed your Surprize at the Order, saying, it was impossible the Duke could mean to break the Line.—My answer was,
that I delivered His Serene Highness's Orders, Word for Word, as
he gave them.—Upon which you asked, which Way the Cavalry
was to march, and who was to be their Guide.—I undertook to lead
them towards the Left round the little Wood on their Left, as they
were then drawn up, where they might be little exposed to the
Enemy's cannonade.

Your Lordship continued to think my Orders neither clear nor
exactly delivered; and expressing your Desire to see Prince Ferdinand,
ordered me to lead you to him; which order I was obeying when
we met His Serene Highness.—During this time I did not see the
Cavalry advance.—Captain Smith, one of your Aids de Camp, once
or twice made me repeat the Orders I had before delivered to your
Lordship; and I hope he will do me the Justice to say, they were
clear and exact.—He then went up to you, whilst we were going to
find the Duke, as I imagine, being sensible of the Clearness of my
Orders, and the Necessity of their being immediately obeyed.—
I heard your Lordship give him some Orders,—What they were I
cannot say—but he immediately rode back towards the Cavalry.

[1] *Lord George Sackville's Vindication of Himself, &c.*, R. Stevens, London, 1759;
also in *Gentleman's Magazine*, 1759, pp. 417 ff.; also British Museum, Political
Tracts.

Upon my joining the Duke, I repeated to him the Orders I had delivered to you, and appealing to His Serene Highness, to know whether they were the same he had honoured me with, I had the Satisfaction to hear him declare, they were very exact. His Serene Highness immediately asked, where the Cavalry was; and upon my making Answer, that Lord George did not understand the Order, but was coming to speak to His Serene Highness, he expressed his Surprize strongly.[1]

Lord George also appealed to Viscount Granby, according to Granby's account in a personal letter to the Duke of Newcastle:

The night after the Duke's orders came out Lord George desired me to come to his quarters, when after complaining of the Duke's cruel treatment of him he shewed me a paper which (as he believed I knew it to be true) he hoped I would sign; I answered him there were many things in it I was quite ignorant of—orders delivered to him that I had never heard of till after the battle. . . . In regard to what I knew myself of matters of fact I differed with him in several things, and I therefore could not possibly sign the paper. He then proposed to me to write a letter to the Duke to clear him of some particular things relating to myself that he said was laid to his charge in regard to his halting the second line. I told him I had already repeated to him several times all I could say in regard to matters of fact concerning the orders for halting which I had received from him. . . . I was then desired to let a letter be indited for me which I might sign if it pleased me—a letter was begun and almost finished, but it was so contrary to my inclinations and way of thinking that I stop't it by declaring I could not sign it; his Lordship has shewn a paper to most of the Field Officers of Cavalry none of whom, I am almost confident, have signed any paper nor, as I know, in any shape given their opinion of it.[2]

News of the victory first reached London without any hint of misconduct by Lord George, and it was on that basis that Lord Holdernesse, the Secretary at War on whom Walpole commented: 'Nature never intended him for anything that he was',[3] wrote to Lord George congratulating him on 'the glorious success of his Majesty's arms', adding with unconscious irony: 'The arrival of Colonel Fitzroy is awaited with the utmost interest.'[4]

---

[1] *Lord George Sackville's Vindication of Himself, &c.*, R. Stevens, London, 1759; also in *Gentleman's Magazine*, 1759, pp. 417 ff.; also British Museum, Political Tracts.
[2] Granby to Newcastle, 29 Aug. 1759; *Newcastle Papers*; also Manners, *Granby*, p. 81.　　　　[3] Walpole to Mason, 31 May 1778; Toynbee, x. 259.
[4] Holdernesse to Sackville, 10 Aug. 1759; *HMC, Stop. Sack.* i. 311.

When reports of Lord George's conduct reached London, followed by the news that on 13 August Duke Ferdinand had asked that Lord George be recalled,[1] excitement over the battle yielded to excitement over the case of Lord George. It is said that the king angrily struck with his own hand Lord George's name from the army list, and personally dismissed him from his post as Master-General of Ordnance.

Duke Ferdinand wrote a personal account of Minden to his cousin George II, and its phrases became general knowledge in the court: 'Son comportement à la journée du prem^r. n'a pas été tel que ni la Cause en general, ni moi en particulier je n'en ai pû etre content, & cela au point que les affaires en auroient pû etre à deux doigts de leur perte & d'un autre cote le Succès de cette journée n'a pas été aussi parfaitement brillant et complet, comme il en avoit tous les moyens possibles en main.'[2]

Generals under criticism traditionally offered their resignations, but did not expect them to be accepted unless a court martial ruled adversely. Lord George followed the convention but Lord Holdernesse did not. He wrote coldly that the king was pleased to comply with Lord George's desire to resign his command, and had appointed Viscount Granby in his place.[3] Lord George was then 'given leave' to return 'forthwith' to London.

Lord George hoped for support from Pitt, the Prince of Wales, Bute, and other powerful friends. The first indication of Pitt's attitude was in an exchange with Bute, who had written to Pitt asking, in effect, clemency for Lord George. Pitt replied on 15 August that giving leave to Lord George to return, rather than ordering him to return, was 'a very considerable softening of his misfortune', and added the rather dubious assurance that 'I shall continue to give him, as a most unhappy man, all the *offices of humanity*, which our *first*, *sacred* object, my dear Lord, the public good, will allow. . . . The King sends the Garter, and a handsome present, to Prince Ferdinand.'[4] Lord George knew nothing of that exchange when he wrote to Pitt asking for his

---

[1] Manners, *Granby*, p. 78.

[2] Clements, *Shelburne Papers*, xxi; *Ferdinand Corresp.*, p. 29.

[3] Holdernesse to Sackville, 14 Aug. 1759; PRO, SP 41/23, no. 285; also *HMC, Stop. Sack.* i. 313.

[4] Pitt to Bute, 15 Aug. 1759; Taylor and Pringle, *Pitt Corresp.*, pp. 417, 418.

support. Pitt replied warning Lord George against demanding a court martial, since 'delusion might prove dangerous', and added that he had not found in Lord George's statement or in Captain Smith's conversation: '. . . room, as I wished, for me to offer my support, with regard to a conduct which, perhaps, my incompetence to judge of military questions, leaves me at a loss to account for'.[1]

The Prince of Wales wrote to Lord Bute his own private reactions: 'I am very much hurt for this officer, as I thought Lord G. would have been a very useful man. I yet hope he will be able to set things right at the army . . . unless P. Ferdinand is very certain of what he alledges, he acts most impiously in this attack, and let the thing be as it will, I think it is pretty pert for a little German Prince to make publick any fault he finds with the English Commander, without first waiting for instructions from the King in so delicate a matter.'[2] But the prince and Bute found public opinion too inflamed to risk flouting it openly, and they gave Lord George very little effective support.

Before Lord George reached England he learned something of the almost universal denunciation he would meet there. In a long letter from Rotterdam to Major-General the Honourable Joseph Yorke, the king's representative at The Hague, Lord George admitted that he was: '. . . but too sensible of the many difficulties I must meet with and the prejudices I have to struggle against; but a good conscience is the greatest comfort and support under such circumstances . . . I cannot yet comprehend why Prince Ferdinand should proceed in so unusual a manner with me. If I have done wrong, why was I to be censured by him complimenting another, and why was that common justice denied me of knowing my crime, my accuser, or being heard before I was condemned.'[3]

In that letter as elsewhere Lord George seemed sincere in his conviction of innocence, but it may have been the sincerity of a man convinced he could not make a mistake. Yorke was either unconvinced or else too cautious to take sides, for he did not reply. The Earl of Hardwicke, Yorke's close relation, kept an open mind and reported the facts as he had heard them to the

---

[1] See Note B, p. 497.
[2] Prince of Wales to Bute, 9 Sept. 1757.
[3] Sackville to Yorke, 2 Sept. 1759; Yorke, *Hardwicke*, iii. 235, 236.

Solicitor-General.[1] Lord George got open support from very
few outside his immediate family, although some men thought
he should be heard before he was dismissed and sentenced by
public opinion. Lord George adopted a vein of martyrdom to
military jealousy and politics, and wrote, probably to Lord
Bute: 'I have nothing further to offer your Lordship but the
poor services of a discarded general, who I flatter myself shld
have been reckoned a good officer had he been less attached to
what he thought the Interest of his own Country.'[2]

Very soon after reaching London in early September, Lord
George reported to Lord Bute that he had written to Lord
Holdernesse, Secretary at War: '. . . requesting a court martial
upon hearing that in the temper his Majesty was in he might
probably as soon as he heard of my arrival in town dismiss me
from his service, especially as I might expect no assistance from
any of the Ministers, because whatever tended to my justification must in a degree reflect upon the character of Prince
Ferdinand'.[3]

A military officer accused of failing to do his duty had two
official recourses. One was to demand a full-dress inquiry by
Parliament sitting as a Committee of the Whole. In Lord
George's case that procedure offered special difficulties. It was
almost impossible to secure a Parliamentary Inquiry if the
Ministry opposed it, and in this case the Ministry did. The very
fact that Parliament was holding a full-dress inquiry, as though
there were any doubt about Duke Ferdinand's conclusions,
would be an affront to the duke and Britain's German allies.
An inquiry would also give the Opposition a chance to say
everything possible to embarrass the Ministry. The Opposition,
on the other hand, had no special interest in defending a man
who had deserted it for the greener fields of Ministry favour.

The alternative was to demand a court martial, to which
every officer was by tradition entitled. A court martial was more
likely than a Parliamentary Inquiry to produce all relevant
evidence in an orderly and legal manner, and to end in a clear-
cut verdict. It was currently believed that Lord George con-

[1] Hardwicke to Solicitor-General, 16 Aug. 1759; Yorke, *Hardwicke*, ii. 234.
Hardwicke's summary was accurate and fair as far as it goes, but it does not
include all the relevant facts as the court martial produced them.
[2] Sackville to (?), 10 Sept. 1759; Clements, *Germain Papers*, ii. 138 ff.
[3] Sackville to Bute, 9 Sept. 1759; *HMC, Stop. Sack.* i. 315, 316.

sulted Lord Mansfield and received that distinguished authority's opinion that a court martial would exonerate him, and
the story is supported by the facts that after the court's adverse
decision Lord George was very bitter against Lord Mansfield.
Lord George must have believed he would be acquitted or he
would not have insisted on a trial, since he recognized that:
'. . . every motive but that of justice must weigh against me'.[1]

Lord Holdernesse replied on 10 September that: '. . . as you
did not demand a Court Martial while in Germany, it must
now be deferred until the officers capable of giving evidence can
leave their posts',[2] a position also taken by Ligonier. Then it
developed that the Solicitor-General and Attorney-General
Charles Pratt were dubious whether a court martial could
properly be held in England under British auspices. No British
charges had been brought against Lord George, and if
Ferdinand's remarks were formal charges they had not been
made within British jurisdiction. Yorke and Pratt advised
Holdernesse that: 'His Lordship, having no other Offices or
commission in the Army, besides those abovementioned, is now
totally removed from all Military Appointments' and therefore
it was doubtful whether he was eligible for or subject to a court
martial.[3] It was an interesting piece of legal logic that Lord
George would make use of in a later case. It would permit the
accusers of any officer to avoid having to prove their accusations
before a court martial, provided they did not make their vili-
fications in the form of official charges, and provided the officer
were promptly dismissed from his commissions.

Lord George protested, but he got small sympathy from some
of his former powerful friends. Lord Ligonier, who had once
been pliable in Lord George's hands, but who was also an uncle
of Captain Ligonier, now '. . . bluntly declared that if Lord
George desired a court martial "he had best go seek it in
Germany" '.[4] But the legal minds were having second thoughts.
On 12 January Yorke and Pratt sent another memorandum to
the Ministry with the conclusion that Lord George could
properly be tried by a court martial, provided he was first

[1] Sackville to Viscount Bateman, brother-in-law, 18 Sept. 1759; Coventry, p. 282.
[2] Holdernesse to Sackville, 10 Sept. 1759; HMC, Stop. Sack. i. 316; also PRO,
SP 41/23, no. 289.
[3] 14 Dec. 1759; PRO, SP 41/23, no. 301.
[4] Walpole to Mann, 13 Sept. 1759; Toynbee, iv. 300; also Manners, p. 85.

officially charged by British authorities with disobedience of orders while under the direct jurisdiction of the king. But no one except Lord George seemed in any haste, despite his urging that the court be convened while the army in Germany was in winter quarters and its officers consequently available as witnesses.[1]

On 22 January, nearly six months after Minden, the king finally directed that a court martial be held, but it was another month before proceedings began by placing Lord George under technical arrest.[2] Meanwhile, the affair had developed aspects worthy of *Alice in Wonderland*. The legal advisers of the Crown instructed Lord Holdernesse that since no charges had yet been brought against Lord George, Holdernesse should write to the accused and ask him what charges he proposed to defend himself against at the court martial. Holdernesse did so, and Lord George replied: 'I can in answer only repeat my humble request to his Majesty that he would direct me to be legally prosecuted for whatever crime I may have been thought guilty of. . . . As I am conscious of no Crime . . . I have nothing so much at heart as the hearing my accusation and the knowing my accusers that I may be permitted to offer such proofs in justification of my conduct as may confute the many expressions thrown upon my character.'[3]

Somehow the contending parties managed to extricate themselves from this legalistic tangle,[4] but even after the trial was well under way the Ministry lawyers had further professional doubts whether it could be continued without a new warrant, since the Mutiny Bill had expired and had not yet been renewed by Parliament. To meet that new crisis of jurisprudence the Secretary at War '. . . proposed that His Majesty should sign a Special Warrant authorizing the Court Martial to continue their Proceedings'.[5]

During those months after Minden, Lord George was without standing in army and government, a pariah in society, and almost a man without a country. The king stripped him of every

[1] 12 Jan. 1760; PRO, SP 41/23, no. 311.

[2] Walpole to Mann, 28 Feb. 1760; Toynbee, iv. 361.

[3] Sackville to Holdernesse, 17 Jan. 1760; original letter in Sackville's hand is PRO, SP 41/23, no. 316.   [4] PRO, SP 41/23, no. 311.

[5] An undated 'Memorandum of Attorney and Solicitor General' in PRO, SP 41/23, no. 29.

commission, honour, and emolument. On 10 September, six
weeks after Minden, he had received a brief communication
from Lord Barrington: 'I have received his Majesty's command
to let you know that he has no further occasion for your services
as Lieutenant General and Colonel of the Dragoon Guards.'[1]
Horace Walpole characteristically speculated on the pecuniary
aspects of Lord George's downfall: '. . . all that can be taken
from him is his regiment, about 2000 a year; his command in
Germany about ten pounds a day; his Lieutenant Generalcy
of Ordnance about 1200 a year and a fort of 300 pounds. He
retains his patent place in Ireland, about 1200 a year and 200
of his wife and himself. With his parts and ambitions it cannot
end here; he calls himself ruined but when Parliament meets he
will probably attempt some sort of revenge.'[2]

Public opinion had long since decided that Lord George was
guilty of disobedience of orders, and that he had disobeyed from
cowardice. Captain Cartwright was one of those who had said
freely about London that Lord George was: '. . . a damned
chicken-hearted soldier—in short, Sir, Lord George was a stink-
ing coward'. There were even suggestions that he had been
bribed by the French. He was burnt in effigy,[3] and by the
irrationality of human hatred was accused of past crimes
probably fictional and certainly irrelevant, including sodomy.[4]
A spate of pamphlets, a few defending him but most denouncing
him and crying for his blood, flooded London. His case engrossed conversation at every social level throughout the winter.[5]
According to Tobias Smollett: '. . . an abhorrence and detesta-
tion of Lord George Sackville as a coward and a traitor became
the universal passion, which acted by contagion, infecting all
degrees of people from the cottage to the throne'.[6] While crying
out to be heard,[7] he was declared worthy of the same fate as

---

[1] Barrington to Sackville, 10 Sept. 1759; HMC, Stop. Sack. i. 316; also PRO,
SP 41/23, no. 291.

[2] Walpole to Mann, 10 Sept. 1759; Toynbee, iv. 300.

[3] 'Poor Lord George! He was burnt this week at Salisbury' (Dodington to
Shirley, 15 Sept. 1759; HMC, v, vi, Matcham, p. 41).

[4] In a scurrilous pamphlet, the author of which was thought to be John Wilkes.

[5] 'What engrosses the most conversation here is the tryall of L. G.S.' (James
Hamilton to ?, 18 Mar. 1760; HMC, Laing, ii (1925), 428).

[6] Smollett, v. 160.

[7] 'As to the unfortunate Lord . . . who offended the great man that has lately been
honoured with a collar of St. George, he leads a most weary life, for more pamphlets

Admiral Byng, who had been shot, as Voltaire put it, in order to encourage the other admirals. Lord George's pamphlets in his own defence did not help and in some circles were '... thought to make against him'.[1] Every Englishman with a hate or frustration could give it an outlet by venting his anger on Lord George; if psychiatrists had then existed they would have invented a word for it.

Only a few men had the courage to maintain that at least the man should be heard before he was condemned. The old Duke of Dorset was so stricken that he retired to Knole and, like one of his forebears in the age of Cromwell, hardly ever left his doorstep again. 'I pity his father, who has been so unhappy in his sons, who loved this so much, and who had such fair prospects for him', wrote the usually unsentimental Horace Walpole; adding that 'The Duchess imputes it all to malice, the Duke sinks under it'.[2] Lord George himself put up so brave a front that a few aristocrats were won to admiration: 'ld. G.S. and his Dear Wife are at Knole & appear in prodigious good spirits', the Duchess of Northumberland reported to her diary, 'just as if nothing had happened. How is that possible? Innocent or guilty his situation is most deplorable & I shd. think he must feel it immensely.'[3] Pitt, who had become one of Lord George's bitterest enemies, wrote with sarcasm that to have 'shown his face at the opera' was the final gesture of Lord George's 'heroic assurance'.[4] All England awaited the court martial.

of abuse appear in a week than I ever saw kites flying in a summer evening in our fields. But they contain little or nothing, and the worst of it is that he is more cruelly dealt with by his advocates than by his adversaries. . . . This man has been condemned and punished too while he is crying out to be heard' (Campbell to ?, 29 Sept. 1759; *HMC, Laing*, ii. 425).

[1] 'Lord George Sackville's reputation is at present, I think, lower than ever, since the publication of his letter to Colonel Fitzroy, and his answer to it, and the declaration of Captain Smith: the facts which are there brought to light are thought to make against him' (Charles Jenkinson to George Grenville, 22 Sept. 1759; *Grenville Papers*, i. 327).

[2] Walpole to Mason, 29 Aug. 1759; Toynbee, iv. 296; Walpole to Selwyn, 29 Aug. 1759; Toynbee, iv. 298.

[3] *Diaries of the Duchess of Northumberland*, 12 Oct. 1759, p. 12.

[4] Chatham to his wife, 19 Nov. 1759; *Life and Letters of Lady Harriet Elliot*.

VI

COURT MARTIAL

HAD Lord George possessed the advantages of historians writing after the fact, he would have seen that he had almost no chance of being exonerated by a court martial. But though he lacked those advantages, he was an astute politician when pride did not obscure his judgement, and he should have recognized how poor his chances were.

Failure of the court to find him guilty would outrage public opinion; failure to sentence him severely would bring down the wrath of the king upon the judges. Even the finding of any extenuating circumstances would reflect discredit on Duke Ferdinand, to whom King and Ministry were heavily committed. A verdict favourable to Lord George might even weaken the alliance against France, lose the war, and discredit the Ministry. The Opposition had nothing to gain by defending so unpopular a man, who was after all an appointee of the Ministry and therefore to be attacked, not defended. Popular opinion was demanding the death sentence, and any man in politics would be risking his own position if he opposed such vehement national emotion. Some years later, wise after the event, Walpole wrote: 'The obvious consequence of a trial was condemnation.'[1]

The judges of the court seem to have made every effort to be fair-minded, but could hardly avoid being influenced by such strong mass opinion. It would have been difficult, too, to find appropriate military judges who had no personal affiliations with men who had already declared against Lord George. The court consisted of eleven Lieutenant-Generals, four Major-Generals, and Charles Gould, acting Judge Advocate. Its chairman, Lord Albemarle, 'was a favourite of the Duke of Cumberland, who was no friend of Lord George. . . . General Cholmondley, with Lord Albemarle the chief examinants, was also much attached to the Duke of Cumberland. . . . To General Balfour, nominated one of his judges, Lord George objected on the score

---

[1] Walpole, *Last Ten Years*, ii. 416.

of former enmity with him',[1] but on the king's order General Balfour continued to sit with the court. Several of its other members were friends of the Marquis of Granby. Among the crucial witnesses Lieutenant-Colonel Ligonier was a nephew of Lord Ligonier, Lieutenant-Colonel Fitzroy was a brother of the adverse Duke of Grafton, Captain Wintzegerode was a German officer long and closely attached to Duke Ferdinand, Colonel Sloper, whose testimony would prove the most damaging of all, had been one of the officers most openly critical of Lord George.

Apart from the king's insistence on the continuation of General Balfour, the court martial seems to have given Lord George every consideration. In late January the Deputy Judge Advocate invited him to name any witnesses he wished the court to hear in his behalf. Lord George submitted the names of eighteen British officers to be summoned from Germany, and all were secured.[2] During the proceedings Lord George was permitted to question directly and freely all the witnesses before the court, and even to interrupt the proceedings, and he made the most of those opportunities.

The trial began on 7 March 1760. Walpole's comments were echoed by others:

Lord George's own behaviour was most extraordinary. He had undoubtedly trusted to the superiority of his parts for extricating him. Most men in his situation would have adapted those parts to the conciliating the favour of his judges, to drawing the witnesses into contradictions, to misleading and bewildering the court, and to throwing the most spectacular colours on his own conduct, without offending the parties declared against him—

a statement that illuminates Hanoverian attitudes toward legal procedures.

Very different was the conduct of Lord George. From the outset and during the whole process, he assumed a dictatorial style to the court, and treated the inferiority of their capacities as he would have done if sitting amongst them. He browbeat the witnesses, gave the lie to Sloper, and used the judge-advocate, though a very clever man, with contempt. Nothing was timid, nothing humble, in his behaviour. His replies were quick and spirited. He prescribed to the

---

[1] PRO, SP 41/23, 20/15; also Walpole, *Last Ten Years*, ii. 417.
[2] Original in Sackville's hand is PRO, SP 41/23, no. 322; also Sackville to Gould, 27 Jan. 1760; *HMC, Stop. Sack*. i. 318.

court and they acquiesced. An instant of such resolution at Minden had established his character for ever.[1]

Thomas Gray the poet corroborated: 'The unembarrass'd countenance, the looks of soveraign contempt & superiority, that his Lp. Bestow'd on his Accusers during the tryal, were the admiration [i.e. astonishment] of all; but his usual Talents & Art did not appear, in short his Cause would not support him.'[2] Lord George's bearing may have reminded some men of a comment passed on his Sackville grandfather: 'who thought he might do anything, yet was never to blame'.

Some ground was cleared at the beginning of the trial. Prince Ferdinand's account of the battle had been printed in the *Gentleman's Magazine* and *The Dublin Journal*, and two charges advanced by Ferdinand were dismissed as not substantiated. One was that Lord George had failed to have the cavalry saddled at the proper hour before the battle; the other that he was late in his own arrival on the scene. On the other hand, Lord George did not challenge the fact that his commission directed him 'to obey such Orders and Directions as should be given him by the said Prince Ferdinand', and he concurred that orders to attack were successively delivered to him by several aides of the prince.

In a pamphlet published soon after the trial, the evidence was reported as close to verbatim as the absence of modern shorthand permitted.[3] Colonel Mauvillon, an officer on the staff of the prince, stated that the order sent to Lord George was to 'advance and charge'. Captain Wintzegerode testified that he was sent with that message:

. . . that he found Lord George at the head of the first Line of Cavalry. He communicated to him his Serene Highness's orders, as they had been given to him by the Prince. Lord Sackville seemed not to understand them, and asked how it was to be done? He endeavored to explain them to him, as well as he could. He made him understand that he was to pass with the Cavalry between the trees, which he saw upon his left; that he would then come upon the Heath, where he was to form with the Cavalry, to advance in order to sustain

---

[1] Walpole, *Last Ten Years*, ii. 430.

[2] Gray, *Corresp.* ii, no. 311, pp. 667, 668.

[3] *Proceedings of a General Court Martial . . . upon the Trial of Lord George Sackville*, London, 1760 (Bodleian Library).

our Infantry, which he thought was already engaged with the
Enemy. Lord George Sackville asked him several questions, how
that was to be done? The Witness then repeated what he had been
saying. Lord George Sackville then turned towards the Officers
attending him, and the Witness, firmly persuaded that he was going
to give the Orders for advancing, went to rejoin his Serene Highness.

Captain Wintzegerode further testified that on his way back
to the prince he met Lieutenant-Colonel Fitzroy coming toward
him at full gallop, '. . . who asked him, why the Cavalry of the
Right Wing did not advance, and gave him to understand, as
he passed him, that his Serene Highness was in the greatest
impatience about it'. Both men hurried toward the cavalry and
found it motionless. Fitzroy went to repeat to Lord George the
message to attack; Wintzegerode went to Lord Granby, 'who
he found at the Head of the second Line of Cavalry, in the
same position as he found him when he passed his Lordship
first'.

Questioned by the court and by Lord George, Captain Wintzegerode said: 'he did not see any reason to hinder . . . the Cavalry
from executing the Orders', and that after he found Lord Granby
the second time, Granby moved his own line of cavalry immediately forward through the trees to the heath.

Lieutenant-Colonel Ligonier testified that he too brought
orders to Lord George to advance with the cavalry: '. . . he delivered him his orders, to which his Lordship made no answer, but
turning about to his troops ordered swords to be drawn and
march; which they did, moving a few paces from the right
forward. He then told his Lordship it was to the left he was to
march.' At that point, said Ligonier, Colonel Fitzroy galloped
up and also delivered the prince's orders for the British cavalry
to advance. Lord George said to Ligonier that the orders were
contradictory. Ligonier answered that: 'they differed only in
numbers, that the destination of the march was the same, to
the left'. 'His Lordship then asked him if he would lead the
column; he said he could not conduct them properly but that
if his Lordship would trust him he would do his best. That was
all that passed between Lord George and Him.' Asked by the
court whether he had insisted to Lord George that his orders
had been correctly delivered, Colonel Ligonier replied: 'Yes,
peremptorily', and that the terrain the cavalry was ordered to

move over was, after passing through an open grove, 'a very fine plain'.

Lieutenant-Colonel the Honourable Charles Fitzroy testified in terms virtually identical with those that had been published in his reply of 3 August to Lord George. When asked whether he had carried any order to Lord Granby that day, he answered: 'Yes—some time after. . . . His Serene Highness said he thought it was not even then too late for the cavalry to advance. The Deponent asked the Prince whether he would have him go and fetch the Cavalry? The answer was Yes, and to deliver the order to Lord Granby. The Deponent found Lord Granby on the enemy's side of the little wood . . . he delivered the Prince's order to Lord Granby, who asked him why he did not deliver it to Lord George Sackville; he told him the Prince had sent the Deponent to him. . . .'

Lieutenant-Colonel Robert Sloper, commanding Bland's regiment of Dragoon Guards, testified that Captain Wintzegerode delivered his orders to Lord George first in French and then in English. Lord George Sackville had said: 'Mais comment?' Captain Wintzegerode had said, moving his hand: 'You must pass through those trees, you will then arrive upon the heath, you will then see our infantry and the enemy.' Captain Wintzegerode then left Lord George Sackville. The Deponent heard his Lordship say: 'I do not comprehend how the movement is to be made.' Being so near his Lordship the Deponent answered: 'It seemed very clear to him, it was to be made to the left by the right wing of the cavalry.' His Lordship said he would make it. For a quarter of an hour after that he did not see his Lordship. His Lordship then returning to the squadron . . . said: 'Colonel, put your regiment in motion.' The Deponent said: 'My Lord, to the left?' His Lordship answered: 'No, straight ahead.' The regiment moved a very few paces. Colonel Ligonier arrived; he said to Lord George Sackville that it was the Duke's orders that he immediately advance with the cavalry under his command and that the movement was to the left. The Deponent then spoke to Captain Ligonier and said: 'For God's sake, sir, repeat your orders to that man (meaning Lord George Sackville), that he may not pretend not to understand them, for it is near half an hour that he received his orders to advance, and yet we are still here . . . but you see what condition he is in.'

The court asked Colonel Sloper: 'What did [you] observe in Lord George when [you] said to Captain Ligonier: "but

you see the condition he is in"?' Colonel Sloper answered:
'Deponent's opinion is that Lord George was alarmed to a
very great degree. When his Lordship ordered the advance he
seemed in the utmost confusion . . . the original orders were to
the left, and the orders his Lordship gave him were "to move the
regiment straight forward".'

Walpole wrote of the Marquis of Granby that in his testimony he 'palliated or suppressed whatever might load the
prisoner', but Granby's statements corroborated those quoted
and added another incident. When Granby received orders
directly from Prince Ferdinand he led his own line of cavalry
through the wood to the attack. Lord George later followed him
with the first line of cavalry, but called to Granby to await him.
Granby said he rode up to Lord George and 'acquainted him
that the Duke's orders were to march up directly; Lord George
Sackville said he was only forming the troops into line.' Granby
said he replied that as his own orders directly from the prince
were to advance, he would order his troops to march on, 'which
they immediately did, with myself 50 or 60 yards in front.
. . . After they had gone about three or four hundred yards he
found his cavalry behind him had halted; he sent immediately
the Major of the Brigade with orders to them to advance as fast
as possible, and to know how they came to halt without his
orders. He was informed that they were halted from the right
by Lord George's orders.' Granby testified that he immediately
gave his own troops orders to continue the advance and not to
halt 'unless by his own orders or by General Elliot, in consequence of orders from him'.

Lord George claimed, though with dubious relevance to the
issue, that on 31 July Prince Ferdinand had given him no intimation of the probability of a battle on the following day, or, on
the morning of the battle, any idea of his intended plan of
action. Lord George said he did not approve the position his
British cavalry were ordered to take that morning, as it exposed
them to the potential fire of several enemy battalions. He stated
that the wood through which the cavalry was ordered to pass
appeared to him so thick as to be impassable, and that it was
only when he rode off to consult the prince about his orders
that he saw the wood to be more open than he had thought. He
maintained that the orders delivered by the various messengers

of the prince were contradictory and unclear, and that when he reached the prince to question him about them the prince gave no sign of being annoyed. Lord George explained that he had halted Granby's troops in order to 'dress the line'; that he had not thereafter pursued the French because no pursuit was ordered or feasible; the battle was already won and the French back under the protection of their guns in Minden.

The court martial ended on 5 April 1760, but before then most men had concluded that Lord George would be found guilty. His old school friend and partner in baiting the Irish Parliament, Primate Stone, still in Dublin, 'retired from town, unable to stand the shock expected by the next post'. Chancellor Howes of Ireland, who reported this to Bubb Dodington two weeks before the final evidence could have reached him, added: 'My inclinations are ever in favour of Innocence, nor could I account for his pressing the trial on any principle but that of conscious innocence on his part.'[1] But when all the evidence was known to him, Chancellor Howes changed his mind, and offered an explanation more plausible than most of those being bandied about: 'Lord G's conduct would be unaccountable did not experience prove that men may deceive themselves in their own affairs, and prove that those of the greatest abilities are most apt to do so, by trusting more to their own powers than the merits of their particular case. Be his fate deserved or not, I feel for him and his family, but presume his dismission may be forgot, and he again become considerable in another walk.'[2]

Walpole offered a variant explanation: 'His real contribution, I believe, was this: he had a high and bold spirit, till danger came extraordinarily near. Then his judgment was fascinated—yet even then he seems not to have lost a certain presence of mind. His quickness in distinguishing a trifling contradiction in the message delivered by two boys in not precisely the same terms, showed that all his senses were not lost.'[3]

Major-General Joseph Yorke and John Almon, the publisher-chronicler, thought Lord George's conduct at Minden was the natural outcome of his previous enmity with Prince Ferdinand,

[1] Howes to Dodington, 21 Mar. 1760; *HMC, Var. Coll., Wykeham Martin*, p. 74.
[2] Howes to Dodington, 17 Apr. 1760; ibid.
[3] Walpole, *Last Ten Years*, ii. 366.

though, as Yorke pointed out, that theory did not justify Lord George's disobedience of orders.[1] Edward Thurlow, later Lord Chancellor, championed Lord George at the time of the court martial, and many years later commented that 'Prince Ferdinand must have been drunk and Lord George the only man who knew anything about the matter'—an explanation too fantastic to have been seriously put by its beetle-browed and dogmatic author.

Lord George's final speech before the court on 3 April seemed eloquent to many.[2] All England awaited the verdict, for '. . . what engrosses the most conversation here is the tryall of L.G.S.'[3] For disobedience of orders on the battlefield many an ordinary soldier had been summarily shot. Officers usually got off with their lives, but were declared incompetent to serve king and country thereafter in any civil or military capacity. The disgrace concomitant with such a sentence was almost as painful as the penalty, and the man's career was ruined for ever.

In Lord George's case there were special considerations. Except for the Minden episode his official military record was spotless. He had high parliamentary abilities and had been considered for ministerial appointment by two governments. He was the son of a powerful and respected duke and had connexions with half a dozen of England's and Scotland's leading families. The Prince of Wales, Lord Bute, and the Leicester House clique, which would assume power when the king died, probably exerted powerful though discreet pressure for an easy sentence. And there were many who wondered whether there were not more in Lord George's conduct than met the eye, or whether Prince Ferdinand had not spoken and acted too quickly. Though such considerations did not influence the court's verdict, they were certainly not ignored in the sentence it recommended. 'It was understood', wrote Lord Shelburne much later, 'that his life was spared out of regard to his family, and to the earnest intercession of his father.'[4]

---

[1] Yorke to Hardwicke, 14 July 1760; Yorke, *Hardwicke*, iii. 245.
[2] *HMC*, v, *Cholmondley*, i (1876), 360. The Cholmondley papers include seven letters from Thomas Cooper discussing the court martial. They are presumably now at Condover Hall, Shropshire, but copies in whole or part are in BM, Add. MSS. 33588 and 34121. [3] James Hamilton to ?, 18 Mar. 1760; *HMC, Laing*, ii. 428.
[4] Fitzmaurice, *Shelburne*, i. 355.

'This court is of the opinion that Lord George Sackville is guilty of having disobeyed the order of Prince Ferdinand of Brunswick when he was, by his Commission and Instructions, directed to obey him as commander-in-chief, according to the rules of war, and it is of the further opinion that the said Lord George Sackville is, and is hereby adjudged, unfit to serve his Majesty in any military capacity whatsoever.'

A few moderate and humane men were relieved. Horace Walpole wrote that: 'Lord George's sentence, after all the annunciations of how terrible it was, is ended in proclaiming him unfit for the King's service—very moderate in comparison of what was intended and desired, and truly not very severe considering what was proved.'[1] 'I am very glad to hear Lord George came off so well', Walpole's friend Montagu replied.[2] Gray the poet reported: 'The old Pundles that sat on Ld. G: Sackville (for they were all such, but two, Gen. Cholmondley, & Ld. Albemarle) have at last hammer'd out their sentence. . . . It is said that 9 were for death, but as two-thirds must be unanimous, some of them came over to the merciful side. I do not affirm the truth of this.' If the report were true, Lord George was saved from death by one vote in fifteen. Gray added, referring to the king, '. . . be that as it will, every body blames *somebody*, who has been out of all temper & intractable during the whole time'.[3]

The king had indeed been determined that Lord George should be severely punished, and was angry that the sentence was not more drastic. 'The King confirmed the sentence, but dissatisfied that it had gone no further, he could not resist the ungenerous impulse of loading it with every insult in his power.'[4] He stripped Lord George of every remaining court affiliation; forbade him attendance at court, and ordered military officers

---

[1] Walpole to Montagu, 19 Apr. 1760; *Walpole Corresp.*, Yale edition, *Montagu*, i. 278.

[2] Montagu to Walpole, 19 Apr. 1760; ibid., p. 281.

[3] Dobree, *Gray Letters*, ii, letter 311, pp. 667, 668.

[4] Walpole, *Last Ten Years*, ii. 431. The king's orders of 23 Apr. 1760 read: 'It is His Majesty's Pleasure that the above Sentence be given out in Public Orders, That Officers being convinced that neither High Birth nor Great Employments can Shelter Offenses of such a Nature; and that Seeing they are Subject to Censures much worse than Death, to a Man who has any Sense of Honour, They may avoid the Fatal Consequences arising from Disobedience of Orders' (PRO, SP 41/23, 20/15).

to read the court's verdict and sentence, with further derogatory statements, before every regiment in the British Army, at home and abroad. Lord George's former friends and sponsors, Pitt and Ligonier, drafted the king's statement.[1] As for the Duke of Newcastle, that old family friend and former political ally, he promptly wrote to the Marquis of Granby, Lord George's successor in Germany: 'I send in confidence, by the King's command, a copy of the sentence of the court martial, so short of what we had reason to expect, and of the merits of the question.'[2] Ten days later he wrote again:

You will receive orders by the post to publish the sentence and the orders *at the head of the line*. That particularly ordered by the King. I hope Prince Ferdinand will see by this that whatever *legerte* there may have been in the sentence of the court martial, His Majesty by the Advice of his Ministers, has taken care to have his sense of it expressed in such a manner and published everywhere so as there can remain no doubt about the King's, and the Nation's mind upon the subject. . . . I have taken some pains in this affair.[3]

The king had further ways of making clear his opinion, and the War Office apparently concurred. Of the witnesses adverse to Lord George, Lord Granby had been immediately made Commander-in-Chief of the British forces in Germany and was soon made Master-General of Ordnance. Lieutenant-Colonel Sloper, who had been a Captain at Minden, was shortly promoted again, and ended his career as a full General. Lieutenant-Colonel Charles Fitzroy, also a Captain at Minden, was promptly appointed aide-de-camp to the king himself.[4] Lieutenant-Colonel Edward Ligonier became a Lieutenant-General in 1777 and other adverse witnesses were promoted or otherwise advanced. Prince Ferdinand was made Knight of the Garter and loaded with presents and praise. On the other hand, Captain Smith, who had been one of Lord George's principal supporting witnesses, 'had no sooner finished his evidence, but was forbid to mount guard, & order'd to sell out'.[5] Even subalterns under Lord George were made to suffer, or so they believed, for personal loyalty to him.

---

[1] Whitworth, *Field Marshal Lord Ligonier*, p. 323.
[2] Newcastle to Granby, 15 Apr. 1760; *HMC, Rutland*, ii. 205.
[3] Newcastle to Granby, 29 Apr. 1760; ibid. The italics are Newcastle's.
[4] Coventry, p. 16.
[5] Dobree, *Gray Letters*, ii, no. 311, pp. 667, 668.

Of all the comments on Lord George's disaster two are the most striking. One came from his political opponent Lord Shelburne: 'I do not conceive that anything but the checks which stopped his military career, could have prevented his being Prime Minister.'[1] The other was the remark ascribed to Lord George's brother, Lord John Sackville, leading under supervision a shabby and melancholy life in Switzerland, when he first heard of Lord George's behaviour at Minden: 'I always told you that my brother George was no better than myself.'[2]

[1] Fitzmaurice, *Shelburne*, i. 345.   [2] Ibid.

VII

PURGATORY

THE fall of Lord George was 'prodigious', for its political and social penalties were as painful as the military verdict. '. . . you will perceive the measure of Lord George's fate is not yet full. I take it for granted that he will be expelled from the House of Commons. When he went there, he went smiling up to the Speaker, who made him a very cold bow, and turning to his son, who was standing by him, said, "Is that man mad to come to this place?".'[1] According to Walpole: 'I, Sir John Irvine and Mr. Brand [were] the only three men in England who . . . dared to speak or sit by Lord George in public places.'[2] 'So finishes a career of a man who was within ten minutes of being the first man in the Profession in the Kingdom.'[3]

Never in their long history had the Sackvilles suffered such a blow to pride and honour. 'The poor old Duke can hardly bear the sight of anybody', according to Thomas Gray,[4] and he lived out the last five years of his life in almost solitary retirement at Knole. But there was a difference between father and son, for though Lord Shelburne wrote that after the verdict 'Lord George sank into obscurity and general contempt. No man would be seen to speak to him in the House of Commons',[5] Shelburne was misleading. Lord George was indeed held in contempt, but it was not universal, and obscurity was the last word to describe him in the aftermath of Minden. Everyone watched him and everyone speculated about him.

Not even the king could prevent Lord George from remaining a Sackville, and Knole provided a social fortress where a disgraced soldier could lick his wounds, gather his few loyal supporters about him, receive the curious as regally as ever, and plan his strategies for rehabilitation. The duke might be broken

[1] Rigby to Bedford, 2 Apr. 1760; Russell, *Bedford Corresp.* ii. 413, 414.
[2] Walpole, quoted by Coventry.
[3] Cox to Weston, 13 Sept. 1759; *HMC*, x. i, *Eglinton* (1885), p. 317.
[4] Dobree, *Gray Letters*, ii, letter 311, pp. 667, 668.
[5] Fitzmaurice, *Shelburne*, i. 356.

in health and spirit, but Lord George showed no outward lack
of either. If the capacity to face social obloquy and the destruction of a career with an outward smile can be called moral
courage, Lord George was, despite the verdict, a brave man.
'With his parts and ambitions', Walpole had written soon after
Minden, 'it cannot end here.'

'. . . you may think perhaps he intends to go abroad, & hide
his head, *au contraire*, all the world visits him on his condemnation. He says himself, his situation is better, than ever it was, the
Scotch have all along affected to take him under their protection; his wife has been daily walking with Lady Augusta', wrote
Gray soon after the verdict. This was a distortion of the other
side of the medal; Lord George was 'in Coventry' with eight-
tenths of England; few men were ever more widely scorned and
socially ostracized. It was not easy for any man under those
conditions to sally forth and meet the overwhelming enemy in
its very heartland of town and court society, but Lord George
attempted it. 'Lord G. S. was last Saturday at the opera, some
say with great effrontery—others with great dejection', Laurence
Sterne reported two weeks after the trial had ended.[1]

Some had thought Lord George had married a little beneath
him, but in this ordeal the former Diana Sambrooke proved not
only a loyal but a surprisingly valuable helpmate. Influential
society women had always liked her, and now she carried herself with such gallantry that they began to admire her as well.
Lord George's wife seen walking in the garden of Leicester
House with the elegant Duchess of Devonshire[2] promised well
for Lord George when, in the eager fullness of time, the Prince
of Wales should become king. Social rehabilitation was a slow
process but steady. By the beginning of 1762 Lady Sarah Lennox,
whom George III had admired with an undemanding passion
rare in princes, recorded another stage in Lady George's progress:
'I was at Lady G. Sackville's last night, & played at quadrille
with Ly. Eliza. Keppel, Ly. Car. Russell, & Lord Carlisle, it
was vastly pleasant I assure you.'[3]

Neither ministers nor leaders of the Opposition could meet

---

[1] Sterne to Stephen Croft, about 1 May 1760; L. P. Curtis, *Sterne Letters*, p. 107.
[2] Dobree, *Gray Corresp.* ii, letter 311, pp. 667, 668.
[3] Lady Lennox to Lady Susan Fox-Strangeways, early 1762; Ilchester and
Stavordale, *Life of Lady Sarah Lennox*, i. 119.

Lord George at an evening soirée and then refuse to recognize him in Westminster or Whitehall the following morning. His wife's social conquests were perhaps more immediately success-ful than his own efforts to recapture the political ground he had lost. Three years after Minden he was still a favourite whipping-boy for John Wilkes's wit in the *North Briton*. 'His *bons mots* are all over the town, but too gross, I think, to repeat; the chief are at the expense of poor Lord George.'[1] But Lord George per-severed 'till men grew weary of showing him contempt which did not Hash him'.[2]

Whatever the failings of the future George III, lack of loyalty to his supporters was seldom among them. Immediately after the Minden verdict Lady Yarmouth of the Leicester House inner circle told the Duke of Newcastle in confidence that the prince intended to continue to receive Lord George. Since no one with Lady Yarmouth's experience would tell anything in confidence to the Duke of Newcastle without the expectation of publicity, her words were probably a planned message from prince to king, and were thus interpreted by George II, who promptly received the news from the duke. The king ordered the Lord Chamberlain to notify the prince that since he had prohibited Lord George from appearing at the Court of St. James, he expected the prince to ban him from Leicester House, 'and lest that should not be sufficient the Vice Chamberlain was sent to acquaint Lord Bute with it'.[3]

The prince's reaction was a mixture of defiance and bad prophecy. He wrote to Lord Bute: 'I think it most injurious that I should receive such a message. I am not under the King's roof and therefore undoubtedly have the right of admitting whom I please without H.M. leave; this harsh affair will be of no bad consequence to Ld. George, on the contrary I think it will open people's eyes, and show that someone is both judge and party.'[4] The prince continued to receive Lord George, but he soon discovered that he could do little to help him. A prince who could defy a king could not openly defy popular sentiment. He continued to patronize Lord George, but more and more cautiously. Even that discreet support troubled some of the

[1] Walpole to Hertford, 18 Nov. 1763; Toynbee, v. 389.
[2] Fitzmaurice, *Shelburne*, i. 356.   [3] 18 Apr. 1760.
[4] 23 Apr. 1760.

prince's advisers, and it was a cause of further bitterness between himself and the king.[1]

Those few men who were openly sympathetic with Lord George could offer him little more than moral support, but he must have welcomed a downright letter from Colonel the Honourable James Murray, serving under General Amherst in Canada: 'I have carefully read the court martial relating to the affair of Minden, and my garrison have studied it, and I may venture to affirm, that there is not an officer in it who does not blush that such a sentence should have been pronounced by a British court. . . . A clear surprize, by the Eternal God . . . everybody will allow, a few months hence, that the commander of the British cavalry acted more like an officer the day of Minden than His Serene Highness did.'[2]

Disgrace sometimes makes a man more sympathetic with the troubles of others. Hugo, a Hanoverian who had been his personal aide in Germany, wrote to Lord George that because of their former affiliation all advancement was closed to him in the British Army, and asked Lord George for help in getting service with the King of Denmark or Sardinia. Lord George replied that all his influence had vanished since 'the resentment of his Majesty has been pleased to show against me and you. . . . On my part I must have recourse to patience till time shall alter my circumstances. . . . I thank God I have sufficient for myself and my friends, and I do insist upon it, if you have the least regard or friendship for me, that you call upon me for whatever may be necessary.'[3] Such words are easily said, but Lord George followed the fortunes of Hugo until Sir Henry Erskine assured him some three months later: 'Your friend can expect no public relief during the war, but a private one may probably reach him through a secret friend.'[4]

One can only guess at what happened to the inner spirit of Lord George when he fell so rapidly from grace. A professional soldier denied for ever a career in which he had risen so close to the top; a promising statesman refused admission to court and shunned by members of Parliament who had once courted his

[1] Walpole, *Last Ten Years*, ii. 400.
[2] Murray to Sackville, 14 July 1760; *HMC, Stop. Sack*. ii. 269; also Clements, *Germain Papers*, ii. 20/49.
[3] Sackville to Hugo, 27 Aug. 1760; *HMC, Stop. Sack*. i. 44.
[4] Erskine to Sackville, 11 Dec. 1760; *HMC, Stop. Sack*. i. 45.

favour—yet still as proud as Lucifer and, outwardly at least, as sure of his superiority as was Milton's Satan. Only a man of unusual sweetness and spiritual strength could have survived such a débâcle emotionally unscarred. Lord George was no such rare spirit. The ordeal left its marks on his character, and perhaps accentuated traits he had kept hidden and controlled. He maintained, most of the time, a stoical front, but there were occasions in those first years after Minden when querulous complaint and bitterness pushed through the façade. An egoism never tempered by serious reversals was now doubly vulnerable. Much of his conduct after Minden can be explained by the assumption that Minden curdled whatever milk of human kindness he had possessed into cynicism and the urge for revenge. But that would be too simple an explanation to account for some episodes in his later life: men do not change their characters overnight, and so complicated a man demands more complicated analysis.

Whatever Lord George's inner fortitudes and from whatever strengths derived, they did not prevent him from cherishing resentments against the men who had been involved in his downfall. Though Granby had done his best to avoid damaging testimony, Lord George never forgave him. When Granby died, a member of the Ministry, a decade later, Lord George wrote of that able and generous-spirited soldier and statesman: 'The death of Lord Granby will, as you say, be of service to the Ministry in point of votes, but of greater service to the army. If real business is to be done what good could ever have happened under such a director?'[1] He never ceased to hate Duke Ferdinand and in 1762 wrote to Irwin with regard to the duke's latest military success: '. . . his Serene Highness will be at the summit of human happiness, that is, so far as so wicked a mind can taste anything that resembles human happiness',[2] and later references were no less bitter.

Most men thus precipitated from the heights to the depths of public esteem would have lacked the fortitude, or perhaps even lost the desire, to attempt the same arduous climb again. Not so Lord George; whatever his downfall taught him it did not rob him of ambition or teach him spiritual humility. His contemporaries, watching his second progress, began to grant him

[1] Sackville to Irwin, 23 Oct. 1770; *HMC, Stop. Sack.* i. 132.
[2] Sackville to Irwin, 20 Aug. 1762; *HMC, Stop. Sack.* i. 88.

grudging admiration for the doggedness with which a proud man accepted humiliations and invented ingratiations in order to win his way back into the seats of the mighty. He must beg favours from men he had once scorned or patronized; he must solicit patronage from men he thought less able than himself. To rise again he first must crawl; to command again he must first obey.

There were various roads to rehabilitation and Lord George essayed all of them that his varied talents would permit. It is probable that he embarked on at least one literary venture soon after the court martial. In 1760 a pamphlet appeared, bitterly attacking George Viscount Townshend, who had commanded at Quebec after the death of Wolfe, and that pamphlet incidentally also attacked Lord George. Viscount Townshend believed the attack had been written or inspired by his political enemy Lord Albemarle, who had been a prominent member of the court that condemned Lord George. Soon afterward another pamphlet appeared, virulently attacking Lord Albemarle, and 'The author of this counterblast was generally believed to be Lord George Sackville'.[1] If so it was a first step, even if only a small one, on the long road back to political power.

But Lord George's main hopes lay in the Prince of Wales. Once king, he could give Lord George high civil employment, and possibly even ignore with royal indifference the verdict of the court martial. In any case, the court's sentence had not excluded Lord George from civil employment, and even a king's First Minister was a civil servant. The public was volatile and had a short memory, or so it was to be hoped. George II might not be long for this world: Lord George with renewed devotion courted the heir to the throne and his favourite Lord Bute, and waited, not too patiently, for his time to come.

At first it seemed the wait might not be long, for after only six months of Lord George's painful purgatory George II died and in November 1760 his grandson became George III. Lord George could contain his impatience no longer; even before the new king was crowned he wrote to Lord Bute inquiring 'whether it were proper to pay his duty at Court as soon as possible'.[2] It

---

[1] Gore Brown, *Thurlow*, p. 30.
[2] Sackville to Bute, late Oct. 1760; *HMC, Stop. Sack.* i. 57; also Clements, *Germain Papers*, ii.

was a daring request and must have embarrassed Lord Bute. The public had by no means forgotten Minden, and many influential men in the new government as well as in its Opposition were bitter against 'the Minden coward'. A paper had appeared one morning, affixed to the board of the Royal Exchange, warning the new king that Englishmen wanted 'No petticoat Government, no Scotch minister, no Lord George Sackville'.[1] This did not promise well for Lord George's suit, but at least it exalted him to equality with the king's inevitable mother and his inevitable Lord Bute. Perhaps Lord George could make himself inevitable too.

Early in November the new king held his first court levee, and to the astonishment of nearly everyone Lord George put in an appearance. He was admitted and kissed the king's hand. A furore of outraged protest followed: Lord Bute was chastened by his fellow ministers and Lord George was given notice not to appear at court again.[2] One of the most angry of the potentates was William Pitt, who never forgave Lord Bute for this offence against the memory of the dead king.[3] Lord George had played his best card too soon; he would have to hold his weak hand and practise uncongenial humility a little longer.

Two years passed before Lord George made another overt move, as startling as the first. He wrote to the king suggesting that he be appointed to a military post. On 18 December 1762 the king commented in a note to Lord Bute: 'I think he would not only drive out Lord North but displease Lord Halifax',[4] and a few days later he added: '. . . sure after he has been censur'd by every foreign nation, he should not wish to get into a situation where he may one day be treated not in a manner he can wish; a civil appointment is what suits him best, and my D. Friend knows that it has been deemed impolitick to do even that till the end of the sessions; how much should we not hear again of the unlucky day of Minden, if he were in the profession again.'[5]

---

[1] Walpole to Montague, 13 Nov. 1760; Toynbee, iv. 454.

[2] Coventry, *Critical Inquiry*, p. 289.

[3] 'The admission of Lord George Sackville to the Court at the accession of George III was the chief cause of the enmity between Mr. Pitt and Lord Bute. The papers now in the possession of the Earl of Harrowby clearly establish this' (Fitzmaurice, *Shelburne*, i. 232, note).

[4] King to Bute, 18 Dec. 1762; Sedgwick, *Letters*, p. 176.

[5] King to Bute, end of Dec. 1762; Sedgwick, *Letters*, p. 179.

It is more than possible that Lord George had astutely asked
for a military appointment in the hope of being placated by a
civil one. Rejected for the former, he then employed the good
offices of Lord Bute's friend Sir Henry Erskine, a military officer
whom George II had ousted and George III reinstated, to gain
the latter. Sir Henry wrote to Lord Bute in April 1763 reminding him of the 'promise' to Lord George 'that he shall have his
rank and a civil employment at the end of the session'.[1] Lord
Bute's reply was statesmanlike in its blending of sympathy and
denial. He reported the king's desire to show Lord George 'some
strong marks of his favour' but that it was clear the time was not
yet ripe. Later 'offices might be open to him that would lead to
higher ones, and . . . what appeared dangerous now would
become easy and palatable'.

But toward the end of his reply Lord Bute dropped his
friendly tone. Sir Henry Erskine, doubtless at the instigation of
Lord George, had hinted that if the king and present Ministry
did not provide a suitable post for Lord George he would go
over to the Opposition—an Opposition detested by the king.
Whether this could be called warning, threat, or blackmail,
Lord Bute dealt with it in no uncertain terms: 'What, join the
greatest enemy man ever had, who aimed at no less than his
blood, because the most benign of princes cannot do for him
now even what the prince himself wishes, without shaking an
administration that is his last resource! If these be Lord
George's sentiments . . . he is the man the enemy took him for,
and unworthy of the opinion I have instilled into the King
about him, and one whose very name he will never suffer to
be mentioned to him again.'[2] Once more the man of Minden
had over-played his hand.

Lord George's reply through his intermediary Sir Henry
repeated the threat but dressed it in the robes of constitutional
freedom, while carefully protesting loyalty and disclaiming any
responsibility for Erskine's hint. Referring to members of the
Ministry who had opposed employing him, Lord George wrote:
'. . . surely I may be allowed to declare in Parliament my disapprobation of the measures of such men as the only constitu-

---

[1] Erskine to Bute, 2 Apr. 1763; Bute MSS., *HMC, Stop. Sack.* i. 57.
[2] Bute to Erskine, 8 Apr. 1763; *HMC, Stop. Sack.* i. 58, 59; Clements, *Germain Papers*, ii. 56.

tional resentment which can be shown by individuals to servants of the Crown'.[1] He could hardly have veiled more thinly his maintenance of the threat. George III was not a man who liked defiant subjects, and Lord George had moved very near the edge of the precipice again.

Renounced for the time by the king, Lord George turned back to Parliament as a medium for gaining power. He braved the frowns and mutterings in the House of Commons in December 1761 when he joined in the debate on the war in Germany, and won praise from two very different sources. Lord John Cavendish wrote to the Duke of Grafton: 'Ld. George Sackville spoke very well and moderately against the expense of it. He was heard as quietly and replied to as civilly by those who answered him, as if nothing had happened, he has since been up twice with equall success.'[2] The reaction of London society was doubtless mirrored by Mrs. Arabella Ramsden in her letter to Mrs. Charles Ingram: 'I hear Lord George Sackville has spoken very well upon the German affairs.'[3] Of all subjects of debate, that was the most tender for Lord George.

Meanwhile, Lord George was also developing the essential machinery of practical politicians—private channels of information and influence. His friend Irwin was, of course, one of them. Another was Alexander Wedderburn, an administration underling but a rising figure as a legal confidence man and who eventually became the Earl of Rosslyn; he had sided with Lord George after Minden and now became his confidant. How useful both men were is hinted in Lord George's letter to Irwin speculating on the government's negotiations with France and Spain: '. . . but we shall have all the particulars from Wedderburne, as the French Ambassador will on Monday communicate his secret instructions to him.'[4]

In spite of discouragements from the king, Lord George appeared at court very soon after his bid for office had been rejected. The king commented to Bute: 'I wish Lord Geo. had staid away today; but he came.'[5] He continued to come, despite the cool welcome, and gradually became accepted there. When

---

[1] See Note C, p. 497.
[2] Cavendish to Grafton, 15 Dec. 1761; Anson, *Life of Grafton*, p. 35.
[3] Ramsden to Ingram, 17 Dec. 1761; *HMC, Var. Coll.* v, vi, Clements, ii. 180.
[4] Sackville to Irwin, 24 Oct. 1762; *HMC, Stop. Sack.* i. 90.
[5] King to Bute, 21 Apr. 1763, Sedgwick, *Corresp.*, p. 229.

the new Grenville Ministry was in formation, gossip assigned
Lord George a minor place in it,[1] or possibly even Secretary
at War, and that idea was indeed in the minds of Grenville and
the king. But there was still too much opposition. What was
more, Grenville had promised the Marquis of Granby a prominent place in the Ministry and Granby had said he would not
take office in a government that employed Lord George.[2] Once
again an enmity created by himself stood in the way of what
Lord George wanted most. Lord Granby was included in the
new Ministry and Lord George was left out, and appeared very
melancholy about his rejection.[3] He would have to wait another
year at least, and meanwhile all he could do was to make his
influence in Parliament so strong that he was too dangerous an
enemy for the Ministry not to make a friend. If, as Lord Bute
thought, Lord George after that rejection: '. . . sank from all
his hopes, and looks on himself as blasted for ever', he soon
recovered and renewed his efforts.[4]

The years after Minden were an ordeal, but Lord George had
some moments of relaxation and even of pleasure; indeed it was
good strategy not to appear unhappy or too dependent on any
man's favour. His family was increasing satisfactorily; his social
position was greatly improved, and in his home he could escape
from the trials of the world into the consoling warmths and
trivialities of domestic life. He had in Colonel Irwin, who was
rising toward military power at Gibraltar and in the War Office,
a friend in whom he could confide, as much as he ever confided,
his political hopes and his private interests. The correspondence
with Irwin gives occasional glimpses of Lord George as friend,
husband, and father. Because they are almost the only human

[1] 'What is Not a little extraordinary, Lord G. Sackville who has long been in
favour, is now coming into place. Some speak of Treasurer of the Household,
others of the Navy, but that he is coming in is not to be doubted. . . . He seems to
bring in only an additional reinforcement of unpopularity to the Administration
without a full, though with some, proportion of ability' (Edmund Burke to John
Ridge, 23 Apr. 1763; Wentworth MSS., Fitzwilliam Museum, Cambridge).

[2] Bute to Shelburne, Apr. 1763; Fitzmaurice, *Shelburne*, i. 230-2.

[3] 'They say Lord G. Sackville looks melancholy upon its being determined he is
not to be Secretary of War; some other place it is supposed he will have, but he
had set his heart on that particular post' (Elizabeth Countess Cornwallis to the
Hon. William Cornwallis, 10 May 1763; *HMC*, v. vi, *Var. Coll.* (1909), *Wykeham
Martin*, p. 301).

[4] Lord Bute summarized his exchanges with Lord George in a letter to Lord
Shelburne in April or May of that year (Fitzmaurice, *Shelburne*, pp. 230-2).

touches the broom of time has left, they assume a significance beyond their rather colourless character.

On 6 July 1762 Lord George wrote to Irwin to announce the birth of a daughter: 'Before five, the young lady was making an uproar in the family, and Di was pacifying it in French, while the nurses kept talking nonsense to it. A more ridiculous scene you never saw.'[1] Four days later he wrote again to Irwin: 'I always was an excellent physician in other branches. I pretend now to some knowledge of midwifery, and I offer my services gratis whenever Mrs. Irwin pleases to consult me.'[2]

A year later the Irwins were planning to visit Lord George at Knole, which with all its magnificence was apparently lacking in certain elementary conveniences, for Lord George wrote: 'I am sorry Mrs. Irvine wants a cold bath, and particularly as we have not the least convenience of that sort here, so that she had better send her bathing tub by the waggon.'[3] The exchange of letters continued as Irwin moved from post to post, and after another five years Lord George descended to sartorial trivia: 'Lady George says nobody understands lace so well as General Irvine, and she insists upon it that I should write you to bring me over some lace ruffles, which order I obey, and if you will be so good as to lay out fifty pounds upon the ornamenting of my shirts I should be greatly obliged to you.'[4]

Gaiety did not rise higher than that, and more often the vein was a wry humour Lord George may have admired in his old acquaintance, that 'madman' Jonathan Swift. It was primarily in letters to Irwin that Lord George gave vent to the saturnine: '. . . we must take men as we find them, and indeed I have seldom seen business done but with much unnecessary parade'.[5] '. . . I cannot believe that the Duke of Rutland will resign unless he is absolutely engaged by a previous concert with the Dukes of N[ewcastle], D[evonshire] etc. The woman who lives with him is too well pleased with the sweets of employment to permit his Grace wantonly to forego them.'[6] Of Prince Ferdinand: '. . . all these things will rise up in judgment against his Serene Highness if he ever lives to see the day of adversity. At present

---

[1] Sackville to Irwin, 6 July 1762; *HMC, Stop. Sack.* i. 87.
[2] Idem, 10 July 1762; p. 87.   [3] Idem, 2 Sept. 1763; p. 92.
[4] Idem, 22 Sept. 1768; p. 128.   [5] Idem, 3 Nov. 1762; p. 91.
[6] Ibid.

nothing can hurt him; success covers a multitude of sins.'[1] Of
Lord Grenville: 'Mr. Grenville, I know not why, has never
shown any inclination to be even on civil terms with me. I
suppose he sees it to his interest to be otherwise', and Lord
George added that he was averse to 'subjecting myself to the
contempt of one who, before he can be my friend, must feel I
can be an enemy worthy of his attention'.[2] Of Irwin's 'good
reception at Court. . . . It is always desirable to preserve that
degree of countenance and civility which makes the necessary
attendance at a levee an act of inclination as well as of duty.'[3]
And, finally, of Grenville again: 'One cannot imagine that love
of talking alone could have induced him to have entered into
such a detail of his situation . . . he held out to me how idle a
pursuit opposition would be against a ministry so resolute and
well supported.'[3]

Such attempts to turn neatly cynical phrases give an impression rather of a man enjoying his unappreciated superiority than
of one writhing under defeat. Lord George was playing his new
role almost as whole-heartedly as he had once played those of
society's darling, brilliant young soldier, and rising statesman.
If he could not expand his own repute he could at least puncture
the inflated reputations of others.

His power in Parliament was mounting—not primarily because he could speak effectively but because his talents as an
astute political broker were increasingly recognized. To that
end he was keeping a foot in each party camp but a faithful
heart in neither. By moving in and out of all the shifting factions
he increased his knowledge of where and when to strike, and
his negative value as a dangerous man to have on the opposing
side. Success in politics often consists of the power to destroy,
and in that game Lord George was an acknowledged expert.
No other concept of political strategy explains his political
infidelities and veerings before 1775.

In January 1764 he flirted with the Grenville administration,
but when it began to weaken he attacked it and supported Pitt,[4]
though Pitt was still adamant against Lord George holding
office. Meanwhile, he cultivated his political intimacy with

---

[1] Sackville to Irwin, 3 Sept. 1762; *HMC, Stop. Sack.* i. 89.
[2] Idem, 5 Sept. 1764; p. 95.   [3] Idem, 2 Nov. 1764; p. 96.
[4] Walpole to Hertford, 22 Jan. 1764; Toynbee, v. 439.

Wedderburn, that shrewd exponent of expediency in court politics.[1] In late 1764 the Whigs, organizing a new Ministry, made overtures to Lord George. He received their approaches guardedly and wrote to Irwin: 'A garrison never surrenders at discretion until deprived of every means of offense and defense. Thank God as yet I have some ammunition left and plenty of provisions.'[2]

The Whigs under Lord Rockingham won their brief place as a Ministry to a reluctant king, but they had no Cabinet place to offer Lord George. If, however, he could be induced to accept appointment at a secondary level, he could be kept from turning his talents to the service of the Opposition. Charles Townshend wrote to him in the flattering terms conventional on such occasions:

I have never lost sight of your interest in any one turn of the last fickle years . . . nothing would make me happier in this present strange time than to find that necessity had removed those prejudices which reason ought to have conquered with respect to you, for it would be a real pleasure to me . . . to see you received and established in a manner you approve. Upon my last mentioning you, as all men do who speak justly of your abilities and consequence in Parliament, I found a disposition to treat with you.[3]

Such a letter, in spite of its mixture of cautious qualification with barefaced flattery, was happily reminiscent of the good old days.

In late 1765 Henry Fox made advances to Lord George: 'I know your Lordship's abilities, and should esteem your friendship and be proud of it',[4] and at last a firm offer came from the Ministry. It was not of an exalted post and it did not come as unsolicited as Lord George later pretended, but it was the fashion for men to say they had accepted only from a sense of duty the very posts they had ardently sought. Lord George must have had to choke down his pride to ask the support of one of the men with whom he had long been at enmity. 'There was another man', wrote Walpole of the aspirants for office in the new Ministry, 'who was early in the most humble application

---

[1] Walpole, *Reign of George III*, ii. 276, note.
[2] Sackville to Irwin, 5 Sept. 1764; *HMC, Stop. Sack.* i. 95.
[3] Townshend to Sackville, 9 July 1765; *HMC, Stop. Sack.* i. 62.
[4] Fox to Sackville, late 1765; Clements, *Germain Papers*, i, photostats.

to the Duke of Cumberland to be received into the new establishment; this was Lord George Sackville. He did not ask, he
said, for anything in the military line. The Duke was disposed
to give him hopes only; but, by more judicious address to Lord
Rockingham, Lord George was not long before he obtained one
of the lucrative Vice-Treasurerships of Ireland.'[1]

It was the first solid fruit of five years of effort, and though
by Lord George's earlier standards it was modest, it was also
sweet. It established acceptance of his right to hold civil office;
it brought him an income without separating him from the hub
of politics and power in London, and it restored him to membership in the Privy Council, a recognition so important that one
contemporary called it 'a somewhat unworthy concession to a
powerful family influence'.[2]

Return to office brought trials as well as satisfactions. Lord
George wrote to Irwin: 'I am now undergoing that kind of
abuse in the newspapers which I knew was to happen whenever
I returned to office.'[3] But the ordeal and the appointment
proved short-lived. Lord George was still anathema to Pitt,
whose contempt was unabated and unconcealed. He regarded
Lord George's restoration to the Privy Council as a personal
insult and threatened to upset the delicately balanced Ministry
so effortfully assembled. He had Lord George in mind when he
wrote to Shelburne that 'Faction shakes and corruption saps
the country to its foundations',[4] and Shelburne, another power
among the Whigs, rejoined that he privately thought Lord
George's advancement 'profoundly distasteful'.[5] But so long as
Pitt was not a member of the Ministry, his disapproval was
dangerous but not fatal.

It was soon apparent, however, that without the support of
Pitt and the Duke of Grafton the Rockingham Ministry could
not survive, and Pitt was approached to join it. Notes of a conversation between Pitt and Grafton, recorded by Grafton's
amanuensis, say that Pitt '. . . condemned much the filling up
the vacant offices, and particularly restoring Ld. G. Sackville
to the Privy Council, at which he would never sit with his Lord-

[1] Walpole, *Reign of George III*, Le Marchant, i. 14.
[2] J. H. Jesse, *Memoirs*, i, xviii. 353.
[3] Sackville to Irwin, 23 Dec. 1765; *HMC, Stop. Sack.* i. 103.
[4] Fitzmaurice, *Shelburne*, i. 369.   [5] Ibid., p. 340.

ship. That he looked upon that measure as reproachful to the late King's memory, to his ministers, to Prince Ferdinand, and the verdict of the court martial that condemned him.'[1] Grafton himself wrote that: 'Mr. Pitt dwelt long on the disgrace that the recall of Ld. G. Sackville had brought on the nation, declaring over and over that his lordship and he could not sit at the Council board together.'[2] By that fact Lord George or else the Ministry was doomed.

Meanwhile, Lord George presented to the public the air of a man pressed into public service against his will, but determined not to lose his independence. Though he could not have obtained his post without having given the Ministry reason to believe he would support it on major issues, he wrote to Charles Townshend: 'I did not give the slightest hint that I should act in support of the administration upon expectation of any subsequent arrangement',[3] though he had been eager for appointment and had confessed to Irwin that: 'I am not sorry I am now once more belonging to the court.'[4] Walpole's explanation probably had some truth in it: 'Lord George . . . was proud, haughty and desperate. Success by any means was necessary to restore his credit; and a court that was capable of adopting him, was sure he would not boggle at anything to maintain himself.'[5]

Lord George had at last regained a place on the political ladder, but neither talent nor influence could keep him there. On 30 July 1776 Pitt joined the Cabinet, and on the same day Lord George was 'rather cruelly removed'[6] from his post as Vice-Treasurer of Ireland. 'Pitt promptly turned Lord George out . . . as he had said he would.'[7] His letter of dismissal was, with another touch of irony, signed by his old military rival General Conway.[8]

It must have been a devastating blow, even though Lord George must have foreseen it from the moment the Ministry determined to save itself by adding Pitt. For once, Lord George

---

[1] The amanuensis was Mr. Stonehewer, 16 Jan. 1766; Anson, *Grafton Corresp.*, p. 66.   [2] 17 Jan. 1766; Anson, *Grafton Corresp.*, p. 67.

[3] Sackville to Townshend, 13 July 1765; *HMC, Stop. Sack.* i. 65.

[4] Sackville to Irwin, 23 Dec. 1765; *HMC, Stop. Sack.* i. 103.

[5] Walpole, *Reign of George III*, iv. 84.

[6] Walpole to Mann, 1 Aug. 1766; Toynbee, vii. 33; also Clements, *Germain Papers*, iii. 133/80.

[7] Walpole, *Reign of George III*, ii. 414.   [8] *HMC, Stop. Sack.* i. 66.

seems to have refrained from open displays of resentment, and wrote a tactfully grateful letter to his sometime chief Lord Rockingham. All his gains had not, in fact, been lost by dismissal. His right to hold office had been established, and if the Whigs stayed in power and Pitt withdrew from failing health, Lord George might be given another office. If the Tories should later form a Ministry and invite Lord George to join it, the Whigs could hardly invoke the ghost of Minden against a man to whom they had themselves once given office. The tide would turn again, though not as soon as Lord George hoped.

VIII

THIS SIDE OF PARADISE

DISMISSAL from office did not mean exclusion from politics. It freed Lord George from any considerations of responsibility to party, from any activities to distract him from the chambers and corridors of Parliament, and from any loyalties except to himself. In politics he was more energetic than ever: a man to be reckoned with by Whigs and Tories alike. Neither party cared to embrace him too warmly, but neither wanted to risk his vehement opposition. Horace Walpole once more wrote of his 'sound ability' and of the 'nervous compactness' of his 'pithy speeches'.[1]

In a society in which social standing was closely related to political success, Lady Diana continued to prove a valuable aid. She was increasingly intimate with influential women like Lady Mary Coke, whom the old king's son would have married but for excessive deference to convention, and whose diary reveals her frequent visits to Lady George Sackville.[2] Powerful men in politics could not deny outward affability to a man whose wife was a friend of their own.

But it was chiefly Lord George's spadework in the House of Commons that made his political position ever stronger. By 1767 he was again recognized as a man with a future, and even felt his position strong enough to give occasional vent to his self-assurance, his animosities, and his talent for invective. He sometimes addressed the House 'with great bitterness and violence'.[3] His methods fostered old and new enmities, but they made his tongue feared and his opinions respected. He did not win men's hearts but he sometimes subjugated their minds, and that served his immediate ends. But he still laboured under the shadow of Minden, for a resentful opponent could still always probe in public that unhealed wound.[4] Even in 1769 there were still men ready to protest any sign of court favour to Lord George. 'I hear

---

[1] Walpole, *Last Journals*, i. 233, 133.
[2] Coke, i. 158; iii. 13, 37; iv. 66, 167, 173, 448.
[3] 15 Dec. 1768; Coke, ii. 427.
[4] Coke, ii. 429, 430.

that Lord George Sackville has been at court, and that the King was civil to him, which has, I find, created a clamour, and it will possibly create still more.' There was nothing the astute Charles Jenkinson enjoyed more than foreseeing trouble, except reporting it confidentially to the king.[1]

Such episodes must have discouraged Lord George, but they did not deter him. If he could not win men's esteem he would ride rough-shod over them, or find some way to force their support. His sporadic attacks upon one after another of the leaders of both Ministry and Opposition seemed erratic but they were calculated strategy. The upward trend of his influence led some observers to wager on his ultimate success in gaining a Ministry post. With the irony that so frequently marked his career, it was a reference to Minden that enabled him to lay the ghost of cowardice that Minden had raised.

In a debate in the House of Commons on 14 December 1770, Lord George referred to the honour of his country. From any lips but his this would have been merely a routine flight of rhetoric, but Captain Johnstone, recently returned from the governorship of Pensacola, rose to remark that: '... he wondered that the noble Lord should interest himself so deeply in the honour of his country, when he had hitherto been so regardless of his own'.[2] No man of spirit would let such an insult pass, and no man with political ambitions could afford to do so—least of all Lord George. He allowed several days to pass before he issued his challenge: his friends said in order to arrange his affairs, but others said he challenged only when he found he could not avoid it and retain a shred of reputation. Captain Johnstone was an expert duellist and, according to Walpole, 'meant mischief'.

The two men met, with all the formalities, in Hyde Park. Both missed at the first exchange of pistol shots. At the second, Captain Johnstone's bullet struck the barrel of Lord George's pistol, and all agreed that honour had been satisfied. 'I am glad it was not yourself', the Captain was reported to have said in a sudden flight of generosity, and he later declared that he never knew a man to behave better in a duel than Lord George had done.[3] Horace Walpole wrote to his friend Horace Mann: 'Lord

---

[1] Jenkinson to Grenville, Nov. 1769; Smith, *Grenville Papers*, i. 356.
[2] Almon, iii. 274.   [3] Almon, iii. 278.

George behaved with the utmost coolness and intrepidity.'[1] The king was less favourably impressed. He wrote to Lord North: 'Lord George . . . permitting so many days to elapse before he called Governor Johnston to an account for the words he made use of on Friday does not give much of an idea of his resolution but that he has at length been persuaded by his Friends to take the step.'[2] But most men accepted the duel as proving that cowardice had not been the cause of Lord George's conduct at Minden.

Lord George, more emphatic and influential than ever, was flirting with several political factions. In 1766 his ally Wedderburn had brought him into amiable relations with the Grenvilles,[3] and in the following year they courted an alliance with him,[4] but Lord George declined to commit himself without equal commitment by the Grenvilles. In the month of the duel London gossiped that: 'Lord George . . . is to take the head of the Rockingham party. This is what they all avow.'[5] That proved a false rumour, but its existence did his reputation no harm, and made him even more self-confident. In 1770 he made a vehement attack on Lord Mansfield,[6] and in December of that year he opposed the king and Lord North in the selection of a new Lord Chancellor.[7] There was no question of Lord George's importance in the Commons, but his independence and forcefulness also militated against his objective. Each party was hesitant to give high recognition to a character at once so dominant and unpredictable.

By 1770, however, Lord George's position was further complicated by the protests of the American colonists against British control and British taxes. On those issues Lord George, who had been inclining toward the Whigs, had strong feelings at variance with them. The right of Parliament and the Crown to rule its colonies arbitrarily seemed to him fundamental to orderly government and British superiority. Everything in his

---

[1] Walpole to Mann, 8 Dec. 1770; Toynbee, vii. 425.

[2] Fortescue, *Corresp. George III*, ii. 425.

[3] 'Sir Fletcher Norton and Wedderburne are hitherto friendly with Grenville, and your humble servant is now upon terms of friendship with him' (Sackville to Irwin, 9 Dec. 1766; *HMC, Stop. Sack.* i. 117).

[4] As a letter to Sackville by Whately, written at George Grenville's instructions, makes clear (Smith, *Grenville Papers*, 21 July 1767; iv. 71).

[5] Coventry, p. 158.　　　　　　　　　　[6] Walpole, *George III*, iv. 54.

[7] Taylor, *Pitt Corresp.* iv. 62, note.

nature was roused by the colonial challenge, which he took to be a revolt against established authority. Lord George had at last bound himself to a principle, and was prepared to maintain it at whatever cost to justice, expediency, and his nation.

In nearly all his speeches before Parliament, Lord George had until then confined himself to subjects on which he could claim experience or authority: Ireland, Germany, military matters, election procedures. Regarding America and Americans he was wholly inexperienced and more ignorant than many of his fellow Parliamentarians. America was a country he had never wanted to visit and would never see: its people had ideas he would never sympathetically comprehend. Yet concerning them he was at his most authoritarian, vociferous, and inflexible. Beneath the outward logic of his arguments lay deeper emotional reasons. He resented American claims because they represented the assertion of the middle and lower classes against their betters. Most of the American colonists, had they remained in England, would not have been members of its governing class; crossing the ocean to America gave them no right to challenge the authority of their established superiors. For such men to question the wisdom and jurisdiction of King and Parliament was not only presumptuous; it was anarchic.

To concede one iota to the demands of the colonials would, in Lord George's opinion, undermine the authority upon which the security and social structure of Britain was based. He dressed his opposition to colonial demands in that constitutional principle, but beneath it was an almost atavistic emotion. The 'ingratitude' of the American peasants struck a fibre in Lord George's feudal being that vibrated with a deep and persistent anger. A political principle alone would not thus have stirred a man whose thirty years of political life had been marked by consistent devotion to no tenet but expediency.

Knole and Ireland provide clues to Lord George's feeling about the Americans. To the scion of Knole only the king was his superior; few men were his equals and the mass of common people were his inferiors. Irishmen were of a still lower breed, because they were not English. Americans were only half English and they renounced that half when they refused to accept the paternal suzerainty of their aristocratic betters. Within the stone walls and oak panels of Knole the divine right of kings was no antiquated anachronism: it was a living conviction, and with it was a corollary, less loudly voiced but equally strongly held: the divine right of the *élite* to govern everyone else. When the Americans first protested Lord George regarded them as misguided children, to be disciplined but not disinherited. But by 1770 the Bostonians, at least, had become rebellious scoundrels. Those of them who promptly admitted the error of their ways might be generously pardoned by the king's grace; those who did not must be brought to penitent submission on their knees. Otherwise the whole orderly world of Lord George would be undermined.

That was very close to the doctrine of the king himself. It was at first supported by a large proportion of vocal Englishmen as well as the Ministry of Lord North. Until the American issue became predominant, Lord George had been opposing that Ministry more often than supporting it. When the case of John Wilkes was at its riotous peak Lord George had goaded Lord North in the House of Commons,[1] and during a debate on the Falkland Islands he had pronounced that: 'Ministers had been guilty of more neglect and inattention, than anyone would think men, who had any regard for their heads would be capable of. But these men have, in fact, no attention whatever to their own characters.'[2] But as the American problem became the paramount one, the Ministry found him so valuable an ally on colonial policy that they overlooked his strictures on other matters. Lord George never failed to speak vigorously whenever the question of America came before the House of Commons. He criticized the limited disposition of British troops in the colonies;[3] urged that each colony be compelled to pay the local costs of British troops sent into it;[4] and supported a motion to establish British troops in interior parts of the colonies as well as in their sea-coast cities.[5]

Ever since the American denunciation of the Stamp Act in 1765, Lord George had been ready to use military force to maintain British policies. In late 1765 he wrote to Irwin: 'Everybody is distressed about America. The spirit that rages there is

---

[1] Walpole, *George III*, iv. 290.   [2] Coventry, p. 297.
[3] Walpole, *George III*, ii. 414; 27 Jan. 1767.
[4] Fortescue, *Corresp.* i. 451; 22 Feb. 1767.
[5] Ibid., p. 453; 24 Feb. 1767.

beyond conception. God only knows how it will end, for as yet
I have heard of no human reasoning that promises a happy
end to it.'[1] A month later he wrote sarcastically of Pitt's more
lenient policy: 'It seems we have all been in a mistake in regard
to the Constitution, for Mr. Pitt asserts that the legislature of
this country has no right whatever to lay internal taxes upon the
colonys. . . . Mr. Pitt says the Stamp Act must be repealed.'[2]
A year later he told Irwin that: '. . . nothing but military power
could make the Americans in their present temper submit',[3] and
that: 'The ministers . . . must perceive how ill they are requited
for that extraordinary lenity and indulgence with which they
treated the last year these undutiful children. . . . These affairs
. . . will afford matter of triumph to those who foretold the fatal
consequences of yielding to riot and ill-grounded clamour.'[4]
Lord George was a member of a committee of the Privy Council
for Plantation Affairs, to which were referred in June 1770:
'. . . the disorders, confusions and misgovernment which have
lately prevailed in the Province of Massachusetts Bay'.[5] In that
committee Lord George's vehement opposition to any leniency
toward the Bostonians weakened the thought that he might
become a leader of the Whigs.[6]

The issue of America filled his mind. 'As to politics I think
little about them', he wrote disingenuously to Irwin, '. . . but
when the time comes I will endeavor to make the best I can of
them, and show that I am not apt to change my sentiments
about men or measures.'[7] There is no doubt what politics and
measures he meant, for his letter turned immediately to the
question of America, and stayed there. 'There is nothing left for
the mob of Boston but to decide between ruin and submission.'[8]
Before the House of Commons he defended in January 1775
all the acts of the Ministry against the Americans, and after

[1] Sackville to Irwin, 23 Dec. 1765; *HMC, Stop. Sack.* i. 103.
[2] Idem, 17 Jan. 1766; *HMC, Stop. Sack.* i. 105, 106.
[3] Idem, 13 Feb. 1767; *HMC, Stop. Sack.* i. 119.
[4] Ibid.
[5] Munro and Fitzroy, *Accounts of the Privy Council of England, Colonial Series*, vol. v,
1766–83, PRO, HMS, 1912, preface, x.
[6] Edmund Burke's letters of 11 Nov. 1772 and 10 Jan. 1773 make it clear that
Lord George's leadership of the Whigs was under serious consideration. See also
Guttridge in *Amer. Hist. Review*, Oct. 1927, no. 1, pp. 23 ff.
[7] Germain to Irwin, 30 Oct. 1774; *HMC, Stop. Sack.* i. 133.
[8] Idem, 2 July 1774; *HMC, Stop. Sack.* i. 133.

Bunker Hill he wrote: 'As there is no common sense in protracting a war of this sort, I should be for exerting the utmost force of this Kingdom to finish this rebellion in one campaign.'[1] He might still be with the Opposition on some issues, but on the paramount one he was with the administration.[2]

On that issue he had begun as early as 1774 to sound in Parliament like a member of the Ministry,[3] and a year later he was known as the ablest supporter of its American policy.[4] He assumed the mantle of an expert on American affairs and was increasingly taken at his own valuation. Thomas Hutchinson, who had been the Crown Governor of the Massachusetts Bay Colony, wrote in his diary in late 1774, after a call on Lord George: 'He has a great knowledge in American affairs.'[5]

Lord George was meanwhile busy strengthening his personal affiliations with the North Ministry, and re-established a working amity with Lord Mansfield, whom he had attacked only four years earlier.[6] He began to exchange long letters on American policy with Lord Suffolk, Secretary of State, who was also a strong believer in no compromise with the American rebels.[7] That association brought Lord George into closer and more confidential relationship with Lord Suffolk's assistant, Lord North's

[1] Idem, 13 Sept. 1775; ibid., p. 137.

[2] Though Lord George supported the Ministry Bill on the Act of Settlement (Walpole, *Last Journals*, i. 45; 9 Mar. 1772), he spoke in agreement with Burke on the India Company (ibid., p. 46; 9 Dec. 1772), though three days later he switched his position on the India Company and opposed Burke (ibid., p. 162; 12 Dec. 1772). Throughout the year 1773 he spoke chiefly against the Ministry, or at least not in clear support of it, on every major issue except America. On West Indian affairs he spoke with 'pith, irony and satire' (ibid., p. 173; 15 Feb. 1773). He spoke against the Ministry regarding the marriage of the Duke of Gloucester (ibid., p. 210; 20 May 1773), and in defending Clive 'he was allowed to have surpassed himself' (ibid., p. 233; 21 May 1773).

[3] He supported Lord North in the debate on the King's Address, 7 Mar. 1774 (Fortescue, *Corresp.* i. 78). Three weeks later he did so again on the Massachusetts Bill, 28 Mar. 1774 (ibid., p. 86), in what Walpole termed 'a much admired speech in favour of the motion—and himself' (Walpole, *Last Journals*, i. 323), and Lord North rose to praise him.

[4] Walpole, *Last Journals*, i. 323.

[5] Hutchinson, *Diary*, i. 294; 15 Nov. 1774.

[6] Walpole, *Last Journals*, i. 325.

[7] 'I think it our duty to exert every nerve to subdue this Rebellion in the most expeditious and effective manner . . . tell me what you think' (Suffolk to Germain, 15 June 1775; Clements, *Germain Papers*, iii; also *HMC, Stop. Sack.* ii. 1). 'I had one long letter from Lord Suffolk. I wrote him my opinion in return' (Germain to Irwin, 29 June 1775; *HMC, Stop. Sack.* i. 135 and ii. 1–3).

private adviser, and the Ministry's handy man, William Eden, later Lord Auckland.[1] With Eden he developed an exchange of confidential information that continued so long as both could profit from it. And there was still Wedderburn, an influential adviser of the Ministry in legal matters—'in the highest degree plausible, insinuating, persevering, dextrous and intriguing'.[2] It was Wedderburn who secretly negotiated Lord George's coming leap into the arms of Lord North.[3] 'It would be the greatest mortification to me to act on different ground from Wedderburn', Lord George had written to Irwin in 1770.[4]

Even then Lord George was reluctant to put all his political eggs into the Ministry basket. Just as he had once courted, at the same time, King George II and his *bête noire* the then Prince of Wales, so now he curried the favour of George III's brother: '. . . he and his wife had been most assiduous in paying their homage at Gloucester House . . . the King hated nobody who paid court to his brother as much as he hated his brother, and was dissembler enough to reward the first when his brother would be the first person punished.'[5] Walpole's phrasing was confusing, but his cynicism was clear.

Lord George won the king's approval by loudly invoking 'fire and sword against the Bostonians'.[6] His pronouncements in support of George III's American policy 'engrossed all tongues', and Walpole, who did not agree with that policy, concocted a new explanation of Minden: 'I think nobody can doubt of Lord George's resolution, since he has exposed himself to the artillery of the whole town. Indeed I always believed him brave, and that he sacrificed himself to sacrifice Prince Ferdinand.'[7] Colonel Isaac Barre even accused Lord George in the House of Commons of dictating to Lord North his harsh policy

---

[1] 'I have this moment had a letter from Eden. They have no later accounts from America' (Germain to Irwin, 13 Sept. 1775; *HMC, Stop. Sack.* i. 136).

[2] Lecky, iv. 89. Alexander Wedderburn (1733–1805) became Solicitor-General in 1771, Attorney-General in 1778, and Lord Chancellor in 1793. In 1780 he was created Lord Loughborough, and in 1781 Earl of Rosslyn. His sister had married Lord George's intermediary with the king in 1760, Sir Henry Erskine, who was a close friend of Lord Bute. Wedderburn 'connected with Lord Suffolk, and paid court to Lord George Germain' (*HMC, Var. Coll.*, 6, *Knox*, pp. 267, 268).

[3] Walpole, *Last Journals*, i. 325.

[4] Germain to Irwin, 23 Oct. 1770; *HMC, Stop. Sack.* i. 131.

[5] Walpole, *Last Journals*, i. 326.

[6] Walpole to Conway, 15 Jan. 1775; Toynbee, ix. 133.

[7] Walpole to Countess of Upper Ossory, 23 Nov. 1775; Toynbee, ix. 285.

toward America. Lord George was not dictating anything to the
Ministry, but by September 1775 he was influencing it as much
as though he were a member of its inner councils, even to the
extent of suggesting the dismissal of the Secretary at War, Lord
Barrington.[1] It was thought only a matter of weeks before a
prominent place in the Ministry would be found for him,[2] thus
realizing the half-prediction Lord Shelburne had made the
previous year: 'He has certainly put himself forward of late,
and met with great encouragement from ministry.'[3]

Arrangements were indeed under way. On 13 October William
Eden sent to Lord George, 'by Lord North's desire', a draft of
the king's proposed speech from the throne at the opening of
Parliament, thus bringing Lord George unofficially into the
First Minister's close confidence.[4] Eden then forwarded a very
extraordinary proposal from Lord North: that Lord George
accept appointment as the king's sole commissioner to arrange
a reconciliation with the Americans, '. . . with ample powers to
settle everything in dispute with any colony. . . . Lord North
. . . thinks you are the fittest man in the Kingdom.' The idea was
so fantastic that one inclines to think Lord North put it forward
more as a feeler than with serious intent. Eden must have
realized the impracticability of the proposal, and since Lord
George's ancient grudge with the Howe brothers was common
knowledge, must have had his tongue in his cheek when he
added that Lord North: '. . . also knows that nothing would
make your friend Howe so happy as to see you in such a
situation'.[5]

Lord North's idea, if it was ever a serious one, came to nothing, but a post in the Cabinet for Lord George was in the
making. In early November 1775 Lord North made several
switches in his Ministry to make room for him as Secretary of
State for the Colonies. According to Lady North this was accomplished without hurting any Minister's feelings. She wrote
to her father-in-law that the Earl of Dartmouth wished to move
from Secretary of State for the Colonies to the less controversial

---

[1] 'I firmly believe with Ld. Geo. G. that the removal of Ld. Ba. from his present
office would be a wise and popular measure pregnant with good consequences'
(Eden to North, 13 Sept. 1775; *Stevens Facsimiles*, ix. 853).
[2] Clements, *Hutchinson Diaries*, p. 297, 12 Nov. 1775.
[3] Shelburne to Pitt, 4 Apr. 1774; *Pitt Corresp.* iv. 340.
[4] Eden to Germain, 3 Oct. 1775; *HMC, Stop. Sack.* ii. 11.   [5] Ibid.

and exacting duties of Lord Privy Seal, but that Lord Weymouth protested that he had been promised the latter post, and would not be bought off by any offer less than one of the older Secretaryships of State. The timely illness and withdrawal of Lord Rochford made that possible: '. . . so now everything is I hope settled to their satisfaction'.[1]

Lord North must have been glossing over to his wife the difficulties of the rearrangement, for Lord Dartmouth's correspondence shows that he protested strongly against being transferred, except to Privy Seal,[2] and was not easily persuaded.[3] Lord North's chief reason for appointing Lord George to a Cabinet post was his need for an effective Ministry spokesman in the House of Commons.[4] Lord Dartmouth was not only a peer and hence unable to speak in the Commons, but he was no more than lukewarm about the king's American policy.[5]

The Bishop of Worcester, brother of Lord North and active in the House of Lords, had reservations about taking Lord George into the Ministry. In a letter to their father, the Earl of Guilford, the bishop commented: 'I hear Fitzpatrick says the Ministry have now got the only two things they wanted, Character and Courage, by taking in Ld. Lyttleton and Ld. G. Germaine. I am not without fears that Ld. George may be an unpleasant partner for Lord North. He is not a popular Man, & is reckoned impracticable and ambitious.'[6]

Lord George's position was strengthened by an event apart from politics and war, and it was this that had led the Bishop of Worcester to refer to him by another name than Sackville. At this new crisis in his life fortune turned in his favour.

---

[1] Lady North to her father-in-law the Earl of Guilford, 10 Nov. 1775; from an original letter in the North Collection, Bodleian Library, d 25, folio 56.

[2] HMC, Dartmouth (1895), ii. 398.

[3] North to King, Fortescue, Corresp. i. 278.

[4] 'Ld. N. thinks it lucky that Ld. G.G. is to succeed him as it will be a great ease to him to have a responsable person in the House of Commons for the three Secretaries being all in the House of Lords made his Situation in the House of Commons more disagreeable' (Lady North to the Earl of Guilford, from an original letter in the North Collection, Bodleian Library, d 25, folio 56).

[5] Lord Hillsborough told Hutchinson that 'Lord Suffolk, Gower, Rochefort, Sandwich & the Chancellor with Lord North were all of one mind for a vigorous push—that Lord Dartmouth was alone' (Clements, Hutchinson Diaries, p. 265; 17 June 1775).

[6] Worcester to Guilford, 11 Nov. 1775; from an original letter in the North Collection, Bodleian Library, d 26, folio 24.

Lady Betty Germain at last left her beech trees, her potpourri, and her philanthropies, and went to her ultimate reward.[1] In 1763 she had begun to fail, to the regret of a society that loved and respected her. Lord Shelburne had written then: 'Her Ladyship is now turned four-score years of age, and as her memory and some of her faculties begin to fail her, she has left off these three years coming to Drayton. . . . It is supposed that she intends this part of her estate for her nephew Mr. Beauclerc, eldest son of my Lord Vere of Hanworth.'[2]

Drayton was an estate worth inheriting. Horace Walpole, touring that same year from country house to castle, described it to his friend Montague:

. . . we hurried away, and got to Drayton an hour before dinner. Oh! the dear old place! You would be transported with it. In the first place it stands in as ugly a hole as Boughton—well! that is not its beauty. The front is a brave strong castle wall, embattled, and loop-holed for defense. Passing the great gate you come to a sumptuous but narrow modern court, behind which rises the old mansion, all towers and turrets. The house is excellent; has a vast hall, ditto dining room, King's chamber, trunk gallery at the top of the house, handsome chapel, and seven or eight distinct apartments, besides closets and conveniences without end. Then it is covered with portraits, crammed with old china, furnished richly, and not a rag in it under forty, fifty, or a thousand years old; but not a bed or a chair that has lost a tooth or got a grey hair, so well are they preserved.[3]

The Beauclercs were Lady Betty's natural heirs, but she was faithful to the wish of her Dutch adventurer husband she had outlived by some fifty years. When she died in late 1769 she bequeathed Drayton, its possessions and rentals, together with a generous capital sum as Sir John Germain had wished—to the youngest son of the Duke of Dorset. The Beauclercs were philo-

---

[1] She had after the Minden disaster written to Lord George letters of cheerful gossip and inconsequence, like that describing meeting at a house party at Lord Temple's the attractive young Miss Coats: 'a mighty pretty woman, a parson's daughter and but a small matter of fortune; I fancy Lord Temple makes pure work with his love for her, for that, you know, comes of course' (Lady Betty Germain to Sackville, 28 Aug. 1760; *HMC, Stop. Sack.* i. 45). The affair was all the more intriguing because it was Lady Temple who 'brought' Miss Coats to the party.

[2] Fitzmaurice, *Shelburne*, 1763.

[3] Walpole to Montagu, 23 July 1763; *Walpole Letters*, Yale edition, *Montagu*, ii. 89, 90.

sophical. Lord Vere wrote to Lord Temple: 'Great part of the world, we hear, are extremely angry at her having left Drayton to Lord George Sackville, and, I conclude, will not believe neither Lady Vere nor I are in the least disappointed, though we can, with the greatest truth, affirm we never one hour in our lives expected it, not only from the ascendant we daily saw the Duke of Dorset had with her, but from its being the wish and desire of Sir John; but in short, he has it, and 20,000 Pounds to lay out, to add to it.'[1]

Lady Betty had set one condition to the bequest. Lord George must take the name of Germain. Perhaps if Lord George had made the name of Sackville more illustrious he would have hesitated to discard it, but he may actually have preferred a new name that did not remind every man of Minden. In 1770, by special Act of Parliament, Lord George Sackville ended his legal life and was replaced by Lord George Germain, the affluent master of Drayton, a property suitable to even the greatest of statesmen.

The Lord George Germain about to take high office late in 1775 was different in more ways than in name from the Lord George Sackville of the smiling years before Minden. He was now fifty-nine, somewhat battered by the years and bearing the emotional scars of his misfortune. The reverse that had toughened his nature had not mellowed it. More men feared his tongue than liked his ways; more men used him than trusted him. Adolphus, a contemporary historian, described him, rather more kindly than many another man of his time would have done: '. . . tall and dignified, his harangues were more argumentative than florid; without resorting to the artificial graces of oratory, he addressed the judgment, constantly confining himself to the subject under debate; he was concise, and as he never rose to speak but on a weighty question, he was always heard with attention and spoke with effect.' But, as often when friend or foe described Lord George, Adolphus added a qualification to his handsome portrait: 'Though he had . . . great dignity of mind and sterling sense, his manners were rather distant than attractive.'[2]

Adolphus was picturing Lord George as a figure in Parlia-

<hr />

[1] Vere to Temple, 19 Dec. 1769; *Grenville Papers*, iv. 491.
[2] Adolphus, *England from the Accession of George III*, ii, xvii. 291.

ment: but, even there, many other men would have been less flattering. They would have said that though his influence in Parliament was great, it was due primarily to his talents as a negotiator, a fixer, a go-between. They would have insisted that he used every trick of the politician's trade, from the pose of simple integrity to the direction of covert manipulations; that he practised chicanery with such noble dignity that he made it seem a justified means to a high end. Augmented wealth and regained social position gave him easy access to men of all parties, and power to make or break all but the strongest.

Sir Nathaniel Wraxall, who knew Lord George with some intimacy, wrote that 'No man better understood the management of Parliament, the prolonging or acceleration of a debate . . . and every detail of official dexterity or address requisite in conducting affairs submitted to a popular assembly'[1]—and the words 'address' and 'dexterity' carried broad implications in Hanoverian politics. Lord Shelburne, a political opponent with less address, wrote perhaps a little enviously of Lord George a few years later: 'The Court itself, and indeed most men, were dupes to his imposing manners, and gave him credit for a great deal more ability than he had.'[2]

On 10 November 1775 Lord George Germain issued from his new office in Whitehall a circular announcing his appointment as Secretary of State for the Colonies.[3] The American rebellion had given that office an importance that would make him a leading figure in Lord North's Cabinet. It was a lucrative post, 'worth 5200 pounds a year clear',[4] but after so long a wait for power it was worth more than pounds sterling to Lord George.

To Whigs like Burke, Fox, Chatham, Shelburne, and Richmond, no Secretary of State for American Affairs could have been a less pleasing choice. They might be divided in their policies toward America, but they were united in opposition to those of Lord George. Once again irony ruled, for it had been the Whigs who had in 1765 first brought Lord George out of

---

[1] Wheatley, *Wraxall Memoirs*, i. 389.   [2] Fitzmaurice, *Shelburne*, i. 357.
[3] PRO, 30/55, no. 85. Coventry wrote: 'On the 7th September 1775 Lord George Germain took the seals of his office' (Coventry, p. 309), but this is incorrect. The official Gazette announcing his appointment appeared on 11 Nov.; and see Hutchinson, *Diary*, i. 556.
[4] Hutchinson, *Diary*, i. 556; also in Clements, original diary, p. 299, 12 Nov. 1775.

disgrace and back into government service, and he had been thought of as a Whig. Yet, in the words of a contemporary Whig historian: 'The most odious of tasks was assigned to the most odious of instruments.'[1]

No man had ever worked harder to obtain a post in government. In the words of Walpole, who had warned others not to trust Lord George, he had 'persisted to act in public till the uncommon excellence of his abilities had surmounted the load of contempt under which he had lain'.[2] General Sir John Irwin, who knew all about Lord George's persistent efforts for appointment, must have been amused when he read Lord George's personal letter: 'When you arrive I fear you will find me in Lord Dartmouth's office as Secretary of State for America. I have try'd and I cannot avoid it. Pity me, encourage me, and I will do my best.'[3]

Irwin knew what Lord George meant by doing his best. He would pursue with dogged inflexibility his forceful, punitive policies toward those 'misguided children' who had turned into 'rebellious scoundrels'. He would indeed show 'that I am not apt to change my sentiments about men or measures'. Lord George had sometimes changed his coat with the political winds, but as regarded America he was always consistent.

Thus, with Bunker Hill already history, the man disbarred by court martial from further military service to king and country had become the chief director of the armies engaged in the most significant war of the century. The disobedient general now had authority over the commanding officers of that war; he would expect unquestioning obedience, and he would become the chief determiner of military strategy. How great was his authority, how wise his strategy, how active the part he played, would soon be revealed. Lord George's 'best' in his new service to king and country would help lose the country an empire, inspire the king to draft his abdication notice, and turn into a great nation the rebels he detested. The spirit of irony had not yet had its laugh out.

[1] Belsham, *Memoirs*, ii. 134. [2] Walpole, *Last Journals*, i. 320.
[3] Germain to Irwin, 4 Nov. 1775; *HMC, Stop. Sack*. i. 138.

IX

SECRETARY FOR AMERICA

THE Secretary of State for the Colonies was often called the Secretary for America, but Lord George did not like that convenient abbreviation. It failed to emphasize his full equality with the other two Secretaries of State.

The issue was not merely a theoretical one. Lord George was immediately faced with the reluctance of other Ministers to recognize his place in the Cabinet's inner circle. Part of this reluctance was personal, for Lord George was still the Man of Minden, and his post-Minden manœuvres had made or consolidated enmities. But it was also a question of rivalries for power, and each of Lord George's predecessors had made concessions to those rivalries. The status of the Secretary of State for the Colonies had never been defined with invulnerable clarity, and the holders of the two 'ancient' Secretaryships had never been willing to treat it as in all respects equal to their own. The reason was obvious. Whatever powers the new Secretary acquired must inevitably be deducted from their own.[1]

Lord George had never been inclined to acquiesce in less authority than he thought his due. He must have realized that if he wanted full equality as a Secretary of State he would have to fight for it. He could do so with some confidence, for the king and Lord North both wanted and needed his forceful energies in office, and his effective services in the House of Commons. He had also the advantage of being generally believed to be an efficient administrator. The Earl of Rochfort, retiring Secretary of State, wrote as Lord George took office: 'The hands of government are certainly strengthened by Lord George Germain.' And he had not been four months in office when the king wrote to Lord North: 'I am much pleased with the letters to M.G.s Carleton and Burgoyne and see in them that precision which it would be to no disadvantage to other Departments if they could imitate.'[2]

---

[1] M. A. Thomson, *Secretaries of State*, p. 60.
[2] King to North, 30 Mar. 1776; Fortescue, *Corresp.* iii. 347.

Previous to 1768 there had been two Secretaries of State, denoted 'as for the North', and 'as for the South', and the regulation of political affairs in the colonies had been their joint though vaguely defined province. Mercantile aspects of the colonial affairs had been largely administered by the Board of Trade, a separate agency without great power or prestige, which had bent a deferential ear to any proposals from a Secretary of State. Each of the two 'ancient' Secretaries had been nearly omnipotent in matters within the assigned geographical purview of his post, with power and prestige second only to those of the First Minister. When Lord George joined the Ministry, the Earl of Suffolk was Secretary of State for the North, and Lord Weymouth the new Secretary of State for the South.

By 1765 it had become apparent that a more unified and attentive responsibility for colonial affairs was badly needed. In 1766 the Earl of Chesterfield, observing with shrewd prescience the mounting importance of the colonies and their growing spirit of independence, had remarked that if the British Government did not soon establish a Secretary with full and undisputed powers over America, then 'in a few years we may as well have no America'.[1] In 1768 a third Secretaryship of State 'for the Colonies' was created, and Lord Hillsborough, who had twice been president of the Board of Trade, became its first incumbent.

To avoid clashes with the 'old' Secretaries, the precise extent of Lord Hillsborough's powers had never been pressed by King or First Minister.[2] On paper he held a warrant identical with those held by the other two Secretaries, except for the insertion of a preamble which stated: 'Whereas the public business of our colonies and plantations is increasing, it seemeth expedient to us to appoint one other principal secretary of state besides our two ancient secretaries.'[3] The two 'ancient secretaries' promptly saw fit to interpret this preamble as a limiting distinction from their own. They had seen to it that in practice the Secretaryship for the Colonies was regarded by the bureaucracy as a junior post. By those denigrating little devices in which bureaucrats are experts, the staffs of the two 'ancient secretaries' had largely

[1] Robson, *Amer. Revolution*, p. 65.
[2] M. A. Thomson, pp. 60 ff.
[3] Basye, *Amer. Hist. Review*, xxviii, no. 1, pp. 13 ff.

established the attitude that Lord Hillsborough was 'only held to be the First Lord of Trade with Seals and Cabinet'.[1] Under Lord Hillsborough the economic aspects of colonial affairs had remained largely in the hands of the Board of Trade, of which he was the presiding officer. Hence the position of the Secretary of State for the Colonies clearly fell far short of that 'full and undisputed power over America' that Lord Chesterfield had thought essential.

When the Earl of Dartmouth, a good man but not a forceful one, succeeded Lord Hillsborough, the offices of the other two Secretaries openly denied his equality, and especially his right to give all orders within his geographic sphere to the Admiralty and the Secretary at War. Lord Dartmouth was too straight-forward and good-natured to compete in political chess games with the Earls of Suffolk and Rochefort, who were not equally handicapped by those qualities.[2] His authority to give orders to Admiralty and War Office was narrowed down from precedent to precedent to a working agreement that he might direct the movement of troops once they were within the colonies, but that all orders to send troops there must come from one of the older Secretaries of State.[3] When the sending of British troops to America became an important matter, then it took, in effect, control of colonial policy away from the Colonial Secretary.

As American affairs became of paramount importance, the king and Lord North felt the need of having them directed by a man more forceful than Lord Dartmouth and in greater sympathy with the king's policy of firmness. Lord Dartmouth was relieved to be pushed aside into the respectable but less crucial office of Lord Privy Seal,[4] and Lord Weymouth, who

---

[1] *HMC, Var. Coll.* 6, *Knox*, p. 256.

[2] Pownall to Knox, 23 July 1773; ibid., p. 110.

[3] PRO, State Papers Dom., M.I., 26; also Basye (see p. 102, note 3 above). Also 'Arrangement Concerning the Troops to be transported to Africa and America', endorsed 'Approved by the King Feby. 1, 1773' (PRO, SP 41/26, 25/17).

The Home Office records show that until the time of Germain's incumbency the primary orders in such cases were usually issued by Pitt and later by Lord Rocheford as 'principal secretary of state', and not by the Secretary of State for the Colonies. It was Lord Rocheford who instructed Barrington, the Secretary at War, to send troops to Boston instead of to 'different places in North America' as previously planned (Apr. 1774, PRO, SP 41/26, no. 16; also 23 Jan. 1775, PRO, SP 41/26, nos. 19, 20, 21).

[4] M. A. Thomson, p. 58; also Rocheford to Sir John Blaquiere, 11 Nov. 1775; *Harcourt Papers*, x. 26.

had been promised a Cabinet post, was invited to be Secretary of State for the Colonies.

Contemporary opinions differed about the character of Lord Weymouth.[1] Horace Walpole had, some years before, pronounced him: '. . . an inconsiderable and debauched young man attached to the Bedfords',[2] but since that time the viscount had become more sober and had displayed considerable ability, and Edmund Burke, more likely than Walpole to be critical of dissipated young viscounts, later called Weymouth: '. . . a genteel man of excellent sense'.[3] Perhaps the noble lord demonstrated some of that good sense by declining the colonial secretaryship and became instead one of the 'ancient' Secretaries of State.

William Knox[4] later gave an account of Lord George's first problem in his new office:

A difficulty had formerly been made by Lord Weymouth of considering the American Secretary as a Secretary of State. Lord Hillsborough had never been considered so by the other Secretaries; he was only held to be First Lord of Trade with Seals and Cabinet; his commission confined his efficiency to the Colonies. Lord Dartmouth's commission was the same, and Lord Weymouth had refused the Department when Lord Dartmouth got it on that very account. . . . A difficulty in giving Lord George such a [full Secretary's] commission, 'twas apprehended, would be made by Lord Weymouth and Lord Suffolk. . . . The Attorney General and Lord Weymouth were supposed to object together.

In the resultant skirmishing Lord George won the first round, or rather the king won it for him. William Knox called it 'one of those minute strokes for which he is so eminent', and thought that it 'removed all difficulty'. When the Privy Council met to install Lord Weymouth as Secretary of State, Southern Department, and Lord George Germain as Secretary of State for the Colonies, 'the lord President opened the business by moving that Lord Weymouth be sworn. The king promptly rejoined: "There are two Secretaries of State to be sworn; let them both be sworn together"', and it was done.[5] By that apparently casual

---

[1] See Note D, p. 498.

[2] Walpole, *Memoirs of George III*, ed. Barker, ii. 126, 127.

[3] Burke, *Corresp.* i. 75.   [4] See Note E, p. 498.

[5] *HMC, Var. Coll.* 6, *Knox*, p. 256.

manœuvre the past was officially wiped clean, and Lord George entered upon his duties with no statutory handicaps, with the demonstrated support of the king, and with only the covert obstructionisms of his colleagues and their staff to cope with.

But powers established by statute can be eroded by lack of co-operation and delimited by working definitions. In that process, one of the leading operators was William Eden, whose friendship to Lord George was secondary to a primary alliance with a more powerful patron, his own chief Lord Suffolk. It is difficult to know how much the part Eden played was in deference to confidential instructions from Lord Suffolk, who was also posing as Lord George's loyal friend, and how much of it was of his own choosing. Eden was also close to Lord North, who was committed to support Lord George's claims for equality. Eden was, however, in the habit of juggling several loyalties judiciously in the air without disaster to himself.[1] From that *mélange* of motivations the events emerge.

After Lord George had been installed, Eden prepared a memorandum which, while purporting to define more clearly the relationships in operations between the three Secretaries of State, would in effect keep the Secretary for the Colonies in an inferior place.[2] Eden's fine Italian hand is revealed in a draft of 'Minutes for a Royal Order touching the Appointment of Lord George Germain as Secretary of State for the Colonies', dated 17 December 1775, written in his own hand, and sent to his 'intimate friend' Solicitor-General Wedderburne.

It proposed that the king order:

That a warrant shall be made out for the Appointment of Ld. Geo. Germaine to be one of my Principal Secretaries of State in the same Form and Manner in which the Secretaries of State for the Northern and Southern Departments have hitherto been appointed: It is my Intention, in order to obviate any Inconveniencies which may arise from this Appointment in the Course of Business *that this sort of Appointment shall make no Difference with regard to the Duties of the third Secretary of State who is always to be considered as separate from the other*

---

[1] 'Mr. Eden is the intimate friend of the Solicitor General, & is now become the most confidential counsellor of Lord Suffolk' (Lord North to Guilford, 21 June 1772; original letter in the North Collection, Bodleian Library, d 24, folio 162). Three years later North was himself using Eden confidentially.

[2] PRO, Patent Rolls, 16 George III, part 2, memo. 4; also Basye (see p. 102, note 3).

two;[1] & that the Ministers filling the Northern and Southern Departments shall *in all Events* be considered as the *two* principal Secretaries of State in whatever Period they may be appointed.

Wedderburne made it clear to Eden that he disagreed emphatically, and Eden then wrote to him again:

I only understand and feel that one or two of Lord George's friends have an Intention and Wish to raise his Department upon the two other Departments, & I begin to believe that they will succeed in so doing, at the same time that they will teach him endless Jealousies & Heartburnings against those who have been his best friends, & who solely contributed to his being in the situation from which they are suffering such Embarrassments[2] . . . if the American Department is to be blended with them in the manner that you wish to propose, it will be the only honourable one of the three; the others will become irksome and inconvenient, & will end in being insignificant & disagreeable. . . . To cut the matter short, I . . . will neither meddle nor make any further . . . and so whether we lose our mizzen mast or only a Hen Coop I do not care a damn, but will not touch another rope unless the Captain orders me, be the cost what it may.

Eden ended by accusing Wedderburne of supporting Lord George against Lord Suffolk.[3]

The controversy reduced these two shrewd and ambitious manipulators to an indiscreet frankness, for Wedderburne replied:

Ld. S has withdrawn from me in this business all that confidence which enables a Man to act the part of a Common friend, & merely as the friend of Ld. Geo.: I should advise him to resign his seals rather than submit to an Explanation not called for, not attempted on two former occasions, that can only be proposed (as you know It only is) to make him submit in the first place to an Indignity, & afterwards hold the exercise of his office at the discretions of the other offices, and at his own risque.[4]

Having achieved by the king's *coup* full statutory authority and parity with the other Secretaries of State, Lord George set out to make that parity real. Having done so, he was not the man to leave well enough alone, and showed an inclination to extend his working powers beyond their own. He gained, on

---

[1] *Stevens Facsimiles*, ix. 857. The italics are Eden's own.
[2] Eden probably meant Lord North, Lord Suffolk, and himself.
[3] Eden to Wedderburne, *Stevens Facsimiles*, ix. 858.
[4] Wedderburne to Eden, *Stevens Facsimiles*, ix. 859.

paper, no authority beyond that of his colleagues, but the importance of the American war, his standing with the king, and his own positive personality resulted in his directing for several years a major British war, more single-handedly than any man of his time except Pitt.

Lord George attacked his new work with great energy and optimism. He was so aggressive in office that the Opposition soon began to look for ways in which he might be curbed. In 1779 Sir Joseph Mawbery even raised in the House of Commons the question whether, as the holder of a 'new office', Lord George could legally retain his seat in that House. By tradition and statute Sir Joseph had something of a case, but he raised the point too late. It was more than ten years since the third Secretaryship had been created, and over three years since Lord George had been installed in it. Sir Joseph's motion to exclude Lord George from membership in the House unless he resigned his Secretaryship had only one supporter besides himself.[1]

Lord George missed no opportunity to drive home his insistence on his standing, and even implied that although as a Secretary of State he was for the time concentrating on American affairs he was not by his office limited to them. Before Parliament he described himself as 'Secretary of State at large',[2] and when, in 1780, Burke offered an Establishment Bill that provided for the abolition of 'the office commonly called or known by the name of third secretary of state or secretary of state for the colonies', Lord George insisted that he was neither third Secretary of State nor Secretary of State for the Colonies, but 'one of his Majesty's principal secretaries of state'. With the Ministry still in control of Parliament, Burke's motion failed.[3]

Lord George could not have been so potent in office but for Lord North's weakness in Cabinet leadership and the personal support of the king. George III found in Lord George a firm and convinced supporter of his own determination to maintain to the full the royal powers, and to make no concessions to the American rebels. The king was by principle and precedent the head of the armed forces, and was determined to exercise that function. And although in Whig political theory the Ministry

---

[1] *Hansard*, xxi. 250 ff.; also M. A. Thomson, p. 61.
[2] *Hansard*, xx. 266; also Basye, see p. 102, note 3 above.
[3] *Hansard*, xxi. 193, 194; also Basye, pp. 13 ff.

was responsible to Parliament, George III believed it also responsible to him, and tried to determine what man might head a Ministry and what other men might be members of it. 'The rights to choose Ministers and to decide on measures were the main rights claimed by George III.'[1] As the number of administration leaders who sincerely supported the king in these theories diminished, he found Lord George more and more indispensable.

The king kept in close touch with his Secretary of State for the Colonies; expressed his opinions firmly on both major matters and details; supported ministers who agreed with him and sought ways to dispense with those who did not. Had Lord North been a stronger leader the king's influence would not have been so great, or Lord George in such frequent and intimate contact with his sovereign. It was largely as a result of Lord North's lack of assertion that the king took so active a part in the direction of the war, but contrary to some recent opinions, George III did not direct the American war, or insist on having his way in any decision that the Cabinet firmly and openly opposed. Lord Hillsborough, who had long served in the Ministry, told Thomas Hutchinson in 1775: 'The King . . . will always leave his own sentiments & conform to his ministers', though he will argue with them, and very sensibly; but if they adhere to their opinion he will say, "Well! do you chuse it should be so? Then let it be." And sometimes he had known him to add, "You must take the blame upon yourself".'[2]

An added factor in Lord George's administrative power was the king's dislike of committee government. He was never happy with the anonymity of group opinion, and preferred to deal with individuals whom he trusted or whom he could overrule. His attitude toward the Cabinet is illustrated by two sentences in a letter he wrote to Lord North on 18 July 1778. Referring to a matter connected with the navy, he commented: '. . . You have already this morning settled with Lord Sandwich . . . . There can be no reason to delay issuing the orders till a Cabinet is summoned; what is so clear ought never to be delayed for that formality.'[3]

---

[1] Robson, *Amer. Rev.*, p. 25.
[2] Clements Coll., *Hutchinson Diaries* (original), 17 Feb. 1775; p. 203.
[3] *Sandwich Papers*, ii. 125, 126.

In that case Lord North's procedure was typical. Though he had limited ideas of Cabinet leadership, he believed in Cabinet government, and recognized that it would be undermined if he acted as the king proposed. But Lord North never cared to create an issue, especially with the king. He did not call a Cabinet meeting, but wrote to Lord Sandwich two days later: 'Upon a subject on which I am not clear that the opinion of the Cabinet will be uniform, I do not like to have a very material measure depend on mine. Lord Weymouth is I believe in the neighborhood, and Lord George Germain in London as well as my Lord President and Lord Chancellor; could not the sentiments of three or four of us be taken in the course of the day? . . . I desire you not to act upon them [my first thoughts] without taking some other opinion.'[1]

It was seldom, however, that Lord North asserted Ministry leadership even by such gentle indirection. 'The Prime Conductor seems to leave more to other persons than has been usual', Hutchinson confided to his diary.[2] Lord North was not a leader and did not want to be. Frequently during the war years he begged the king to relieve him of his ministerial post, and he remained only because the king insisted. 'A pliant tool, without system or principle', Walpole pronounced him in 1776 when the worst was yet to come.[3] Pliant he was, though in his way he could be stubborn; and without system in any but Treasury affairs and Tory elections, but Walpole was wrong in pronouncing him without principles. Lord North had high private standards of honesty, loyalty, and justice, and in personal relationships he maintained them better than many men of his time.

Lord North openly refused to consider himself or to be considered the king's Prime Minister. In his concept he was the First Lord of the Treasury, directly responsible for Treasury matters but not for the individual actions of his fellow Ministers heading other departments. He recognized that he had been personally commissioned by the king to form a Ministry and to keep it in office, but he did not believe that commission included the duty to direct general policy or the operations of other

---

[1] *Sandwich Papers*, ii. 126.
[2] Clements Coll., *Hutchinson Diaries* (original), 17 Feb. 1775; p. 206.
[3] Walpole, *Last Journals*, i. 513; Jan. 1776.

ministers, once the king had appointed them. His daughter said that he once told her there was no such thing as a Prime Minister in the British constitution, and he told Charles Fox in 1779 that his own obligations to the Government were dual and no more than that: he was 'head of a very important department . . . where I acknowledge I am solely answerable for whatever is transacted', and he was also committed to 'working in concert with others in his Majesty's confidential councils'.[1] 'If the hon. gentleman . . . supposes me to be the first, or sole, minister I do assure him he is mistaken; I know of no such minister in this country.'[2] 'He was so far from leading the opinions of the other ministers that he seldom gave his own and generally slept the greater part of the time he was with them.'[3]

It was this attitude of Lord North's that made the Cabinet even less efficient and responsible than its own low level of competence predicated. When Thomas Hutchinson returned to London after some years as Governor of Massachusetts Bay Colony, he concluded:

I had not a right idea when in America of the state of administration. In matters of moment the prime minister is much less the factotum than I imagined. Such matters come entire before the cabinet, the King himself being more his own minister than any of his predecessors have been in the present century. The minister of the department which such matters particularly respect, it is natural to suppose, will have some additional weight, but no one seems to have a right to guide, & therefore no one ought to be particularly responsible.[4]

Hutchinson was correct in the main, but he overrated the importance of the Cabinet, which met on an average of less than once a week, dined all too well, discussed matters casually without official minutes or often formal votes, and included men hardly on speaking terms.

---

[1] Robson, 'Lord North', in *History Today*, ii. 8. 532, 533.

[2] *Hansard*, xx. 948. In the debate in Parliament on the army estimates in December 1778, when the Ministry (primarily Lord Sandwich) was criticized for failure to support Admiral Keppel, Lord North 'declared that he by no means deemed himself responsible. He was not, nor could be consulted upon it. The affair arose in another department, with which, in point of official business, he was totally unconnected. Whatever, therefore, might be the issue of the inquiry, he thus publicly laid in his claim not to be considered as any partaker of the consequences' (14 Dec. 1778; *Hansard*, xx. 88).   [3] See Note F, p. 499.

[4] Clements Coll., *Hutchinson Diary* (original), p. 171; Jan. 1775.

A man like Lord George would naturally rush to fill the vacuum of leadership created by Lord North's *laissez-faire* policy.
In character and personality Lord North and Lord George
were in striking contrast. Lord North was liked even by his
political enemies; Lord George was disliked by many of his
political allies. Behind an ugly face and figure Lord North was
genial, modest, witty, and cultivated; beneath Lord George's
impressive façade there was little that was winning. Yet in fair-
ness to Lord George, he and the king together gave the only
firm and consistent leadership that Britain had during the years
of the American war. The tragedy was that their leadership
was so wrong-headed.

Not even a Pitt or a Churchill could have welded the members
of the North Ministry into a unified and efficient government.
'In private, that Cabinet was unanimous in only one thing,
dislike of each other.'[1] Robinson, Lord North's Treasury aide
and the king's confidential adviser, wrote of the Cabinet that it
was '. . . totally disjointed . . . hating, I may say, but I am sure
not loving, each other, never acting with union even when they
meet'.[2] Members of the Cabinet took long weekends even in
crises; often retired to the country during the long parliamentary
holidays; were not regularly at their desks when Parliament was
in session; and when they did meet over dinner and wine their
talk was reported to be not always businesslike or edifying. 'Every
minister is out of town', wrote Lieutenant-Colonel Smith in
London to Eden in America in August 1778, when Britain was
at war with France as well as America.[3]

The composition of the Cabinet was vague. It consisted not
of a specific list of *ex-officio* members, but of those ministers whom
the king and Lord North found it desirable or expedient to
include. It usually included the three Secretaries of State,
Lord Privy Seal, Lord Chancellor, and, after 1778, Lord Amherst as Commander-in-Chief. Others were sometimes co-opted.
Lord George and Thurlow, Lord Chancellor after 3 June 1778,
were the only members regarded by their contemporaries as of
more than average administrative ability.

The recommendations of the Cabinet were sometimes carried
to the king by Lord North, but several of the Ministers might

---

[1] Robson, 'Lord North', in *History Today*, ii. 8. 533.   [2] Ibid., p. 534.
[3] Smith to Eden, Most Secret, Aug. 1778; *Stevens Facsimiles*, v. 513, 514.

report directly to George III the opinion or variant opinions in the Cabinet, not always very accurately. If a Cabinet consensus had the strong support of Lord North, the king was likely to approve it. If Lord George Germain pressed a point and Lord North did not openly oppose it, the king usually found it acceptable. And by a peculiar and rather touching loyalty, he supported Lord George and the Earl of Sandwich all the more strongly when they were most condemned in Westminster and the country. Under these circumstances, as anyone with administrative experience would predict, the Cabinet seldom opposed the wishes of its two or three most influential members. Such a government was not likely to wage a winning overseas war.[1]

The Secretary at War has not been mentioned. That post was held by Lord Barrington until December 1778 and after that by Charles Jenkinson, later Lord Liverpool. One might reasonably assume that in war-time the Secretary at War would be a man of Cabinet importance and power, but that assumption would underestimate the magnificent illogicality of the Hanoverian system. The Secretary at War was not even a member of the Cabinet and rarely met with it even during the greatest crises of the war. He played no part in formulating military strategy and had no share, at the upper levels, in its direction. In modern business terms, his function gave him less discretionary power than that of a Vice-President for Operations in a large modern manufacturing company. And even in implementing the decisions of others, his powers were restricted by the quite separate, independent, and uncoordinated activities of the Ordnance, Treasury, and Navy Boards, the Paymaster's Office, and the Board of Trade.

This peculiar situation was so important in augmenting the powers of Lord George Germain that it must be looked at more closely. Until Germain took office the two Secretaries of State and the First Minister determined military strategy and the disposition of troops, and then directed the Secretary at War what orders to issue for their movement and provenance. The Secretaries of State even ruled on many minor details and military appointments.[2] In the war against America, the powers previously exerted by the two 'ancient' Secretaries devolved

[1] See Note G, p. 499.   [2] M. A. Thomson, pp. 73 ff.

upon Lord George Germain, and under his jurisdiction those powers tended to expand, in details as well as in major matters. One example should suffice. When in February 1777 Daniel Weir became 'Commissary General of Stores, Provision and Forage to Our Forces serving within Our Colonies in North America', the appointment was made and the commission signed on behalf of the king, not by the Secretary at War but by Lord George.[1] It was not until after 1783 that the Secretary at War became a Minister responsible to Parliament.[2]

Both Lord Barrington and Charles Jenkinson insisted upon their own impotence with a modesty that would seem almost neurotic if each had not a good reason. Lord Barrington did not want to implement a land war on his own responsibility because he did not believe in its efficacy. He 'had distinctly informed his brother ministers as early as 1774 that he disapproved the whole policy of coercing the colonies, that he believed the military enterprises which he organized could lead to nothing but disaster'.[3] He steadily asked to be allowed to resign,[4] and his half-heartedness in filling Lord George Germain's orders brought him bitter criticisms from that belligerent Minister.[5] The American letter-books in the British War Office 'show that the Secretary at War interfered but little in the management of military affairs in America';[6] and in fact that is an understatement; there is nothing in those papers to show that he ever did more than ask a few polite and apologetic questions of Lord George Germain. 'Augmenting the forces', Lord Barrington wrote in his own hand, 'is purely a matter of State, and the functions of the War Office do not begin till both the measure and the manner of executing it have been settled in the cabinet.'[7]

Barrington's successor Charles Jenkinson did not disapprove the war, but he had a strong personal reason for proclaiming the

---

[1] E. E. Curtis, *The Organization of the British Army*, p. 205.

[2] Ibid., p. 34. Until July 1794 no Secretary at War ever sat in the Cabinet except Henry Fox for a few months in 1746 (Fox-Strangeways, *Henry Fox, Lord Holland*, i. 237). [3] Lecky, iv. 71.

[4] E. E. Curtis, p. 179. [5] Gee, *The British War Office*, p. 126.

[6] Andrews and Davenport, *Guide to MS. Materials, &c.* ii. 282.

[7] Barrington to the Earl of Antrim, 18 Dec. 1777; *HMC, Lothian*, p. 324. On 3 May 1773 Barrington forwarded to Rochefort, then a Secretary of State, a letter which he said had been 'improperly addressed to the War Office which has nothing to do with Irish promotions' in the British Army (PRO, SP 41/26, no. 12).

limited powers of his office. By the time he became Secretary
the American war was unpopular and half-lost, and both
Parliament and people were searching for scapegoats for the
military failures. Jenkinson had no wish to claim responsibility
and therefore share the blame. He declared before the House of
Commons that as Secretary at War he was no Minister, and
therefore could not be supposed to have a competent knowledge
of the destination of an army in America or of how the war was
carried on.[1] By unanimous consent the functions of the Secretary
at War were 'limited in scope and entirely administrative in
nature'.[2]

Nevertheless the spade-work of military operations had to be
conducted largely through the office of the Secretary at War.
That office contained the only machinery, primitive though it
was, for co-ordinating the military operations with the mani-
fold activities of transport and supply. The decentralization of
government administrative processes made the size and efficiency
of the staff of the War Office of the utmost importance. Consequently only two government departments, the Treasury and
the Admiralty, possessed larger staffs. Yet in 1777, at the height
of the war effort, the total personnel of the office of the Secretary
at War consisted of one combined Deputy Secretary and first
clerk, a paymaster of widows' pensions with one deputy, an
examiner of accounts with one assistant, an office-keeper, ten
or twelve clerks, a messenger boy, and a 'necessary woman'—
a total of not more than twenty. Lord George's office staff was
enlarged during the war, but it never exceeded two undersecretaries, six clerks, and a porter.[3]

By the most charitable of modern standards office efficiency
was low.[4] As for consistency of office policies and procedures,
they rested chiefly on continuity of office personnel, and until
shortly before the war most employees in government departments changed with each Ministry. In the War Office that
system had been altered, but any gains in continuity of procedure

---

[1] *Hansard*, xx. 1253; Gee, p. 124, note.   [2] Gee, p. 136.
[3] Court and City Register, 1775, quoted by E. E. Curtis, p. 36; Spector, p. 34;
Thomson, p. 21.
[4] On 14 May 1777 the Secretary at War sent a note to the Secretary for America
'enclosing the last Return of the Forces under Sir William Howe', a most important
document. At the foot of the note, in the same hand, was this addition: 'Inclosure
mislaid' (PRO, CO/5, v. 169, no. 84).

were probably offset by the red tape that develops in any civil service.[1] So far as the Government's overall organization for administering an overseas war was concerned: 'Efficiency, in the sense of the word today, was positively unknown throughout British officialdom at the time of Germain and North.'[2] Since efficiency in war is never better than relative, the British system had been good enough to defeat the French a decade earlier, and in the American war it was competing with the Continental Congress, which set no higher standards. But the Americans did not have to transport and supply 40,000 men for a war 3,000 miles away.

Until 1777 the direct responsibility for taking men and supplies across the Atlantic was divided between the Ordnance, Navy, and Treasury Boards. The Ordnance was, in general, responsible for the transport of artillery, engineers, guns, and ordnance stores. The Navy Board was in charge of the transport of infantry, cavalry, clothing, hospital stores, tents, and camp equipment. The Treasury Board was charged with securing and delivering nearly all food and other consumer supplies for the armed forces. But there were exceptions to these general arrangements, and peripheral areas in which the responsibility was uncertain or divided. After February 1779 the Navy Board took over most, but not all, the functions of transport of the Treasury Board, which had contracted such work to private merchants and shippers under terms often very lucrative to both parties. This change was strongly opposed by Lord George Germain, and his opposition caused great friction with the Admiralty and Lord Sandwich.[3]

When there were not jurisdictional disputes there were jurisdictional confusions and delays. Queries and memoranda moved

[1] Before he resigned in 1778 Viscount Barrington had served nineteen years as Secretary at War, and during that unusually long period of service he kept careful records and also developed a staff of principal clerks with twenty or thirty years of experience (PRO, WO, ii. 42 ff.; also Gee, p. 125). This had great advantages but it also encouraged the statics of bureaucracy. At least Sir Gilbert Elliott, for some time Speaker of the House of Commons, thought so when he complained of Lord Barrington in a letter to his son: 'Your old friend sticks to rules, tape and packthread. Procrastination is the ruin of business; dispatch in everything is half the battle' (Elliott to Hugh Elliott, 1777; Hon. Hugh Elliott, *Life of Lord Minto*, p. 78; also quoted by Gee, footnote, p. 126).

[2] E. E. Curtis, p. 149.

[3] Ibid., pp. 120, 121, quoting Treasury 64: 200, 4 Aug. 1780; Treasury 64: 201, 27 Mar. 1779; Treasury 29: 49, 316.

with cumbersome dignity at foot-messenger speed between departments and offices. Lord George and Lord Barrington corresponded personally about the selection of a medical officer for General Howe's troops in New York;[1] the War Office consulted the Secretary of State about tents for a single regiment;[2] the Secretary of State, the Lords of the Admiralty, and the Secretary at War were all involved in determining the embarkation date of a certain regiment of Foot Guards.[3] The discussions were not always amiable, and Lord George had not been two months in office before he was openly criticizing at least one of his most important colleagues. In conversation with Hutchinson, who had no office or claims to confidences, Lord George '. . . condemned Lord Sandwich for appointing such an Admiral, & for supporting him when every body else gave him up'.[4]

That was the administrative machinery with which George III and his ministers essayed to direct and service the fighting men and ships Britain would need for its first trans-ocean major war. What was the condition of the armed forces? The answers must be drawn chiefly from the events of the war, but the joint conclusions of two distinguished students of those military forces will come as no surprise:

'Parallel ignorance of the conditions of war controlled the military operations. The movements of troops were badly prepared and ill concerted, the organization and equipment unsuited to the character of the campaign, the officers in command lacking in energy and resources.'[5] Despite his optimism Lord George Germain had not assumed a Cabinet post likely to bring him success and esteem.

---

[1] Barrington wrote to Germain to assure him that '. . . it was never my intention to give any Directions in a matter which is so foreign to my Department as the appointment of Hospital Physicians, Surgeons or Apothecaries' (PRO, CO/5, v. 168, no. 57; Barrington to Germain, 19 Feb. 1776).

[2] It was Lord George who gave the final ruling (Lewis to Pownall, Pownall to Lewis, 21 Feb. 1776; PRO, CO/5, v. 168, nos. 71, 72).

[3] For the sending of a small reinforcement to Howe in 1777, and apart from other arrangements made with various Boards and agents, Germain's office specified certain troops and officers to the Secretary at War; ordered supplies, guns, equipment, and ships separately from Treasury, Admiralty, Ordnance, and Navy. A separate order went from Germain to Barrington to 'give orders for the Parties to proceed immediately to the Place of Embarkation', in the case of 'four Commissioned Officers and forty Non Commissioned Officers with private men of the Foot Guards, with four Officers' servants' (15 Feb. 1777; PRO, CO/5, v. 169, no. 38).   [4] Clements Coll., *Hutchinson Diaries* (original), p. 309; 6 Jan. 1776.

[5] J. Munro and Sir A. W. Fitzroy, *The Privy Council*, Preface, p. x.

X

DIRECTING A WAR

No one in modern times has completely directed a major war. Not even Napoleon or Hitler controlled every aspect and event of his nation's military effort. In that sense no single person directed Britain's military and naval operations during the American Revolution. But if one man's word and will were largely dominant, history can justly give him the chief onus for defeat. And if the war machine he tried to steer was inadequate to the demands he made upon it, he is still to blame; having grasped the sword he should have used it according to its strength.

The word 'direction' implies an organization or a machine that can be guided toward a desired end, but toward the end of subjugating the American people Britain was neither a unified organization nor an efficient war machine. Though ten years earlier Britain had defeated France and taken Canada, that was a different kind of war from one against her own colonies, and the British people viewed it differently. In 1775 British society lacked the spiritual impulse, and its fighting forces lacked the power, to win a new kind of war in which both national unity and efficient centralized control were most needed.

There were many reasons for this. The British Army was deficient in numbers, leadership, supplies, transport, imagination, and fighting methods for a war to be fought against men of its own breed 3,000 miles from its home base. The British Navy, too, was inadequate to unprecedented demands for long-distance patrolling, fighting, and transport. To lead and organize such a war, Britain needed a government unusually competent, unified, and generally supported, but the opposite was the case. The American Revolution was Britain's first ideological external war since the Armada. A war of ideas required a British people convinced of the righteousness of its cause, yet many an Englishman sympathized with the Americans, and many another Englishman who did not, nevertheless doubted the wisdom of trying to convert Americans by fighting them. Even winning the war would not solve the conflict of ideas, or win back the loyalty of Americans to principles they had outgrown. Britain was opposing a trend in history in trying to stem a surge toward self-government that has endured to trouble our own times.

A war for principles could not be won unless those principles were shared by Ministry, Opposition, and people, yet nearly all the Whig leaders were sympathetic with the political concepts supporting the American cause, and within the Ministry some men were dubious of the policy they collectively professed. Lord Dartmouth, Secretary of State for the Colonies until after the war began, so disliked coercion of the Americans that he withdrew from that post. Lord Barrington, Secretary at War, openly declared land warfare against the colonials to be hopeless, and for two years urged his resignation on those grounds until it was finally accepted. Adjutant-General Harvey, then the highest staff officer in England, agreed with Barrington and said so very openly: 'Taking America as it at present stands, it is impossible to conquer it with our British army. . . . To attempt to conquer it by our land force is as wild an idea as ever controverted common sense', he wrote to General Irwin about the time of Bunker Hill.[1] General Amherst, Commander-in-Chief after 1777, also advocated only naval operations. Yet other men —a clear majority when the war began—were vehement that Britain must and could subdue the insubordination in its colonies. The struggle between the two factions led a literary gentleman named Beaumarchais, serving in London as personal observer for Foreign Minister Vergennes, to report that 'The war is raging more ferociously in London than in Boston'.[2]

In another way Britain was a house divided against itself. In his efforts to bring government back into the balance it had lost under the long domination of a Whig oligarchy, King George III raised fears that he would undermine the rights of the people. The liberal elements in England suspected his motives for every act, and saw a connexion between the Americans' struggle for political rights and what might soon be a similar struggle in England. Firm in all his policies and inflexible toward America, George III could find few men whom he would trust to serve as ministers on his own terms.

[1] Harvey to Irwin, 30 June 1775; Fortescue, *HBA*, 2, iii. 167.
[2] Graham, *Considerations on the War*, pp. 22–34.

These administrative liabilities for war were augmented by lack of strategic realism. Military men had too little experience in the kind of war that must be fought in America, and too much devotion to the kind of war that could not be. The traditions and organization developed on the battlefields of France and the Low Countries hampered the imagination and flexibility essential on the battlefields of rugged America. The logistics that had led to victory at Blenheim and Minden would lead to defeat at Saratoga and Yorktown. Nearly every aspect of the British military code—the selection of officers in which nepotism and birth played important parts, the training of men, their uniforms, equipment, transport, and fighting methods—was ill adapted to the stone walls of Concord, the forest trails of Saratoga, and the hot, sandy plains of the Carolinas. In military methods Britain was looking backward fifty years as it attempted to conquer a forward-looking people. The surprise lies not in the fact that the British armies did not fight better in America, but that they fought so well.

American fighting methods were not according to the European 'Rules of War', for Americans had not heard of them, or if they had they saw no sense in them. To them a war for freedom was a serious business that left no place for the sport of kings, and their realism was a step toward modern total war. The American contest would not prove a gentleman's game, or show deference to traditional amenities the British armies expected even in a primitive land. British armies on the Continent had by custom included many wives and some children, not to mention other less orthodox camp comforters. It did not, apparently, occur to many British high officers that women and children would be much more difficult to protect and maintain on campaigns in the American back country. When two battalions of Fraser's 71st Royal Highlanders embarked for America in 1776 they took with them 160 women, 32 servants, and 280 tons of personal baggage.[1] That illustration is typical, and the custom continued, only a little less extensively, throughout the war.[2]

[1] PRO, CO/5, v. 170, p. 108.
[2] Burgoyne's 16th or Queen's Light Dragoons, totalling 490 men and officers, sailing to relieve Quebec in the spring of 1776, took with them 42 women, 54 servants, and officers' baggage of 26 tons (PRO, CO/5, v. 170, 168). Three years later, when the Liverpool Regiment embarked, provision was made for

Recent historians have emphasized such military mistakes more than they have stressed an equal hazard beyond the control of strategists and generals—American geography and climate. It was one thing to transport and maintain an army on the cultivated plains of Flanders or Westphalia across only 25 miles of English Channel, but quite another to do so on the far side of the Atlantic. The latter required more and better ships, more provisions, more planning, more time, more risks from storms, adverse winds, and enemy privateers. Long sea trips meant hundreds or thousands of sick soldiers on arrival at the place where they were supposed to fight. Cavalry horses died by scores and hundreds on the way, since even in summer time troopships sometimes took two months to make the crossing.[1] The expectation that British troops in America could buy food and supplies from friendly loyalists, or live off the country, usually proved false. British armies could not even get forage for their cart horses and cavalry mounts; hay had to be sent from England and there was often not room for it in the ships. The width of the Atlantic was as good as a second army to Washington—and less expensive.

The Atlantic was not the only hazard that geography presented to Europeans fighting in America. Few Englishmen had travelled far enough in the colonies to appreciate their distances and difficulties of their terrain. Braddock and Amherst had learned the hard way, but they had led armies chiefly through friendly country where colonial companies joined them, local merchants supplied them, and Americans like Washington guided and advised them. American geography brought with it the American climate, and that too proved an enemy of the British troops. It was hard for them to say which experience they found more trying—fighting and marching in the broiling summer of the Carolinas or in the frozen winters of Quebec. Whitehall and the War Office could have eased this problem

1,169 officers and men, 80 women, and 16 servants (21 June 1779; PRO, CO/5, v. 171, p. 7).

[1] In the spring of 1776 'all the victualling ships' from England to Howe's army were blown off course to the West Indies and had to work north again from there, and it took some of them several months (Robinson to Howe, 21 May 1776; PRO, 30/55, no. 177). Troops often arrived too late to take any active part in the campaign for which they had been primarily sent. This was the case with German troops in the ship *Garland*, which sailed from Spithead on 26 June 1776 but did not reach Quebec until 19 Sept. (PRO, CO/5, v. 253, p. 123).

by proper clothing and equipment but they failed to do so.[1] Grenadiers and Hessians dressed and outfitted as for the Rhineland were cold and over-burdened in winter and sweltering and over-burdened in summer. Much of this was due to extraordinary ignorance in the highest places. When Lord George Germain, newly in office, got news that General Carleton was penned up in Quebec, he rushed to the Admiralty and said he 'must have four ships to send to Canada. Palliser said they could not get up the river, which was frozen, and it was given up.'[2] Howe ignored Clinton's warning that he would be slowed by prevailing headwinds when southbound along the Atlantic coast in summer, and as a result he wasted a precious month and sailed an extra seven hundred miles in taking his army from New York to Philadelphia in 1777—and also cast away the last possibility of saving Burgoyne from capture.

Geography delayed communications and created misunderstandings fatal to British military plans. Howe and Clinton have sometimes been blamed by historians for slowness or lack of aggressive spirit when the real cause was the late arrival of expected troops, supplies, or orders. In winter it was almost certain to take at least three months for Howe or Clinton to send a dispatch to Lord George Germain and receive his reply, and it often took much longer. Even though most dispatches were carefully numbered and acknowledged, the recipient could not always be certain whether the message he received was written before or after the relevant one of his own had reached its destination. At the crisis of affairs in Boston in 1775 the knowledge of the Government in London was nearly three months behind events, and General Gage had been nearly four months behind in receiving pertinent orders.[3] At the time Howe

---

[1] The corruption or slackness was often on the part of private contractors, but those contractors had been hired by the Government, whose officials were parties to such episodes as that of the army tents in 1775. On 6 Oct. 1775 the Quartermaster-General in North America reported to the Secretary at War: 'The tents brought out this year were made of such bad stuff that they would not turn the Rain, and the men in bad weather were constantly wet.' General Gage supported the complaint, and on 22 Jan. 1776 Barrington reported to Lord Weymouth, Secretary of State: '. . . the badness of the tents issued last year from the Ordnance . . . points out that the Tents in store have not been surveyed since the year 1759', and added that his Majesty 'was pleased to direct that they should be forthwith inspected' (PRO, SP 41/26).

[2] Walpole, *Last Journals*, i. 503; 23 Dec. 1775.

[3] 'It is certainly remarkable that Government has not had any account from

evacuated Boston on 17 March 1776 he was unaware that the dispatches he had been sending to the Secretary of State for the Colonies since 10 November of the previous year were being read not by the Earl of Dartmouth but by Lord George Germain. And it was only on 1 May that the Ministry learned that Howe had evacuated Boston.[1] Quebec and its army were wholly out of communication with London for as much as six months during the long Canadian winters. When General Haldimand took over the command in Canada in July 1778 he wrote home that: 'There have been no accounts from Great Britain for nine or ten months, except but what were conveyed by Rebel Newspapers.'[2] The rebels aided nature: though more ships carrying dispatches were slowed by weather than by American privateers.[3]

Much of this delay was of course inevitable, but lack of system made it worse. Thomas Hutchinson wrote in his diary for 8 May 1776:

In my business as a merchant I never wrote a letter of consequence but I tracked the ship it went by from the hour she sailed, and was anxious to inquire by every opportunity after her arrival; but the way here is to send letters from the office of the Secretary of State to the Admiralty, to go as soon as may be. Some little thing or other hinders the sailing of the ship, and the Admiralty do not consider, or perhaps do not know, the importance of the Secretary of State's despatches; the ship lies five or six weeks, and the despatches answer to no purpose. . . . This shows the want of one great director to keep every part of the operations of government constantly in his

---

that army since the end of August, but this had better not be proclaimed in Parliament' (Bishop of Worcester, brother of Lord North, to their father the Earl of Guilford, 13 Nov. 1775; original letter in North Collection, Bodleian Library, Oxford, d 25, fol. 60).

[1] On 2 May 1776 John Robinson of the Treasury wrote to General Howe that 'since yesterday' advice had been received of his quitting Boston (PRO, 30/55, 177). PRO, CO/5, v. 253, no. 100.

[2] Hudleston, *Gentleman Johnny Burgoyne*, p. 125, note.

[3] Germain explained to Carleton in his letter dated 26 Mar. 1777, which reached Carleton on 20 May 1777, that his letter dated 22 Aug. 1776 had been sent in the ship of Captain Le Maitre, who: '. . . after having been three times in the Gulph of St. Lawrence, had the Mortification to find it impossible to make the passage to Quebec and therefore returned to England with it' (PRO, 30/55, 462; also *HMC, Stop. Sack.* ii. 60 ff.; also Hudleston, p. 125). Howe, too, suffered from delays. On 16 Feb. 1776 he wrote from Boston acknowledging the recent receipt of Dartmouth's dispatch of 22 Oct. 1775 (PRO, CO/5, v. 253, p. 175).

head. . . . I sent a packet this winter to Lord G. G.'s office to go in the government box, & after 6 weeks Mr. Knox told me it was sent back to London, the ship not proceeding.[1]

'One great director' of the war would have had to cope with handicaps not remedial by administrative efficiency alone. In 1775 the British Army had known no insistent genius of logistics and organization for several decades, and was the victim of creeping corruption. It was suffering from antiquated organization, poor administration, internal rivalries, nepotism, fiscal carelessness, over-confidence, and routine graft. It contained men of bravery, ability, and integrity, but their efforts, seldom very heroic, had been largely nullified by the dead weight of time-servers, intriguers, casual officers on purchased commissions, and many private soldiers recruited or dragooned from the dregs of society. Its corruption was not dashing and downright but insidious and often picayune; custom hallowed or overlooked vices like petty malingering, favouritism in promotions, special privileges for young lords, and discreet avoidance of active duty. 'It was an army descended from the great Marlborough, who received a handsome percentage from the contractors who supplied his army.'[2] It was an army more immediately derived from the one of which Lord Chesterfield wrote just before Minden: 'Unfortunately the point of profit is more important than the point of honour with our Military dignitaries. Provided they can avoid defeat, they are also ready to avoid victory, as either event would deprive them of their incomes.'[3] That was literary exaggeration, but it was indeed an army in which an officer was routinely paid £800 a year for work he got done by a clerk assistant who was paid 5s. a day.[4]

It was also an army in which the incentive of pay was largely illusory. Men at the top received large stipends and many extra allowances when on active duty, but junior officers were, by their social standards, underpaid, and common soldiers got

---

[1] Hutchinson, *Diary*, ii. 44, 45; Clements, *Hutchinson Diaries* (original), p. 335; 9 July 1776.

[2] De Fonblanque, *Administration and Organization of the British Army*, p. 36.

[3] Belsham, *Memoirs*, i. 268.

[4] 'Viscount Irwin was commissary-general of stores at Gibraltar in 1750 with a salary of 800 pounds a year, while a clerk with 5/– a day did his work' (De Fonblanque, *Admin. Brit. Army*, p. 37).

pittances. General Gage received an extra £10 a day while Commander-in-Chief in Boston, compared with the £2. 10s. a day received by his Major-Generals Howe, Clinton, and Burgoyne.[1] A Captain received an extra £1 a day for service in America, but his gunner's total daily wage was 1s. 4d. and his driver's 1s.[2] To an officer with no other income, no inheritance on which to borrow, and a desire to advance his standing, the temptations for judicious grafting were great and the opportunities almost routine. The financial fortunes sometimes made by men high in the military service did not reflect on their ethics alone; they could not have been acquired without frequent connivance by civilian merchants and bureaucrats. The British commanding officer in America had entire control of the public funds provided to supply his army,[3] and the pressures as well as the temptations were very great. No army has ever been free from peculation and favouritism, but in Hanoverian armies they were common practice.

Apart from these deficiencies in quality, the British Army was inadequate in quantity for the war it had undertaken. Even the overall figures—always more impressive on paper than in reality —seem surprisingly small. In 1775 Britain's total land forces numbered on paper 48,647 men of all categories, of which some 8,000 were then in America. There were 15,000 in England, which at no time during the war could be completely denuded of troops, as the Gordon riots and the French declaration of war made evident. There were 12,000 men in Ireland, which could not be left unchaperoned by British might. The remaining 13,000 had to be scattered at essential military posts from north Scotland to Africa. Gibraltar and the West Indies, for example, could not be left vulnerable to France and Spain. And of the paper total of 48,000, by no means all were 'effectives' or even more than names on a roster.[4]

The war brought enlistments and that rough and ready ancestor of the modern military draft called 'the press', but from the beginning fewer Englishmen than were needed could be

---

[1] PRO, 30/55, no. 9796, Royal Warrants to Pay, 23 Oct. 1776.

[2] The Hessians in the American war were usually 'rented' by a single payment of £25 apiece for an indefinite period. The total cost of an entire company was estimated at £13. 1s. 6d. per day (PRO, CO/5, v. 169, p. 56).

[3] De Fonblanque, Admin. Brit. Army, p. 46.

[4] E. E. Curtis, pp. 2, 51.

secured for this none too popular war.[1] After the French declared open war in 1778, strenuous private as well as public efforts to raise new regiments (headed sometimes by the noble lords who raised them, regardless of military capacity) were made, with some success, but men in some of them mutinied when commanded to embark for America.[2] As early as 1775 it was apparent that Britain would have to hire foreigners to fight her battles in America. Queen Catherine of Russia dallied with the proposal to rent troops to George III but finally declined. Early in 1776 Lord George Germain was hiring troops from petty German states, and he continued to do so until hired mercenaries composed from a third to a half of all the troops Britain had in America.[3]

One episode is revealing. The East India Company was in the habit of recruiting Englishmen to serve in its own private army, and continued to recruit them during the American war. This competition with the Government was so successful that both Lord North and the king did their best to get the Company to desist until the army quotas had been filled. The Company declined to honour the king's request beyond a pledge to restrict its recruiting to the London area.[4]

By 1777 the Secretary of State for America had managed to provide Generals Howe and Clinton with a paper total of some 34,000 men, including those at Halifax and other way stations; Burgoyne with 6,000, and Carleton with a residue in Canada of 3,000. Not one of these generals regarded those numbers as adequate to the assignments given him by that same Secretary,

[1] The records of the War Office show weekly reports of the total number of recruits raised in the British Isles, and those reports for 1777 total 8,610 new enlistments (PRO, CO/5, v. 169).

[2] In April 1779 a draft of men for Frazer's Highlanders mutinied and refused to embark, and the mutiny did not end until half of them had been killed or wounded. Later in the same month a regiment in Edinburgh similarly refused and had to be surrounded and disarmed.

[3] The records of the Secretary for America show that on 20 Jan. 1778 General Howe was nominally in command of 33,186 men, rank and file, in New York, New Jersey, and Rhode Island, and that more than 11,000 of these were hired Germans. A year later, official reports as of 21 May 1779 show that Clinton's army, on paper, including troops in New York, Rhode Island, Halifax, Newfoundland, Florida, Georgia, the West Indies, and in passage, totalled 47,561 and that of these 13,835 were German. In the same month General Haldimand had 8,090 men in Canada of which 3,200 were German (PRO, CO/5, v. 170, no. 43 and v. 171, p. 35).

[4] Fortescue, Corresp. iii, no. 1708.

yet their total was almost as great as the entire effective British Army had been in 1775.[1] After 1778 Britain had also to find men to defend it against France, Spain, and Holland. By drastic efforts it doubled its totals, including hired troops, to 110,000, but of these only half could be allotted to America, Canada, and the West Indies. With the doubling of the armed forces came a great increase in taxes and the national debt, and most Englishmen thought the bargain a bad one.[2]

The war with America demanded closer co-operation than ever before between the British Army and the Royal Navy, but from the beginning there was friction and distrust between them.[3] Navy efficiency was at its lowest point under its current First Lord the Earl of Sandwich, 'whose supreme talents', wrote the caustic Walpole, unjustly, 'were the artifices of a spy'.[4] It is difficult to be sure of the character of the earl, since he was a chief target of Whig virulence, but in a weak and devious Ministry he was one of the most devious and perhaps though not the weakest deserved the later description of Sir John Fortescue as 'a politician of evil reputation and an inveterate jobber'.[5] Though a hardy perennial in office, he was as unpopular as any man in England, and after his denunciation of his former friend John Wilkes he was widely known as Jeremy Twicher,[6] and was, according to a popular couplet:

> Too infamous to have a friend,
> Too bad for bad men to commend.[7]

The effect on the navy was tragic. 'It had become a point of honour that no Whig Admiral should accept command from Lord Sandwich; and this was a serious matter, since by chance the ablest flag officers, with the notable exception of Rodney, were Whigs almost to a man',[8] though after France entered the war some Whig naval men relented. Even if the earl's reputation was deserved it would not be just to hold him solely responsible for the shocking state of ships and navy morale. That had been a cumulative decay over more administrations

[1] E. E. Curtis, pp. 2, 51.   [2] Ibid.
[3] Robson, *Amer. Rev.*, p. 108.
[4] Walpole, *Last Journals*, ii. 11; Mar. 1777.
[5] Fortescue, *HBA*, 2, iii. 170.
[6] The notorious character in Gay's *Beggar's Opera*.
[7] Hudleston, p. 59, note.   [8] Fortescue, *HBA*, 2, iii. 287.

than his own. He was probably no less efficient than some of his predecessors,[1] and was 'by no means solely to blame for the state of the Navy'.[2]

Probably not even its own officers realized how literally rotten were many of the navy's ships of war. In 1778, when Admiral Keppel took command of the fleet against the French, he found that instead of thirty-five ships of the line fit for duty, as Sandwich had officially stated, there were not more than six, and Fox said that the earl's greatest crime lay in concealing such facts when he must have known them.[3] As the demands on the navy increased, its shocking condition became ever more apparent. In the engagement off the Chesapeake on 5 September 1781 that prefaced Cornwallis's surrender, the *Terrible* sank less from enemy action than from her own decayed condition. The *Royal George* went down in calm waters at Spithead when a piece of her bottom simply fell out. Several of the ships engaged at Doggerbank on 5 August 1781 were in similar condition.

Officers as well as ships were in many cases far below standard efficiency. Clinton believed Admiral Arbuthnot so incompetent that he threatened to resign as Commander-in-Chief unless the Admiral were immediately relieved from his command in American waters—but the Admiral remained for more than a year thereafter. Lord George said of another admiral that only Lord Sandwich believed in his competence. Admiral Lord Howe was able, but he was so bitterly at odds with Sandwich that his effectiveness was greatly reduced.[4]

Under all these conditions it is clear that no single man could direct the British war effort in America to a successful end. But one man was more dominant than any other. From the records of operations, from the opinions of his contemporaries, and from his own public statements, it is evident that man was Lord George Germain.

Contemporary correspondence shows how extensively Lord George determined the strategy and ordered the details of

---

[1] Graham, *Considerations*, p. 27.   [2] Fortescue, *HBA*, 2, iii. 170.

[3] *Hansard*, xx. 179; *DNB* under John Montagu, Earl of Sandwich.

[4] 'What makes this so extraordinary is that Lord Howe both hates and despises Lord Sandwich and he has not spoken to Lord George Germain since the expedition to the coast of France in 1758, although these two preside at the head of the two offices through which he must transmit all business' (Captain J. Leveson-Gower to Captain William Cornwallis, 27 Feb. 1776; *HMC, Var. Coll.* vi. 314).

American operations, and the fact that he did so in the king's name and sometimes with official Cabinet approval did not mean that the decisions were not primarily his own. The overall strategy was almost invariably of his formulation, approved routinely or reluctantly by Cabinet and King.[1] In the implementation of strategy, and often in its alteration by the expression of personal wishes that were not orders but could not be wisely ignored, there was almost no limit to his recognized or pre-empted authority. Subject only to the king's approval, Lord George appointed, assigned, and dismissed generals.[2] He even decided in some cases whether and when they should be given leaves of absence.[3] He ruled on the promotions of officers in America,[4] and even regarding the commissioning of an ensign.[5] He went deeply into other minor matters, such as urging the Assembly of Antigua to raise the provisioning allowance of British troops sent to the Island,[6] ordering hospital stores sent to New York,[7] ruling on the exchange and promotion of artillery officers in Clinton's army,[8] and determining the filling of vacancies on the staff of General Howe.[9]

In fact it is difficult to understand how he and his tiny office staff could have kept a ruling finger in so many assorted pies. He approved and arranged the provision of new boots for the hired Brunswick troops;[10] he ordered stores, horses, wagons, and

[1] Olive Gee, 'The British War Office', *Jrnl. Mod. Hist.*, June 1954, vol. xxvi, no. 2, pp. 123–6. The records indicate that before the Burgoyne plan had been submitted to Cabinet or King, Germain had begun to make assignments of regiments to implement it. Both Howe and Clinton, as their dispatches show, regarded Germain's repeated pressures for raids on the New England coast as his pet scheme, not that of King or Cabinet. The letters of Clinton and Cornwallis in 1780 and 1781 seem to confirm that they thought Germain's pressure for a campaign in the Carolinas was his personal wish and not a result of Cabinet deliberation.

[2] King to North, 24 Feb. 1777; Germain to Barrington, 29 Nov. 1778; PRO, CO/5, v. 174, no. 154; Fortescue, *Corresp.* iii. 421; Amherst to Germain, 20 Mar. 1779; PRO, CO/5, v. 174, no. 47.

[3] PRO, CO/5, v. 174, no. 7.

[4] Amherst to Germain, 4 Nov. 1780; PRO, CO/5, v. 174, no. 181.

[5] PRO, CO/5, v. 174, no. 185; see also, for recruiting in Carolina, PRO, CO/5, v. 174, no. 185.

[6] Germain to Barrington, 6 Jan. 1777; PRO, CO/5, v. 169, no. 2.

[7] Barrington to Germain, 14 Jan. 1777; PRO, CO/5, v. 169, no. 14.

[8] Amherst to Germain, 14 Jan. 1779; PRO, CO/5, v. 174, no. 3.

[9] Pownall to Barrington, 13 Jan. 1776; PRO, CO/5, v. 168.

[10] And insisted that the new boots be made in Britain. PRO, CO/5, v. 92, pp. 555–9.

provisions from the Board of Ordnance;[1] he authorized hospital
and jail arrangements at Halifax;[2] he assigned funds to pay for
the hospital and commissary staffs of the Hessian troops;[3] he
procured tents for both regular and provincial loyalist troops;[4]
and he ordered that the clothing provided for provincial loyalist
soldiers be inspected (after complaints voiced in the House of
Commons) to ensure its quality.[5] The 'Precis of Measures for
reinforcing the Army under General Howe' of 1776 illustrates
the extent to which Lord George issued orders to the Admiralty,
the Board of Ordnance, the Lords of the Treasury, and the
Secretary at War.[6]

To a considerable degree he directed the American operations of the navy as well as the army, to the increasing ire of the
Earl of Sandwich. Since only the Secretary of State could order
ships to transport troops to America, Lord George gained a
voice in all kinds of navy operations far beyond those of previous
Secretaries of State, new or 'ancient', whose wars had been
fought nearer home. No one had anticipated the extent to
which a war against the Americans would enlarge the claims of
the Secretary for America to command, or to share in the
command of, general naval operations, but Lord George made
the most of the situation.

His first orders to the Admiralty were clearly within the scope
of his agreed jurisdiction but they were, inevitably, on an unprecedented scale. He had hardly established himself in office
before he sent categorical orders directly to Admiral Palliser of
the Admiralty Office to be ready with 20,000 tons of transports
by 7 February 1776 and with another 32,000 tons by 7 April,

[1] Letters of orders signed personally by Germain in early 1776 included orders
for 500 horses, 3 trains of artillery, provisions for 38,000 men, clothes and blankets
for General Howe's army. PRO, CO/5, v. 253, nos. 114 ff.

[2] Matthew Lewis to DeGrey, 10 Nov. 1778; PRO, CO/5, v. 170, no. 142.

[3] Osborne to Mackenzie, 3 Mar. 1777; PRO, 30/55, no. 438.

[4] Jenkinson, Secretary at War, wrote to Germain: '. . . your Lordship will
receive [i.e. secure] His Majesty's commands thereupon, they not falling within
the Consideration of my Department' (Jenkinson to Germain, 29 Jan. 1779;
PRO, CO/5, v. 171, no. 9).

[5] Germain to Knox, 12 Mar. 1780; HMC, Var. Coll. 6, Knox, p. 156. This was
shortly after Whigs in Parliament had charged that contractors, and officers in
connivance, were making larger personal profits from army supply contracts.

[6] PRO, CO/5, v. 253, pp. 223 ff. Communications and summaries from
Germain's office used phrases such as: 'Orders were given to the Ordnance', 'Lord
Barrington was directed', and 'Orders were given to the Admiralty'.

and those mandates were accepted. At the same time he ordered
the assignment of one frigate to Bermuda waters, and two more
ships to join the Newfoundland squadron by the end of February.[1] Lord George's established responsibility for armed troops
in transit to America soon led to his issuing specific orders to the
commanding naval officers of the ships that conveyed them.[2]
He had not been a year in office before he complained directly
to the king of Lord Sandwich's disposition of the fleet.[3] It became
Lord George's regular procedure to requisition ships from the
Admiralty; then to inform the War Office of their availability;
then to direct when and where what regiments were to be embarked in them and what stores provided, and, finally, to issue
the sailing order.

The entry of the French into the war in 1778 further widened
the vaguely defined area of Lord George's right to 'advise' on
naval operations. If the safety of troops in transport to America
or the West Indies was his responsibility, then should he not
have a compelling voice in any naval operations against the
French in the Mediterranean which might jeopardize those
troops while on the Atlantic? It is difficult to think of any
British naval operations anywhere which might not indirectly
affect the war in America and consequently, the Secretary for
America might argue, come under his jurisdiction.

It was recognized by his associates that in many such matters
Lord George had the right to give orders, or at least advice.
Lord Sandwich wrote to Lord North in 1778 that the plan of
operations under Admiral Byron 'must not be retarded a
moment unless prevented by a counter order from the Secretary
of State'.[4] Lord Amherst inquired of Lord George regarding the
Lady Townshend, an armed transport at Plymouth: 'I beg to
know if it is your Lordship's Intention she should proceed with
the Convoy to Quebec.'[5] In the joint expedition against the
West Indies by Admiral Rodney and General Vaughan, Lord
George sent orders not only to the General but to the Admiral,
and he took open issue with the Earl of Sandwich and other

[1] PRO, CO/5, v. 253, pp. 114 ff.; 1776.
[2] Germain to Admiralty, 1 Apr. 1776; PRO, 30/55, no. 150; also *HMC*,
Dartmouth, ii. 461, 467; also PRO, CO/5, v. 254, no. 5.
[3] Walpole, *Last Journals*, i. 570; 21 Aug. 1776.
[4] Sandwich to North, 8 May 1778; *Sandwich Papers*, ii. 52.
[5] Amherst to Germain, 6 Sept. 1781; PRO, CO/5, v. 174, no. 232.

Lords of the Admiralty as to whether the fleet should be ordered back to home waters for the winter of 1778–9.[1]

So far as Lord George's relations with the Secretary at War were concerned they resembled, except for the polite official phrases, the attitude of a managing director toward his works foreman. It was Lord George and not the Secretary at War who was informed, first and directly, of the results of the operations of troops in America and of their condition there. Throughout most of the war the Secretary at War did not even receive copies of the State of the Army reports sent from America to the office of Lord George Germain, or the monthly returns. In April 1779 Charles Jenkinson, the new Secretary at War, suggested to Lord George that it would be a convenience if the War Office could receive such reports directly, and not have to request permission to see those sent to Lord George. After a delay of over six months, Lord George declined politely to alter the established procedure to that extent.[2]

The claim has often been made that the king was the real director of the strategy of the war, and that men like Lord George acted only as agents of his dominant will. It is true that the king did far more than ratify the recommendations of his Cabinet and Ministers. He took a personal interest in every aspect and detail of the war; he saw most of the dispatches; he discussed nearly every important measure with Lord George Germain, Lord North, and sometimes other Ministers; he had definite opinions on measures and men and sometimes swayed the actions of his government. In the cases of Carleton and Howe, he circumvented Lord George to some extent in his plan to bring disgrace to one and the full measure of blame upon the other. And since Lord North often avoided the leadership the king sometimes assumed it, substituting for him in the attempt to co-ordinate the acts of the Ministers. There is validity in the verdict of a close modern student of the king's inner councils that 'The recently published correspondence of George III shows that the King thus exercised a great control over policy'.[3]

---

[1] *Sandwich Papers*, ii. 41, 42; May 1778.

[2] Matthew Lewis to DeGrey, 20 Apr. 1779; PRO, CO/5, v. 171, no. 49; and De Grey to Lewis, 13 Nov. 1779; ibid., no. 92.

[3] Thomson, *Secretaries of State*, p. 18.

But the records show that the king yielded to the collective opinion of the Cabinet, and also that some of the decisions he thought he was making had actually been made inevitable by the judicious removal of any palatable alternative. In any case, direction of the war by the king would have been a usurpation of the powers of Parliament and Ministry, and though George III was determined to preserve the powers of the Crown as he interpreted them, he was also careful not to exceed them. The royal correspondence shows an untiring attention to the affairs of State, and strong opinions on some issues, but it shows no attempts to force his Ministers into any actions they collectively opposed. In the American war he insisted on only one general principle: the rebellious colonists must not be allowed independence. If the king had really been directing the war, Fox and Burke would have known it and denounced it vehemently in Parliament. Instead they denounced the Ministry, and most specifically of all Lord North, Lord Sandwich, and Lord George Germain. When the Ministry finally decided that peace must be made at any price, the king said he would abdicate rather than approve independence. But when the Ministry and Parliament negotiated terms that freed America, the king did not abdicate. He merely went mad.

There was no doubt in the minds of contemporary Englishmen who was the presiding manager of the American war. Many personal letters and references were in terms that showed their writers took Lord George's direction for granted. Others, like John Almon the chronicler and publisher, stated the matter more formally. He recorded that Lord George Germain: '... was appointed Secretary of State for the American department; by which the conduct of the war against America was, in a great degree, put into his hands'.[1] William Knox, Lord George's undersecretary, wrote: 'Every one who is at all acquainted with the constitution of this government must know that all warlike preparations, every military operation, and every naval equipment must be directed by a Secretary of State before they can be undertaken. Neither the Admiralty, Treasury, Ordnance nor victualling boards can move a step without the King's command so signified.'[2] The conclusions of a man's contemporaries may be

---

[1] Almon, *Biog., Lit. and Polit. Anecdotes*, ii. 133.
[2] Knox, *Extra-official Papers*, i. 14.

discounted as lacking detachment, but they must also be credited with a special validity, for they were present and saw directly what later generations could see only through documents. The historian has a broader view, but cannot recapture the atmospheres and relationships which were more real than the misty mirror of the recorded word alone.

The leaders of the Whig Opposition had no doubt that Lord George Germain was the man most responsible for operations in America and for that reason condemned him first of all when the war went badly. After Saratoga, Charles Fox centred his attack on Lord George: '. . . the secretary of state who had the direction of it'.[1] The Earl of Shelburne dilated in the House of Lords not only upon Lord George's primary responsibility but upon the excessive and all-embracing detail in which he instructed his generals: '. . . they have been directed in their operations, not in the field but in the cabinet. The orders that have been sent out have extended even to the minutiae of the profession, and have furnished objects of ridicule to the subalterns of the army.' There was no doubt in Shelburne's mind who sent out those orders. 'There is a man it seems in this country who has so great confidence in his military talents as to think he can command an army, and ensure victory in his closet, at 3000 miles distance from the scene of the action.'[2] Other Whig leaders were equally specific that Lord George was the directing force.

So were informed observers outside the inner circle of politics. Sir Nathaniel Wraxall wrote of Lord George that: ' . . . the responsibility of the American war reposed principally on his shoulders'.[3] Horace Walpole recorded that: 'Not long after the commencement of the fatal American War, he was hoisted to the management of it',[4] and busied himself in ' chalking out, dictating the measures'.[5] The *Annual Register* usually expressed the point of view of the informed public, and in 1777, before the débâcle at Saratoga was known in London, it commented with unconscious irony: 'We have already seen that the northern expedition was looked upon as the favorite child of government . . . the noble Lord who conducted the American affairs has all

---

[1] 19 Mar. 1778; *Hansard*, xix. 953.   [2] 18 Nov. 1777; *Hansard*, xix. 385.
[3] Wraxall, i. 383–6.   [4] Walpole, quoted by Marlowe, p. 2.
[5] Walpole, *Last Journals*, i. 510, 511.

the applause of this measure, which was considered entirely his own. . . .'[1]

One or two historians of the present century, when reputations are sometimes most easily established by challenging the conclusions of predecessors, have denied that Lord George led in the direction of the war. Their arguments are more stimulating than convincing; their statements stronger than their evidence. Lord George himself would have disagreed with them. In the debate on 31 October 1776, when the Whigs were attacking the Ministry for the failure of the Parker–Clinton attack on Charleston, Lord George rose to say: 'Sir Peter Parker's expedition failed from arriving too late: I am not responsible for its lack of success, for it was planned before I came into office.'[2] The inference was clear. For events in the American war planned after he took office, Lord George was prepared to claim the primary credit or accept the primary blame. Later, while Howe, Burgoyne, and Cornwallis were successively, so it seemed, marching to victories, Lord George told the Opposition that he was pleased to have been the prime mover of each campaign. In 1778, when the Saratoga fiasco was being anathematized in the House of Commons, Lord George announced in proud defiance that: '. . . the failure or success of the American war was solely imputable to himself',[3] and that 'he was ready to submit his conduct in planning the late expedition to the judgment of the House. If it appeared impotent, weak, and ruinous, let the censure of the House fall upon him.'[4] Admiral Lord Howe made it quite clear before Parliament that in his opinion Lord George had absorbed too much of the Ministry's authority. The Admiral '. . . charged the noble Lord at the head of the American department with acting sometimes on his own account, independent of every other member of the administration', in ways 'which tended to dismantle the fleet and make it inferior to that of France'.[5] As for the opinions of the generals

---

[1] *Annual Register for 1777*, p. 38.

[2] Force, *American Archives*, Series V, Book III, p. 938.

[3] *Hansard*, xx. 80.

[4] *Annual Register for 1778*, p. 69.

[5] Admiral Howe's immediate complaint was that Lord George had signed 'an order to New York, authorizing the people there to fit out privateers and letters of marque', which 'drew support, provisions and enlistments away from the regular fleet' (14 Dec. 1778; *Hansard*, xx. 69, 70).

who commanded major armies in America, each was in turn emphatic in protest against Lord George's over-direction.

The Saratoga defeat shook Lord George's power throughout 1778, but he regained it and until late 1781 was in military operations almost as dominant as before. It was not until after the news of the surrender of Cornwallis at Yorktown reached London that Parliament, people, and other members of the Ministry refused to accept his virtual dictation. The change is pointed up by two notes from Lord Amherst, Commander-in-Chief of the armed forces, to Lord George. Three months before Yorktown he had deferentially inquired of Lord George what were his orders for sending reinforcements to America on the ship *Lady Townshend*. Immediately after the news of Cornwallis's surrender, Lord Amherst replied to a routine order from the American Secretary to send certain detachments to America, that such an order must first be confirmed by the Cabinet.[1] By that time the war was lost.

[1] Amherst to Germain, 11 Dec. 1781; PRO, CO/5, v. 174, no. 252. The news of the surrender at Yorktown had reached London on 25 November.

XI

MEN AT ODDS

CLOTHED in his new name and authority, Lord George began with confidence and surprisingly little public criticism. 'I met with no abuse, and all passed as I could wish', he wrote to General Irwin a week after his installation.[1] There were even a few friendly reactions. Blunt Admiral Sir George Rodney wrote to him in characteristically unrestrained terms that his appointment would in some degree make amends for the 'gross, cruel, base, unjustifiable persecution' that Lord George had suffered during the last king's reign.[2] Thomas Hutchinson confided to his diary: 'I don't know of any person more to general satisfaction than Ld. George Germain. He has the character of a great man, and I verily believe is a true friend to both countries and would have no inducement but a regard to the publick interest, to accept of a post attended with so many difficulties.'[3] Many other men were far less enthusiastic, but for the moment most of them held their tongues.

Once again Lord George's contemporaries formed strongly variant opinions of his spirit and conduct. George Selwyn, who recorded his political judgements as assiduously though less acidly than Horace Walpole, wrote to the Earl of Carlisle: 'I am more desirous myself of hearing Lord G. G. than anybody. He looks very confident, and I take it for granted is prepared for all kinds of abuse.'[4] A month later Selwyn reported that: 'Lord G. Sackville seems in very great spirits—is quite persuaded that all this will end after the first campaign, and that he himself, as I take it for granted, shall establish his reputation as a Minister by it.'[5] But the fact that Selwyn still called Lord George by the name Sackville after five years of being Germain boded no good for the new Minister; it showed how easily his earlier mistakes might be recalled.

[1] Germain to Irwin, 18 Nov. 1775; *HMC, Stop. Sack*. i. 138.
[2] Rodney to Germain, 12 Nov. 1775; *HMC, Stop. Sack*. ii. 19.
[3] Hutchinson, *Diaries*, ii. 11; 27 Jan. 1776.
[4] Selwyn to Carlisle, 16 Nov. 1775; *HMC*, xv (1897), 5, 6, *Carlisle*, p. 302.
[5] Selwyn to Carlisle, 20 Dec. 1775; ibid., p. 306.

Selwyn got a different impression of Lord George when he listened to his first speeches as a king's Minister in Parliament. 'He seemed to speak with more weight, before he was in office. The ghost of Minden is for ever brought in neck and shoulders to frighten him with.'[1] Walpole thought Lord George 'at first much flustered'[2]—a weak shadow of his aggressive self. When General Conway attacked his over-optimistic reports of affairs in America, as published in the official *Gazette*, 'Lord George Germaine answered him in a poor abject manner, confessing the misfortune at Boston'.[3] Three weeks later Walpole wrote that Lord George was '. . . dragged up to speak, and never made a poorer figure . . . so grossly dismayed that he had the desperate courage to tell a gross untruth—he denied ever having said that he should insist on implicit obedience from the colonies, which all the House had heard from him'.[4] Hutchinson called on Lord George after three months in office and wrote in his diary: 'I never saw him more dull.'[5]

The explanation may lie in the change in his relation to Parliament. His reputation had been made there as an independent. Now, as a Minister, he could no longer speak or not speak as he pleased. He must when called upon defend his own acts and also those of the Ministry he served. He had built up his influence by the sharpness of his attacks; now he was faced with the more difficult and uncongenial duty of defence. He had previously enjoyed the destructive irresponsibility of the dissenter; now he must be constructive and responsible. As Hutchinson noted: 'It would have been impossible on Lord Dartmouth's going out to have found a successor who would have escaped abuse',[6] but Minden made Lord George the most vulnerable of war ministers. Early in May 1776 Temple Luttrell abused him 'in the grossest terms, and for a long time, in the House of Commons. He said "flight was the only safety that remained for the royal army, and he saw one who had set the example in Germany, and who was fit to lead on such an occasion". Lord George said not a word in reply.'[7]

[1] Selwyn to Carlisle, 12 Dec. 1775; ibid., 310.
[2] Walpole, *Last Journals*, i. 495.   [3] Ibid., p. 540; 6 May 1776.
[4] Ibid., p. 552; 22 May 1776.
[5] Hutchinson, *Diaries* (original MS.), Clements, p. 309; 6 Jan. 1776.
[6] Ibid., p. 313; 28 June 1776.
[7] Walpole, *Last Journals*, i. 541; 10 May 1776.

In his Whitehall office, despite the impression of dullness he gave his admirer Hutchinson, Lord George was 'only too ready to undertake the control of military operations'.[1] Though he had 'always treated Lord Chatham's magnificent plans as visions of a madman', he 'now seemed to have taken that daring and inconsiderate Minister for his own pattern, chalking out, dictating the measures'.[2] He would have been happier if he could have chosen his commanding officers, but when he entered office the four leading generals in America had already been given their commissions. William Howe had succeeded Gage as commanding officer for the colonies, and General Carleton held the governorship and military command in Canada. Clinton and Burgoyne were the next two ranking officers in America, each ambitious to lead a major operation.

In any war, mutual confidence between military leaders in the field and their civilian chiefs in government is highly desirable. In that war of vast distances it was essential to military success, for British generals in America must know what they were expected to do during the long delays in communications, while circumstances sometimes underwent drastic change. The war also required closer co-ordination of military and naval operations than had ever been achieved before. The Secretary for America would obviously have to be on terms of great sympathy with his overseas generals, and ready to give each of them a high degree of discretionary power. One military historian has stated: 'It was quite certain that to attempt to direct operations from London was simply to court disaster',[3] and another concluded that of all the blunders England could make in the American war, 'that of endeavouring to direct the war from London was undoubtedly the greatest'.[4]

Before Lord George came into office he had recognized this

[1] Walter Fitzpatrick, *HMC, Var. Coll.* 6, *Knox Papers*, Preface, p. xviii.
[2] Walpole, *Last Journals*, i. 510, 511; Jan. 1776.
[3] Fortescue, *HBA*, 2, iii. 206.
[4] Lt.-Col. F. E. Whitton, *Prince of Wales' Leinster Regt.*, Murray, London, 1931. One historian of the present century differed, and stated: 'Contrary to accepted belief, British commanders in America were given great latitude in both their planning and their actions . . . this was a convenient umbrella under which mediocre commanders took shelter, which is not borne out by an examination of circumstances' (Robson, *Amer. Rev.*, pp. 134, 138). Mr. Robson's argument would have been more convincing if he had supported it with evidence. No 'examination of circumstances' can ignore the clear record.

and had written to Lord Suffolk that: '. . . the distance from the
seat of government necessarily leaves much to the discretion and
the resources of the general'.[1] Irony runs through the words and
events of the war with America, and never more pungently than
in that statement. Not only did Lord George vacillate between
too much and too little direction of the generals, but he began
with enmity toward his two commanding officers and ended
with the enmity of all four.[2]

Ever since St. Malo he had been openly at odds with the
Howe brothers. Before he had been six months in office one
military man wrote to another: 'Lord George Germaine was
taken into great favour, and was to take the lead in the management of all this American war. . . . What makes this yet more
extraordinary is that Lord Howe . . . has not spoken to Lord
George Germaine since the expedition to the coast of France
in 1758.'[3] Lord Howe would soon be put in command of the
fleet for America, and would at first try, unsuccessfully, to
restore friendly terms with Lord George.[4] His brother William
had made no attempt to conceal his dislike of Lord George
at St. Malo and Minden, but he made similar efforts to repair
the breach during the first year of their new association. Lord
George had not been pleased on entering office to find that
General Howe had been given not only the command in
America but also orders to evacuate Boston. His dislike of the
Howes was personal, but he could dress it in more impressive
reasons. Partly because a brother of the Howes had fought and
died with Americans against the French and had been loved
by the colonists, the Howes had not concealed their dislike of
making war on the Americans, and had assured their parliamentary constituents that they would not fight against the
colonists. But if Lord George thought that, having taken up the
sword, the Howe brothers would not use it with their reputed
vigour, he was wrong. General Howe had already demonstrated
the contrary at Bunker Hill.

[1] Germain to Suffolk, 16 June 1775; *HMC, Stop. Sack.* ii. 2.

[2] Carleton and Clinton wrote bitter protests to Germain; Burgoyne and Howe
demanded Parliamentary Inquiries to justify themselves and condemn Germain's
mistakes.

[3] Capt. J. Leveson-Gower to Capt. the Hon. Wm. Cornwallis, 27 Feb. 1776;
HMC, Var. Coll. 6, *Cornwallis-Wykeham-Martin*, p. 314.

[4] Lord Howe to Germain, 22 and 29 July and 25 Sept. 1775; Clements, *Germain
Papers*, iii, and *HMC, Stop. Sack.* ii. 3, 4, 5, 6, 9.

Nearly all military men had approved the appointment of General William Howe as commanding officer in America. He had seen more successful active service than any eligible British general except Amherst, who had declined the appointment.[1] 'It was generally believed in 1775 that a better appointment . . . could scarcely have been made',[2] and even Howe's professional rival Burgoyne had warmly credited the hollow victory at Bunker Hill to 'the conduct and spirit of my friend Howe'.[3] Lord North was notably friendly to the Howe brothers.[4] Lord George, eager to demonstrate his ability by conducting a short, successful war, and perhaps mellowed for the moment by his new appointment, was apparently ready to overlook his old enmity with Howe, for he began by giving him full support and compliments so elaborate that they sounded suspiciously insincere. He never badgered Howe as much as he later badgered Clinton. Perhaps the outspokenness of the Howe brothers and their strong position in Court and Parliament made him a little afraid of them.

Howe replaced General Gage on 2 August 1775;[5] was gazetted Lieutenant-General[6] and given the rank of full General in America.[7] Before Lord Dartmouth retired from the Secretaryship he had raised with Howe the question of evacuating Boston before winter and moving to New York or 'somewhere else'.[8] When Lord George took office he claimed he discovered that Lord Dartmouth had actually ordered withdrawal from Boston and immediately raised the matter with the king. The king '. . . said the order was conditional, but he assured his Majesty it was absolute. He then wrote not only a publick but a private letter to Genl. Howe, placing however his great confidence in

[1] Fisher, *True History*, p. 201.

[2] T. S. Anderson, *The Howe Brothers*, pp. 4, 117 (thesis pagination).

[3] Burgoyne to Germain, 20 Aug. 1775; *HMC, Stop. Sack.* ii. 16.

[4] North to General Howe, 25 June 1776; PRO, 30/55, no. 221. The tone of this letter, and the fact that it was one of the few letters that North wrote personally to a general in America, is indicative of his friendliness.

[5] PRO, 30/55, no. 24. But Gage's official letter of dismissal from Germain was dated 18 Apr. 1776. Clements, *Gage Papers*, English Series, xxx.

[6] *HMC, Amer. MSS.* (1904), p. 6.

[7] Barrington to Howe, 23 Mar. 1776; PRO, 30/55, no. 144.

[8] Dartmouth to Howe, 5 Sept. 1775, no. 31. At the Parliamentary Inquiry in 1779 Howe said he had regarded Dartmouth's dispatch, which he received on 9 Nov. 1775, as an order, which he could not then fulfil for lack of adequate transport (*Hansard*, xx. 667).

the improbability of carrying the order into execution.'[1] That, at least, was what Thomas Hutchinson recorded that Lord George had told him.

Howe had not evacuated Boston during the winter, partly because adequate transport had not reached him. Possibly Lord George did not hurry the transports. Howe thought Lord Dartmouth was still Secretary of State for America when he wrote in December that he had got six of his companies into ships but was holding them in Boston harbour until more transports came to take all the troops to Halifax. Howe was already complaining of slowness in the arrival of ships and supplies.[2] A little later he wrote (he still thought to Dartmouth) that he could not obey the order to evacuate until more transports arrived from England,[3] and settled in at Boston for the winter.

Lord George wrote approving a withdrawal to Halifax if Howe believed it necessary; promising Howe large reinforcements to take New York, and then inconsistently urging him to use a large part of those reinforcements to occupy Rhode Island. Howe, meanwhile, wrote to the Secretary for America warning him that: '. . . the apparent strength of his army for the Spring did not flatter him with the hope of bringing the rebels to decisive action'.[4] That was not the kind of talk Lord George wanted to hear from his commanding General; he refused to believe that rebel resistance could be other than weak, and ascribed Howe's statement to over-caution or lack of initiative.

Before Howe learned that he was dealing with a new Secretary, a sudden event compelled him to evacuate Boston. For some time he had feared the American forces might occupy Dorchester Heights overlooking Boston and thus make the city untenable, and had planned to remove that danger by taking the Heights himself. But a spell of bad weather kept him from doing so, and suddenly, on 5 March 1776 Washington captured the heights. Howe evacuated Boston on 17 March and moved

---

[1] *Hutchinson Diaries* (original MS.), Clements, p. 316; 2 Mar. 1776.

[2] Howe to Secretary of State for America, 13 Dec. 1775; PRO, CO/5, v. 253, no. 7.

[3] Ibid., no. 92.

[4] Howe to Germain, ibid. Germain to Howe, 28 Mar. 1776; ibid., no. 94; also PRO, 30/55, no. 461.

his troops to Halifax to await supplies, reinforcements, navy support, and further orders.[1]

When that news reached Lord George he voiced no open criticism of Howe, though he hinted his disappointment and his doubts of Howe's aggressiveness to a few confidential friends. His letters to the General continued their unctuous flatteries. So did Howe's replies: there seems no doubt but that at this stage each man was trying hard to get along with the other. Lord George sent Howe at Halifax all the reinforcements and supplies he had promised and did his best to get the Admiralty to send the needed ships.

Both men had, on the whole, grounds for satisfaction with each other and for optimism. When Howe left Halifax he had with him or in transit the most powerful army Britain had ever sent to America. Its 25,000 trained British and German soldiers outnumbered by two to one Washington's untrained regulars, most of whom were on very short enlistments. To Lord George complete victory seemed imminent as well as inevitable, and he could not help feeling annoyed with Howe's letter of 26 April, which was dubious about an early and complete victory over the rebels and confessed 'apprehensions that such an event will not be easily brought about'.[2]

Other irritations developed during Howe's stay at Halifax. Lord George wrote urging him to provide some honourable and lucrative post for one Colonel Christie, 'as a man of merit and a great sufferer by unhappy disputes'. Whatever Colonel Christie's merits, in Lord George's eyes one of the chief of them was his support of General Sackville after Minden. Howe did not take kindly to the suggestion, with the result that Lord George was soon urging Christie upon an equally reluctant General Carleton in Canada. Lord George also sent out his friend Sir Henry Erskine, and demanded to know precisely what exalted use Howe would make of him. And forgetting his earlier pronouncement to Lord Suffolk about the necessity of giving generals in America discretionary latitude, Lord George began to display a '. . . foolish ambition to direct all operations from Whitehall'.[3] He sent Howe detailed suggestions and instruc-

---

[1] Howe's dispatch reached Germain's office on 2 May 1776 (PRO, CO/5, v. 253, no. 98).   [2] Howe to Germain, 26 Apr. 1776; *HMC, Stop. Sack.* ii. 30.
[3] Germain to Howe, 27 Apr. 1776; PRO, 30/55, no. 119; also *HMC, Amer. MSS.* vi (1904), p. 36; Fortescue, *HBA,* 2, iii. p. 397.

tions that were not quite orders but were difficult not to follow. There were minute directions regarding plans, promotions, recruiting of loyalists, control of transports, and even the handling and destination of certain 'rebel prisoners'. Howe dealt with these as best he could, but Lord George's attitudes on promotions and transports made him angry and he showed it.[1]

Few traditions were more cherished by British commanding officers in the field than the rights to fill vacancies in their field staffs, to make promotions within their own ranks, and to control the use of transports while they were engaged in the movements of troops. So far as the first two of these were concerned, Howe recognized that if his army were merged with that in Canada, then General Carleton as the ranking officer would properly command the united force. Anticipating that possibility, Howe asked, reasonably enough in view of the tradition, concurrent authority to continue making promotions within the ranks of the regiments assigned to him. With regard to the transports then in Halifax harbour waiting to be joined by other transports with men and supplies, Howe felt the need to control their use and to maintain proper discipline of their crews while on land.[2]

He asked Lord George for assurance on these questions and received replies that seemed to him so equivocal that he pronounced them to be 'a deliberate affront', and on 25 April wrote to Lord George offering his resignation.[3] Barrington supported Howe on the promotion issue, but Lord Sandwich opposed having any navy men even temporarily under the control of the army commander. Lord George was not prepared to risk the furore Howe's resignation would rouse, so he did his best to solve the transport problem by a compromise, and made just enough grudging concessions on the promotion issue to restore Howe to reasonable good humour.[4] A little later Lord North took the unusual step of writing a cordial personal letter to

---

[1] PRO, 30/55; also PRO, WO, 10, 11, 678, 683, 684; also PRO, CO/5, vols. 167, 73, 253, 263; also *HMC, Amer. MSS.* vi.

[2] *HMC, Stop. Sack.* ii. 31–34.

[3] Howe to Germain, 25 Apr. 1776; *HMC, Stop. Sack.* ii. 31.

[4] Barrington to Wm. Gaull, 1 July 1776; PRO, WO, i, 10; also Robson, 'Purchase and Promotion in the British Army in the Eighteenth Century', in *History Today,* xxvi. 57–72.

Howe, which also encouraged him as to the future: 'We expect
before the end of August to have shipped from England and
Ireland a sufficient quantity of provisions to feed your army
(computed at 36,000 men) till May 1777.'[1] That was a larger
army than Howe had yet asked for, or would ever, in effective
fighting men, get.

The ultimate arrival of ships and men at Halifax turned Howe
from uncongenial cerebration to military activity. He left
Halifax on 7 June; began his disembarkation near New York
about 1 July; beat the Americans on Long Island on 27 August;
took New York on 15 September; won again at White Plains in
October, and helped the Marquis of Cornwallis push across
New Jersey.[2] Howe was at the peak of his success and reputation.
The king made him a Knight of the Bath, though Lord George
somewhat took the edge of satisfaction from this award. He
wrote to Sir William Howe that he had himself thought some
other award would be more 'agreeable to you' than one so
recently also given to General Carleton; Lord George '. . . could
have wished there had been any other method of shewing the
high sense the King has of your merit and services'.[3]

Lord George never thought so highly of Howe as immediately
after his capture of New York, but Lord Cornwallis had become
his special favourite. On the same day that Lord George had
written to Howe about his knighthood, he also wrote to Cornwallis: 'Your Lordship I presume will be desirous of remaining
under General Howe if we are to have another campaign, but
whatever your commands are upon that head, when you signify
them to me I shall with pleasure obey them.'[4] There is no better
way to undermine a commanding officer than to promise one
of his aides unqualified support and a choice of appointments.

After that first campaign Howe seemed to lose his energetic
drive. A number of reasons were suggested. It was whispered
in London and shouted in America that the pleasures of New

---

[1] North to Howe, 25 June 1776; PRO, 30/55, no. 221.

[2] Lecky, iv. 2 ff.

[3] Belcher, ii. 219; and Germain to Howe, 18 Oct. 1776; HMC, Stop. Sack.
ii. 43.

[4] Germain to Cornwallis, 18 Oct. 1776; Clements, Germain Papers, v. 48. Members
of Cornwallis's family were in powerful positions: one was Archbishop of Canterbury.

York and a new mistress made Howe reluctant to take the field.
A popular ditty of the day began:

> Awake, awake, Sir Billy;
> There's forage on the plain,
> Oh leave your little filly
> And open the campaign!

It is also possible that Howe's sympathy with the Americans
tempered, even if only subconsciously, his martial energies, but
this seems unlikely. Howe was first of all a soldier and a fighting
man. He was also a man of simple mental processes, who,
though he could suffer from indecision, was not capable of
playing a successful double game. When called upon to fight
he fought hard and shrewdly, without reservation. Any sympathy he may have had with the Americans did not prevent
him from winning hard battles at Bunker Hill, Long Island,
White Plains, Brandywine, and Germantown.

There were more likely reasons for the periods of apparent
apathy that interlarded Howe's brief spurts of energy after
1776. One was his appointment, with his brother, the Admiral,
to negotiate peace with the Americans. No general can be
expected to charge into battle with a sword in one hand and an
olive branch in the other, or to win a successful peace while
waging an aggressive war. Subtler men than Sir William Howe
would have been thrown into confusion by that dual commission. There is some evidence that after the capture of New York
Howe hoped that by not pressing the Americans too belligerently
he might win them back to loyalty, or at least increase the
chance of successful peace negotiations. If so, he was soon dis-
illusioned. The Americans did not want peace without freedom:
Lord George did not want peace without their subjection. As
the months in New York drew into a year, Howe's own
experiences convinced him that he could not conquer America
without larger forces than Lord George would—or perhaps
could—send him. But a still more convincing reason has come
to light. Howe was no strategist or administrator. He was a
man of action, and in that capacity as competent in his last
battles as in his first ones. He could fight better than he could
direct and organize, but he had been placed in a position where
strategy, logistics, and politics were as important as leading a

charge up Bunker Hill. What was more, he realized, as Lord George did not, that Britain's cause would be lost in America if his own force was destroyed by piecemeal attrition. He had to keep it together and use it cautiously. He could not risk cumulative losses in a series of indecisive battles, or even by expensive and not final victories. To keep his force in being was more important than to win every battle except the last one. Lord George was constantly urging Howe to draw Washington into a pitched battle on favourable ground; Howe knew Washington would not be drawn. This was not the type of warfare that suited Howe's temperament, talents, or experience, or suited Lord George's desire that he attack vigorously in all directions at one time. Howe was miscast in America and he knew it.

That is revealed in a letter his brother, Admiral Lord Howe, wrote to Lord George ten days after Howe's greatest success in capturing New York. Lord Howe wrote that General Howe: '. . . professes his plan to be of greater compass than he feels himself equal to direct, and judges it proper that a chief officer in the character of a viceroy with unlimited powers should be chosen for the occasion'.[1] The Howes were as proud in their way as Lord George was in his, and both brothers must have suffered in making this confession, particularly to a man they disliked. Their sacrifice of pride brought no tangible results.

Whatever the causes of General Howe's caution, it did not please Lord George. Though he continued to handle Howe more delicately than any other general in America except Cornwallis, he increasingly showered him with orders and urgent suggestions. The capture of New York had made Lord George so certain of quick victory that he wrote to Howe expressing the hope 'that you may pay a visit to Philadelphia before this Campaign ends. The punishing that seat of the Congress would be a proper example to the rest of the colonys.'[2] By 'punishing' Lord George meant destruction or burning: he had already suggested the burning of Boston. Lord George also pretended to be sending Howe reinforcements to the full number requested, but he reduced the numbers and then failed to supply even that quota. He held forth promises of the dates when

[1] Admiral Howe to Germain, 25 Sept. 1775; *HMC, Stop. Sack.* ii. 9.
[2] Germain to Howe, Oct. 1776; Clements, *Germain Papers*, v.

reinforcements could be expected and did not meet them. He frequently urged upon Howe that very dissipation of forces that Howe thought dangerous, if not fatal to success.

These were problems in which friction between the commander in the field and his superior in London was almost inevitable. Few generals in any war have felt that they were receiving full understanding and support from the civilian officials at home. If Britain had not the resources to provide Howe with everything he needed to win the war, it was not the fault of Lord George Germain. Britain's supply and transport problems were, in proportion to its capacities, even more demanding than those upon the United States in its later war in the far Pacific. Had Lord George admitted to Howe the inevitable shortages, he might have stood better with that general and with history. Instead he gave Howe false hopes, half-promises, and then disappointments.

In December 1776 Howe complained to Lord George of the inadequate naval forces at his service, and the lack of large ships of the line, which Lord George had given him reason to expect. The fact was that the Earl of Sandwich had refused to send any ships of the line, chiefly for a reason he would not admit—that so few were fit for active ocean duty, and they might be needed to protect England. Lord George's reply to Howe was unsatisfactory partly because it was evasive: 'All that I need say to you at present, concerning the ten ships of the line which you solicit, is that Lord Sandwich will write fully to Lord Howe upon that subject . . . it gives me pleasure to acquaint you that I have reason to hope that such a force will be sent as will be deemed sufficient by yourself and Lord Howe.'[1] Admiral Howe and Sandwich were at odds, but even had they been the best of friends all the ships needed could not have been produced. The General's campaigns suffered accordingly; on more than one occasion he revised or postponed his plans for reasons derived from delays or shortages of ships.

Lord George in turn was irritated by Howe's demands for more men and ships than Lord George thought could be needed. He was also annoyed by Howe's repeated warnings

---

[1] Germain to Howe, 14 Jan. 1777; PRO, 30/55, nos. 213, 371; also *HMC, Stop. Sack*. ii. 50, 52, 57. Howe's dispatch complaining was: Howe to Germain, 18 Dec. 1776; *HMC, Stop. Sack*. ii. 52.

that the number and value of loyalists was not as great as Lord George chose to believe, and that the war would not be quickly or easily won by a single great campaign. When Howe wrote in August that he was not: '. . . so sanguine in my expectations as some of the friends of Government here are for getting recruits in this country for the Army',[1] Lord George ignored the conclusion; continued to count largely on loyalist enlistments, and blamed Howe when they were disappointing. The more Howe's predictions proved true, the less Lord George liked the man who made them.

By early 1777 the laboured politeness of the official exchanges did not conceal the fact that each man was resentful of the other. Explanations became more brief and compliments more hollow. When Howe asked Lord George to send him 300 cavalry horses, Lord George replied crisply that he was sending a hundred. When Howe wrote that since he could not get hay or forage in New York it must be sent him by ship, Lord George answered that there would be no room for forage in the next lot of transports and Howe would have to get it in America. But such minor differences paled before the issue of reinforcements. In late 1776 Howe requested what amounted to an added 15,000 men for the 1777 campaign, making it clear that his ability to embark on his proposed plans depended on receiving them. Lord George replied that men would be sent to approximately that number, but it was perfectly clear that his arithmetic was specious and that Howe's request was being drastically reduced.

Howe was angry as well as discouraged, but he kept his anger to himself. He reduced his ambitious campaign plans, but then Lord George complained that 'the King' was greatly disappointed that Howe was not conducting punitive raids along the coast of New England, and sent Major Balfour to New York to persuade him. When on 2 April 1777 Howe wrote that the opening of his campaign would be delayed because of the slow arrival of men and supplies,[2] Lord George disregarded the reason, deplored Howe's inactivity, and later told the king and others that he could not understand why Howe was so late in opening his campaign. By June 1777 Lord George's misunder-

---

[1] Howe to Germain, 10 Aug. 1776; *HMC, Stop. Sack.* ii. 38.
[2] Howe to Germain, 2 Apr. 1777; *HMC, Stop. Sack.* ii. 63, 64.

standings with Howe had become a major cause of the coming disaster at Saratoga.

Meanwhile, Lord George's relations with his commanding officer in Canada had reached the breaking point. General Guy Carleton was, of all available British generals, the one best qualified to head the British forces in Canada. He was a professional soldier of the best type, with some of the qualities of a great statesman, and those qualities were especially needed in Canada during the American war. The British task in Canada was not only to defend it against American attack, or even to use it as a base for aggressive action, but to hold the Canadians to loyalty to a Crown to which they had been attached for only a decade. Carleton realized this as Lord George did not, and acted with integrity, caution, and vision. Canadians have appreciated Carleton, as soldier and as statesman, more than most Englishmen and Americans. One leading Canadian historian wrote:

> Of Carleton's merits as a soldier there can be no question. No one ever gauged a military situation better. No one ever displayed more firmness and courage at a time of crisis, made more of small resources, or showed more self-restraint. But he was more than a good military leader; he was also a statesman of high order, and, had he been given a free hand and supreme control of the British forces and policy in America, he might well have kept the American colonies as he kept Quebec. . . . Above all, he had a character above and beyond intrigue. Had he not been ousted by malign influence . . . .[1]

Most of Carleton's contemporaries would not have thought of replacing him. One unidentified Englishman took it upon himself to send a long letter directly to Lord George's office in late 1775, analysing the situation in Canada then, and assuring the American Secretary that Quebec '. . . will be defended to the last Extremity for there is not perhaps in the world a more experienced or more determined officer than General Carleton'.[2]

Some of the very qualities most needed in a commander in Canada were qualities Lord George disapproved in Carleton, as lack of firmness and aggressive energy. Carleton combined experience and understanding of the pioneer Canadian mind

---

[1] Lucas, *History of Canada*, p. 115.
[2] Clements, *Germain Papers*; dated Quebec, 30 Nov. 1775.

with common sense and patience. Generous to a defeated foe,
a severe disciplinarian but a considerate leader of his men, he
would not charge into the colonies on a dangerous or futile
campaign; he would not play politics for personal advancement,
or flatter a superior he did not respect.[1]

In 1775, with only a handful of British troops and an uncertain
Canadian constituency, Carleton had successfully resisted the
combined attack of two small American armies: one led by the
able General Montgomery down Lake Champlain to Montreal
and the other led by the brilliant Benedict Arnold across the
frozen wastes of northern Maine toward Quebec. Carleton had
been forced to yield Montreal, where he had only 600 men of
all sorts,[2] and had barely escaped in a small boat at night down
the St. Lawrence to Quebec. To defend Quebec he had only
160 trained British soldiers and such Canadians as he could
enlist and trust, with no artillery and not a single armed vessel.[3]
When Montgomery attacked on New Year's Eve with some
1,200 men Carleton had assembled an almost equal number,
but a large proportion of them were 'anything but trustworthy'.[4]
He held Quebec against a siege all winter, and repulsed a desperate final attack in which Montgomery was killed. Arnold
continued the siege until Burgoyne arrived from England with
strong reinforcements on 6 May 1776 and helped Carleton
drive the Americans out of Canada.[5]

Those reinforcements gave Carleton an army which on paper
numbered 9,984 British and German troops,[6] but he could
attack no further without ships to move his troops up Lake
Champlain, where Arnold had assembled a considerable fleet.
Carleton spent from 19 June to early October building the
necessary craft,[7] and then swept the Americans and their ships
from the lake. By that time he had added enough volunteers
to bring his total force to a nominal 13,000 men,[8] but the hard
winter would soon make any troop movements almost impossible. Carleton reluctantly decided it was too late to attack
Ticonderoga, where Arnold was strongly established.[9] And

[1] See Note H, p. 499.   [2] Fortescue, *HBA*, 2, iii. 162.
[3] Tracy, *History of Canada*, ii. 578 ff.   [4] Fortescue, *HBA*, 2, iii. 163.
[5] PRO, CO/5, v. 253, nos. 18, 30.   [6] Ibid., nos. 23–41.
[7] Ibid., no. 24.
[8] Fortescue, *HBA*, 2, iii. 179; also PRO, CO/5, v. 253, no. 44.
[9] Lecky, iv. 12.

'. . . on the 15th of October he quitted Crown Point & returned to Canada with his whole force'.[1]

For all this Carleton was thanked and knighted by his government, but only over the protest of the new Secretary of State for America. Lord George had expected more from the 1776 campaign; he believed Carleton should have captured Ticonderoga and thus brought to a glorious end the first year of the new Secretary. In any case Lord George would have been alert to find fault with Carleton, for the two men strongly disliked each other. The enmity went back at least as far as Minden. 'Lord George Germaine hated him as one who, by his friendship with the Duke of Richmond, and by his own firmness, he concluded or knew, was not favorable to his Lordship on the affair of Minden.'[2] Now Lord George had a chance for revenge.[3]

It was true that Carleton's manners were not always ingratiating; he was spoken of as 'a man of strong resentment, as prejudiced against Lord George, & dissatisfied at not having a general command, Howe being his Junr. in the army'.[4] Even if those statements were true they would not justify the treatment Carleton received from Lord George.

Whatever the causes of the enmity, Lord George never missed an opportunity to discredit Carleton. 'I remarked to the King how extraordinary a conduct the Commander in chief . . . held in letting so many ships arrive from thence without a single line

---

[1] PRO, CO/5, v. 253, 55.

[2] Walpole, *Last Journals*, i. 527, 528. Walpole stated elsewhere (ibid. ii. 47; 6 Oct. 1777) that Carleton had been a witness against Lord George at the Minden court martial, but there is no record of that in the *Proceedings*. Walpole probably realized his mistake, for in his later *Memoirs on the Reign of George III* he referred to Carleton's connexion with the Minden affair as through his friendship with the Duke of Richmond. Tracy stated that one of Carleton's friends had appeared against Lord George at the trial, but does not name the man (Tracy, ii. 605).

[3] A summary probably prepared in Germain's office and reflecting his attitudes contains the following passage: 'It was expected that not only Canada would be recovered, but a Communication opened with the King's forces on the side of the Atlantic, and by that means place the Rebel Army between two Fires. It was also expected that the King's Forces would be joined by great Numbers of loyal subjects who it was represented by Gov. Tryon, Col. Skene, Proprietor of Skeenesborough . . . groaned under the Oppression of the Rebel Committees' (PRO, CO/5, v. 253, nos. 37, 38).

[4] Hutchinson, who wrote that, was an admirer of Germain, a frequenter of his office, and at once a victim and a disseminator of his propaganda (*Hutchinson Diaries*, 25 Nov. 1776; Clements (original MS.), p. 326).

for this office'—that was a typical remark of Lord George where
it might do the most harm to Carleton.[1] Nor would he forgive
Carleton for refusing to give an important post in Canada,
already committed to another with the approval of Lord
Barrington and the king, to one of his own protégés. The man
Lord George favoured was that same Colonel Christie whom
General Howe had declined to appoint to a high post in his own
army. The Colonel may have been a friend of Lord George or
the friend of a friend: Horace Walpole disposed of him in the
single phrase 'an obscure Scot'. At any rate Lord George had
determined that Carleton should make Christie his Quartermaster-General. It was bad luck for Carleton that the man appointed to that post only a few weeks before was his own brother,
an able Major,[2] for the relationship made him vulnerable.
Carleton refused to appoint Christie to that or any other office
satisfactory to the Colonel. Lord George was insistent, and
charged Burgoyne, who was to lead the reinforcements to
Canada, to urge Christie's case again on Carleton.

Burgoyne apparently developed a sympathy for Carleton. His
report to Lord George, though diplomatic, made clear his hope
that Christie would be recalled from Canada: 'I found Major
Carleton acting as Quartermaster General for the army, by an
appointment dated some months ago. I perceived also in my
first conversation that the General was determined not to employ Col. Christie . . . the General . . . I understand means to
request that they may never serve in the same army . . . [I hope
that] the two parties may be speedily separated.'[3]

Lord George did not take the defeat gracefully. He wrote to
Burgoyne of Christie: 'As he is disagreeable to the General, it is
impossible they should remain together, but when an officer has
been employed by me for the benefit of the public, I cannot
consent to his disgrace to gratify the humour of any individual.'[4]
Lord George wrote that letter to Burgoyne the day after he
had written one to Carleton that not only drastically reduced
Carleton's military scope, but was also a preface to an attempt
to disgrace him.

---

[1] Germain to Knox, 12 Oct. 1776; Clements, *Knox Papers*, ii. 55.
[2] Walpole, *Last Journals*, i. 528; 15 Feb. 1776.
[3] Burgoyne to Germain, Clements, iv. 34; also *HMC, Stop. Sack*. ii. 36, 37.
[4] Germain to Burgoyne, 23 Aug. 1776; *HMC, Stop. Sack*. ii. 40.

Fortified by awareness of Lord George's support, Colonel Christie attacked Carleton. In his report to Lord George, he wrote that Carleton's decision not to attempt Ticonderoga in late October was '. . . beyond all human comprehension', and that: '. . . my real belief is that he is totally unfit for such a command, and must ruin his Majesty's affairs . . . in either a civil or a military capacity'.[1] This would have been merely funny if it had not given Lord George a further excuse to put the worst possible interpretation on every dispatch from Canada. Perhaps Lord George had forgotten a letter he had received in 1758 from his former regimental officer James Wolfe, then with Carleton at the capture of Louisburg and loud with praises of Carleton: 'Can Sir John Ligonier allow his Majesty to remain unacquainted with the merit of that officer? . . . If I was in Carleton's place I wouldn't stay an hour in the army.'[2] What would Wolfe have thought in 1777, when, while Carleton was 'doing his best work, Germain was planning to humiliate and supersede him'?[3]

Carleton's downrightness had given Lord George one or two other minor points to bring against him. In his haste after having driven the American forces out of Montreal and his annoyance at several failures of supply from England, Carleton had reported to Lord George in a letter less elaborately unctuous and deferential than was the military tradition. Several of Carleton's phrases were earthy and Walpole called them 'obscene and ill-written', though Hutchinson only commented: 'The Gazette gives Carleton's letter; short, & it is generally said, written as if he were out of humour.'[4] Lord George might have commented, somewhat as Lincoln later did of Grant, that he would not object to his other generals writing so poorly if they would fight as well, and the usual procedure would have been to prune the letter before printing it in the official Gazette. But Carleton's letter was published unaltered, and Walpole suggested that: '. . . it is not improbable that Lord George

---

[1] Christie to Germain, 26 Oct. 1776; HMC, Stop. Sack. ii. 44 ff. Christie and Carleton may have had an earlier enmity, for a decade earlier Christie had hoped to be made Quartermaster-General under Wolfe but Carleton had received the appointment (Clements, *Germain Papers*, i).

[2] Wolfe to Sackville, July 1758; HMC, Stop. Sack. ii. 266.

[3] Tracy, *History of Canada*, ii. 604.

[4] *Hutchinson Diaries*, Nov. 1776; Clements (original MS.), p. 361.

Germaine, out of hatred, had suffered it to appear in that manner'.[1] Walpole was right: Lord George specifically ordered that the letter be printed as written.[2] The episode did Carleton no great public harm, but it enabled Lord George to criticize him to Cabinet and King.

Carleton had also become involved in another teapot tempest that Lord George did his best to inflate into a hurricane. In 1775 Lord Dartmouth had appointed Peter Livius to be Chief Justice of the Province of Quebec.[3] Livius was soon charged with improper conduct in office, and after formal hearings Carleton as Governor dismissed him. Livius protested and made counter-charges against Carleton. Few men believed Livius or supported him, but Lord George did, and ultimately got the affair before the Privy Council. By that time few people knew or cared about a minor squabble in Canada some years before; Carleton was serving with credit in another post, and nothing further was done. Taken separately each of those episodes was trivial, but together they showed what a cold east wind was blowing from Lord George's Whitehall office toward Carleton in Canada.

Meanwhile it was widely believed that Lord George was placing his own secret agents covertly around Carleton, and engaging in correspondence with some of Carleton's subordinates in a way calculated to undermine any general's authority and the morale of his staff.[4] Lord George's desire to humiliate Carleton became common gossip in London's inner circles, and few were surprised when he openly condemned Carleton's decision not to attempt to capture Ticonderoga in 1776 as a major military blunder. Lord George was ignorant of Canadian winters, and what he found it inconvenient to recognize he often refused to believe. He may even have been right about Ticonderoga, though most of the expert opinion supports Carleton's decision.

Another matter which Lord George chose to interpret as 'failure' on Carleton's part was really greatly to his credit.

---

[1] Walpole, *Last Journals*, i. 565.

[2] 'You will put Carleton's letter in the Gazette' (Germain to Knox, 27 July 1776; *Knox Papers*, Clements; also *HMC, Var. Coll.* 6, *Knox*, pp. 123, 124.

[3] Dartmouth to Carleton, 23 May 1775; Clements, *Shelburne Papers, Amer. Affairs*, i. 219.

[4] Guttridge, *Germain in Office*, p. 34.

Carleton had not acceded to Lord George's repeated pressure
to employ Indians to terrify, scalp, and kill American men,
women, and children.

Lord George found various ways to indicate his lack of confidence in Carleton. One of them was to avoid recognizing him
in 1776 as the senior ranking officer on the American continent
—a fact that had been pointed out by the king himself. While
General Gage was still in command at Boston, the king had
written in his own hand that: 'G. Carleton must be apprized that
if any accident should happen to L. G. Gage he is then immediately to repair to the Army, and M. G. Howe must (if such
an event should happen) conduct affairs until the arrival of his
senior M. General.'[1] Howe himself, a year later, had reminded
Lord George that he was outranked by Carleton, and had
volunteered his ready acceptance that if the two armies should
join he would be subordinate to Carleton.[2] There is no evidence
that Lord George took notice of Howe's suggestion, and Howe's
promotion a few months later altered the situation.

Lord George was at that very time opposing the king's determination to honour Carleton for his successful defence of Canada
by making him a Knight of the Bath. His opposition failed and
the king conferred the Red Ribbon on Carleton on 6 July 1776.[3]
Lord George could not have voiced his disapproval in a more
improper way than by writing to Burgoyne in Canada hinting
that the award was made not on Carleton's merits but because
the king wanted to please Carleton's wife,[4] and by his dog-in-
the-manger letter to Howe.[5]

To the king, Lord George continued his campaign of detraction of Carleton: 'Lord George Germain has the honor to send
to your Majesty Sir Guy Carleton's Letter by which your
Majesty perceives he has abandon'd Crown Point. Genl. Burgoyne was strongly in opinion against that measure. Lord George
is glad your Majesty will permit him to make his report on what

---

[1] Memo. dated 1 Apr. 1775; Fortescue, *Corresp. Geo. III*, iii. 195.

[2] Howe to Germain, 7 June 1776; *HMC, Stop. Sack.* ii. 33.

[3] *DNB*, under Carleton.

[4] 'I suppose the King could not forbear granting so agreeable a commission to
Lady Maria as the carrying such a mark of his royal approbation to her husband'
(Germain to Burgoyne, 23 Aug. 1776; *HMC, Stop. Sack.* ii. 39). The letter may have
had some bearing on Burgoyne's declining, through his friend the Earl of Derby,
Germain's suggestion of a Red Ribbon for himself a year later.

[5] See Note I, p. 500.

pass'd between him and General Burgoyne before your Majesty honors him with an Audience.'[1]

The king commented to Lord North: 'That there is a great prejudice perhaps not unaccompanied with rancour in a certain breast against Governor Carleton is so manifest to whoever has heard the subject mentioned, that it would be idle to say more than that it is a fact; perhaps Carleton may be too cold and not so active as might be wished . . . but should the proposal be to recall Carleton from his Government or censure his conduct that would be cruel and the exigency cannot authorize it.'[2]

Two months later Lord George showed a little more of his hand, and urged that Carleton be dismissed from his military command and governorship. The king wrote again to Lord North: 'He wants Carleton to be recalled, but I have thrown cold water on that and Ld. Suffolk and Ld. Gower will oppose it at your meeting.'[3] It was one of the few times that the king worked covertly, in advance of a Cabinet meeting, to circumvent Lord George.

The third ranking officer on the American continent was General Henry Clinton. Clinton had first arrived at Boston in the ship *Cerberus*, in company with Howe and Burgoyne, in time to aid General Gage at Bunker Hill, and he had acquitted himself well there. He had then been assigned to land command of an expedition with Sir Peter Parker to harry the rebels in the South and perhaps capture Charleston. That expedition had been a failure, partly because no clear-cut plan had been given its joint commanders, and partly because neither Admiral nor General was given authority over the other if they disagreed.

Clinton had decided that it would be unwise to attempt to take Charleston: if it could be captured it could not be held without a strong garrison for which no provision of men had been made; if it were taken and later abandoned the southern loyalists who had openly declared themselves would be endangered and any further loyalist help discouraged. But Admiral Parker was eager to attack Charleston and Clinton rather weakly deferred. Clinton failed to discover in advance that the island on which he landed his men for the attack was separated

[1] Germain to King, 10 Dec. 1776; Fortescue, *Corresp.* iii. 405.
[2] King to North, 13 Dec. 1776; ibid., pp. 406, 407.
[3] King to North, 24 Feb. 1777; ibid., p. 421.

from his first objective by a channel not one foot deep but, at high tide, seven, and Sir Peter charged about with his ships quite independently of Clinton's knowledge or needs. After many days of futility and cross-purposes the attempt was abandoned and in July Clinton went by sea to New York[1] and was made second in command to Howe.

Clinton and Parker soon redeemed their reputations by a well-organized and well-managed occupation of Rhode Island, though the achievement might not have been so impressive had they met more than trivial resistance.[2] But the Charleston fiasco had raised Clinton's ire against Lord George Germain. The report he had sent Lord George, which explained his own difficulties and was frankly critical of the naval operation, appeared in the official Gazette in a form that seemed to reflect on Clinton's military competence. Clinton believed that Lord George had done this deliberately, or had allowed it to be done to protect the navy at the expense of Clinton's good name. He got leave from Howe to go to London and protest. There he had many sympathizers and the support of the Whigs, who successively championed every general whom Lord George successively belittled.[3] Charles James Fox made Clinton's protest the occasion for a severe attack on the Ministry: 'Something has been said on the case of General Clinton: I wish that matter had been more explained; as it stands at present, the Gazette account is an infamous libel on the character of that gallant officer. Let the Administration stand forth, and avow that representation; they will not do it; they dare not do it; they skulk from an open and fair representation.'[4]

Lord George and the Ministry maintained their anomalous position, but did their best to mollify Clinton. They offered him a knighthood as compensation and evidence of the king's good opinion, and, his silence thus purchased, Clinton reluctantly consented to return to New York as second in command to Howe, whom he disliked and with whom he seldom agreed. But

---

[1] Lecky, iv. 12.

[2] Lecky, among others, doubted that the military advantages of holding Rhode Island 'justified the British commander in detaining at least 6000 soldiers for nearly three years' inaction on the island'. Lecky was right, but the move was made and the area held at the repeated urging of Germain.

[3] Walpole, *Last Journals*, ii. 10; 28 Feb. 1777.

[4] Force, *Amer. Archives*, Series V, iii. 1004; Oct. 1776.

Clinton never liked or really trusted Lord George thereafter. He arrived in New York early in July 1777 to find matters there in a situation that alarmed him, and a month later confided to young Colonel Charles Stuart, who reported it to his father the Marquis of Bute, that: 'The Minister has used me so ill that I can no longer bear with life.'[1]

Thus matters stood between Lord George and his senior officers in America at the beginning of 1777. He was at odds with all three, and determined to recall and humiliate the ablest of them. Yet at that very time Lord George was also formulating elaborate and complicated campaign plans, involving all three, which he was confident would bring devastating victories and win the war before the year was out.

[1] Charles Stuart to Bute, Aug. 1777; Wortley, p. 148.

XII

PLANS AND MOTIVES

DISREGARDING the realities of logistics and American resistance, Lord George set out confidently to direct the quick and complete suppression of the American Revolution. In his optimism he was at first by no means alone. Englishmen fed one another on pleasant fictions: that the rebellion was fostered by a mere handful of radicals and rascals who had overawed the rest; that the loyalists were in the majority and eager to fight for the Crown; that Americans were cowards or tyros in warfare, and that only in New England was there any real resistance.

General Percy, who had been at Minden and was now with Howe in America, wrote to Lord George after the capture of New York that: '. . . this Business is pretty near over'.[1] General Murray encouraged Lord George to believe that: 'The native American is an effeminate thing, very unfit for and very impatient of war.'[2] To such men, as to Lord George, any conciliatory gestures would only strengthen the position of the rebels and weaken that of the loyalists. Suggestions that France or Spain might join the war against Britain did not shake their confidence. When Colonel Barre spoke in the House of Commons of the danger that France would support the rebels, Lord George replied loftily: 'How, do you suppose, would the House of Bourbon like to have the spirit of Independence cross the Atlantic? Would they not fear that their own colonists would catch fire at the unlimited rights of mankind?'[3] In that statement Lord George was disingenuous, since only two weeks earlier he had written to General Howe suggesting the entrance of France on the side of the Americans as a likely and imminent event.[4] And a little later he admitted its likelihood to Clinton.[5]

No government ever indulged more blindly and persistently

[1] Clements Coll., *Germain Papers*, v. 44; also *HMC, Stop. Sack.* ii. 40.
[2] Murray to Germain, 6 Sept. 1776; Clements, *Germain Papers*, vi. 88; also *HMC, Stop. Sack.* i. 370.　　　[3] *Hansard*, 31 Oct. 1776, p. 1429.
[4] Germain to Howe, 18 Oct. 1776; Clements, *Germain Papers*, v.
[5] Clements, *Clinton Papers*, F. 146, Apr. 1777.

in wishful thinking than Lord North's Ministry with regard to America, and no member of that Ministry was so obdurate in his myopia as Lord George Germain. The King and Cabinet found his confidence reassuring and his firmness compelling, and in the twenty-two months before Saratoga Lord George often moved without troubling to ask for Cabinet approval, confident of the king's support and Lord North's acquiescence. It would be the events of 1777 that would measure his capacities, and he was determined to make those events overwhelmingly successful. He set out with confident energy to raise or hire adequate troops, ships, and supplies, and to develop a grand strategy that would win the war that year.

Quick success was at first taken for granted by most men in the field. In late 1776 Howe wrote from New York that with adequate reinforcements and naval support the war could be won in a single campaign, for Howe had not yet outgrown his own age of innocence. General Carleton first offered to supply General Gage with two regiments to be recruited in Canada, and was later forced to report that they could not be enlisted to that number. But aided by large reinforcements and Burgoyne, Carleton had driven the Americans out of Canada by the summer of 1776 and was planning an aggressive move the following summer. All seemed ripe for a strategy of the juncture of massive forces that would settle the issue and, not altogether incidentally, prove to the world the military genius of Lord George Germain.

That strategy was already half formulated in half a dozen military minds. In April 1775, four days before Lexington, Lord Dartmouth had suggested a military action that would cut off New England from the rest of the colonies.[1] Later Howe had written from Boston that the rebels would be more distressed by British occupation of the line of the Hudson River than by any other activities in or from Canada.[2] In May 1776 Howe had suggested from Halifax that the capture of New York would make possible a joint action by the northern and southern British armies along the Hudson River, '. . . if the Canadians are hearty',[3] and Howe was already speculating on his authority

[1] Dartmouth to Gage, 15 Apr. 1775; PRO, CO/5, v. 92, pp. 197–221.
[2] Howe to Secretary for America, Dec. 1775; Fortescue, *HBA*, 2, ii. 174.
[3] Howe to Germain, 12 May 1776; *HMC, Stop. Sack.* ii. 327.

relative to Carleton's when the two armies coalesced. And even
from remote Malta General James Murray had written to Lord
George that the conquest of the colonies should be '. . . pushed
from the side of Canada. . . . Sir Guy Carleton will have it in
his power to reinforce his army with 10,000 Canadians, and the
Indians to a man are at our direction. . . . The summer will be
very well employed in establishing the Army at Albany.'[1] After
Arnold and Montgomery were defeated at Quebec the same
general idea was rife in military circles.

Carleton was in fact understood to be planning to attack up
Lake Champlain and take Ticonderoga, as Lord George had
hoped he would do in 1776.[2] In the summary of military events
in 1776 in Lord George's office: 'It was expected that not only
Canada would be recovered but a Communication opened with
the King's forces on the side of the Atlantic', and 'by that means
place the Rebel Army between two fires'.[3] Howe's letters in
late 1776 seemed to take it for granted that his junction
with Carleton's army would be the main strategy of the 1777
campaign.[4]

Burgoyne was hurrying back from Canada with a memorandum from Carleton proposing in general terms just that kind
of campaign. Carleton asked for only another 4,000 men and
an increase in his regimental companies to 100 men each. With
those additions and some freshly recruited Canadians he proposed to send a diversionary force by way of Lake Ontario into
the Mohawk Valley; to lead his main force up Lake Champlain;
take Ticonderoga; make a junction with the troops from the
Mohawk, and establish a strong base for attacks on Massachusetts and Connecticut. But Carleton made no specific mention
of moving as far south as Albany, or of meeting there a force
moving northward from New York, though that may well have
been in the back of his mind.[5] Burgoyne had been with Carleton
and was familiar with his proposals: his sanguine brain expanded

---

[1] Murray to Germain, 27 Aug. 1776; *HMC, Stop. Sack*. i. 370.

[2] 'The plan of Lord George Germaine had uniformly been to pour an army from
Quebec on the back of the colonies; and he resumed that purpose with all his
activity' (Walpole, *Last Journals*, i. 527).

[3] PRO, CO/5, v. 253, no. 21.

[4] '. . . nor have I any dependence upon General Carleton's approach to act with
influence this year upon the main rebel army opposed to us' (Howe to Germain,
25 Sept. 1776; *HMC, Stop. Sack*. ii. 41). The key words are 'this year'.

[5] PRO, CO/5, v. 42, p. 36; also Kingsford, *Hist. Canada*, vi. 120.

them, and his ambition envisaged an important place for himself in the undertaking. Thus in November 1775, in spite of enmities and slow communications, the minds of Howe, Carleton, Burgoyne, and Germain seemed to be moving along closely parallel lines.

In a letter to Lord George dated 30 November 1776, Howe embodied his previous ideas into specific and complicated proposals. If Lord George wanted an elaborate programme of aggressive operations, Howe was prepared to provide it—if Lord George would supply the men, materials, and ships. Howe asked that his force be augmented to 35,000 men—8,000 of them to 'cover New Jersey'; 20,000 to comprise two armies for two separate moves northward, and the remainder to garrison New York and other bases of operations. One of his armies of 10,000 would '. . . act on the side of Rhode Island . . . to be commanded by Lieutenant General Clinton'. The other would move up the Hudson River to Albany, where Howe assumed that Carleton would surely arrive by September 1777. Howe added that: 'South Carolina and Georgia must be objects for winter, but to complete the plan, not less than ten ships of the line will be absolutely requisite, and a reinforcement of troops to the amount of 15,000 rank and file.'[1]

Since Howe did not like to disperse his forces, his proposal to divide his proposed attacking force of 20,000 into two armies was probably in deference to Lord George's repeated desire for an attack on the New England coast. Howe's letter crossed in mid-ocean one from Lord George on that very matter, again urging an attack on Rhode Island as '. . . the first object of your attention, as soon as you could with propriety separate your force. That post still seems to me so essential. . . .'[2] Despite his own failure in 'buccaneering', Lord George was unable, throughout the war, to resist the paper attractions of diversionary attacks.

To understand the confusions that followed it is essential to bear in mind the intervals between the sending and the receipt

---

[1] 'By a consideration of the difficulties that Army must meet with before it reaches Albany in the course of the next campaign, it is reasonable to conclude that this will not be effected earlier than the month of September' (Force, *Amer. Archives*, 5th series, iii. 926; also Fortescue, *HBA*, 2, iii. 199; also *HMC, Stop. Sack*. ii. 49; also summarized in PRO, CO/5, v. 253, pp. 272 ff.; Howe to Germain, 30 Nov. 1776). Howe obviously meant Sept. 1777.

[2] Germain to Howe, 18 Oct. 1776; *HMC, Stop. Sack*. ii. 42.

of dispatches. In summer a one-way crossing from England seldom took less than a month, and in winter at least twice as long.[1] Under such conditions, the date on which a dispatch was received is more important than the date on which it was written or sent. The message from Howe dated 30 November 1776, outlining his proposals for a campaign in 1777, crossed the Atlantic in almost record time for the winter months, since it was recorded as having reached Lord George's office on 30 December. Meanwhile other plans were being made in London. Burgoyne arrived there from Canada before Christmas, and before New Year's Day he had discussed directly with the king his hope to return to lead an aggressive campaign from Canada.[2] Burgoyne probably soon learned of Howe's idea of a juncture at Albany, and his own proposals were in line with it. The king and Lord George were acquainted with Burgoyne's thoughts long before they were formally presented to the Cabinet, and before Howe's detailed plan reached them.

In fact there is reason to believe that as early as late December Lord George had encouraged Burgoyne to believe he would be put in command of the northern army his plan proposed. That arrangement would have been only an extension of orders Lord George had sent to Carleton on 22 August 1776, but which Carleton did not receive until the following May. What is more, a bet recorded at Brooks' Club on Christmas Day 1776 was this: 'General George Burgoyne wagers Charles Fox one pony that he will be home victorious from America by Christmas Day 1777.'[3] A pony was fifty guineas, and there can be no doubt that General George Burgoyne was simply a mistake for General John. There was no General George, and Gentleman John had placed other bets in Brooks' Club in the past. In a statement to his parliamentary constituents two years later, Burgoyne wrote: 'My endeavors in the campaign under Sir Guy Carleton, in 1776, were also thought worthy commendation, and before my return I was pitched upon for the command of the troops destined to make a junction with General Howe from Canada.' If by 'my return' Burgoyne meant his return to England, then he must have been told by Germain of his dispatch to Carleton

---

[1] See p. 161, note 1.
[2] Burgoyne to Germain, 1 Jan. 1777; Clements, *Germain Papers*, v.
[3] Frothingham, p. 179, note.

of 22 August 1776. If Burgoyne meant his return from England
to Canada in March 1777, his statement is meaningless. If he
meant that he was told of his new command before the end of
February 1777, then Lord George not only antedated Cabinet
approval in the selection of Burgoyne, but, for reasons which
will emerge, deliberately deceived the Cabinet in the matter.

Burgoyne's memorandum entitled 'Thoughts for Conducting
the War from the Side of Canada'[1] was not formally presented
to the Cabinet until 25 February. The Cabinet recommended
the plan to the king on 28 February, though all concerned may
well have discussed it during previous weeks.[2] The king had, in
fact, outlined a similar plan in a letter to Lord North in mid-
December.[3] Burgoyne's plan was promptly approved by the
king. The Cabinet then recommended '. . . that Lieutenant-
General Burgoyne should be again employed in Canada'.[4]

Those unaware of Lord George's aversion to General Carleton
would assume that able and successful soldier to be the natural
choice to head the northern army that would attack the rebels
from Canada. But Lord George had already taken steps to
prevent that choice. In August 1776 he had persuaded the
king that the Governor of Canada would be needed within its
boundaries to defend and administer it, thereby precluding
Carleton from leading any troops into New York state.[5] General
Amherst was then approached to head the northern army but
declined; he had already said he would not lead troops against
the Americans. General Clinton, who had priority rank over
General Burgoyne and had come to London boiling with a sense
of injustice at the reports of his conduct in the Charleston campaign as published in the official Gazette, was then approached.
Clinton's memorandum of his conversation with the Secretary
was illuminating:

His L.ship began by saying that the other day being with the
King, he asked his Majesty whether he had come to any determina-

---

[1] Burgoyne's 'Thoughts' are in manuscript form in Clements, *Germain Papers*,
v, 63. His Letter to his Constituents was published in pamphlet form in 1779, and
the statements on his selection are on pp. 5 ff.

[2] *Sandwich Papers*, i. 285.

[3] King to North, 13 Dec. 1775; Fortescue, *Corresp.* iii. 406, 407.

[4] *Sandwich Papers*, i. 285.

[5] Fonblanque, pp. 221, 225; also see Burgoyne's statement before Parliament in
1779.

tion in regard to the time of my going back to America; that the King made answer, he had come to no determination that he understood I was still hurt, that he had ever declared his public & private approbation of my conduct on all occasions. Ld. G. told me, he then said to his Majesty, that if I had his Royal approbation he submitted whether it would not be right to give me some immediate publick mark of it, that he knew of none so proper as the red ribbon; that my Family, Rank, & Character intitled me to it. the King said he had no objection, therefore desired it might be signify'd to me, that notwithstanding there was no vacancy, I might be invested with it immediately. I told his L.ship that nobody could be more sensible than his Humble Servant of the King's most gracious goodness on all occasions. his L.ship said the King seemed to doubt whether Sr. William Howe might not be offended at the Ribbon being given to me in so particular a manner, upon which I looked very grum; & his L.ship told me his answer was, that Sir W.H. would of course be pleased, that an officer he approved of, should receive such a mark, besides which, Mr. H. had no right to monopolize all the red ribbons nor anything else.

His L'ship then proceeded telling me, *that* ceremony over, he took it for granted I should have no objection to return to America; I said, that with that publick mark of Royal approbation . . . I should have none. . . .[1]

Lord George then asked Clinton's opinion on American matters, but, according to Clinton, answered most of his own questions. He '. . . asked me whether I thought the Rebels would ever be able to raise an Army, expatiated largely upon their inability to do it, that they grew less able every day, & that they would be at last drain'd. I answered all this by one short remark: was, is, or will their inability be greater than ours, certainly no.'

But although Clinton was not wholly disarmed by Lord George, he was silenced by a knighthood and by assurances that if he returned to America under Howe: '. . . it was intended that I should be commander-in-chief if any accident happened'. Lord George also sounded out Clinton about taking command of the proposed northern army, but Clinton declined on the grounds that he would not displace Carleton in any way that would reflect on that officer's service and abilities. The interview ended, Clinton recorded, with Lord George saying

[1] Clements, *Clinton Papers*, Apr. 1777, fol. 146.

'. . . a thousand civil one two threes, & I as many polite four five sixes'.

Another version makes Lord George no more than a reluctant collaborator in the award of the knighthood to Clinton. 'Clinton had let it be known among the officers in America that he insisted on publication of his entire despatch about Sullivan's Island. . . . Lord George and Lord North agreed that publication would be unwise, and decided on a Knighthood as the only means of re-establishing Clinton's prestige.'[1] Walpole's comment was: 'General Clinton was pacified by a supernumerary red ribbon—a paltry way of retrieving his honor, which he had come so far to vindicate.'[2]

Whether or not Burgoyne had received covert advance assurances, he was then the natural next choice to command the northern army. He was eager; his energy and optimism appealed to Lord George; and his appointment would further undermine Carleton. It was true that Lord George had been somewhat critical of Burgoyne for returning to England without his own express permission,[3] but the death of Burgoyne's wife was an extenuating fact, and soon after Lady Charlotte's death Lord George had written to Burgoyne in Canada: 'You have no friend who has felt more sincerely for you than I have done.'[4] Burgoyne had, in fact, been courting Lord George's favour and had written to him in August 1775 as: '. . . the man who my best judgment tells me is the most capable of any in England to redeem America by his counsels'.[5] Lord George could not

---

[1] Clements, *Clinton Papers*, fol. 146.

[2] According to a later statement from Clinton, he was at that time or possibly a little later approached by Germain regarding replacing Carleton not only as commanding officer of the northern army but also as Governor. If so, Lord George must have done so without the knowledge, or at least the approval, of Lord North and the king. If Lord George did make the proposal of both posts to Clinton, then he broke his own rule that the Governor of Canada should not leave the province. Clinton wrote later: 'It is true, indeed, that I was offered a very high command. . . . I could not by any means accept before the very able General in possession should think proper of himself to resign' (Clements, *Clinton Papers*, 'Historical Detail'; also Willcox, p. 65).

[3] 'I am surprised at Clinton's coming home. Burgoyne will not be sorry to see that he is not the only General, second in command, who takes that liberty without the King's leave' (Germain to Knox, 31 Dec. 1776; *HMC, Var. Coll.* 6, *Knox*, p. 128). Burgoyne had been given leave by Carleton and Clinton by Howe.

[4] Germain to Burgoyne, 23 Aug. 1776; *HMC, Stop. Sack.* ii. 39.

[5] Burgoyne to Germain, 20 Aug. 1775; Clements, *Germain Papers*, iii; also *HMC, Stop. Sack.* ii. 6, 8.

too whole-heartedly approve any man who admired and praised
Carleton as warmly as Burgoyne had done in early 1776, when
he had written to Lord George: 'I found General Carleton very
much satisfied with the plans of Government relative to the war
in Canada; very warm in the pursuit of the duties to which he
is called.'[1] But when Burgoyne returned to England openly
critical of Carleton for not having attempted to take Ticonderoga, Lord George was pleased. He was, or pretended to be,
shocked at Carleton's caution, and had written to General
Howe: 'It was a great mortification to me to be informed that
the army from Canada had thought it right to leave Crown
Point unoccupied and repass the Lake.'[2] Lord George had
sent off a letter to Carleton on 22 August 1776 saying that as
Governor of Quebec he must not move out of his boundaries.
That letter reached Sir Guy in May 1777.[3]

In the appointment of a commander of the northern army,
Lord George was juggling several balls, for on 24 February the
king wrote to his First Minister, Lord North: 'Lord George
Germain will tomorrow propose Clinton for Canada and Burgoyne to join Howe. I thoroughly approve of this.'[4] But only
three weeks later Thomas Hutchinson wrote in his diary: 'At
Mr. Knox's in the evening. It looks as if Burgoyne was to take
command of the army, at least out of Carleton's hands. And
Knox said the Indians would certainly be employed this summer,
& that there was no danger of Carleton's hindering it.'[5] William
Knox was Lord George's undersecretary.

Burgoyne of course accepted, and seemed in the happy position of commanding an army in a campaign he himself had
planned, although his 'Thoughts' merely co-ordinated the ideas
of other men.[6] The northern army was to move from Montreal
southward by way of Crown Point and Lake Champlain, take
Ticonderoga, and then move on to Albany. A smaller diversionary force would go by way of the eastern end of Lake
Ontario into the Mohawk Valley; clean out resistance there,

---

[1] Burgoyne to Germain, early 1776; Clements, *Germain Papers*, iv. 34; also
HMC, Stop. Sack. ii. 36, 37.
[2] Germain to Howe, 14 Jan. 1777; *HMC, Stop. Sack.* ii. 56.
[3] See p. 164, note 5.
[4] King to North, 24 Feb. 1777; Fortescue, *Corresp.* i. 421.
[5] 11 Mar. 1777; Clements, *Hutchinson Diaries* (original MS.), pp. 388, 389.
[6] PRO, CO/5, v. 43, p. 36.

and then move eastward to rendezvous with the main force
north of Albany. Thus far the plan was pure Carleton. But
Burgoyne made the joining of the two chief armies an integral
part of the plan. A strong force under Howe was to come up
the Hudson River or possibly through western Connecticut, and
effect a junction with Burgoyne's army at Albany. If that line
were taken and held, so the strategists agreed, New England
would be completely cut off from the other colonies.

In view of later events, several points stressed by Burgoyne
in his 'Thoughts' are significant. He stated that: 'These ideas
are formed upon the supposition that it be the sole purpose of
the Canada army to effect a junction with General Howe, or
after co-operating so far as to get possession of Albany and open
the communication to New York, to remain upon the Hudson's
River, and thereby enable that general to act with his whole
force to the southward', and he emphasized the same objective
of meeting Howe in another paragraph. He urged that the
commander of the northern army be given 'latitude' to determine his operations as far as Albany in the light of conditions
as they might develop during the campaign. That latitude was
even to include the possibility of shipping his entire army by
water from Quebec to New York, or to move eastward from
a captured Ticonderoga into Vermont, western Massachusetts,
and Connecticut. Three thousand men should be left in Canada
for its defence; stores should be assembled at Crown Point—
'one of the most important operations of the campaign because
it is upon it that most of the rest will depend'; Ticonderoga
should be taken early in the summer and then become the main
base, with Crown Point becoming a secondary one.

It was also apparent that in February 1777 Burgoyne was not
so naïve about the extent and methods of American resistance as
some of his later critics have maintained. He predicted that the
enemy would be in force at Ticonderoga and estimated that the
fortress could accommodate some 12,000 defenders. He showed
that he was aware of the alternate routes by way of Lake George
or Skenesborough, and had weighed the merits of each. He
predicted that the Americans would have a strong naval force
on Lake George, and would block the trail from Skenesborough
to Albany by destroying bridges and fortifying strong points
for delaying actions. Therefore, he argued, the northern army

must have 'a weight of artillery', with at least 8,000 regulars, 2,000 Canadians, 1,000 or more 'savages', and a corps of water-men. In fact 'Burgoyne indicated the purely military difficulties of the advance so clearly that a wise man might well have hesitated to incur them'.[1]

In his notes on the proposals he had brought from Carleton, Burgoyne had warned Lord George not to expect much military help from the Canadians, who, he wrote: '. . . are under no discipline, and continually desert or pretend sickness'.[2] This was not an original conclusion. Six months earlier Carleton had reported it, and Francis Maseres had written to Lord Shelburne that: 'The Canadians persist in refusing to act offensively against the Americans, but they say they are ready to defend their own province against any incursions.'[3] But Lord George remained confident that Burgoyne could easily enroll as many Canadians as he could possibly need.

All the available contemporary comments on Burgoyne's plan assume that the first objective of both northern and southern armies was to make a junction at Albany. There is not one recorded reference to what the northern army might do after reaching Albany, except as instructed there on arrival by General Howe. Notes on the Burgoyne plan in the king's own hand state that: '. . . the outlines of the plan seem to be on a proper founda-tion', and that: '. . . the force from Canada must join Howe at Albany'.[4] And in the king's correspondence was a memorandum, unsigned, dated 5 March 1777, probably written by the king or Lord Amherst: 'As Sr. W. Howe seems to think that he can't act in the Massachusets from Rhode Island, It may probably be the most adviseable to Force to Albany and Join at that place, Instead of Going to the Connecticut River. The Numbers which are proposed for this Expedition, seem to be but Small.'[5]

[1] Fortescue, *HBA*, 2, iii. 206; Hudleston, pp. 124 ff.
[2] Clements, *Shelburne Papers, Amer. Affairs*, i. 151.
[3] Maseres to Shelburne, 25 Aug. 1775; Clements, *Shelburne Papers, Amer. Affairs*, i. 113.
[4] Fonblanque, p. 487; also Whitton, p. 169; also Greene, *Rev. War*, p. 78.
[5] Fortescue, *Corresp.* iii. 444, 5 Mar. 1777. The style and spelling are similar to those of the king in his personal notes to Lord North, and the script is said to resemble his. The content is in keeping with the king's marginal notes quoted above. But Amherst was one of the few possible commentators who was as familiar with the geography of the area as the writer appears to be. It is not in the hand or style of North or Germain.

It was left to the Secretary of State for America to implement the decision of Cabinet and King in all necessary ways: to draw up relevant orders and see that they reached all the military officers involved. There must have been further conversations between Lord George and Burgoyne, for Burgoyne did not leave London for Quebec until 27 March. But those conversations could not have been very long or very frank, for when Burgoyne's official orders reached him just before embarking they contained some unpleasant surprises. The orders for the campaign—the only ones Burgoyne ever received—were in the form of a dispatch which Burgoyne was to take to General Carleton containing orders for Carleton to pass on to Burgoyne. In one important respect, Burgoyne found, his plan had been emasculated, for the discretionary powers of the commanding officer of the northern army had been completely removed. He had recommended 'latitude' in the choice of route to Albany, but the orders were specific and mandatory that he was to 'force' his way to Albany, and there place himself and his troops under the command of General Howe, who would be ordered to meet him there. Burgoyne was also disturbed to find that the total of trained troops he would receive would fall below the 8,000 he had stated as the necessary minimum.

In his initial enthusiasm over this great opportunity Burgoyne was not minded to make serious protests, or to fear disaster. If he was, without any deference to obstacles, opposition, or casualties, to 'force' his way to Albany, he would, by God, do so. His troops were well-trained men from Britain and Germany; his officers were first-rate; the artillery was plentiful and included larger guns than were usually taken on such an expedition. Deficiencies in numbers, if not in quality, could probably be made up by recruiting more than the proposed 2,000 Canadians and, if necessary, more Indians. And since Lord George's dispatch said that appropriate orders, including a copy of those to Carleton including his own, were being sent to Howe, everything seemed reasonably satisfactory. Howe was a good fighter, and could be counted on to force his way, too, to Albany. Burgoyne was still optimistic when, on 6 May 1777, his ship dropped anchor under the high cliffs of Quebec. On that same day he wrote to General Frazer: '. . . being called upon at home for my opinion on the conduct of the war on this side I gave it freely; the material parts of it have been adopted by the Cabinet'.[1]

Burgoyne would have been less confident had he known what other papers and plans had been passing through the office of the Secretary for America while he was still in London, and what had transpired since. Some of Howe's letters to Lord George and Lord George's replies, during February and March, must have been deliberately kept from Burgoyne, although it would have been natural and proper that he should hear of any other plans significant to his own undertaking. If he had known all that had been written and arranged he would certainly have demanded explanations or resigned his command. Why Lord George kept him ignorant is a mystery. Howe's intentions and Lord George's approval of them were apparently also kept from Clinton, and not even mentioned in Clinton's conversation with Lord George in April.

On 20 December 1776 General Howe had written to Lord George a dispatch received at his office, according to its endorsement, on 23 February 1777.[2] In that dispatch Howe proposed an utterly new plan for his own activities in 1777: an attack on Philadelphia. By implication it discarded any direct aggressive participation in or responsibility for the campaign from the north that he had proposed only 21 days earlier. Howe's letter made only two references to that plan or to any activities of the army in Canada:

> By this change, the offensive plan towards Boston must be deferred until the proposed reinforcements arrive from Europe, that there may be a corps to act *defensively* upon the *lower* part of Hudson's river, to cover Jersey on that side, as well as to facilitate *in some degree*, the approach of the army from Canada. . . . We must not look for the northern army to reach Albany before the middle of September; of course the subsequent operations of that corps will depend upon the state of things at the time.

Howe then specifically proposed to leave '4000 men on York Island and posts adjacent, and 300 on Hudson's River'.[3]

---

[1] Burgoyne to Frazer, 6 May 1777; Robson, *Amer. Rev.*, p. 139.
[2] PRO, CO/5, v. 253, no. 142; and *Hansard*, xx. 685.
[3] Howe to Germain, 20 Dec. 1776; Force, *Amer. Archives*, 5th series, iii. 1318; also PRO, CO/5, v. 253, pp. 278 ff. The italics are mine.

Nothing in Howe's letter, or in his later letters on his plans, specifically precluded the possibility that he might have thought that he could take Philadelphia so quickly that he would have time to get to Albany with a strong force to meet Burgoyne there as early as September. Had Howe left New York in early June; had he then taken the direct course and several weeks less in reaching Philadelphia, he might conceivably have been able to lead or send an adequate force to Albany in time to meet or rescue Burgoyne. But nothing in Howe's later letters hints that he had the remotest idea of doing so. And nothing in Lord George's replies to Howe indicates that he thought that was Howe's intention—except one clause in one dispatch to be quoted later. If either man had had the hope that Howe could in less than three months take Philadelphia and then move his army quickly to Albany he was carrying optimism to absurdity. It is highly unlikely that Howe at least, who after 1776 moved slowly and cautiously, was so unrealistic.

Howe planned to march by land to Philadelphia with 10,000 men. Though hoping for reinforcements to the number requested in his dispatch of 30 November, he had on 20 December received no assurance to that effect. He indicated that unless those reinforcements, to the full number requested, reached him promptly he would abandon the operations of the second aggressive army of 10,000 he had recommended in his proposals of 30 November 1776. If Lord George did not send him the men to make up that army, Howe in effect washed his hands of any responsibility for inaugurating a forceful campaign northwards. If a British army were to move southward from Canada—and Howe had received no official word to that effect—it could not count on any major aid from him.

Why had Howe so drastically altered his proposals between 30 November and 20 December? He never gave a clear explanation, but it can be assumed that he concluded his first plan was too ambitious unless he was in possession of all the reinforcements, ships, and supplies he had requested. He had received no assurance of them. And Howe was finding Washington a more skilful and dangerous enemy than he had expected, and support from loyalist Americans less great. His plan to attack Philadelphia was, in the light of his situation and knowledge when he made it, at least defensible.

Lord George's reaction to it was less so. On 23 February, when Lord George received Howe's second proposals, he was within four days of presenting Burgoyne's plan to the Cabinet, and a week later he was instructed to inform Howe what would be expected of him in the Burgoyne plan. Lord George also knew that he was not going to send Howe all the reinforcements Howe had requested, and had written to Howe to that effect on 24 January 1777.[1] In view of the adoption of the Burgoyne plan, Lord George could not let Howe decline all responsibility for supporting the Burgoyne army. With some 7,000 fewer men than he had hoped for, Howe would be even less able to capture Philadelphia quickly enough to move, afterwards, north to meet Burgoyne.

Lord George knew all this late in February, and a little later he knew still more. For he received another letter from Howe, dated 20 January, which made Howe's intentions, and lack of them, still more clear. Howe summarized the contents of that letter to the House of Commons two years later: 'I pressed for more troops. . . . I observed that if the reinforcements were small the operations would of course be curtailed. This letter also arrived in England prior to General Burgoyne's departure.'[2]

Lord George had been somewhat staggered by the size of the reinforcements Howe had requested. He could not believe that so many men would be needed to put down the rebels, and it was very doubtful that he could provide them or that Lord North could pay for them.[3] But apparently Lord George could not bring himself to write those painful facts clearly to Howe.

---

[1] Germain to Howe, 14 Jan. 1777; *Hansard*, xx. 684; and PRO, CO/5, v. 253, pp. 278 ff.

[2] *Hansard*, xx. 685. Germain acknowledged the receipt of Howe's letter in his reply dated 3 Mar. 1777. Germain also received a letter from Cornwallis, also dated 20 Jan., urging a reinforcement to Howe of at least 15,000 men.

[3] 'The military establishment voted for 1777, including 24,000 foreign troops, was just short of 89,000 men, which, after deducting a very insufficient force for the Mediterranean stations, left but 57,000 men for the service of the colonial garrisons and for the prosecution of the war . . . these figures, though small in themselves, existed on paper only and were very far from realized in fact' (Fortescue, *HBA*, 2, iii. 196). That paper 57,000 would include Burgoyne's 7,000 Europeans, Carleton's residue of 3,000, the troops at Newfoundland, St. Johns, Halifax, the West Indies, Ireland, and in transit, as well as the sick, wounded, deserted, and captured. It did not include loyalists enlisted in America, but Howe and Clinton never had more than 8,000 loyalists ready to fight, and Carleton probably less than 2,000 at any one time. The army figures also did not include Indians, but they were negligible in numbers and of very dubious value.

Instead, in his reply dated 14 January, he had used specious
arithmetic to pretend that the 7,800 men he proposed to supply
were in reality the 15,000 men Howe had said he needed. He
called Howe's plan well-digested, but deferred royal approval
and was non-committal about the ten ships of the line.[1]

When Howe received that dispatch he was not fooled, but
angered and discouraged. Howe naturally counted only such
of his men as were physically fit for field duty; Lord George
counted every man, sick, wounded, captured, deserted, untrained, administrative, or otherwise unavailable for active
fighting, as listed in the original regimental rosters. 'This misconceived calculation can no otherwise be accounted for, as
I apprehend, than by his Lordship's computing the sick, the
prisoners with the rebels, as part of the real effective strength
of the army', Howe told the House of Commons in 1779.[2] The
difference turned a paper 15,000 men into an actual 8,000.

Lord George replied on 3 March to Howe's revised campaign
plans of 20 December. Although the Burgoyne plan had been
approved only a week before, Lord George approved Howe's
plan, further detailed and somewhat amended by his dispatch
of 20 January, for a campaign against Philadelphia,[3] and Howe
received that dispatch on 8 May.[4] But Lord George also gave
Howe further bad news about his reinforcements. The 15,000
men that had previously been reduced to 8,000 was now to be
diminished to an initial 3,000 to be sent 'as soon as the season
will permit'.[5] Yet Lord George not only approved plans based

---

[1] HMC, Stop. Sack. ii. 56; Trevelyan, Amer. Rev. iv. 70.

[2] Howe to House of Commons, 29 Mar. 1779; Hansard, xx. 684.

[3] 'I am now commanded to tell you that the King entirely approves of your
proposed deviation from the plan which you formerly suggested, being of the
opinion that the reasons which have induced you to recommend this change are
solid and decisive' (Germain to Howe, 3 Mar. 1777; HMC, Stop. Sack. ii. 58; also
summarized in PRO, CO/5, v. 253, p. 286).

[4] Hansard, xx. 685.

[5] 'I begin to fear that it will not be possible to send you more new forces than
about 820 Hessian Chassures; do. Hanau about 400. [Written in the margin of the
dispatch at that point is: 'A mistake, they are being sent to Quebec.'] . . . two
regiments of Anspach Infantry consisting of about 1280, and four companies of
Highlanders amounting to about 400. . . . I flatter myself they will be duly furnished
in proper time, and that these (together with the others) will be ready to sail for
New York as soon as the season will permit.' Fortescue concluded that this reduced
the total of 8,000 previously promised to some 3,000 (Fortescue, HBA, 2, iii. 207;
also Hansard, xx. 686).

on the larger number, but also urged that Howe undertake
a 'warm diversion' on the coasts of Massachusetts and New
Hampshire.

Lord George's dispatch to Howe made no reference whatever
to the established plan for a meeting of the northern and
southern armies at Albany, approved by the Cabinet the week
before. There is a possible indirect reference: Lord George
wrote of Howe's 'proposed deviation'. He almost certainly meant
the revisions of Howe's 20 December plan in Howe's 20 January
plan, but it is within the bounds of Lord George's military
optimism and geographic ignorance that he thought of the
capture of Philadelphia as a mere deviation in the route from
New York to Albany. Howe, who knew nothing of the Cabinet's
approval of the Burgoyne plan, could reasonably assume that
whatever campaign was to be undertaken by the army in
Canada would not involve him.

There is still no answer to the mystery why Lord George did
not inform Howe that Burgoyne expected to be met in Albany,
and why he did not tell Burgoyne, who was still in London, anything of Howe's new plan. But even if Lord George deliberately
withheld this information, it is equally baffling why other men
in London, who must have known the facts, also failed to do so.
The king had approved both the Burgoyne plan and Howe's
move on Philadelphia, and so, presumably, had the Cabinet.
Undersecretaries in the office of Lord George must have known
of both. Did none of them foresee confusion and disaster and
feel a responsibility to prevent it? Did they all think that Howe
could take his army to Philadelphia, capture and garrison it,
and then get to Albany in September? Or did they think that
Clinton would be left with enough men in New York to meet or
rescue Burgoyne? If so, why did no one mention this expectation
to Howe, or to Clinton, who was in London throughout the
spring? Clinton later said that he had not known until he
rejoined Howe in New York in early July that Howe intended
to move to Philadelphia BEFORE he made his rendezvous at
Albany. And Howe had already written to Lord George that he
would leave in New York only enough troops to defend it and
its essential outlying points. The only reasonable explanation
of the whole fantastic situation is that it developed from a variety
of causes: delay and lack of clarity in dispatches, unjustified

optimisms, misunderstandings, carelessness, ignorance, and irresponsibility of many men. But of all these men, the least pardonable was the responsible co-ordinator, Lord George Germain.

Lord George took two steps, and only two, to inform Howe of the Burgoyne plan as approved. In the orders that Burgoyne carried to Carleton was the instruction to send a copy of them to Howe. Carleton did so, and Howe acknowledged receipt of them in a letter to Carleton dated 5 June 1777.[1] Lord George's dispatch to Carleton also stated that he was sending a copy of his orders to Carleton directly to Howe from London. What happened to that dispatch, if it was ever sent, was later a subject of impassioned discussion. Howe acknowledged his receipt of that dispatch in a letter to Lord George dated 5 July 1777,[2] but by that date it was unimportant. He had seen the copy from Carleton a month earlier, and he had long since taken steps to clear himself of any responsibility for Burgoyne, and was almost ready to embark his troops for a long cruise to Delaware and Chesapeake Bays.

Howe had made it clear to Lord George in his letter of 30 November 1776, and in later dispatches, that his own movements would depend on the number and time of arrival of reinforcements. When Howe discovered that his requested 15,000 men had been reduced to 2,900,[3] he wrote to Lord George that: '. . . owing to his receiving only one fifth of the reinforcements asked for, he would be obliged to go more slowly'.[4] After receiving Lord George's dispatch of 3 March, Howe was justified in assuming that Lord George had abandoned all thought of Howe's making an expedition in force up the Hudson in time to be of any use to Burgoyne.[5]

Howe's reply, dated 2 April, to Lord George's dispatch of

[1] PRO, CO/5, v. 94, pp. 299–303; also *Hansard*, xx. 688; also *HMC, Stop. Sack.* ii. 63; also *Whitton*, ii. 63.

[2] The ship that carried the copy of Carleton's orders to Howe from London was the *Somerset*, which, according to the journal of its captain, anchored off Sandy Hook on 3 June (*Sandwich Papers*, i. 281). Howe did not acknowledge the receipt of that dispatch until 5 July. The dispatch did not include a word of directions to Howe in connexion with its contents (Fortescue, *HBA*, 2, iii. 210).

[3] Trevelyan, *Amer. Rev.* iv. 70; see also p. 174, note 5 above.

[4] Guttridge, p. 29.

[5] Fortescue, *HBA*, 2, iii. 207.

3 March is significant. He began by expressing regret at the further reduction of his reinforcements, and then continued:

In these circumstances I find myself under the necessity of relinquishing a principal part of the plan before proposed for an offensive corps on the side of Rhode Island etc., and to adopt one on a smaller scale, which the enclosed distribution points out.

From the difficulties and delays that would attend the passage of the Delaware by a march through New Jersey, I propose to invade Pensylvania by sea, and from this arrangement we must probably abandon the Jerseys, which by the former plan would not have been the case. . . . From these considerations . . . it is probable the campaign will not commence as soon as your Lordship may expect . . . but your Lordship may be assured the operations will be forwarded as expeditiously as the nature of the service will admit, and meanwhile I shall anxiously await his Majesty's commands by Major Balfour. . . . Restricted as I am from entering upon more extensive operations by the want of force, my hopes of terminating the war this year are vanished. Still I think it probable that by the latter end of the campaign we shall be in possession of New York, the Jersies, and Pensylvania, tho' this in some measure must depend upon the success of the northern army. . . . Your Lordship will receive inclosed a copy of my letter to Sir Guy Carleton, which goes in a few days by frigate. . . . And I send this letter that I may have the honor of his Majesty's commands upon it in time, if the contents should not meet with the royal approval.[1]

In the enclosed copy of a letter to Carleton Howe had written:

. . . having little expectation that I shall be able, from the want of sufficient strength in this army, to detach a corps in the beginning of the campaign to act up Hudson's River consistent with the operations already determined upon, the force your Excellency may deem expedient to advance beyond your frontiers after taking Ticonderoga

---

[1] That letter was endorsed in Germain's office: 'Recd. 8th May. No. 7. This plan of operations, written after the receipt of No. 2, but before No. 5 or 6 had reached him' (Howe to Germain, 2 Apr. 1777; PRO, CO/5, v. 253, no. 146; also *Hansard*, xx. 686; also *HMC, Stop. Sack.* ii. 63). Washington's effective counter-strokes at Trenton and Princeton and his constant menace of British troops in New Jersey may have influenced Howe's decision to go to Philadelphia by sea. His letter to Germain dated 2 Apr. revealed a distaste for taking his army across the Delaware. A more determining cause was probably the constant diminution of his hopes for reinforcements. In his plan of 30 Nov. 1776 Howe planned to use 35,000 men; in his plan of 20 Dec. 1776, 19,000 men; and in his plan of 2 Apr. 1777, 21,000 men, in the last case leaving only '3200 men and 3000 Provincials' in and about New York (PRO, CO/5, v. 253, no. 299).

will, I fear, have little assistance from hence to facilitate their approach; as I shall probably be in Pensilvania when that corps is ready to advance into this province it will not be in my power to communicate with the officer commanding it so soon as I could wish; he must therefore pursue such measures as circumstances be judged most conducive to his Majesty's service, consistently with your Excellency's orders for his conduct. . . . I flatter myself . . . that it will prove no difficult task to reduce the more rebellious parts of the province. In the meanwhile I shall endeavor to have a corps on the lower part of Hudson's River sufficient to open the connection for shipping through the Highlands, at present obstructed by several forts erected by the rebels for that purpose, which corps may afterwards act in favour of the northern army.[1]

Howe thus put the issue of his own responsibility for the northern army clearly before Lord George. If Lord George approved Howe's letter to Carleton, then Howe had no obligation to move up the Hudson beyond the very limited assistance he proposed, and that only if he found it convenient. If Lord George declined to approve Howe's letter to Carleton, it followed that because of Howe's insistence that his reinforcements were inadequate, an order to Howe to support Burgoyne would result in Howe's giving up his attack on Philadelphia.

Lord George replied: 'As you must from your situation and military skill be a competent judge of the propriety of every plan, his Majesty does not hesitate to approve the alterations which you propose, trusting, however, that whatever you may meditate, it will be executed in time for you to co-operate with the army ordered to proceed from Canada and put itself under your command.' That was the only reference to the northern army. Whatever responsibility for its welfare that reference might have thrown on Howe was immediately nullified by Lord George's further sentence: 'I have the pleasure to acquaint you that his Majesty entirely approves of your letter to Sir Guy Carleton.'[2]

[1] Howe to Carleton, 5 Apr. 1777; PRO, CO/5, v. 94, pp. 299–303; also HMC, Stop. Sack. ii. 65 ff. In his testimony before Parliament on 22 Apr. 1779, Howe said that his letter of 2 Apr. 1777 had been written: '. . . spontaneously to Sir Guy Carleton; I say spontaneously because I had not at that time received any official information concerning the plan of the northern expedition, which I conceived was to take place that year' (Hansard, xx. 688). That statement was correct.

[2] Germain to Howe, 18 May 1777; Clements, Germain Papers, vi; also PRO, CO/5, v. 94, pp. 339–44; also PRO, 30/55, 529, 530; also Hansard, v. xi; also HMC, Stop. Sack. ii. 66, 67; also summarized in PRO, CO/5, v. 253, 292.

When Howe produced his copy of that dispatch before the House of Commons in 1779 it bore the endorsement: 'No. 8, written in consequence of the receipt of No. 7. This letter was received by Sir William Howe on the 16th August on his passage up Chesapeake Bay, being the one numbered 11.' By 16 August it was far too late for Howe to take any action that could help Burgoyne effectively, unless he abandoned his attack on Philadelphia. But when he had sailed from New York some three weeks before he had had no reason to think Burgoyne would need help. Burgoyne's dispatch received then had reeked confidence.

Before he started with his army for Crown Point, Burgoyne knew the purport of Howe's letter of 5 April to Carleton, and later said that letter had not troubled him, since he had assumed that soon after writing it Howe had received orders from Lord George to meet the northern army at Albany. That was a reasonable assumption by Burgoyne in view of what he did and did not know. Burgoyne also assumed that Howe would leave with Clinton in New York a force strong enough to meet him at Albany and draw off, if necessary, any strong rebel attack on the northern army.

If Burgoyne had known the whole truth he would probably have begun his own campaign just the same. He was ebulliently sure of himself and his men; he underestimated the fighting capacity though not the numbers of the Americans who might oppose him. He was unaware of all the difficulties of supply in a region where the natives proved, to his surprise, almost universally unfriendly. On these matters Carleton could perhaps have warned Burgoyne more strongly, but Burgoyne was in no mood to welcome cautionary advice, and after Lord George's treatment of him Carleton was certainly under no obligation to volunteer it.

Lord George had written to Howe on 14 January that as soon as the king had made up his mind about Howe's proposal to attack Philadelphia: 'Major Balfour will be immediately dispatched to you with all the necessary instructions.' Can the mystery of Lord George's procedure be explained by his having sent Major Balfour to impart orally to Howe some instructions that do not appear on the written record and contraverted those that do? That was almost certainly not the case. If all the records and personal correspondence of the time can be trusted, Major Balfour's messages were limited to urging the Howe brothers to change their minds and include in their summer activities the punitive raids on the New England coast that were so dear to Lord George's heart.[1] And none of the principals involved ever offered that explanation.

Thus on 1 June 1777 Burgoyne had been in Montreal three weeks and was almost ready to start southward with his army, confident that Howe had received mandatory orders to meet him in force at Albany as early as might be, perhaps in September. Burgoyne did not know that Howe had received Lord George's repeated approval of his plan to take his own army in the opposite direction; he did not know that Howe had left with Clinton an army too small to hold New York and at the same time give Burgoyne any real help if he should need it. He also did not know that the Americans could produce any army except Washington's capable of putting up powerful and determined resistance to trained European troops.

On 1 June Howe had just received reinforcements bringing his total strength to 27,000 men instead of the 35,000 he had said would be necessary to his original proposals—the only proposals in which he had included any aggressive move northward. With all his letters and plans officially approved, Howe had no reason to expect that Burgoyne was still counting on him, in force, at Albany. Howe, too, was ignorant of the capacity of the Americans, without Washington, to resist Burgoyne. Howe in fact had every argument for his own defence except the use of common sense.

Meanwhile in London on 1 June, Lord George had, twelve days before, sent to Howe the king's approval of Howe's letter to Carleton disclaiming any ability or intention to help Bur-

---

[1] 'Major Balfour, who carried the despatches of 3rd March, containing the approbation of the Plans of Operations, and proposing the Attack upon the Coasts of New England, arrived at New York the 8th May, in the *Augusta* Man of War' (PRO, CO/5, v. 253, no. 213). On 31 May Admiral Howe wrote from New York to Germain acknowledging a letter he received there through Major Balfour, concerned with the naval aspects of the proposed New England raids (Admiral Howe to Germain, 31 May 1777; *HMC, Stop. Sack.* ii. 68). The Whitehall summary states that on 3 June 1777 General Howe wrote to Germain that he had received the despatches by Major Balfour, but that he and Admiral Howe agreed that no raids could be attempted on the New England coast 'without distressing other parts of the service' (PRO, CO/5, v. 253, no. 294).

goyne. Lord George must have known that Burgoyne was still counting on Howe, yet he had taken no steps to disillusion Burgoyne. Howe had made his plans very clear to Lord George, who had no justification for complaining to the king that Howe was an unsatisfactory correspondent and that it was: '. . . surprizing that the General should be so fond of concealing his operations'.[1]

Thus on 1 June 1777, in the words of the leading historian of the British Army: 'Howe was left with directions to attack Philadelphia, and Burgoyne with positive and unconditional commands to advance to Albany and there place himself under Howe's orders. . . . Never was there a finer example of the art of organizing disaster.'[2]

---

[1] Germain to King, 5 June 1777; Fortescue, *Corresp.* iii. 451. Germain also complained to Knox: 'I hope that Balfour will have convinced Sir William Howe that he distresses us by not communicating his ideas more frequently and more explicitly' (Germain to Knox, 11 June 1777; *HMC, Var. Coll.* 6, *Knox*, p. 180). And again to Knox two weeks later: 'I cannot guess by Sir William Howe's letters when he will begin his operations, or where he proposes carrying them on. His saying that Lord Cornwallis is obliged to use the old camp equipage, the new not being yet arrived, inclines me to think that he may wait for the *Isis* before he takes the field in force' (Germain to Knox, 24 June 1777; *HMC, Var. Coll.* 6, *Knox*, p. 208).

[2] Sir John Fortescue, *HBA*, 2, iii, p. 210.

XIII

FRUITS OF ENMITY

THE dispatch from Lord George Germain that Burgoyne delivered to Carleton on his return to Canada in early May of 1777 contained strong criticisms of Carleton's military conduct and orders 'insulting in their minuteness' to turn over his army and campaign to Burgoyne.[1] No man of sense could regard the orders as other than a virtual dismissal. No man of self-respect could fail to protest.

That was the first dispatch Carleton had received from Lord George since the previous autumn, and the first Lord George had sent off to him since 22 August 1776, several weeks before Carleton drove the American forces from Lake Champlain.[2] That August dispatch had never reached Carleton, though a copy of it had reached General Howe,[3] who consequently knew throughout the winter and spring what Carleton did not. For the dispatch of 22 August 1776 was a preface to the virtual dismissal in the orders of 26 March 1777.

In the March dispatch Lord George enclosed a copy of the August one, and explained that the ship which carried its original had been unable to enter the St. Lawrence river because of ice, and had returned to England.[4] The August dispatch had ordered Carleton to turn over his attacking force immediately to Burgoyne or some other subordinate; to instruct that officer

---

[1] Fortescue, *HBA*, 2, iii. 207.

[2] Force, *Amer. Archives*, 5th series, vol. iii.

[3] Howe acknowledged its receipt in his dispatch of 28 Nov. 1776 (ibid.).

[4] The complete dispatch dated 26 Mar. 1777 is available as PRO, CO/5, Quebec, 13; also as PRO, 30/55, Carleton Papers, no. 462; also as *HMC, Stop. Sack*. ii. 60 ff.; also as BM, Addit. MSS., 21697, fol. 158, and 21698, fol. 3; also as Clements, *Germain Papers*.

'Mr. Ellis says that Capt. Mattaire, who was sent with despatches of importance to Quebec, after being 90 days at sea, & near the coast of America is returned to Falmouth, which was scarce ever known before. Mr. E. supposes that they were orders to Carleton to retain sufficient forces to defend Quebec, & to deliver the rest to Burgoyne to force his way with them to Albany if possible' (Clements, *Hutchinson Diaries* (original MS.), p. 363; 2 Dec. 1776). Wellbore Ellis was a Tory placeman with an ear constantly to the ground.

'to put himself as soon as possible under the command of General Howe'; to send most of his recently received artillery and military stores to Howe; and to exert himself 'as successfully in your civil capacity as you have always done in your military command'[1]— an empty compliment from a man who was at the same time robbing a general of his army. The dispatch written the following March revised these orders, but in ways still more distressing to a commanding officer.[2]

Since last hearing from Lord George, Carleton had driven the invading forces from Canada; built ships and defeated the American flotilla on Lake Champlain; and taken Crown Point. Lord George's dispatch of 26 March offered not a word of appreciation of those achievements. Instead it sharply criticized Carleton for having failed to take Ticonderoga, and expressed 'mystification' at his withdrawal from Crown Point. It even stated, with dubious truth, that by failing to capture Ticonderoga Carleton had freed American forces to go to the aid of Washington and had thus made Howe's fighting around New York more difficult.

These galling statements were embroidery around the even more devastating orders themselves. The Governor of Canada and Commander-in-Chief of its armed forces was ordered to turn over all but 3,000 men, including all reinforcements and new artillery, to Burgoyne, a subordinate officer, for a major campaign which Carleton himself had proposed to Lord George in a dispatch carried to him by that very officer. And although Carleton was instructed to 'consult with' Burgoyne on the plans for the campaign, the orders were so specific and mandatory that they left little room for suggestions and advice. Burgoyne would not only take over the greater part of Carleton's army, but on reaching Albany he would put that army under the command of General Howe, also junior to Carleton in seniority. The whole arrangement was out of line with normal military procedure or courtesy. It seemed not only a studied insult, but an attempt to break Carleton's career for ever.

With a further disregard of military good sense, Lord George ordered Carleton to recruit Indians and 'to employ them in

---

[1] Force, *Amer. Archives*, 5th series, vol. iii; Clements, *Germain Papers*, v. 41.
[2] This shows the Burgoyne plan of 1777 to be merely an elaboration of plans made in August 1776.

making a Diversion and exciting an alarm upon the Frontiers of Virginia and Pennsylvania'.[1] Since Carleton might not cross his provincial boundaries, he could not, even if he had adequate troops, lead the Indians in terror raids in remote western Pennsylvania and Virginia, by which Lord George must have meant modern Ohio and Kentucky, several hundreds of miles away. The scheme was so absurd that it must have been intended as a wanton gibe at Carleton's avoidance of using Indians.

Those were the orders to a general who, in the opinion of most of his contemporaries, was the man best qualified to govern Canada and command the northern army. It was true that Carleton had failed to attack Ticonderoga in October 1776, but Lord George's letter of 22 August 1776 could hardly have been based on that disappointment. It was true that Carleton had refused (though certainly his refusals were well within his rights) to gratify Lord George's wishes with regard to Colonel Christie and Peter Livius, and had even sent an uncomplimentary dispatch to Lord George. It was true that, when placed in contrast with Burgoyne's genial ebullience, Carleton seemed stern and remote. Young Lieutenant Digby, for example, had served in Canada under Carleton and admired him, but when Burgoyne arrived in 1776 Digby lost his heart to Gentleman John, and wrote home that:

General Carleton is one of the most distant, reserved men in the world, he has a rigid strictness in his manner very unpleasing and which he observes even to his most particular friends and acquaintances. . . . He was far from being the favorite of the army. General Burgoyne alone engrossed their warmest attachment. From having seen a great deal of polite life, he possesses a winning manner in his appearance and address (far different from the severity of Carleton) which causes him to be idolized by the army, his orders appearing more like recommending subordination than enforcing it. On every occasion he was the soldiers' friend.[2]

Digby was correct in his contrast but he exaggerated Burgoyne's charms and failed to appreciate Carleton's virtues or their special necessity in Canada at that time. Carleton needed to instil discipline into raw troops and also, perhaps, into socially inclined young officers drawn from English country house circles.

---

[1] Clements, *Germain Papers*, v.
[2] Hudleston, *Gentleman Johnny Burgoyne*, pp. 120, 121.

Carleton might not have charmed his men, but he took very good care of them in the essentials: he did not expose them to needless risks and hardships; he saw that they had adequate food, blankets, and ammunition, and was probably more tactful than Burgoyne in handling the independent Canadians. The criticisms of Anburey, another young officer in Carleton's army, were just the opposite of those of Digby. Anburey thought Carleton should have been more severe and less long-suffering with the Canadians, and deplored Carleton's having such a 'good-natured, affable disposition, that he always listens to their complaints'.[1]

A more detached and expert opinion of Carleton came from Major-General Baron Riedesel, who commanded the German troops under Carleton in 1776 and under Burgoyne in 1777. Riedesel wrote after the war that: '. . . a great mistake was undoubtedly made by the British ministry. Carleton had, hitherto, worked with energy and success; he knew the army thoroughly and enjoyed the confidence of the officers and men. It was a great risk to remove a man, who was so peculiarly fitted for so important a position, without a better cause.'[2]

Lord George differed sincerely with Carleton on one point of military strategy. From the beginning he insisted that Indians should be recruited not only to fight against the Americans but by their savagery to 'strike terror into their hearts'. Lord George repeatedly urged his generals to enlist and use Indians more energetically, and showed no great concern at the shocking barbarities they could hardly be prevented from perpetrating.

Carleton knew the Indians and the settlers as Lord George did not. He was aware how undependable most Indians were; that although useful for scouting they were of little value in an open fight; that they were difficult to fit into an organized army and impossible to control unless thus integrated. They were usually more trouble than they were worth. His reservations did not stop there. He deplored, because he knew, the savagery Indians were capable of, and he had too high a concept of Britain's honour and his own to be willing to sponsor that kind of war. Nothing, Carleton believed, would be more certain to add to the colonials' resentment against Britain than British use of the Indian terror against them. Lord George's advocacy of

---

[1] Thomas Anburey, *Travels*, i. 43.   [2] Kingsford, vi. 176.

such methods can be excused, if at all, only by crediting him with lack of imagination to envisage what Indians were like when turned loose with tomahawk and scalping-knife on some defenceless hamlet of old men, women, and children, or among wounded enemies on the battlefield.

The Colonial Office summary of the year 1776 gave another reason for Carleton's refusal to use the Indians extensively: '. . . his sole object appears to have been the prevailing on the Canadians to defend their Country, & it is highly probable that his repeated Orders to restrain the Savages within the limits of the Province, was with a view to avoid giving Occasion to the Canadians to charge him with being the Aggressor, and on that account to excuse themselves from taking up arms'.[1]

Carleton had been faced with the Indian issue early in 1775 and had by various devices avoided employing them. In July of that year Colonel Guy Johnson, a great friend of the seven Iroquois tribes, arrived in Montreal with about 200 Indians and urged upon Carleton 'the necessity of immediately employing them against the rebels; but General Carleton informed him that as his Body of Regular Forces was but inconsiderable he must depend, for the defense of the Province, on the Canadian Militia, a good Body of which he hoped to assemble shortly, & in the mean time that Col. Johnson should amuse the Indians in the best manner he could, but not to suffer them to go beyond the 45th Degree of Latitude, the Boundary of the Province.'[2]

When the Indians, stimulated by Colonel Johnson and others, wanted to attack the Americans on Lake Champlain, General Prescott, acting under Carleton's instructions, told them: 'His orders were such as would not allow him to suffer the Indians to act beyond the Line of the Province, but directed them to send Parties to gain Intelligence of the Rebels' Motions.'[3] In the summer of 1775 Lieutenant-Governor Hamilton at Detroit enlisted Indians there to join Carleton, but then received a letter from him '. . . acquainting him that he had sent back some Ottawas who had offered their services, desiring them to hold themselves in readiness next Spring'.[4]

[1] PRO, CO/5, v. 253, no. 18.
[2] Ibid., no. 7; reporting Carleton to Johnson, 17 July 1775.
[3] Ibid., no. 8.
[4] Ibid., pp. 131 ff.; 19 July 1775.

When reports of these rejections reached Lord George he was openly angry with Carleton. He instructed Burgoyne, who was about to leave for Quebec, that '... the assistance of the Indians and Canadians would be highly necessary, and that their Tempers and Dispositions were to be cultivated with particular attention'.[1] This was an order, and to support it Lord George secured £5,000 from the Treasury to buy 'gifts' for the Indians in Canada.[2] What these presents were to be is indicated by receipted bills for tomahawks and scalping-knives supplied to other Indians elsewhere.[3] The British Treasury records show that £87,484 was expended officially for 'presents to Indians' from 1775 to 1779 inclusive. Probably a larger sum was used unofficially for the purpose.[4]

After Burgoyne had joined Carleton in 1776 Lord George wrote to him: 'I hope every precaution has been taken to secure the Indians to our interest. The Congress is exerting all their influence to debauch them from you. . . . The dread the people of New England etc. have of a war with the savages proves the expediency of our holding that scourge over them. The Indians report that had General Carleton permitted them to act last year, Canada would not have been in the hands of the rebels.'[5] Burgoyne appears to have begun his American experience in agreement with Lord George, but he had not been long in Canada before he wrote to him that the Indians were '... ignorant of the use of arms, awkward, disinclined to the service, and spiritless'.[6] By then he was less critical of Carleton for having dismissed most of the red men who had been with him before he attacked Arnold on Lake Champlain.[7] But to Lord George,

[1] Ibid., no. 34; Spring, 1776.   [2] Ibid., no. 20.
[3] Though some Tories as well as many Whigs protested, Lord George continued to urge and finance the use of Indians. In the Florida campaign in 1780 Indians were recruited, armed, paid, and transported for attacks on local inhabitants. A bill dated 8 May 1780 to 'The Crown for Indian presents furnished by order of Major Campbell' by John Falconer and Company, and receipted by that company as paid in full 'by the Lords Commissioners of the Treasury', totalled £9,987 and included: 49 dozen knives, 11 dozen hatchets, and 12 dozen tomahawks. A similar bill shows that 'sundries supplied for the use of the Indians', receipted as paid by the Commissary of the Indian area on 4 Mar. 1780, included '60 scalping knives' (PRO, 30/55, v. 88, nos. 9857, 9870).
[4] HMC, Var. Coll. 6, Knox, p. 293.
[5] Germain to Burgoyne, 23 Aug. 1776; HMC, Stop. Sack. ii. 40.
[6] Burgoyne to Germain, 14 May 1777; Fonblanque, pp. 231, 232.
[7] PRO, CO/5, v. 253, nos. 26, 46.

Carleton's continued obstinacy in not using Indians seemed close to insubordination.

Lord George did not find Howe much more co-operative with regard to the use of Indians. Before Howe took New York, Lord George had written to him that '. . . the securing the assistance of the Indians was an important consideration',[1] three weeks later he ordered Howe to '. . . make use of the friendly Indians in such a manner as may be most serviceable in the Prosecution of the War';[2] and just before Howe took Philadelphia Lord George urged him again to '. . . secure the future affection of the savages'.[3] Howe must have felt as Carleton did, for Indians were very few indeed in his regular army.

Indians were not an important military factor in a single major battle. The British use of Indians in the South was a main source of resentment by Americans, and doubtless led many Americans originally thought loyalist not to support the British forces'.[4] The *Annual Register* of London gave its opinion in 1777 that the barbarities practised by Indians in Western Virginia and North Carolina, sponsored by British military men, had been a great influence in alienating loyalist sentiment in the southern colonies.[5]

Lord George never abandoned his Indian policy. In 1779 he wrote to Clinton, then commanding in New York, of his plans for the troops in Canada: '. . . a considerable Diversion will also be directed to be made on the side of Canada by a succession of Parties of Indians supported by Detachments of the Troops there, alarming and harassing the Frontiers, and making Incursions into the Settlements'.[6] Carleton was no longer in Canada to circumvent Lord George's designs.

The Americans used Indians too, but not so many and not so often as the British, in spite of the lack of enthusiasm for the practice of every British commanding officer. 'England obtained in consequence much the larger share of the benefit and the discredit of their assistance.'[7] And such use as the Americans made of Indians was directed against armed British, German,

---

[1] Germain to Howe, 28 Mar. 1776; PRO, CO/5, v. 253, no. 4.
[2] Germain to Howe, 19 Apr. 1777; Clements, *Germain Papers*, vi.
[3] Germain to Howe, 3 Sept. 1777; Clements, *Germain Papers*, vi. 88.
[4] Lecky, iv. 14, 15.   [5] *Annual Register*, London, 1777.
[6] Germain to Clinton, 23 Jan. 1779; PRO, CO/5, pp. 55 ff.
[7] Lecky, iv. 14.

or loyalist soldiers: the British Government used them with the specific intention of bringing terror to the civilian population.[1] The person clearly responsible for that government policy was Lord George Germain.

Carleton delayed several days before he replied to Lord George's dispatch of March 1777. Then his answer was worthy of the occasion. He sharply denied and refuted Lord George's charges of sloth or over-caution in failing to attack Ticonderoga, yet: 'For these things I am so severely censured by your Lordship, and this is the first reason assigned why the command of the troops is taken from me.' He mixed sarcasm with wrath in pointing out the absurdity of the excuse that his Governor's duties would prevent his leading an army into New York state.[2] Two days later he sent another letter to Lord George, saying that he had been treated with 'Slight, Disregard and Censure' because of Lord George's 'private Enmity'.[3]

In his reply to Lord George's devastating orders of 26 March 1777, Carleton added that he would give Burgoyne 'every assistance in my power', and he did. Burgoyne was, then and later, unqualified in his praise of Carleton's co-operation. Since no arrangement could have been better calculated to breed difficulties between two soldiers, it is greatly to the credit of Carleton that under the circumstances he and Burgoyne remained on sympathetic terms.

Lord George did not at first show Carleton's acid replies to the king and Lord North. Had he done so they might have asked to see Lord George's dispatch that had roused Carleton's ire. Though the king had approved the nature of the orders to be sent to Carleton, he valued Carleton highly and had insisted over Lord George's protest on awarding him the Red Ribbon of the Bath. It seems very unlikely that the king would have

---

[1] In theory the Indians were to create terror without barbarities, but to an Indian this was inconsistent. Colonel Guy Johnson wrote to Germain: 'The terror of their name without any acts of savage cruelty will tend much to the speedy termination of the rebellion.' A year later Johnson wrote to Germain: 'I am persuaded . . . that I can restrain the Indians from acts of savage cruelty' (*Documents related to the Colonial History of New York*, viii. 699; also quoted by Lecky, iv. 14). Few British leaders actually prevented Indian barbarities. In spite of Burgoyne's sincere efforts, his few remaining Indians perpetrated one shocking murder of an officer's wife shortly before Saratoga.

[2] He had a competent Lieutenant-Governor. For the entire dispatch see Kingsford, vi. 129 ff.   [3] Carleton to Germain, 22 May 1777; Hudleston, p. 127.

approved the actual text of Lord George's crucial dispatch. But Carleton wrote also to Lord North, enclosing his request to be relieved of his appointments in Canada, and Lord North sent to the king Carleton's request to resign a post: '. . . which, indeed, it could hardly be expected he ever meant to hold, when he wrote to Lord George Germain the letters which are brought in by the same conveyance'.[1]

In his reply to Lord North's note and enclosure, the king ranged his personal sympathies on the side of Carleton: 'Any one that will for an instant suppose himself in the situation of Sir Guy Carleton, must feel that the resigning the Government of Quebec is the only dignified part, though I think as things were situated the ordering him to remain in the Province was a necessary measure, yet it must be owned to be mortifying to a soldier. The General seems at the same time to have facilitated as much as possible the steps necessary for enabling Burgoyne to cross the Lakes.'[2]

Burgoyne himself reported to Lord George: 'I should think myself deficient in justice and in honour, were I to close my letter without mentioning the sense I entertain of General Carleton's conduct; that he was anxiously desirous of leading the military operations out of the province, is easily to be discerned; but his deference to his Majesty's decision, and his zeal to give effect to his measures in my hands, are equally manifest, exemplary and satisfactory.'[3] Five days later Burgoyne wrote from Montreal to General Harvey that though Sir Guy: '. . . thinks he has some cause for resentment for the general tenor of treatment he has received from some of the ministers, he had done everything possible to assist him'.[4]

Lord George insisted even to his undersecretary Knox that Carleton's 'ill-humour' was entirely his own fault. 'I shall wait with impatience for Carleton's dispatches. I do not wonder he is displeased at receiving such particular directions from hence, as he must see that they proceed from the inactivity of the past campaign.'[5] His first reply to Carleton's angry rejoinder was

[1] North to King, 2 July 1777; Fortescue, *Corresp*. iii. 457.
[2] King to North, 2 July 1777; ibid.
[3] Burgoyne to Germain, 14 May 1777; Hudleston, p. 138.
[4] Burgoyne to Harvey, 19 May 1777; ibid., p. 144.
[5] Germain to Knox, 10 July 1777; *HMC, Var. Coll.* 6, *Knox*, p. 132.

dated the same day.[1] He wrote to Carleton that the orders sent him (and, by implication, the comments that accompanied the orders) came directly, and 'after mature deliberation', from the king, though: '. . . if the manner of conveying them is improper, I alone stand responsible for it . . . the last letter', Lord George wrote, 'was particularly directed by the King'. Lord George declined: '. . . to enter into an ill-humoured altercation with you', and insisted that reports of: '. . . my having any personal dislike to you are without the least foundation'. But he belied that last assurance with a final gibe: 'I cannot finish this subject without expressing my astonishment at your supposing that I could descend so low as to encourage faction and cabal in your government. I trust you did not so lightly give credit to intelligence when you were to decide upon measures relating to the public service.'[2] Depending on intelligence far more faulty than Carleton's was a habit of Lord George himself.

Before Lord George had composed that condescending dispatch, Carleton had again written pressing his resignation. He said he could no longer be of use to the king's service, in either a civil or a military capacity, under Lord George's administration.

On the contrary, apprehending that I may occasion no small detriment to it, for all the marks of your Lordship's displeasure affect not me, but the King's service and the tranquility of his people; I therefore flatter myself I shall obtain his royal permission to return home this fall, the more so that from your first entrance into office, you began to prepare the minds of all men for this event, wisely foreseeing that, under your Lordship's administration, it must certainly come to pass, and, for my own part, I do not think it just that the private enmity of the King's servants should add to the disturbance of his reign. For these reasons I shall embark with great satisfaction, still entertaining hopes and ardent wishes that after my departure, you may adopt measures tending to promote the safety and tranquility of this unfortunate Province; at least that the dignity of the Crown may not appear beneath your Lordship's concern.[3]

Lord George did his best to convince the king that Carleton's acidulous comments on a king's minister were attacks on the

[1] Clements, *Germain Papers*, vii. 72.
[2] Germain to Carleton, 10 July 1777; *HMC, Var. Coll. 6, Knox*, p. 132.
[3] Carleton to Germain, 27 June 1777; Kingsford, vi. 127.

king himself, but it was not until August that he sent, perhaps on request, Carleton's letters to the king, with the written comment: 'The ill-humour of the General continues in its full force, and Lord George is not Conscious of deserving any of the imputations laid to his Charge, and therefore bears it with great indifference.'[1]

The king knew better, but it looked as though Lord George had been successful in bringing a sad end to Carleton's distinguished military career. If Carleton's resignation were accepted he would come home with the imputation of failure, almost of disgrace. If he were compelled to remain a while in Canada he would be in the degrading position of a general relieved of command of his army by an officer junior to him, a discredited civilian governor in a province dominated by military issues. It was decided, apparently by the king, that Carleton could not be spared from Canada for another year, and he remained until replaced by General Haldimand on 27 June 1778. But Lord George had reckoned without changing circumstance and the king's strong sense of justice. Events during that last year in Canada led public opinion to honour Carleton on his return to London as a mistreated hero. He was welcomed by the king, praised by the Opposition, and consulted as an expert by Parliament, where he had the satisfaction of watching the increasingly drastic discomfiture of Lord George Germain.

In his entire correspondence with Carleton during that final year in Canada, Lord George only once enunciated an appreciative sentence. In his dispatch of 3 August 1777, he informed Carleton that: 'All the letters from General Burgoyne and the other officers of the northern army are full of the warmest acknowledgments of the cordial, zealous and effectual assistance they have received from you'.[2] Lord George could hardly have conceded less, since Carleton's generous conduct had become a matter of general knowledge. Carleton left Canada with the warm praises of most Canadians, but Lord George wrote to General Howe: 'I fear Sir. G. Carleton will do nothing but scold all winter',[3] and was busy preparing instructions for Carleton's successor, General Haldimand, who had been a

---

[1] Germain to King, 3 Aug. 1777; Fortescue, *Corresp.* iii. 464.
[2] Germain to Carleton, 3 Aug. 1777; Hudleston, p. 137.
[3] Germain to Howe, 9 Oct. 1777; *HMC, Var. Coll.* 6, *Knox,* p. 139.

witness favourable to Lord George at his court martial after Minden.[1]

Carleton was not a man to be bullied without risk. Even verbally he could give as good as he got. Writing to Lord George in line of duty on 6 November he merely added the personal hope that his successor would arrive soon, since Lord George had manifested to all the world that he no longer trusted his Governor in Canada to execute the duties of his appointment.[2] Carleton was also writing less restrained letters to his friends in Parliament. All the inner circle in London knew the story, and most men sympathized with Carleton. Members of the Whig party made him one of their favourite examples of the Ministry's incapacity, injustice, and ingratitude. Colonel Barre told the House of Commons on 20 November that the Ministers had disgraced General Carleton because he would not hire Indians to commit savageries, and because Carleton had been humane to American prisoners of war.[3] In its record of the events of the year the *Annual Register* said of Burgoyne's appointment to head the northern army that though his 'ability was unquestioned' it 'could hardly be expected not to give umbrage to General Carleton, to whose abilities, and resolution, this nation in general acknowledged, and the world attributed, the preservation of Canada'. It was said, the *Register* continued, that 'his powers had been diminished in proportion to the greatness of his service'.[4] As for the king, he was not always deferential to the wishes of his Secretary of State for America, for on 29 August 1777 Major-General Carleton was promoted to the rank of permanent Lieutenant-General.

When a statesman uses his power to indulge his personal rancours, the results may injure him more than his victim. Lord George's attempts to destroy Carleton's career and reputation

[1] Knox had apparently prepared a draft of instructions to Haldimand, and included a proposed letter to Carleton saying that the advice Carleton could give his successor would be very useful to Haldimand. When Lord George had gone over the draft he wrote to Knox: 'I had rather not have said that the information Haldimand was to receive could not fail of being of the greatest use to the conduct of his Administration. As I do not believe a word of that sentence, you must absolve me of the crime of signing what I do not think true' (Germain to Knox, 19 Sept. 1777; *HMC, Var. Coll.* 6, *Knox*, p. 138).

[2] Carleton to Germain, 6 Nov. 1777; *HMC, Amer. MSS., Dartmouth,* ii. 446. Carleton's letter was to confirm reports that Burgoyne was in difficulties.

[3] Walpole, *Last Journals,* ii. 78.   [4] *Annual Register* for 1777.

unquestionably helped to undermine his own. His dearest public objective was to win the American war, but by mid-1777 he had alienated Carleton, roused resentments in Howe and Clinton, and would soon reap the whirlwind with Burgoyne.

If mutual respect and confidence between military leaders in the field and their civilian chiefs back home were essential in that war of great distances, then Lord George, after only eighteen months in office, had lost three-quarters of the battle. Yet in spite of the facts, many of them common knowledge in London; in spite of even more disastrous misunderstandings during the interval, Lord George was capable of standing before the House of Commons six months later and bestowing 'the highest encomiums on the abilities of the generals'—Howe, Carleton, Clinton, and Burgoyne.

XIV

THE CONQUERING HERO

LIEUTENANT-GENERAL JOHN BURGOYNE left London on 27 March 1777; reached Quebec on 6 May and Montreal on 12 May.[1] Fortune seemed at last to be smiling on his ambitions. He was about to lead an army to a crushing victory that would win the war.

It was a good army, almost equally divided between trained British and German regulars, and it was well staffed. No such brilliant collection of well-born officers had ever been assembled in America. More than thirty of them would in time attain the rank of General, and nearly as many more would sit in the House of Lords or the House of Commons. Among the younger officers were the Earl of Balcarres, then aged 25, Viscount Petersham aged 22, the Earl of Harrington then 24, Lord Torpichen and Lord Napier, then aged 19. At least four of Burgoyne's officers were currently members of Parliament, and Major-General Phillips, Major-General Baron Riedesel, Colonel Fitzroy, Colonel Viscount Ligonier, and Captain Edward Fay had all been at the Battle of Minden. Much was expected of them, for Lord George Germain was already assuring the House of Commons that 'Washington's army was very weak' and that 'he had great hopes from the campaign'.[2]

Burgoyne believed the Americans might oppose him in numbers superior to his own, and young Lieutenant Anburey doubtless reflected his chief's opinion when he wrote home to his family in June: 'By all accounts that can be collected, the Americans are in great force at Ticonderoga, nearly to the number of 12,000, and a considerable number occupy Lake George, sustained by a naval power.'[3] But Burgoyne also believed the enemy's fighting quality and leadership to be greatly inferior, and he was certain that if Washington should come north to oppose him Howe would pursue Washington,

---

[1] *Hansard*, xx. 786.   [2] Walpole, *Last Journals*, ii. 27; 15 May 1777.
[3] Anburey, i. 158; 14 June 1777.

who would then be caught between the two armies and destroyed.

He took every possible step to remind Howe of that expectation. He had written to Howe from Plymouth just before sailing, and twice from Quebec:[1] '. . . wherein I repeated that my orders were to effect a junction with his excellency',[2] and gave Howe 'intelligence of my situation at the time'.[3] Burgoyne was still troubled by the rigidity of his orders—not that he feared their inflexibility would endanger his ultimate success but because it might prevent him from wider conquests and greater honour, and 'honour' was a word that came often and passionately to Burgoyne's lips. Just after he reached Montreal he wrote to Lord George a hint that he would like to stretch his orders just a little: 'It is my design, while advancing to Ticonderoga, and during the siege of that post, for a siege I apprehend it must be, to give all possible jealousy on the side of Connecticut.'[4] That desire was so strong in Burgoyne's mind that he elaborated on it in a letter to General Harvey a week later:

My intention is, during my advance to Ticonderoga, and siege of that post, for a siege I apprehend it must be, to give all possible jealousy on the side of Connecticut. If I can by manœuvre make them suspect that after the reduction of Ticonderoga my views are pointed that way, it may make the Connecticut forces very cautious of leaving their own frontiers, and much facilitate my progress to Albany. I mention this intention only to Lord George and yourself, and I do it lest from any intelligence of my motions that may reach England indirectly, it should be supposed I have suffered myself to be diverted from the main object of my orders. The King and his Majesty's ministers may rest assured that whatever demonstrations I may endeavor to impose upon the enemy, I shall really make no movement that can procrastinate my progress to Albany.[5]

He also wrote to Howe in the same vein, taking occasion once more to emphasize his expectation of a 'junction' with Howe at Albany: 'I wish a latitude had been left me for a diversion

[1] *Hansard*, xx. 786; also Burgoyne's statement before Parliament, published by Almon, 1779.

[2] Burgoyne, *A State of the Expedition, &c.*, Almon, London, 1780.

[3] *Hansard*, xx. 787; also Burgoyne, *Statement before Parliament*.

[4] Burgoyne to Germain, 12 May 1777; also Hudleston, p. 146. Burgoyne meant chiefly the area which is now Vermont.

[5] Burgoyne to Harvey, 19 May 1777; Hudleston, p. 144.

toward Connecticut, but such an idea being out of the question
by my orders being precise to form a junction . . .'[1] These letters
make it clear that long before it became expedient for Burgoyne
to defend his actions by blaming the inflexibility of his orders,
he conceived them as leaving him no alternative to 'forcing his
way' straight to Albany.

In Montreal Burgoyne encountered various problems and
minor disappointments, but that was to be expected in campaigns, and he was not too greatly troubled. He confided, however, to General Harvey: 'I had the surprise and mortification
to find a paper handed about at Montreal, publishing the whole
design of the campaign, almost as accurately as if it had been
copied from the Secretary of State's letter. My own caution has
been such that not a man in my family has been let into the
secret. Sir Guy Carleton's, I am confident, has been equally
discreet. I am therefore led to doubt whether imprudence has
not been committed in private letters from England.'[2] Burgoyne
may well have suspected the same man as a later historian did,
who stated categorically regarding those indiscretions: 'The
blame must accordingly lie with Lord George Germain or his
confidential assistants.'[3] Burgoyne's complaint was echoed by
young Anburey: 'We have more dangerous enemies at home
than any we have to encounter abroad: for all transactions that
are to take place are fully known before they are given out in
orders . . . the whole operations of the ensuing campaign were
canvassed for several days before he [Burgoyne] arrived, while
he supposed he was communicating an entire secret.'[4]

Lord George had assured Burgoyne that he could count upon
recruiting all the Canadian fighters he would need, though
Burgoyne, having been in Canada with Carleton the year before,
should have been a better authority. But Burgoyne found
few Canadians ready to enlist or accept military discipline.
Lieutenant Anburey wrote: 'The lower class of Canadians are
exceedingly insolent and insult their officers upon every occasion. . . . I should attribute it to the very great indulgence
shewn them by General Carleton.'[5] Anburey had praised

---

[1] Burgoyne to Howe, May 1777; Fonblanque, p. 233.
[2] Burgoyne to Harvey, 19 May 1777; Fonblanque, p. 242.
[3] Kingsford, vi. 206.   [4] Anburey, i. 121; 20 May 1777.
[5] Anburey, i. 108; 27 Feb. 1777.

Carleton's treatment of American prisoners: '. . . the humanity of General Carleton, who had cloathed all those who were taken prisoners, they being almost in a state of nakedness; many of them he suffered to return to their homes on the paroles of not bearing arms during the war. Those who are here . . . fare the same as our own soldiers.'[1] Carleton had treated the Americans well not only from humanity but in order to hold the Canadians to loyalty by avoiding severity to the Americans, with whom Carleton knew many of them were sympathetic. As for Canadian insolence, it was an aspect of the pioneer spirit, and Carleton knew it must be endured until their independence could slowly be disciplined. Most of them, of course, were of French descent.

Quebec had been a British province for less than fifteen years, and the French among its population had no great urge to fight for Britain. On the whole they 'remained loyal to the King, but would not serve . . . in the militia' against the Americans.[2] Those who did resented the restrictions of British parade-ground army regulations, especially when imposed by British officers and subalterns who seemed arrogant and in their own way provincial. Many refused to enlist under Burgoyne unless he would commission as their immediate superiors Canadians with rank and authority equal to the British officers. This Burgoyne would not do, and his contingent of Canadians proved less numerous and less dependable than he and Lord George had expected. 'Only 150 would serve as soldiers, while even for employment in the matter of transport they were backward and unwilling.'[3] As for the Indians, Burgoyne became less and less enthusiastic about their value. But some would be useful for scouting at least, and not to enlist them would be to incur the strong displeasure of the Secretary of State for America. Burgoyne did his best to prevent them from savagery and attacks on women and children and to keep them under regular army discipline. Under those restraints the Indians too were not eager to serve, and Burgoyne enrolled only a few.

Such supplies and equipment as Burgoyne had not brought from England were, it developed, almost unobtainable in Canada. When Burgoyne set out, he was short of the horses

---

[1] Anburey, i. 88; 18 Jan. 1777.   [2] Fortescue, *HBA*, 2, iii. 163.
[3] Ibid., p. 223.

and carts he needed to transport food and supplies, haul his heavy artillery, and carry more than 200 wives and children of his British and German officers. Among these were Baroness Riedesel and her three daughters, one aged four, one aged two, and the third born after the baroness had come to Canada. They went through the whole campaign including Saratoga and then into the prisoner-of-war camp at Cambridge, Massachusetts. When it was all over, the baroness published her journal of the campaign, and provided historians with many interesting details, including her unverified references to Burgoyne's affair with 'the wife of a commissary'.[1]

Burgoyne wrote to Lord George Germain only two weeks after his arrival in Canada that: 'The army will fall short of the strength computed in England, and the want of camp equipage, clothing and other necessary articles will cause some inconvenience.'[2] Burgoyne had yet to discover that in Adirondack warfare inconvenience could also be caused by equipment of the wrong kind. The British and German regiments, including the 20th Foot which had fought at Minden, began the campaign with the same elaborate uniforms they would have worn in the Low Countries. Each British grenadier carried a musket, sixty rounds of ammunition, a blanket, a hatchet, a haversack with four days' rations, and some part of a tent, to a total of over sixty pounds. The Brunswick dragoons wore tall jackboots, stiff leather breeches, enormous leather gauntlets, and a hat heavy with plumes. Their long perukes trailed from the backs of their heads, and each carried a broadsword weighing almost four pounds, a heavy carbine, and a pouch of flour to make bread. These troops were in the habit of marching in close order, and very few of them had ever fought in primitive, rough country.

Burgoyne knew his objective must be achieved by late October, for after that the cold would make sleeping in tents by

[1] Curtis, p. 11, note. Officers' wives and sometimes their children were often permitted by the commanding officer to accompany British troops on active duty. Apart from any special luxuries they provided at their own cost, their food and bedding were usually provided by the Quartermaster. Burgoyne, after Saratoga, was charged by political enemies with letting his army be followed by a thousand unauthorized women, but his hot denials were unanimously supported by all his officers and by other evidence. The contingent of women in Burgoyne's army was smaller, rather than larger, than in comparable cases.

[2] Burgoyne to Germain, 14 May 1777; Fonblanque, *Pol. and Mil. Episodes, &c.*, London, 1876, p. 231.

inexperienced men unendurable if not fatal, and the snows would make communications and supplies from Canada almost impossible.[1] He consequently had little time to train his troops in what he thought he knew of the fighting and maintenance methods peculiar to North America; to organize transport, and to wait for more ammunition from England. He realized that as sharpshooters in the woods his men could not equal the best of the Americans, but he doubted the desire or ability of the rebels to stand up to close formation attack. In the last analysis, he told his officers, battles could be won in America as they were won in Europe—by trained, disciplined troops; well organized, well artilleried, and well led. 'Our success in any engagement must rest greatly on the bayonet, the great utility of which General Burgoyne pointed out in an order a few days since, strongly recommending to officers to inculcate that idea in the minds of the men', wrote Anburey on 20 May.[2]

Burgoyne had heard nothing directly from Howe, and 'during the movement of the different corps to the general rendezvous', he found time to write to Howe once again, and to repeat 'my expectation of being before Ticonderoga between the 20th and 25th instant. . . . I repeated . . . my assurance that I would make no manœuvre that could procrastinate the great object of a junction'.[3]

Having done his best to inform Howe and to avoid keeping him waiting in Albany, Burgoyne set out, though still short of men, draught animals, and ammunition. Instead of the 8,000 his plan had stated to be the necessary minimum, he had 6,740 regulars, of which 3,724 were British and 3,016 were German. He had some 150 Canadians and about 500 Indians—numbers well below those he had counted on. Colonel Barry St. Leger, who set out at almost the same time on his diversionary expedition to the Mohawk Valley, had about 1,700 men, also less than the 2,000 or more specified in Burgoyne's 'Thoughts'. Of these nearly half were Indians, led by the famous Joseph Brand, known to the Indians as Thayendanegea. St. Leger was to go by way of Lake Ontario and Oswego to the Mohawk River, and then work back east to meet Burgoyne.

[1] His own experience made Burgoyne less critical of Carleton for declining to accept the risks of winter by an attack on Ticonderoga in 1776.
[2] Anburey, i. 126; 20 May 1777.
[3] *Hansard*, xx. 787; also Burgoyne, *Narrative before Parliament*.

Fortified by confidence, martial music, and, in the case of the Indians, firewater, the brightly uniformed and heavily laden northern army proceeded on foot to the northern end of Lake Champlain by way of St. Johns on 17 June,[1] and embarked at Cumberland Bay on 20 June.[2] All began auspiciously. 'To the great praise of General Carleton', wrote Anburey on 30 June, 'very little delay has yet occurred, for he forwards the stores very expeditiously, and however ill-treated many people suppose he is . . . in not having command of this army . . . he lets no pique or ill-will divert him from doing all the real service in his power.'[3]

The urge to drama and elocution was strong in Burgoyne, and he gave full vent to both in his proclamation on 23 June. His purposes were to inspire his men; to attract and encourage American loyalists; to weaken rebel morale by promising lenient treatment to Americans who yielded without resistance and severe treatment of those who did not, and to restrain his Indians from barbarities. One sentence is an adequate example of his style: 'Animated by these considerations, at the head of troops in the full power of health, discipline and vigor, determined to strike when necessary and anxious to spare when possible, I by these presents invite and exhort all persons, in all places where the progress of this army may point (and, by the blessing of God, I will extend it) to maintain such a conduct as may justify in protecting their lands, Habitations and Families.'[4]

Burgoyne continued with a warning to his Indians that Lord George might not have approved: 'I positively forbid bloodshed when you are not opposed in arms. . . . Aged men, women and children must be held sacred from the hatchet, even in time of actual conflict. . . . You will be called upon to account for scalps.' And he added: 'This army will not retreat.'

How much of this harangue the Indians understood and accepted the record does not show, but it did not prevent them from becoming a problem to the decently humane Burgoyne. The proclamation brought strong reactions in British and American circles. Most of its critics ignored its intentions and mocked its style. Horace Walpole pronounced it: '. . . a

---

[1] PRO, CO/5, v. 253, nos. 170, 172.   [2] Kingsford, vi. 177 ff.
[3] Anburey, i. 183; 30 June 1777.
[4] Fonblanque, pp. 489 ff.; Hudleston, pp. 153 ff.; Anburey, i. 168; 23 June 1777.

rhodomontade in which he almost promises to cross America in a hop, step and jump'. Francis Hopkinson, a colonial wit, produced a parody that caused mirth in London as well as Boston. Edmund Burke made a joke of it in the House of Commons, picturing a riot among the animals in the zoo on Tower Hill, with the Keeper of his Majesty's Lions addressing them: 'My gentle lions, my humane bears, my sentimental wolves, my tender-hearted hyenas, go forth: But I exhort ye as ye are Christians and members of a civilized society, to take care not to hurt a man, woman or child.' Walpole wrote that when Lord North heard this burlesque he '. . . almost suffocated with laughter'. Hutchinson, who had lived in New England, called Burgoyne's speech: '. . . flowery, but on the whole much to the purpose'.[1]

Burgoyne's men loaded into all kinds of small craft their food, supplies, and the special tents and conveyances for officers' baggage, women and children. They pushed and dragged their big guns aboard large flat-bottomed rafts called radeaux. Some of them packed themselves into open gun-boats hurriedly built or reclaimed from the fleet Carleton had spent the previous autumn constructing. The generals were in pinnaces, and Burgoyne and his personal staff aboard the new Lake frigates *Royal George* (24 guns) and *Inflexible* (20 guns). The Indians paddled independently in long birchbark canoes that carried from fourteen to twenty braves. The fleet moved slowly, with contingents of scouts working their way by land along both shores of the Lake.[2] Thus strung out and moving only some twenty miles a day, the convoy would have been vulnerable to attacking craft, but the worst foe the army met was a constant swarm of voracious mosquitoes.

Burgoyne took Crown Point after only token resistance from a few settlers. He remained there for three days to organize a supply depot and hospital;[3] to await supplies, and to allow the Indians to recover from having celebrated the end of their long paddle by getting enthusiastically drunk. Then he left 200 men to maintain the base and moved briskly by land and water over the short distance to Ticonderoga.[2]

Those who moved by land got their first taste of the roads they

<hr>

[1] Hudleston, pp. 160, 161; Clements, *Hutchinson Diaries* (original MS.), p. 394, 6 Aug. 1777.   [2] Kingsford, vi. 177 ff.
[3] Fortescue, *HBA*, 2, iii. 224; also Anburey, i. 184.

might expect for the balance of the way to Albany. Burgoyne had been prepared for rough trails, but not for the transportation problems that promptly developed. One-third of the teams promised by the Canadian contractors did not appear, and Burgoyne asked all his officers to leave some of their heavy personal luggage behind. The order was not received happily, and the Germans in particular demurred, so the burdens of the already heavily laden carts and horses were augmented. But on the whole spirits were still high and the troops in excellent condition. On 1 July they encamped before Ticonderoga, and the next day Burgoyne wrote once again to Howe:

I wait only some necessaries of the heavy artillery which have been retarded by the contrary winds on Lake Champlain, to open batteries upon Ticonderoga. The army is in the fullest powers of health and spirit, I have a large body of savages, and shall be joined by a larger in a few days. Ticonderoga reduced, I shall leave behind me proper engineers to put it in an impregnable state; and it will be garrisoned from Canada, where all the destined supplies are safely arrived. My force therefore will be left complete for future operations. The enemy do not appear to have the least suspicion of the King's real instructions relative to the campaign after the reduction of Ticonderoga. . . . I shall explicitly follow the ideas I communicated to your Excellency in my letters from Plymouth and Quebec.[1]

Howe could be pardoned if Burgoyne's highly optimistic dispatch fortified his own wishful thinking that the northern army would need no help to get to Albany. Howe was once again reminded that Burgoyne expected to be met there, but he did not change his plans. On 5 June he had sent a dispatch to Lord George once again washing his hands of any responsibility for Burgoyne: 'General Howe . . . trusts his Lordship may expect a successful campaign to the southward, but fears little can be done to the northward more than to give security to this province.'[2] But Howe's view on the opposition Burgoyne might meet was highly inconsistent. In some dispatches he said Burgoyne would need no help at all beyond, perhaps, the opening of the Hudson from New York to Albany. But on 7 July he sent Lord George a curious letter that can be interpreted only as thinking that Burgoyne would meet such strong resistance

[1] Burgoyne to Howe, 2 July 1777; HMC, Stop. Sack. ii. 72.
[2] Howe to Germain, 5 June 1777; HMC, Stop. Sack. ii. 68.

that he could not achieve a juncture with the southern army 'this campaign':

> I beg leave to observe upon the order given to General Burgoyne for discontinuing the junior lieut-colonels as brigadiers, that it seems only intended to take place when the two armies absolutely join, which I do not suppose to happen this campaign, as I apprehend General Burgoyne will find full employment for his army against that of the rebels opposed to him. . . . The instructions I have taken the liberty of leaving with Sir Henry Clinton are to be upon the defensive with power to act otherwise according to concurrent circumstances without losing sight of the principal object in the security of this place, which I hope may be approved.[1]

Burgoyne knew nothing of this. He expected hard fighting and probably a siege at Ticonderoga, but since the fort had never been attacked with guns so heavy as those he had brought for the purpose, he was confident. Ticonderoga had been built on the foundations of the original French fort, but greatly elaborated and strengthened. The main works were on the west side of the river, but a hill on the east side had also been strongly fortified and the two connected by a bridge some 300 yards long, protected by a massive boom and the guns of the fort. Ethan Allen and his Green Mountain boys who had taken Ticonderoga from the handful that was then the British garrison could not have done so except by surprise. In spite of repeated warnings from General Philip Schuyler and efforts by Washington, however, the Continental Congress had allowed the fort to fall into serious disrepair, and when on 21 May 1777 Washington sent John Patterson to inspect it the resultant report was most unfavourable.[2] Its garrison, commanded by General St. Clair, consisted of about 2,000 men 'sick and well', woefully short of clothing, blankets, food, and supplies. Many of them had no shoes and stockings, and there was only one bayonet for every ten men. The tents were in poor condition and the powder magazines so badly decayed that much of the powder was found to be useless. Little had been done to improve that state when Burgoyne encamped before it on 1 July.

[1] Howe to Germain, 7 July 1777; *HMC, Stop. Sack.* ii. 70 ff. This letter was written sixteen days before Howe sailed from New York and eight days before he received the account of Burgoyne's being before Ticonderoga. It bears the endorsement, apparently made in Germain's office: 'Rd. 22nd August No. 10'.

[2] Hudleston, p. 162.

St. Clair and his little army were good men, and Burgoyne might have had a long expensive siege but for one fact. A steep eminence called Sugar Hill overlooked the fort from the west. It had not been fortified or even manned because the fort had never been attacked with guns big enough to make their presence on that hill (if they could possibly be got there) a menace to the fort. Burgoyne had such guns, though he had to wait several days for them to come up the Lake, and he had in General Phillips one of the best artillery engineers in the British Army.

General Phillips immediately saw the possibilities of Sugar Hill and, before the American garrison could prevent them, his men managed to drag their heavy guns up its steep ascent. That made the defence of Ticonderoga by so weak a force almost hopeless. 'General Phillips', wrote Anburey, 'has as expeditiously conveyed cannon to the summit of the hill, as he brought it up in that memorable battle at Minden.'[1] St. Clair, a brave man but a sensible one, concluded it was better to lose the fort but save his army than to lose both. He evacuated Ticonderoga on 6 July so neatly that most of his men got clean away. Burgoyne had taken, almost without firing a shot, the key position in the north.[2]

---

[1] Anburey, i. 191; 5 July 1777.   [2] PRO, CO/5, v. 253, nos. 170, 172.

XV

CONTRETEMPS

THE threads in the fabric of time have seldom been more difficult to unravel than in the events of the American Revolution. Its generals as well as its later chroniclers were handicapped by the complications of its chronology. For this the Atlantic Ocean is largely to blame. The delays it caused upset men's plans and obscured the sequences of cause and effect. War planners and war makers could not base their decisions on what had just happened but on what they had just heard had happened, or hoped had happened, several weeks before. To understand their reasoning and their actions one must place himself in their situations; forget one's hindsight and share their ignorance. The modern American who, by time's greatest joke, can learn at lunch what happened in London that day at tea, must constantly remind himself that what Lord George Germain thought in London in 1777 was based on events already outdated in America.

Burgoyne took Ticonderoga on 6 July, but the news did not reach London until 22 August, and then uncertainly.[1] It was received there with elation but not with surprise, for reports of Burgoyne's easy progress up Lake Champlain had previously reached England. The king had written to the Earl of Sandwich: 'Appearances cannot be more favourable than those of success at Ticonderoga, which will I trust enable Burgoyne to get soon to Albany.'[2] Burgoyne became the toast of the hour, and although the public did not know the final objective of his campaign it could easily be guessed. The war seemed almost won. Some American loyalists who had fled to England engaged passage or chartered ships to take them back to the colonies as

[1] On 15 July Howe, still in New York, sent to Germain a copy of Burgoyne's confident dispatch of 2 July, written before Ticonderoga fell, and added that later unofficial intelligence convinced him that Burgoyne had taken the fort. That letter from Howe was endorsed in Germain's office: 'Rd. 22 August. no. 11. This letter was written eight days before the fleet sailed from New York' (*HMC, Stop. Sack.* ii. 72; also *Hansard*, xx. 694).

[2] King to Sandwich, 3 Aug. 1777; *Sandwich Papers*, i. 293.

soon as Howe and Burgoyne had tidied up the fag-ends of American resistance.

There were some Englishmen who were less optimistic and a few who were not pleased. Fox, openly sympathetic with the rebels, deplored Burgoyne's success, partly because it strengthened a Ministry he detested. Other men, eager for British victory, were confused and troubled by the apparent lack of co-ordination between Howe and Burgoyne. Some of them knew, or thought they knew, that Howe was supposed to move north to meet Burgoyne, but he had not, apparently, even started up the Hudson, and there were rumours that he was setting out for Philadelphia. Did that mean that Burgoyne would be left to win his way to Albany unaided, and then to New York? And when it was learned that in taking Ticonderoga he had not captured its defenders, it seemed almost certain that they and other Americans would gather to oppose Burgoyne elsewhere; that the crucial battle lay still ahead. Perhaps Burgoyne's easy good fortune at Ticonderoga would make him over-confident: everyone knew he was given to optimism and superlatives. Commenting on the delay in receiving Burgoyne's official dispatch about Ticonderoga, Walpole wrote: 'I suppose the silent, modest, humble General Burgoyne has not yet finished his concise description of the victorious manner in which he took possession of it.'[1]

These men would have been even more troubled had they known the whole truth. They, as well as Burgoyne, would have been startled by Howe's renunciation of any intention or responsibility to move northward, and by his statement to Lord George that he did not expect a junction with the northern army that year.[2] They would have been mystified by Lord George's official approval of Howe's plans that would take him farther from Burgoyne. They would have been alarmed to find that Lord George had made no attempt to disillusion Burgoyne on that score.

Reason is baffled by Lord George's apparently casual attitude toward the whole affair. How could a man who had written such instructions to Burgoyne, and who had exchanged so many dispatches with Howe, write to Knox in late June: 'I cannot guess by Sir Wm. Howe's letter when he will begin his operations,

---

[1] Walpole to Mason, 18 Sept. 1777; Toynbee, x. 113.
[2] Howe to Germain, 7 July 1777; HMC, Stop. Sack. ii. 70.

or where he proposes carrying them on'?[1] Lord George joined in the general joy over the capture of Ticonderoga and accepted the credit for planning it. Burgoyne became for the moment his personally sponsored hero. To the suggestion that Burgoyne be immediately awarded the Red Ribbon he was as cordial as he had been opposed to a similar award to Carleton, though Burgoyne had not yet fought a single battle. Within a week after hearing of Ticonderoga Lord George wrote to Burgoyne's friend, the Earl of Derby, that: 'Burgoyne's conduct is so meritorious and the approbation of his services is so general ... the King speaks of him as an officer of distinguished merit, and immediately declared he would honour him with the vacant red ribbon. I trust he will hereafter receive more substantial marks of honour.'[2]

'The red ribband was offered to Lord Derby for Burgoyne, but the latter, who had expected it before he had done anything to deserve it, had left directions with Lord Derby to refuse it', according to Walpole.[3] Perhaps Burgoyne was more modest than Walpole gave him credit for being; perhaps he had noticed that six months after Carleton had received his Red Ribbon he had been insulted, robbed of his army, and in effect replaced; perhaps Burgoyne hoped that the postponement of the honour would more surely bring him 'more substantial marks of favour'. Lord Derby replied to Lord George that Burgoyne would prefer to have his Red Ribbon postponed.[4] His wish was observed. Burgoyne did not receive it then, or ever.

Whatever Lord George's inner feelings, he realized a month before the news of Ticonderoga that by letting Howe go to Philadelphia he had left Burgoyne to sink or swim unaided, for he confided to Knox on 27 July: 'If Burgoyne's army is not able to defeat any force that the rebels can oppose to it we must give up the contest.'[5] After his one weak plea to Howe in his dispatch of 18 May, Lord George had made no further references to any aid by Howe to Burgoyne. Writing to Howe on 6 August he did not even mention the northern campaign.[6] In fact Lord

[1] Germain to Knox, 24 June 1777; *HMC, Var. Coll.* 6, *Knox*, p. 131.
[2] Germain to Derby, 29 Aug. 1777; Fonblanque, pp. 248, 249.
[3] Walpole, *Last Journals*, ii. 42; 22 Aug. 1777.
[4] Derby to Germain, 31 Aug. 1777; *HMC, Stop. Sack.* ii. 75.
[5] Germain to Knox, 27 July 1777; *HMC, Var. Coll.* 6, *Knox*, p. 133.
[6] Germain to Howe, 6 Aug. 1777; *HMC, Stop. Sack.* ii. 73.

George's military aspirations were questing beyond Albany and Philadelphia, for in another dispatch to Howe he wrote that: '. . . the King was concerned that he should find the proposed diversion on the Coast of New England not consistent with his other Operations'.[1]

Immediately after London heard of the capture of Ticonderoga, Lord George wrote to General Irwin a letter that showed no apparent concern over Burgoyne's future. 'Burgoyne is fortunate and deserves it. His account of his success is not exaggerated, and we have reason to hope his progress will be rapid.' Anticipating any sure news, Lord George also told Irwin that Howe had sailed for Philadelphia, but was aware of Burgoyne's situation and would doubtless keep himself in a position to cope with it if necessary—though Germain did not suggest how.[2] But just at that time he confessed some concern to Knox: 'I hoped our letter would have given us some reason why the campaign began so late, but we are to remain in ignorance.'[3]

There are three possible explanations of Lord George's bold front during August and September. He may have thought that Burgoyne could win through to New York unaided; he may have thought that somehow Clinton or Howe could get help to him if necessary, or he may have recognized his blunder but refused to face its results. The first two of these in combination seem more likely. There are several indications that Lord George thought Washington's army the only effective one the rebels could produce, and that if, by going to Philadelphia, Howe drew Washington in that direction, then Howe would be aiding Burgoyne almost as much as if he had gone up the Hudson to meet him. That was the explanation many amateur strategists were offering one another as reports of Howe's move to the southward reached them. Henry Ellis had written on 4 August to Knox, speaking of Howe: 'By seeming determined to march thro' the Jerseys, he has obliged Washington to collect and retain the principal part of the rebel army there, whereby no considerable body of troops could be detached either to obstruct the landing of the troops sent southward or the army from Canada.'[4] That was the strategy Howe himself had suggested

---

[1] Germain to Howe, PRO, CO/5, v. 253, no. 150.
[2] Germain to Irwin, 23 Aug. 1777; *HMC, Stop. Sack.* i. 138.
[3] Germain to Knox, 22 Aug. 1777; *HMC, Var. Coll.* 6, *Knox,* p. 136.
[4] Henry Ellis to Knox, 4 Aug. 1777; ibid., p. 134.

in a dispatch to Lord George on 16 July, a day after reports had reached him of the capture of Ticonderoga:

... if General Washington should march to the defense of Pensilvania, I shall in such event order them [Clinton's reserves] to join me in that province. The enemy's movements taking this turn, I apprehend General Burgoyne will meet with little interruption otherwise than the difficulties he must encounter in transporting stores and provisions for the supply of his army ... on the other hand, if General Washington should march with a determination to force General Burgoyne, the strength of General Burgoyne's army is such as to leave me no room to dread the event, but if Mr. Washington's intention should be only to retard the approach of General Burgoyne to Albany he may soon find himself exposed to an attack from this quarter and from General Burgoyne at the same time, from both which, I flatter myself, he would find it difficult to escape. Under these circumstances, I propose going up the Delaware, in order to be nearer the place than I should be by taking the course of Chesapeak Bay, provided the enemy had discovered a disposition to defend Pensilvania.[1]

At that point Clinton entered the field, as usual too late and on the losing side. While in London during the spring he had learned of the northern campaign and the part Howe was expected to take in it. He had also heard some loose talk of a plan of Howe to attack Philadelphia, and had told Lord George that any move on Philadelphia should end and not begin the year's campaign. Until he arrived at New York he had no idea that Howe intended to move on Philadelphia before he made juncture with Burgoyne. When he found Howe about to embark for the Delaware or Chesapeake Clinton was appalled.[2]

'I lost no time,' Clinton wrote later, 'when asked, in delivering to Sir William Howe my opinion on the southern move with the same freedom I had done in England to the Minister. I stated the probable risks and delays ... from sickness and southerly winds in the summer months, and with all deference suggested the many and superior advantages to be derived at the present moment from a cooperation of his whole force with General Burgoyne on the River Hudson.'[3]

[1] Howe to Germain, 16 July 1777; *HMC, Stop. Sack.* ii. 72; also Fortescue, *Corresp.* iii. 462. 　　　　　　[2] Willcox, *Amer. Rebellion*, p. 59, note.
[3] King to John Robinson, 11 Mar. 1777; BM, Addit. MS. 37,833, fols. 155, 159; Willcox, *Amer. Rebellion*, pp. 59 note, 61, 62; Clinton, *Historical Detail*; Clements.

Howe produced the counter-arguments he had sent to Lord George. Clinton tried to convince him that if he should move north Washington would have to follow him and could not avoid being drawn into battle. Howe had been trying to manœuvre Washington into precisely that position; by moving toward Burgoyne he could not only force Washington to fight but to fight both Howe and Burgoyne at the same time. The result should be a devastating British victory. But Howe pointed out that the die was cast: Lord George had in the king's name approved the attack on Philadelphia, approved his plan to go there by sea, and approved his letter to Carleton saying that Burgoyne could expect little or no aid from New York. Clinton pointed out that Burgoyne's dispatches made it very clear that Burgoyne still expected Howe, in force, at Albany, and in fairly short order. Howe replied that if, later, as seemed most unlikely, Burgoyne needed the help of a diversion or the opening of the lower Hudson river, Clinton in New York could see to it—provided he took no risks of losing New York or the British outposts there. Lord George had promised to send reinforcements to New York very soon; when they arrived Clinton could keep them in New York if Howe did not need them in the Philadelphia area. Howe thus evaded the problem by turning it over to Clinton, who remained dubious, unhappy, and protesting.[1]

The arrival of Burgoyne's dispatch, confirming his capture of Ticonderoga and exuding confidence in the future, ended Clinton's hopes of persuading Howe, who had already begun to embark 13,799 men in transports in New York's lower bay.[2] According to Clinton, every one of Howe's chief officers except Cornwallis thought Howe should be moving to the north and not to the south. One officer recorded his impression of Howe's men as they went aboard ship: 'Nothing but being present and seeing the countenances of the soldiers could give an impression adequate to the scene; or paint the astonishment and despair that reigned in New York when it was found that the North River was deserted, and Burgoyne's army abandoned to its fate.

---

[1] Clinton wrote his account largely to defend himself against critics. He never liked Howe, and though his account of Howe's indifference is substantially true it is probably overdrawn.

[2] Fortescue, *HBA*, 2, ii. 211. Later reinforcements, largely drawn from Clinton, would bring Howe's total troops for the Philadelphia campaign to 18,000 (Greene, p. 83).

. . . The ruinous and dreadful consequences were instantly foreseen and foretold; and despondence or execration filled every
mouth.'[1]

Clinton was left, angry and frustrated, with nothing but
vague orders, heavy responsibilities, and troops inadequate to
meet them. While Howe and Burgoyne were charging about
with fine armies and a chance to win great victories for Britain
and honour for themselves, he was left weakly on the defensive,
excluded from glory, but expected to save both if need arose. It
was true that on paper, by Lord George's accounting, he had
9,000 men, but some were undependable loyalists and only
4,527 were regulars reported fit for action.[2] That was barely
enough to defend New York if Washington seriously attacked it.
And soon Clinton received a letter from Howe, written on 30
July while at sea: 'I cannot positively determine when I shall be
able to send you reinforcements. But if you can in the meantime
make any diversion in favour of General Burgoyne's approaching Albany (with security to King's Bridge I need not point out
the utility of such a measure.'[3] That message brought Clinton's
dislike of Howe almost to the boiling-point. He had spent hours
trying to convince Howe of the necessity as well as 'the utility
of such a measure', but Howe had disregarded him, gone off
with most of the troops, and now left the responsibility to him.
Clinton wrote in his memoirs: 'It could not . . . but appear
singular that he should now propose to me an offensive operation though he knew very well no change had happened since
his departure to put me in a fitter condition for it.' He talked
of immediate resignation. 'Clinton was much dissatisfied with
General Howe, and said it was only from a point of honour that
he did not ask to be recalled.'[4]

Howe's departure by sea puzzled men on both sides of the
Atlantic. Few men in either camp could believe that Howe
intended to leave Burgoyne wholly to his fate. Henry Ellis,
former Crown Governor of Georgia and an ardent loyalist,
wrote to William Knox: 'People here are greatly puzzled by
General Howe's conduct, but if he can get between Washington

[1] C. F. Adams, *Studies Military, &c.*
[2] PRO, CO/5, v. 253, no. 215.
[3] Howe to Clinton, 30 July 1777; *Hansard*, xx. 695; Willcox, *Amer. Rebellion*,
p. 66; Clements, Clinton, *Hist. Detail.*
[4] Walpole, *Last Journals*, ii. 46; 6 Oct. 1777.

and his magazines, by possessing himself of Philadelphia, his last motion will have decisive consequences. Washington cannot then move northward to obstruct Burgoyne.'[1]

Howe's transports were delayed, as Clinton had predicted, by south-west headwinds, and did not reach the entrance to the Delaware until 29 July, six days after leaving Staten Island. His ships stood off Newcastle, and Howe could have landed his men there, unopposed by any significant resistance by land or sea, only a long day's march from the outskirts of Philadelphia. Howe later said his naval officers had advised him that the river off the landing-places was dangerously shallow and that the shores were too marshy for landing large guns. John Fiske the American historian called Howe's explanation 'trumped up and worthless', but Fiske was chronically scornful of British generals. Fortescue the British military historian took no position in the matter. One who knows the Delaware must be inclined to doubt, even after allowing for later dredging, that Howe would have encountered any great difficulties in landing somewhere on the west bank of the Delaware. In any case Howe's naval officers should have informed themselves and him on that point before they planned their course and landing. And it is relevant that a year later the British naval commander chose Newcastle as the best place to embark that same army in their retreat. Howe did not attempt the landing and put out to sea again. He vanished from the ken of friend and foe for over two weeks.[2]

Once again he was impeded by headwinds and did not work his way up Chesapeake Bay and begin to discharge his troops at its headwaters at the Little Elk river until after 20 August. He was then a short day's march from the point on the Delaware where he might have landed three weeks before. He had made a sea trip of what would normally be some 350 miles but in sailing distance probably proved twice that, in order to arrive at a point twenty miles farther from Philadelphia. He had spent nearly six weeks in order to get only sixty miles nearer Philadelphia than he had been when he left Staten Island. The previous year Howe had fought his way over most of those sixty

---

[1] Ellis to Knox, 4 Sept. 1777: *HMC, Var. Coll.* 6, *Knox*, p. 137. Most of Washington's ordnance was being made in the small iron-foundries of south central Pennsylvania.

[2] Fortescue, *HBA*, 2, iii. 212.

miles to Trenton. This time he had also cut himself off for six
weeks from any messages from Clinton, Burgoyne, or Lord George
Germain.[1]

From the head of the Elk River Howe acknowledged receipt
of the dispatch from Lord George dated 18 May, in which Lord
George had voiced the polite hope that: '. . . whatever you may
meditate, it will be executed in time for you to cooperate with
the army ordered to proceed from Canada and put itself under
your command'. Howe replied in two separate letters. In one
he wrote that not having heard from General Burgoyne[2] he did
not know what credit was to be given to the rumoured successes
of the rebels in that quarter, but that as rebel accounts of their
successes were in general much exaggerated, he hoped that even
should these be true, General Burgoyne would still be able to pursue the advantages he had already gained with so much honour
to himself. Lord George received that letter on 12 October,
the day before Burgoyne decided to capitulate.[3]

In his other letter Howe disposed once more of any responsibility for Burgoyne.

Your Lordship has been pleased to signify that my alterations in
the plan of this campaign have been approved by the King, but that
his Majesty trusts that the operations of this army, intended for the
recovery of the province of Pensilvania, will be finished in time for
me to co-operate with the northern army. It is with much concern
that I am to answer that I cannot flatter myself I shall be able to
act up to the King's expectations in this particular, as my progress,
independent of opposition from the enemy's principal army, must
be greatly impeded by the prevailing disposition of the inhabitants,
strongly in enmity against us; many having taken up arms, and by
far the greater number deserted their dwellings, driving off at the
same time their stock of cattle and horses.[4]

It took Howe only ten days after landing to become disillu-
sioned as to the reported friendliness of the natives of Delaware
and south-east Pennsylvania. Howe's reactions were correct,
though another man, determined to see what he wanted to see,

[1] Robson, *Amer. Rev.*, p. 107.
[2] How could a message from Burgoyne have reached him during those weeks?
[3] Howe to Germain, 30 Aug. 1777; *HMC, Stop. Sack*. ii. 74.
[4] Howe to Germain, 30 Aug. 1777; PRO, CO/5, v. 253, no. 151; also *HMC,
Stop. Sack*. ii. 74. The two letters were endorsed as received 28 Oct., 'and had heard
of Gen. Burgoyne's misfortune at Bennington'.

denied it. Howe was accompanied by that ardent, voluble, influential loyalist Joseph Galloway, who had been an important
citizen of Pennsylvania. In his later testimony before Parliament
Galloway said nearly all the natives he saw with Howe after the
landing at Elk River were friendly to the Crown.[1] But that was
when Galloway was trying to defend Lord George by discrediting Howe.

Howe's movements baffled Washington as much as anyone
else. In the autumn of 1776 Washington had assumed that
Philadelphia would be the next chief object of the British Army,
for Howe was crossing New Jersey with that obvious objective.
Washington was distressed that the citizens of Philadelphia were
not being more helpful to the revolutionary cause: '. . . nor do
I see any liklihood of their stirring to save their own capital,
which is undoubtedly General Howe's great object'.[2] A few days
later Washington wrote: 'I have no doubt but General Howe
will still make an attempt upon Philadelphia this winter.'[3] But
the defeats at Trenton and Princeton had led Howe to withdraw
his forces toward New York.

That had been in late December, and as 1777 began,
Washington and Congress began to hear rumours that the
British would make a major attack from Canada. Washington
saw immediately that if an army from Canada should take
Ticonderoga and continue southward, Howe should strike up
the Hudson to meet and join it. But the reports were so persistent
that Washington feared a British move from Canada might be
only a feint to draw him northward while Howe, able to move
freely by sea, suddenly attacked Philadelphia or some other port
on the seaboard farther south. And even if the northern British
Army should take Ticonderoga, it might merely leave a garrison
there; draw back quickly to the St. Lawrence River; take ship
and join Howe somewhere along the Atlantic coast. Washington
had interior land communications, but no navy, and the British
could land an army almost at will anywhere from Philadelphia
to Charleston.

Washington's problem was augmented by his dependence on

---

[1] T. Balch, Galloway, Examination etc., 16 June 1779.

[2] Fitzpatrick, *Washington, Works*, iv. 213; also Lecky, iv. 19. Pennsylvania was
largely inhabited by Quakers and other pacifist sects and by Germans disinterested
in politics.

[3] Fitzpatrick, *Washington, Works*, iv. 234; also Lecky, iv. 20.

Congress for approval of his strategy as well as pay for his
soldiers. Most of the members of the Continental Congress
were self-appointed military strategists, and many of them based
their strategy upon a desire to keep their home constituencies
well guarded by Washington's army. Members of the Congress
from New England were consequently sure that Boston or Providence was the real objective of Howe and Burgoyne, and urged
Washington to stay close to that area. Pennsylvanians were
certain that he should be near Philadelphia. In contrast: 'Of
twenty-four opinions recorded by Washington and the ablest
and best informed of his general officers, Greene, Knox and
Sullivan, thirteen were that Howe's objective was Philadelphia,
eight were that the target was Philadelphia or the Hudson, and
three that the British would try to subjugate New England.'[1]
In late 1776, when Howe was crossing New Jersey, the Congress
took no chances as to its own safety and retired from Philadelphia to Baltimore, and did not return until after Washington's
victories at Trenton and Princeton.[2]

In early April 1777 Washington wrote to his brother expressing his 'utter astonishment at the continued inactivity of
General Howe'.[3] He would have awaited developments more
happily if Congress had been taking steps to strengthen its
defences and his own army, but the American Government was
suffering from the same diseases as the British. Intrigues,
bickering, and sincere differences of opinion had turned Congress
into a debating society, yet it still insisted on directing Washington and controlling every military plan and operation. Washington knew that committees cannot win wars, but Congress
was his master and his paymaster. He could try to persuade it
but must in any case obey it, even in the choice of generals.
That meant that until Howe showed his hand Congress would
talk, and Washington could only wait.

The American forces in up-state New York were under the command of the able and energetic Philip Schuyler, a descendant
of the Dutch patroons; a man of aristocratic traditions and old-
fashioned manners among English and Scots settlers who had
broken with the traditions and lacked the manners. His army

---

[1] Freeman, *Washington*, iv. 403, note.
[2] Walpole, *Last Journals*, ii. 9; 24 Feb. 1777.
[3] Fitzpatrick, *Washington*, *Works*, iv. 387.

consisted of only a few thousand half-trained short-term volunteers, with little equipment and less money. That was not Schuyler's fault; he had done his best, but geographically and politically he was at the end of the line.

The threat of invasion from Canada suddenly made that force important and awakened the ambitions of General Horatio Gates. Gates was a man with less military good sense than Schuyler but greater 'address', and he had many friends in and about Congress. He had served as a colonial in Braddock's ill-fated parade into western Pennsylvania, under Cornwallis in Nova Scotia, and briefly in command at Ticonderoga in 1776, and fancied himself as a military genius. During the winter he had been manœuvring to replace Schuyler as commander of the forces in the north.

When that doughty Dutchman heard of Gates's endeavours and innuendoes he went post-haste from Albany to Philadelphia to demand an inquiry into his own conduct and Gates's. He arrived just after Congress had voted appointing Gates to replace him. Gates started north to his new command while Schuyler remained and insisted on a hearing. As a result Congress reversed itself, fully exonerated Schuyler, and restored him to his former command. Gates declined to serve under Schuyler, and soon made his way back to the ears of Congressmen.[1]

When Schuyler got to Albany he was shocked to find how little had been done in his absence to prepare resistance to Burgoyne. It was too late to do very much to strengthen the defences, and Congress had still made no appropriations and sent no supplies. The people of New York state and nearby New England were over-confident, or apathetic, or at odds with one another. Some thought St. Clair could hold Ticonderoga without gunpowder or bayonets; some did not believe in the imminence of serious attack; some were immersed in getting in their crops; some cared only what happened within their own immediate areas, and many were busy arguing politics with their neighbours, or disagreeing who should captain the local militia. Most of these men would get out their squirrel guns when the redcoats and Indians were almost upon them, but not before. Few of them realized how weakly their great bastion, Ticonderoga, was held.[2]

[1] Tracy, ii. 6, 7.   [2] Freeman, *Washington*, iv. 416.

Washington did his best to rouse Congress, and sent Schuyler a few men he could ill spare from his own inadequate army. Howe's failure to move still baffled him. Before 7 June he heard nothing that threw decisive light on Howe's plans, but on that day word reached him that 'many vessels' at New York were being fitted out as transports for men and horses. That led Washington to conclude—tentatively—that a move by sea to Philadelphia or Charleston was more likely than a move up the Hudson. But Howe made neither. He simply sat in New York.[1]

Even the loyalists in America began to wonder whether Howe was as capable as he had seemed at first. Nicholas Cresswell, a young Englishman who had been caught in Virginia on a business trip to the colonies when war broke out, and had managed to get to New York, wrote in his journal on 2 June: 'The Commander in Chief is either inactive, has no orders to act, or thinks he has not a force sufficient to oppose the rebels.'[2] Few were as certain of Howe's intentions as General Heath, who was heading the revolutionary troops in Boston, and who through the spring and summer repeatedly wrote to his associates: 'I think the enemy will if possible effect a junction on Hudson's River. This has all along been my opinion.'[3] But, Washington asked himself, if Heath were right, why was Howe still assembling and fitting out transports off Staten Island?[4] If this was only a bluff it was an elaborate one, expensive in time as well as money. Surely Howe was not foolish enough to neglect co-operating with Burgoyne, who was reported to have taken over Carleton's army and to be embarking it at the northern end of Lake Champlain!

In early June Congress, in its crystal-ball wisdom, sent word to St. Clair that though Burgoyne might threaten Ticonderoga his main objective was elsewhere. But a few days later, on 15 June, St. Clair's men captured a British spy and extracted from him the dependable news that Burgoyne intended to take Ticonderoga and then move south to meet Howe at Albany. St. Clair relayed this report to Schuyler, who sent it on to Washington in northern New Jersey. It almost convinced

---

[1] Freeman, *Washington*, iv. 427, 428.
[2] Cresswell, *Journal*, p. 229; 2 June 1777.
[3] Mass. Hist. Socy., *Heath Papers*, part ii, vol. iv, p. 119.
[4] Freeman, *Washington*, iv. 424.

Washington that he must be ready to move north on a moment's notice.

Washington still shrank from any irrevocable move. Everything that Howe was doing meant, at face value, a move by sea. Washington's spies in New York unanimously reported that Howe's goal was Philadelphia. But Washington was still unconvinced. He decided to remain a little longer in northern New Jersey, prepared to move either way. Howe would certainly have to show his hand soon. But another two weeks passed and still the situation was not clear. Howe was wasting half the summer, and he was more likely to be doing that if he were waiting for Burgoyne to near Albany than if he were planning to capture Philadelphia before snowfall. On 1 July Washington wrote to General Putnam, commanding the troops along the Hudson: '. . . it appears almost certain to me that General Howe and General Burgoyne design if possible to unite their attacks and form a junction of their two armies . . . there is the strongest reason to conclude that General Howe will push up the river immediately to co-operate with the army from Canada'. On 2 July he wrote to Governor Trumbull to the same effect.[1] He even risked a chip or two on that bet, and ordered Putnam to send two of his brigades to Schuyler, who ultimately received four Massachusetts regiments from the defences around Peekskill on the Hudson.

Though still woefully weak, Schuyler felt he could wait no longer before moving northward from Albany. He started with only half the 10,000 men he had asked for, and most of those he had were untrained and poorly equipped—some of them mere boys. He reached Fort Edward, which was little more than an entrenched camp, on 8 July to receive the shocking news that Ticonderoga had fallen. This changed the picture, and Schuyler withdrew south again as far as Stillwater, and there began to build what defences he could.

On that same day Washington got reports that Burgoyne had settled down before Ticonderoga in a way that committed him to attack. From that news Washington at last decided that Howe would certainly move up the Hudson, and very soon. His opinion was fortified when he received, probably the following day, a letter from General Heath, more certain than ever that a move

[1] Freeman, *Washington*, iv. 436; also Whitton, p. 195.

by Howe on Philadelphia would be '. . . repugnant to every principle of sound military policy. . . . I think his real object is if possible to form a junction with Carleton.'[1]

On 10 July Washington heard from Schuyler that Ticonderoga had fallen. It was an unexpected and devastating blow.[2] Two days later he wrote to the President of Congress that the loss of the fort was: '. . . among the most unfortunate that could have befallen us',[3] and to Schuyler that: '. . . the whole affair is so mysterious that it baffles conjecture'.[4] 'It is an event of chagrin and surprise, not yet comprehended within the compass of my reasoning. . . . This stroke is very severe indeed, and has distressed me much.'[5] Washington seldom confessed to being so badly shaken, and the event strengthened his conviction that Howe and Burgoyne would try to meet. But he was still too cautious to risk everything on that belief.[6] 'The complexion of things to the Northward and preparations lately made by General Howe, leave little room to doubt that their intentions are to form a Junction up the North River', Washington wrote to Governor Livingston of New York on 12 July.[7] Burgoyne, he thought, would not risk moving much farther south, extending his supply line and unnecessarily battling Schuyler alone, until he knew Howe was on his way up the Hudson.

Yet there was still no sign of a northward move by Howe, whose troops, it was reported, were embarking on the transports. If Howe attacked somewhere between Cape May and Charleston Washington was helpless to defend against him. But if Howe, strategically fantastic as it seemed, moved away from Burgoyne to Philadelphia, Washington could and should get his army there first. He did not dare to cross the Rubicon of the Delaware River, but as the last half of July wore on and Howe made no northward gesture, Washington began to move his troops, now increased to about 14,000 men (mostly untrained and on short enlistments), a little nearer to Philadelphia. But he did so with

[1] Heath to Washington, Mass. Hist. Socy., *Heath Papers*, ii, vol. iv, p. 147, 9 July 1777.   [2] Freeman, *Washington*, iv. 442.
[3] Ibid., p. 444; also Fitzpatrick, viii. 384.
[4] Washington to Schuyler, 13 July 1777; Fitzpatrick, viii. 393.
[5] Freeman, iv. 444; also Fitzpatrick, viii. 428.
[6] Washington's dispatches to the President of Congress during the seven weeks before Howe's appearance in the Chesapeake are in Sparks, iv. 479–505.
[7] Fitzpatrick, viii. 300.

trepidation,[1] for he still shared the opinion of his brilliant young aide Alexander Hamilton, who could not conceive '. . . upon what principle of common sense or military propriety Howe can be running away from Burgoyne to the southward'.[2]

At the very end of July word came that Howe had embarked, and that his fleet was apparently heading southward. On the 30th Washington wrote to Gates: 'Howe's in a manner abandoning General Burgoyne is so unaccountable a matter that till I am fully assured it is so, I cannot help casting my eyes continually behind me.'[3] Washington knew how wrong John Adams was in his belief that 'Howe is unable to do anything except by stealth. Washington is strong enough to keep Howe where he is.'[4]

By doing the unpredictable Howe had gained the military initiative. He kept it by doing the unaccountable. On 31 July Washington heard from the President of Congress that Howe's fleet had appeared in Delaware Bay.[5] Relieved that at last he was certain of Howe's objective, Washington hurried his men toward Philadelphia. But the next day word came that Howe's transports had vanished out to sea again.[6] For the two weeks that Howe's ships and army then remained invisible, Washington could do nothing but stand in his tracks north of Philadelphia and wait, though he did order Sullivan's and Sterling's brigades back to Peekskill on the Hudson.[7] As late as 11 August Washington believed that joint action by Howe and Burgoyne was 'so probable and of such importance' that he could 'with difficulty give in to a contrary belief'.[8]

Howe's fleet was seen in Chesapeake Bay a few days after that, but word of it did not reach Washington before he had decided, with the endorsement of Congress and his own council of officers, to leave Bucks County north of Philadelphia and move northeastward toward New York and Burgoyne.[9] Just as his troops were breaking camp on 22 August, Washington got definite news that Howe was making a landing at the head of Chesapeake

[1] Greene, p. 83.   [2] Freeman, iv. 446, note.
[3] Washington to Gates, 30 July 1777; Fitzpatrick, viii. 499; also Fonblanque, p. 281.
[4] Adams to Abigail Adams, 27 May 1777; Adams, *Family Letters*, p. 278; also Freeman, iv. 403.
[5] Freeman, iv. 447.   [6] Ibid., 448.   [7] Greene, p. 83.
[8] Washington to Ward, 11 Aug. 1777; Fitzpatrick, ix. 57; also Freeman, iv. 451.
[9] Freeman, iv. 459.

Bay.[1] If so he must intend Philadelphia after all, though by a curiously roundabout and time-wasting route. Washington hurriedly cancelled his orders to move north and started south again, reaching Philadelphia and Wilmington about 25 August.[2]

Washington had written to Schuyler a comment of remarkable prescience: 'As I suggested before, the successes General Burgoyne has met with may precipitate his ruin. From your account he is pursuing that line of conduct which of all others is most favorable to us. I mean acting in detachments. Could we be so happy as to cut off one of them, though it should not exceed four, five or six hundred men, it would inspirit our people.'[3]

American defence in the north was again demoralized by another change in leadership. While Schuyler was busy with his command, Gates had again been busy with Congress, whose members inclined to blame Schuyler for the fall of Ticonderoga. The legislators again reversed themselves and replaced Schuyler, for the second time in six months, with Gates, who arrived at Stillwater and took command on 19 or 20 August.[4] Schuyler was willing to serve under Gates though Gates had declined to serve under Schuyler, but Gates ignored his rival and Schuyler retired to Albany and took no further active part in the proceedings. Had Gates not been joined by abler and more aggressive generals than himself, the results at Saratoga would have been different.

Schuyler, in spite of all his vicissitudes, had done what he could and done it well. His urgent pleas for troops were bringing results from which Gates would profit. In late July General Lincoln arrived at Stillwater with 2,000 men from New Hampshire. General Golver came in with part of his brigade, and Benedict Arnold, in active fighting a host in himself, appeared with a considerable detachment. Schuyler had promptly sent Arnold off to the west to cope with Colonel St. Leger, whose Indians had ambushed and killed the old warhorse General Herkimer and a thousand local recruits, and who was apparently about to capture Fort Stanwix. Most important of all to the final result at Saratoga had been Schuyler's work in impeding

---

[1] Fitzpatrick, *Washington, Works*, iv. 466–501; also Greene, p. 83; also Fortescue, *HBA*, 2, iii. 212; also Freeman, iv. 459.

[2] Freeman, iv. 460; also Greene, p. 83.

[3] Washington to Schuyler, 22 July 1777; Fitzpatrick, viii. 448; also Fonblanque, pp. 277, 278.   [4] Stone, p. 39.

Burgoyne's path southward from Skenesborough. He had sent
a thousand skilled woodsmen to this task, and they had performed it expertly.

There was no longer any question in Washington's mind that
the objectives of Howe and Burgoyne were quite different. Their
failure to co-ordinate was still a mystery, but Washington's
course was at last clear. He must oppose Howe at Philadelphia
and leave Gates and his men to deal with Burgoyne. It would
rest with a few detachments of troops around the New York
area to keep Clinton, with his limited force, too busy to take
significant aid to Burgoyne. When, on 22 August, Washington
received the news that Howe was landing his army at the Head
of Elk, he wrote: 'Now let all New England turn out and crush
Burgoyne.'[1]

[1] Fitzpatrick, *Washington, Works*, iv. 466–501; also Fortescue, *HBA*, 2, iii. 212.

XVI

THE PLOT THICKENS

THE easy capture of Ticonderoga and ninety-six American cannon but almost no Americans[1] was not without cost to Burgoyne. As the key to his sole supply route it had to be strongly held. He sent a message back to Carleton asking him to send men to garrison Ticonderoga.[2] Though Burgoyne had written to Howe that Ticonderoga would be 'garrisoned from Canada',[3] he later told Parliament of Carleton: 'I was apprehensive he would not think himself authorized by the King's orders to comply.'[4] His fears were justified. Carleton replied that his orders confined his scanty troops within the boundaries of his province.[5]

So Burgoyne had to leave about 950 of his men at the fort and nearby 'carrying place',[6] and a little later another 200 at Diamond Island on Lake George for supply transport.[7] With the 200 men previously left at Crown Point, his attacking force was reduced by one-fifth, while most of the former Ticonderoga garrison joined General Schuyler.

This was an inevitable price of conquest, but there were other prices less inevitable that proved equally high. The easy victory at Ticonderoga encouraged Howe to assume Burgoyne would need no help from him, and misled Burgoyne into underestimating future American opposition. Had Burgoyne been less confident he might not have risked dissipating his strength by sending off a detachment to Bennington. He might even have halted his advance at Ticonderoga until he reached a clearer understanding with Howe and Clinton. A delay there would have been less expensive than the later delay at Fort Edward.

The taking of Ticonderoga also roused at long last the Continental Congress to give real support to the defence of the

---

[1] Lecky, iv. 60.   [2] Burgoyne to Carleton, 11 July 1777; Lecky, iv. 60.
[3] Burgoyne to Howe, 2 July 1777; HMC, *Stop. Sack*. ii. 172.
[4] *Hansard*, xx. 788; 20 May 1778.
[5] Carleton to Burgoyne, 29 July 1777; Fonblanque, p. 202; also Hudleston, p. 170.
[6] Kingsford, iii. 177 ff.   [7] PRO, CO/5, v. 253, no. 337.

north, and frightened the settlers of northern New York and New England into serious resistance.[1] After Ticonderoga, the farmers, trappers, and small townsmen of upper New York and New England set out, singly and in local companies, along the roads and trails toward Schuyler's encampment. And the number of loyalists Burgoyne had expected to find seemed to diminish still further as the spirit of the revolutionaries was roused by the menace of invasion.

Burgoyne did not delay at Ticonderoga. He immediately sent Generals Frazer and Riedesel to pursue St. Clair and his troops. Frazer caught up with some of them at Hubbardtown and there was a brisk action in which the Americans fled but the British lost 183 men including Major Grant.[2] Burgoyne's men also overtook St. Clair's flotilla of 200 small boats loaded with supplies salvaged from Ticonderoga: '. . . burnt three galleys, captured two others, and took or destroyed the greater portion of the stores and provisions',[3] but St. Clair and most of his men got safely to Fort Edward.[4] At almost the same time Lieutenant-Colonel Hill and the ninth British regiment had a spirited action near a primitive entrenchment dignified by the name of Fort Anne, which resulted in the Americans burning its defences and retiring to Fort Edward. Meanwhile Burgoyne's main force broke the log boom across the narrows at Ticonderoga and in small boats paddled and rowed up the narrow headwaters of the South River to Skenesborough, where they drove off its few defenders.[5]

At Skenesborough, now Whitehall, Burgoyne waited for nearly a week for his supplies from Canada to catch up with him, and made a crucial decision. A road ran southward through Fort Anne and Fort Edward toward Albany, but there was an alternate route. Burgoyne could return by boat the few miles to Ticonderoga and then march the short distance by land to the northern end of Lake George. There he could embark his troops and go down that Lake to Fort George at its southern end, from which there was a moderately good wagon road to Fort Edward. By that course, his way would be less hindered by barriers and his men less harassed by enemy snipers.

[1] It also led Americans to unjust criticisms of Schuyler and St. Clair, who was accused of treachery and cowardice.
[2] Stone, p. 23.   [3] Lecky, iv. 60.
[4] Hudleston, p. 168.   [5] Kingsford, vi. 187–200; also Lecky, iv. 60.

Later critics have blamed Burgoyne for not going that way, but they have neglected to estimate how long it would have taken him to drag his boats overland to Lake George, or neglected to recognize that Burgoyne needed all his boats on Lake Champlain to bring him supplies from Canada. He had been present when Carleton had spent most of the previous summer building boats to take his troops up Lake Champlain, and could not afford a similar delay. It was not only inconsistent with his orders but unpalatable to his temperament and danger-ous to his ultimate success, since Schuyler's army was increasing every day. To take the Lake George route Burgoyne would also have had to back-track a few miles, lowering the spirits of his men and raising those of Americans who might regard it as a retreat.

There were other objections to the Lake George route. It would give his men less chance to 'commandeer' the food, horses, and forage they badly needed; and the country was more rugged than the road from Skenesborough south. At Skenes-borough he had not yet been rejoined by Frazer and Riedesel; if he continued southward they could meet him easily; if he turned north toward Lake George they would have to turn back still farther. There was yet another point. Burgoyne was casting a longing eye on western New England as an alternate route, or at least as a threatened course that would keep the enemy uncertain.

In his defence of his decision before Parliament a year and a half later, Burgoyne gave most of those reasons, and in view of what he knew and did not know at Skenesborough they were valid.[1] What he did not feature before Parliament was another factor which may have influenced his choice of route. He was accompanied by Colonel Philip Skene, a Scot who had been a Major in the British force that took Ticonderoga from the French in 1758, and who had then acquired a royal grant of some 34,000 acres around the south end of Lake Champlain. He had built at Skenesborough a stone manor house which Burgoyne made a headquarters, and an enormous barn.[2] The

---

[1] Burgoyne's Narrative before the House of Commons, as printed in *A State of the Expedition &c.*, 2nd edition, Almon, London, 1780. See also *Hansard*, xx. 793; also Fonblanque, pp. 267–70.

[2] For Skene see Van Doren, *Secret History*.

more the road between his holdings there and others near Fort Edward was improved, as it certainly would be if Burgoyne took that route, the better it would be for Colonel Skene. Colonel Skene strongly recommended that route to Burgoyne.[1]

Skene's advice may have been impersonal, but he was not above embellishing facts with misinformation. On 15 July he wrote to Lord Dartmouth from Skenesborough that the people of the area were hurrying in large numbers to pledge loyalty to the king; that he himself as Burgoyne's commissioner was about to set out for the nearby village of Castleton to receive the happy submission of its inhabitants, and that the Indians were 'under the greatest order'.[2] Skene was also assuring Burgoyne that: '. . . large numbers of the yeomanry of the county would flock to his standard'.[3]

As the heavily laden troops sweltered southward, they found the countryside provided less food and forage than they had hoped. Most of the horses, cattle, and grain had been removed, hidden, or destroyed, and in spite of Skene's report the inhabitants were almost to a man antagonistic.[4] The transport of the large guns, the baggage, provisions, and women slowed down the march, and the German troops in particular did not take easily to conditions so unlike those in the cultivated landscape and comfortable villages of Westphalia, where peasants were used to war and adjusted to it in a civilized manner, selling goods cheerfully to both sides, and not indulging in strong personal feelings about politics. Burgoyne's Indians were becoming intractable or simply vanishing into the woods. As supplies grew short, a raid into New England looked more attractive than ever, and just after leaving Skenesborough Burgoyne wrote to Lord George: 'Your Lordship will pardon me if I a little lament that my orders do not give me the latitude I ventured to propose in my original project for the campaign, to make a real effort instead of a feint upon New England. As things have

---

[1] Stone wrote that although Burgoyne was influenced in many ways by Skene, he did not choose the route to please Skene (Stone, pp. 29, 30).

[2] Skene to Dartmouth, 15 July 1777; *HMC, Dartmouth*, ii (1895); *Amer. Papers*, xiv. 10.

[3] Stone, p. 29.

[4] Burgoyne suffered considerably, and not only on the expedition to Bennington, by the infiltration of shirt-sleeved locals who pretended to be loyalists and were not (Stone, pp. 29–40).

turned out, were I at liberty to march in force immediately by my left, instead of to my right, I should have little doubt of subdueing before winter the provinces where the rebellion originated.'[1]

But Burgoyne was still confident; he had lost almost no troops in action except the 183 at Hubbardtown, and he did not fear defeat in battle by any enemy he might encounter *en route* to Albany. His men, however, were experiencing new annoyances distinctly lowering to their morale. Lieutenant Anburey, who had seen an officer shot down by an invisible marksman, wrote back to England with obvious nostalgia: 'This war is very different from the last in Germany.'[2] Two days later he wrote again from Skenesborough of a problem that was becoming more serious every day, and quoted a recent order from Burgoyne:

It is observed that the injunction given before the army took the field, relative to the baggage of officers, has not been complied with, and that the regiments in general are encumbered with much more baggage than they can possibly be supplied with means of carrying, when they quit the lakes and rivers: warning is therefore given again to the officers, to convey by the bateaux which will soon return to Ticonderoga, the baggage that is not indispensably necessary to them, or upon the first sudden movement it must inevitably be left on the ground. Such gentlemen as served in America in the last war may remember, that the officers took up with soldiers' tents, and often confined their baggage to a knapsack, for months together.[3]

No general's proclamation can prevent soldiers not under actual fire from making themselves as comfortable as possible, and gentlemen officers like their little comforts. Burgoyne's second warning was not enough. A month later, after the ardours of the road to Fort Edward should have shaken off all superfluous personal baggage, General Phillips found it necessary to issue a General Order to his own men: 'Major General Phillips has heard with the utmost astonishment that notwithstanding his most serious and positive orders of the 16th instant that no Carts should be used for any purpose whatever, but for the Transport of Provisions, unless by particular orders from the Commander

---

[1] Burgoyne to Germain, 11 July 1777; Fonblanque, p. 256.
[2] Anburey, 12 July 1777; i. 197.
[3] Anburey, 14 July 1777; i. 209.

in Chief etc. as expressed in the Order, there are this day about thirty Carts on the Road loaden with Baggage. . . .'[1]

In his original 'Thoughts' Burgoyne had predicted that the Americans would impede the way with fallen trees, but neither he nor his men anticipated what a thorough job of road-blocking General Schuyler's woodsmen would do. Anburey wrote again from Skenesborough on 17 July: 'We are obliged to wait for some time in our present position, till the roads are cleared of the trees which the Americans felled after their retreat. You would think it almost impossible, but every ten or twelve yards great trees are laid across the road, exclusive of smaller ones.'[2] Grenadiers, Hessians, and artillerymen, toiling with heavy equipment, heavier guns, too few horses, and diminishing supplies, found their way impeded not only by fallen trees but by the destruction of all the bridges over the innumerable little streams and marshy places. Between Skenesborough and Fort Edward they had to build or repair forty bridges and a corduroy causeway nearly two miles long over flooded land, and even Baroness Riedesel had to descend from her tumbril-like vehicle and walk with the common soldiers. The country around them was wasted of all support to a passing army, in places even the grass had been burned. Horses and cattle had vanished and the houses were deserted of all save silent and unfriendly old men, women, and children. And though Burgoyne's men seldom saw an enemy rifleman, bullets that occasionally came from nowhere, though they caused very few casualties, were distinctly upsetting.

Anburey was referring to drill-book discipline when he wrote: 'I found all manual exercise is but ornament',[3] and Sergeant Lamb discovered that: 'In fighting in the wood, battalion manoeuvers and excellence of exercise were found of little value.'[4] More than one of Burgoyne's men must have recalled General Braddock's experience along similar trails in western Pennsylvania. What had been saved from that disaster had been saved by a young colonial officer named George Washington. Now Washington was on the other side.

Burgoyne waited nearly two weeks at Skenesborough for supplies from Canada, for the way ahead to be cleared, and for

[1] Lamb, *An Original Authentic Journal*; 19 Aug. 1777.
[2] Anburey, 17 July 1777; i. 212, 213.
[3] Anburey, 12 July 1777; i. 198.   [4] Hudleston, p. 168.

the opening of communications to Lake George for later transport of artillery and stores down that lake.[1] In spite of his
advance guard's efforts to clear the way, it took his army twenty
days to cover the twenty miles to Fort Edward, and even that
was 'no mean feat'.[2] On 31 July he found Fort Edward 'pre-
cipitately abandoned', and on the same day the American force
consolidated its position near Stillwater, thirty miles south of
Fort Edward and another thirty miles north of Albany.[3]

Burgoyne remained at Fort Edward for six weeks, until
12 September.[4] There were reasons to justify the pause. On
his march from Skenesborough Burgoyne had been able to ac-
cumulate only supplies enough to give him a four days' reserve.
Before he went farther into enemy territory he needed food and
ammunition from Canada. The Canadian contractors had still
not produced horses to the number promised, and Burgoyne did
not want to move too far ahead of his heavy artillery.[5] Above all
he hoped to hear from Howe or Clinton just when and where he
would be met. It was not easy for messengers to get through to
New York and several had been captured. Burgoyne sent more.

But he weakened his case for immediate co-operation by
writing too confidently of his situation. Clinton recorded later:
'I was at last relieved from my suspense by a letter from General
Burgoyne dated from Fort Edward on the 6th August, wherein
was described his march thither from Skenesborough and his
expectation of reaching Albany by the 23rd at farthest. This
letter showed him to be in the highest spirits, and did not contain
an expression that indicated either an expectation or desire of
cooperation from the southern army.'[6] Clinton's words were
literally true, but he was being disingenuous. Burgoyne had
made it clear ever since he first wrote to Howe from Plymouth
that he expected to be met in force, and every letter to Howe or
Clinton was implicit in that assumption.

If, while at Fort Edward, Burgoyne had known that he was
to be left wholly dependent on himself, he might have moved
several weeks earlier, risking all while the odds were less against
him. Or he might have concluded that Howe's abandonment
freed him from the shackles of his orders, and struck off eastward

---

[1] Fortescue, *HBA*, 2, iii. 226.   [2] Ibid.   [3] Hudleston, p. 169.
[4] Kingsford, vi. 234–7.   [5] Fortescue, *HBA*, 2, iii. 226.
[6] Clements, Clinton, *Historical Detail*; also Willcox, *Amer. Rebellion*, p. 70.

and then south, flanking the Schuyler–Gates army and moving toward New York down the easier route of the Berkshire Valley. Or he might have pocketed his pride and retreated to Canada, holding Ticonderoga as a warrant of a successful campaign. But from Burgoyne's point of view his actions were still dependent on getting specific instructions from Howe. 'I have spared no pains to open a correspondence with Sir William Howe, but of the messengers sent out at different times and by different routes, not one is returned to me, and I am in total ignorance of the situation or intention of that General', he had written to Lord George the day before he entered Fort Edward.[1]

No general should be expected to follow orders so literally as to make their final objective impossible. If Burgoyne concluded that he could not 'force his way to Albany' single-handed, he could quite properly take some other course. Nor could any general be expected to move forward in enemy territory without adequate food, transport, and ammunition. Burgoyne's scouts had reported that the Americans were assembling stores at Bennington, not far south-eastward in Vermont as the crow flies, though a much longer distance up and down the steep wooded foot-hills between the Adirondacks and the Green Mountains. The Bennington stores were said to include horses, and Riedesel badly needed horses if his dragoons were to be effective in a coming battle.[2] Colonel Skene approved sending a detachment to bring back the supplies, and assured Burgoyne that: '. . . the country swarmed with men who wished to take up arms for the King'.[3] On 13 August Burgoyne sent off 500 men, including Colonel Skene, to Bennington.

A small force raiding deep into enemy territory should move fast, but to heavily accoutred grenadiers in rough and strange country there is no such thing as speed. Burgoyne made the mistake of sending German troops under Colonel Baume.[4] Blundering through the forests, dragging two field guns up and down the hills, their progress and numbers in their absurd uniforms were well heralded by enemy scouts, for Colonel Baume had the bad judgement to allow what appeared to be friendly Americans to follow their files and even pass through their camp at night.

[1] Burgoyne to Germain, 30 July 1777; Fonblanque, p. 270.
[2] Hudleston, p. 174.   [3] Fortescue, *HBA*, 2, iii. 228.   [4] *HMC, Stop. Sack.* ii. 74.

Three days later, nearing Bennington, they were attacked by some 1,800 men under General Stark, and the friendly guides and visitors proved to have been enemy scouts. Baume's men managed to dig in on a hilltop and send runners back to Burgoyne for immediate aid. The message got through, but Burgoyne compounded his first mistake by sending more German troops, under Colonel Breyman, to relieve their countrymen. It rained hard; the guide lost or said he lost his way, and Breyman's relief party sometimes made no more than a mile an hour. Before it arrived Baume and most of his men had been killed, wounded, or captured. Breyman, Skene, and most of the relief detachment got back to Burgoyne, but the loss was a severe one.[1] Burgoyne could ill afford to lose 600 men.[2] Precisely what Washington had hoped for had come about, and the defeat served to 'inspirit' the Americans out of all proportion to its size.

Burgoyne explained the defeat in a dispatch to Lord George Germain as due to: '. . . the credulity of those who managed the department of intelligence and who suffered great numbers of rebel soldiers to pass and repass, and perhaps count the numbers of the detachment, and upon an ill-founded confidence that induced Lieutenant Colonel Baume to advance too far to have a secure retreat'.[3] The near future would add irony to Burgoyne's criticism of Colonel Baume for an incautious advance. And whatever the blunders of others, Burgoyne had used bad judgement in sending so ill-adapted a force on so risky a foray. His spirits fell after that disaster and never fully recovered their former ebullience.

Other developments added to Burgoyne's uneasiness. The few loyalists proved reluctant to fight, and of the four hundred he had attached to his army less than half had brought any arms. Ammunition was already one of Burgoyne's most serious short-

[1] According to Stone, Burgoyne in the two actions near Bennington lost about 360 men killed, about 700 as prisoners, four brass cannon, and some hundreds of guns, and after these losses had only twenty German mounted dragoons as his entire cavalry force (Stone, pp. 34–36). Fiske said there were 207 killed and 670 taken prisoner. The latter figures coincide fairly well with Burgoyne's reported numbers at the beginning and end of the campaign, allowing for other losses. In order to avoid overstatement a smaller figure is arbitrarily given here.

[2] PRO, CO/5, v. 253, no. 172.

[3] Ibid., no. 336; also Hudleston, p. 180.

ages. In contrast, the enemy was reported to be multiplying daily. 'Wherever the King's forces point, militia to the amount of three or four thousand assemble in twenty-four hours, they bring with them their subsistence etc., and, the alarm over, they return to their farms. . . . The great bulk of the country is undoubtedly with the Congress in principle and in zeal.'[1] And news from St. Leger indicated that his progress was at best slow.

As for letters from the south [Burgoyne had written to Lord George] only one from General Howe has come to hand,[2] . . . the Highlands have not even been threatened. The consequence is that Putnam has detached two brigades to Mr. Gates, who is now strongly posted near the mouth of the Mohawk River, with an army superior to mine in troops of the Congress, and as many militia as he pleases. Had I a latitude in my orders, I should think it my duty to wait in this position, or perhaps as far back as Fort Edward, where my communication with Lake George would be perfectly secure, till some event happened to assist my movement forward, but my orders being positive to '. . . force a junction with Sir William Howe', I apprehend I am not at liberty to remain inactive longer than shall be necessary to collect twenty-five days provisions and to receive the reinforcement of the additional companies, the German drafts and recruits now (and unfortunately only now) on Lake Champlain.[3]

That was a different Burgoyne from the orator of the embarkation and the optimist of Ticonderoga, one who was learning things about fighting in America that Lord George Germain would never quite believe. Burgoyne's letter did serve one useful purpose: it proved that long before he was in serious trouble he believed he had no alternative to obeying orders that forced him straight forward.

Others shared Burgoyne's change of spirits. Colonel Skene, who had managed to get safely back from Bennington, wrote to Lord Dartmouth in far more sober terms than his effusion of some six weeks earlier. He blamed Colonel Baume as responsible for the defeat at Bennington and supported Burgoyne as 'unluckily circumstanced' in not having heard from General Howe

---

[1] Fonblanque, p. 275.
[2] Hudleston, p. 181.
[3] Burgoyne to Germain, 20 Aug. 1777; Fonblanque, pp. 275 ff.; also Hudleston, p. 181.

or having had assistance from 'any army on the North River to open the communication'.[1]

All the news seemed bad. By the end of August Burgoyne must have heard the whole disappointing story of his diversionary force in the Mohawk Valley. St. Leger had arrived at Fort Stanwix, the key to the Mohawk Valley, on 3 August. It was defended by Colonel Gansevoort with some 700 men, very little gunpowder, beef that had gone bad, and bullets many of which did not 'suit the firelocks'. But the fort was a square, solid log structure, strongly resistant to any fire except from larger guns than St. Leger had, and its defenders were not lacking in courage. While St. Leger was besieging it, General Herkimer, the veteran of the French and Indian wars, was hurrying with 1,000 men to relieve it. St. Leger managed to waylay him and in the battle of Oriskany, in which St. Leger's numerous Indians certainly ignored Burgoyne's rules, Herkimer was fatally wounded and his men routed. But the fort still held out. Then St. Leger received reports that Benedict Arnold was on his way to relieve Gansevoort. That was true, but the rest that St. Leger heard was artful propaganda spread by Arnold: that Arnold's force was large; that Burgoyne had been heavily defeated,[2] and finally that Burgoyne's whole force had been cut to pieces.[3] Deceived and alarmed, St. Leger abandoned the siege and returned to Oswego and ultimately to Montreal.[4]

In all that followed it is essential to remember how uncertain and slow were the communications between the chief actors of the drama. A message from Burgoyne to Carleton had to be carried on foot or horse from Fort Edward to Skenesborough (or to the southern end of Lake George, then by ship up that Lake, and then by land to Ticonderoga). From there it would go by boat, when a boat was available, the length of Lake Champlain, and thence by land to Montreal or Quebec. A message to Germain in London would take the same route to Quebec, there await a ship to England, and with luck reach its destination, in the ice-free months, six weeks after leaving Quebec. Return messages would take almost as long. Dispatches from Burgoyne to Clinton would go by foot messengers who had to work their way through enemy country for nearly 200 miles. A message to

---

[1] Skene to Dartmouth: *HMC, Amer. Papers, Dartmouth*, ii. xiv, 443.
[2] Lecky, iv. 627.   [3] Fortescue, *HBA*, 2, iii. 230.   [4] Hudleston, p. 148.

Howe, after he had landed and could be reached at all, would go to Clinton and then be forwarded by him. At least half of all the messages from Burgoyne to Clinton and Howe did not reach their destinations.

Those vicissitudes of communication determined the various times when men in Quebec, New York, Philadelphia, and London changed from confidence to worry and from worry to alarm about the state of the northern army. Clinton, nearest to Burgoyne, was the first to feel real concern, but Clinton had never been optimistic. The news of Bennington, which first reached him through enemy channels, confirmed his earlier fears, but did not alter his conviction of his own inability to do anything really effective for Burgoyne. He had no greater strength than when Howe had left him in mid-July, for instead of sending back men to New York Howe was asking for more. Clinton dared not attempt even a token diversion up the Hudson until the long-overdue reinforcements arrived.

On 11 September he wrote to Burgoyne that: '. . . if he thought his operations could be assisted by it, I should in about ten days make an attempt on the forts in the Highlands with about 2000 men, as I was in hourly hopes of receiving a reinforcement from Europe of about that amount'.[1] By the time Burgoyne received that dispatch on 21 September, he was in still deeper waters. Two days before he had met Gates's army in their first engagement and had learned its strength. He sent off an immediate reply to Clinton, reporting his technical success in that battle but adding that: '. . . an attack or even the menace of one upon Fort Montgomery would be of very great use'.[2] In the days that followed he sent further messages, each more urgent than the last. Not all of these reached Clinton, but those dated 23 and 24 September got to him on 29 September.[3] By the time he made his desperate position clear to Clinton, it was too late. The fault was partly Burgoyne's; he failed to recognize or report his deteriorating situation.

It is not so easy to trace the growth of alarm in the mind of Lord George Germain. Either he was fluctuating from confidence

[1] Clinton to Burgoyne, 11 Sept. 1777; Clements, Clinton, *Hist. Detail*; also Willcox, p. 70; also Fonblanque, p. 286; also Hudleston, p. 194.
[2] Burgoyne to Clinton, 21 Sept. 1777; Clements, Clinton, *Hist. Detail*; also Willcox, p. 72.
[3] PRO, CO/5, v. 94, no. 715.

to trepidation and back again from day to day, or else he was concealing, most of the time, the fears he hoped would prove unnecessary. Once Howe had embarked to go southward, there was little that Lord George could have done to save Burgoyne. He could not have got word to Carleton or Clinton in time for either to have done anything really effective with the limited troops at their disposal. And once Howe had started out on his six-week sea voyage, aid in time from his troops was out of the question.

Lord George continued to profess optimism, especially to the king and even to his friend General Irwin. On 22 August he wrote to the king that 'Lt. General Burgoyne's short letter is most satisfactory',[1] though on the following day he whistled a little less loudly through the woods to Irwin: 'I confess I feared that Washington would have marched all his forces to Albany, and attempted to demolish the army from Canada, but the last accounts say he has taken up his quarters at Morristown after detaching 3000 men to Albany. Sir William Howe has gone up the Delaware leaving a strong force with Clinton at New York.'[2] Even to Irwin he was being disingenuous, for he knew how few men Howe had left with Clinton. When news of Saratoga reached London, Lord George suddenly sang quite a different tune. He then '. . . regretted that Sir Henry was not earlier in a condition to help Burgoyne'.[3]

As soon as Lord George realized Burgoyne was in serious trouble he apparently began to build his fences against charges that he had mismanaged the campaign. The only defence he could offer would be the mistakes of his generals, and at first he selected Howe as the potential scapegoat. He had for some months expressed criticisms of Sir William. On 11 June he had written to Knox his hope that Major Balfour had convinced Howe that he distressed Lord George '. . . by not communicating his ideas more frequently and more explicitly'.[4] Four days later he was sarcastic about the Admiral: 'Lord Howe is the most disinterested man I know, in permitting the trade of Charleston to be carry'd on without interruption, when he might avail

[1] Germain to King, 22 Aug. 1777; Fortescue, *Corresp.* iii. 469.
[2] Germain to Irwin, 23 Aug. 1777; *HMC, Stop. Sack.* i. 138, 139.
[3] Jane Clark, p. 559.
[4] Germain to Knox, 11 June 1777; *HMC, Var. Coll.* 6, *Knox*, p. 130.

himself of so many rich prizes.'[1] By late August he was voicing his criticisms of General Howe to the king by careful innuendo. In the same letter in which he praised Burgoyne's progress 'Lord George Germain has the honor of sending your Majesty all the letters he has received from Sir William Howe. The Private letter Confirms the opinion Lord George always had of the General's pursuing his intended operations to the Southward. Your Majesty will be pleas'd to remark, that no reason is assigned for the Campaign opening so late.'[2]

The 'private letter' from Howe was the one which, read carefully in its context, disclaimed any intention to meet Burgoyne. By some omission, that was the letter that was not included in the correspondence from Howe that Lord George sent to the king. Was it deliberately overlooked? If so, it must have been because Lord George did not want the king to know how completely Howe had been allowed to wash his hands of any responsibility for Burgoyne. Without a knowledge of that letter Howe's actions might later seem indefensible; with a knowledge of that letter and of Lord George's reply approving it, it was Lord George's position that was indefensible.

On 9 December, a few days after the reports of the Saratoga surrender had been confirmed, Lord George wrote to the king explaining that he had just discovered (some four and a half months after it had been received) that he had neglected to enclose one of the letters from Howe. The king therefore did not read the letter in which lay Howe's chief justification for his conduct until nearly five months after Howe had written it; until six weeks after Burgoyne had surrendered, and until a week after that news had reached London.[3] By the time the king read that letter he had long been exposed to Lord George's hints of dissatisfaction with Howe, and had had a full week after the bad news to reach the natural conclusion that Howe or Burgoyne had been chiefly to blame. Lord George saw fit to add his own comment with his enclosure: '. . . it plainly shows that Sir William Howe thought Lt. General Burgoyne's army in safety even if it had been attacked by all Washington's forces'.[4]

Whether or not the king had thought Howe was supposed to

---

[1] Germain to Knox, 15 June 1777; *HMC, Var. Coll. 6, Knox*, p. 131.
[2] Germain to King, 22 Aug. 1777; Fortescue, *Corresp*. iii. 469.
[3] Germain to King, 9 Dec. 1777; Fortescue, *Corresp*. iii. 507.   [4] Ibid.

meet Burgoyne at Albany, nearly everyone else thought so. Even in remote Minorca Governor James Murray assumed it in September when he wrote to Lord George that: 'When Burgoyne gets over the Lakes, and Sir John Johnstone penetrates with his Indians, Sir William Howe's detachments co-operating with them, must . . . accomplish your most sanguine wishes.'[1] Lord George did not enlighten General Murray.

Lord George's undersecretaries, who must have known the truth, were sometimes no more frank than their chief. A week after Howe had sailed for Philadelphia, Hutchinson wrote in his diary that he: 'Went to the Secretary of State's office. From Mr. D'Oyley I am satisfied that Howe did not intend Philadelphia. . . . I suppose he is gone with a great part of the army & fleet to New England.'[2] It was a full month later that another undersecretary, William Knox, told Hutchinson: '. . . that Howe certainly intended to go to Philadelphia when he left New York'.[3]

Reports of Burgoyne's earlier difficulties must have crossed the Atlantic briskly, for on 1 September Lord George wrote in a memorandum to Knox: 'I hope your intelligence about Burgoyne has no foundation.'[4] The worst that could then have been reported were Burgoyne's supply troubles, his failure to destroy St. Clair's forces, his disappointment in recruiting loyalists, and his difficulty in clearing the road to Fort Edward.

The news that Howe had sailed from New York could not be kept from Parliament and hence from the public, and before the end of September questions were echoing in London clubs and Parliament corridors. William Knox, who probably knew all that Lord George knew, wrote that: 'People here are greatly puzzled by General Howe's conduct.'[5] Horace Walpole wrote on 27 September that: 'The Howes are gone the Lord knows whither',[6] and a month later: 'Since we know nothing certain of the state of affairs in America; the very existence where, of the Howes, is a mystery. . . . Burgoyne [is said] to be beaten.'[7]

---

[1] Murray to Germain, 6 Sept. 1777; HMC, Stop. Sack. i. 370.
[2] Clements, Hutchinson, Diaries (original MS.), p. 393; 30 July 1777.
[3] Ibid., p. 398; 1 Sept. 1777.
[4] Germain to Knox, 1 Sept. 1777; HMC, Var. Coll. 6, Knox, p. 137.
[5] Hudleston, p. 186.
[6] Walpole to Countess of Upper Ossory, 27 Sept. 1777; Toynbee, x. 121.
[7] Walpole to Mann, 26 Oct. 1777; ibid., p. 143.

Walpole also recorded a story that is significant even though almost certainly inaccurate: 'The ministers were so confounded by Howe's expedition, when they wished he should have gone north to get Washington between him and Burgoyne, that they sent orders to Burgoyne not to advance beyond Albany till he could hear from and concert with Howe.'[1] One Minister, at least, could not have been confounded by that news. If other Ministers were, it proves what a lone hand Lord George had been playing.[2]

Three statements by Lord George at about that time, taken together, allow of no explanation except disingenuousness. One was a private note to William Knox: 'I am sorry to find that Burgoyne's campaign is so totally ruined; the best wish I can form is that he may have returned to Ticonderoga without much loss. His private letter to me, 20th of August, contains nothing material about the affair at Bennington, but what alarms me most is that he thinks his orders to go to Albany to force a junction with Sir William Howe are so positive that he must attempt at all events the obeying them.'[3] Yet Lord George wrote to the king nine days later: 'The progress of General Burgoyne is as rapid as could be expected, and the difficulties he has surmounted do him great honor . . . in a private letter he complain'd of not hearing from Sir W. Howe, or of not knowing anything of his operations. He had dispatched Ten Messengers to New Yorke, and not one of them had returned.'[4] Only four days after that Lord George sung still another tune: 'I am sorry the Canada army will be disappointed in the junction they expect with Sir William Howe, but the more honour to Burgoyne if he does the business without any assistance from New York.'[5]

Further disingenuousness is indicated in a report from other sources a month later: 'Lord George Germaine owned to Lord Hertford that General Howe had defeated all his views by going to Maryland instead of waiting to join Burgoyne. Clinton has not force sufficient at New York to send him any relief.'[6] Lord

[1] Walpole, *Last Journals*, 10 Sept. 1777; ii. 44; also Fonblanque, p. 343.
[2] There is no record of any such Cabinet action or any such order to Burgoyne. Had an order been sent him about the time Walpole wrote it would not have reached him before his surrender. [3] Hudleston, p. 182.
[4] Germain to King, 25 Sept. 1777; Fortescue, *Corresp.* iii. 480.
[5] Germain to Knox, 29 Sept. 1777; *HMC, Var. Coll.* 6, *Knox*, p. 139.
[6] Walpole, *Last Journals*, ii. 9.

George was probably also the 'very great man' in the Duke of Richmond's letter to the Marquis of Rockingham: 'I believe it is also true that a very great man said within these few days that he expected accounts of a general defeat very soon.'[1] To complete the fantasy, Lord George wrote to Knox: 'If Sir Wm. Howe would carry any part of his army into the Southern Provinces this winter I should have no doubt of his success.'[2]

By October London was talking of little else but the military situation in America. Irwin wrote to the Earl of Buckinghamshire in Dublin: 'Not a word from Sir William Howe. I need not add that our impatience is great',[3] and between the lines of that correspondence it is clear that Irwin's fears were as great as his impatience. Viscount Townshend, Master of Ordnance, hoped that a victory by Howe in Philadelphia might somehow save Burgoyne: '. . . the decisive stroke I hear Sir William Howe has struck will, I hope, be followed by so general a dismay that Burgoyne's progress will be clear'.[4] Reports of St. Leger's withdrawal from the Mohawk Valley reached London on 28 October to add to the general dismay.[5]

While Lord George was whistling in the woods and London seethed with confusion, Burgoyne was facing immediate and concrete problems. His orders urged him forward, and whatever common sense might plead, his temperament concurred with his orders. On 13 September, with every show of confidence and determination, he led his little army westward across the Hudson on a bridge of hurriedly built pontoons. That was at Batten Kill, $10\frac{1}{2}$ miles south of Fort Edward.[6] He was some 200 miles from Montreal, with 40 miles of land transport between himself and Lake Champlain, and some 45 miles from Albany.[7] His army totalled not more than 5,500, sick, well, and wounded. It was now almost entirely an army of Europeans; the Canadians who had not been left at way stations or simply vanished were few, and only fifty Indians crossed the river.[8] The Hudson was Burgoyne's Rubicon.

---

[1] Richmond to Rockingham, 2 Nov. 1777; Baxter, *British Invasion from the North*, p. 65.
[2] Germain to Knox, 13 Sept. 1777; Clements, *Knox Papers*, iii. 37.
[3] Irwin to Buckinghamshire, 30 Sept. 1777; *HMC, Lothian*, i. 316.
[4] Townshend to Knox, 5 Nov. 1777; *HMC, Var. Coll.* 6, *Knox*, p. 140.
[5] Walpole, *Last Journals*, ii. 69.   [6] Kingsford, vi. 234–7.
[7] Greene, p. 109.   [8] Kingsford, vi. 177 ff.

At that point Burgoyne received his first dispatch from Howe since he had left Lake Champlain. It was written in very small characters on a narrow strip of thin paper inserted in a quill. It bore no date and was in other ways unhelpful. Howe congratulated Burgoyne on taking Ticonderoga without loss, and continued:

My intention is for Pennsylvania, where I expect to meet Washington, but if he goes to the north, contrary to my expectations, and you can keep him at Bay, be assured I shall soon be after him to relieve you. After your arrival at Albany, the movements of the Enemy will guide yours, but my wishes are, that the enemy be drove out of this province before any Operation takes place in Conecticut. Sir Henry Clinton remains in the command here, and will act as occurences may direct. Putnam is in the highlands with about 4000 men. Success be ever with you.[1]

That message was obviously written before Howe left New York on 23 July, seven weeks before Burgoyne received it. Howe's confidence in Burgoyne's unassisted powers was flattering, but it destroyed his last flickering hope of any aid except Clinton's cautious and limited endeavours. Had Howe's dispatch reached him only a week earlier at Fort Edward, Burgoyne might have considered withdrawal to Ticonderoga. But now the die was cast.

The next day Burgoyne led his men a little farther south, and that night they encamped 'on the heights and in the plains of Saratoga'.

---

[1] Clements, *Howe Papers* (photostat and original); also Fonblanque, pp. 280, 281. The original in the Clements Collection is in excellent condition and though in a very small script quite legible, except that the final words at the end of each long line (and the end of the paper strip) are obscured. Each of the two strips of paper is about 17 by $\frac{3}{8}$ in., and the ink letters, though tiny, are beautifully inscribed.

XVII

SARATOGA

ON 19 September Burgoyne advanced in three columns, leading the centre one himself.[1] He knew the Americans outnumbered him by at least two to one, and he may have known that Benedict Arnold, one of the most aggressive of leaders, was back from outwitting St. Leger, and that Gates had also been joined by Morgan and his rangers, the best regiment of marksmen in the world. But he did not know, because no one knew, how grimly the local militia would defend their homeland, or how much the American spirit had been roused 'to madness by an outrage of the Indians', who had killed the young wife of an American officer despite Burgoyne's orders.[2] He did not realize, either, the effect upon the Americans of learning at Bennington that Burgoyne's troops were by no means invincible; that: '. . . a spirit of resistance had arisen wholly unlike anything the British had yet encountered during the war. . . . The almost certain prospect of capturing a British army elated the Americans to the highest degree, and new volunteers rapidly poured in.'[3]

Burgoyne did not believe the bulk of the Americans would stand up against his disciplined professionals and large guns in an open fight, and in this opinion he was justified, for nothing in his experience in Boston, Canada, or Ticonderoga had demonstrated otherwise. What was more, Clinton, he thought, would soon be near enough to distract or divide Gates's army. But even if Burgoyne had realized how great were the odds against him, he would probably have sought battle just the same. Had he tried to withdraw the Americans would have been on his retreating columns with all the dash of Arnold and all the arts of backwoods guerrilla warfare. And there were still his orders to force his way to Albany. If he were to fight he must fight immediately, for his supplies and ammunition were dwindling and the enemy were multiplying.

[1] Stone, p. 43.   [2] Fortescue, *HBA*, 2, iii. 227.
[3] Lecky, iv. 61, 63.

The British troops marched in close formation directly on the American position. Gates wanted to receive them behind his earthworks, but Arnold, defying his commanding officer, led his regiment out to the attack, and most of the American troops followed. There was hard fighting from noon to darkness. Burgoyne led his centre steadily forward, displaying masterful leadership as well as great personal bravery—according to his men he was everywhere at once. His courage was equalled by Arnold's and most of the troops on both sides. All afternoon the opposing companies, soon irregular and disordered among the trees and rocks, swayed back and forth, but, as young Lieutenant Anburey wrote that night by camp-fire: 'Just as the light closed, the enemy gave ground on all sides, and left us completely masters of the field.'[1]

It was technically a British victory, but of what real value was mastery of the battlefield when the enemy was master of almost everything else? The Americans could afford their losses of the day, and as many more tomorrow, but Burgoyne could not. The day's fighting had demonstrated that Gates's army was a far more formidable opponent than Burgoyne and his men had expected. 'The courage and obstinacy with which the Americans fought, were the astonishment of everyone, and we are now become fully convinced, that they are not that contemptible enemy we had hitherto imagined', Anburey added to his letter home.[2]

Burgoyne was a good enough general to realize all that. The Americans had not been beaten but lay undismayed between himself and his destination. All the strategic advantages lay with them. To drive through their lines was, he thought, still possible, but it would be at best a very expensive operation and might bring disaster, especially since: '. . . from the thickness of the wood it was impossible to catch a view of any part of their position, and they knew the terrain far better'.[3] Unless Clinton drew off the enemy very soon, everything was in their favour.

Everything but determination. There is no evidence that after that revealing day's fighting Burgoyne seriously considered retreat. But he did change his plans. He decided to avoid major engagements for a few days in the hope of relief by Clinton.

---

[1] Anburey, i. 245; 24 (19) Sept. 1777.   [2] Ibid.
[3] As Burgoyne told the House of Commons later. *Hansard*, xx. 798.

Though on 10 August Clinton had written of his 'present inability to make a diversion',[1] that was nearly six weeks ago,
and he must long since have started up the Hudson in considerable force. It was important at least to find out where Clinton
was before Burgoyne committed his battered little force to
another trial of strength. He sent off messages to Clinton,[2] and
began to fortify his new position at Freeman's Farm.[3] There he
remained for nearly three weeks, observed and harassed by the
nearby enemy, but avoiding large-scale action.

Two days after that first battle Burgoyne received Clinton's
dispatch of 11/12 September. It was not encouraging. Clinton
stated his intention to move up the Hudson as soon as possible,[4]
but said his start depended on reinforcements not yet arrived,
and that he proposed to bring only 2,000 men no farther than
the Highlands of the Hudson, well below Albany. Burgoyne
sent off a reply the next morning, reporting the success of the
recent battle, but urging haste. He sent further messages on each
of the following days. Not all of them got through to Clinton, but
those of 23 and 24 September reached him on 29 September.[5]

After the campaign had ended, men began to point out many
things that might have been done differently, and among them
one has seldom been stressed. It was the failure of Clinton to
receive reinforcements at the time he had been given good
reason to expect them that kept him from operations that might
have saved Burgoyne's army. If Clinton had started three weeks
earlier with 4,000 men, when Burgoyne was stronger and Gates
was weaker, the story might have ended very differently.
Clinton's expectation of reinforcements was based on assurances
from Lord George Germain.

Every day of that three weeks' wait at Freeman's Farm diminished Burgoyne's food and supplies, and the ammunition
that had never been too plentiful. 'We have gained little more
by our victory than Honour', wrote Anburey in melancholy
second thoughts, using a word often on the lips of his commanding general. 'The desertion of the Indians, Canadians and
Provincials, at a time when their services were most required,
was exceedingly mortifying.'[6]

[1] Clements, Clinton, *Historical Detail*; also Willcox, *Amer. Rebellion*, p. 70.
[2] Kingsford, vi. 234–7.   [3] Stone, p. 52.
[4] Clinton to Burgoyne, 12 Sept. 1777; Hudleston, p. 194.
[5] PRO, CO/5, v. 94, no. 715.   [6] Anburey, i. 248; 6 Oct. 1777.

Finally, on 30 September, the ships with Clinton's reinforcements dropped anchor in New York's lower bay, but the condition of the men was a shock to Clinton's hopes and plans. There were less than the expected 3,000, and only 1,700 were fit for duties of the lightest kind.[1] Soon after their arrival, however, Clinton received Burgoyne's dispatches of 23 and 24 September, convincing Clinton that he needed immediate help. Clinton moved as fast as could be reasonably expected. On 2 October he set Tryon's corps in motion northward, and the next day started himself with the rest of 3,000 men, sending word to Burgoyne that at last he was on the way.[2] He risked leaving in New York a weaker force than he thought really cautious, for many of the men there were ill, and at Howe's request he had felt constrained to send him another five battalions.[3]

While still on the outskirts of New York city, at Verplanck's Landing, Clinton received another dispatch from Burgoyne, dated 28 September.[4] Burgoyne's note was short, and referred Clinton to its bearer, Captain Campbell, for further information that he dared not put into writing so likely to fall into enemy hands. Clinton later recorded Captain Campbell's account:

Burgoyne's army did not exceed 5000 men, having lost 500 or 600 in the action on the nineteenth; that the rebel army was very strongly posted to the amount of above 12,000 men within a mile a and half of his army, and had perhaps another considerable body hanging in the rear; that his provisions would not last him longer than till the 20th of October; his communication with Canada being entirely cut off; that altogether he had no doubt of being able to force his way to Albany, yet, being uncertain he could subsist after he got there, he wished before he attempted it to know whether I could open a communication with that town, at what time I expected to be there, and whether I could procure supplies from New York for him afterwards, requesting I would send him as soon as possible by triplicates

---

[1] Clements, Clinton, *Hist. Detail*; also Willcox, *Amer. Rebellion*, p. 63. The records illustrate the usual contrast between the way heads were counted in Germain's office and in the field. Germain's office summary stated: 'The reinforcement Sir H. Clinton had received before he attacked Fort Montgomery amounted to about 3000' (PRO, CO/5, v. 253, no. 215).

[2] Jane Clark, p. 556.

[3] PRO, CO/5, v. 253, no. 215.

[4] The Colonial Office summary said Burgoyne's letter dated 20 Sept. was received by Clinton on 4 Oct. (ibid., no. 357). It seems clear that the dispatch received then was Burgoyne's plea for immediate aid, brought and amplified by Captain Campbell (Clements, Clinton, *Hist. Detail*; also Willcox, p. 74).

my most explicit orders, either to attack the enemy or to retreat across the lakes while they were still clear of ice—hinting at the same time that he would not have relinquished his communication with them had he not expected a cooperating army at Albany. This account of General Burgoyne's real condition, which I had neither heard of nor suspected until the present moment, filled my mind with the most anxious reflections. . . . As matters were circumstanced, I greatly feared it was too late. . . . I therefore dispatched a messenger to General Burgoyne to let him know where we were.[1]

That so proud and confident a general as Burgoyne should ask Clinton to make the crucial decision for him revealed Burgoyne's new uncertainty and dismay. He was fully justified in asking for orders from Clinton, who represented Howe in Howe's absence, but to Clinton Burgoyne's request seemed something of a trap. If he should send Burgoyne orders and Burgoyne met disaster after following them, Ministers and Parliament might place the blame on Clinton. And how could Clinton, only vaguely instructed by Howe and only vaguely informed of Burgoyne's situation, send him explicit orders? Clinton was a responsible soldier, personally as well as professionally dismayed by Burgoyne's danger, but he was also human. Perhaps there flitted across his mind memories of those days in the *Cerberus* in 1775, when Howe and Burgoyne had been so confident and perhaps a little patronizing of the silent, sensitive, and socially defensive Clinton. And now that 'shy bitch' of 1775 was being supplicated for orders by Burgoyne, and left by Howe to pull his chestnuts, as well, out of the fire.

Whatever Clinton's personal feelings, there is not the slightest reason to think they influenced his military decision. He declined to give Burgoyne any orders or advice: '. . . Not having received any instructions from the Commander in Chief relative to the Northern army, and unacquainted even of his intentions concerning the operations of that army, excepting his wishes that they should get to Albany, Sir Henry Clinton cannot presume to give any orders to General Burgoyne. General Burgoyne could not suppose that Sir Henry Clinton had any idea of penetrating to Albany with the small force he mentioned in his last letter of the 11th September.'[2]

---

[1] Clements, Clinton, *Hist. Detail*; also Willcox, p. 74.
[2] Clinton to Burgoyne, 6 Oct. 1777; Clements, *Clinton Papers*; also Willcox,

Clinton did assure Burgoyne that he was moving northward as fast as possible and would do all he could to help him. He hurried his small force up the Hudson, landed at Stony Point and took Fort Montgomery and Fort Clinton on 6 October with competent dispatch and the loss of only forty-one men.[1] He wrote to Burgoyne of those successes: '. . . and let him know that all of the obstructions on the river between us and Albany were removed. But I told him likewise that I must hold myself excused from either ordering or advising, though I should not relax in my exertions to facilitate his operations.'[2]

Even before Captain Campbell had reached Clinton, Burgoyne had put his men on reduced rations[3] and ordered them to conserve their ammunition. On 5 October he called his general officers to a council of war. He told them what his orders were and that he regarded them as positive.[4] He reported all that he had recently learned of Howe's activities and remoteness, of Clinton's situation and presumed progress up the lower Hudson. He said it was now evident that from the first his army had been intended to be risked and if necessary sacrificed in the interests of other undertakings.[5] Then he asked his officers, one by one, whether the Army could with honour retreat. Generals Frazer and Riedesel advocated immediate withdrawal to Ticonderoga; General Phillips would offer no opinion, and most of the rest thought the situation justified 'honourable withdrawal'. But Burgoyne repeated the mandatory nature of his orders and said he believed they required one more attempt to break through to Albany, where he still hoped they would find Clinton and essential supplies. What the Army would do if, battered and starving, they got to Albany and found no Clinton and no supplies, he did not say, but his officers deferred to his judgement and it was agreed to attack.

pp. 379, 380; also Hudleston, p. 196; and partly in Anderson, *Howe Brothers*, p. 261). [1] Freeman, iv. 520.

[2] Clements, Clinton, *Hist. Detail*, vi. C; also Willcox, p. 77 and note. This message was sent in a silver bullet and intercepted (Willcox, p. 77, note). It read: '*Nous y voila*, & nothing now between us but Gates. I sincerely hope this little success may facilitate your operations. In answer to your Letter of the 28th Septr. by C. C. I shall only say I can not presume to order, or even advise, for Reasons obvious. I heartily wish you Success, and am, etc., H. C.'

[3] Fonblanque, p. 291.

[4] 'Burgoyne's instructions were undoubtedly positive' (Fortescue, *HBA*, 2, iii. 241). [5] Burgoyne's Account before Parliament.

What advice would that council have received had it been honoured by the presence of the former Lieutenant-General Lord George Sackville? Would he have exuded as much optimism at Freeman's Farm on 5 October as was still emanating from Lord George Germain at Whitehall? On 12 November, when it was all over though he did not know it yet, Lord George wrote to his Cabinet colleague Lord Sandwich: 'Clinton's going up the Hudson is most probable, and a most interesting event for the success of the campaign.'[1]

At noon on 7 October Burgoyne renewed the fight.[2] He led some 1,500 of his best men, with ten guns, from his entrenched camp to feel out the enemy's strength and if possible drive Gates's left flank from the hills that menaced the British position. Gates, immediately informed of the movement, ordered General Morgan to 'begin the game'. In the fighting against Carleton in Canada and elsewhere, the gigantic hulk of Morgan and the marksmanship of his picked men from the back hills of Virginia and Pennsylvania had become famous. They co-ordinated their efforts with deadly effect—shooting from the treetops, signalling to one another with turkey calls, and sensing the unvoiced commands of their general. They began the game with deadly effect.

It was a game that Benedict Arnold insisted on joining immediately, again in spite of Gates's restraining order. He followed up Morgan with great vigour, and Burgoyne's men, though fighting well, were driven back into their camp. By that time the battle was general. Arnold attacked the British entrenchments and though wounded kept his horse and overwhelmed one section of Burgoyne's German troops who, not at their best in these unorthodox fighting conditions, retreated all too quickly. Lieutenant-Colonel Breyman of the Bennington relief party was killed; the Brunswick troops, according to Anburey and Morey, 'bolted', and General Riedesel and his officers had to draw their swords on their own men to get them back into line. Night ended an action that was unquestionably a defeat for the British troops. General Frazer, conspicuous in

---

[1] Germain to Sandwich, 12 Nov. 1777; *Sandwich Papers*, i. 311.

[2] The account of the second battle is drawn from many sources, but chiefly from Lecky, iv. 63 ff.; Stone, pp. 56 ff.; Fonblanque, pp. 292 ff.; Hudleston, pp. 200 ff.; Kingsford, vi. 210 ff.; Fortescue, *HBA*, 2, iii, and Burgoyne's dispatches and later statements.

full uniform on a large grey horse, was a natural target for
Morgan's men; he fell mortally wounded and was replaced by
young Lord Balcarres. Sir Francis Clarke was killed and Acland
shot through both legs and taken prisoner. Burgoyne emerged
from the thick of the fight with one bullet-hole through his hat
and another through his waistcoat, but according to his officers
displayed nothing but the most reassuring cheerfulness then and
throughout the dark days that followed.

That night it was evident that the British camp was no longer
tenable. Burgoyne must have undergone mental agony as he
yielded to the necessity of even a short retreat in the face of the
enemy, but to remain in his present position would have been
foolhardy. He fell back nearly to the place where his troops had
first crossed the Hudson, obliged to leave his sick and wounded
in the abandoned camp with a note to Gates from Burgoyne
asking that they be given care and protection. The request was
honoured.

The new camp was near Schuylerville, the home of the discarded general unhappily chafing at the bit in Albany. His mill
and barns overlooked Burgoyne's position and would also
impede the fire of Burgoyne's remaining artillery if the enemy
attacked from that direction. Burgoyne ordered them burned,
a military necessity for which Schuyler forgave him when the
two men met, assuring Burgoyne that he would have done the
same thing. There the British Army once again licked its wounds
—outnumbered, short of provisions, horses, powder, and guns,
and constantly compressed into a smaller and smaller area.
Baroness Riedesel wrote of the first night in that new camp:
'The greatest misery and confusion prevailed; the Commissaries
had forgotten to distribute provisions; there were plenty of
cattle but none had been killed. More than thirty officers, driven
by hunger, came to me. I had tea and coffee made for them and
shared my food with them.'[1] One wonders what the ordinary
soldiers got that night.

They got very little in the days that followed. The camp was
soon completely surrounded and so overlooked by snipers that
it was dangerous to light even the smallest fire after dark, and
the men lived chiefly on salt pork and an uncooked paste of
flour and water. The only water in the camp came from a single

[1] Baroness Riedesel, *Journal*, quoted by Hudleston, p. 206.

spring soon so muddied by heavy rain and constant use that many of the men drank only the rainwater they could catch in their busbys. They could not even relieve their feelings by firing back at the snipers, for Burgoyne had ordered them to save what little was left of their powder for a battle yet to come.And there were over two hundred women and children huddled in the camp.[1]

During those days Burgoyne received Clinton's message that he had cleared the way from Albany to New York, but by that time not New York but survival had become Burgoyne's objective. Clinton also said he could come no farther, and Burgoyne's last hope of relief vanished. As he read that message, his camp was being compressed within an area only a mile and a half long and half a mile wide, and General Lincoln had completely severed his communication line with Canada; harried the garrison at Ticonderoga, and captured some 300 men and most of Burgoyne's boats. Retreat to Canada was now out of the question.

On that very day Howe, who had entered Philadelphia on 26 September,[2] wrote to Clinton to send him 'without delay' three regiments, three battalions, and any new reinforcements he had under his command in New York, except, as Clinton later quoted Howe's order: '. . . I should be on the eve of accomplishing some very material and essential stroke, being at liberty in that case to proceed upon it, provided I judged it might be executed in a few days after the receipt of his letter'.[3]

Even had Clinton received that dispatch while leading a force briskly to Albany, Howe could not have left his old friend Burgoyne more in the lurch if he had planned it that way. But unfortunately for Burgoyne, Clinton was 'on the eve' of no such 'material and essential stroke'. Howe's order reached him on 15 October, not while Clinton was moving up the Hudson but after he had returned to New York. He had hurried back there on receiving word that his two senior generals, Robertson

---

[1] The official returns of the British regiments on 22 Nov. 1777 when captive in Cambridge, according to the Heath papers, indicate that there were then 215 women with the British captives, and a provision return of the German troops at the same time included another 82 women. This was a larger female contingent than that officially reported at the start of the campaign. An interesting speculation.

[2] Clements, Clinton, *Hist. Detail*; also Willcox, p. 80.

[3] Fonblanque, pp. 304, 305.

and Leslie, had fallen ill. That meant the command would devolve upon 'an unworthy Hessian . . . nobody but drunken General Schmidt. . . . I therefore determined to return myself'. He sent Howe most of the men he had requested, and, as it turned out, Howe's order had no effect on Burgoyne's situation.

Clinton had left most of his 3,000 men up the Hudson under the command of General Vaughan, with orders to do what he could to create a diversion in favour of Burgoyne and thereafter return to New York without delay. Vaughan got no nearer to Albany than 45 miles, and from Burgoyne's point of view might as well have been back in New York, to which Vaughan and his small force soon returned.

On 12 October Burgoyne called another council of his officers, at which it was decided to attempt a further retreat by night, leaving behind most of the remaining guns and baggage. But at that point Burgoyne's scouts returned to report that no move, even at night, could be made without immediate and fatal discovery. The plan was abandoned and another council held on 13 October, at which Burgoyne said that: '. . . should General Clinton be where reported, yet the distance is such as to render any relief from him improbable during the time when our provisions could be made to last'.[1] He then asked whether there was any alternative to capitulation, and whether to capitulate would be dishonourable. At that point a cannon-ball whizzed through the tent where the council of war was assembled.[2] It was promptly agreed that to capitulate would not be dishonourable.

Burgoyne began negotiations with Gates, using all his literary skill to avoid officially admitting the obvious facts that he was beaten and must surrender. In this he was remarkably successful. Gates was not in a mood to quibble over words if he could capture the whole British Army without the risks and losses of a final desperate battle. He too was uncertain of Clinton's exact location, strength, and intentions, and wanted to get Burgoyne's surrender before his own rear might be threatened. He agreed to very generous terms, and in the final negotiations Burgoyne extracted further face-saving concessions. The British troops would be permitted to march out of their camp with their colours flying and need ground their arms only at the command

[1] Hudleston, p. 208.   [2] Kingsford, vi. 234-7.

of their own officers. Passage would be granted to the 'Army under Lieutenant General Burgoyne to Great Britain upon condition of not serving again in North America during the present contest, and the port of Boston is assigned for the entry of transports to receive the troops whenever General Howe shall so order'. The word 'surrender' was not used: the agreement was a 'convention' and Burgoyne would never allow it to be called anything else. No army in such dire straits could have hoped for better terms, and, so long as Gates and his men determined the matter, the terms were observed and the treatment of the captured British soldiers was extremely humane.

The Convention was signed by Gates and Burgoyne on 16 October.[1] Gates himself was a pattern of chivalry to Burgoyne and the officers' ladies, and when Burgoyne handed him his sword Gates returned it with compliments. General Schuyler made Burgoyne his house-guest for some days in Albany, and Washington, in later correspondence with Burgoyne, addressed him as an equal brother officer. The Continental Congress was not, however, equally gallant or complacent about the terms arranged by Gates. It considered them too generous, and later, perhaps with justification, revoked them.

As for Burgoyne, he consoled himself that though he had lost an army he had at least not lost his honour or that of his country. His ordeal in America, brief but agonizing, was nearly at an end. His ordeal in England, longer and perhaps no less painful to a man of his pride, would soon begin, and in that ordeal his chief antagonist would be Lord George Germain.

---

[1] Fortescue, *HBA*, 2, iii. 241.

XVIII

RECRIMINATIONS

BURGOYNE's men admired him too much to blame him for their captivity. They also largely exonerated Clinton (except, perhaps, from excess of caution) as soon as they learned how, under the limitations of his orders and his manpower, he had done all he could. They could not so easily hold Howe blameless for his apparent bad judgement, or disobedience of orders, or indifference to their fate. Yet military men liked Howe: he had been a friend of Burgoyne, and was not the kind of man to leave comrades in arms unassisted. They concluded, with Burgoyne, that there must have been some blunder among the politicians of Whitehall. Anburey probably voiced the captive army's consensus of opinion when he wrote from internment in Cambridge, on 17 November:

It was universally understood throughout the army, that the object of our expedition was to effect a junction with that under General Howe. . . . You can easily conceive the astonishment it occasioned, when we were informed that General Howe's army had gone to Philadelphia. . . . I am too much afraid those at the head of our affairs too implicitly credited every report, and are continually led away by the false information of men who are interested in the deception, and are profiting by the common calamities of England and America.

Three days later Anburey added: 'That some great error has been committed, either unintentional or designed, must be evident to everyone—where to fix it is impossible to say. But time, that great discloser of all secrets, will no doubt reveal this.'[1]

A loyalist previously devoted to Howe sounded the same note when he wrote from New York, on 10 November:

There has been a strange fatality in this affair. We had an army of about 30,000 men, lying idle here till the latter end of July; yet no attempt was made to open Hudson's River, through which channel only, provisions and other necessaries could be sent to

---

[1] Anburey, ii. 4, 19; 17 and 20 Nov. 1777.

Burgoyne. . . . When General Howe went to the Southward he left no more troops here than were barely sufficient to defend the place, so that nothing could be undertaken, offensively, against the Rebels, till about the beginning of October, when General Robertson arrived, with a reinforcement of near 2000 men. General Sir Henry Clinton, immediately after this, formed an expedition against the Highlands.[1]

The mystery remained, and men rushed to explain it as nature rushes to fill a vacuum. Every American, loyalist or rebel; every Englishman, Whig or Tory, chose his explanation and his scapegoat according to his passions more than his knowledge. Burgoyne again told his officers that the Powers in London must have intended to sacrifice the northern army, if necessary, to assure the success of some larger strategy. Howe had taken Philadelphia: was that the larger aim, and was it worth the price of Burgoyne's surrender? Clearly not, and it was rumoured that the Saratoga débâcle might lead the British to evacuate Philadelphia. What sort of strategy was that?

Meanwhile every British general who had played a major part in the events began to erect his own defences against blame. Burgoyne knew he would have to justify every step he had taken between Crown Point and the final surrender, and that to defend himself he would have to point elsewhere to the cause of his defeat. He was in no doubt that the fault lay in the inflexibility of his own orders and in some confusion in Howe's mind or Howe's orders. To exonerate himself he must point that out, and he lost no time. While a guest in the home of General Schuyler in Albany, a few days after the surrender, Burgoyne began to put his pen to work. As soon as possible he sent Lord George Germain a detailed report of those final weeks; and, wise in the ways of politics, he sent a copy to his friend the Earl of Derby. If Lord George suppressed Burgoyne's report, then Derby could make it public. Lord George did withhold, at first, parts of Burgoyne's report that were critical of his orders, until he found that Lord Derby was showing his copy widely about London. To Lord George and his supporters, that was a further reason for condemning Burgoyne. Lord George's attitude was doubtless reflected in his friend Irwin's letter to the Earl of Buckinghamshire on 20 December:

. . . Gen'l Burgoyne's letter does him harm in the publick. His

[1] J. Bew, *Historical Anecdotes*, London, 1779, p. 26.

charge against ministers with regard to his orders, is thought unfair; those who are in the secret of them say it is unjust; however the ministers are determined to let the blame lie at their doors till his return, before they expose his orders to the publick view. You will I presume be astonished to know that Genl. Burgoyne sent a duplicate of his letter to Lord George to Lord Derby, and that his Lordship was actually reading to the company at Almack's that letter, much about the time Lord George sent the original to the King at the Queen's house. This makes much conversation.[1]

It did indeed make conversation, though by no means as adverse to Burgoyne as Irwin reported. The Opposition embraced the opportunity Burgoyne's letter gave them to criticize the Ministry and especially Lord George. Most sophisticated Englishmen knew that Burgoyne had sent a copy to the earl to make sure that his own defence was not quietly interred in the files of the Secretary for America. His procedure was not unusual in such circumstances and it almost certainly did him more good than harm. He was not in London to speak for himself, and had no other recourse, but his letter was a declaration of war on Lord George and the Ministry, which was by no means content to 'let the blame lie at their doors'. Cabinet discussions were immediately held as to how Burgoyne could be prevented, upon his eventual return to England, from gaining a public hearing to air his embarrassing views.

Burgoyne had also taken a prompt step to make his position clear to the king. On 20 October he had written to Colonel Phillipson, aide to George III:

. . . I foresaw, and believe expressed to you, that passing Hudson River was putting the fate of the army upon a chance, but that the precision of my orders, the season of the year, and other circumstances of the time, made the step unavoidable. I enclose to Lord Derby a copy of my dispatches to Lord George, in order that it may be published by him in case the Ministry should mangle or curtail any part of it in their Gazette. . . . I do it to furnish you with means of defending your friend against the attacks that necessarily follow unsuccessful events. I expect ministerial ingratitude will be displayed, as in all countries and all times has been usual, to remove the blame from the order to its execution . . . .

It was the will of the State to risk a corps of troops to assist the great general arrangement of the campaign. This army . . . has been

---

[1] Irwin to Buckinghamshire, 20 Dec. 1777; *HMC, Lothian*, i. 324.

totally unsupported by Sir William Howe. When my conduct for proceeding so far as to leave my communication with Canada is arraigned, face the accusation with the wording of my instructions, and ask the accusers what they would have said had I remained supine at Fort Edward ... orders, in the construction of which there was neither latitude nor alternative, compelled me to lay by, in consequence, the general maxims of military reasoning upon securing a retreat. ... I am impatient, you may imagine, to be at home to undertake my own cause, but I think it indispensable to be directed entirely by Sir William Howe.[1]

Burgoyne was indeed eager to get to London to speak in his own defence, and he was still a member of the House of Commons. That was the chief reason for his prompt request to Howe, his superior officer in America, for authorization to sail for England. Burgoyne's health had suffered during the last gruelling weeks of his ordeal, and he gave that as the primary reason for his wish to get home. He may have felt privately that Howe had let him down badly, but he did no more than hint at that in his letters to Howe. He needed Howe's help, and he had already decided that the real villain of the piece was Lord George Germain.

Howe and Clinton had similar fears of being blamed and misrepresented at home, and similar convictions about Lord George. Each shared Burgoyne's belief that no general 3,000 miles from London could defend himself against the kind of whispering campaign of detraction Lord George might organize. The only way to get back to London soon was to resign; it was also customary for commanders in the field to offer their resignations when something went seriously wrong, though not customary to accept them out of hand. To both men resignation had other attractions. Clinton was so frustrated and disgusted with Howe as well as Lord George that he did not want to continue to serve in America under either man. He had hardly reached New York from his raid up the Hudson before he 'renewed my solicitation for leave to return home, as I plainly saw that my continuance in America was not likely to contribute to the service of my country or the advancement of my own honour ... but I was obliged to submit to the mortification of enduring my situation somewhat longer'.[2]

---

[1] Burgoyne to Col. R. B. Phillipson, 20 Oct. 1777; *Sandwich Papers*, i. 306–9.
[2] Clements, Clinton, *Historical Detail*; also Willcox, *Amer. Rebellion*, p. 84.

Aware that his conduct was vulnerable, Howe may have thought it wise to offer his resignation before it was requested, but he was disgusted by what he believed was Lord George's failure to support him properly and Lord George's tendency to over-advise him. On 22 October, almost immediately on hearing news of Burgoyne's surrender, he wrote to Lord George a letter that served three purposes. It stated his own defence; it warned Lord George that if he put the blame for Saratoga on General Howe, then General Howe could prove that all his actions had been approved in advance by Lord George, and it offered his resignation in terms that, if read by others, would challenge Lord George's management of the war:

I was surprized to find the General's [Burgoyne's] declaration in his message to Sir Henry Clinton by Captain Campbell 'that he would not have given up his communications with Ticonderoga had he not expected a co-operating army at Albany', since in my letter to Sir Guy Carleton, a copy of which was transmitted to your Lordship in my dispatch of 2nd April, No. 47, and of which his Majesty was pleased to approve, I positively mentioned that no direct assistance could be given by the southern army. This letter I am assured was received by Sir Guy Carleton and carried by him to Montreal before General Burgoyne's departure from thence.

And Howe ended his letter with this request:

From the little attention, my Lord, given to my recommendations since the commencement of my command, I am led to hope I may be relieved from this very painful service, wherein I have not the good fortune to enjoy the necessary confidence and support of my superiors, but which I conclude will be extended to Sir H. Clinton, my presumptive successor, or to such other servant as the King may be pleased to appoint. By the return therefore of the packet I humbly request I may receive his Majesty's permission to resign the command.[1]

While Howe was composing that letter, one from Burgoyne was on its way to him. That letter summarized the final weeks of the campaign, the final exhaustion of his provisions and ammunition, the undependability of his Indians, Canadians, and loyalists, and the reduction of his regular troops to 3,500 of

---

[1] Howe to Germain, PRO, 30/55, no. 74; also PRO, CO/5, v. 94, 729–34; also PRO, CO/5, v. 253, no. 155; also *HMC, Stop. Sack.* ii. 80.

which 'not 2000' were British. It told of his encirclement by an enemy army of 16,000 men, and then continued:

Conscious that the precision of my orders both in letters and in spirit left me no latitude in abandoning my communications on the 13th of September, that the corps of troops I commanded was in the interest of the Government a corps to be hazarded for the great purpose of effecting a junction, or at least of making a powerful diversion in your favour, by employing forces that would otherwise join General Washington, convinced that I can justify myself to my profession and to the world upon these points, I am in no pain concerning them. . . . But I think it necessary to give my own account of my own conduct at home, and to precede the troops if it can be done with propriety.[1]

Five days later Burgoyne again wrote to Howe:

It is now demonstrated that even a relief from famine would not have effected any junction with Sir H. Clinton. His strength and his situation were not such as to oblige Gates to desist, and my force was too inadequate, and the country much too strong to cut my way thro' the whole . . . if ministers blame me for this devotion of myself and troops upon the principle and spirit and letter of their measures and their orders, and such ingratitude in Cabinets is not uncommon —I am called by the feelings of personal honour to exhibit my defense to my profession and the world.

He called on Howe 'as my friend . . . to furnish me with means to effect my passage to England for these great personal reasons'.[2] A few days later he repeated his 'impatient desire' to return to England,[3] and on 21 November he wrote once more from Cambridge to say he had requested a passport from Congress to embark on a frigate at Rhode Island, since both his 'business and his health' required his immediate presence in England.[4]

Howe replied to most of Burgoyne's letters in friendly terms, though without special warmth.[5] There is no evidence that he greatly bestirred himself to help Burgoyne get to England, or that he put any impediments in Burgoyne's way. Meanwhile

---

[1] Burgoyne to Howe, 20 Oct. 1777; PRO, 30/55, no. 707 (marked 'recd. 30 October'); also summarized in HMC, Stop. Sack. ii. 78.

[2] Burgoyne to Howe, 25/27 Oct. 1777; PRO, 30/55, no. 716.

[3] Burgoyne to Howe, ibid., no. 740.

[4] Burgoyne to Howe, 21 Nov. 1777; ibid., no. 753.

[5] Howe to Burgoyne, 14 Nov. 1777, 19 Dec. 1777, 5 Feb. 1778, and 21 Feb. 1778; ibid., nos. 744, 813, 928, and 958.

Burgoyne was coping with more immediate problems, and some of his actions showed why he was known as Gentleman John. To ameliorate the personal difficulties of his troops in captivity in Cambridge, he advanced twenty thousand pounds from his own modest fortune, which brought his affairs to a 'distressed condition'.[1] Among the beneficiaries may have been Colonel Philip Skene, who had been made a prisoner at Saratoga.[2]

Clinton was more sympathetic than Howe in a letter which addressed Burgoyne as 'my dear friend', and did not disguise his disagreement with Howe's decision to move on Philadelphia:

> I feared indeed, and I was not silent on the subject, that when our force was removed out of the power of cooperating with you, such numbers would press upon you from the four contiguous provinces as might overwhelm you. I had still, however, a hope that the Commander in Chief might get possession of Philadelphia and send me reinforcements from thence early enough to enable me to do something in your favour; that I should have succeeded, had he sent me those reinforcements, I will (now that I have seen the country) by no means assert. . . . I should at least have had the satisfaction of having endeavored to assist you, though, in truth, report at that time did not represent you as in need of any succours. As it was, I cannot but flatter myself that the stroke which the late and scanty reinforcement of recruits enabled me to make was of service to you in your Convention, which I agree was most favourable.
>
> Could you with reason, my dear friend, expect that I should form the most distant idea of penetrating to Albany? Had I thought that with the small number I could have spared from thence I could have been equal to forcing the Highlands, I should not have conceived myself justified in detaching part of my garrison further, without extraordinary motives. . . . As for having applied to me for orders, I could never be expected to give any, ignorant as I was of your plans and those of the Commander in Chief.[3]

Among Clinton's private papers lay a memorandum with the imprint of his own hand and style. Perhaps it was written in the bitter moments after Saratoga; perhaps a few months later: the date does not alter its significance:

Had Sir William fortified the hills around Boston he could not have been disgracefully driven from it; had he pursued his victory at

[1] Pigot to Howe, 12 Jan. 1778; ibid., no. 868.
[2] Ibid., no. 904.
[3] Clinton to Burgoyne, 16 Dec. 1777; Fonblanque, pp. 324, 325.

Long Island he had ended the rebellion; had he landed above the
lines at New York not a man could have escaped him; had he co-
operated with the Northern Army he had saved it, or had he gone
to Philadelphia by land he had ruined Mr. Washington and his
forces; but, as he did none of these things, had he gone to the D . . . l
before he was sent to America, it had been the saving of infamy to
himself and indelible dishonour to his country.[1]

Carleton too wrote to Burgoyne in commiseration at his victi-
mization by 'ministers', and left no doubt at all that he meant
Lord George Germain: 'This unfortunate event, it is to be
hoped, will in future prevent ministers from pretending to direct
operations of war in a country at 3000 miles distance, of which
they have so little knowledge as not to be able to distinguish
between good, bad, or interested advices, or to give positive
orders in matters which from their nature are ever upon the
change.'[2]

While the generals were exchanging post-mortems over Saratoga, men in London were still unaware of the surrender, but
increasingly apprehensive. The Opposition had begun in late
September to harry the Secretary for America with questions,
criticisms, dire predictions, and embarrassing demands for
copies of orders and dispatches to the generals. Bad news travels
faster than good, and rumours faster than truth, especially on
the pen of an alert gossip like Horace Walpole, who had written
as early as 26 October: 'Burgoyne is said to be beaten.'[3]
Walpole was a Cassandra, for all he could then have known was
of the Bennington disaster some six weeks before. But premoni-
tion was in the air. Early in November the Opposition demanded
to be given the facts about the plans and the current situation
in America, and moved for all papers connected with Burgoyne's
campaign. The Ministry's majority voted down the motion,[4]
and dodged further trouble by getting Parliament adjourned
for a week. 'They could not meet', said Shelburne, 'the force of
their opponents' objections. Talk to them about the truth! Like
Pilate they waived the question and adjourned the court.'[5]

When Parliament reconvened on 18 November, it was opened
by a speech from the throne. During the intervening week

---

[1] Clements, *Clinton Papers*.
[2] Carleton to Burgoyne, 12 Nov. 1777; Fonblanque, p. 318.
[3] Walpole to Mann, 26 Oct. 1777; Toynbee, x. 143.
[4] Fitzmaurice, *Shelburne*, iii. 12.   [5] *Hansard*, xix. 614.

unconfirmed reports had reached London that Burgoyne was in serious trouble, but the address made no mention of that, and was full of optimistic clichés. Lord Sandwich of the Admiralty seemed especially confident, and as late as 20 November Lord George declared: 'There was every reason to hope for success in America.'[1] It was moved by the supporters of the Ministry to accept and approve with thanks the speech from the throne, but Pitt, now the frail and invalid Earl of Chatham, moved an amendment which in effect discredited the Ministry for its failures in America. In the debate that followed, the Earl of Shelburne, who claimed to have from military sources authoritative information of Burgoyne's disaster, castigated the Ministry for its misleading account of present and future successes:

The issue of Mr. Burgoyne's expedition is too melancholy to be made a subject of conversation; his army, by every appearance, is destroyed; but supposing the contrary, and that not finding it practicable to push forward, he has been so fortunate as to effect a retreat to Ticonderoga, or any of the other posts he left behind him; nay, granting more than the modesty of the Administration will permit them even so much as to suggest, that by subsequent successes he has formed a junction with General Clinton and has reached New York; what end would this answer, but that at the expense of many millions, and two campaigns, he has reached a place by land, which he could without the least trouble or interruption have reached by sea, in almost as many weeks.[2]

On the same day Charles James Fox put his finger on the mistakes the Ministry had made in its strategy and management of the American war, and his ideas resembled those of Carleton in his letter written to Burgoyne just four days earlier:

There was a fundamental error in the proceedings which would for ever prevent our generals from acting with success; that no man with common sense would have placed the two armies in such a position as from their distance made it absolutely impossible that the one should receive any assistance from the other. That the war carried on by General Burgoyne was a war of posts; that the taking one did not subdue the country, but that it would be necessary to conquer it inch by inch: that his army was not equal to the task.[3]

[1] *Hansard*, xix. 434.
[2] *Hansard*, xix. 384; 18 Nov. 1777; also Fitzmaurice, *Shelburne*, iii. 12; see also Shelburne to Price, 24 Sept. 1777, and Carleton to Shelburne, Aug. and Sept. 1777.
[3] J. Wright, *Speeches of Fox*, Longmans, London, 1815; i. 93.

The burden of reply fell largely on Lord George, since other members of the Ministry were, or seemed to be, remarkably un-informed regarding strategy and operations in America. Some of them had not shared the optimism Lord George professed. Lord Barrington, for example, had written confidentially to the Earl of Buckinghamshire in Dublin on 1 November: 'We are full of anxious expectation of news from Howe and Burgoyne',[1] but Barrington, though Secretary at War, did not seem very clear just what instructions had been sent to either general.

In his statement to the House of Commons on 20 November, Lord George was on the defensive. He implied that Burgoyne was largely to blame. 'The whole of the plan was suggested by Genl. Burgoyne who came hither authorized by Carleton to explain his Ideas, little Alteration was made and the Instructions sent to Carleton were seen and approved by the General who was to execute them.'[2] Lord George did not see fit to mention that, from the time he first saw his orders, Burgoyne repeatedly expressed discomfort at their inflexibility.

When the Opposition suggested that the Ministry had failed to instruct Howe and Burgoyne properly, Lord George replied:

With regard to the Canada expedition, the honourable gentleman was under a mistake when he imagined that General Burgoyne had orders to fight his way to New York, there to join Sir William Howe: that his orders were to clear the country of rebels as far as Albany, which town was prescribed to him as the boundary of his expedition, unless circumstances might make it necessary to cooperate with General Howe, in which case he was to assist him to the utmost of his power.[3]

Lord George did not mention that Burgoyne's orders were certainly 'to force his way to Albany', which was the real question, and he was fortunate that Opposition members of the House could not see the actual orders and compare them with Lord George's interpretation of them. In a memorandum he had himself written shortly before his speech, Lord George had stated: 'Burgoyne in his plan does not require or expect any assistance in facilitating his approach to Albany.'[4] Every letter

---

[1] Barrington to Buckinghamshire, 1 Nov. 1777; *HMC, Lothian*, i. 318.
[2] Memo. in Germain's hand in Clements Coll., *Germain Papers*, viii. 8/67.
[3] *Hansard*, xix. 434.
[4] Memo. in Germain's hand in Clements, *Germain Papers*, viii. 8/67.

Burgoyne had written to Lord George and to Howe since leaving Plymouth contradicted Lord George's statement.

Lord George's assurances to Parliament were a nice example of the distortion of the full truth by statements of partial truth. By the time a listener had sifted out Lord George's confusions of phrase, he must have concluded that if Lord George's orders to his generals were no clearer than his explanations, disaster was indeed in the making. The House got no clarification on its paramount immediate question: Had Howe been ordered to meet Burgoyne at Albany, or at least to assist him if necessary to get there? And, if 'circumstances made it necessary to co-operate with General Howe', in what ways were the two armies, one at Philadelphia and the other at Albany, expected to co-operate?

The Opposition also questioned Lord George's reiterated insistence on the great numbers and devotion of loyalists in America. Most Englishmen were reaching Walpole's conclusion of 1 September: 'In one thing alone all that come from America agree, that the alienation from this country is incredible and universal.'[1] But the Ministry maintained its majority and voted down Chatham's amendment to the reply to the king's address by 243 to 86. The historian Gibbon, who supported the Ministry, confessed to Walpole that: '. . . if it had not been for shame, there were not twenty men in the House but were ready to vote for peace'.[2]

The vote did not silence the Opposition, and the Ministry seemed uncertain whether to defend itself by fixing the blame on Howe or on Burgoyne. The Opposition's chief target was Lord George Germain. Fox led the attack. He declared that:

. . . ever since the day that nobleman forced himself into adminis-tration, our affairs began rapidly to decline. That it was the measures which he dictated to the ministry, that drove the Americans to a declaration of independence; and that as he was the cause of the continuance of the war, so he ought not only to be removed from the management of our officers, but be made to know, that a minister was accountable to the nation for the orders he gave, and the measures he advised.[3]

[1] Walpole to Mann, 1 Sept. 1777; Toynbee, x. 103.
[2] Walpole, *Last Journals*, ii. 76; late Nov. 1777.
[3] Wright, *Speeches of Fox*, i. 94; 18 Nov. 1777.

A little later Fox accused Lord George of being chiefly responsible for the barbarities perpetrated by Indians under British
sponsorship: 'For the past two years that certain noble lord has
presided over American affairs, the most violent scalping, tomahawk measures have been pursued—bleeding has been his only
prescription.'[1]

Lord George occasionally turned so quickly from his usual
confident superiority to apology that it is hard to believe he did
not adopt humility as an expedient pose. He seemed to wilt
under Fox's attack, and most of his contemporaries thought his
dismay genuine. Horace Walpole wrote that Fox's attack
'. . . was felt in the deepest manner by Lord George, who rose
in the utmost consternation, and made the poorest figure . . .
pleaded having been invited into the service by Lord North,
and declared himself ready to quit it . . . his confusion led him
into a wretched defense. . . . Lord North handsomely defended
Lord George.'[2] A few days later Lord George made a statement
so inconsistent with all his previous professions and actions that
it must have seemed an aberration: 'Lord George Germaine, to
the astonishment of everybody, confessed that, if America was
to be conquered by force, it would be of no utility.'[3]

That statement came from Lord George the day after the
rumours of disaster at Saratoga had been unofficially confirmed.
On 1 December General Irwin wrote: 'There are bad reports,
however they are still but reports, about General Burgoyne.
I find Howe knows nothing more of him than we do.'[4] On that
day, too, Lord George informed the king that: 'The news from
Sir Henry Clinton and Major General Vaughan is much to their
honor. Lt. General Burgoyne's situation is bad at any rate but
it is to be hoped not so very bad as reported by the rebels.'[5]

According to Colonel Leland, Lord George began the next
day cheerfully: 'I saw Lord George Germain this morning, who
seemed serene and in good spirits.'[6] But on 3 December the
news was confirmed in letters from Carleton and all England
was shocked and angry—all the more so because most men did

---

[1] Wright, *Speeches of Fox*, i. 99.
[2] Walpole, *Last Journals*, ii. 76; late Nov. 1777.
[3] Ibid., p. 80; 2 Dec. 1777.
[4] Irwin to Buckinghamshire, 1 Dec. 1777; *HMC, Lothian*, i. 324.
[5] Germain to King, 1 Dec. 1777; Fortescue, *Corresp.* iii. 501.
[6] Leland to Bute, 2 Dec. 1777; *HMC, Lothian*, i. 326.

not know whom to be angry with. 'The consternation at first was great, and it was generally thought the Administration would be changed.'[1] Stocks fell and did not recover.[2] A few days later Anthony Morris Storer, later Minister to France, wrote to George Selwyn: 'You have no idea what an effect this news has had on the minds of people in town. Those who never felt before feel now. Those who were almost indifferent to American affairs are now awakened out of their lethargy, and see to what a dreadful situation we are reduced. Everyone is at fault at this dreadful check. Where the blame is, nobody can fix; all seem, however, to be willing to excuse Burgoyne.'[3]

At first Howe was thought chiefly to blame. 'Howe's going round to Chesapeak instead of going to join Burgoyne, is censured much, and it now begins to be said, that he has not capacity for the place he is in', the Loyalist Thomas Hutchinson wrote in his diary on 1 December,[4] and some two weeks later he added: 'The clamour increases against the Howes, who ought to be heard before they are condemned.'[5] For the first time the nation as a whole realized that it was likely to lose its American colonies altogether; that its Ministry was of very doubtful competence, and that the defeat at Saratoga would probably induce France to give active military and naval aid to the Americans, and thus create a major war in Europe as well. The public mood changed from initial confidence to confusion, from confusion to frustration, and from frustration to what Hutchinson called 'universal dejection'.

The Opposition had reached such heights of vituperation before the bad news was confirmed that they had few superlatives of denunciation left, and the speeches of Fox, Burke, Barré, Shelburne, and Richmond were less effective because they were repetitive. Even Fox could not improve on his attack of 18 November:

An army of 10,000 men destroyed through ignorance, the obstinate willful ignorance and incapacity of the noble Lord called loudly for vengeance. . . . A gallant general sent like a victim to be slaughtered, when his own skill and personal bravery would have

---

[1] Walpole, *Last Journals*, ii. 80.   [2] Lecky, iv. 74.
[3] Storer to Selwyn, 11 Dec. 1777; Jesse, *Selwyn*, iii. 248.
[4] Hutchinson, *Diaries*, ii. 169; 1 Dec. 1777.
[5] Hutchinson, *Diaries*, ii. 172; 18 Dec. 1777.

earned him laurels, if he had not been under the direction of a
blunderer, which circumstance alone was the cause of his disgrace.
. . . The General and the House had been imposed on and deceived;
Burgoyne's orders were to make his way to Albany, there to wait the
orders of Sir William Howe and to cooperate with him; but General
Howe knew nothing of this matter, for he had gone to a different
country, and left the unhappy Burgoyne and his troops to take care
of themselves.

Lord George Germain, Fox concluded, was 'solely responsible'
for the 'lamentable situation'.[1]

Lord George remained silent before most of the attacks. But
when on 3 December Colonel Isaac Barre rose in Commons and
directly addressing him: '. . . called upon the noble Lord to
declare upon his honour, what was become of General Burgoyne
and his brave troops, and whether or not he had received
expresses from Quebec informing him of his having surrendered
himself, with his whole army prisoners of war',[2] that noble Lord
replied lamely that the surrender of Burgoyne was not officially
confirmed,[3] and that he hoped the House would not be 'over-
anxious in condemnation, nor decide on the propriety or impropriety of the concerted plan that led to this unhappy event.
He hoped they would suspend their judgments both on the
conduct of the general and of the minister on this occasion. For
his part he declared he was willing to submit his conduct in
planning the expedition to the judgment of the House.'[4]

A long debate followed, which Lord North ended by expressing 'his sorrow at the unhappy news', his assurance that
no man would do more than he to obtain peace—but he also
talked of his need for more funds to continue the war until
peace could be arranged. He added the somewhat elliptical
comment: 'As to the noble Lord in the American department,
he trusted he had acted on the soundest principles of candour and
deliberation.'[5]

Fox then moved for 'Copies of all Instructions and other
Papers, relative to the expedition from Canada under lieutenant
general Burgoyne, and also a copy of such parts of the instructions

---

[1] Wright, *Speeches of Fox*, i. 94; 18 Nov. 1777.
[2] *Hansard*, xix. 533; 3 Dec. 1777; also Fitzmaurice, *Shelburne*, iii. 12.
[3] But Carleton's dispatches reached him some time that day.
[4] *Hansard*, xix. 534.   [5] Ibid.

given to general sir William Howe, as relate to any intended co-operation with lieut.-general Burgoyne'. That motion was defeated by the Ministry forces,[1] and Walpole commented: 'The Parliament was so thoroughly corrupted and stanch that the Court took heart.'[2] But individual members of parliament continued to volunteer opinions on the American situation and the Ministry's blunders. Commenting on the Ministry's defeat of Fox's motion, David Heatley, who seldom spoke in the House, told its members that: 'Since the noble lord at the head of the American department came into office, his Majesty has been advised not to lay the least scrap of information before the House. . . . We know that he is responsible.'[3] Colonel Barre returned to the attack. He was '. . . shocked at the cool, easy manner in which the noble lord related the state of the brave Burgoyne. . . . Nobody could say that Burgoyne had failed through his own misconduct; the minister who had planned the expedition was to blame; it was an inconsistent scheme, an unpracticable one, and rather too absurd for an Indian chief.'[4]

The situation was saved, for the time, when the Ministry arbitrarily adjourned Parliament earlier than usual before Christmas, and kept it adjourned for six weeks.[5] But though Lord George had been able to prevent the relevant papers from getting before the Whigs in Parliament he could not refuse them to the king. When he sent them to George III in mid-December he included a note of his own that hinted what his personal defence would be:

'Lord George Germain has the honor of sending to your Majesty the Dispatches from Lt. General Burgoyne and Sr. Guy Carleton . . . the positive orders which Lt. General Burgoyne refers to, your Majesty will remember, but it was never understood that at such a distance any order would be positive, in the present case the words of the order will not bear the strict construction the General put upon them.'[6] What the king thought of Lord George's actual phrasing of the orders when he saw them on 15 December was not revealed, but what he thought of

---

[1] *Hansard*, xix. 541, 542.
[2] Walpole, *Last Journals*, ii. 81; early Dec. 1777.
[3] *Hansard*, xix. 555.
[4] *Hansard*, xix. 534.
[5] Lecky, iv. 75; also, Pitt, *Corresp*. iv. 454 ff.
[6] Germain to King, 15 Dec. 1777; Fortescue, *Corresp*. iii. 514.

Lord George's attacks on Carleton, and of the efforts to silence
Burgoyne on his return from America, emerged in time.

Thus ended the eventful year of 1777. The fortunate imminence of Christmas saved Lord George from a climax of condemnation that might have forced his resignation or dismissal.
It gave Lord George and Lord North six weeks to plan their
defences before Parliament met again. But what defences could
Lord George build; what scapegoat could he find upon whom
he could successfully load all the blame for Saratoga? It was not
a pleasant holiday problem, and Lady Germain was ill.

The people of England were also not in a holiday mood.
Anger was blended with mortification at how low the power and
repute of British arms had fallen. Their Government seemed
incompetent, and the Opposition more noisy than effective. It
won every debate but lost all the crucial votes. How could it be
otherwise when the party in power had such advantages in
patronage, and made full use of them? Britain was losing a war
and the richest colonial empire since the halcyon days of Rome.
And new crises might lie ahead. In a month or so England might
find itself invaded by France or Spain and perhaps by both.
England's sons were being enlisted, pressed, wounded, captured,
killed; and all to what avail? Taxes were rising, prices mounting,
and stocks and bonds declining.

On the other side of the Atlantic, Burgoyne found little solace
in the dull alien society of Cambridge, and writhed in a series
of frustrations. He was concerned about the treatment and
welfare of his troops, and about the slowness of Congress to
implement Gates's promise that they might be taken home to
England. He was even more concerned to get to London quickly
himself. He had asked Congress and General Washington to
grant him parole, but Congress had not acted, and Howe was
not being too helpful. Meanwhile Howe awaited news regarding
his offer to resign, and Clinton, who was never really contented,
was even more unhappy. His own offer of resignation had been
declined with cordial praise of his conduct by Lord George, but
praise from that source had been demonstrated an unstable
foundation for the future. If Howe left, Clinton would probably
be made Commander-in-Chief, but he did not know whether
to be glad or sorry at that prospect. It was doubtful wisdom to
accept command of an army that might be badly supported, in

a war that could not be won. As for Carleton, even a Quebec winter was no more coldly bitter than his resentment against the man who had ruined his career and sent his army to be captured.

It was not a merry Christmas or a promising New Year for any of them.

XIX

EXPLANATIONS

No British government was ever more bitterly and persistently attacked than Lord North's Ministry over its conduct of the American war. No Ministry ever defended itself so weakly yet stayed in power so long. When it could, the Ministry evaded issues, and even tried to withhold the facts or discredit key witnesses for the Opposition. That strategy seemed to its critics a confession that the Ministry knew that, if revealed, some of its proceedings would be damning. The areas where the Ministry was most vulnerable, and tried to conceal the most, were those in which Lord George and the Earl of Sandwich were primarily responsible. To evade a difficult issue was characteristic of Lord North, but to discredit witnesses was more typical of Lord George and the First Lord of the Admiralty.

Even some devoted Ministry supporters were troubled or confused, and as the Opposition thundered they winced, sat silent, or left the House. But loyalty to the king, to Lord North, to their own faction or their own interests, kept them with the Ministry in the crucial votes. Lord North was the only member of the Cabinet who consistently defended Lord George, and then chiefly in the crises when Lord George's fall might pull down the Ministry as well. Other Ministers gave the impression of being reluctant to risk their own standing by defending Lord George, or else of being genuinely ignorant of the precise orders and events that led to Saratoga or, later, to Yorktown. Since the truth might be dangerous, it was safer to seem uninformed.

Some members of the Government, like Dartmouth and Gower, revised their opinions in deference to the facts. So did William Knox, Lord George's most trusted undersecretary, whose ownership of lands in the southern colonies had fortified his ardour against the American rebels. Soon after Saratoga he prepared a memorandum that began: 'The mode adopted for carrying on the war was founded on misinformation. It was represented that the root of disaffection lay in the Town of

Boston, and that if Rebelion could be crushed there it would die in all other parts. Experience has shewn the disaffection was general.'[1] But experience brought no such enlightenment to Lord George, and he did not adopt the principles of Knox's memorandum.

When Parliament reconvened about a month after Christmas, the Opposition promptly renewed its inquisition. The attackers had more talent, more eloquence, and better arguments than Lord North and his supporters, but one hard fact kept them from upsetting the Ministry: Lord North had the votes.

This did not mean that the majority of Englishmen in 1778 necessarily approved the Ministry's conduct of the war, or even the war itself. As the Duke of Richmond concluded before the news of Saratoga: '. . . the people begin to feel the continuance of the war, the losses, the taxes, the load of debt, and the impossibility of such success as to re-establish permanent tranquility'.[2] But Parliament was not so constituted as to represent the British people. Lord North's parliamentary strength lay not in those members of the House who reflected or even valued public opinion, but in the support of certain blocs which, in the main, did not. First of all were the hundred-odd adherents of his own organization and beneficiaries of his patronage. But they alone could not make a majority in the House of Commons.

The continuation of the North Ministry, and of the war, depended upon its ability to hold the support of two nominally independent groups, and only one of these was in the House of Commons. It consisted of the rural estate-holders who were not peers but were 'of independent fortune', known as the country gentlemen. By temperament and interest opposed to change, they preferred the monarch's leadership to that of the old Whig oligarchy or of any new régime that might alter the hegemony of country over town, farm over factory. Intellectually remote from the issues of the American war, they supported His Majesty's Government because they supported from habit the traditions inherent in the royal person; they thought and voted, in the words of Theodore Roosevelt, 'from the hips'. In 1775 they had wanted 'a greater exertion of power to reduce America

---

[1] Clements, *Knox Papers*, ix. 21.
[2] Albemarle, *Life of Rockingham*, ii. 348; also Lecky, iv. 74.

to its former state of order'.[1] After Saratoga they stood firmly by the Ministry, as its large majorities rejecting the motions of Chatham and Fox indicated.[2] But they did so with less conviction and not quite so automatically, for they were beginning to be uncomfortable about the American war and the competence of the Ministry either to win it or to end it satisfactorily. The *Annual Register* for 1778 recorded the change in their attitude: 'The country gentlemen were unusually blank. They saw not only an end to all their hopes of obtaining a revenue from America, but they found themselves saddled with the burthen of a war, which in point of expence proportional to the service or force expended, was infinitely more ruinous than any other in which the nation had ever been involved, without even a remote prospect of its being brought by any means to a conclusion.' They gave 'their silent votes, but nothing more than their silent votes to the Minister'.[3] But that description came from the pen or the followers of Burke, and was not without wishful thinking. It would better describe the attitude of the country gentlemen after Yorktown in late 1781 than after Saratoga in 1778.

Men's principles are sometimes unconsciously consistent with their interests, and the country gentlemen were losing enthusiasm over sustaining the principle of Parliament's rights over its colonies not only because the war was going badly, but because it was threatening to impair their comforts and their incomes. They were large landowners, and taxes on land were going up. They derived most of their revenue from crops, rents, and government bonds, and income from land and securities was going down. So was the market value of government bonds, the country gentleman's measure of the nation's credit and

[1] 'When there are 400 members in the house of commons, it may be assumed that 250 of them are ready in all questions *pedibus ire* after the premier. About 40 are as determined in all cases to go a contrary way, & in what relates to America there are about 30 Americans who always go with the 40. The remaining 80 are gentlemen of independent fortunes who have only the general good to make their object. Seven eighths of the last have upon principle always gone with administration in American matters, but in general they wish that there was a greater exertion of power to reduce America to its former state of order' (Clements, Hutchinson, *Diaries* (original MS.), p. 211; Feb. 1775).

[2] Richard Pares, *Limited Monarchy in Great Britain in the 18th Century*, a pamphlet published for the Historical Association by Kegan Paul, London, 1957, pp. 22, 25.

[3] *Annual Register for 1778*, p. 48.

society's stability. In January 1778 government three per cents.
were eight points lower than at the end of the fifth year of the
last great war with France.[1] Lord North was devoting all his
considerable financial skill to trying to pay for the war in ways
that would not arouse his constituents, but its increasing cost
made that impossible. The new excises he was compelled to
impose had not yet directly injured the country gentlemen, but
they were beginning to have painful indirect effects.

A second group whose support Lord North needed and cultivated was less important only because it had no place in the
House of Commons. But it could and did influence many a vote
there. This group consisted of the bishops, who were members
of the House of Lords. They had wide influence upon the clergy
at all levels, and the local clergymen often guided the political
thinking of their local communities. The hierarchy of the Church
derived their clerical promotions from the Ministry and the
Crown, and their futures depended upon the continued good
will of King and Court. The prelates did not hesitate to see that
their subordinates supported the North Ministry, for bishops
are not always ardent exponents of freedom of thought within
their own profession. 'Clergymen who in the fast-day sermons
distinguished themselves by violent attacks on the Americans
. . . were conspicuously selected for promotion.'[2] Lord North's
brother, Brownlow North, was then Bishop of Worcester by
grace of the recommendation of the First Minister, and that
grace would soon move him upward to become Bishop of
Winchester. He was an active supporter of the Ministry in the
House of Lords, and Lord North and his father the Earl of
Guilford corresponded intimately with the Archbishop of
Canterbury. Edmund Burke wrote of the clergy in general that
they were 'astonishingly warm' for the American war, and 'what
the Tories are when embodied and united with their natural
head, the Crown, and animated by their clergy, no man knows
better than yourself'.[3]

With the votes of placemen, country gentlemen, and followers
of the clergy, Lord North could count on keeping his Ministry
in office. 'The majority, both in and out of Parliament, continued
in blind support of the measures of administration', wrote the

---

[1] *Hansard*, xix. 617.
[2] Lecky, iv. 72.
[3] Burke, *Works*, ix. 152, 153; also Lecky, iv. 66.

Duke of Grafton.[1] The duke did not mean the majority of
British citizens, for neither Whig nor Tory aristocrats gave much
weight to the opinions of ordinary men who did not vote. He
meant the majority of those who controlled the votes.

In 1778 the Opposition hoped that the Saratoga revelations
would weaken Lord North's hold on the country gentlemen,
but since the government files were not made available, Burke,
Fox, and Barre could not support their vituperations with facts
and documents. Their attacks lost effectiveness by repetition.
So long as the 'blind support' of the Ministry continued in
Parliament, the Opposition cause was almost hopeless and the
Opposition leaders knew it. 'The language of the Opposition in
their private correspondence, and sometimes in public, was that
of extreme despondency.'[2]

Fox continued to lead the Opposition attack. He told the
House: 'The principal and indeed the sole design of sending
general Burgoyne from Canada was that of forcing his way to
Albany, and making a junction with general Howe . . . the whole
disconcertion and failure of general Burgoyne's expedition was
owing either to the ignorance or negligence of the secretary of
state who had the direction of it.'[3] Fox even condemned General
Conway as 'the avowed advocate of so soiled a character as
Lord George Germaine's'.[4]

Fox was supported not only by the Opposition's other big
guns, but also by its lighter artillery. Sir Alexander Leith said
of the British use of Indians in the war that Lord George
Germain was

. . . the sole author and contriver of those barbarous measures. He
was astonished that the noble lord, considering several circumstances
which he refrained from mentioning, could presume to intrude himself into an office he was unqualified to fill; and he was still much more
astonished that he dare continue in it, when his own experience must
have long since convinced him, that he was totally unworthy of it.
Every single measure he had recommended himself, or adopted from
others, exhibited many proofs of his incapacity.[5]

John Wilkes, a villain to conservatives but a hero to the arti-
sans of London, invoked the ghost of Minden once again in

[1] Lecky, iv. 66, note.   [2] Lecky, iv. 66.
[3] *Hansard*, xix. 955; 19 Mar. 1778.
[4] Walpole, *Last Journals*, ii. 8.   [5] *Hansard*, xix. 700; 6 Feb. 1778.

Lord George's mismanagement 'of a second battle in a second war'.[1]

Burke was equally specific in placing the blame: 'Ignorance has stamped every step during the course of the expedition, but it was the ignorance of the Minister for the American department, not to be imputed to General Burgoyne, of whose good conduct, bravery and skill he did not entertain a shadow of a doubt. . . . The intended measure was a conjunction between Howe and Burgoyne; it was to be produced in the strangest way he ever heard of; the armies were to meet—yes; Howe was travelling southward and Burgoyne in the same direction.'[2] Somewhat later Burke returned to the attack: 'He begged to say to the noble lord, who had denied himself to be the cause of our disasters in America, that if he would not confess that he had, through wilful blindness, lost that continent, he must be forced to acknowledge that he had been the dupe of interested individuals, that he had been misinformed, mis-advised, and had misconducted the whole affair. The noble lord had not intended, perhaps, to lose America, but he had certainly lost America.'[3]

In the House of Lords Shelburne and Richmond led the attack with equal vehemence. Shelburne denounced 'the Pall Mall planners of the expedition', and said that if Burgoyne's orders were before the House they would reveal the incapacity of the Ministers in the most glaring colours. Lord Chatham, returning from invalid retirement to the parliamentary fray, paid compliments to the courage, zeal, and abilities of Burgoyne but condemned the campaign as 'a most wild, uncombined project'.

Most men liked Lord North personally, and he was only a secondary target. Some Whigs also knew or suspected that he was supporting the king's policy more from loyalty than conviction. They believed Lord George to have been the chief initiator and guide of the campaign plans in a casual, disunified, and irresponsible Cabinet. It is difficult to agree with Lecky that 'the bitterness with which the Opposition attacked Lord North was always considerably aggravated by the very

---

[1] *Hansard*, xix; 13 Feb. 1778.
[2] Hudleston, p. 224.
[3] *Hansard*, xix. 1224; 28 May 1778.

prevalent belief that he was not seriously convinced of the wisdom of the war'.[1]

Except when goaded beyond endurance Lord George said as little as possible in reply to these attacks. Lord North said still less, and the other Ministers almost nothing. The Ministry doubtless hoped that, given silent treatment, the Whig diatribes would soon wear out themselves or their audience. The Ministry's general line of defence was that: '. . . the northern expedition was . . . a wise and necessary measure . . . that it was capable of success; and that Lord George Germain had omitted nothing which could be done by an attentive minister to insure its success'. Lord George himself insisted that Burgoyne's orders allowed 'a discretionary latitude of conduct'.[2] This threw the blame squarely on Burgoyne, and the Opposition could do little to disprove that explanation until Burgoyne returned or they could see the actual orders and exchanges.

Burgoyne was doing his best to accommodate. He persisted in his pleas to Congress and to Washington. Washington was sympathetic and probably supported Burgoyne's request, and on 11 March he wrote to Burgoyne that Congress had granted him permission to go to England, provided he would return if summoned. It was a remarkable action by Congress, and a still more remarkable letter from Washington:

> Viewing you in the light of an officer contending against what I conceive to be the rights of my country, the reverse of fortune you experienced cannot be unacceptable to me, but abstracted from consideration of national advantage, I can sincerely sympathize with your feelings, as a soldier . . . and as a man, whose lot combines the calamity of ill-health, the anxieties of captivity and the painful sensibility for a reputation, exposed, where he most values it, to the assaults of malice and detraction. . . . And wishing you a safe and agreeable passage, with a perfect restoration of your health, I have the honour, etc. G. Washington.[3]

With Burgoyne hurrying home to bring new life to the Opposition's waning fury, Lord George was faced with added problems of strategy. Ever since mid-December he had been preparing his defences against just such an event, and he had not disclosed his full hand to Parliament. The strategy he

---

[1] Lecky, iv. 72.   [2] Wright, *Speeches of Fox*, i. 121.
[3] *Hansard*, xix. 1185; also Fonblanque, pp. 329, 330.

formulated was to keep Burgoyne, as well as the records, from the curiosity of Parliament. To do this he would have to muffle Burgoyne. Since no one could wholly silence the voluble and popular Gentleman John, he must be so discredited that his words would carry no weight. Lord George took both objectives promptly in hand.

If this strategy failed, however, and Parliament in effect exonerated Burgoyne, then Lord George would have to see that the blame was thrown on General Howe. This would be more difficult. Could Parliament and public be convinced that Howe had disobeyed orders to meet Burgoyne, or had at least ignored a clear understanding and expectation that he would do so? That would be a ticklish business if the Opposition gained access to all his correspondence with Howe. Better, perhaps, to establish that Howe was expected to salvage Burgoyne after taking Philadelphia, and that Howe could have done so if he had not unaccountably wasted half the summer doing little or nothing in New York.

Unfortunately for Lord George, Howe could give several answers to that criticism. He could point out that he had had to wait in New York because his supplies and reinforcements had reached him much later than Lord George had led him to expect. He could say that he had postponed his start for Philadelphia until he had received from Burgoyne assurances that he could continue to Albany unassisted. Howe could also claim, though with less cogency, that he had left Clinton with orders to help Burgoyne if Burgoyne needed help, and that Clinton would have had adequate force to do so if the promised reinforcements had arrived at New York when expected. These would be effective rejoinders because they were all at least partly true, and some of them could be proved. It would be safer to make Burgoyne the victim, but it would do no harm to go carefully over the Howe papers and to prepare a subtly discrediting interpretation of Howe's letters and conduct. Meanwhile there was Howe's tender of resignation to be dealt with. Howe had probably made it *pro forma* rather than with the expectation that it would be accepted, for after all, had he not just taken Philadelphia? If the king should curtly accept Howe's resignation, the public would assume that Howe must have been responsible for Burgoyne's failure. On 11 December, ten days after the news of the Saratoga surrender reached him, Lord George sent a dispatch to Howe regarding his offer to resign: '. . . as the particulars of Lieut. General Burgoyne's situation are still unknown, and your own campaign is not finished, I am not authorized to signify his Majesty's commands on this subject . . . a material alteration in the plan of carrying on the war must necessarily take place . . . until the effect of your operations this campaign is fully known, it is impossible for his Majesty to come to any determination, or to send you any particular instructions.'[1]

That letter, with its pointed omission of any commendation for Howe's considerable achievement in taking Philadelphia, was in contrast to Lord George's superlatives to Howe after he had taken New York. Howe must have recalled his copy of Lord George's letter to Carleton eight months earlier, for there were similarities in the coolness of tone. Soon after Carleton received his letter he had been relieved of his command and treated in a way which threatened an end to his military career. Would Howe shortly find himself similarly dealt with? He was left in uncertainty for nearly three months before he received orders from Lord George to give up his command to Clinton as soon as feasible.[2]

With Howe temporarily dealt with, the problem of Burgoyne remained. He too had powerful friends, and the king liked him and had ridden with him regularly in Hyde Park. He would surely demand a full hearing by the king, by Parliament, and perhaps by a martial court. Lord George knew from experience something of the ways in which a man could be prevented from gaining a royal audience, a parliamentary hearing, or a court martial. As one of the most skilful political managers in Britain, Lord George should be able to forestall Burgoyne.

The question of how to deal with Burgoyne on his return was discussed in the Cabinet and with the king before Christmas of 1777, despite the fact that no one knew when, or indeed whether, Burgoyne would return from America. The king maintained that Burgoyne should be given a fair hearing, and Lord George

[1] Germain to Howe, 11 Dec. 1777; Clements, *Clinton Letter Book*, pp. 398–400; also *HMC, Stop. Sack.* ii. 84. This letter was endorsed: 'Recd. at Philadelphia, 27th February, 1778, No. 16'.
[2] PRO, CO/5, v. 253, no. 16; also Clements, *Clinton Letter Book*, p. 405, 18 Feb. 1778; also *HMC, Stop. Sack.* ii. 92.

consequently found it expedient to profess the same opinion. But he also implanted in the king's mind certain suggestions. One was that the Opposition, who were anathema to the king, would make use of a Parliamentary Inquiry into Burgoyne's conduct to attack Lord North and the Ministry; to express opposition to the American war, and to disseminate their levelling doctrines through England. Another was that until Burgoyne had been heard and cleared of blame by the military authorities, it would be improper for him to see and talk with the king.

On Christmas Day the Adjutant-General presented to the king a draft of a possible procedure that: '. . . will not preclude Lt. General Burgoyne from the extensive Enquiry in any mode he pleases to request on his arrival'.[1] The king was pleased, but he had not reckoned with certain political subtleties. Two days later he discovered some of them, and wrote not very happily to Lord North: 'I cannot help expressing some surprise that so many of the Cabinet have doubted of the propriety of bringing the unhappy fate of Lt. G. Burgoyne's Expedition to an Enquiry, though I thought there might be a diversity of opinion as to the mode and extent of such an inquiry; in the state of it yesterday I think Lord G. Germain judged right in not for the moment pressing the affair further.'[2] Lord George may have been playing a double game, but if so the king was soon aware of it, for he had expressed his opinion of the whole issue with frankness and perception in another letter to Lord North: 'I confess I am still of the opinion that I threw out yesterday, that if on consideration it should be thought right to inquire through the medium of a Board of General Officers, into the defense laid down by General Burgoyne that his orders were positive (which I must incline to) the reference ought to extend to the failure of the expedition.'[3]

Even before 1777 had ended, a plan was in the making to substitute a hearing *in camera* for a parliamentary inquiry or a public court martial. A Parliamentary Inquiry could be held only by a motion in Parliament, but early in 1778 the Ministers were not sure of holding their majority on such an interesting

[1] Adjutant-General to King, 25 Dec. 1777; Fortescue, *Corresp.* iii. 522.
[2] King to North, 27 Dec. 1777; ibid., p. 527.
[3] King to North, 25 Dec. 1777; ibid., p. 520.

issue. Again the Government's legal technicians were called upon. William Knox recorded the helpful activities of the ablest of them:

When the failure of Burgoyne's expedition was threatened to come under discussion in the House of Commons, Thurlow, who was the Attorney General, came to me at the office one day and told me he was informed by all the Ministers that I could give him the information he wanted about this expedition. There were three things he wanted to know: the motives and reasons of the expedition, the measures that were concerted for its execution, and the occasion of its failure. I told him I would put into his hands a paper I had drawn up for the Cabinet Ministers according to my annual custom,[1] which was a *precis* of the whole correspondence of the preceding year, which would give him much of the information he desired, and accordingly brought him one of the copies. He turned over the sheets and examined them, and then said, 'Why, this is the very thing I wanted, and you have done it already; pray, do the Ministers know of this?' 'Yes, Sir, they have all had copies of it'. 'Then, by God, they have never read it, for there is not one of them who knows a tittle of the matter.'[2]

Thurlow from that point directed the strategy of the Ministry's defence, and did it so well that according to Walpole it was the cause of his being made Lord Chancellor.[3]

Among Lord George's papers was found a memorandum outlining that strategy, probably the product of those overnight researches by Thurlow:

To withstand the communication of papers relative to the expedition under General Burgoyne would be a very difficult point after all that has already passed on that subject, and yet if General Burgoyne had not in the first instance appealed to the public, I think it would have been a right measure in administration to have opposed it. His conduct requires and ought to undergo an inquiry, but it should be an inquiry by officers, and it should await his arrival.
. . . The defense of the expedition, so far as it relates to the administration, depends upon shewing that the object to be attained

[1] These may well have been the annual summaries of events found in PRO, CO/5 in volumes like 253, which by internal evidence seem to have been prepared in Germain's office and are sometimes given a slant in his favour.

[2] *HMC, Var. Coll.* 6, *Knox*, p. 270.

[3] 'It was said that he obtained the Seals at last by the difficulties the Court was in by General Burgoyne's arrival. He, in one night, went through all the papers that had passed between that officer and the Ministers' (Walpole, *Last Journals*, ii. 218; 4 Dec. 1778).

was important, that it was attainable with the force employed, that the necessary preparations were made, that the orders left a sufficient discretion to the commander. The first and second points are left very imperfect in the papers produced for the House, and it will be necessary to add to them General Carleton's letter of the 2nd October 1776, referring to General Burgoyne for information and General Burgoyne's plan for the expedition of the 28th February 1777. This last is absolutely necessary, because it accounts for the conciseness of the instructions which did not require to be very ample when they only related to a plan formed by the person to whom they were addressed. It appears also from this paper that a co-operation of Howe's army was not expected, but the expedition taken up as an independent enterprise by the force allotted for it.[1]

The last sentence was an extremely curious interpretation of Burgoyne's 'Thoughts', and only a legal genius could have made it seem convincing. Since the papers in question were withheld from Parliament as long as possible, it is not unreasonable to suppose that the members of the Cabinet did not find their contents sufficiently convincing of the above doctrine to make them public unless forced to do so.

The Opposition was confident that the Ministry would not be withholding the papers unless it had something to conceal. Other events suggested the penchant of the Ministry for concealment to the public detriment. Long before Saratoga the country had feared that France would enter the war, and knew Benjamin Franklin was in Paris to gain that end. The day before Parliament reopened after its Christmas recess, the French Government informed Franklin that France would sign on 6 February a treaty acknowledging and supporting the independence of the Americans.[2] The British intelligence service, whose members in Paris were numerous and reasonably efficient, reported what half Paris knew or suspected. So did Lord Stormont, the British ambassador there. Yet the North Ministry gave no hint to Parliament of the French intention, and took almost no steps to prepare its army, navy, and people for this new threat. On the contrary, the Ministry disclaimed until mid-March having any certain knowledge of the Franco-American treaty. The Opposition accused it of having withheld the news because it might endanger its own continuance in office.[3]

[1] *HMC, Stop. Sack*. ii. 88.   [2] Lecky, iv. 64.
[3] *Hansard*, xx; also Walpole, *Last Journals*.

There were other events, less important but curious, that throw some light on the Saratoga fiasco and its aftermath. Christian D'Oyley, one of the important secretaries in the office of Lord George, resigned on 6 February 1778, and did it so suddenly that Lord George commented to William Eden: 'D'Oyley's manner of leaving my office was not the most polite, and I might express surprise that I was not among the first that was inform'd of his intention, when you know the real cause perhaps you will think as I do upon this subject.'[1]

What was the real cause to which Lord George referred so mysteriously? Walpole had, as usual, an answer: 'Mr. Doyley, Secretary to Lord George Germaine, resigned, professing he had accepted his employment from friendship to the Howes, and quitted because he could no longer be of any use to them. This more than implied, it spoke, that Lord George Germaine was their enemy.'[2] The dates support Walpole's explanation. Lord George's letter of dismissal to General Howe was dated 4 February. D'Oyley almost certainly knew its contents, and he resigned two days later. According to Thomas Hutchinson, D'Oyley himself confirmed Walpole: 'Called on Mr. D'Oyley. He has put himself out because he sees that he does not please Lord George. He shews his attachment to the Howes more than ever.'[3]

D'Oyley may have had another reason more significant than personal loyalty to the Howes. Suppose he realized that Sir William Howe's dismissal would almost certainly result in an inquiry by Parliament which would make available the correspondence of the American Secretary's office with Howe? Suppose that correspondence should reveal a blunder in Lord George's office, in which D'Oyley had been involved, which explained the military misunderstanding that led to Saratoga? If so, D'Oyley might think it well to clear out while he could.

Some of the stories later volunteered by contemporaries give that possibility credence. One of them was advanced by Lord Shelburne, and cannot be ignored even though his strong political aversion to Lord George makes him a dubious witness:

Among many singularities [Lord George] had a particular

---

[1] Germain to Eden, 10 Feb. 1778; Stevens, *Facsimiles*, iv. 370.
[2] Walpole, *Last Journals*, ii. 109. Clements, *Germain Papers*, iv. 33/36.
[3] Clements, *Hutchinson Diaries* (original MS.), p. 424.

aversion to being put out of his way on any occasion; he had fixed
to go into Kent or Northamptonshire at a particular hour, and to
call on his way at his office to sign the dispatches, all of which had
been settled, to both these generals. [Shelburne was referring to the
original orders of co-operation to Howe and Burgoyne.] By some
mistake those to Howe were not fair copied, and upon his growing
impatient at it, the office, which was a very idle one, promised to
send it to the country after him, while they dispatched the others
to General Burgoyne, expecting that the others could be expedited
before the packet sailed with the first, which however by some mistake sailed without them, and the wind detained the vessel which
was ordered to carry the rest. Hence came Burgoyne's defeat, the
French declaration and the loss of the thirteen colonies. It might
appear incredible if his own Secretary and the most responsible
persons in office had not assured me of the fact; what corroborates
it is that it can be accounted for in no other way.[1]

Burgoyne's biographer de Fonblanque, writing in 1876, offered
a variant account, but one similar enough to Shelburne's to
suggest that both were drawn from a common source. Without
quoting his authority, de Fonblanque stated categorically: 'The
dispatch with full and explicit instructions was found after the
Convention of Saratoga, pigeon-holed and carefully docketed,
only wanting the signature of the Minister.'[2]

If those two accounts were the only ones, it would be reasonable to assume that they were fabrications after the fact, and to
agree with Sir G. O. Trevelyan that the Shelburne story should
be received 'with caution, if not with incredulity'. But that
eminent historian made no reference to a third account which
has only in recent years become easily available. Who was Lord
George's 'own Secretary' who, Shelburne said, assured him of
the fact? Lord George's chief undersecretary and most trusted
office confidant was William Knox, and in Knox's papers was
found a memorandum offering another and far more plausible
variant. There were several reasons why Knox would not have
been likely to fabricate his story. He was an able and responsible
civil servant, loyal to Lord George so long as Lord George was
his chief, and he was occasionally personally consulted and apparently trusted by Lord North. He was also 'a very strenuous
and persevering advocate of the British measures against

---

[1] Fitzmaurice, *Shelburne*, i. 358 ff.
[2] Fonblanque, pp. 232, 233.

America. . . . To his zeal and suggestions many of the unfortunate measures against America were ascribed.'[1] Knox did not
tell his story in 1778 when it would have been a political bomb-
shell and cannot therefore be accused of inventing it to play
politics, or to advance any personal interest of his own:

There certainly was a weak place in Lord Sackville's defense,
which was the want of any official communication to Howe of the
plan, and Burgoyne's instructions, with orders for his cooperation;
of which I was not only innocent, but it was owing to my interference
that Howe had any knowledge of the business. Mr. D'Oyley, my
then colleague, having been some time Deputy Secretary at War,
and the particular friend of Howe, had the entire conduct of the
military business, and Burgoyne and he had settled the force and
Instructions, and Burgoyne had gone in to the King and obtained
his consent for having the command and everything in his own way;
even the specific detachments and corps were all named and not
left to Carleton to select.

When all was prepared, and I had then to compare and make up,
Lord Sackville came down to the office to sign the letters on his way
to Stoneland, when I observed to him that there was no letter to
Howe to acquaint him with the plan or what was expected of him in
consequence of it. His Lordship started, and D'Oyley stared, but
said he would in a moment write down a few lines. 'So', sayd Lord
George, 'my poor horses must stand in the street all the time, and
I shan't be to my time anywhere.' D'Oyley then said he had better
go, and he would write himself to Howe and inclose copies of
Burgoyne's Instructions, which would tell him all that he would
want to know; and with that his Lordship was satisfied, as it enabled
him to keep his time, for he could never bear delay or disappointment; and D'Oyley sat down and wrote a letter to Howe, but he
neither shew'd it to me or gave me a copy of it for the office, and, if
Howe had not acknowledged the receipt of it, with the copy of the
Instructions to Burgoyne, we could not have proved that he ever
saw them. I applied upon this occasion to D'Oyley for a copy of his
letter, but he said he had kept none. I then desired he would get
one from Howe, who had the original, but he would not ask for it,
and Lord Sackville did not call upon Howe for it. Thurlow would,
however, have called for it, if the enquiry had gone on, as I had
told him all the circumstances.[2]

That story seems too circumstantial not to have been based,

[1] Almon, *Biog. and Lit. Anecdotes*, ii. 112–15.
[2] HMC, *Var. Coll.* 6, *Knox*, p. 277; also *English Review*, Edgerton, xxv, 1910.

at least, on the truth, though not all its details can be accepted verbatim.[1] But the essential facts fit so well with D'Oyley's sudden resignation, with the concealment of the facts, and with Howe's insistence that he never received specific orders to co-operate with Burgoyne, that one is inclined to accept its main points. It received further circumstantial support from the fact that Howe acknowledged in a rather pointed way his receipt 'by the *Somerset*, transmitted by Mr. D'Oyley, copies of your Lordship's letter to Sir Guy Carleton of 26th March'.[2]

But, true or not, none of these stories has important bearing on the main course of events that led to Saratoga. For whether or not Howe received any specific order to co-operate with Burgoyne, such an order would have been replaced by Lord George's dispatch approving the plan to go to Philadelphia, and adding only the codicil: 'Trusting, however, that whatever you may meditate, it will be executed in time for you to cooperate with the army ordered to proceed from Canada and put itself under your command.' Howe did not receive that dispatch, dated 18 May, until 20 August, when he was already landing troops at the head of Chesapeake Bay, and he acknowledged its receipt on 30 August. Had Howe then immediately returned to New York, he might have got to Albany in time to save Burgoyne, but he would have had to abandon the elaborate campaign on which he had already embarked. It was that 18 May dispatch, too, that contained Lord George's approval of Howe's letter to Carleton disclaiming responsibility for meeting the northern army—an approval that put Howe in the clear. Thus in one dispatch Lord George trusted that Howe would co-operate, but also approved Howe's intention of not co-operating. Confusion could not have been more ingeniously confounded.

Though the Knox and D'Oyley stories do not account for the Saratoga disaster, they help to explain the conduct of Lord George after Saratoga. To defend himself against his attackers, Lord George must have gone very carefully through all his records, and could not have failed to see that in the hands of the Opposition those records would reveal his own carelessness.

---

[1] Burgoyne did not settle in their final form the instructions to be sent to Carleton which included his own orders, or he would not immediately upon receiving them have expressed to Lord George his surprise and disappointment at their inflexibility.   [2] Howe to Germain; Clements, *Germain Papers*, vi. 75.

A final gnomic contribution by D'Oyley supports that conclusion. In a private letter to Sir Philip Francis in India (who may
have been the author of the Junius letters), D'Oyley wrote:
'I last Friday asked and obtained leave to retire from my situation in the Lord G. Germain's office, and at the moment various
are the speculations upon it, as it is not generally known that
leave is gone to Howe to give up his command. My reasons for
giving up are many, but must not be trusted in a letter. The
friends of opposition increase, and we are now in the midst of
an enquiry into the state of the nation, in short, we are in a
damned bad way, and I wish I was in Calcutta, or anywhere
but here.'[1]

At the peak of this particular crisis in Lord George's career
he had the misfortune of a personal loss that temporarily
weakened his will to defend himself or continue in office. On
15 January 1778 Lady Germain died 'of the measles'. '. . . as
she was a good wife and mother and a sensible woman, her
death was a great blow to him at this moment'.[2] Lord George
retired to Knole for over a week, missing important meetings
of the Cabinet on 17 and 18 January at which the future of the
war, the Ministry, and probably of Lord George were discussed.
His position and the Ministry were jeopardized by his absence,
as Lord Suffolk hinted in a letter dated the day of Lady George's
death: 'Zeal for the public welfare urges me to endeavor to
rouse your attention even in the first agonies of grief . . . we
can't go far without your assistance.'[3]

Lord George's reply contained an offer to resign that was
probably the most sincere of such offers that he made during
the various crises of four years. But it was only an unofficial
offer and was never presented directly to Lord North or the
king, and his recovery from so drastic a sacrifice to his grief was

---

[1] Parkes, *Memoirs of Sir Philip Francis*, ii. 134, 135; 19 Feb. 1778.

[2] Walpole, *Last Journals*, ii. 91; 15 Jan. 1778; also *Annual Register for 1778*, p. 225.
There were later troubles. The London *Public Ledger* of 22 July 1778 contained a
report: 'respecting Lady George Germain having burst her coffin & of her being
reburied. Steps were taken to hush up this catastrophe. The state of mind in which
Lord George finds himself whenever that unhappy subject of Lady George's death
is brought back to his mind makes Mr. de G[rey] anxious to prevent his Lordship
from seeing it in any other paper', and Mr. de Grey, Lord George's office assistant,
asked publisher Almon to try to prevent any further publication (BM, Addit.
MS. 20,733, fol. 38).

[3] Suffolk to Germain, 15 Jan. 1778; *HMC, Stop. Sack*. ii. 90.

rapid. On the same day that he wrote to Suffolk of his wish to resign, he also wrote to Knox referring to his possible retirement in far more equivocal terms. Though he mentioned to Knox that he had offered his resignation to Lord Suffolk, he proceeded to political matters in a way that discounted his proposal, and advised Knox to withhold even from Lord Suffolk the papers on Saratoga, at least until his return. 'I hope Lord Suffolk will want no explanation of the papers which you will not be able to give him.'[1] And a week later he sent Knox a letter which indicated that his mind had moved some way from insistence on resigning:

. . . as to the measure of carrying on the war from that quarter, it was the opinion of every officer and every American I ever conversed with that an attack from Canada was the only method of crushing the Rebellion and of bringing the New England Provinces to their senses.[2] Whether the force was adequate or that force properly conducted, were, I thought, the great objects of inquiry. What papers may be asked for, or what Lord North may give, I know not; but for my own part I should wish soon to come to a decision, for nothing is so disagreeable as to have enquiries of this sort hanging over the heads of the Administration. . . . If I find myself unequal to the dutys of my office, I trust I shall be relieved from it.[3]

The 'if' was already bulking large in Lord George's mind.

Ten days later Lord George informed Knox, probably with relief, that Sir John Irwin had told him that: 'Lord North did not chuse to consent to the papers from my office being laid before the House till I had been acquainted with the particulars of the motion.'[4] Meanwhile Lord Suffolk had replied to Lord George's talk of resignation in terms Lord George must have found reassuring: 'Allow me now to express my hopes that calmer and maturer reflection will have convinced your lordship that it can neither be for the King's advantage or your own credit that you should retire at such a moment. On the contrary, I await with anxious expectation to hear that you mean shortly to come amongst us again, and avail yourself of the best relief

[1] Germain to Knox, 16 Jan. 1778; *HMC, Var. Coll.* 6, *Knox*, p. 141.
[2] But Fortescue said General Harvey, the top officer in Whitehall, opposed it, and General Amherst believed the war should be a naval one.
[3] Germain to Knox, 23 Jan. 1778; *HMC, Var. Coll.* 6, *Knox*, p. 142.
[4] Germain to Knox, 25 Jan. 1778; *HMC, Var. Coll.* 6, *Knox*, p. 142.

from private affliction, public busyness.'[1] Nothing further was said about that particular proposal to resign, and the sympathy that went to Lord George for his bereavement may have worked a little to strengthen his fragile political standing.

Even during that retreat at Knole the Secretary for America did not neglect his defences, or the Opposition cease its attack. 'Lord George Germaine justified himself in writing against Burgoyne, and suffered his defense to lie in his office and be perused.'[2] The Whigs began their tirades again, though Fox at least had little hope that the Ministry could be driven out. He wrote to Richard Fitzpatrick in Canada on 3 February:

> We shall soon go into an enquiry upon the Canada expedition, in which how Lord G. will defend himself, is much above my comprehension. They mean to be hard upon Burgoyne, which is a business beyond what even you or I would have expected from them. . . . I am convinced we shall so far succeed as to get great decisions in the House of Commons, and to convince all the world that the Ministers deserve all possible contempt; but when we have done that, I think we shall have done all we can do, and that the Ministers, though despised everywhere, will still continue Ministers.[3]

Fox was no more cynical than Walpole, who wrote in his journal six weeks later: '. . . though the Ministers had endeavoured to stir up persecution against Burgoyne and the Howes, I have no doubt but as fast as they come over, the court from its natural cowardice, will endeavor to bribe and pacify them'.[4]

In mid-March the Opposition formally moved for a full-dress inquiry into the surrender of Burgoyne. Fox tried to extend the motion still further into an inquiry into the entire conduct and direction of the war in America, but this was voted down by 164 to 44. A bitter debate on the original motion followed. During the first day Lord George said nothing except when called upon to answer specific questions, and some of these he avoided. According to Walpole, Lord George had told a friend the day before: '. . . that he was ready to resign . . . but that he would be acquitted first by the House of Commons'.[5] His friend

---

[1] Suffolk to Germain, 20 Jan. 1778; *HMC, Stop. Sack.* ii. 91.

[2] Walpole, *Last Journals*, ii. 91.

[3] Fox to Fitzpatrick, 3 Feb. 1778; Russell, *Life of C. J. Fox*, i. 168. Fitzpatrick was a brother of the Earl of Upper Ossory, and Fox married his sister.

[4] Walpole, *Last Journals*, ii. 129.   [5] Ibid., p. 142.

Wedderburn, Solicitor-General, was the chief Ministry spokesman in Lord George's defence, but not a very effective one.
Thurlow came to his aid with his heavy oratorical guns.

On the following day the debate continued and:

Lord George Germaine at last defended himself in a good speech
. . . though many thought he did not clear himself, he had, however,
had the precaution to tell General Howe, in a letter, that he hoped
to be in time to assist Burgoyne. . . . Wedderburne moved an acquittal of his friend, which was voted with a small majority under forty.
. . . Lord George . . . contrary to all precedent, voted in his own
case for himself . . . Charles Fox said to many that he would attend
the House no more.[1]

Fox was so angry at the vote against his motion that he
declared he would not propose his next motion, which was to
have been a vote of censure of Lord George, 'but, taking the
resolution of censure out of his pocket, tore it in pieces and
immediately quitted the House. As soon as Mr. Fox was gone,
the Solicitor-General moved: "That it does not appear to this
Committee, that the failure of the Expedition from Canada
arose from any neglect in the Secretary of State." The resolution
was agreed to by the Committee, but was never reported to the
House.'[2]

Thanks to the support of the Ministry's placemen and the
somewhat unhappy country gentlemen, Lord George survived
that crisis. For the moment he and the Ministry were saved to
send more generals to fight and lose again. But it could not be
said that Lord George's honour was saved or that his post was
permanently secure. Burgoyne and Howe had not yet been
heard by Parliament and the court of public opinion, and more
men of both parties than were yet ready to admit it had reached
the conclusion of a later historian: 'The ultimate cause of the
disaster was Lord George Germain.'[3]

[1] Ibid.
[2] Wright, *Speeches of Fox*, i. 121, 122.   [3] Lucas, p. 182.

XX

SCAPEGOAT

'THE King of England has promised Lord George Germain to uphold him and sacrifice Burgoyne, but the people and the Opposition will uphold the latter, and his arrival and the re-assembly will decide everything.'

With that New Year's Day message from London to Foreign Minister Vergennes, his confidential adviser Beaumarchais announced the next act of the parliamentary tragi-comedy.[1] It was an analysis that did credit to the perception of that literary gentleman, but as prophecy it was optimistic. No Parliament ever decided everything, and the Parliament of 1778 less than most.

Burgoyne sailed from New England about 3 April,[2] and arrived at Portsmouth on 13 May 1778. He immediately sent to Lord George a cautious letter in which he stated his desire to '... lay before the King's ministers in person what could not be conveyed by any other means'.[3] He reached London a day or two later.

Burgoyne had always been popular with society and public. Many Ministry supporters liked him better than their own Secretary of State for America, whom they would have been glad to see removed if it could be done without danger to the North régime. Uncertain how to treat Burgoyne, they received him with caution that varied from the cordial to the cool. The Opposition, however, welcomed him warmly, some for his own sake and many because they saw him as a useful tool for discrediting the Ministry. The public was divided in its reactions, but there was a widespread feeling that he was a courageous soldier badly maligned, and that even if he had made mistakes there were deeper causes of the Saratoga disaster nearer home.

---

[1] Beaumarchais to Vergennes, 1 Jan. 1778; French Archives, Angleterre, v. 528, fol. 5; also *Stevens Facsimiles*, xxi. 1815.

[2] PRO, 30/55, no. 1122.

[3] Burgoyne to Germain, 13 May 1778; Clements, *Germain Papers*, vii. 43.

There is a story that when Burgoyne reached London he was uncertain whether to throw the chief blame for his misfortune on Lord George Germain or Sir William Howe. Thomas Hutchinson recorded it in his diary: 'At Lord Townshend's. It is said when Burg. arrived Charles F asked him his plan? "To charge Howe with leaving him to be sacrificed." "If that's your plan we must forsake you, we are determined to support H." '[1] That story was so much to the advantage of the Ministry that one suspects Ministry propaganda, of which Hutchinson was more than once the tool. Hutchinson was even suspected of being on Lord George's private payroll and later attacked the Howe brothers. 'Never', he wrote on one occasion, 'were two men more universally condemned than the Howes. It was even said, two men of less ability could not be found.'[2] That was certainly a canard: every part of the statement was untrue. There are good reasons to doubt the truth of his account of Burgoyne's conversation with Fox. Burgoyne's first dispatches after Saratoga to Lord George, Lord Derby, and Colonel Phillipson show that he blamed the orders from the Ministry for the débâcle. Although in his first letter to Howe after the surrender he was plaintive about not being met and aided, his later letters indicated no reproach of Howe.

It was the first aim of Lord George's defence to silence criticisms from returning generals. On a recent visit to London, on leave from New York, Cornwallis had talked too freely about the Ministry's strategy in America, and, according to Walpole, '. . . was suddenly ordered back thither, and with . . . little civility'.[3] It was much more important to muffle Burgoyne. In that endeavour the king had, apparently somewhat reluctantly, agreed to co-operate, as Beaumarchais had reported. It was almost certainly in agreement with previous plans that Lord George wrote to the king just as Burgoyne arrived in England: 'Your Majesty will be pleased to give the orders you shall think proper with regard to any enquiry that may be made into the conduct of Lieutenant General Burgoyne.'[4]

There is no reason to doubt the substantial accuracy of

[1] Hutchinson, *Diaries*, Clements (original MS.), p. 455; also printed edition, ii. 210; 22 June 1778.
[2] Hutchinson, *Diaries*, printed edition, ii. 184; also W. C. Ford, p. 125.
[3] Walpole, *Last Journals*, ii. 161.
[4] Germain to King, 13 May 1778; Fortescue, *Corresp.* iv. 241.

Burgoyne's account of his first interview with Lord George after his return.

I was received with much apparent kindness; explanations passed, but they were friendly; I was heard attentively, through a report of all the transactions subsequent to the Convention of Saratoga, and I was led by degrees, and without suspicion of insidiousness, to the most confidential communication, on my part, of facts, observations, and opinions, respecting very important objects. . . . It was not until after the matter of my communication was exhausted, that the Secretary of State drew from his pocket an order, that I should prepare myself for an enquiry: at which I expressed my fullest satisfaction, till he followed the order with the information, of the *etiquette* I before mentioned, that I was not to appear at Court.[1]

Burgoyne also learned that the inquiry was not to be a regularly constituted court martial; but was to be held *in camera* and limited to the events of the operations themselves, rigidly excluding the strategy or the orders to other generals. This was wholly unsatisfactory to Burgoyne. He insisted on his right to a court martial, to an inquiry by Parliament and an interview with the king. Lord George continued to refuse all three. Echoing his own experience after Minden, he told Burgoyne that since no servant of the king had charged him with any improper conduct there were no charges for a court martial to consider. As for a Parliamentary Inquiry, it would not be needed, since a military inquiry had already been arranged. Neither man would yield, and the interview ended less cordially than it began.

The plans to silence Burgoyne did not end there. A rumour went about London that he had agreed not to take his seat in Parliament until after the special board of inquiry had completed its business. He promptly wrote to Lord George 'contradicting the rumor'.[2] In effect he declared open war against the Ministry and threw himself into the welcoming arms of the Opposition. Public interest in the controversy threatened to keep Parliament in session longer than the Ministry desired.[3]

Burgoyne then received a formal notice from the Judge Advocate to appear before five general officers appointed 'to

---

[1] Burgoyne's *Letter to his Constituents*, 1779; pp. 5 ff.
[2] Burgoyne to Germain, 18 May 1778; Clements, *Germain Papers*, vii. 144; also *HMC, Stop. Sack*. ii. 110.
[3] *Hansard*, xix. 1176, footnote.

examine and inquire into the causes of the failure' at Saratoga.
The following day the Board of Officers convened, and began
by asking Burgoyne to explain 'with precision' the nature of
his parole. This seemed a curious question upon which to put
initial emphasis, but the reason for it emerged soon enough.
Burgoyne explained:

. . . that he has never been considered as a Prisoner of War, and
that he holds himself a free man in every Circumstance except that
he is restricted by the Convention of Saratoga not to serve in
America during the War; with the further Parole on his leaving
America, that should the Embarkation of the Convention Troops
be by any means prolonged beyond the time apprehended, he will
return to America upon demand and due notice given by Congress,
and will redeliver himself into the Power of the Congress, unless
regularly exchanged.[1]

This was almost the exact phrasing of the parole he had signed
on 2 April, as recorded in the papers of the Continental Congress
now in the Library of Congress.

The board wasted no time on other considerations but made
its report to the king the very next day.[2] It held that Congress
had a lien on Burgoyne's person, and that consequently any
proceeding by the board or the British Government: '. . . which
may in any wise tend however remotely to restrain or affect his
Person, until such Parole is satisfied' might 'operate to the
prejudice of Your Majesty's Service and possibly have very
serious Consequences respecting the Troops included in the
Convention made at Saratoga'. Three days later the king
approved the board's report. The military inquiry into the
Saratoga campaign was ended.

Lord George's plan to prevent a court martial had worked
perfectly, but his plan to keep Burgoyne from being heard in
Parliament got somewhat out of hand. On 21 May Burgoyne
took his seat in the House of Commons and no one challenged
his right to do so. He 'said nothing, nor was anything said
to him' in the debates of that day.[3] But two days later, with
Burgoyne present: 'Mr. Vyner declared he should desire leave
to ask him some questions. Burgoyne replied he should be very
ready to answer any, and should even declare some things that
would astonish everybody. He had intended to have Charles

[1] PRO, CO/5, v. 253. [2] Walpole, *Last Journals*, ii. 176. [3] Ibid.

Fox question him in order to bring out what he wished—a step
that showed he thought himself, as it made him, desperate with
the Ministers.'[1]

Consequently, on the very day that the king approved the
report of the special Board of Officers, Burgoyne was heard in
the House of Commons. Walpole's report of that event is substantially corroborated by other sources: 'General Burgoyne
appeared in the House of Commons, which was so exceedingly
crowded that they were forced to turn out the strangers, though
Burgoyne begged that they might stay and hear his defense.
Vyner, after asking him some questions on the affair at Saratoga,
moved for a Committee to inquire into his conduct.'[2] Burgoyne
seconded the motion, and in doing so gave an account of his
campaign; 'said nothing hard on General Howe'; 'did great
justice to the Americans, and complained much of his being forbidden the King's presence'. Richard Rigby, an unblushing
Ministry placeman, who had made a fortune from his post as
Paymaster of the armed forces, 'contested the possibility of
Burgoyne's being examined by a Committee, being a prisoner'.[3]
Wedderburn supported Rigby, but Burgoyne claimed that
Congress had let him come to England to clear his character.
'Lord George observed that the word *permitted* proved his being
a prisoner. Charles Fox wondered there could be any doubt of
trying the General when the Minister, Lord George, had been
tried; and his conduct had appeared so unsatisfactory that the
Committee had made no report to the House; and he moved to
extend the inquiry to the whole measure of the expedition.'[4]

The debate on Vyner's motion and Fox's amendment gave
Burgoyne a chance to amplify his statement, and he made the
most of it:

The plan as originally drawn I have no reason to be ashamed of,

[1] Walpole, *Last Journals*, ii. 176.

[2] Vyner's motion was: '. . . that this House will now resolve itself into a committee of the whole House to consider the state and condition of the Army which
surrendered themselves on Convention at Saratoga, and also by what means
lieutenant general Burgoyne, who commanded that army, and was included in
that Convention, was released and is now returned to England' (*Hansard*, xix. 1176;
26 May 1778).

[3] 'Mr. Rigby said, that the honourable gentleman being a prisoner, was in fact
dead to all civil as well as military purposes, and, as such, had no right to speak,
much less to vote in that House' (Wright, *Speeches of Fox*, i. 126).

[4] Walpole, *Last Journals*, iii. 179; 26 May 1778.

because it underwent the inspection of some of the first and ablest officers of this country; but the plan, as it stood when orders were framed, can with no more propriety be called mine, than others formed by the cabinet for the distant parts of America or any other quarter of the globe where I had no participation or concern. . . . A latitude to act against New England was erased, a power to embark the troops in case of unforeseen impediments and to make a junction with the southern army by sea was not admitted . . . by cutting off every proposed latitude and confining the plan to only one object, the forcing of a passage to Albany, the orders framed upon that plan could in no wise be understood than as positive, peremptory and indispensable.[1]

Burgoyne insisted that from the beginning he had been given to understand that he would be met at Albany with appropriate forces, supplies, and further orders:

I expected co-operation; no letter from sir W. Howe removed that expectation. That to sir Guy Carleton had never weighed on my mind; because it was dated early in April, and consequently long before the secretary of state's instructions, which I must have supposed to relate to co-operation, could be received. The letter [from Howe] of 17th July mentioned that general's return to my assistance, should Washington turn his force against me; indicated as I thought an expectation of my arrival at Albany; and informed me that sir Henry Clinton was left at New-York, and would act as occurences might direct; I did not know sir Henry Clinton's force.[2]

Burgoyne also answered several anticipated criticisms. He defended his return to Europe before his troops as necessary for his health; 'for the purpose of settling large and complicated accounts . . . and to lay before the government important truths, not to be communicated by other means, and to supply, as far as in me lay, by an assiduous and honest exertion in this House, the misfortune that had disenabled me from performing my duty in the field'. He read to the House the letter from Washington authorizing his departure from America. He denied the charge that he should have used Indians more effectively, and the opposite charge that he should not have used them at all:

I ever respected the Indian alliances as a necessary evil. I believe their services to be over-valued; sometimes insignificant, often

---

[1] 'The Substance of Gen. Burgoyne's Speeches on Mr. Vyner's Motion, etc., on 26 May 1778'; a pamphlet, Exshaw, Dublin, 1778; also *Hansard*, xix. 1178 ff.
[2] *Hansard*, xx. 796, 797.

barbarous, always capricious, and that employment of them was only justifiable when being united to a regular army so that they may be kept under control, and made subservient to a general system. . . . Barbarity was prevented . . . if to restrain [them] from murder was to prevent them from having done greater service, I take with pride the blame.[1]

Burgoyne denied that his army was overloaded with the baggage of its officers, and said that: 'All baggage of bulk had been cheerfully left behind by the officers, to the abridgement of many material comforts; some of them had not beds, many lay in soldiers' tents, and I know of none that had more than the common necessaries for active service.'[2] He defended his delays of two weeks at Skenesborough and six weeks at Fort Edward, as well as the long interval between the first and second battles at Saratoga, and his choice of the land route to Fort Edward. These were points of which Lord George had made special criticisms, and opinion on them remained divided.[3] Burgoyne ended by citing the experiences of Generals Gage, Carleton, Howe, and himself: '. . . for the instruction of all those who might be hazardous enough to attempt to serve their country under the auspices of men who were obliged to cover their ignorance and inability, and screen themselves from ignominy and contempt, by throwing blame upon the men who were unwise enough to act as they were instructed'.[4]

Burgoyne's speech produced words and scenes that led Horace Walpole to describe the House as '. . . a scene of folly and Billingsgate', where Burgoyne '. . . bullied, and Lord G. Germaine scolded like two oysterwomen',[5] and to add rather unjustly that: 'Burgoyne has tried to be the pathetic hero.' Sir Alexander Leith, defending Burgoyne, said that Lord George Germain was 'not fit to serve the King', and this inspired Temple Luttrell, a brother of the Duchess of Cumberland, to give the House his version of Lord George's appointment and services:

Lord North did then seize the glorious opportunity to recommend

---

[1] *Hansard*, xx. 796, 797.   [2] Ibid.

[3] Germain's writing in his own memorandum read: 'His taking the road by Skenesborough instead of Lake George was not only a delay but caused much unnecessary fatigue to his army. His halting afterward . . . gave the Rebels every opportunity of preparing for defense' (Clements, *Germain Papers*, viii. 8/67).

[4] Wright, *Speeches of Fox*, i. 128.

[5] Walpole to Mason, 31 May 1778; Toynbee, x. 254.

to his sovereign a minister whose loss of a nation's confidence and his own character is a matter of public record. . . . What plan of his, since in his office, dare he expose to the public eye, and say it has succeeded? Why then should we give him partial acquittal to the prejudice of a gallant officer whose only crime has been that he was too zealous, too brave, too enterprizing, too anxious for the good of his country; had strictly obeyed his orders; and done all that British valour was capable of, to carry the minister's plan into execution? . . . [If Burgoyne had] receded from his colours, disobeyed the commands of his superiors and hid himself from danger, such conduct would have given him pretensions to the honours and emoluments of the American Secretaryship.[1]

Horace Walpole reported what happened then:

Lord George started up in the most violent rage, and clapping his hand to his sword, said, though he was an old man, he would not hear such an insult from a young man, who was an assassin and of the most wretched character. This produced the highest warmth and clamour. Luttrell went out of the House that they might not be prevented fighting; but they forced him back by an order of the House, when he would not retract a syllable, said he had said nothing but what was on the record, and declared he would be sent to prison rather than to retract. Lord North said a few faint words for Lord George, though he owned he had been disorderly. Mr. Buller was for committing Luttrell, but most condemning Lord George; the latter made apologies, and called Luttrell *his noble friend*, which the latter rejected with great indignation. The confusion lasted above two hours, when Luttrell was forced to disclaim any further resentment. The Board of Officers dropped. Burgoyne would not submit to it, and it was allowed to have been improperly appointed.[2]

'Lord George grasped his sword—and then asked pardon for having been so grossly insulted', Walpole commented with gleeful sarcasm to Mason.[3]

Vyner's motion for an inquiry was lost by 144 to 96, but Burgoyne's statements were widely accepted as exonerating him of at least the chief blame. The virulence with which the Ministry's men attacked Burgoyne was an indication that his charges had struck home. Lord George's defenders denied that, and when Burgoyne published his defence in pamphlet form[4]

---

[1] *Hansard*, xx. 1200–3.   [2] Walpole, *Last Journals*, ii. 179.
[3] Walpole to Mason, 31 May 1778; Toynbee, x. 254.
[4] Walpole, *Last Journals*, ii. 186; 16 June 1778.

and it was widely read and reprinted in Dublin, Hutchinson could do no better than to write in his diary: 'Much talk of Burgoyne's publication. Some say he has ruined himself by it.'[1]

Burgoyne had had his brief day in court but was unsatisfied because he had received no formal exoneration, and the Ministry were equally discontented that he had been given an informal one by public opinion. But the Ministry had still not yielded up the relevant papers to Parliament.[2] The issue was not closed, since Howe was still to be heard from, and the legal authorities of the Ministry, Thurlow and Wedderburn, bent their expedient minds to finding further ways in which both generals could be prevented from making speeches to Parliament. They also studied how Burgoyne's charges could best be answered if they were repeated, and among the papers in Lord George's files was one, prepared soon after Burgoyne's first speech, summarizing his main points.[3]

Wedderburn presented a new theory to the House of Commons. Since Burgoyne was in the power of the American Congress he obviously did not exist as a free Englishman, and therefore could not take his place in the House. The argument failed to win the support of any but the most devoted of the Ministry's placemen. The memory of the storm that nearly unseated the Ministry when Wilkes was excluded from the Commons was still fresh, and other members thought that if Ministers were allowed to exclude one duly elected member from Parliament, it might later find arguments to exclude any other member whose conduct embarrassed them. Burgoyne, if excluded, might, like Wilkes, be promptly re-elected, and raise a popular constitutional issue. Walpole simply pronounced Wedderburn's argument 'most absurd',[4] and it was abandoned.

Reasonably impartial men concluded that the Ministry had shown itself both incompetent and gullible about America. With masterly understatement James Hare reported: 'The Ministry have been so frequently and fatally misinformed by

---

[1] Hutchinson, *Letters and Diaries*, ii. 210; 22 June 1778.

[2] On the very day that Burgoyne addressed the House, the Judge Advocate sent official word to William Knox that: '. . . the inquiry into the causes of the failure of success in the Expedition from Canada would not proceed at this time, and consequently that no papers would be wanted' (PRO, CO/5, v. 170, no. 82; 26 May 1778).

[3] *HMC, Stop. Sack.* ii. 110.   [4] Walpole, *Last Journals*, ii. 182.

their friends in America of late, that I do not give quite implicit belief to all they say.'[1] The issue refused to be interred, and feelings were as strong among the Lords as the Commoners. 'Lord Derby, whose aunt General Burgoyne had married, and who resented his disgrace so much that he would not go to court, moved the Lords to address for all the papers relating to the convention of Saratoga, but it was rejected without a division.'[2]

Burgoyne's persistent efforts to see the king continued to fail, for his co-operation with the Opposition had made the king lose sympathy with his old riding companion of Hyde Park. The king thought it '. . . rather particular that Mr. Burgoyne should wish to take a lead in Opposition at a season when his own situation seems to me to be far from either pleasant or creditable'.[3] A general reaction was expressed with characteristic succinctness by the tenth Earl of Pembroke, a Lord of the Bedchamber, to his son Lord Herbert: 'Burgoyne in my mind allways carried more sail than ballast, but he is gallant and honest; and such ought not to be sacrificed to a Minden B . . . g Hero.'[4]

If the Ministry could not get the vocal Burgoyne out of Parliament perhaps they could get him out of hearing distance. According to General Amherst, Lord George did not directly 'develop' the next move, but it is not unreasonable to suspect he inspired it.[5] An action by the Continental Congress unwittingly provided the opportunity. It declined to honour General Gates's Convention agreement to permit the captured troops of Saratoga to return to England, and not without some justification.[6] In 1778 Congress formally denounced that clause of the agreement,

[1] Hare to Selwyn, 27 June 1778; Jesse, *Grenville*, iii. 288.

[2] Walpole, *Last Journals*, ii. 184; 2 June 1778.

[3] Donne, *Letters of George III*, ii. 198; also W. C. Ford, p. 129.

[4] Herbert, *Pembroke Letters and Diaries*.

[5] Amherst to Germain, undated except 'Wednesday evening, Whitehall'; Clements, *Germain Papers*, viii. 75; also *HMC, Stop. Sack*. ii. 121.

[6] Some of the British and German officers had broken their paroles. The Congress was also angered by the refusal of the British Government to regard or treat men captured from the ships of the new United States Navy as prisoners of war, or to permit their exchange in the usual way (see S. Morison, *John Paul Jones*, 1959). France's entry into the war had also made the return of the Saratoga captives diplomatically difficult for the Congress, since although they were pledged not to fight in America, they were not pledged not to fight elsewhere, and could thus be used against France and relieve other men to fight against the Americans as well.

and this gave the Ministry a new and plausible way to attack
Burgoyne. On 5 June 1778, after Burgoyne had been less than
a month in England, Lord Barrington, Secretary at War, wrote
to him: 'The King, judging your presence material to the troops
detained prisoners in New England, under the Convention of
Saratoga, and finding in a letter of yours to Sir William Howe,
dated April 9, 1778 that "you trust a short time at Bath will
enable you to return to America", his Majesty is pleased to order
that you shall repair to Boston as soon as you have tried the Bath
waters, in the manner you propose.'[1]

With the magnificent inconsistency of bureaucracies, a government which had denied Burgoyne an inquiry 'which may
in any wise tend, however remotely, to restrain or affect his
person', and which had questioned his legal existence and therefore his right to sit in the House, was now ordering him to
replace himself in the hands of an enemy government that had
not sent for him. But when a king is 'pleased to order' it is a
rash man or a brave one who openly resists. But to Burgoyne
it was not an order given by his old friend the king but a punitive
move by his enemies in the Ministry. In a later letter to his constituents Burgoyne wrote: 'Though it bore the King's name, it
was avowedly a Letter of the Cabinet, and there remained no
longer a doubt in my mind that my ruin was a measure of state.'[2]
Under the circumstances Burgoyne was justified in being a little
disingenuous. He replied to Lord Barrington that his doctor
had ordered him 'repose, regimen of diet and repeated visits to
Bath'.[3] Five days later Barrington wrote that the king attached
much importance to Burgoyne's presence with his captive troops
and that it was '. . . His pleasure that you return as soon as you
can, without any risk of material injury to your health'.[4]

There the matter rested for a year. Burgoyne remained in
England, in good enough health to harass the Ministry at every
opportunity and again to present his case effectively at the
Parliamentary Inquiry for Howe. Then, on 24 September 1779,
the Ministry returned to the attack through Charles Jenkinson,
who had replaced Barrington as Secretary at War. Hutchinson

[1] Barrington to Burgoyne, 5 June 1778. This and later exchanges quoted in
this controversy are in Burgoyne's *Letter to his Constituents* and/or Hudleston,
pp. 285–300.   [2] Burgoyne's *Letter to his Constituents*.
[3] Burgoyne to Barrington, 22 June 1778.
[4] Barrington to Burgoyne, 27 June 1778.

had written of Jenkinson that he 'has the King's ear, and deserves it, for he is exceedingly clever'.[1] Walpole described him less favourably as '. . . the director or agent of all his Majesty's secret counsels . . . able, shrewd, timid, cautious, and dark; much fitter to suggest and digest measures than to execute them',[2] and later as a man '. . . that would have fixed a bowstring round the throat of the Constitution'.[3] Jenkinson wrote officially to Burgoyne: 'I am commanded by the King to acquaint you that your not returning to America and joining the troops, prisoners under the convention of Saratoga, is considered as a neglect of duty, and disobedience of orders, transmitted to you by the Secretary at War, in his letter of 5th June, 1778.'[4]

Burgoyne, who was as ready with pen as with tongue and sword, and almost as rash, replied: 'The time in which I am charged with neglect of duty, has been employed to vindicate my own honour, the honour of the British troops and those of his Majesty's allies, under my late command, from the most base and barbarous aspersions that were ever forged against innocent men, by malignity supported by power.' Since, Burgoyne asked, he had been deprived of an inquiry by the argument that he was not amenable to British law while on American parole, how could British law now order him to return to a foreign country that had not asked for him? His enemies were

very systematically desirous of burying my innocence and their guilt, in the prisons of the enemy, and by removing my person, to the other side of the Atlantic Ocean, the means of renewing Parliamentary proceedings which they have reason to dread. . . . if not allowed an early trial, or by the King's grace, upon this representation, restored to a capacity of service . . . accept my resignation of my appointment upon the American staff, of the Queen's regiment of light dragoons; and of the government of Fort William, humbly desiring only to reserve my rank as lieutenant general in the army to render me the more clearly amenable to a court martial hereafter, and enable me to fulfil my personal faith, should I be required by the enemy to do so.[5]

[1] Clements, *Hutchinson Diaries* (original MS.), p. 5; 5 July 1774.
[2] Walpole, *Memoirs of George III*, iv. 135, note.
[3] Walpole, *Last Journals*, i. 513.
[4] Jenkinson to Burgoyne, 24 Sept. 1779; Hudleston, pp. 287, 288.
[5] Burgoyne to Jenkinson, 9 Oct. 1779; Hudleston, p. 288.

Jenkinson replied within the week:

. . . Having laid your letter before the King, I am commanded to acquaint you, that for the reasons submitted to his Majesty by the Board of Officers, in their report, dated May 23, 1778 (which reasons subsist in the same force now as they did at that time) his Majesty does not think it proper that any part of your conduct should be brought before a military tribunal, so long as you shall continue engaged to re-deliver yourself into the power of Congress upon their command and due notice being given by them. Nor does his Majesty think proper, in consequence of the representations contained in your said letter, to restore you, circumstanced as you are, to a capacity of service. Neither of these requests can therefore be granted.

I have it further in command from the King to acquaint you, that his Majesty considers your letter to me a proof of your determination to persevere in not obeying his orders . . . and for this reason, his Majesty is pleased to accept your resignation of the command of the Queen's regiment of Light Dragoons, of the Government of Fort William, and of your appointment to the American staff, allowing you only to reserve the rank of Lieutenant General in the army, for the purposes you have stated.[1]

Burgoyne stuck by his guns:

I must persist in denying that I have received any other order, than an order subject to my own discretion. I must persist in my claim to a court martial. I apprehend, that if I am not subject to a trial for breach of orders, it implies that I am not subject to the orders themselves. I do not admit that I cannot legally have a court martial, I must request you to assure his Majesty, with all humility on my part, that though I have reason to complain heavily of his Majesty's Ministers, my mind is deeply impressed, as it ever has been, with a sense of duty, respect and affection for his royal person.[2]

Jenkinson's answer was brief: 'Sir: I have the honour to acknowledge the receipt of your letter, dated the 17th instant, and to acquaint you, that I took the first opportunity of laying it before the King. I have the honour to be, etc.'[3]

No further attempt was made to force Burgoyne to America, and he never again set foot there. He paid a high price in honours and income for his independence, but he made the most of it. His pamphlet seeking the support of his constituents

---

[1] Jenkinson to Burgoyne, 15 Oct. 1779.
[2] Burgoyne to Jenkinson, 17 Oct. 1779.
[3] Jenkinson to Burgoyne, 22 Oct. 1779.

at Preston, which told the whole story of his tribulations, won him re-election and a wide reading. He continued, in Parliament and in public, to broadcast the sins of the Ministry. Fashionable society had never deserted him, and he was soon as popular as ever in most of the best clubs and country houses, and an influential member of the Opposition.

His obligation to the Continental Congress remained, and on 3 April 1781 Thomas Bee moved, Thomas McKean seconded, and the Congress voted a resolution recalling Burgoyne under his parole. Washington explained to General Clinton that Burgoyne's high rank had made an exchange impossible, but did not add that the Congress had been angered by the continued imprisonment in the Tower of London of the captured Henry Laurens, former President of the Congress, and that the recalling of Burgoyne was in partial retribution.

Washington was probably not sympathetic with the action of Congress, for he proved amenable to the proposals of Burgoyne's friends in both parties. Burgoyne's departure for America was postponed while new negotiations for an exchange were undertaken, though not, apparently, with the active help of the Ministry. Edmund Burke wrote to Benjamin Franklin in Paris urging an exchange and praising Burgoyne as a man who always behaved 'with the Temper that becomes a great military character, that loves nothing so much in the profession as the means it so frequently permits of generosity and humanity'.[1] This must have seemed to Franklin a unique first motive for a professional warrior, but he helped to cut the knots of the diplomatic tangle. The American victory at Yorktown helped still more, since it made the possession of Burgoyne unimportant to an America that had won the war.

The matter was settled when Washington accepted Clinton's suggestion that the American and British Commissioners General of Prisoners meet and 'adjust the exchange', and on 2 February 1782, and after four and a half years of being a prisoner on parole, Burgoyne was exchanged for 1,047 enlisted men and lesser officers of the American Army. 'It was taking a quantity of silver in exchange for a piece of gold', Edmund Burke told the House of Commons.[2]

[1] *Hansard*, xxii. 860.
[2] Ibid.

Burgoyne had fought the enemy and though captured he had not been contained. He had returned to his own land to fight a second war against his own government at almost equal risks, and though badly injured he had not been silenced or exiled. Freed at last from parole, not even Lord George Germain could question his rights as an Englishman. Especially Lord George, for the same week that brought Burgoyne his freedom brought to the Secretary of State for America a less welcome relief from the powers and pains of office.

XXI

DIGRESSION ON PEACE

IT is impossible to be certain what the majority of Englishmen really thought about the American war. Votes in Parliament could not reveal, since Parliament did not represent, the opinion of all the common men of England. But the number of military and naval officers who openly opposed the war is impressive.[1] Sir Jeffery Amherst, one of the nation's most experienced and respected soldiers,[2] and Admiral Keppel, one of its ablest naval officers,[3] both refused to command against the colonists, and accepted active service only after France had entered the war.[4] General Conway, one of Britain's most prominent soldier statesmen, told the House of Commons in late 1779 that: 'He still, as he always had done, abhorred and detested that war. He thought it unjust in principle, oppressive and unconstitutional, and had it proved successful, big with danger to the liberties of this country.'[5] General Harvey had from the beginning opposed any attempt to coerce the Americans by a land force as a 'wild' idea.[6] Admiral Howe and General Howe had, before Lexington, told their constituents at Nottingham that they would not fight against the Americans.

Other men in less powerful military positions had also sacrificed their careers to their principles. The Earl of Effingham resigned his commission rather than take up arms against the Americans.[7] So did Lord Pitt, heir to the Earl of Chatham,

---

[1] Turberville, *Lords*, p. 361.

[2] 'They had offered a peerage and everything else he could ask to Sir Jeffery Amherst to take the command . . . but his wife dissuaded him and he gave for answer that he could not bring himself to command against the Americans, to whom he had been so much obliged' (Walpole, *Last Journals*, i. 433; 7 Feb. 1775).

[3] 'Admiral August Keppel was an active follower of the Marquis of Rockingham. . . . He refused to serve against the Colonists' (*Sandwich Papers*, ii. 3).

[4] Amherst as Military Adviser to the Cabinet and later as Commander-in-Chief of British armed forces, in 1778; Keppel in command of the home fleet against France in April 1778.

[5] *Hansard*, xx. 1251; 8 Dec. 1779.

[6] Harvey to Irwin, 30 June 1775; Fortescue, *HBA*, 2, iii. 167.

[7] Turberville, *Lords*, p. 361.

X

perhaps at his father's orders.[1] So did Captain Peregrine Bertie, member of Parliament for Oxford, and young Hugh Percy, who in a later war would become a Lieutenant-General. Their general attitude was expressed by the Earl of Chesterfield, a worldly but by no means unprincipled man: 'I never saw a froward child mended by whipping.'[2]

Major-General William Phillips exemplified a larger group of military men who, like General Clinton, consented to serve, but with troubled hearts or inner confusion. Phillips was a professional soldier and one of Britain's best artillery officers. By bringing his guns rapidly into action at Minden he had helped defeat the French; by dragging them up Sugar Hill to command Ticonderoga he had ensured its capture. After Saratoga he became a prisoner of war; was finally exchanged; joined Clinton to fight again, and sickened and died while leading a force into Tidewater, Virginia, in 1781. Yet in the spring of 1778 he wrote to Clinton from internment at Cambridge: 'Rumour in many tongues, cries out a French war. Should it be so, I shall hope to join you in Fields where we have fought and conquer'd. There conquest becomes a gratification and the mind exults. Here pity interposes and we cannot forget that when we strike we wound a Brother.'[3]

Lord George Germain, however, was troubled by no such doubts or such fraternal sympathy for the colonists. As Secretary for America he was as clearly charged with leadership in making peace as in making war, but he initiated not a single serious move toward negotiation. He had not assumed his post to conciliate the Americans but to subjugate them. He stood openly for unconditional surrender and dictated terms. When others insisted on peace overtures he seems to have done his best to prevent them from being successful.

Soon after Bunker Hill the Opposition demanded a serious attempt at conciliation, and before Lord George had been six months in office Lord North supported a proposal to appoint Commissioners to discuss peace with representatives of the Continental Congress. When compelled as a member of the Ministry to co-operate in that endeavour, Lord George was outwardly amenable but covertly obstructionist. William Knox,

---

[1] Hudleston, p. 62.　　　　　　　　　　　　　　　　[2] Ibid.
[3] Phillips to Clinton, 20 May 1778; PRO, 30/55, no. 1186.

who probably understood his chief as well as any man, wrote that: 'The truth was, Lord George having now collected a vast force and having a fair prospect of subduing the Colonies, he wished to reduce them before he treated at all.'[1]

When the terms to be offered the Americans were under discussion in March 1776, Lord George insisted on conditions so inflexible that Lord North openly opposed him.[2] Lord George threatened to resign if he did not have his way, and Lord North and Dartmouth threatened to resign if he did.[3] However much the king hated the idea of overtures to the colonists, he hated the idea of losing Lord North still more, and Lord North won the duel. Lord George gave in, but only outwardly. Since as Secretary for America he was the chief intermediary between the new Commissioners and the Cabinet, he continued to make their mission difficult.

The Commission, appointed on 6 May,[4] had a curious membership in view of its objective. The original idea had been to have one Commissioner—Admiral Lord Richard Howe, but after some discussion a second commissioner was added—his brother General Howe, who had just become Sir William as a Knight of the Bath. Lord George liked the idea of a Commission still less when he heard the Howe brothers were to head it, and though he could not prevent their appointment he bargained for the addition of his political crony William Eden.[5] Eden was

---

[1] *HMC, Var. Coll.* 6, *Knox*, p. 259.

[2] See letters of Suffolk and Wedderburn.

[3] Germain insisted that the Americans should be required to acknowledge the complete authority of Parliament, in which he proposed that they not be directly represented. He regarded the Commission merely as empowered to accept submission. . . . Dartmouth, desiring conciliation, threatened to resign forthwith, and North stated he would not continue in office if such a condition were insisted upon. Germain retorted by suggesting that he should resign himself (*HMC, Stop. Sack.* ii. 23–25).

[4] PRO, CO/5, v. 253, no. 128; also Clements, *Knox Papers*, ix. 9, the latter an original copy dated 6 May 1776, with a copy of the 'Additional Instructions' that made the Howes' task more difficult.

[5] 'Lord George had no liking for the Commission more especially for Lord Howe being sole Commissioner . . . altho' he was content that he should go a Commissioner if others were joined with him, [or] if it was agreed that he should be tied down by Instructions such as Lord George should think proper. Lord Howe insisted upon what had been promised only he consented that his Brother the Genl. should be joined with him, nor would he go Commander of the Fleet if he was not Commissioner also . . . . Lord Sandwich did not chuse to give him the Command of the Fleet but all the other ministers having set upon him he at last gave way' (Clements, *Knox Papers*, x. 23).

a member of the Board of Trade, Undersecretary and general factotum to Lord Suffolk, and undercover handyman to Lord North. He was a man always on the inside of things, whose influence exceeded his official positions and whose ambition matched his considerable ability. The Howe brothers were members of a prominent Whig family; they could not well refuse service in the cause of peace, and they were appointed by Lord North partly in hope of disarming Whig opposition. But to have as Peace Commissioners the commanding officers of the land and naval forces opposing the Americans; to ask them to merge the sword and the ploughshare, placed the Howe brothers in the difficult position of trying to act the lion and the dove at the same time. Some men in Westminster disapproved their appointment for another reason. 'Could no abler men be found to conduct a business of such moment?' Henry Ellis inquired.[1] Eden, with his political astuteness, might temper their military minds, but Lord George had other reasons for including him. He shared at that time Lord George's inflexibility toward the rebels, and would see that the Howe brothers were not too soft; and as an adviser to Lord North he could be counted upon to restrain the First Minister's urge toward undue conciliation.

Lord Howe was soon at odds with Lord George regarding the peace terms that could be offered. The Ministry, after some vague consultations with Parliament, had outlined general instructions to the Commissioners, but the closer definition of the peace terms fell largely into the hands of the Secretary for America. It soon became apparent to Lord Howe that Lord George was interpreting the Ministry's instructions in a far different spirit than Lord North and Parliament had intended. If Lord George's instructions were adhered to, the Commissioners could offer the Americans only peace terms they would certainly declare unacceptable and probably regard as offensive. Lord George wrote in irritation to Lord North that the Admiral, though reasonable enough in other matters, seemed to have no understanding of the delicate complications of peacemaking, and: '. . . it always ends in the same story. I beg Lord North would see and finally settle with him'.[2]

---

[1] Ellis to Knox, 15 May 1778; *HMC, Var. Coll. 6, Knox*, p. 143.
[2] Germain to North, 18 Feb. 1776; *Stevens Facsimiles*, v. 465.

But Lord North dodged the issue and Lord Howe threatened to resign. He wrote to Lord George that:

He always flattered himself the instructions of Government were that he should be authorized upon his arrival to hold forth to the Americans, in the mildest tho' firmest manner the most favorable terms the Government meant to grant. . . . But observing that a method directly the reverse is now ordered to be pursued, it is with infinite concern that he finds himself obliged to confess that he is disqualified from engaging as a Commissioner in the execution of Instructions formed in that plan.[1]

The controversy dragged on for another month, though even Wedderburn warned his friend Lord George that the instructions he was forcing upon Howe were too restrictive. 'I should think the whole business much safer if . . . his powers were not totally restrained, than from any limitation that could be penned in an Instruction which he accepted reluctantly. . . . I really think the best security for the good execution of it will be the idea that he is confided in.'[2]

With other Ministers and most of Parliament insistent on more latitude for Admiral Howe, and the Howes threatening not to serve otherwise, Lord George backed down again, and the Commission began its efforts. On 20 June 1776 the Howe brothers issued their first proclamation, offering pardons to Americans who would pledge loyalty to the Crown.[3] Even at that time 'General Howe's opinion was that the declaration would produce no effect'.[4] The General was correct, but the Howe brothers dutifully issued further proclamations on 14 July, 19 September, and 1 November 1776.[5] The 1 November proclamation offered absolute pardon to all Americans who within sixty days took an oath of allegiance to the Crown. Lord George did not approve that continued solicitation, and wrote to Knox: 'Sir Wm Howe finished his campaign honourably and advantageously; but I cannot approve of the general pardon from the Commissioners. It is poor encouragment for the friends of Government, who have been suffering under the tyrany of the rebels, to see their oppressors without distinction put upon

[1] Lord Howe to North, 26 Mar. 1776; *HMC, Stop. Sack*. ii. 29.
[2] Wedderburn to Germain, 24 Apr. 1776; ibid.
[3] Clements, *Germain Papers*, iii; also *HMC, Stop. Sack*. ii. 36.
[4] Henry Strachey, *Journal*, 12 July 1776; *HMC*, vi, *Strachey*, p. 402.
[5] Clements, *Germain Papers*, v.

the same footing with themselves.'[1] He instructed the Howes to proclaim that all Americans who had not subscribed allegiance within the sixty-day period would then be promptly visited with the 'punishment their crimes merited . . . it will be incumbent upon you to use the powers with which you are entrusted in such a manner that those persons who have shown themselves undeserving of the royal mercy may not escape that punishment which is due their crimes, and which it will be expedient to inflict for the sake of example and futurity'.[2]

To insist that men like Hancock, Jefferson, Franklin, and Washington must be treated like war criminals was to make peace negotiations futile, as the Howe brothers knew and Lord George should have known. On 25 March 1777 the frustrated Howes wrote to him to inquire: 'Are we required to withhold his Majesty's pardon, even though the withholding of such a general pardon should prevent the termination of the war?'[3] Lord George never gave the Howes a clear answer; he could not do so without making himself vulnerable to Parliament and his own colleagues, but his private answer would almost certainly have been Yes. Their letter crossed one he sent them urging them not to be soft in their peace talks.[4]

Lord George was counting on a smashing victory by Burgoyne and another by Howe before the winter of 1777 set in, and thought it would be well to keep the peace talks from committing Britain to any terms more generous than the ones which could be dictated after those defeats of the rebels. He had no sympathy with the Howe proclamation of 15 March 1777, which again offered pardon to Americans bearing arms against the Crown, if they surrendered before 2 May.[5] This repetitive offering of pardons had lost any original effect, but the Howes had nothing else to offer. There was nothing of conciliation in a pardon for renouncing rebellion, and the Howes were forbidden by the terms of their instructions to propose any real concessions. The Committee of Congress appointed 'to hear such propositions as Lord Howe should think fit to make',[6] reported that: 'His

[1] Germain to Knox, 3 Dec. 1776; *HMC, Var. Coll.* 6, *Knox*, p. 128.
[2] Germain to Lord Howe, 14 Jan. 1777; *HMC, Stop. Sack.* i. 56.
[3] Howe to Germain, 25 Mar. 1777; Clements, *Germain Papers.*
[4] Germain to the Howes, 25 Mar. 1777; PRO, CO/5, v. 177, 147, 148.
[5] PRO, 30/55, no. 444.
[6] Resolve of Congress, 6 Sept. 1776.

Lordship's Commission contained no other authority of importance than that of granting pardons ... and of declaring America,
or any part of it, in the King's peace, upon submission.'[1]

It was obvious that any punitive or destructive actions by
British ships, soldiers, or mercenaries would impair the chances
of Howe's success in the peace talks. Yet during the life of the
Peace Commission, Lord George urged on the Howe brothers
'a warm diversion upon the coasts of Massachusetts Bay and
New Hampshire', whose ports he wanted occupied or destroyed.
Descents of the same kind on Rhode Island and Charleston
were often in his mind and in his letters. It was not easy for the
Commissioners to attempt to gain peace while the Secretary
of State was known in America to be saying that he longed to
see Boston in flames. To Lord George's repeated proposals of
raids on New England Sir William Howe replied in June 1777:
'. . . it is not practicable without interfering with the more
important operations of the campaign, that have received the
royal approbation and which are already too much curtailed
by the want of land force'.[2]

Lord George's peace procedures widened the split in the
Cabinet and made that split apparent to all. Almost at the same
hour on 30 May that he was stating to the House of Commons
that the policy of the Government was unconditional surrender
of the Americans, Viscount Weymouth, another Secretary of
State, was denying that very policy in the House of Lords.[3]
On that issue Lord George had the support of the king; and
Lord North, who never openly opposed his sovereign, did his
best to placate his resentful colleagues. It is no wonder the Peace
Commission failed.

Six months later, after the news of Burgoyne's surrender
reached London, sentiment for a negotiated peace mounted
rapidly. Even Israel Maudit, a writer who sometimes sold his
pen to the Ministry, declared for independence in early 1778.
Not only because Lord George seemed to have lost the war but
because he insisted on continuing it, 'The unpopularity of the
American Secretary was . . . great and manifest.'[4] Lord North

[1] Balch, *Galloway*, p. 10, note.
[2] Howe to Germain, 3 June 1777; *HMC, Stop. Sack*. ii. 68.
[3] Walpole, *Last Journals*, ii. 29.
[4] Adolphus, ii, ch. 23.

tried to save both the colonies and his Ministry by a second and
more urgent effort to negotiate peace, and to see that this time
it was offered on terms the Americans might accept.[1] He even
told the king that he had never really approved the war; certainly Saratoga convinced him that it was futile. But the king
would not agree, and was always 'deeply hurt' at what he
called such disloyalty or desertion. Lord North continued to act
in opposition to his own sentiments, though they were known to
a few and suspected by many. 'Lord N is for peace at any rate',
Lieutenant-Colonel Smith wrote in his secret report to Eden in
America.[2]

Had Lord North not anticipated the Opposition leaders in his
move for peace, they might have forced it or forced out his
Ministry, for even the country gentlemen were beginning to
waver. The astute Beaumarchais reported to Vergennes: 'Be
certain also that the English Ministers restrain the universal
resentment only by assuring all their friends that they are
working sincerely for peace with America.'[3] The peace terms
Lord North proposed to Parliament surprised the Opposition
by their liberality. They included repeal of the duty on tea to
the colonies, no colonial taxes for revenue, the income of any
taxes to regulate commerce to be used for public purposes
within the colony from which they came and only with the
approval of the Assembly of that colony. 'Everything', as
devoted followers of the Ministry explained, 'except independence, was conceded.'[4] Such terms gave the Whigs, the
more liberal Tories, and the public, little excuse for opposing
the Ministry on the peace terms, and they rather grudgingly
approved the very measure they had wished to initiate. Though
he had done it too late to achieve peace, North had at least
stolen a march on his British opposition.

This time Lord North practically ignored Lord George
Germain in the formulation of a peace programme and in the
selection of Peace Commissioners. It would certainly not have
been helpful to the cause to take Lord George's advice, for even
after Saratoga he was opposed to any concessions to the rebels,

[1] *Hansard*, xix. 762 ff.; 16 Feb. 1778.
[2] Smith to Eden, Aug. 1778; Stevens, *Facsimiles*, v. 513, 514.
[3] Beaumarchais to Vergennes, 1 Jan. 1778; French Archives, Angleterre, v. 528,
f. 5; also Stevens, *Facsimiles*, xxi. 1815.
[4] Lecky, iv. 76, 77.

and said, according to report, that Lord North's proposals would make 'a disgraceful peace'. But Lord George complained bitterly at not having been consulted:

. . . when I consider [he wrote to Irwin on 3 February] that this whole matter of conciliation, the choice of commissioners etc. has been carried on not only without consulting me but without the smallest degree of communication, and when I reflect upon the Chancellor's conduct towards me . . . I cannot doubt but that my services are no longer acceptable. I wish to take my ground as well as I can, and to show that I cannot submit to neglect and ill-usage, at the same time that I would avoid distressing those with whom I have acted; though perhaps I might be justified if I looked only at my own situation.[1]

Yet after Lord North had guided his conciliation bill through the House of Commons: 'Lord George Germaine rose and said a few words, and declared he looked upon himself as responsible for those pacific measures.'[2] Had Charles Fox been in the House at the time he could hardly have resisted puncturing that pretence.

As First Lord of the Treasury, Lord North had special reasons for initiating peace proposals. He hoped 'partly to get rid of the inquiry', and also to enable the Ministry 'to get back the votes they had lost, as the most conscientous would be glad of peace'.[3] But he also knew that Britain could not continue to finance so expensive a war. In another year there would be, on the payroll if not on active duty, over 300,000 men, including mercenaries, in the British land and naval forces.[4] The national debt had risen nearly 50 per cent. during the past three years, and if the war could be won at all, it obviously could be won only by even more expensive efforts. New excises were bringing mounting complaints from every level of British society. And who could tell how much a war with France, and perhaps with Spain as well, would add to this staggering bill? 'The stocks, the political pulse of the nation, were so low they plainly demonstrated the weakness of the state', Burke told the House of Commons on 16 March 1778.[5] Thomas Coutts, moneylender to kings as well as merchants, and head of the banking enterprise that still bears

---

[1] Germain to Irwin, 3 Feb. 1778; HMC, *Stop. Sack*. i. 139.
[2] Walpole, *Last Journals*, ii. 124. [3] Ibid., p. 109.
[4] Lecky, iv. 14. [5] *Hansard*, xix. 908.

his name, wrote a week after the news of Saratoga: 'I hear the
Ministry still talk of going on with the war. I daresay they will
be as long as they can, but it cannot go on very long. Burgoyne's
army being taken prisoners made the Stocks fall. I think it
should have had a contrary effect since it was likely to have
drawn matters to an end. Probably Howe's army may next
year be in the same situation, or sooner.'[1] When bankers declare
a war a bad risk, ministers and kings must cut their losses or
else fall from power, as Lord North recognized if the king did not.

In the peace effort of 1778 the terms the new Commissioners
might offer were discussed in Parliament, but the orators were
too busy shooting off their own fireworks to achieve clear-cut
agreements in specific detail, as one example illustrates. 'James
Luttrell proposed that the Commissioners for Peace should be
authorized to promise the removal of any Ministers to whom the
Americans should object. It occasioned a long debate but was
rejected.'[2] A motion to give the rebellious colonies veto powers
in the choice of British Ministers was fantastic, and the fact that
it was discussed did not mean that Parliament was seriously
considering the motion on its merits. The proposal was a stick
with which to beat Lord George and other Ministers, and the
Whigs grasped it with enthusiasm.

Parliament finally granted the Peace Commissioners large
powers to treat with Congress, to proclaim the cessation of
hostilities by land and sea, to grant pardons to all descriptions
of persons, and to suspend the operation of all Acts of Parliament relating to the American colonies which had been enacted
since 1763.[3] Two years earlier such terms might have ended
the rebellion, but after Saratoga and the French declaration the
American mood had changed. It is unlikely that the Congress
would have accepted any terms short of full independence.

When the Opposition discovered that the new Peace Commissioners were to be briefed and directed by the Secretary of
State for America, they raised strong objections and threatened
to vote against the Bill. Spencer Stanhope pointed out that Lord
George Germain had:

. . . observed the most profound silence concerning the peace

---

[1] Coleridge, *Life of Thomas Coutts*, i. 86; 10 Dec. 1777.
[2] *Hansard*, xix. 898; also Walpole, *Last Journals*, ii. 131.
[3] Lecky, iv. 76; from 18 George III, c. xi, xii, xiii.

terms. . . . What, shall we trust the correspondence with the commissioners, the instructions to be signed, the principal direction of
this great work of conciliation, to a man, whose sentiments, the last
at least that he has thought proper to declare upon the subject here,
were that he would sooner cut off his right hand than sign a treaty
with rebels with arms in their hands? Has he changed his opinion
in that respect, or does he hold this House too cheap to tell them
whether he has or not?[1]

Lord George, who was present, continued silent, and Lord
North's Bill of Conciliation was passed.[2]

It was not easy to secure men of competence and standing,
satisfactory to Opposition as well as King and Court, to serve
on the Peace Commission. Whoever had fought or negotiated
in America had returned with diminished stature, except a few
lucky ones.[3] William Eden angled for appointment and secured
it. Richard Jackson, a member of Parliament with good reputation and a knowledge so pompously encyclopedic that he was
known as 'omniscient Jackson', agreed to serve, but after conversations with the Ministers withdrew at the eleventh hour.
Eager for real conciliation, Jackson apparently concluded there
was no alternative to giving the colonies full independence,
and this the Ministry would not consider.[4] He was replaced
by Captain George Johnstone, former Crown Governor of
East Florida, 'brave, brutal, rash, overbearing, litigious and
rather clever',[5] who had fought a duel with Lord George
Sackville;[6] 'was an excellent example of the time-serving member of Parliament, who would stickle at nothing in support
of the Ministry',[7] and had the special qualification of having
once been found guilty by a court martial of insubordination
and disobedience.

The third member and head of the Commission was a far
more winning character. When he was appointed on 13 April
1778 Frederick Howard, fifth Earl of Carlisle, was only thirty.
In his earlier youth he had been a stripling of fashion who had

[1] *Hansard*, xix. 802.   [2] *Hansard*, xix. 815.
[3] Walpole, *Last Journals*, ii. 129; 6 Mar. 1778.
[4] Van Doren, *Secret History*, p. 68.
[5] Walpole, *Last Journals*, ii. 127, note.
[6] Ibid., p. 157; 4 Apr. 1778.
[7] C. F. Adams, 'Contemporary Opinion on the Howes', *Proc. Mass. Hist. Socy.*
xliv, Nov. 1910, pp. 94 ff.

run up large debts by spectacular gambling and written an ode to the odeist Thomas Gray. More recently he had put aside such youthful indiscretions; renewed his friendship with his Eton schoolmate William Eden; formed another with Charles Fox, and taken soberly to politics. Lord North was eager to win him to support the Ministry and had him in mind for further appointments.[1] He had developed such seriousness of purpose that Burke pronounced him: '. . . a young man of considerable promise and accomplishments . . . an eminently honest and well-meaning man',[2] and even the critical Horace Walpole pronounced him: '. . . very fit to make a treaty', but added ironically, 'that will not be made'.[3]

It was not long before the Commissioners began to wonder whether the Ministry really wanted them to achieve a peace. Immediately after his appointment to what men with more arrogance than diplomacy called 'The Commission for Restoring Peace to the Colonies', Eden took it upon himself to offer a suggestion, with an implied criticism well wrapped inside it, to Lord George Germain. He knew of Lord George's treatment of Clinton and suggested that Clinton could not be of real help to the Commissioners if his morale were too shattered by frustrations from Whitehall. Eden wrote from Downing Street to Lord George:

You will be sick of my letters before I begin my mission under your command; but I must say one more word for poor Clinton. I think the slight he now suffers may have decisive consequences against the success of our business, which cannot be conducted well unless we have the cordial co-operation of the actual Commander-in-Chief of his Majesty's forces for the time being. Lord Suffolk, to whom I found all the rest of this story quite new, agrees with me in this.[4]

There is no indication that Lord George took this advice to heart, and his Undersecretary Knox later wrote:

. . . all attempts to negociate with the Congress or any body of men in the exercise of authority arising out of Independency must be vain, because the giving up Independency is giving up themselves. For a similar reason our General and Admiral are the most unfit persons

[1] Van Doren, *Secret History*.   [2] Lecky, iv. 518, 542.
[3] Walpole to Mann, 4 Mar. 1778; Toynbee, x. 197.
[4] Eden to Germain, 12 Apr. 1778; *HMC, Stop. Sack*. ii. 106.

to be entrusted with the powers of negociation, for Peace must put
an end to their command & proffits & deprive all their favourites
and dependents of their emoluments, and it ought not to be expected
of any men to act against their own interest and the advice and
persuasion of all the people around them.[1]

Eden then underwent an experience which shook the confidence of even so experienced a public servant. He wrote to
Lord North of: 'the coolness with which this business has been
from the first treated by the Cabinet'.[2] It was probably the
same experience that Lord Carlisle described in a personal
letter to an old friend and mentor:

These preliminary arrangements being settled, we were desired to
meet at Lord North's on the 13th of March, to receive the outlines
of our instructions and compare our different ideas of the business
in which we were to be employed. At this meeting were present
Lord North, Lord Geo. Germain, the Attorney General, the Solicitor
General, Mr. Eden, Mr. Jackson, and myself. Little passed of any
real importance, and I confess I came away a little shocked at the
slovenly manner in which an affair so serious in its nature had been
dismissed.[3]

Somewhat deflated by this and other indications of their secondary importance in the eyes of the Ministers, the three members
of the Commission took ship at Portsmouth on 22 April 1778.[4]
They were surprised to discover at the last moment that they
were to be landed at New York when the main British force
was established at Philadelphia, and their protests induced the
captain to take them to Philadelphia instead. The Earl of Carlisle wrote back to a friend his comments on that episode and
on an even greater surprise that followed:

The day before our departure from London I thought it necessary
to call upon the Secretary of State for the American department, in
order to receive any further instruction that his Majesty might
honour me with. My visit was very short, and consequently not
difficult to recollect everything that passed.
    One thing fell from him that, if I had been more upon my guard,

---

[1] Germain to Knox: Clements, *Knox Papers*, ix. 29.
[2] Eden to North, 30 Mar. 1778; Stevens, *Facsimiles*, iv. 411.
[3] Carlisle to the Rev. Mr. Ekins, 'Private', from America, 29 Oct. 1778; *HMC,
Var. Coll.* 5, 6, *Carlisle*, pp. 377–9.
[4] Walpole, *Last Journals*, ii. 168.

might have induced me to have pursued him with more pressing interrogation; but at that time it did not occur to me that in order to *ensure* our departure, care was to be employed that we should have no intimation of the extraordinary plans laid down for the Naval and Military Commander whom we in our ignorance believed were either instructed or of themselves would act in that manner as might tend to facilitate our endeavors, I confess it made little impression upon me . . . .

Finding that New York was particularly marked out for the place of our destination, I wished to know the reason why that place was preferred to Philadelphia; the only answer I obtained was, *perhaps that city may not by your arrival be in our hands*. . . . I own I did not conceive anything further could be hid under those expressions, but that it was not insisted upon that city should be retained at all events, but that it should be relinquished, if other pursuits made the measure justifiable.

Upon our arrival in the River we found to our great surprise all the naval armament collected together with evident preparations for the immediate evacuation of the city . . . Immediately upon our landing the two Commanders in chief Lord Howe and Sir Henry Clinton, lost no time to display the embarrassment they were under & the difficulties that were to attend our undertaking. We were greatly astonished to find that they were both under the irresistable influence of *Positive* and repeated orders; which orders had industriously been kept a secret from us, tho' sent out long before our departure, and which when they are laid before you will clearly convince you are calculated to render the Commission both ineffectual and ridiculous.[1]

No action short of a drastic military defeat could more substantially have reduced the bargaining power of the Commissioners than the British withdrawal to New York. It was, in reality, a retreat. Not to have informed the Peace Commissioners of a move so important to their work was unpardonable. While Lord North and Lord George briefed the Commissioners, the evacuation of Philadelphia had already been ordered. Eden had warned Lord George that to show lack of confidence in Clinton might impair that general's services; now Eden himself, the trusted working associate of Lord North, Lord Suffolk, and Lord George Germain, had been refused their confidence in a matter crucial to the success of his work for them. Uncertain of the privacy of his letters, Eden first wrote very cautiously of the

---

[1] Carlisle to Ekins, Oct. 1778; Stevens, *Facsimiles*, i. 101; from Carlisle MSS. at Castle Howard.

matter to his brother in England: 'As to Politics, I must be excused at present,—I cannot in any degree trust this conveyance—If some steps had not been taken at Home which we never learnt till we arrived here I have little doubt that the Commission for Peace might in two or three months have made a great impression.'[1]

Eden believed he knew who had concocted the deceit, and did not hesitate to say so to Wedderburn in a letter marked Private:

Now what am I to think of this treatment I have personally received in this Transaction. L. G. Ger. *on the 12th March* communicated to me a Plan for carrying on this Campaign of a totally different Import. . . . *from the 17th of March to the 31st* Ld. North wd. never let me see Him: on the 31st it was arranged that the present Commission shld. be appointed & from that day to my departure on the *12th of April* I saw Him frequently & tho this important order was again in discussion with the Cabinet, He never said one syllable in Allusion to it.[2]

The next day Eden put restraint behind him and wrote to Lord George:

Having had very little claim to be honour'd with your Lordship's confidence, I cannot trouble you with any personal complaints respecting your reserve and secrecy in the extraordinary change of measures which makes the river at this moment as vast and mortifying a spectacle as any Englishman ever saw. Your Lordship might well suppose that if I had been thought proper from any established pretensions either of friendship or official confidence to be entrusted with the purport of the instructions of the 21st March, I might naturally have met with that attention from Lord Suffolk or Lord North. In my private capacity, therefore, I cannot complain of your Lordship, tho' perhaps I may think, that after you had communicated to me your first dispatch to Sir Henry Clinton . . . you had tacitly engaged yourself to communicate also any change in your plan so extremely decisive as that which was transmitted by your Lordship on the 21st of March, and again confirmed by you on the 9th of April, during which your Lordship had several long conversations with me, and never dropped a single expression that could lead me to conjecture what was passing.

[1] Eden to Morton Eden, 15 June 1778; Stevens, *Facsimiles*, v. 499.
[2] Eden to Wedderburn, 18 June 1778; from ship off Newcastle, Delaware, 'Private'; Stevens, *Facsimiles*, v. 500.

My only complaint, therefore, is that being appointed one of his Majesty's Commissioners, I was not entrusted with a measure essential to the conduct of that Commission, but was made a sacrifice to an official charge which the Parliament intended to be important and honourable, but which the King's ministers from subsequent motives thought proper to deprive of all the support that could add either effect or weight to it.[1]

Lord George commented in a note to Knox that: 'The Commissioner's letter and Mr. Johnston's protest are a melancholy beginning of our negotiations with America. I cannot say I expected much good from that quarter, but the Commissioners begin by taking care of themselves in laying the blame upon the Administration, and will soon declare that peace would have been settled had Philadelphia been held by our troops.'[2]

In due course Eden got his explanations. His confidential informant Lieutenant-Colonel Smith wrote to him: '*The fact is*, Lord S[uffolk] was absent from that meeting & never knew of it; Lord N[orth] thought you knew it, & Ld. G. G. says he had orders to communicate to no one, but his own Secretary.'[3] If Lord North thought Eden had been informed, from whom could orders have come to Lord George not to communicate the decision to the Commissioners?

Lord George also wrote to Eden what he doubtless regarded as a satisfactory explanation:

I was surprised when I rec'd your Letter to hear that you had left England without being informed of the order given for evacuating Philadelphia. I was not at liberty to mention that Measure to any Person whatever (excepting to Mr. Knox who was to be employed in writing the Dispatch). Even Mr. de Grey in whom I place entire Confidence was not acquainted with it, and I was not permitted to communicate with Him upon that Subject. I can make no apology to any other Person for having obeyed the Orders I received. . . .

You will know how little I was consulted either about the Act of Parliament, or the appointment of the Commissioners, or the Powers

---

[1] Eden to Germain, 19 June 1778, from the ship *Trident* of Newcastle, Delaware; *HMC, Stop. Sack*. ii. 115. The evacuation orders to Admiral Howe and General Clinton were dated 21 Mar. and a second set of orders dated 9 Apr. confirmed them. The Peace Commission was officially constituted on 13 Apr. and left England on 22 Apr.

[2] Germain to Knox, 23 July 1778; *HMC, Var. Coll.* 6, *Knox*, p. 144.

[3] Smith to Eden, Aug. 1778, 'Most Secret'; Stevens, *Facsimiles*, v. 513, 514. The italics are Smith's.

to be trusted to them. My part in all that transaction was merely official, and as I was no stranger to the unreserved Confidence shewn to you upon that, and every other Business of Importance, I could not suppose that any Information from me could have been necessary; even if I had been at Liberty to have given it to you.[1]

While Clinton, starting on 18 June, led his army, closely pursued by Washington, across New Jersey and back to New York,[2] the Peace Commissioners went to New York by sea. They were unable even to enter into any official negotiations with the American Government: '. . . the American demands being in excess of the powers vested in the Commission'.[3] Congress refused to discuss any reconciliation that was not based on British recognition of America's full independence.

Before the end of July the Commissioners realized the futility of their position and in a letter to Lord George recommended their immediate return to England. 'Under the present state of affairs to persist any longer in our pacifick advances either to the Congress, or to the People at large, would be to expose his Majesty and the State of Great Britain to Insults; of which we should be sorry to be the occasion.'[4] But Lord George, who had done much to lessen the hopes of the Commissioners, now urged them to remain a while longer. Perhaps he did so in deference to the wishes of his colleagues; perhaps to prevent an uprising in Parliament fostered by the Opposition; perhaps because, in a mood so critical of the Ministry and himself, the Commissioners would be a political menace in London. Carlisle and Eden were placed in an impossible position. Half of London condemned them for not offering the Americans more; the other half for offering them too much.

[1] Germain to Eden, 3 July 1778; Clements, *Germain Papers*, vii. 51; also Stevens, *Facsimiles*, v. 511.
[2] Clinton reached Sandy Hook, across outer New York Bay from Manhattan, on 2 July 1778, after 14 days *en route*. He said he brought the troops back by land because the transports were late in reaching Philadelphia; because the naval officers said they could not embark the troops nearer than Newcastle, Delaware; and because there was not room in the transports for his cavalry and provisions. (Clinton to Germain, 5 June 1778; Clements, *Clinton Letter Book*, pp. 4, 5). Newcastle was the very spot that Howe had found inadequate to land the same army some ten months earlier.
[3] *DNB*, Carlisle.
[4] Peace Commissioners to Germain, end of July 1778; Clements, *Germain Papers*, vii. 49.

In October the Commissioners, as a final effort, published a manifesto appealing to the people of America, and offering peace terms to each state separately; threatening a desolating war if those offers were not widely accepted.[1] There were no affirmative results. Meanwhile two of the Commissioners had got into trouble in very different ways. Lord Carlisle was challenged to a duel by Lafayette and declined with dignity and good sense.[2] Commissioner Johnstone attempted 'private bribery' of American leaders; was disavowed by his fellow Commissioners and discredited on both sides of the Atlantic.[3] A year later, however, he was busily defending Lord George Germain in Parliament.

Lord George continued to deflate the spirits of the Commissioners. In early August he wrote to them to be careful to make no concessions without his express advance approval;[4] in September, in yielding to their urgent pleas to return, he gave them '. . . the discretionary Leave desired, confiding they would not use it improperly'.[5] With this qualified support and encouragement Carlisle and Eden had made their final effort in October and then returned to London. They doubtless would have agreed that: 'For the failure of the Carlisle peace mission Germain was more responsible than for its initiation.'[6]

Eden did not find Lord George as cordial as before his departure. 'Lord George was determined to get rid of him, and did everything to prevent his continuance' at the Board of Trade.[7] Carlisle was not less outraged at the treatment the Commissioners had received from the Ministry. Eden wrote to inform Lord North that Carlisle proposed to move in Parliament

---

[1] Lecky, iv. 78, 79.

[2] Of the Earl of Carlisle: 'Lafayette enraged at some strong expressions reflecting on the conduct of the French, which had been published in one of the proclamations of the commissioners, challenged Carlisle, as the principal commissioner, to a duel. Carlisle very properly declined the meeting, and informed Lafayette in a letter that he considered himself solely responsible to his country and his King, and not to any individual, for his public conduct and language' (*DNB*, Carlisle).

[3] Johnstone: '. . . so conducted himself that his colleagues disavowed his acts and he was forced to retire from the Commission, for having attempted to bribe some of the American leaders. He returned to England; attacked the Howe brothers and defended Germain' (C. F. Adams, *Mass. Hist. Socy.* xliv, Nov. 1910, p. 100, note).

[4] PRO, CO/5, v. 253, no. 201.

[5] Germain to Peace Commissioners, 2 Sept. 1778; PRO, CO/5, v. 253, no. 202.

[6] Guttridge, p. 13.   [7] *HMC, Var. Coll.* 6, *Knox*, p. 266.

that the House be given all the orders from Germain and
Sandwich that had bearing on the evacuation of Philadelphia
and the dispersion of British ships and troops 'to different and
distant services'.[1] This was obviously an attack on the Ministry,
to whom such a move could be highly embarrassing. Eden made
it quite clear to Lord North that he supported Carlisle's intention, thus risking a break with his old confidential chief. The
king, informed by Lord North of this proposed move, replied
that '. . . it does not require great penetration to discover that
Lord Carlisle is pressed to the step [he] is taking, either by his
relations or by Mr. Eden, in hopes it may drive you to give up
Lord George Germain'.[2]

Lord North wrote very promptly to Eden that he could not
approve: '. . . a motion which, if carried, will be more pernicious
to the general interest of the country. . . . From the moment that
this enquiry is gone into, I shall give up all hopes of reconciliation with the Colonies. . . . I write this in a hurry, & trust that
you will either burn it or send it back to me'.[3] Eden did neither.
The king commented to Lord North the next day: 'Lord North
. . . must now have his eyes fully opened to Mr. Eden's character.'[4]

Something more would have to be done to silence Lord
Carlisle. Perhaps an immediate offer of a post in the Ministry
would keep him from playing into the hands of the Opposition.
Carlisle thus became a pawn in a new duel between Lord North
and Lord George. Lord North, with the king's approval,
decided to separate the office of the Board of Trade from that of
the Secretary of State for America,[5] and appoint Lord Carlisle
Commissioner of Trade. Lord George threatened to resign if
this were done, for it would be a diminution of his prestige and
would seem a sign of disfavour from the king and Lord North.
But even Lord George's old ally and defender Wedderburn
manœuvred against him in the matter, for Wedderburn had
hitched his wagon to the rising star of young Lord Carlisle.[6]

---

[1] Eden to North, 10 Feb. 1779; Stevens, *Facsimiles*, v. 555.
[2] King to North, 11 Feb. 1779; Donne, *Letters*, p. 226.
[3] North to Eden, (?) 11 Feb. 1779; Stevens, *Facsimiles*, v. 556.
[4] King to North, 12 Feb. 1779; Stevens, *Facsimiles*, v. 557.
[5] Germain had begun his Secretaryship with an active attendance of the meetings
of the Board of Trade. But, though by 1778 he had become less regular in attendance and consequent influence, he had no wish to be shorn of any of his powers or
prestige.   [6] HMC, *Var. Coll.* 6, *Knox*, p. 268.

Wedderburn dearly craved a peerage, and did not welcome competition. He: '. . . felt himself little obliged to L. G. G., who had asked for a peerage'.[1]

During the last months of 1775 Wedderburn had been Lord George's most confidential political ally and source of inside information. Eden had been a close second and the intermediary between Lord North and Lord George. Now, in 1778, Lord George had lost the support and liking of both. Eden wrote to Wedderburn: 'It is but too true also, that the man who presides in the American office, at the same time that He precludes every accession of strength from any other quarter to the King's Government, has continued to lose the Esteem & Reliance of every description of men Civil and Military, who are to serve with Him or under Him.'[2] The Board of Trade was reorganized and Carlisle put at its head. Having insisted he would resign if that were done, Lord George sulked but did not resign.

The Opposition were critical of some of the actions of the Peace Commissioners, but they were much more critical of the Ministry that had mis-instructed and deceived them. Lord George was under the complicated necessity of defending himself by seeming to be eager for peace; of conceding that the Americans were more united than he had always claimed, and of undermining the Ministry's Commissioners while appearing to support them. There were plenty of embarrassing questions the Opposition could ask. Fox demanded regarding the evacuation of Philadelphia: '. . . if it was to be done, Sir, why did not the commissioners know it? Why were they sent out in ignorance, and exposed as wanting the confidence of their employers?'[3] The Ministers gave no satisfactory reply, but they could still muster a majority of votes in both Houses. Six months later Sir William Meredith—an honest man of great seriousness, good intent, little subtlety and less influence—pointed out that Lord George's records proved that: '. . . at the very time when ministers had talked so loudly of their desire to conciliate with America . . . the American Secretary had instructed the commander by sea, and the commander in chief by land, to carry on the war with as much severity as possible'.[4]

[1] Smith to Eden, 'Most Secret', summer of 1778; Stevens, *Facsimiles*, v. 513.
[2] Eden to Wedderburn, 17 Jan. 1779; Stevens, *Facsimiles*, v. 552.
[3] Wright, *Speeches of Fox*, i. 135.   [4] *Hansard*, xx. 836.

But by that time new events had made Lord George's management of the Peace Commission a less crucial subject. The war seemed to be going rather better in America, and public fears were concentrated on the intentions of the French and on mounting taxes and prices. American resistance, indeed, appeared less vigorous; Clinton was holding his own against Washington, and there were reports that he and Cornwallis had hopes of winning the southern states back to the Crown. Lord George's standing in the court profited by these diversions and apparent improvements. In September 1779 the Earl of Pembroke wrote disgustedly to young Lord Herbert: 'Ld. G. Germain seems in higher favor than ever at Court . . . proof of how very abject we have become.'[1]

But beneath the surface of this somewhat calmer sea, the currents of opposition to the war and to Lord George, the most forceful of its advocates, were gaining force. Englishmen were listening more sympathetically to Opposition insistence that the American war was not only wrong but futile. On 12 June 1780 young William Pitt, just beginning his great career, told the House of Commons that the American war was '. . . a most accursed, wicked, barbarous, cruel, unnatural, unjust and diabolical war, conceived in injustice, nurtured and brought forth in folly',[2] and his words won more applause than protest. More and more members of Parliament began to nod their heads as Burke reiterated the futility of the struggle,[3] which Rockingham called '. . . the horrid, wicked and abominable American war'.[4] Yet it was just at that time that Lord George confided in a note to Knox: 'I dread nothing so much as the hurrying out of this war before we are prepared for peace.'[5]

Whatever Lord George's failings, vacillation in his attitude toward America was not one of them. His opposition to conciliation was the one political principle he never abandoned; even after he had lost all power and nearly all influence he remained faithful to it. In July 1782, when hardly another man in England thought that the Americans could be kept from full independence, Lord George expressed the hope that

---

[1] Herbert, *Pembroke Letters*; Apr. 1779.
[2] Adolphus, iii. 375; 12 June 1780. [3] Christie, p. 139; 6 Sept. 1780.
[4] Rockingham to the Rev. Henry Zouch, 11 Sept. 1780; *HMC, Lonsdale*, no. 138.
[5] Germain to Knox, 7 Aug. 1780; *HMC, Var. Coll.* 6, *Knox*, p. 169.

Lord Shelburne in his peace negotiations would maintain '. . . the
sovereignty of this country over America'.[1] A year later, as he
saw that hope vanish, Lord George wrote bitterly: 'I did not
expect that the Cabinet would have proceeded with so much
firmness and vigor in preferring the interest of America to that
of Great Britain.'[2] A month later still, the importance of the
new nation angered him: 'It is ridiculous to keep all the powers
in Europe in suspense till thirteen provinces can agree upon
what form of government they will adopt.'[3]

Whether the cause was egotism or pure misfortune, Lord
George had ended his own military career in 1759 with notable
failure. Then, by arduous efforts, he had reached high rank as
a statesman. The great statesman leads his country to increased
power or peaceful prosperity. In his second career Lord George
had done neither. He had failed again.

[1] Germain to Knox, 9 July 1782; *HMC, Var. Coll.* 6, *Knox,* p. 185.
[2] Germain to Knox, 4 July 1783; ibid., p. 191.
[3] Germain to Knox, 16 Aug. 1783; ibid., p. 192.

XXII

OLD SCORES AND NEW HAZARDS

WHILE Parliament was debating paths to peace, Lord George Germain was firmly continuing down the road of war. That road no longer led narrowly to the rebellious thirteen colonies alone. It widened and branched to Gibraltar, to the West Indies, to the coast of Africa, and even to India, as France and Spain became imminent and then avowed enemies. Lord George widened his own purview accordingly, until it included all the seas and sea-coasts from the home Channel to the Mediterranean and across to the Caribbean. He had always claimed that as one of his Majesty's principal Secretaries of State his powers and duties were not necessarily limited to Britain's colonies, and when France entered the war he put that claim to the test. His participation in the larger strategy led him into new areas of controversy with his Cabinet colleagues.

In expanding his influence he was partly justified, since Britain's use of men, ships, and resources in any part of the world affected its prosecution of the war in America. But Lord George's insistent participation in European strategy and naval affairs had several unfortunate results. It irritated his fellow Ministers and especially Lord Sandwich and his associates in the Admiralty, upon whose close co-operation the success of the British armies in America depended. It led to confusions, delays, and cross purposes in Britain's military and naval operations, and it distracted Lord George from concentrating on affairs in America—a problem to tax all the talents of any statesman.[1]

Despite these widened activities, Lord George still had inclination and made time to pursue his enmity against the sturdy and unyielding Carleton; to develop new animosities against the Howe brothers; to harass the insecure Clinton into deeper frustrations, and to urge the eager Cornwallis on toward projects pregnant with further disaster.

[1] Clements, *Germain Letter Book*, *Misc.* iv.

Many men were disturbed by what they thought was the unjust and unwise dismissal of Carleton, and the king was one of them. In February 1778 Lord George sensed that the king and Lord North were planning to make what amends they could to Carleton, and he did not like it. He inquired of his friend General Irwin, then in the War Office, whether Carleton was under consideration for some new appointment.[1] On 6 March the king appointed Carleton to the honourable though inactive post of Governor of Charlemont in Ireland, with a pension of £1,000 a year that would continue through the lives of his wife and sons.[2] The appointment was quite outside Lord George's province, but he reproached Lord North for conniving against him by aiding Carleton, and told Eden he would resign. Eden relayed that news to Lord North, who received it with more equanimity than would have pleased Lord George, and replied to Eden:

The intelligence you send me is quite new to me. I trust that L.G.G. has no reason to complain of me. Carleton's promotion is certainly not my act, though I have so good an opinion of Sr Guy that I am glad to hear of it. This resolution must have been lately taken. It would have been more convenient if it had been taken before. I believe there has been long a determination to avail himself of the first favourable opportunity of quitting his station, & he thinks Carleton's promotion has provided it.[3]

Once again Lord George did not make good his threat, perhaps because he thought the hour not a sufficiently 'favourable' one. He wanted to leave his post 'with honour', sweetened by 'some mark of the King's favour', and at the moment the king did not seem to be in a cordial mood. The king would probably have welcomed his resignation, but would not buy him out. Lord George swallowed his threat and his defeat, but not his animosity toward Carleton.

Carleton reached England about 5 July 1778,[4] where he was cordially received by the Opposition, by most military men, and by the increasing group of men of both parties prepared to like any enemy of Lord George Germain. Carleton, unlike

---

[1] Germain to Irwin, 3 Feb. 1778; HMC, Stop. Sack. i. 139.
[2] Walpole, Last Journals, ii. 129.
[3] North to Eden, 3 Mar. 1778; Stevens, Facsimiles, iv. 387.
[4] PRO, 30/55, no. 1239; 5 July 1778.

Burgoyne, was not refused attendance at court, and unlike Burgoyne he did not call promptly on the Secretary for America. Lord George wrote to Knox two months after Carleton's return: '. . . I conclude he will not do me the honor of reporting to me the state of his late Government before he has related all his grievances to his Majesty.'[1] In private conversation Carleton did not conceal his low opinion of Lord George Germain.

The Opposition did not let the country forget their own poor opinion of that noble Lord or of his shabby treatment of one of Britain's ablest generals. Fox told the House of Commons that: 'The manner in which that other gallant officer, Sir Guy Carleton, had been treated, needed no comment; it was upon the record, and would stand an example in the future, for the instruction of all those who might be hazardous enough to attempt to serve their country under the auspices of men who were obliged to cover their ignorance and inability . . . by throwing blame upon the men who were unwise enough to act as they were instructed.'[2] Six months later Burke reverted to: '. . . the affront put upon General Sir Guy Carleton, and the illiberal abuse thrown out against the Howes by the runners of administration. If Ministers did not speak out in direct terms of abuse of those able and injured officers, it was well known they heartily approved of it.'[3] Lord North rose and 'exculpated himself from having ill-used General Carleton: he bestowed the highest encomiums on his abilities'; personally deplored the abuse of Carleton that had appeared in the newspapers, and said he wished a stop could be put to it.[4] That made it doubly clear that the persecution of Carleton came from Lord George Germain.

Lord George had not succeeded in discrediting Carleton as a soldier, but concluded it might be possible to impugn his past conduct as a civil servant. In 1779, a year after Carleton had ceased to be Governor of Quebec, Lord George obtained the appointment of a committee of the Privy Council to investigate the charges Peter Livius had brought against Carleton when Governor of Quebec. Carleton treated this political manœuvre with calm disdain, and when invited by the committee to come

[1] Germain to Knox, 14 Sept. 1778; *HMC, Var. Coll.* 6, *Knox*, p. 150.
[2] *Hansard*, xix. 1220; 28 May 1778.
[3] *Hansard*, xix; 26 Nov. 1778.   [4] Ibid.

before it and defend his dismissal of Livius replied by letter that
he had stated his reasons at the time, in a dispatch to Lord
George Germain, and felt no need to repeat them.[1] The committee, shepherded by Lord George, ultimately reported that:
'. . . there does not appear to us good and sufficient cause for
displacing Mr. Livius', and on 29 March the reinstatement of
Livius was ordered. Few men took the affair as a serious reflection on Carleton. Colonel Christie, whom Carleton had refused
to have as his quartermaster general, encouraged by Lord George,
continued to air absurd charges against Carleton's general competence, but no one paid much attention. The long duel between
Lord George and Carleton did not end there; its climax was
intertwined with other events still to come.

Lord George's devotion to old animosities did not end with
Carleton. Of the three ambitious generals who had stared at a
rebellious Boston from the deck of the *Cerberus* in the spring of
1775, Howe and Burgoyne had already ended their American
services ingloriously, and each blamed his failure primarily on
Lord George. The third member of the *Cerberus*'s 'precious
freight' remained, though by no means happily, in America.
Clinton had observed with foreboding the trials of his two companions in arms and Lord George's part in them, and had
himself experienced the administrative methods of the Secretary for America. He had not trusted Lord George since 1776,[2]
when he had come to London to: '. . . pursue his anger against
Lord George Germain for having misrepresented his conduct at
Charles Town, in the Gazette'.[3]

After Saratoga, Lord George had emulated the technique of
Prince Ferdinand after Minden: impugning the conduct of a
superior officer by ignoring him while praising his subordinate.
Lord George told the House of Commons of: '. . . the gallant
behaviour of sir Henry Clinton, in an expedition up the North
River, in which services had been performed scarcely entitled
to credit [i.e. belief], if they had not been authenticated beyond
a possibility of doubt'.[4] He also praised Clinton in a letter to

---

[1] PRO, Accounts of the Privy Council, Colonial Series, v. 5, pp. 464 ff.

[2] 'In June 1776 General Clinton, at the head of some troops which had lately
arrived from Ireland, and supported by a fleet under Sir Peter Parker, attempted
to capture Charleston . . . after several attempts the difficulties of the enterprise
were found to be so great that it was abandoned' (Lecky, iv. 12).

[3] Walpole, *Last Journals*, ii. 10; 28 Feb. 1777.   [4] *Hansard*, xix. 529.

Howe which contained no praise for Howe,[1] but Clinton was already wondering how long his sun would shine.

Saratoga forced the Ministry to a reappraisal of its military policy, and Amherst was again urged by the king and Lord North to take the command in America. No better choice could have been made. That tall, slender professional soldier, silent but forceful, coldly distinguished in appearance but hotly colloquial in argument, had a military reputation second to none in Britain. Amherst declined,[2] and told the Cabinet that: '... forty thousand men would be required for offensive operations by land in America', and recommended a naval war only,[3] but after France entered the war in March 1778, he agreed to become Commander-in-Chief in London, with Cabinet membership.[4] As a result Lord George lost his domination of military policy for America, though he was able to prevent the adoption of Amherst's strategy of a purely naval blockade. In so far as the Cabinet made any clear-cut determination of military policy it did so in the meetings which led to Lord George's second dispatch on 21 March to Clinton, but in general the Cabinet favoured operations too defensive to please Lord George and the king, and too aggressive to suit Amherst and Lord North. And since the Secretary for America was still in the key position of conveying Cabinet decisions to the generals in America, he was able to interpret them along lines more satisfactory to himself.

Shortly before the Cabinet discussed fully the implications of the French declaration, Lord George sent Clinton a long letter marked 'Most Secret' on 5/8 March 1778. Peace gestures, Lord George wrote without marked enthusiasm, would be made toward the Continental Congress, but if they should fail the war would be continued and it would be:

... his Majesty's firm purpose to prosecute it with the utmost vigor. ... It is therefore proper that I should now acquaint you with his Majesty's intentions respecting the operation of the next campaign, should another campaign become necessary, as far as his Majesty has determined upon them. The unfortunate issue of the

---

[1] Germain to Howe, 11 Dec. 1777; *HMC, Stop. Sack.* ii. 85.
[2] J. C. Long, *Amherst*, pp. 189, 238.
[3] Fortescue, *HBA*, 2, iii. 249; also J. C. Long, *Amherst*, p. 238.
[4] J. C. Long, *Amherst*, p. 243.

Canadian expedition and the unbroken state of the rebel force would make it necessary to have at least as great an army in the field to effect anything of importance in the next campaign, as that which Sir William Howe commanded in the last. . . . Every possible effort will be made to send reinforcements. . . . I am not without hopes we shall be able to send out, in the course of the summer, ten or twelve thousand British soldiers, to which I expect will be added a regiment or two of Germans. . . . A large supply of arms will . . . be sent for the purpose of arming such of the [loyalists] as shall join the King's troops.

Lord George then presented elaborate and ambitious campaign plans.[1] This was the dispatch which Lord George showed William Eden when discussing the plans of the Peace Commission.

The dispatch was on the whole encouraging to Clinton, though he was suspicious of Lord George's large hopes and half-promises. That suspicion was justified very soon, when another 'Most Secret' dispatch from Lord George, dated only two weeks later, informed him of a complete change in the plans so recently outlined. During the interval France had officially declared war, and Lord George gave that fact to account for the change, a very adequate reason if Lord George had known or suspected nothing of the intentions of France before he wrote his dispatch of 5 March. But if so, his ignorance was unique. Paris had been gossiping about it for months, and men in London had been placing bets on the date of the French declaration.

Lord George's second dispatch to Clinton represented the decisions of the Cabinet at its meeting of 18 March, when those present were North, Sandwich, Weymouth, Amherst, Dartmouth, and Germain.[2] Lord Suffolk was absent, and so were Thurlow and Wedderburn. Lord George had urged that '. . . unless the Attorney and Solicitor General are there we shall make very little progress', but North did not grant his wish to have present those two supporters of all-out war. In a chastened mood, Lord George wrote to Lord North five days before the meeting: 'I have not presumed to take any steps about commission, ship or any other matter till I have heard what I must

[1] PRO, 30/55, no. 996; also Stevens, *Facsimiles*, v. 1062, 1068, 1069; also Clements, *Clinton Letter Book*, Suppl. iv. 1; also *HMC, Stop. Sack.* ii. 94; 5/8 Mar. 1778.
[2] Clements, *Germain Letter Book*, p. 15.

do. . . . There shall not be a moment's unnecessary delay and I shall expect all the assistance you can give me that everything may be done as well as possible and as much to your satisfaction.'[1] Lord North must have been gratefully surprised to find his Secretary of State for America suddenly so docile.

The Cabinet told Lord George quite definitely what he must do, and Lord George's second dispatch reflected the Cabinet verdicts. He informed Clinton that the new demands of the French war on Britain's troops, ships, and resources would require a defensive strategy in America. Clinton was to evacuate Philadelphia and withdraw to New York as soon as possible. If the Peace Commission failed, Clinton might then need to abandon New York as well, in which case he would hold Rhode Island and Halifax and send the rest of his troops to Canada. Lord George was much more vague about his earlier hopes of sending Clinton another 12,000 men during the coming summer.[2] This was the dispatch the contents of which were kept secret from the Peace Commissioners.

The same dispatch that projected those drastic withdrawals also, however, contained instructions more in keeping with Lord George's personal opinions than those of the collective Cabinet. Lord George's further orders would effect the very dissipation of forces that Clinton was to give up Philadelphia and New York to consolidate. Clinton was to detach 5,000 men, with artillery and stores, for an attack on St. Lucia in the West Indies; he was to send 3,000 more, with guns and stores, to Florida by sea; he was to do his best to keep up an 'alarm' on the coast of the New England provinces.

Clinton could hardly have failed to be confused and shaken by these inconsistencies of defence and attack. Why give up hard-won Philadelphia for the sake of St. Lucia and an empty and remote Florida? Why, if it became necessary to abandon New York, should the garrison at Rhode Island be strengthened? 'Rhode Island could not be held if New York were evacuated because it depended on New York for fuel.'[3] So also, to a great extent, did Halifax. Lord Howe had long since complained of

---

[1] Germain to North, 13 Mar. 1778; Clements, *Germain Papers*, vii.

[2] PRO, 30/55, no. 1031; also PRO, CO/5, v. 253, no. 215; also *HMC, Stop. Sack*. ii. 151 ff.; also Fortescue, *HBA*, 2, iii. 250 ff.; also Stevens, *Facsimiles*, v. 1068, 1069; also Clements, *Germain Letter Book*, pp. 17–25.

[3] Fortescue, *HBA*, 2, iii. 250.

the Rhode Island beachhead that its 'Troops were kept inactive to no purpose, the station being as much a distraction to
the British Navy as to the American generals'.[1] And why send
troops in large numbers to Canada, which was very unlikely
to be attacked, and from which Burgoyne had demonstrated
aggressive action to be impracticable?[2] If Halifax were to be
used for future attacks on the mainland, why not hold New York
instead of having to retake it? If Halifax was to be a centre for
defence, the question arose: defence of what? There would be
nothing to defend but Halifax and Canada, and both depended
less on land troops than on the Navy.[3] Lord George's dispatch
of 21 March must have made Clinton a little more sympathetic
with the problems Howe had faced in dealing with Lord George.

Clinton took over officially as Commander-in-Chief when
Howe left for England about 1 May 1778.[4] Philadelphia was
evacuated and the Peace Commission failed. The letters of
Lord George through the rest of 1778 made it clear to Clinton
that the Secretary for America still laboured under delusions as
to the number and usefulness of loyalists in America; as to the
capabilities of a relatively small British army in a large, unfriendly continent, and as to his own capacity to direct in detail
military operations 3,000 miles away in country he had never
seen. Clinton was by that time in deep anxiety not only about
lack of supplies of all sorts but lack of money to pay his troops.[5]
Yet in addition to the formal orders in March, Lord George
urged Clinton to send troops to recover Georgia and the
Carolinas.[6] Clinton protested,[7] but in September Lord George

---

[1] Lord Howe to Admiralty, 31 Mar. 1777; Fortescue, *HBA*, 2, iii. 251.

[2] Fortescue, *HBA*, 2, iii. 250.

[3] PRO, 30/55, no. 1031; also PRO, CO/5, v. 253, no. 215; also Fortescue,
HBA, 2, iii. 250.

[4] PRO, 30/55, 1031 ff.

[5] Clinton to Germain, 25 Dec. 1778; Fortescue, *HBA*, 2, iii. 280.

[6] Germain to Clinton, *HMC, Stop. Sack.* ii. 151 ff.

[7] Clinton pointed out that after sending 8,000 men to the West Indies as ordered,
and being subject to any requisition of men that General Haldimand had been
authorized by Germain to draw from Clinton to serve in Canada, 'which I am to
suppose will be little less than 6000 men', he would then have about 12,000 men
left: 'a very inadequate number for the defense of this place, which alone would
require at least 15,000 men even if we had the exclusive command of the Sea'
(Clinton to Germain, 27 July 1778; Clements, *Germain Papers*, vii. 50). Germain
replied that he did not think Haldimand would need to draw on Clinton for as
many as 6,000 men.

wrote to him: 'I suppose that if you evacuate anything, it will be Rhode Island,'[1] thus reversing his previous top priority on holding Rhode Island. Lord George had become to the harassed Clinton both the cause and symbol of frustration.

One reason for Lord George's volatile advice and ineffective support to Clinton was his partial inattention. He was no longer concentrating on a land war on the American continent. Unable to conduct the war against the colonists as aggressively and successfully as he had hoped, he sought larger outlets for his ambitions. If he could not immediately beat the Americans in America he could perhaps be credited with beating the French in the West Indies, Africa, and the Atlantic. After 1778 he must have given as much time and thought to operations peripheral to America, including the Irish situation, as to the problems of Clinton and his army. As early as April 1778, when his position was far from secure, Lord George plunged into naval strategy in the Mediterranean and the Atlantic with a memorandum to the King and Cabinet, urging operations far outside his statutory jurisdiction.[2]

Clinton's failure to attack successfully in all directions at the same time increasingly irritated Lord George, as did the fact that Clinton, like Howe, insisted on counting his men in terms of effectives and realities instead of paper records and expectations. Lord George complained to Knox: 'I do not like Clinton's dispatches as well as I had expected; he is magnifying the force of the rebels and diminishing his own by the new-fashioned way of computing his army by the number of rank and file fit for duty.'[3]

Before Clinton had held his command six months he asked to be allowed to resign: '. . . you cannot wish to keep me in this mortifying command', where I 'remain a mournful witness of the debility of an army whose head, had I been unshackled by instructions, might have indulged expectations of rendering serious service to my country'.[4] His second in command Lord Cornwallis also asked to be relieved. Reports of these complaints and requests brought questions in Parliament, but Lord George

[1] Fortescue, HBA, 2, iii. 250 ff.; Sept. 1778.

[2] Clements, Germain Papers, vii; 29 Apr. 1778.

[3] Germain to Knox, 14 Sept. 1778; HMC, Var. Coll. 6, Knox, p. 150.

[4] Clinton to Germain, 8 Oct. 1778; Clements, Clinton Letter Book, i. 71; also Stevens, Facsimiles, ii, no. 1175; also Willcox, Amer. Rebellion, p. 390.

passed them off as trivial in the House of Commons: '. . . nor had that officer desired to be recalled in August, for want of reinforcement; on the contrary, in his last letter in which he asked leave to return . . . he wished to state ideas of the future conduct of the war in person; and that if leave should be granted him to come to England, he would be ready to return to his army in a week after he should have conferred with the administration'.[1] Lord George replied to Clinton that in view of '. . . the great military talents so discoverable in all your movements' the King 'cannot at present comply with your request'.[2] Clinton continued, but his frustration affected the morale of his staff and the operations of his army. It also assumed added forms. Howe had fought a skirmish with Lord George for the sacred right of commanders in the field to promote worthy officers, and had finally secured grudging acquiescence. Now Clinton had reason to fear that he was to be robbed of the same traditional privilege, and nothing hurt Clinton's sensitivity more than any hint of inequality with Howe. In January 1779 he wrote to Lord George in unusually brief and belligerent terms: 'I send you duplicates of my Letter to Lord Barrington & Lord Amherst, relative to the Appointment of a Captain in the 7th. I must request that they may be delivered immediately; & if my appointment is reversed, I must request an immediate permission to quit this command as I cannot submit to remain a moment in it, curtailed of powers my Predecessor had, and maintained in similar cases.'[3]

Somehow that difficulty was adjusted, but Clinton no longer seriously hoped for any change in Lord George's methods. During 1779, in spite of the fact that his army had been greatly reduced by detaching nearly 10,000 men to the West Indies, Florida, and the South, Clinton received urgent instructions to embark on new ventures. In January 1779 Lord George ordered him (though almost always after the experience with Burgoyne he inserted a covering phrase that the general must use his own judgement) to bring Washington to a pitched battle or else chase him into 'the highlands of the Jersies or New York'; to

---

[1] *Hansard*, xx. 75.

[2] Germain to Clinton, 3 Dec. 1778; Clements, *Clinton Papers*, viii; also Willcox, p. 397.

[3] Clinton to Germain, 10 Jan. 1779; Clements, *Germain Papers*, ix. 3.

keep in New York an army of about 12,000 men and at the same time detach two corps of about 4,000 men each to act in destructive raids on seaport towns along the New England and Chesapeake Bay Coasts.[1] In March he suggested that Clinton open a communication with the people of Vermont and offer them separate peace terms, apparently overlooking the fact that though the Vermonters hated the 'Yorkers' they hated the British more, and that it was the Vermonters who had taken Ticonderoga from the British and destroyed Burgoyne's detachment at Bennington.[2] Four weeks later Lord George urged Clinton to detach a force; send it by ship to South Carolina, and take Charleston.[3]

From Lord George's point of view Clinton was in command of nearly 50,000 fighting men. Lord George's records of 31 May 1779, for example, indicated that Clinton's men totalled 47,661, but Lord George's figures included every man, trained or untrained, sick or well, missing or captured, whose name had once been put down on the regimental returns. This was the method of computation that Howe had denounced in Parliament only a few months before, when, speaking of Lord George's failure to send him the requested troops in 1777, he said: 'This misconceived calculation can no otherwise be accounted for, as I apprehend, than by his lordship's computing the sick, and the prisoners with the rebels, as part of the real effective strength of the army.'[4]

---

[1] Germain to Clinton, 23 Jan. 1779; PRO, 30/55, nos. 1706, 1707; also Clements, *Germain Letter Book*, pp. 61–67; also *HMC, Stop. Sack*. ii. 151 ff.

[2] Germain to Clinton, 3 Mar. 1779; PRO, 30/55, nos. 1789, 1791. Germain had received reports that Ethan Allen and other leading Vermonters would consider changing sides. There was certainly such a rumour, but whether Allen and the others were sincere or merely feeling out the enemy is a debatable question.

[3] Germain to Clinton, 31 Mar. 1779; PRO, 30/55, no. 1870; also *HMC, Stop. Sack*. ii. 151 ff. See also PRO, 30/55, no. 1981, 5 May 1779; and Fortescue, *HBA*, 2, iii. 280 ff., for above and for Germain's dispatches of 11 Apr. and 5 May.

[4] The figures in the Colonial Office return were:

at New York	17,871
at Rhode Island	6,581
at Halifax	3,900
at Newfoundland	320
in Florida and Georgia	7,875
in passage	5,261
under Gen. Grant in the West Indies . .	5,853
TO A TOTAL OF	47,661

of which 13,835 were Germans and 6,371 were Provincials.

To Clinton, Lord George's computations were absurd, and to base expectations upon them was unjust—a deliberate attempt to belittle his own problems and mislead the Parliament and people. Over the troops in Florida and Georgia, in Halifax and Newfoundland, he was only nominally in command, and they were useless to him in any of the campaigns he might undertake from New York to Charleston. The 5,000 troops recorded as his because they were 'in passage' were of no value to him until they arrived—if they ever did. And to have the 6,000 men in the West Indies under General Grant included in his available forces was the most irritating of all; he had had almost nothing to say about sending them, no real command over them while there, and no certainty when they would be returned. In the event, it was not until August 1779 that Admiral Arbuthnot brought them back, but instead of the 6,600 men originally promised they proved to be in all but 3,800 men. 'But even of these', Clinton recorded, 'the numbers fit for duty were few, and they brought with them a malignant jail fever, which soon spread itself among the rest of my army and sent above 6000 of my best men to the hospital.'[1]

At the end of 1779 Clinton's actual effectives on the mainland did not exceed 27,000 trained men,[2] and that number included the troops in Florida and Georgia. Excluding those, Clinton had a working army of not more than 20,000 Europeans during most of the four years of his command. The defence of New York and its outposts was judged to require nearly half of these. When Clinton went with Cornwallis to Charleston he took with him every man he thought he could spare from New York, and the total was 7,600.[3]

Clinton later wrote of those days in 1779: 'The promises repeatedly made me of early reinforcement from Europe and the West Indies had been so unequivocal that they could not be doubted. My plan of operation had been formed on that ground. . . . The American Secretary had assured me in his letter of April that besides the whole European reinforcement, the whole of General Grant's command should be returned to me from the West Indies as soon as the season for offensive

---

[1] Clements, Clinton, *Hist. Detail*; also Willcox, pp. 140, 141.
[2] Fortescue, *HBA*, 2, iii. 305; *Hansard*, xx. 684; 29 Mar. 1779.
[3] Ibid.

operations in that climate was over.'[1] But though through the summer of 1779 Clinton received no reinforcements, Lord George was privately encouraging Cornwallis to push him into a major campaign in the Carolinas. Clinton's urgent pleas for men and money sometimes got no answers except notes requesting the promotion of somebody's favourite son, or inquiring why new campaigns or punitive raids were not being undertaken, or even why the commissary stores which sold goods to Clinton's men had not paid their last bills for goods received.[2] The answer to the last was the easiest of all: no one in the British forces in New York had received any money for some months.[3]

Clinton claimed with some justice that not one of the promises made to him in 1778 had been fulfilled. On 14 May 1779 he wrote to Lord George:

In the plan of operations which your Lordship has chalked out for me in your Secret and Confidential Dispatch of the 23rd of January[4] your Lordship has supposed that I shall be able to employ much larger detachments than I fear will correspond with my Force. . . . My real force for the Field will not gain by the nominal strength attributed to my Army. . . . I believe the Force with which your Lordship seems to apprehend that I might drive Washington from his present situation and oblige him to retire to the Mountains is in my idea by no means equal to the task.[5]

He pointed out that Lord George had used one method of counting men when giving orders, and a different method to magnify Howe's successes near Philadelphia to Parliament. In dealing with Clinton, Lord George counted as available to him many men reported not fit for duty, but: '. . . when your Lordship in the House of Commons stated the Force of Sir William Howe at Brandywine, you went upon a different rule', and gave only the 'rank and file fit for duty in the Field'.[6] A few days later Clinton's anger reached the boiling point, and for once he discarded the polite indirections that were protocol in military

---

[1] Clements, Clinton, *Hist. Detail*; also Willcox, p. 138.
[2] R. G. Adams, *Papers of Germain*, Clements, 1928, p. 43.
[3] Clinton to Robinson, 11 May 1779; PRO, 30/55, no. 1995.
[4] See p. 337, note 1.
[5] Clinton to Germain, 14 May 1779; PRO, 30/55, no. 2000.
[6] Clinton to Germain, 11 May 1779; Clements, *Clinton Letter Book*, ii. 139.

correspondence with a superior, and wrote with unvarnished directness:

When I was ordered to this difficult command (under circumstances much less eligible than those in which it had been undertaken by my predecessor) I was flattered with the hope of having every latitude allowed me as the moment should require. . . . After I had assumed the command, difficulty arose on difficulty. I, notwithstanding, struggled through them with a zeal and activity which I think your Lordship cannot arraign. This surely, my Lord, ought to have increased the confidence which I was taught to believe was imposed in me. How mortified then must I be, my Lord, at finding movements recommended for my dehabilitated army which your Lordship never thought of suggesting to Sir William Howe when he was in his greatest force and without an apprehension from a foreign enemy.

It is true your Lordship does not bind me down to the plan which you have sketched for the ensuing campaign. Your Lordship only recommends. But by that recommendation you secure the right of blaming me if I should adopt other measures and fail.

I am on the spot; the earliest and most exact intelligence on every point ought naturally, from my situation, to reach me. . . . Why then, my Lord, without consulting me, will you adopt the ill-digested or interested suggestions of people who cannot be competent judges of the subject, and puzzle me by hinting wishes with which I cannot agree yet am loath to disregard? For God's sake, my Lord, if you wish me to do anything, leave me to myself and let me adapt my efforts to the hourly change of circumstances![1]

Clinton stayed angry for a good two months, for it took that long for his protest and the reply to cross the Atlantic. In early July the harassed commander expressed himself to General 'Flintlock' Grey:[2] 'The Month of July is arriv'd and no Reinforcements, No Camp Equipage, nor anything to enable me to continue my move, inadequate as I fear the Reinforcements will be, they ought at least to have been here by the last of May . . . not a word from Europe this month, not a farthing of money, no information, no army. Good God!'[3]

[1] Clinton to Germain, 22 May 1779; Clements, *Clinton Letter Book*, ii. 269; also Willcox, p. 408.

[2] After the battle of the Brandywine, Grey was known as 'General Flintlock' because at that battle he ordered every man under his command to remove the flintlock from his gun to ensure that he would use only the bayonet, with effective and horrible results.

[3] Clinton to Grey, 3 July 1779; Clements, *Shelburne Papers, Amer. Dispatches*, i. 9.

Lord George must have recognized the validity of Clinton's complaint, but to a friend he protested it with a bland air of injured innocence:

I have received letters from Sir Henry Clinton very different from those I expected. You were witness to my poor endeavors in making his command not only honourable but agreeable to him. He complains of not being left sufficiently at liberty in the plans of operations, when every caution was used to prevent the least inconvenience to him by anything like positive orders. All was left to his judgment. But it is impossible . . . that government must not express a wish in general to what point operations of the campaign should be directed.[1]

This was a disarmingly plausible defence but a disingenuous one. Lord George's wishes developed into almost mandatory pressures, and not to follow them was to court the displeasure of one of the most powerful and unforgiving men in England.

In his reply to Clinton, Lord George ignored the real issues and substituted new flatteries and new half-promises.

Your own determination to take the field . . . is conformable to that vigor and zeal which have distinguished your operations in every instance since you were appointed to the chief command; and his Majesty has the firmest reliance that no opportunity will be lost, nor any exertions omitted . . . it is not the present intention to make any reduction in the forces under your command until the great object of the war in America, the recovery of the revolted provinces, is attained.[2]

Lord George could not afford to face the criticism certain to be poured upon him if he allowed Clinton to resign in anger. He could not pretend that Clinton was incompetent, for the king and the War Office thought highly of him. He could not claim that Clinton was unable to get on with anyone, or that most of his associates did not admire him greatly. Admiral Collier, for example, had very recently written directly to Lord George to report: '. . . my entire Satisfaction & Pleasure, in serving with this Gentleman; *one* Mind has animated us on every occasion when our Royal Master's Service could be promoted; We are neither of us *Land* or *Sea* Officers, but *both* . . . . He wants

---

[1] Germain to Major Drummond; Clements, *Clinton Letter Book*, ii.
[2] Germain to Clinton, 25 June 1779; PRO, 30/55, no. 2082; also *HMC, Stop. Sack*. ii. 130; also Clements, *Clinton Letter Book*, pp. 79–82.

no Stimulative to promote Enterprize.'[1] Lord Sandwich recorded that: 'The government was evidently loath to lose the services of Sir Henry Clinton, notwithstanding Germain's opinion of him.'[2]

Clinton continued as Commander-in-Chief into the year 1780, and so did his problems.

---

[1] Collier to Germain, 15 June 1779; Clements, *Germain Papers*, ix. 17.
[2] *Sandwich Papers*, iii. 241.

XXIII

THIRD BATTLE OF SARATOGA

WHILE Sir Henry Clinton was forced to the defensive in America, Sir William Howe was taking the offensive against less open enemies in England. Another battle of Saratoga was soon to be fought in London, though it would cover the same ground. It was Lord George and the Ministry that were on the defensive, for by May of 1778 it was evident that they had failed to get Burgoyne accepted as the chief cause of the Saratoga disaster. To save themselves, it was essential to establish the blame elsewhere. The next logical scapegoat was General Howe.

It would not be easy to prove Howe the villain. He stood well with military men; he had many friends in powerful places; the king liked him and was by scandalous and probably false report an unofficial blood relation. What was more, Howe had achieved the only two major successes of the American war—the captures of New York and Philadelphia. The King and Cabinet had only reluctantly approved Lord George's acceptance of Howe's proffered resignation, and were voicing concern at Lord George's 'cool' treatment of him. In February the Cabinet urged that Howe, who was after all still Commander-in-Chief until he left America, should not be so pointedly ignored by Lord George, who confessed to Knox: 'The lords have advised some little alterations in the two drafts, and they think that some general intimation of the plan of the campaign should be given to Sir William Howe.'[1]

Lord North and the king had another reason for preventing Lord George from placing the blame on General Howe. Lord North was eager to bring his brother Admiral Lord Howe into the Ministry; partly because the Admiral was able, partly to silence his criticisms of the Ministry, and partly as a sop to the Opposition, for the Howes had been Whigs. Lord Howe would certainly make Ministry exoneration of his brother a condition

---

[1] Germain to Knox, 18 Feb. 1778; *HMC, Var. Coll.* 5, 6, *Knox*, p. 143.

of his acceptance, and if he failed to secure it would attack Lord George Germain with the enthusiasm of twenty years of accumulated distaste.

But in making Sir William the culprit of Saratoga, the greatest difficulty lay in the records, so it would be highly desirable to keep them from the eager eyes of the Opposition. So long as the Ministry majority held firm, that could be done—if Lord North would agree. If Parliament did see those records, Lord George would have to confuse them by apt interpretations, obfuscations, and the timely production of red herrings. In this he would be helped by the fact that the more one studied the dispatches the more confusing they became.

And after all, Lord George could point out to Parliament that he had supplied Howe with the most powerful army that had ever taken the field in America, reaching by 1777 a total of 33,186 British and German fighting men.[1] Sir William might reply that even they were not adequate to the need, and that as early as 1776 he had warned Lord George that the colonies could not easily be won back.[2] But Howe could not prove any important instance in which the Secretary had failed to support him within the limits of the men, materials, ships, and money England could supply. It would take a closer study of the papers than Parliament should be allowed to give, to conclude that in innumerable little ways Lord George had misled and failed General Howe.

On the very day the authenticated news of Saratoga reached London, Lord George inserted a significant sentence into his letter to the king: 'Sir William Howe's complaint of want of support is very unjust, but his desire of being recalled does not come unexpected.'[3] Ten days later he wrote with portentous coolness to Howe that: '. . . as the particulars of Lieut. General Burgoyne's situation are still unknown, and your own campaign is not yet finished, I am not authorized to signify his Majesty's commands on this subject'.[4]

---

[1] According to War Office records, Howe had 19,071 men in the Philadelphia campaign, 10,426 in the New York area, and 3,687 in Rhode Island (PRO, CO/5, v. 170, no. 43).

[2] Howe to Germain, 26 Apr. 1776; *HMC, Stop. Sack.* ii. 30.

[3] Germain to King, 1 Dec. 1777; Fortescue, *Corresp.* iii. 501.

[4] Germain to Howe, 11 Dec. 1777; *HMC, Stop. Sack.* ii. 83, 84. That dispatch was endorsed: 'Recd. at Philadelphia. 27th February 1778. No. 16.'

Meanwhile London opinion was being manipulated by attacks on Howe which were certainly not discouraged by Lord George. They were especially notable in the *Morning Post*, 'a paper notoriously paid by the Court',[1] and in pamphlets written by Israel Maudit, a journalist of considerable ability and standing who moved in the society of Hutchinson and Knox. Though Maudit often talked privately of the need to conciliate the colonists, Hutchinson was probably correct that: 'Maudit . . . appears to be employed by the Ministry.'[2] In this case he was probably employed personally by Lord George, since detraction of the Howes in such bitter terms would certainly not have suited Lord North while he was trying to add the Admiral to the Ministry. 'Maudit, if a tool of North, could not afford to attack Howe; but if he was a tool of Germain, he might run the risk in behalf of his patron.'[3]

The Opposition was certain that the propaganda campaign against Howe was sponsored by the Ministry. Thomas Townshend asked rhetorically in Parliament:

Were not the runners of administration, their tools and emissaries, in the House and out of it, constantly employed in this dirty, treacherous and insidious occupation? Were not a whole legion of newspaper writers and pamphleteers in constant ministerial pay, in order to effect this base purpose? For his part there was not a week but some scurrilous pamphlet, composed of a mixture of plausible reasoning, pompous expressions, misrepresentations, and artful invectives against the conduct of the commander in chief was left at his house. The authors were known, and well known to be under the wing of government; payed and caressed, placed and pensioned by them. . . . Such were the men, such were the affected language and insidious arts of administration. They basely endeavored to effect

[1] Walpole, *Last Journals*, ii. 95.

[2] These sentences, purporting to express American opinion, are typical of Maudit's efforts: 'It is a unanimous sentiment here, that our misfortunes this campaign have arisen, not so much from the genius and valour of the rebels, as from the misconduct of a certain person. Our Commander in chief seems not to have known, or to have forgotten, that there was such a thing as the North River; and that General Burgoyne, with his small army, would want support in his attempt to penetrate to Albany; . . . In fact, there is not a common soldier in the army but knows, that deserting the North River lost Burgoyne and his army' (From Maudit's pamphlet 'View of the Evidence Relative to the Conduct of the American War', 2nd edition, London, 1779).

[3] W. C. Ford, *Parliament and the Howes*, Mass. Hist. Socy., xliv. 121, 130.

in private, what they dare not own in public. They heaped com-
mendations in that House on the hon. commander in chief, while
they exerted every effort by indirect means to disrobe him of his
honours and reputation.[1]

The campaign was expanded by the publication of pur-
ported loyalist letters from America, critical of Howe. Some
of these were probably fabricated, but authentic ones certainly
existed.

Nicholas Cresswell, a sober and decent young Englishman
who had gone to America on business and been caught there
by the war, wrote in his journal at Leesburg, Virginia, in July
1777: 'Poor General Howe is ridiculed in all companies and all
my countrymen abused. I am obliged to hear this daily and dare
not speak a word in their favour. It is the Damd Hessians that
has caused this, curse the scoundrels that first thought of sending
them here.'[2] But a few months later Cresswell was shaken in his
esteem for Howe when he talked with him in New York: 'His
Excellency asked me about affairs in Virginia and whether I
thought there was a great many friends to Government there.
To both questions I answered him with truth to the best of my
knowledge. But I think his information has been bad and his
expectations too sanguine.'[3]

Other loyalists, in their dismay over Saratoga, turned against
Howe and found various reasons to explain his conduct. A letter
from America in the files of Lord Dartmouth said Howe had
always been jealous of the superior military ability of Burgoyne
and Clinton, and had deliberately made a sacrifice of Burgoyne
and a catspaw of Clinton by leaving Clinton too few troops to

---

[1] *Hansard*, xx. 732; also W. C. Ford, p. 135.

[2] Cresswell, *Journal*, p. 181; 17 July 1777.

The British Government was almost as severely criticized for using German
troops and allowing them to plunder as for using Indians and not preventing them
from scalping. Robert Morris, in a report to the American Commissioners in Paris,
wrote on 21 Dec. 1776: 'We are told the British troops are kept from plunder, but
the Hessians and other foreigners, looking upon that as the right of war, plunder
wherever they go . . . and horrid devastations they have made' (*Amer. Diplomatic
Corresp.* i. 233–46; quoted by Lecky, iv. 24). '. . . a deep and legitimate indignation
was created by the shameful outrages that were perpetrated by the British and
German troops' (Lecky, iv. 27). 'The Hessians, encouraged by plunder, had at
first behaved with great cruelty to the Americans; but, the English imitating them,
General Howe had been forced to restrain marauding' (Walpole, *Last Journals*,
ii. 9; 24 Feb. 1777).

[3] Cresswell, *Journal*, p. 219.

aid Burgoyne.[1] Henry White, one of the loyalist Council in New York, wrote that:

... the series of blunders and mismanagement will be better known to the world when the transactions on this side come to be more generally understood. . . . We find a great deal said about the Canada expedition, most certainly it was badly conducted, but the expedition to Chesapeak Bay is the real occasion of all the mischief that has happen'd; had it been left to Congress, they cou'd not have plan'd a more destructive measure to the King's affairs; and it was foreseen and foretold by every man of sense who was well acquainted with the country. This unaccountable movement is well deserving of a national enquiry. . . . There was time enough to have open'd Hudson's River, fixt the Canadian army at Albany, and taken possession of Philadelphia as soon as they did.[2]

By the time Howe reached London with dispatches from Clinton on 2 July,[3] Lord George had done his best to set the stage. In the Clements Library is a long memorandum headed 'Hints for the Management of an intended Inquiry'. It proposed to attack Howe by pointing out that: 'The Numbers of the British Troops often four and sometimes six Times the Numbers of the Rebels with those of the latter being ascertained by Proof.' The document listed questions to be put to General Howe; anticipated his answers and then supplied rejoinders to demolish them. The questions were largely concerned with Howe's management at White Plains, Trenton, Brandywine, Red Bank, and Philadelphia, and references to Burgoyne and Saratoga were notably missing. There was also a long summary in Lord George's own hand of his correspondence with Howe beginning in 1776, with detailed analyses of all the exchanges bearing on the campaign plans for 1777.[4]

The persistent attacks on Lord George during the previous months had prevented him, however, from perfecting his arrangements for dealing with Howe.[5] 'It was very uncertain how he would be received, but he had an audience with the King on the 3rd, and was received favourably.'[6] The king reported the

---

[1] HMC, Dartmouth, ii (1895), 447; 11 Nov. 1777.
[2] Henry White to William Knox, 17 Aug. 1778; HMC, Var. Coll. 5, 6, Knox, p. 147.
[3] Hutchinson, Diaries, ii. 211.
[4] Clements, Germain Papers, xi. 110 ff.
[5] Ibid. vii. 48.
[6] Walpole, Last Journals, ii. 189.

interview immediately to Lord North: 'I had a long conversation today with him the Substance of which was his very strongly declaring nothing shall make either His Brother or Him join Opposition, but that Lord G. Germaine and his Secretaries Nox and Cumberland have everywhere loaded him with obloquy that he must therefore be allowed some means of justifying himself.'[1]

The king's sympathy for Howe, and Lord North's desire to attach his brother to the Ministry, kept matters at a stalemate, '. . . with Lord George squeaking, wanting some feathers, afraid to stay, more afraid to go, in confidence no where', as the irreverent Lieutenant-Colonel Smith reported it to Eden, wisely marking his letter 'Most Secret'.[2] Lord North's approaches to Admiral Howe to join the Ministry,[3] or to give it his implied support by accepting command of the Western Squadron,[4] brought the prompt reply that Howe would consider the offer after the Ministry had given public exoneration of his brother and himself from all the insinuations which were being circulated, he said, with the connivance of Lord George Germain. 'The Howes never gave out that they expected thanks or approbation but only exculpation', according to Knox.[5] Lord Howe '. . . sent Lord North a resolution to that purpose which Lord North returned, saying he would not consent to it, and if he did, his friends would not'.[6] Lord Howe remained adamant, and Lord North ultimately abandoned his hope of securing him. Ministry supporters then had no option but to support Lord George by condemning the Howes, and James Hare, an independent member of Parliament, wrote to George Selwyn that all the ministerial people were abusing General Howe unmercifully.[7]

During the negotiations the members of the Opposition also held their fire, for they had no reason to champion the Howes if the Howes were about to ally with the Ministry. But when the negotiations failed they promptly opened their attack,[8] and

[1] King to North, 3 July 1778; Fortescue, *Corresp.* iv. 176.
[2] Smith to Eden, summer of 1778; Stevens, *Facsimiles*, v. 513/10.
[3] North to King, 31 Dec. 1778; Fortescue, *Corresp.* iv. 239–41.
[4] *HMC, Var. Coll.* 5, 6, *Knox*, p. 262.
[5] Ibid.   [6] Ibid.
[7] James Hare to George Selwyn, 27 June 1778; Jesse, *Grenville*, iii. 288.
[8] Russell, *Corresp. C. J. Fox*, i. 208.

moved that the Germain–Howe correspondence be made available to them.[1] The Ministry, according to Knox, had previously agreed that such a motion should be opposed, on the grounds that no accusation had been made against either of the Howes, '. . . and a negative vote was put upon the question for calling in Lord Cornwallis in the committee'.[2]

Charles Fox told the House: 'Ministers have hitherto evaded every thing which could possibly lead to an inquiry upon their conduct, by refusing every document necessary for their acquittal or conviction; everything that might lead to proofs of their guilt or innocence.'[3] Some weeks later he added: 'A refusal to admit such evidence was a clear acknowledgement of their guilt; they dare not face the enquiry, because they know it would lead to their conviction.'[4] Meanwhile Howe criticized the Ministry in Parliament, 'to which no reply was made'.[5]

London boiled with partisanship, but many members of its society were doubtless as much confused as Lady Sarah Lennox, who wrote to Lady Susan O'Brien:

You surprise me by saying you don't know what Sir Wm Howe can be accused of; why, don't you know that it's the fashion to say he saved the Americans? Can there be a greater crime in these days? 'Tis true they say he did it to prolong the war, & put money in his pocket, so they don't even allow him the merit of being a little humane, & on the other side, the Opposition tax him with permitting cruelty towards the Americans to keep up his popularity. I hope and believe he will clear himself of every fault but that one of undertaking an unjust & an absurd war; which I wish he had never done for his own sake, poor man.[6]

Lord George was as non-committal as possible, but at times he was goaded into replies that were not always consistent. On one occasion he tried to hide behind the Cabinet and King. 'He declared . . . it was not his intention to skulk behind the Throne, but fairly to stand forth responsible for his own conduct; at the same time repeating that whatever he had done, was with

---

[1] *HMC, Var. Coll.* 5, 6, *Knox*, p. 262.
[2] Ibid.
[3] Wright, *Speeches of Fox*, i. 143; 3 Mar. 1779.
[4] Ibid., p. 172; 29 Apr. 1779; also *Hansard*, xx. 178.
[5] Pembroke to Cox, 27 Apr. 1779; *Pembroke Diaries*, p. 176.
[6] Lennox to O'Brien, 23 Nov. 1778; *Life and Letters of Lady Sarah Lennox*, i. 285.

the advice and approbation of the other branches of administration.'[1] Sometimes he implied that his generals in America faced
heavy odds; at others that the American enemy was very weak.

The Opposition pierced Lord George's armour when they
pointed out that he had not been able to keep the confidence or
respect of a single leader of British troops in America. One
member of the House said it was general knowledge that '. . . all
our Commanders had desired to leave their commands, and
were come home dissatisfied with the conduct of our Ministers'.[2]
No one could deny that, but few if any knew how widespread
were the military's irritations with Lord George. Major-General
Sir Eyre Massey, for example, commanding at Halifax, wrote
to Clinton in 1778: 'Had a letter from Lord G. Germain; it
contains no orders but desires I may supply the inhabitants of
Halifax with coals, a measure I ever pursued since I commanded
this province.'[3]

The king's attitude toward Lord George was indicated by his
desire to find a good 'military preferment' for Sir William Howe.[4]
But a formal inquiry might bring down not only Lord George
but the entire Ministry, and the king viewed the loss of Lord
North with a distaste only second to the prospect of a Whig
Ministry. By personal efforts Lord North could probably have
marshalled enough votes to prevent any inquiry, but he
made no great effort to do so. When Howe himself moved on
17 February: 'That there be laid before this House, copies or
extracts of all letters and correspondence that passed between
his Majesty's secretary of state for the American department
and Sir William Howe, from the 2nd of August 1775 to the
16th of May 1778',[5] the motion was agreed to, though no papers
were forthcoming,[6] and it was not conceded that witnesses
might be called.

A Committee of the Whole House consequently began to sit
in Inquiry on 29 April 1779.[7] Lord Pembroke summarized the
first act of the drama in a letter to his son's tutor, the Reverend

---

[1] *Hansard*, xx. 80; 14 Dec. 1778.
[2] Cadell (publisher), *A Speech on some Political Topics, to be made 14 Dec. 1778*,
Cadell, London, 1779, p. 22.
[3] Massey to Clinton, 20 Aug. 1778; *HMC, Amer. Mass.* i (1904), 281.
[4] King to North, 13 Feb. 1779; Fortescue, *Corresp.* iv. 277.
[5] *Hansard*, xx. 139; 17 Feb. 1779.
[6] *Hansard*, xx. 144.   [7] Fortescue, *Corresp.* iv. 331.

William Coxe: 'Sir William Howe desired to be heard & examined in Parliament, as he found Ministers were whispering away his character. Administration opposed it, but, for once, Honor prevailed, & the papers . . . etc. were granted; it went accordingly for two days, at the end of which, Ministry mustered all their forces, & crushed it.'[1]

The king was relieved. He wrote to Lord North:

I am glad to find by Lord North's letter that the examining Witnesses on the Military conduct of Sir Wm Howe in North America hath been negatived, and that it is probable this business will not be further agitated, My reasoning on this affair has proved false, for I imagined when once it had been brought before the House of Commons that Lord G. Germain would have thought his Character had required its being fully canvassed but to my great surprise on Wednesday I found him most anxious to put an end to it in any mode that could be the most expeditious.[2]

The king apparently still did not know that Lord George had reason to fear full revelations regarding Saratoga.

On the very edge of this victory Lord George made a false step, and turned victory into defeat. In Parliament he: '. . . had observed a profound silence about the conduct of Howe, no answers made to any of Howe's charges nor any attempt to attack him while the examination was open'. But just as the Inquiry was being finally muffled, '. . . and without any fresh provocation from Howe who had not said a word upon the motion of this day',[3] Lord George, who '. . . still meant no witness should be examined',[4] rose and '. . . complained on Friday that the Inquiry had been stopped without his being heard, tho we know it was his own choice'.[5]

He could not resist a final blow at Howe, but he misjudged the reaction of one of his own party supporters. Richard Rigby, an adherent of the Bedfords, had always been ready to support the Ministry in return for its favours. But Rigby was also a friend of Howe, and 'had stayed away & not voted against the enquiry before'. Now he was present, and Lord George failed

---

[1] Pembroke to Coxe, 27 Apr. 1779; *Pembroke Diaries*, p. 176.
[2] King to North, 30 Apr. 1779; Fortescue, *Corresp.* iv. 332, 333.
[3] Wedderburn to Eden, 3 May 1779; *HMC, Stop. Sack.* i. 139.
[4] *HMC, Var. Coll.* 6, *Knox*, p. 262.
[5] See above, note 3.

to allow for personal loyalty when he let slip the remark: '. . . that he did not think that the Howe conduct *had* been *quite* right'. This was too much for Rigby, who '. . . got up and said that tho' till then he had not seen the absolute necessity of an enquiry, when there was no accusation, yet now there was, since one of the Administration accus'd him publickly, it would be no longer fair to refuse an enquiry, & therefore made a Motion for it, & Ld. North upon that got up and seconded his motion, & the enquiry is to come on immediately'.[1] Irony never asserted itself more neatly. The man most opposed to an inquiry had inadvertently brought it about: the motion that achieved it was made by one of the Ministry's most dependable placemen and seconded by the First Minister. Charles Jenkinson, the king's confidential adviser, did not mince matters in reporting to his Majesty:

I cannot help mentioning in what a very disgraceful light the Government appeared in the House of Commons yesterday. Lord George Germain was indiscreet beyond description, and gave ground to the Opposition which it was very difficult to resist. . . . I would at present only humbly advise that when your Majesty sees Lord North tomorrow you would urge Him to have a meeting with Lord George Germain, the attorney and the Lord Advocate and Mr. Rigby . . . and get them to agree on some mode of conducting this Enquiry so that your Majesty's Government may not be disgraced by it. . . . I very much fear from what I heard last night that we shall lose our Majorities.[2]

The king expressed his irritation to Lord North: '. . . to crown all Ld. G. Germain chose to bring a specific disapprobation of the landing at the head of Elk, it was impossible to resist the examining of witnesses'.[3]

Howe, and with him Burgoyne, thus got the chance to be heard in full and to call supporting witnesses. Though Walpole characteristically belittled Burgoyne,[4] that irrepressible gentleman made the most of the chance. He repeated his complaint

---

[1] Lady Pembroke to her son Lord Herbert, 4 May 1779; *Pembroke Diaries*, p. 178. William Knox's account corroborated that of Lady Pembroke on the main points (*HMC, Var. Coll.* 6, *Knox*, p. 262).

[2] Jenkinson to King, 4 May 1779; Fortescue, *Corresp.* iv. 334.

[3] King to North, 10 May 1779; Donne, *Letters*, ii. 248.

[4] 'Burgoyne thrust himself into the altercation with his usual self-sufficiency and ill-success' (Walpole, *Last Journals*, ii. 219).

of having been denied an interview with the king, 'whose ear was daily poisoned against him'. He forced Lord George to make defensive statements that many thought specious: for Lord George denied that: '. . . he took any particular part in preventing the hon. general from seeing his sovereign'.[1] 'As for the orders for the hon. general's return to his captive army, he asserted, that the order was framed in cabinet, and did not originate with him, as an individual.'[2] Burgoyne's witnesses gave evidence that was 'unusually clear, plain, accurate, and direct in its matter. It went uniformly to place the character of General Burgoyne in a very high point of view.'[3]

Howe was less eloquent than Burgoyne and a less skilled Parliamentarian. His prepared statement was not well organized or delivered, but its content and the supporting testimony of his witnesses made a strong impression on Parliament and public. He denied that he had ever received orders to meet or support Burgoyne; produced all the dispatches he had received from Lord George to prove it, together with Lord George's approval, in the king's name, of Howe's letter of 5 April to Carleton. Howe testified that he had sent that letter to Carleton, with a copy to Lord George: '. . . spontaneously, because I had not at that time received any official information concerning the plan of the northern expedition. . . . On the 5th of June I received a copy of the Secretary of State's letter to Sir Guy Carleton, dated the 26th of March', which included the campaign orders to Burgoyne. 'I must observe', Howe continued, 'that this copy of a letter to Sir Guy Carleton, though transmitted to me, was not accompanied by any instructions whatsoever, and that the letter intended to have been written to me by the first packet, and which was probably to have contained some instructions, was never sent.'[4]

Howe accused Lord George of having acted independently of the rest of the Ministry in his direction of the American war, and the Ministry with having: '. . . treacherously and traitorously deceived this country; inasmuch as they had declared to the house of commons, that they had reason to expect a successful campaign, when they had it in their pockets, under the general's

---

[1] *Hansard*, xx. 714, 715.   [2] *Hansard*, xx. 716.   [3] *Hansard*, xx. 801, 802.
[4] Howe's Narrative before a Select Committee of the House of Commons, London, 1870. Howe's speech was on 22 Apr. 1779 (PRO, CO/5, v. 94, no. 299).

A a

own hand, that nothing was to be expected'.[1] He produced all the correspondence that proved Lord George had more than once approved Howe's proposals to attack Philadelphia, and had done so without a single reference to any obligation to meet Burgoyne, except the weak statement in a dispatch which did not reach Howe until he was disembarking his troops at the head of the Elk River. He challenged Lord George to disprove any of these statements and Lord George failed to do so.

Had I [said Howe to Parliament] adopted the plan of going up Hudson's River, it would have been alleged that I had wasted the campaign . . . merely to ensure the progress of the northern army, which could have taken care of itself, provided I had made a diversion in its favour by drawing off to the southward the main army under General Washington. Would not my enemies have gone further, and insinuated, that, alarmed at the rapid success which the honourable General had a right to expect when Ticonderoga fell, I had enviously grasped at a share of that merit? Would not the ministers have told you, as they truly might, that I had acted without any orders or instructions from them; that General Burgoyne was instructed to force his way to Albany, and that they had put under his command troops sufficient for the march? . . . And would they not readily have impressed this House with the conclusion, that, if any doubt could have arisen in their minds of the success of such a well-devised plan, they should, from the beginning, have made me a partner to it, and given me explicit instructions to act accordingly?[2]

Howe '. . . imputed his own desire of being recalled to Lord George Germaine, who had not co-operated with him, nor treated him with confidence, nor taken his recommendation of officers, for preferment'.[3] Admiral Howe testified to the same effect, and said that he had been: '. . . deceived into his command; that he was deceived while he retained it; that, tired and disgusted, he desired permission to resign . . . that, on the whole his situation was such, that he had, in the first instance, been compelled to resign; and a thorough recollection of what he had suffered, induced him to decline any risk of ever returning to a situation which might terminate in equal ill-treatment, mortification, and disgust'.[4]

[1] C. Stedman, *History of the Origin, Progress and Termination of the American War*, 2 vols., London, 1794, i. 394. Stedman served under Howe.
[2] Howe, *Narrative*, see p. 353, note 4.
[3] Walpole, *Last Journals*, ii. 219.   [4] *Hansard*, xx. 218.

By that time: 'the inquiry had reached a stage where it could be described as a struggle between Sir William Howe and Lord George Germain'.[1] In the first exchange Lord George, according to Walpole, came off the better: 'Lord George answered him very ably, and, being as clear-headed as Howe was confused, turned the applause of the House against him, particularly on recommendations, of which he had received but three, two of which he had complied with, and the third was in favour of an officer notoriously unworthy.'[2] Few of Walpole's contemporaries agreed with him that at any point Lord George came off better. As the Inquiry continued, the inner circle of the Ministry certainly grew more and more alarmed.

Howe's supporting witnesses were more startling than himself regarding the futility of the war in America. Lord Cornwallis, Major-General Grey, Sir Andrew Hannard, and Sir George Osborne gave testimony that:

. . . went to the establishment of the following points of fact, or of opinion:—That the force sent to America was at no time equal to the subjugation of the country—That this proceeded, in a great measure, from the general enmity and hostility of the people, who were almost unanimous in their aversion to the government of Great Britain, and also from the nature of the country. . . . That this latter circumstance rendered it impossible for the army to carry on its operations at any distance from the fleet.[3]

The officers who appeared for Burgoyne supported these conclusions. They included Sir Guy Carleton, Captain Money his acting Quartermaster-General, the Earl of Harrington, Major Forbes, Captain Bloomfield of the artillery, and Lieutenant-Colonel Kingston, all of whom except Carleton had been through the Saratoga campaign.[4]

Cornwallis was very cautious in his replies, '. . . and on the question of the failure to assist Burgoyne he was brief, vague and evasive. On the vital point of Howe's reasons for all his movements, he declined to answer questions, because, having been Howe's confidential officer, it would, he said, be improper for him to reveal in Parliament what he had learned in that capacity',[5] but his testimony implied criticism of Ministry

---

[1] W. C. Ford, p. 139.
[2] Walpole, *Last Journals*, ii. 219.
[3] *Hansard*, xx. 749.
[4] *Hansard*, xx. 801, 802.
[5] Fisher, *True History*, p. 364.

management and he was downright in praise of Howe's military capacities and of the personal affection he won from his officers and men.

Carleton had already made quite clear where he stood, but in giving opinion on matters of military judgement he was as reticent as Cornwallis. He held Lord George responsible for the plan of campaign and for its failure, and when asked with insistent repetition what he would have done had he been in Burgoyne's place with Burgoyne's orders, he finally replied: 'I really don't know.'[1] The implication was obvious.

After Carleton's testimony Lord George could not resist making a thrust or two at his old enemy. He said that the selection of Burgoyne to lead the campaign, '. . . however displeasing to you, was particularly directed by the King . . . so that all my business consisted in putting his Majesty's commands into the form of a dispatch'.[2] The Opposition must have wished it were possible to cross-examine the king on that point.

Once again Lord George, by yielding to personal enmity, gave his opponents a rare opportunity, and Charles Fox grasped it promptly. He accused Lord George of hiding behind the robes of the king. If, as Lord George had implied, the king was dictating measures to the Cabinet, then he was exceeding his constitutional powers. The Ministry was eager to avoid any discussions of that tender point, and Lord North intervened to say that the Ministry was not hiding behind the throne and that he himself, as First Minister, would lay claim to an equal part of any blame assigned to the Secretary for the Colonies for the recent events in America. This was regarded as a generous gesture by Lord North but did not silence Fox, who finally forced Lord George to admit, reluctantly but explicitly, that in such matters the king could act only on the advice and responsibility of his Ministers. That admission demolished his previous defence.

General Grey had: '. . . declared so positively that the American people were so generally indisposed to the Government of this country, that it was judged absolutely necessary for the justification of the administration to examine evidences to take off the impression Grey had made'.[3] Lord George produced

---

[1] See note K, p. 500.   [2] Hansard, xx. 804.
[3] HMC, Var. Coll. 6, Knox, p. 262.

counter-witnesses, but Edmund Burke belittled their statements
by pointing out that they were mostly Loyalist refugees, ad-
venturers with private axes to grind, or former petty officials
and contractors making profits on war supplies.[1] The Earl of
Pembroke wrote to his son Lord Herbert that Lord George:
'. . . is now endeavoring to invalidate what Genl. Grey, Sir Guy
Carleton, Lord Cornwallis, & all the officers have sworn, by the
evidence of a set of thieves, contractors, Commissaries etc.'[2]
Pembroke was a vehement critic of Lord George, and delighted
in his own linguistic excesses,[3] but his conclusions in this matter
were widely shared. One of the Ministry witnesses thus charac-
terized was Joseph Galloway, a reformed revolutionary who had
once been Speaker of the Pennsylvania Assembly.[4] He told
Parliament that from two-thirds to four-fifths of the Americans:
'. . . were zealously attached to the government of this country[5]
. . . that the force sent out from this country was fully competent
to the attainment of its object', and that: '. . . the British troops
were better at bush fighting than the Americans'.[6] Another
witness for the Ministry claimed that: 'The force that was got
together against Burgoyne was only 10,000 men of which 2000
were sick at Albany and 1200 sick at New City near Stillwater'
at the time of the battles.[7] No one took these witnesses very
seriously.

General Robertson, an honest and unimaginative military
wheelhorse, told Parliament that General Grey's statements
were inaccurate, but he too failed to convince his hearers, since
most of his experience in America had been twenty years
earlier. His honesty, in fact, turned him into a witness embarrassing to the Ministry that had put him on the stand. Under
questioning he said of the Saratoga campaign: 'I conversed with
many officers on the subject; many of them feared that General
Burgoyne's army would be lost, if not supported. I wrote myself,
on being informed of the situation of the different armies, to a
gentleman in this House, telling him, that if General Burgoyne
extricated himself from the difficulties he was surrounded with,

---

[1] *Hansard*, xx. 758.
[2] Pembroke to Herbert, 20 May 1778; *Pembroke Diaries*, p. 183.
[3] See p. 359, notes 5 and 6.
[4] Clements, *Knox Papers*, ix, *Misc.*, p. 34.
[5] *Hansard*, xx. 805.   [6] *Hansard*, xx. 866.
[7] Clements, *Germain Papers*, xi.

that I thought future ages would have little occasion to talk of
Hannibal and his escape.'[1]

The Opposition pointed out that Galloway was receiving
a regular stipend from the Treasury, and Thomas Townshend
said Galloway was: '. . . a man who remembered every military
manoeuver that had, as well as those which had not, taken
place; but who recollected nothing of his own conduct in the
American Congress'.[2] The Opposition also charged that some
of the witnesses for the Ministry had been coached in advance
by Lord George Germain or his assistant de Grey. Lord George
denied this accusation, but de Grey, called to the stand, admitted having sent for some of the men who were to testify,
as he: '. . . thought it due from him as a matter of courtesy
to see each, in order to converse with them on the subject of
American affairs'.[3]

No effective effort was made by the members of the Ministry
to disprove Howe's statements. Lord George insisted that he
had: '. . . no disposition to accuse General Howe . . . but that
he wished to present evidence to refute some statements made
by Howe and others, especially to the effect that the Americans
were almost unanimous in the opposition to Britain'. But again
Lord George made mistakes that weakened his case. He said
that he had not sent Howe in 1777 the added 15,000 men Howe
had requested, because Howe did not need them:

. . . against an enemy flying on every side, scarcely a battalion in
any one body . . . combined with the information of persons well
informed on the spot, and on his own judgment, he thought then,
and now, that such a requisition on the part of the commander in
chief ought not to be complied with, and to show that his opinion
was not peculiar to him and the rest of his Majesty's servants, it was
well known, that at the very period alluded to, such was the low,
desperate state of the rebels, that they secretly sent a deputation of
three persons to the general, to inform him that they had consulted
the Congress on the occasion, who had consented to permit them to
receive the King's troops into Philadelphia.[4]

Howe replied quickly: '. . . respecting the pretended invitation
from the inhabitants of Philadelphia, which, he said, had been

---

[1] W. C. Ford, p. 123; citing *Parl. Register*, xiii. 281.
[2] *Hansard*, xx. 818.
[3] *Hansard*, xx. 811, 812.   [4] *Hansard*, xx. 742.

fabricated by himself, in order to deceive the enemy'.[1] The House of Commons had evidence that in this case at least Lord George's 'well informed' secret agents in America had misled him.

Lord George also told the House that: '. . . the hon. general first proposed the expedition to the southward on May 8, 1777'. The dispatches showed that Howe had proposed that expedition on 20 December 1776; that Lord George had acknowledged on 3 March 1777 the receipt of that proposal and on 18 May had written to Howe his Majesty's approval of the expedition on Philadelphia. When his mis-statement was partly pointed out, Lord George replied airily that: '. . . it could hardly be expected, that in the heat of debate, he could carry in his memory the contents and dates of every letter and paper which related to the present enquiry'.[2]

Lord George was also on dubious ground when he said that Howe's long silences as to his plans and operations had caused him to lose confidence in his Commander-in-Chief, and that during much of 1777 he knew no more: '. . . of the hon. commander, nor what he was doing, than any person walking the streets'.[3] The correspondence disproved that statement. Lord George's dispatch of 3 September 1777 to Howe stated that it was in reply to eight dispatches received from Howe during June and July.[4]

By that time most men had made up their minds as to the conclusions to be drawn from the Inquiry. Even before the most significant parts of the testimony had been presented, Lord Pembroke had written to his son: 'Does it not look, without exaggeration, as if being villainous was a sufficient recommendation' to power in the Ministry?[5] and that: '. . . the Howe Inquiry has perfectly cleared Burgoyne also'.[6]

Within the Ministry there were dismay and forebodings. Early in May Lord North predicted to the king that the Howes would be not only exonerated but complimented by Parliament, and that: '. . . some resolutions may be prepared against the continuance of the War, which though not carried will be supported

---

[1] *Hansard*, xx. 745.
[2] *Hansard*, xx. 761.
[3] *Hansard*, xx. 761.
[4] PRO, 30/55, no. 660.
[5] Pembroke to Herbert, 20 May 1779; *Pembroke Diaries*, p. 183.
[6] Pembroke to Herbert, 9 July 1779; *Pembroke Diaries*, p. 204.

by so many votes as to leave it almost impossible to remain in office'.[1] Lord Barrington, recently resigned as Minister at War, wrote privately to the Earl of Buckinghamshire a condemnation of his former colleagues perhaps more truthful than his estimate of the Opposition. After referring to: '. . . the disagreements which appear in Parliament among the ministers now in office', Barrington continued: 'No wonder . . . that an Administration which has no system, no steadiness and little concert should appear sometimes to differ. . . . I am told that Lord North and Lord George Germain managed the debate to which you allude so unfortunately, that even their warmest and best friends supported them with great reluctance, and openly blamed their conduct. Happily for the Ministry, the opposition is so universally detested and feared, that they find a support in the nation to which they are not entitled but from *comparison*.'[2]

The Ministry, in fact, appeared to be falling apart. Lord Gower, President of the Privy Council, '. . . who had hitherto been one of the staunchest supporters of the Government, resigned his post on the ground that the system which was being pursued must end in ruin to his Majesty and the country'.[3] Lord Bathurst had resigned as Lord Chancellor on 3 June 1778, largely in protest against American policies and Lord George Germain's management of them.[4] Lord Dartmouth, as Lord Privy Seal, had never been in agreement with them. Even Lord North, who continued those policies under pressure from the king, confessed to being personally out of sympathy with them. In a private letter to the king he described the efforts he had made to dissuade Gower from resigning and then added: 'In the argument Lord North had certainly one disadvantage, which is that he holds in his heart, and has held for three years past, the same opinion with Lord Gower.'[5] Lord Weymouth a little later resigned as Secretary of State, and the death of the other Secretary, Lord Suffolk, removed from the inner circles of the Cabinet one of the firmest supporters of the non-conciliatory policy toward America.[6]

---

[1] North to King, 10 May 1779; Fortescue, *Corresp.* iv. 337.
[2] Barrington to Buckinghamshire, 17 May 1779; *HMC, Lothian*, i (1905), 351.
[3] Fox, *Corresp.* i. 212; also Lecky, iv. 73.
[4] *HMC, Var. Coll.* 6, *Knox*, p. 144.
[5] Lecky, iv. 73.
[6] Lecky, iv. 73 ff.

The prediction of Lord North was not realized, for the Ministry did not fall. The king's fear that Parliament would declare that the war must be promptly ended on any terms did not materialize. What may have been the hope of both men— that Lord George Germain would resign voluntarily—also failed of realization. Toward the end of the Inquiry the Howe brothers demanded that the Ministry make an unqualified statement whether or not their conduct had: '. . . furnished cause of crimination', but the Ministry declined to oblige. In most men's minds, Burgoyne and Admiral Howe had cleared themselves; General Howe had not technically disobeyed or done wrong but had shown bad judgement and poor strategy. The Dean of Canterbury wrote that: 'Lord Howe's character is as much respected as ever, but General Howe's has suffered much by the enquiry.'[1]

Spain's declaration of war diverted popular interest. As the best way to end the Inquiry, Lord North and Lord George simply declined to speak or even to answer questions. 'Not one of the ministers said a word, and thus the Enquiry was put an end to, without coming to a single Resolution on any part of the Business.'[2] But the Inquiry presaged the final ending of the American tragedy. George Grenville, son of the Minister who had imposed the Stamp Tax, told the House of Commons that: 'He was now convinced, that the measures respecting America were wrong at the outset; that they were worse conducted', and that Fox's motion of censure on the conduct of the war 'met with his most hearty approbation.'[3]

Lord George Germain, however, seemed to be as far as ever from that conclusion. The end of the Inquiry seemed to bring him no emotion beyond relief that he had once again survived a very *mauvais quart d'heure*. If his inmost reactions included a shred of contrition for any past action, he concealed it well. But he must have realized that he could no longer consider himself a faultless manager of political or military manœuvre, and that only the Spanish Declaration and the stubborn loyalty to Lord North of the country gentlemen kept him a Minister.

---

[1] Rev. James Cornwallis, Dean of Canterbury, to Hon. Wm. Cornwallis, 3 Oct. 1779; HMC, *Var. Coll.* 5, 6, *Cornwallis-Wykeham-Martin*, p. 320.
[2] *Hansard*, xx. 818.
[3] *Hansard*, xx. 232.

The reactions of Sir William Howe are also obscure, though for a different reason. One does not find deep-sea fish in a shallow pool. Howe's character lacked depth. Charles Lee, discredited General in the American forces but not without talents, lived for some time as an exalted prisoner of war in easy intimacy with Howe in New York. After that close acquaintance he wrote to Benjamin Rush of Howe's character: 'He is naturally good-humoured, complaisant, but illiterate and indolent to the last degree, unless as an executive officer, in which capacity he is all fire and activity, brave and cool as Julius Caesar. His understanding is . . . rather good than otherwise, but was totally confounded and stupified by the immensity of the task imposed on him.'[1] This appears to be a far more fair and considered judgement than one from Lee more frequently quoted: 'Howe shut his eyes, fought his battles, drank his bottle, had his little whore, advis'd with his Counsellors, receiv'd his Orders from North and Germaine.'[2]

It is unlikely that Sir William suffered greatly from the criticism through which he had passed. He was more capable of hurt pride or downright anger than any more complicated spiritual pain, and was reasonably indifferent to the opinion of the common man, so long as it did not intrude on his habits or his military career. He had no reason to think that career was ended, and no remaining clouds of criticism could prevent him from succeeding in time to the title and privileges of the fifth Viscount Howe. As a commanding officer in America, popular tradition has given Howe less credit than he deserved. More than a century ago Lord Melbourne described him to Queen Victoria as: '. . . brave as a lion, but no more of a commander than a pig'. No man can be reduced to two similes, and as a commander Howe was a victim of more weaknesses than his own. His virtues and vices were those of his age and his caste: his misfortune was to be called to a role too big for him. But whatever his faults, most men, after 1779 as well as before it, would rather have followed and trusted Sir William Howe than Lord George Germain.

---

[1] Langworthy, *Memoirs of Lee*, 4 July 1778; also quoted by T. S. Anderson, *Command of the Howe Brothers*.
[2] Hudleston, *Warriors in Undress*, Castle, London, 1925, p. 100.

XXIV

ROADS TO NOWHERE

NEWS of the Inquiry in London reached Clinton some weeks later. Since he had poor opinions of both Howe and Lord George, his satisfaction at the discomforture of both must have tempered his other chronic griefs. From Clinton's point of view, however, Howe and Lord George were still impairing his own position, since the Inquiry distracted a tottering Ministry and a discordant Parliament from the immediate needs and problems of the Army in America. Clinton's requests and complaints seemed to fall on increasingly indifferent ears.

During the summer of 1779 Cornwallis returned to New York as Clinton's second in command. Clinton was glad to have so competent a soldier, but considerably less glad to find that Lord George had given Cornwallis a dormant commission to succeed Clinton whenever the Secretary gave the word. That was not an unusual arrangement: Clinton had been given a similar reversion of Howe's command on 26 April 1776 and again in July 1777.[1] But Clinton was especially sensitive and insecure, and he had seen Carleton, Burgoyne, and Howe all summarily treated; Cornwallis was the current favourite and his dormant commission might be a preface to comparable treatment of Clinton whenever Lord George found it convenient. No arrangement could have been better calculated to shake Clinton's confidence in Lord George and in himself, or more likely to set him at odds with Cornwallis. It was one thing to resign voluntarily and with honour, but quite another to have one's junior officer conscious that at any moment he might become one's successor. It was not long before Clinton had convinced himself that Cornwallis was playing his cards to replace him.

That was unjust to Cornwallis, who, at least in that summer of 1779, was playing no such game, as a letter to his brother

---

[1] Clements, *Clinton Letter Book*, p. 327.

made very clear: 'I am now returning to America, not with views of conquest and ambition, nothing brilliant can be expected in that quarter. . . . I hope Sir H. Clinton will stay, my returning to him is likely to induce him to do so. If he insists on coming away, of course I cannot decline taking the command, and must make the best of it.'[1]

Clinton wrote to Lord George almost immediately after Cornwallis's arrival:

To say truth, my Lord, my spirits are worn out by struggling against the consequences of so many adverse incidents . . . had even the feeble reinforcements which I am still expecting arrived as early as I had thought myself secure would be the case, I should have found myself enabled to attempt measures perhaps of serious consequences. Under my present circumstances, if I shall not have fulfilled the expectation which may have been indulged for the army, I trust I shall always find the failure attributed to its just cause, the inadequacy of my strength to its object. . . . Thus circumstanced, and convinced that the force under my command at present, or that will be during this campaign, is not equal to the services expected of it . . . permit me to resign the command of the army to Lord Cornwallis.[2]

Clinton was more than hinting that if failure were blamed on him he would turn the attack on those who had failed to give him adequate support. Lord George took the hint; he could not risk another Inquiry inspired by Clinton's disgruntled return to England, and his reply was placatory: 'Though the King has great confidence in his Lordship's abilities, his Majesty is too well satisfied with your conduct to wish to see the command of his forces in any other hands. . . . You have had too many proofs of his Majesty's favor to doubt of his royal approbation. The reinforcements sent you have been as ample as could be afforded in the present situation of the country.'[3]

Once again Clinton continued, but disconsolately, with mounting apprehensions of mistreatment and futility. The French Navy had begun to challenge Britain's control of the

---

[1] Cornwallis to the Hon. Wm. Cornwallis, 5 May 1779; *HMC, Var. Coll.* 6, *Cornwallis-Wykeham-Martin*, p. 319.

[2] Clinton to Germain, 20 Aug. 1779; PRO, 30/55, no. 2209; also *HMC, Amer. MSS.* ii. 13.

[3] Germain to Clinton, 4 Nov. 1779; PRO, 30/55, no. 2408; also *HMC, Amer. MSS.* ii. 51.

American seaboard and, aided by American privateers, was making more and more uncertain the arrival of replacements and supplies. Clinton was again compelled to operate an army without money, and under the circumstances was remarkably restrained about it. He had written to Lord George in February: 'I am extremely sorry that I should be again under the disagreeable necessity of representing to your Lordship the distress that we still labor under for want of a Remittance of Specie from England. There is not a single Shilling in the Military Chest.'[1]

Admiral Arbuthnot, in charge of keeping the sea lanes open, was generally known as a blustering, foul-mouthed bully, destitute of even a rudimentary knowledge of naval tactics, and favoured only by Lord Sandwich. He was a sore trial to Clinton, and a constant menace to his plans and safety. But Clinton's strong complaints of Arbuthnot to Lord George brought no results. It is difficult to know how much, at that juncture of the war, Clinton's inactivity was due to these and other handicaps, and how much to a nature easily discouraged or excessively cautious. Admiral Rodney, who was a better judge of ships than men, spent a few days in New York late in 1780 and then wrote with typical vehemence to Lord George:

'Tis with real grief when I say that the language of the *Chief* savours too much of procrastination, and in confidence to your Lordship I must confess that my high ideas of the great abilities and superior activity of the General to my own deceived me upon the proof, and though I believe him and am assured that he is a brave and honest man, I am convinced nature has not given him an enterprizing and active spirit . . . when success has crowned his arms an immediate relaxation takes place, and his affection for New York (in which he has four different houses) induces him to retire to that place, where without any settled plan he idles his time . . . and suffers himself to be cooped up by Washington with an inferior army . . . permitting the officers of the army to act plays.[2]

But as evidence that Rodney's judgements were not always dependable, the same letter assured Lord George that: 'Washington is certainly to be bought.' Rodney himself was not beyond criticism. Admiral Arbuthnot complained to Lord George of his high-handedness on almost the same day that

---

[1] Clinton to Germain, 27 Feb. 1779; Clements, *Clinton Letter Book*, ii. 49.
[2] Rodney to Germain, 22 Dec. 1780; *HMC, Stop. Sack*. ii. 191–4.

Rodney was complaining of Clinton: 'All I can say is that
Admiral Sir George Rodney displayed the most wanton un-
presedented abuse of power that ever was exhibited, has striped
the storehouses of all the necessaries both for ships and men; he
has carried away two frigates and impressed 400 [of my] seamen.'[1]

Rodney's report may account in part for Lord George's impatience with Clinton. But whoever was right about Clinton's
character, Lord George was certainly wrong in his concept of
loyalist enthusiasm in the former colonies. He accepted at face
value assurances from a few loyalists in Georgia and the Carolinas
that those provinces could very easily be won back to the Crown.
'. . . whenever the King's troops move to Carolina, they will
be assisted by very considerable numbers of the inhabitants',[2]
James Simpson wrote, and Joseph Galloway, undismayed by
his deflation at the Inquiry, was still insisting that America was
full of eager loyalists, and was writing long letters to Lord
George outlining the course to be followed after the rebels were
completely defeated.[3]

The conquest of the southern states was especially attractive
to Lord George for a practical reason. Lord North had told the
Cabinet that he could not raise funds to finance the American
war for more than another year. If the Carolinas could be set
free to send their valuable indigo and tobacco to England it
might more than pay for the cost of the operation.[4] Lord George
ignored all information and advice contrary to his desires.
Among his papers, for example, lay a letter from Jonathan
Boucher, who wrote: 'that North Carolina was the poorest
country in the revolted colonies . . . of its people even the most
loyal could hardly declare themselves, for they live so dispersed
that they would be an easy prey'.[5]

Clinton resisted Lord George's urgings to a campaign in the
South, and expressed doubts regarding the help the southern
loyalists would give. In early 1779 he wrote to Lord George:
'I have the honor to transmit to your Lordship. . . . Intelligence
from the Rebel Country divested from the too Sanguine Reports

---

[1] Arbuthnot to Germain, 19 Dec. 1780; *HMC, Stop. Sack.* ii. 190.
[2] Simpson to Germain, 28 Aug. 1779; *HMC, Stop. Sack.* ii. 137.
[3] Galloway to Germain; *HMC, Stop. Sack.* ii. 124.
[4] Fortescue, *HBA*, 2, iii. 250 ff.
[5] Boucher to Germain, Nov. 1775; *HMC, Stop. Sack.* ii. 19, 20.

of the zealous friends of His Majesty's Government.'[1] Clinton also doubted the wisdom of extending his limited forces so far from their key position in New York; he had withdrawn his troops from Rhode Island to centralize his resources.[2] In view of that strategy he was not inclined to deploy them again at a far greater distance, on what might easily prove an abortive venture, especially with the French fleet an increasing menace along the seaboard.

Clinton's reluctance led Lord George, in defiance of good military and administrative procedure, to correspond directly and privately with Cornwallis, who was eager to lead a campaign in the South, and accepted the reports that as soon as a British army appeared there the natives would flock to support it. Without taking any official action that would show on the records, Lord George worked to put a good part of Clinton's army under the strategic and operational control of Cornwallis. Lord George's methods were less harsh and overt than when he had turned Carleton's army over to Burgoyne, but they proved almost as effective, and equally unfortunate.

Whatever Clinton's 'lassitude', he had good reasons for reluctance, and advanced some of them to Lord George: 'I have as yet received no assurances of any favourable temper in the province of South Carolina to encourage me to an undertaking where we must expect so much difficulty. . . . The small force which the present weakness of General Washington's army would enable me to detach might possibly get possession of Charleston . . . but I doubt whether they could keep it . . . [the move] would reduce me to the strictest defensive in this country.'[3]

The pressures from Lord George and from Cornwallis continued, and toward the end of 1779 Clinton gave in. Since a campaign in the South was insisted upon, there was always the chance that it might be successful, and redeem his years in America by a striking success. In any case it was better to lead the campaign, at least in its first stages, than to see all the credit go to a subordinate. Clinton's only intention was to capture and

---

[1] Clinton to Germain, 11 Jan. 1779; Clements, *Germain Papers*, ix, 1/a.
[2] *HMC, Amer. MSS.* ii. 48; 7 Oct. 1779.
[3] Clinton to Germain, 4 Apr. 1779; PRO, 30/55, no. 1885; also *HMC, Stop. Sack.* ii. 124, 125.

if possible hold Charleston, and perhaps to venture somewhat into its immediate hinterland. At the very end of 1779 he took ship with Cornwallis and some 7,000 men, 2,000 of whom were American provincials.[1]

Nearly all his cavalry horses died on the voyage,[2] but that was not unusual, and otherwise the sea trip to Charleston was safely accomplished. Clinton captured Charleston on 12 May 1780, far more quickly and easily than he had expected, and with impressive results. He took 5,000 prisoners, 800 cannon of various sizes, ages, and degrees of utility, and eight small ships—all at a loss he said was not more than 400 British killed and wounded.[3] It was a most impressive victory, though strategically far less important than was at first believed when the news reached England. Lord George interpreted it as evidence that he had been wholly right, and assumed that the complete conquest of the entire South would shortly follow.

Clinton was less impressed by his own success; and he was worried about the security of New York and the movements of Washington during his absence. The presence of a French fleet in the New York area concerned him still more, for he was losing confidence in the ability of Admiral Arbuthnot to do anything effective. He left some 4,000 men with the confident Cornwallis,[4] and hurried by ship to New York, reaching there on 9 June 1780.[5] While he was at sea, the former Crown Governor of South Carolina was writing to Lord George that all accounts from North Carolina indicated that the majority of its inhabitants were ardently loyalist.[6]

Clinton's instructions to Cornwallis were to hold Charleston; to rouse the loyalists in Georgia and South Carolina and supply them with arms, and then, if all were propitious, to raid northward into North Carolina. Cornwallis was above all to keep open his communications to his base in Charleston, since he was wholly dependent on it for men, supplies, communications, and withdrawal.

The capture of Charleston, and Cornwallis's later apparent victorious progress, turned British opinion from discouragement

---

[1] Lecky, iv. 119. [2] Fortescue, *HBA*, 2, iii. 307.
[3] Lecky, iv. 120. [4] Lecky, iv. 211.
[5] *HMC, Stop. Sack.* ii. 168; also Lecky, iv. 121.
[6] Martin to Germain, 10 June 1780; *HMC, Stop. Sack.* ii. 168.

to something approaching confidence and then, as nothing much further seemed to be happening, to disinterest that moved toward apathy. The Earl of Chatham's daughter, Lady Harriet Eliot, wrote to her mother from London in April 1780: 'There is very little news at present. I think America seems to be quite forgot.'[1]

Clinton, in New York, grew more and more uneasy. He seldom received reports from Cornwallis, and although those that reached him told of minor victories, they also indicated dangerously extending lines of communication. Clinton wrote a prescient sentence to Lord George that August: 'An inroad is no countenance, and to possess territory demands garrisons.'[2] But Clinton's pessimism only made Lord George more ready to ignore him and support Cornwallis directly. Lord George's dispatches to Cornwallis, who still carried the dormant commission as Commander-in-Chief, took from Clinton any real control of the operations of his subordinate. Some time in late 1780 a change came over Cornwallis, who had until then worked loyally under Clinton. Whether because of his early victories in the Carolinas or the praises and encouragement he was getting from Lord George, Cornwallis began to treat Clinton with indifference.

The less highly Lord George thought of Clinton, the less he was inclined to go to troublesome lengths to gratify him by getting rid of Admiral Arbuthnot. It was not a unilateral dislike; Arbuthnot's letters show that he was irritated by Clinton, though he pretended to endure it with noble forbearance: 'To say the truth my Lord, my task is not easy, nor my road pleasant; so many circumstances occur in the course of business, that I submit to only for peace: that keeps my command of temper so continually upon the stretch that I am apprehensive that I shall not be able much longer to possess philosophy sufficient.'[3] Two weeks later his philosophy had clearly begun to desert him: 'I cannot submit to such irregular proceedings. . . . Somebody must set this Gentleman right . . . I dare not, for I will not quarrel.'[4]

---

[1] Lady Harriet Eliot to Countess of Chatham, 18 Apr. 1780; Headlam, *Letters of Lady Harriet Eliot.*
[2] Clinton to Germain, 25 Aug. 1780; Fortescue, *HBA*, 2, iii. 331.
[3] Arbuthnot to Germain, 31 May 1780; Clements, *Germain Papers*, xii.
[4] Idem, 4 June 1780.

Clinton's concern about Arbuthnot's incompetence was enhanced by Cornwallis's dependence on Arbuthnot's squadron. If the seas could not be kept open Cornwallis could not be supplied or, if necessary, rescued. But that argument carried little weight with Lord George, who was developing other ideas for Cornwallis. While Clinton seemed to be doing little or nothing in New York, Cornwallis was sweeping through the Carolinas, and on the maps of Whitehall securing thousands of square miles to the Crown. He won decisively over Gates and DeKalb and some 6,000 rebel militia at Camden and had other lesser victories, while his minor defeats and losses seemed at the time insignificant. Exhilarated by his progress, Cornwallis moved nearer and nearer to the Virginia line and farther and farther from his base at Charleston. He was beginning to fix his eyes on the conquest of Virginia and to write to Clinton and Lord George that, with co-operation from an army moving into Virginia from the North, he could conquer the entire South.

Beneath the surface of that success there were disturbing facts that Clinton saw more clearly than Cornwallis, but Lord George declined to see at all. The farther Cornwallis moved the weaker his strategic position became. His little army was constantly being diminished by trivial losses that cumulated into a large one. Sickness, defections, detachments for garrisons, communications, and forage all took their toll. The countryside proved remarkably unproductive of food and even elementary supplies, and by April it was already unbearably hot for plodding British infantrymen not acclimated to temperatures of eighty degrees in the shade.

At first Cornwallis was all confidence about the loyalists as well as about military success. On 4 July 1780 he wrote to his brother: 'The people of the back country seem most sincerely happy at returning to their union with Great Britain, and execrate the tyranny of their late rulers.'[1] But three months later he was confessing that the loyalists were disappointing him, and that conclusion was supported by his officers. Lord Rawdon reported in several letters to Lord George and to Clinton that even in South Carolina, reported to be the most loyalist of the

---

[1] Cornwallis to the Hon. Wm. Cornwallis, from Charleston, 4 July 1780; *HMC, Var. Coll.* 6, *Cornwallis-Wykeham-Martin*, p. 325.

colonies, the inhabitants were of very little help, even in providing dependable information.[1]

On one occasion Cornwallis called on all local citizens to join him, but failed to enlist a single man. On another: 'One whole corps, which had been entrusted with the protection of sick soldiers, went over to the enemy, giving up their officers and the sick soldiers as prisoners.'[2] On another: 'A rebel, who had sworn allegiance and obtained from Cornwallis not only a certificate of loyalty but a commission in the loyal militia, seduced his regiment from the colonel and led them to join Sumter.'[3] Some who took the loyalty oath proved to be traitors and had to be shot, a denouement that did not encourage further enlistments. Cornwallis was by 1781 obliged to admit that: 'Our experience has shown us that their numbers are not so great as has been represented, and that their friendship was only passive.'[4] He was also beginning to recognize that his conquests were impermanent, and in one of his infrequent dispatches to Clinton wrote that: 'The troops here have gained in reputation but lost in numbers.'[5]

Lord George preferred to accept other and more favourable reports that were still coming to him from Tory merchants and planters in and about Charleston, and from British officers in his special confidence. One of these was Lieutenant-Colonel Balfour, who wrote to him that many of the chief citizens of North Carolina had sworn allegiance to the king, and from this inferred that most other North Carolinians would promptly do so. Lord George grew still more critical of Clinton's caution and inactivity in contrast to Cornwallis's striking progress. He wrote to Knox: 'Clinton is of all men the most jealous, and when he has not the whole credit of a measure is apt to dislike the plan, however well concerted.'[6] Clinton was also annoying because he kept insisting that he would resign unless Lord George got the Admiralty to replace the bumbling Admiral Arbuthnot. Lord George had promised Clinton to do so, but: '. . . the old Admiral still remained in command of the fleet, constantly

---

[1] *HMC, Stop. Sack.* ii. 185, 186; 24 and 28 Oct. 1780.
[2] Lecky, iv. 123.
[3] Ibid.
[4] Cornwallis to Germain, 18 Apr. 1781; Ross, *Cornwallis Letters*, i. 90.
[5] Cornwallis to Clinton, Aug. 1781; PRO, 30/55, no. 2976.
[6] Germain to Knox, 5 Sept. 1780; *HMC, Var. Coll.* 6, *Knox*, p. 171.

changing his plans and completing none of them, and hampering
the General in a fashion which kept Clinton in terror of losing
supremacy at sea'.[1]

It would not be easy to get the Admiral transferred to a lesser
post, and after all, why do a service for a general who was
constantly critical, at a cost to an admiral who was effusively
protesting to Lord George his gratitude for: '. . . all your goodness to a perfect stranger. My head may err but my heart will
ever acknowledge very great partiality'.[2] Even if Lord George
had not been at odds with the Earl of Sandwich, it was natural
that a First Lord of the Admiralty should not welcome pressures
to cashier one of his admirals simply because one of Lord
George's generals did not like him. Yet there was very little
doubt that Clinton was the better man of the two, and William
Eden was urgent that something would have to be done. Eden,
who seemed to know everything that went on within the
Ministry, had taken it on himself once more to act the almost-
honest broker, and had written to Lord George that letters from
Clinton proved the absolute necessity either of removing him or
sending a new commander of the naval squadron without delay.
Eden had added regarding Clinton: '. . . I must do him the
justice to add that he writes with good humour, and as much
cheerfulness as could be expected.'[3]

Knox was advising Lord George to take a firm hand in naval
affairs. He wrote to him regarding Lord Sandwich and his fellow
Lords of the Admiralty: '. . . to the insufficiency of their
Instructions, when no directions are given them, much of our
delays & disappointments are owing and if your Lordship does
not determine to give the orders yourself insted of leaving it to
Lord Sandwich . . . things will never be better'.[4]

Lord George was not so potent in such matters as he had been
in earlier days, and he had to take up with the Cabinet Clinton's
virtual ultimatum. He wrote to Clinton: 'I have judged it
improper to receive any Commands from His Majesty upon
the Subject without first laying the whole before the King's
other Confidential Servants and submitting their opinion to his

---

[1] Fortescue, *HBA*, 2, iii. 388.
[2] Arbuthnot to Germain, 17 Dec. 1779; Clements, *Germain Papers*, xi. 51/5.
[3] Eden to Germain, 4 Oct. 1780; *HMC, Stop. Sack.* ii. 183.
[4] Knox to Germain, 31 Oct. 1781; Clements, *Germain Papers*, 42/127; also
HMC, Stop. Sack. ii. 215.

Majesty.'[1] At long last, on 11 October 1780, but just a week after Eden had prodded Lord George, the minutes of the Cabinet recorded agreement that Admiral Arbuthnot be transferred, but added: 'If this arrangement, together with assurances of such a reinforcement of troops as can be spared from this country, does not induce Sir Henry Clinton to think that he can continue in the command, his Majesty though unwillingly does in that case permit him to resign his command to Lord Cornwallis.'[2]

That codicil, which was obviously a bargain with Sandwich, led that noble earl to write to Arbuthnot five days later: 'I am much inclined to think that Sir Henry Clinton will resign his command, as most of the points he has urged as a condition of his remaining have been refused.'[3] Sandwich did his best to achieve this face-saving solution, and even suggested to Lord George that he treat Clinton so cavalierly that he would resign and thus let Arbuthnot remain—the successful prosecution of the war being, apparently, a secondary matter. Sandwich added: 'I throw this out only for your consideration.'[4]

Lord George was only a lukewarm advocate of Clinton, but he could not afford to lose him or to rouse Parliament by openly alienating him, so he sang one tune to Clinton and another to the Earl of Sandwich. He wrote to Clinton: 'His Majesty has been pleased to appoint Admiral Arbuthnot to relieve Sir Peter Parker in the command at Jamaica, and another Flag Officer now on the list will immediately be named to the Command in North America.'[5] But he wrote to Sandwich:

. . . the distance is so great, and Sir H. Clinton acting more from caprice than common sense, it is impossible to guess what effect the concessions made to him will have upon his mind . . . . In the conversation I had with Colonel Bruce, who carried my letter to the General, I explained very freely to him the impossibility of the service being carried on if Sir H. Clinton would not act steadily and confidentially with the King's servants; and the only favour I had to beg of him was either to come home directly or to continue in his command with good humour.[6]

---

[1] Germain to Clinton, 4 Oct. 1780; Clements, *Clinton Letter Book*, pp. 222–7.
[2] *Sandwich Papers*, iii. 255; 11 Oct. 1780.
[3] Sandwich to Arbuthnot, 18 Oct. 1780; *HMC, Stop. Sack*. ii. 185.
[4] Sandwich to Germain, 18 Oct. 1780; *HMC, Stop. Sack*. ii. 185.
[5] Germain to Clinton, 13 Oct. 1780; Clements, *Clinton Letter Book*, p. 229.
[6] Germain to Sandwich, 19 Oct. 1780; *Sandwich Papers*, iii. 258.

Had Clinton received such a message he would probably have resigned on the spot, and he would certainly have made some reference to it in his papers and later accounts of the war. He did none of these. And though Sandwich wrote to Arbuthnot that the Cabinet had refused most of Clinton's conditions for remaining, Lord George implied to Clinton that they had been granted. Neither was the truth; most of them were promised but not performed.

Lord George had described the change to Clinton as immediate, but in the lexicon of the North Ministry there was no such word. Arbuthnot continued for some months his command of the American fleet, and Lord George continued to assure Clinton that Arbuthnot was on the point of transfer.

Late in 1780 Clinton foresaw a disastrous possibility that Lord George declined to face, and wrote to Arbuthnot, who was about to send Rear-Admiral Graves and six ships of the line to the Leeward Islands, that the plan gave him the greatest concern. Only if the fleet could be held together in the waters near New York, Clinton explained, could it maintain superiority over the French Navy in that area; without that superiority the enemy would be at full liberty to take a French army to the Carolinas 'without leaving me power to render Lord Cornwallis my assistance against them'.[1] Arbuthnot yielded to this warning[2] which would be even more significant in retrospect a year later.

Another four months passed and Arbuthnot was still in command of the fleet in American waters, moving his ships busily but unprofitably up and down Long Island Sound or scattering them ineffectively from Rhode Island to Bermuda. Clinton confided to General Phillips, whom he had sent with a force to the Chesapeake area: 'Our Admiral is grown, if possible, more impracticable than ever. He swears to me, he knows nothing of his recall. To others, he says he is going home immediately. If the next packet does not satisfy me in this particular, I shall probably retire and leave him to Lord Cornwallis' management.'[3] Clinton was always hoping against hope that the 'next packet' would bring solutions: it almost never did.

[1] Clinton to Arbuthnot, 9 Dec. 1780; *HMC, Stop. Sack*. ii. 199, 200.
[2] *HMC, Stop. Sack*. ii. 200.
[3] Clinton to Phillips, 30 Apr. 1781; Clements, *Shelburne Papers, Amer. Dispatches*, i. 68.

Thus as the year 1780 drew to an end, Lord George Germain had reduced his last commanding general in America to something like psychotic and military impotence. He had also aroused and stimulated enmity between Clinton and Cornwallis, and had encouraged Cornwallis to feel almost independent of his military commander.[1] For several months there was almost no communication between the two generals and Clinton professed to being: '. . . in the dark as to the real scope and intention of Cornwallis' movements'.[2] According to Walpole, the two men: '. . . were so ill together that Sir Henry had owned to Conway that he was determined to challenge Lord Cornwallis after the campaign'.[3]

Lord George did not see the situation thus, or see himself as the generals saw him. In a note to Knox in 1780 he wrote of the generals and admirals: 'How miserably we have been served in the war.'[4] If mutual trust and goodwill between statesmen and generals are essential to victory, Lord George had chosen a curious way to win a war.

[1] Fortescue, *HBA*, 2, iii. 358.   [2] Ibid., p. 376.
[3] Walpole, *Last Journals*, ii. 377; 3 Nov. 1781.
[4] Germain to Knox, 13 July 1780; *HMC, Var. Coll.* 6, *Knox*, p. 168.

XXV

THE INNER CIRCLE

LORD GEORGE GERMAIN had never been schooled in the
art of compromise. He had risen in the Army less by self-
discipline than by self-assertion, and he had gained power
in Parliament less by working with others than by personal
manœuvres and personal defiances. The aftermath of Minden
had not made him a warmer lover of his fellow men, whom
he trusted no more than they trusted him. Through the long
decade that followed he had learned how to be obsequious, but,
restored to power, he put humility behind him except as a
forensic device. He was loyal to the king, but his primary loyalty
was to Lord George Germain.

Nearly all the Cabinet Ministers of George III lacked the
sense of collective responsibility and co-operation expected of
Ministers today, and Lord North demanded even less unity in
his Cabinet than his predecessors had done. Yet Lord North
knew that no government can function without reasonable give
and take between its leaders, and expected that in crucial
matters of common welfare each Minister would adjust himself
to the interests of government and party. He would hardly have
admitted Lord George to his Ministry's inner circle without
that assumption, yet Lord George told young Mr. Roberts, an
emissary from Sir Edward Walpole, '. . . that from the moment
he had entered the King's service, he had declared himself an
independent man, and had told Lord North he would be so, and
should be ready to resign his post at any time'.[1]

In the loose structure of Lord North's Government, Lord
George was not the only Minister who sometimes acted independently of the collective will, but he was the only Minister
who for the first two years did so with such casual consistency.
Until after Saratoga he treated the Cabinet as an organism to
which it was expedient to pay lip service, a tool he might
conveniently use, a shield behind which it might be expedient

---

[1] Walpole, *Last Journals*, ii. 48.

to retreat, and sometimes an inconvenient impediment to his independent operations. He could take the Cabinet thus lightly because it was not upon the Cabinet that his own power depended. So long as he could make himself seem indispensable to the king and Lord North he felt secure.

In view of the special strengths and weaknesses of Lord North and the king, Lord George's tactics kept him in office longer than would seem possible today. This was partly because his abilities, though not exceptional, stood out among the members of a weak Cabinet: his single-mindedness was compelling, and his confidence reassuring. And to a strong-minded king he became so identified with the royal will that to have dismissed him without honours would have seemed a public confession of the weakening of that will.

Such a Minister could hardly expect to be popular with his fellows, and Lord George was not. 'He seems to have been a man who could work kindly with no one.'[1] 'With Lord Sandwich he had been at variance ever since he received the seals; he had bullied all the Admiralty. All the Ministers had kept aloof from him, and did even at St. James.'[2]

The breach with Sandwich was greatly deepened after the French entered the war, for Lord George then insisted on a naval strategy at odds with the opinions of the Earl and the Admiralty.[3] His only alliances were with Lord Suffolk and two or three of the lesser but influential members of the Ministry, and even those lasted only so long as they were mutually expedient. Once, amid the attacks and personal losses of early 1778, Lord George seemed to show some dependence on another Minister. 'If Lord Suffk. continues ill & impossible to go on, Lord G. will certainly resign', Colonel Smith predicted to Eden.[4] But Smith was wrong.

---

[1] Fortescue, *Corresp.* iv, Intro., p. vi.

[2] Walpole, *Last Journals*, ii. 67; 25 Oct. 1777.

[3] Lord North, caught between two men more opinionated and forceful than himself, vacillated between them, and even the king was uncharacteristically undecided. These divided inner councils were a main reason for British naval inefficiency during the war (see G. S. Brown, 'The Anglo-French Naval Crisis', in the *William and Mary Quarterly*, xiii. 3–25, 1956). Germain wanted the Navy to take aggressive action against the French fleet in the Atlantic; Sandwich favoured keeping the fleet together for the protection of Britain, and his Admiralty supported him.

[4] Smith to Eden, Aug. 1778, 'Most Secret'; Stevens, *Facsimiles*, v. 513, 514.

Without Lord George there would have been disagreements and factions in the North Ministry, but he inspired and augmented many of them. Under his hand purely political differences soured into personal enmities,[1] until the disunity within the Cabinet was exposed to public view.[2] Hillsborough, Lord Lieutenant of Ireland, wrote: '. . . the ministry were never so disunited. They would not even speak to one another on public affairs.'[3] It was characteristic of the times and the man that a little later Hillsborough rejoined that Ministry. It was also characteristic that the king accepted him after having said of him in 1776 that he 'did not know a man of less judgment'. Firm opposition to conciliation with America had become so rare among men eligible for ministerial appointments that with the king it outweighed all other factors.

Lord George and Lord North would not under any circumstances have been really congenial, for few men were more unlike in temperament and manner. Lord North, in spite of his puffy face and figure, was a far more likeable person than the concepts handed down to posterity by his political opponents in England and America. He was as affable as Lord George was reserved, as modest as Lord George was egoistic, as amenable as Lord George was immutable. No matter what a man's politics, Lord North was prepared to like him as a man, and no matter how great the excuse for bitterness, he would avoid it if possible. To the king he gave a painful loyalty worthy of better ends; to his fellow Ministers great patience, and to the rest of the world an easy tolerance. His reputation for personal integrity (as distinguished from his skilful management of electoral purchases) was never seriously questioned in a Parliament given to personal attacks, and his wit in the House drew from his most vituperative critic Charles Fox the tribute that Parliament '. . . had no more complete master of language'.[4] Burke, another chief opponent, described him as '. . . a man of admirable parts,

[1] '. . . there were several factions in the Ministry: Lord North and Dartmouth were one, the Bedfords were divided into two, and Lord Mansfield, Jenkinson, Wedderburn, Lord Suffolk and Lord George Germain were another, and were most trusted by the King; and yet Lord George could not be well with the King' (Walpole, *Last Journals*, ii. 103, note; 4 Feb. 1778).
[2] Walpole, *Last Journals*, ii. 29; 30 May 1778.
[3] Hillsborough to Hutchinson, 5 Aug. 1778; Clements, *Hutchinson Diaries* (original MS.), p. 525.
[4] Christie, *End of Lord North's Ministry*, p. 64.

of general knowledge, of a versatile understanding, fitted for every sort of business, of infinite wit and pleasantry, of a delightful temper, and with a mind most perfectly disinterested', but '. . . he wanted something of the vigilance and spirit of command that the time required'.

As First Minister Lord North had the defects of those virtues. He was reluctant to make unpleasant decisions and prone to accept without corroboration the statements of others. He lacked a capacity for organization even when he saw how essential it was. He allowed his fellow Ministers to steer separate and sometimes contradictory courses, and disclaimed responsibility for their actions in the affairs of their own departments, unless previously approved by the Cabinet. He seldom urged his own opinions on his colleagues and sometimes napped soundly at Cabinet meetings. His loyalty to the king led him to maintain the king's American policy against his own judgement. Few men were more eager to see the American war 'terminated with honour to this country', as he informed General Howe in 1777,[1] yet he led in its continuance until the termination was without honour. He held together a weak Ministry far longer than its policies and performance merited; telling the king that his continuance was a public disservice but continuing at the king's insistence.

George III's devotion to Lord North was equally impressive and equally unfortunate. Had he accepted one of Lord North's many pleading resignations and reconciled himself to almost any other possible Ministry, the war would have ended sooner. But, apart from personal loyalty to Lord North, the king would not release him for fear of that very result. Yet George III, with all his tragic lacks in vision and understanding, was a man of character and integrity—within the narrow range of his comprehension he was a better leader and judge of men than most of his Ministers, and had higher ethical standards. He was a devoted admirer of the English system of government and was determined to maintain it, but unfortunately the system he admired was that of the time of George I, and hopelessly outdated. He failed to allow for the inevitable political changes required by Britain's social and economic development, for the rise of the lower classes, the complications of overseas government,

[1] Robinson to Howe, 5 Mar. 1777; PRO, 30/55, no. 432.

the inevitable additions to the powers of a Ministry, and to the freedoms of the common man. His lack of imaginative insight brought disaster to his nation, yet few men exceeded him in stubborn courage to do what he thought was right. It was his tragedy and Britain's that he saw his duty so myopically, and took it so seriously.

Those were the two men upon whom Lord George's power and position rested: yet he had not been six months in office before he risked offending both of them, and all for the sake of a sinecure worth £600 a year to which he was almost certainly not entitled. On 30 March 1776 he wrote to the king: 'Lord George Germain begs leave to inform your Majesty, that by the death of Baron Muir the office of Receiver General of Jamaica becomes vacant. Lord George would be infinitely Obliged to your Majesty if you would be graciously pleased to grant that office to his youngest son George Germain it is said to be worth six Hundred pounds a year.'[1] Lord George's younger son was at that time less than seven years of age.[2]

On the same day Lord North also sent a note to the king:

Lord North begs leave to trouble his Majesty about a considerable sinecure place vacant in Jamaica by the death of Baron Muir. It is a revenue place, &, therefore, I believe, by law is given by a Warrant countersigned by the Treasury. By some mistake, however, some of the Warrants have been issued by the American Secretary, & it is probable that his Majesty will have an application for the disposal of it; Lord North hopes that his Majesty will not countersign any Warrant till the Point is clear'd up. The name of the Office is, Receiver General of Jamaica.[3]

On the same day that he received the two letters the king replied to Lord North:

I am sincerely obliged to You for acquainting Me that You look upon the Receiver General of Jamaica as a Treasury Appointment, and shall be ready to give any assistance in this business, provided the Appointment be made out in favour of one of Your Sons. As You seemed to expect Lord George Germain wrote to Me in favour of his Second Son; but I instantly answered that I was apprized of the vacancy, but could not think of any Appointment untill it was clearly proved that it had been usually prepared in his Office, as

---

[1] Germain to King, 30 Mar. 1776; Fortescue, *Corresp*. iii. 346.
[2] The boy was born in 1770.
[3] North to King, 30 Mar. 1776; Fortescue, *Corresp*. iii. 348.

I believed as other *Receivers* that it ought to be filled up by a Warrant of the Lords of the Treasury. You will never find any occasion of providing for Your Children that I shall not be more happy if possible than Yourself to provide for them. It has not been my fate in general to be well served, by You I have, and therefore cannot forget it.[1]

Lord George must have realized that Lord North would resent this covert raid upon his perquisites. No shrewd politician would have risked the loss of Lord North's goodwill for £600 a year: no man as wealthy as Lord George Germain need have done so.

There were other episodes that revealed Lord George's singular obtuseness to the reactions of Lord North and the king. He deliberately embarrassed them by forcing Lord Harcourt, who had offered a merely *pro forma* resignation, from his post as Lord Lieutenant of Ireland.[2] On at least one occasion he did not follow the form of requesting the Cabinet to meet, but 'summoned' it.[3] He and Lady George gave a great ball to which nearly everyone of social and political importance in London was invited—except Lord and Lady North.[4] Horace Walpole recorded that six months after he had taken office 'Lord North's friends grew very sick of Lord G. Germaine's assuming ascendancy'.[5]

Lord George was not above misleading his Cabinet colleagues. When in late 1776 Howe's request for 15,000 more men to raise

---

[1] King to North, 31 Mar. 1776; Fortescue, *Corresp.* iii. 348.

[2] Lord Harcourt had offered his resignation in a conventional situation; he did not mean or think that it would be accepted (Fortescue, *Corresp.* iii. 298, 333). Sir John Blaquiere reported to Lord Harcourt: 'Lord G. Germaine, I found, was one of the loudest men at St. James last Friday, to cry shame that you had not got your recall when you had so earnestly pressed for it. His object, together with that of the Suffolk clique, is notorious. It distressed Lord North, and, if they can prevail, they think that their cousin of Buckingham stands foremost' (Blaquiere to Harcourt, 18 Nov. 1776; *Harcourt Papers*, x. 204). The Earl of Buckinghamshire later became Lord Lieutenant of Ireland.

[3] 'Lord George has summoned the Cabinet to meet at nine o'clock this evening. . . . If your Majesty had any particular Commands Lord George will remain at home to receive them until he goes to the meeting' (Germain to King, 2 May 1776; Fortescue, *Corresp.* iii. 365). It was only the first minister or the king who 'summoned' a meeting.

[4] Pemberton, *Lord North*, p. 86; Bodleian North Collection (original letter of Lady North to Guilford).

[5] Walpole, *Last Journals*, i. 562; 8 June 1776. 'Lord G. Germaine . . . dictating the measures, and leaving the whole burthen of supplies on the shoulders of Lord North, whom at the same time, without reserve in his most public conversations, he spoke of as a trifling and supine Minister' (Walpole, *Last Journals*, i. 510–11).

his total to 35,000 came before the Cabinet, its Minutes read: 'Lord George Germain read General Howe's demand of men for the next campaign', and proposed to submit to his Majesty the advisability of 'taking into his pay about 4000 German troops, which number will complete the 35,000 rank and file which the General proposes for his operations.'[1] Lord George could not have failed to know that the 4,000 Hessians, together with all the other reinforcements he proposed to send, would not bring Howe's total of new troops to more than 10,000 or his grand total to more than 30,000.

That was not the only occasion when Lord George did not take the Cabinet fully into his confidence. The Minutes of another Cabinet meeting record the decision '. . . that Lieutenant General Burgoyne should again be employed in Canada'.[2] Several months earlier Lord George had given Burgoyne reason to expect that assignment,[3] and Burgoyne later testified that long before that Cabinet meeting Lord George had promised him not only re-employment in Canada but the command of the northern army in the coming campaign.

Howe's successes in and about New York in 1776, and the prospect of a great victory by Burgoyne, enabled Lord George to ride roughshod in 1777 over his critics in Ministry and Parliament. His stock was at its highest, and he had become a figure all Europe was watching. The Marquis de Noailles wrote to Minister Vergennes: 'As this individual seems to be becoming a person of importance, all eyes will necessarily be fixed on him, and it will thenceforth be easier to discover what may more particularly concern him.'[4]

Burgoyne's surrender and the resultant revelations unleashed the repressed enmity against Lord George within as well as without the Ministry. Immediately after the news of Saratoga reached London, Lord North wrote to the king: '. . . the consequences of this most fatal event, both in America and foreign parts may be very important and serious, and will certainly require some material change in our system'.[5] There was no doubt what most of Lord George's associates thought the first

---

[1] *HMC, Dartmouth* (1895), ii. 432.
[2] *Sandwich Papers*, i. 285; Feb. 1777.
[3] Germain to Burgoyne, 23 Aug. 1776; *HMC, Stop. Sack.* ii. 39.
[4] Noailles to Vergennes, 5 Sept. 1777; Stevens, *Facsimiles*, xviii. 1676.
[5] North to King, 4 Dec. 1777; Fortescue, *Corresp.* ii. 504.

change in the system should be. He had no decent alternative to offering his resignation, though he did it half-heartedly, and the king postponed action upon it. But in 1778 the king and Lord North appear to have decided that at the first expedient opportunity Lord George must go,[1] especially since other ministers were threatening to leave if Lord George did not. Lord North informed the king that the Lord Chancellor, Bathurst, '. . . is inclined to leave the administration. . . . Indeed this is to be expected from other quarters.'[2]

The king promptly appealed to Bathurst to remain, and reported to Lord North that he thought he had persuaded the Lord Chancellor to continue, for the Chancellor '. . . expresses great esteem for all the Members of the Cabinet except Lord George Germain'.[3] But Bathurst and Gower shortly left the Ministry, and Lord Barrington, after two years of insistent resignations, escaped from the war office, where he was succeeded by Lord Bute's former private secretary Charles Jenkinson, '. . . who could always be trusted to act as a mere clerk fulfilling the directions of the King'.[4] When Lord Suffolk died, Lord George lost his only political ally in the Cabinet. Suffolk was eventually succeeded by Lord Hillsborough, '. . . whose American sentiments make him acceptable to me', the king wrote to Lord North.[5]

By the latter half of 1778 Lord George seemed to have weathered the storm, since the king was unwilling either to force him out with no honour, or to buy him out with too much honour. And as other Ministers began to hint doubts of the wisdom of continuing the king's implacable American policy, Lord George's devotion to that policy made him seem more valuable to the king. Steps were taken, however, to curb Lord George's independent operations. One of these was to insist that all major military and naval plans and operations be brought before the Cabinet in advance of the issuance of orders implementing them. Lord North informed his Ministers that henceforth: 'Any particular measure respecting our preparations

---

[1] Fortescue, *Corresp.* i, Preface.
[2] North to King, 16 Feb. 1778; Fortescue, *Corresp.* iv. 38.
[3] King to North, 17 Feb. 1778; Fortescue, *Corresp.* iv. 38, 39.
[4] Lecky, iv. 108.
[5] King to North; Donne, *Corresp. George III and North*, ii. 200; King to John Robinson, 15 Oct. 1776; *HMC*, x, part vi, p. 15.

must be settled in a Cabinet',¹ and though that order also affected the Earl of Sandwich, it was aimed primarily at Lord George.

As a further safeguard, Lord (Jeffery) Amherst was appointed as Commander-in-Chief in Britain and military adviser with Cabinet rank. Amherst had been a favourite protégé of the Duke of Dorset. 'Lord Amherst and Lord George Sackville had always lived on the most intimate terms from childhood. Sir Jeffery was born within a mile of Knowle Park. . . . At the time when the Duke of Dorset was lord lieutenant of Ireland and his son, Lord George Sackville, was his Secretary, Sir Jeffery Amherst formed a part of the household.'² But the appointment of Amherst did not please Lord George, not only because it curbed his power, but because Amherst had recently declined to replace Howe as Commander-in-Chief in America. Lord George had then written angrily to the king: 'From a Boy he had a degree of what some people thought firmness, and others called obstinacy, in his Tempers, which made reasoning with him, upon points he had resolved, of no effect. How he or any officers can decline service when so honourably and so directly offer'd by his Sovereign is beyond all conception. Lord George will omit no opportunity of telling Lord Amherst his opinion on so interesting a subject.'³ Years later Lord George insisted that as a young man Amherst had been his father's postilion and would have remained so but for the duke's good offices.⁴ Every part of that statement was untrue.⁵ Amherst had been the duke's military aide in Ireland, and if there were anything demeaning about that, Amherst's

---

¹ North to Sandwich, 2 Mar. 1778; *Sandwich Papers*, i. 347.

² Coventry, p. 62. Amherst was from a good family and his father was an attorney of standing at Gray's Inn, but compared to nearby Knole the Amherst country home—'Brooks Place'—was small and unimpressive (J. C. Long, *Amherst*).

³ Germain to King, 3 Jan. 1778; Fortescue, *Corresp.* iv, Intro., p. xvi.

⁴ Actually Amherst had been treated as a member of the Dorset household and the duke's private assistant. His only service as 'postilion' was when, at the duke's official installation ceremonies as Lord Lieutenant, young Amherst rode in full military regalia on the shafts of the duke's coach (J. C. Long, *Amherst*).

⁵ In 1743 Colonel Lord George Sackville, aged 27, had written to his father from Spire in the Rhineland: 'You cannot imagine how well everybody speaks of Jeff. Amherst. He is of great use to General Ligonier, and the General is very sensible of it. He cannot be long before he is promoted in his turn, for he is now the eldest lieutenant in the regiment, and there can be no danger of any body's being put over his head' (Sackville to Dorset, 1 Oct. 1743; *HMC, Stop. Sack.* i. 286; also Clements, *Germain Papers*, i).

shame was shared by Lord George's close friend Sir John Irwin.

Lord Amherst was not a man to be pushed around by anyone. The king and Lord North may have hoped that his appointment would bring Lord George's resignation, but it did not. It did not even curb his private campaign against General Carleton. When Lord George heard that the king proposed to give Carleton a reasonably lucrative and honourable appointment, he again threatened to resign if the plan were completed. The king proceeded to appoint Carleton, and wrote to Lord North:

I owne, I think Lord G. Germaine's defection a most favourable event, he has so many enemies, that would have made him a heavy load whenever the expedition under Lt. G. Burgoyne came to be canvassed in Parliament, yet I should never have recommended his removal unless with his own good will now he will save us all the trouble, the laying it on my bequeathing the Government of Charlemont on Carleton is quite absurd and shews the malevolence of his mind. Carleton was highly wrong in permitting his pen to convey such asperity to a Secretary of State, but his meritorious defense of Quebec made him a proper object for a Military award and as such I could not think of providing for any other General till I had repaid the Debt his services had a right to claim.[1]

Once again Lord George thought better of his threat to resign, and a new attack upon him by the Opposition so angered the king that Lord George seemed to him a tolerable minister by comparison. Lord North, since the king would not release him, tried to save his Ministry by adding to it, as a concession to the Opposition, the ailing but influential Chatham. Even Bute, the Old Tory favourite of the king, broke his long silence and spoke of Chatham as indispensable; Lord Mansfield, a bitter political enemy of Chatham, said with tears in his eyes that unless the king sent for Chatham the ship would assuredly go down. George Grenville, the son of the author of the Stamp Act, and Lord Rocheford, Secretary of State, employed the same language, and public opinion loudly declared itself in the same sense.[2]

Pitt and Pitt's policies were anathema to the king, but under Lord North's pressure he half acquiesced, though with conditions. Lord North must remain at least the nominal head of the

[1] King to North, 3 Mar. 1778; Fortescue, *Corresp.* iv. 45.   [2] Lecky, iv. 80.

821295   C C

Ministry, and the proposed new government must function in such a way that the king would never have to deal with Pitt. 'I solemnly declare that nothing shall bring me to treat personally with Lord Chatham', the king wrote to Lord North on 16 March,[1] and he added a little later: 'Before I will ever hear of any man's readiness to come into office I will expect to see it signed under his hand that he is resolved to keep the empire entire, and that no troops shall be subsequently withdrawn from America nor independence ever achieved.'[2]

Like seconds arranging a duel between their principals, William Eden, as spokesman for Lord North, and Lord Shelburne, as agent for Pitt, met to discuss terms. Pitt insisted that as a first step toward his joining the Ministry Lord George Germain must be removed from office.[3] No matter how much the king would have welcomed Lord George's withdrawal, he would not force him out of office in deference to the demand of the hated Pitt, and he would not purchase Lord George's resignation with as exalted an honour as Lord George was certain to demand. This left Lord North, who had only two days before again begged the king to release him from office, in an almost helpless position.[4] He made a final effort: 'Lord North has the honour of troubling his Majesty again upon the subject of his last letter in which he omitted one article, viz: a Peerage for Lord G. Germaine who is not in the Catalogue of Ministers.[5] Lord North thinks himself bound to duty to repeat that (although he is ready to sacrifice every consideration to his Majesty's wishes) the present Ministry cannot continue a fortnight as it is.'[6] The king replied on the same day: 'My sole wish is to keep you at the head of the Treasury and as my Confidential Advisor.'[7] On that same day or the following one the king further dashed Lord North's fading hopes of an arrangement with Pitt and the Opposition by writing to him: 'I would far rather lose the Crown I now wear, than bear the ignominy of

[1] King to North, 16 Mar. 1778; Donne, *Corresp.* ii. 149.
[2] King to North; ibid., p. 298.
[3] Fitzmaurice, *Shelburne*, iii. 23.
[4] North to King, 15 Mar. 1778; Fortescue, *Corresp.* iv. 56.
[5] Lord North meant that Lord George was not listed for inclusion in the proposed revised Ministry.
[6] North to King, 15 Mar. 1778; Fortescue, *Corresp.* iv. 56.
[7] King to North, 15 Mar. 1778; Fortescue, *Corresp.* iv. 57.

possessing it under their shackles.'[1] Lord North's only hope was to try to get Pitt to relax his terms, but Pitt insisted on the dismissal of Lord George, and the king wrote to Lord North that he would be willing to: '. . . strengthen the Administration by an accession from any quarter, but I will never consent to removing the members of the present Cabinet from my service'.[2]

Lord North essayed a more desperate approach, and wrote the king that '. . . peace with America, and a change in the Ministry are the only steps which can save the country'.[3] The king would not accept that conclusion. Pitt, who had held his hand and voice from condemnation of the Ministry, then rejoined the Opposition in attack, and the fall of Lord North seemed certain. It was saved by a power greater than King or Parliament. Pitt had been far from well; he had emerged from invalid retirement to take the helm and save England from her ancient enemies France and Spain. At the height of the crisis, just before the crucial vote that might have unseated the Ministry, Pitt rose on 7 April, '. . . wrapped in flannel, supported on crutches', and embarked on the speech calculated to carry all before it and himself into the leadership of a new Ministry. 'His sunk and hueless face, rendered the more ghastly by the still penetrating brilliancy of his eyes, bore plainly in it the impress of approaching death, and his voice was barely audible in the almost breathless silence of the House', wrote Lecky, moved to dramatic licence by the significance of the scene.[4]

Pitt completed his address, but when he rose to reply to the Duke of Richmond he faltered and fell. To all appearances he was dying. Confusion broke out; men crowded about the stricken hero but no one did much to help him, and he was finally half-pushed and half-carried, semi-conscious, from the hall. In this distrait mêlée the crucial vote was taken. The collapse of Pitt had disorganized the Opposition, which lost the issue by the narrow margin of 17 votes.[5] Pitt died a month later;[6] and Lord North, with Lord George a lucky appendage, was forced to reluctant continuation in an office he did not want.

[1] King to North, 15 (?) Mar. 1778; Fortescue, *Corresp.* iv. 58.
[2] King to North, 22 Mar. 1778; Fortescue, *Corresp.* iv. 72.
[3] North to King, 25 Mar. 1778; Fortescue, *Corresp.* iv. 78.
[4] Lecky, iv. 85.   [5] *Hansard*, xix. 1012; also Fitzmaurice, *Shelburne*, iii. 31.
[6] On 11 May 1778; Lecky, iv. 85.

Nothing had been really changed by this dramatic ending of a great man's career, and just a few days before Pitt died Lord North again appealed to the king: 'If your Majesty does not allow me to retire, you and this country are ruined',[1] and he repeated his pleas to resign in later letters. The king was adamant. Burgoyne's arrival led Parliament once more to voice violent criticisms of the Secretary of State for America, and for a few days Lord George was so shaken that he was prepared to sell his office for something less than a peerage. On 12 May he wrote to Lord North with reference to the Wardenship of the Cinque Ports, a lucrative honour held by the ailing Lord Holdernesse:

I understand Lord H. is dying. I should be happy in succeeding him as W of C Pts, it has long been the object of my wishes. If your Lordship thinks of asking for that office for yourself I can have no pretensions to it: the truth is that when I consider my age I cannot expect to have health and activity much longer to discharge the duty of my present situation. Indeed I have found attendance of the House of Commons this session too fatiguing and almost intolerable . . . if any new arrangement is to be made for the convenience of his Majesty's Government, I am ready to return to the private station from which I was called; most undoubtedly it would be most satisfactory to me to receive such a mark of his Majesty's favour as might show the public that my poor endeavors in his Majesty's service had met with his royal approval.[2]

As Lord George probably knew, Lord North had himself looked forward to becoming the Warden of the Cinque Ports. He was far from rich and had a wife and children to provide for: he had never pressed the king for any material gains from his loyal political service, and there was every reason to believe that the king planned to give him the Cinque Ports. Lord George was in reality proposing to Lord North: 'If you want me out of the Ministry badly enough to sacrifice this plum to me, and the King shares your desire, I will go. Otherwise you will have to force me out, with all the loss of face that effort would bring the King and Ministry.' Lord George was rich and though somewhat troubled by stone, in reasonably good health; at 62 he was at an age when some statesmen have embarked on

---

[1] North to King, 7 May 1778; Fortescue, *Corresp.* iv. 135.
[2] Germain to North, 12 May 1778; HMC, *Stop. Sack.* i. 78.

their greatest public service. Lord North would probably have made the sacrifice but the king was in no mood to let him do so, and when Lord Holdernesse died he made Lord North Warden of the Cinque Ports. Lord George once again remained in office, and with the help of Lord North weathered the storms raised afresh by Burgoyne's disclosures in Parliament.

In the latter half of 1778 there were no further disasters in America, and Parliament and public turned to concerns more immediate than the dismissal of Lord George Germain. The efforts and dangers of a new war with France tended to draw all Englishmen closer together. Lord North, however, did not dismiss his concerns and his pleas. He informed the king again in November that: 'He considers his continuance in Government in his present situation as highly prejudicial to his Majesty's affairs, &, therefore, he intreats his Majesty to continue his search after a better arrangement . . . the Public business can never go on as it ought, while the Principal & most efficient offices are in the hands of persons who are either indifferent to, or actually dislike their situation.'[1]

Ever since Saratoga Lord North had been in an impossible situation. His Ministry was weak and divided. He was leading in the support of a war in which he did not believe. The war had revealed that the British Navy was in a shocking condition, yet it was now faced with the French and perhaps the Spanish fleet, as well as with American privateers and the alarming raids of John Paul Jones. Although Lord Sandwich was not wholly to blame for this, he was the responsible Minister and the Opposition and public were clamouring for his dismissal as loudly as for that of Lord George Germain. As for the Army, it had been in relatively good condition at the end of the previous war, and its failures could be traced directly to the mistakes of the Ministry. But the more Lord Sandwich and Lord George were attacked, the more determined was the king to stand by them. 'Unable or unwilling to enter into a defense of their conduct, and unable to make a change in the heads of those two great administrative departments, North could only strive to quiet criticism, to divert attacks and to get along as best he could.'[2] But the more he tried to smooth matters over, the more

---

[1] North to King, 10 Nov. 1778: Fortescue, *Corresp.* iv. 215.
[2] W. C. Ford, p. 134.

valid became Burke's charge that: 'Ministers, conscious of their
incapacity and criminal neglect in conducting the American war,
endeavored to stifle all inquiry.'[1]

The Ministry was literally falling apart. Thurlow, who
replaced Lord Bathurst as Lord Chancellor, was the only
member of more than average ability and his personality did
not increase the popularity of the Ministry. He had gained his
advancement by directing the Ministry's strategy during the
Burgoyne debates, but many regarded him as 'the Moloch of
his profession . . . not a great lawyer, but he was a most powerful
and ready debater, a man of much rugged sense and indomitable
character, coarse, violent, shameless and profane',[2] who had
gained advancement by attaching himself to the king.[3] Thurlow
was an asset, but this was not a situation where the Ministry could
be saved, or the war won, by a legal bullyboy. William Eden,
himself almost a member of the Ministry's inner circle, confessed
his own dismay to another of his ilk, the astute and ambitious
Wedderburn: 'In short we are entering upon the last struggle
of the Empire under infinite disadvantages, & I own frankly to
you that I think the Cabinet, as at present constituted, totally
unequal to the undertaking.'[4]

Lord North was telling the king as much. The only hope was
to bring new men of ability and influence into the Ministry.
There were few such men available among its supporters, and
the addition of further die-hards would not conciliate the
Opposition or the public. Admiral Viscount Howe was no Pitt,
but he was able, respected, and came from an old Whig family.
If he could be induced to join the Ministry its position would be
a little more hopeful. But if Admiral Howe accepted he would
create a new problem or, rather, renew an old one. Lord North
consulted the king:

Lord George Germain certainly cannot remain in office a moment
after one of his accusers is introduced into the Cabinet. Whether
Lord George can in honour, at such a moment, accept of any favour
from the Crown may be questioned. . . . If he may with credit, & I
should hope he may, accept of a mark of your Majesty's approbation,
that mark must be considerable, & such as shall convey to the world

---

[1] *Hansard*, xiii. 65; also W. C. Ford, p. 138.   [2] Lecky, iv. 88, 89.
[3] Who later used him to negotiate a new Ministry.
[4] Eden to Wedderburn, 17 Jan. 1779; Stevens, *Facsimiles*, v. 552.

that your Majesty is satisfied with his services. . . . He has asked us at different times, the Wardenship of the Cinque Ports, & a Peerage, & I should think that his having ask'd any particular favour would render such a favour the most honourable to him. . . . If he has a peerage, his last request, & which certainly would be the most honourable to him, It is highly to be apprehended that the Attorney General, & many other aspirers to peerages, would be out of humour, & that the promotion would not meet with a very general popularity. I do not know whether any thing else can be thought of for him, but whatever is given to him on such an occasion ought to be very creditable, & very distinguishing.[1]

When the question of accepting Sir William Howe's resignation had been raised, '. . . the King was divided in his mind whether Lord George or General Howe should retire'.[2] Lord George had won that round, but the king continued to regard him, privately, as a liability to the Government.[3] Lord North would have been glad to see Lord George removed in order to secure Admiral Howe, but the king would not have his hand forced by any man, and Lord Howe's insistence that Lord George must be dismissed made George III as stubborn as only a man who is being stubborn on principle can be. Nor would he buy Lord George's resignation at the price of a peerage.

To exchange the Cinque Ports for Lord George's voluntary resignation would be a serious personal sacrifice to Lord North, but he wrote to the king to '. . . submit to his Majesty the absolute necessity of offering to Lord George (as he cannot have a peerage) the Wardenship of the Cinque Ports, made up to the value of the place when held by Lord Holdernesse. He would not mention this again but that he really thinks that any disgrace to Lord George would be both unjust and impolitick.'[4]

The king's acceptance of Lord North's offer was highly qualified: '. . . if on the whole it should be thought to offer it to him, I will not object to his having the Same Salary as Lord Holdernesse, but only during Pleasure.'[5] And the king insisted that he

---

[1] North to King, 31 Dec. 1778; Fortescue, *Corresp.* iv. 239–41.

[2] Fortescue, *Corresp.* iv, Intro., p. vi.

[3] 'Lord George Germaine was as desperate. . . . He had not a friend but Lord Suffolk, either at Court or in the Opposition. He was fallen as low as could be, except by dismission. None of his plans had succeeded, and his parts were sunk in esteem as low as his character' (Walpole, *Last Journals*, ii. 245).

[4] North to King, 29 Jan. 1779; Fortescue, *Corresp.* iv. 262.

[5] King to North, 29 Jan. 1779; Fortescue, *Corresp.* iv. 263.

would give the Cinque Ports to Lord George only on the condition that Lord North would continue indefinitely as First Minister.[1] Apparently the king was confident that both Lord George and Lord North would accept these conditions, for he added to Lord North: 'You may therefore now sound out Lord Howe.'[2] But Lord George held out for a peerage after all, and Lord Howe was firm that not only must Lord George go but that he and his brother must have formal public exoneration from the Ministry. The complicated deal failed, and the Howe brothers angrily joined the Opposition. The king no longer hid from intimates like Lord Sandwich his opinion of his American Secretary: 'Lord Sandwich's note confirms my former opinion, that Lord George Germain lets his imagination run too far on half words he picks up and then reasons upon very slight foundation.'[3]

By June 1779 the Parliamentary Inquiry had built up such a case against Lord George that he once again raised the hopes of the king and Lord North, who discussed what arrangements they would make '. . . upon the resignation of Ld. George Germain, if the information we have received of his intention proves true'.[4] As a further incentive to the king not to haggle over the price of this desired purchase, Lord North once again urgently offered his own resignation. The king was always a brisk correspondent and replied on the same day. He would be glad to be rid of Lord George, but in view of the disclosures of the Inquiry was more determined than ever not to do Lord George too great an honour. 'It would be an endless repitition to state my objection to decorating Lord Geo. with a Peerage: He has not be of use in his department, and nothing but the most meritorious Services could have wiped off his former misfortunes.'[5]

Lord North could at least clip Lord George's wings a little and thus demonstrate to the world that the Secretary for America was not in high favour. Since it was also desirable to

---

[1] Otherwise 'The new head of the Treasury *Must be* Lord Weymouth and the Warden of the Cinque Ports remain with Lord North' (King to Weymouth, 1 Feb. 1779; Fortescue, *Corresp.* iv. 265).   [2] King to North, 9 Feb. 1779; ibid., p. 267.
[3] King to Sandwich, *Sandwich Papers*, iii. 30.
[4] North to King, 15 June 1779; Fortescue, *Corresp.* iv. 355.
[5] King to North, 15 June 1779; ibid., p. 356. The spelling is as in the original.

enlist the support of the young Earl of Carlisle, urged by Gower,
who had served with devoted futility as head of the recent Peace
Commission but was now threatening to make his own revelations of Ministry machinations, Lord North suggested to the
king that the Board of Trade be taken from under the suzerainty
of the Secretary of State for the Colonies, and that Lord Carlisle
be appointed its independent head.[1] Lord North had drafted a
letter on the matter to Lord George, and the next day the king
approved the project and the draft, except that he desired Lord
North to '. . . alter the first paragraph which looks too favourable: I certainly have no intention to confer a peerage on Lord
George'.[2]

Lord North apparently revised the draft accordingly, for the
letter he sent to Lord George, dated the same day, was certainly
not encouraging regarding 'the other part of your request',
which was the peerage.

> . . . upon receiving about a twelvemonth ago a letter from your
> Lordship I immediately laid your letter before the King and have
> several times since mentioned the same subject to his Majesty. I have
> never yet been able to bring your Lordship any answer, his Majesty
> having always appeared desirous of your Lordship's continuance in
> your office, and having always declined to signify his pleasure with
> respect to the other part of your request. . . . I believe that Lord
> Gower has it at heart to introduce Lord Carlisle into public business,
> and no way of doing it occurs to me so proper and convenient as the
> separation of the Board of Trade from the American Seals, and the
> appointment of Lord Carlisle to be First Commissioner of Trade.
> This must, however, be done entirely with your good will or not at
> all, and it must not even be mentioned to any other person til it has
> been submitted to your consideration and decision. . . . To the
> accomplishment of these objects nothing can more essentially con-
> tribute than your Lordship's compliance with the proposal I have
> taken the liberty to suggest.[3]

Despite its verbal decorations, Lord North had never written

[1] North to King, 9 Sept. 1779; Fortescue, *Corresp.* iv. 431. The Secretary of
State for the Colonies had never been *ex officio* the Chairman of the Board of
Trade. The records show that during the year 1776 the board met weekly when
Parliament was in session, and that Germain attended all its 37 meetings. In 1778
he missed only five meetings, two of which were immediately after the death of his
wife on 15 Jan. (PRO, Minutes of the Board of Trade for 1776 and 1778).
[2] King to North, 10 Sept. 1779; Fortescue, *Corresp.* iii. 432.
[3] North to Germain, 10 Sept. 1779; *HMC, Stop. Sack.* ii. 138.

a firmer letter to Lord George, who apparently recognized the futility of any reply but acquiescence. But his acquiescence was grudging. Lord George made it quite clear that if the king and Lord North wished to get him out of the Secretaryship altogether they could not hope to do so without open dismissal or open compensation. His language was elaborate but his meaning was clear:

When I had the honor of writing to your Lordship last year I was really apprehensive that I should not have been able to have undergone the fatigue of the attendance in the House of Commons added to the business of my office. I by no means wished to convey the most distant idea of declining the King's service so long as I was able to discharge the duty of it to his Majesty's satisfaction. . . . It was natural of me to hope that I might have deserved some mark of his Majesty's favour. As that is not the case, I can only lament it as a misfortune, but I shall never presume to complain of it as the least injustice.

Lord George then wrote that he had no reply to the suggestion regarding Lord Carlisle: '. . . but humbly to submit to what he may think most for his service, though I feel it as degrading to me'.[1]

Lord North and the king stood firm, and two weeks later Lord North informed Lord George that: '. . . having laid the contents of your Lordship's letter before the King . . . the arrangement regarding Carlisle will go into effect.' Lord North ended this announcement with compliments to Lord George for setting so fine and unselfish an example of sacrifice of personal interests to the public good.[2]

In reply Lord George posed two questions, each insulting to Lord North. 'I beg you to inform me whether the King read your letter to me and my answer to it, and if his Majesty . . . upon that state of the business . . . approves of the proposed arrangement.'[3] Lord North replied on the same day, and without further diplomatic compliments: 'The King read both your Lordship's letter to me and mine to you before he gave me those commands which I executed in the letter I wrote to your Lordship on Wednesday.' It was clear that the subject was closed. Lord

[1] Germain to North, 13 Sept. 1779; *HMC, Stop. Sack.* ii. 141.
[2] North to Germain, 29 Sept. 1779; *HMC, Stop. Sack.* ii. 145.
[3] Germain to North, 1 Oct. 1779; *HMC, Stop. Sack.* ii. 146.

George did, however, extract one compensatory assurance. The king told him that in standing and power he would remain '. . . in every respect on the same line as the two ancient Secretaries'.[1]

Lord George had not gained a political friend in the accession to the Secretaryship at War of Charles Jenkinson: '. . . unobtrusive, his long lantern-like face expressionless as a board, his eyes invariably downcast', moving observantly through the corridors of court and Parliament, saying little and hearing everything.[2] Jenkinson, whom someone called 'the King's jackall', reported to his sovereign that '. . . nothing would satisfie the Opposition but a Sacrifice of Lord North, Lord Sandwich, & Lord G. Germaine'.[3] Within the Ministry the discords were sharper and more apparent than ever. Lord Lyttelton told the House of Lords that: 'Ministers talked of the necessity of being united, in the very moment that their own conduct was an example of the most jarring councils, and the most divided opinions.'[4]

The two Ministers most cordially hated outside court circles still seemed to have the special favour of the king. Lord Pembroke, who was certainly no fool and in a position as a Lord of the Bedchamber to observe intimately, made several reports to his son Lord Herbert in September 1779: 'Ld. Sandwich, & Ld. G. Germaine seem in higher favor than ever at Court, & their being suffered to be so is a proof of how very abject we are grown . . . there is no favorite at Court equal to the First Lord of the Admiralty except the Minden hero perhaps.'[5] And Lord Herbert informed his old tutor two months later: 'Everybody and everything seems to totter except those two infamous favorites the Lords S . . . . . h and G . . . . . n.'[6] The king was at least successful in concealing his private efforts to get rid of 'the Minden hero'.

The constant skirmishes between Lord Sandwich and Lord George became more bitter and open. Lord George took issue with Sandwich as to whether the western fleet should winter in West Indian or British waters; as to whether the Navy should

---

[1] Donne, *Corresp.* ii. 283.   [2] J. C. Long, *Amherst*, p. 300.
[3] Jenkinson to King, 7 Nov. 1779; Fortescue, *Corresp.* iv. 477.
[4] *Hansard*, xx. 1038; 25 Nov. 1779.
[5] Pembroke to Herbert, 24 and 30 Sept. 1779; *Pembroke Papers*, pp. 267, 269.
[6] Herbert to Coxe, 24 Dec. 1779; *Pembroke Papers*, p. 363.

seek battle with the French near Gibraltar or in American
waters; and as to whether the French Navy was on its way to
America or would sweep the waters from the Azores to the
Lizard.[1] In each of these issues, which some claimed were not
his business, Lord George carried the controversy to the Cabinet
and King, and in each of them he failed to get his way. He also
introduced his private espionage agents into the Navy, and
incurred a complaint from Sir Peter Parker, Vice-Admiral in
command of the Jamaica area, who wrote to the Earl of
Sandwich: 'I understand, my Lord, that copies of some of the
letters that have passed between the Governor and myself have
been transmitted to Lord George Germain, and representations
made with a seeming intention to prejudice me in the opinion
of those whom it is my duty as well as inclination to please. . . . It
would have been almost impossible to have withstood such
duplicity of conduct if I had not been honoured with your Lordship's friendship.'[2]

To the Lords of the Admiralty such interferences seemed
intolerable. About the time that Admiral Parker's letter reached
the Earl of Sandwich, Malone wrote to the Earl of Charlemont:
'There is, it is said, a violent quarrel between Lord Sandwich
and Lord George Germain.'[3] But to the earl's protest Lord George
was ready with counter-attacks: 'If Lord Sandwich proposes or
fully approves of any plan we seldom want resources; on the
other hand, if he does not heartily adopt what other Ministers
think right, official difficulties occur, and the state of our fleet
is such that no new measure can be pressed.'[4]

This battle within the Cabinet angered the king, whose idea
of unity was all for one and that one himself. His attitude toward
Lord George was distinctly less cordial as 1780 moved into 1781.[5]
When Lord George made a personal attack on Sandwich in the
House of Commons the king, according to Walpole, forced him
to offer an apology to the earl, though it was a half-hearted one.[6]
The irony of the situation escaped almost no one when, only a
week later, in the House of Commons: 'Lord George Germaine

---

[1] *Sandwich Papers*, ii. 7.
[2] Parker to Sandwich, 3 June 1780; *Sandwich Papers*, iii. 152.
[3] Malone to Charlemont, 18 June 1781; *HMC, Charlemont*, i (1891), 383.
[4] Germain to Knox, 1 Nov. 1781; *Sandwich Papers*, iv. 17.
[5] *Greville Diaries*, p. 16.
[6] Walpole, *Last Journals*, ii. 381–3; 3/4 Dec. 1781.

talked of the great unanimity amongst the Ministers, in which no mortal believed him',[1] and then, three days later, confessed to the Commons: '. . . that he did not know what was the opinion of the other Ministers' with regard to the independence of America.[2] Amid this collapse of even the semblance of order and reason, Lord North continued his plaintive supplications to the king. Lord North '. . . considers it his duty to inform his Majesty that he finds his spirits, & his frailties both of body & mind much less equal to his situation then they were this time twelve-month. He will do what he can, but thinks it not improbable that he may fail in the midst of his Majesty's most important business, for which he humbly suggests to his Majesty that it will be right for his Majesty always to be prepared.'[3]

Once again Lord George had ridden out the storms that began after Saratoga, and had out-manœuvred his sovereign and his First Minister as well as his enemies. He could even edify his undersecretary with protestations of his freedom from self-interest. He wrote to Knox that if England could triumph over its enemies, what became of a few individuals like himself would be of very little consequence: '. . . and I should be very happy to see the administration in those hands which could most effectually relieve us from our present distresses'. But, he added: '. . . if I was to be asked where the men were capable of such exertion I must confess I know no such'.[4]

Though 1780 brought Lord George and Britain no great losses, it brought them no great gains, and left Britain no nearer victory over the Americans and Lord George apparently no nearer his peerage. Many observers were surprised that the king would not pay Lord George that price for his resignation. On 14 September Horace Walpole wrote: 'Seven new Barons created. . . . The late Speaker, Sir Fletcher Norton, and Lord George Germaine, were not made Peers as expected.'[5]

Lord North tried to escape all other problems and responsibilities by plunging into the difficult financing of a hopeless war, but was successful in neither. In April he repeated his old plea

---

[1] Walpole, *Last Journals*, ii. 388; 11 Dec. 1781.
[2] Walpole, *Last Journals*, ii. 389; 14 Dec. 1781.
[3] North to King, 24 Oct. 1780; Fortescue, *Corresp.* v. 142, 143.
[4] Germain to Knox, 2 Jan. 1780; *HMC, Var. Coll.* 6, *Knox*, p. 155.
[5] Walpole, *Last Journals*, ii. 328, 329. Sir Fletcher's ship ultimately came in, for in time he became Baron Grantley.

to the king: 'I humbly submit once more to your Majesty that it is absolutely necessary that I should be permitted to retire at the end of the Session, & some other arrangement take place.'[1] In May he tried again: 'Lord North finds himself so weak and unable to go on for any time, that he cannot help reminding his Majesty of the request he has lately had the honour more than once of submitting to his Majesty's goodness.'[2] But on the question of losing Lord North, pathos moved the king no more than reason.

It was in that state of confused and reluctant misgovernment that the Ministry weathered the first ten months of 1781. The rises and falls in the court standing of Lord George Germain were the fever chart of the Government and nation; by his chances of survival those of the Ministry could be measured. It was the misfortune of Britain that its welfare was so closely bound up with Lord George's personal fortunes. His ambitions in Ireland had so upset Anglo-Irish relations that they did not recover for several decades. His conduct at Minden had robbed his country of a great victory. His political manœuvres before 1775 had prevented the creation of a coalition Ministry that might have avoided a war with the colonies. Under his direction of the American war, the British cause in the colonies moved from the decent and possible to the indefensible and hopeless. His ambitions and methods had exacted from his nation a high payment for disservices rendered.

[1] North to King, 7 Apr. 1780; Fortescue, *Corresp.* v. 39.
[2] North to King, 18 May 1780; Fortescue, *Corresp.* v. 60, 61.

XXVI

REBELLION AT HOME

IN 1778 the menace of disaster in America and invasion from France had stimulated a new patriotic urgency in British society at all levels. But it had not brought unity. Parliament was almost riotous with recriminations, and the nation's stability was rudely shaken by manifestations of discontent and even revolt at home. The restiveness of the London masses had asserted itself in challenges to established authority that were alarmingly reminiscent of the rioting over Wilkes and the Middlesex elections a few years before. Wilkes had encouraged the discontented to defy government in the name of freedom, and the experience was too heady a one not to enjoy again. In February 1779, aroused by the controversy between Admiral Keppel, the Opposition hero, and Admiral Palliser, the right-hand man of Lord Sandwich, the mobs of London rioted again.

Lord George Germain, an outstanding representative of much that the lower classes most disliked, was one of their chief targets. They broke the windows of his London house; 'got in and threw the furniture out of the windows', and left his daughters cowering in their beds, 'terrified to death'. Then came the impetuous and bigoted demagoguery of young Lord George Gordon, who inspired the religious intolerants, the dissatisfied, and the criminal elements to combine in riots so serious that men feared for their lives and the safety of their families. Martial law was declared; troops were called out night after night; ministers and other men of mark turned their houses into fortresses. Lord George, '. . . having assembled some friends for the purpose, barricaded the passages and entrance to his house in Pall Mall, which was very susceptible of defense, after which he coolly waited for the attack of the populace.'[1] This time the mob was repelled without injury.

The rioting worked indirectly to the advantage of the Ministry and Lord George. When mobs threatened the foundations of

[1] Wraxall, i. 240; Lady Pembroke to Lord Herbert, 18 Feb. 1779; *Pembroke Diaries*, p. 141.

social order, most Englishmen decided that law in the form of
the existing government must, for the nonce, be supported, and
even Burke and Fox agreed. The attacks on Lord North and
Lord George brought them sympathy from men who opposed
the first and hated the second. Such reactions did not turn
politics into a love-feast, but it made attacks on the Ministry
less vicious and less effective.

After Spain declared war and the Howe Inquiry ended in
June 1779, the surface of politics and social unrest seemed to
become less storm-ridden, perhaps from the nation's emotional
exhaustion, perhaps from its frustration. In Parliament the
Opposition might fulminate but they could not win; they could
discredit the Ministry but they could not oust it; they could
condemn the American war but they could not end it. Rockingham and Shelburne privately confessed their impotence, just as
Charles Fox had done earlier by walking out of the House in
the angry futility of defeat.

When Parliament recessed on 1 July 1780, it was after a year
in which '. . . no material change had taken place, either in the
general temper of the nation or in the political state of the contending parties. A total indifference to the desperate situation
of affairs, or at least the means of retrieving them, seems to have
marked, at the time, the character of the people, beyond any
former period of history.'[1] They appeared confused, baffled,
even apathetic. The Earl of Chatham's daughter summarized
the outward aspects of London society when she wrote to her
mother that: 'America seems to be quite forgot.'[2] The war was
in the doldrums: both Britain and America were a little too
strong to be defeated and a little too weak to win. Americans
failed to maintain the first fervour of enthusiasm, unity and
sacrifice; Englishmen slackened in their determination to put
down colonial rebellion when vigorous measures began to
demand personal austerities. Americans were waiting for France
to win their war for them; Englishmen were waiting for France
and Spain to show their hands in some major sea or land attack.

Yet beneath the calmer surface the tides of national dissatisfaction were running strong and deep. Englishmen were not
really apathetic, they were merely uncertain how to move, whom

---

[1] *Hansard*, xxii. 634; *Annual Register for 1781*.
[2] Headlam, *Letters of Lady Harriet Eliot*, 18 Apr. 1780, p. 54.

to blame, and how to overcome the depression of their personal impotence. Many who doubted the competence of a government headed by Rockingham or Shelburne, Fox or Burke, were nevertheless concluding that North, Sandwich, and Germain must go. If Parliament had accurately reflected public opinion, the Ministry would almost certainly not have survived the year 1780.

The Opposition suffered, however, from internal pains of their own: from the extremist positions of Richmond and Fox, from rivalries within their ranks, and from a lack of unified aims. Their leaders were abler than the king's Ministers, but their only real solidarity was in antipathy to the men in power. The Opposition was not, in the modern sense, a political party. It was not well organized, well disciplined, or possessed of common objectives. It was a loosely knit association of separate 'factions' which allied with other factions only toward some immediate and specific end. Even on the issue of the American war there was wide difference of opinion. By 1780 Fox, Rockingham, and Richmond would probably have been willing to make peace on the basis of independence for the colonies, though they would have disagreed whether to do so from principle or expediency. But Chatham had vehemently opposed full independence, and so had Shelburne, Burke, and Barre.[1] Fox and Richmond were led by eloquence into extremes, and Englishmen did not trust extremes. The Earl of Buckinghamshire wrote with some truth to General Clinton: 'The nation have no confidence in the Administration and full as little, perhaps less, in the Opposition.'[2]

Whatever was the actual will of the people, the North Ministry was securely in power so long as it could hold its parliamentary majorities, which did not necessarily represent popular opinion. Those few aristocrats and politicians who really cared what the will of the people was, had no sure way of determining it. Parliamentary elections did not reveal it, or even encourage Englishmen below a certain social and economic level to think or talk politics. A minority controlled the plebiscite, and Whig as well as Tory members of that minority had no real desire to yield that power to the common man.

In 1780 Lord North thought it expedient to strengthen the

---

[1] S. G. Fisher, *True History*, p. 199.
[2] Buckinghamshire to Clinton, 1 Mar. 1782; *HMC, Lothian*, p. 412.

position of his Ministry by calling a general election. His announcement was made at the last possible moment in order to take the Whigs by surprise, and in spite of earlier speculation it did so. The North supporters had been quietly at work exchanging favours and even guineas for votes, but the Opposition had only a few weeks to campaign. The party in power had further advantages. As a Ministry it was weak, but as a political party it was better organized than the Opposition, which consisted of Old Whigs, New Whigs, Tories who were no longer conservatives, and various kinds of independents. Lord North's supporters were held together, in an election at least, by self-interest, patronage, and hope for further favours, and he made the best of his opportunities to distribute appointments, honours, favours, pensions, and contracts where they would do the most electoral good. He invented no new corruptions not familiar in the time of Sir Robert Walpole, but he used the old ones with great efficiency and little compunction—just as Whig Ministries had done before him and would do again. Unless some drastic military or political setback intervened, the Opposition had little chance of returning a majority to either House, and their leaders knew it. Only four months before the North Ministry finally fell, Lord Rockingham, the leader of the largest Opposition junto, confessed to a friend: 'I make as little doubt that a majority in Parliament composed of some credulous fools and as many corrupt knaves, will assent to whatever is desired to be re-echoed in the [King's] speech.'[1]

By the canon of simple arithmetic the North Ministry won the 1780 elections, but analysis of the returns indicates that within the shell of their victory lay the seeds of coming defeat. The parliamentary seats the Ministry held or won were mostly those that least reflected public opinion; the seats they failed to win represented a rising tide of popular opposition to themselves and to the war. Of the 405 borough seats in the House of Commons, some 220 were controlled by 119 men, most of whom were Ministry supporters or ready to become so if the reward were good enough.[2] Bubb Dodington had 'commanded' at least six seats in the House of Commons and the Duke of Newcastle had 'owned' four and influenced many more. The Sackvilles con-

[1] Christie, *The End of Lord North's Ministry*, pp. 269 ff.
[2] Ibid.

trolled the two seats for East Grinstead and Lord George had 'given' one for a while to his friend General Irwin. Many other nobles and rich squires similarly determined local elections.[1] Lord North typified another form of electoral influence in the fact that he had family connexions with at least twelve of the members of Parliament most active in support of his Ministry.

In the controlled constituencies, the number of voters was small and they took their instructions from the lord or squire on whom they were economically or socially dependent. The men elected consequently had no powerful incentive to know or care what the residents of the area they 'represented' really thought. Daniel P. Coke, campaigning in Nottingham in 1780, told his constituents from the hustings: 'I decline then entering into the discussion of political questions as they so frequently cause confusions',[2] and few thought the remark peculiar.

As London and other cities grew in population they did not grow comparably in parliamentary representation. A thousand urban citizens sometimes carried less electoral weight than ten men in certain rural boroughs. The County of Middlesex, including the city of London, paid more than one-seventh of the land taxes of all England, but had only eight representatives in the House of Commons, and those eight were largely selected by the London liveried companies. The Duchy of Cornwall, in contrast, paid one-seventieth of England's land taxes but elected forty-four members—over one-tenth of the borough membership of the House.[3] As taxpayers, the average Londoner was only one-fiftieth as well represented as the average man of Cornwall.

The system inevitably lent itself to corruption, especially by the party in power, which never used its chances more thoroughly than in 1780. Four months before that election, North's Treasury assistant Robinson studied each constituency and its controlling forces and made bargains, appointments, exchanges, and promises accordingly. The king himself was a close ally: he supplied funds for electoral needs; urged the royal tradesmen and court suppliers to support the Ministry candidates, and ordered the houses he had had erected at Windsor to be placed

---

[1] Unless otherwise specified, the facts on the composition of Parliament and the elections returns in 1780 are derived from Christie.

[2] Christie, pp. 131, 132.

[3] Christie, p. 134.

on the parish rate lists in the names of certain of his servants, thus creating helpful new Ministry votes in a doubtful area.

Government appointments and contracts were persuasive tools. The Parliament of 1774 had included 70 peers and 170 members of the House of Commons who held profitable posts or contracts from the Ministry.[1] In the 1780 elections a quarter of the members of both the outgoing and incoming Parliaments held some place of honour or remuneration from the government.[2] A song of the election ran:

> 'Tis money makes the member vote,
> And sanctify our ways:
> It makes the patriot turn his coat,
> So money we must raise.[3]

The party in power also had the advantage of being able to use public money for election purposes, for although Parliament in theory held the purse-strings, there were certain funds the Ministry could draw upon without public accounting. Ministry expenditures from such funds for the 1780 elections, as recorded in the government books, cost the tax-payer over £50,000, but probably much larger sums were actually spent,[4] from sources like the king's privy purse, the Civil List Fund, and the Secret Service Fund.[5] Lord North's talents as a practical politician were a chief source of his power. In the 1774 elections he bought seats in Parliament by flat payments of £2,500 to £3,000 each, and there is no reason to think the price of seats, or the funds to buy them, had declined in 1780.[6] Individual voters were also subsidized. 'I learnt that there are about 400 voters for Members in Aylesbury: that, upon an election, all, except about 70, who are above it, receive from each of the two members, between seven and eight pounds a man. . . . Alderman . . . . . recd. a letter offering him a Borough in Cornwall for £2000', wrote Thomas Hutchinson in 1774.[7] The enormous sums, up to

---

[1] D. M. Clarke, p. 236. [2] Ibid. [3] Ibid., p. 240.
[4] Ibid., p. 234. [5] Lecky, iv. 183.
[6] On 5 Oct. 1774 Lord North wrote to Cooper in his Treasury department regarding Lord Falmouth: 'His Lordship must be told in as polite terms as possible that I hope he will permit me to recommend to three of his six seats in Cornwall. The terms he expects are 2,500 Pounds a seat to which I am ready to agree.' At the same time North told Robinson of the Treasury to let Cooper know whether he had promised £2,500 or £3,000 for each of Lord Edgecombe's seats (D. M. Clarke, *British Opinion*, p. 231).
[7] Hutchinson, *Diary and Letters*, i. 249; 24 Sept. 1774.

£50,000 and more, reported to have been spent by individual candidates for Parliament indicate another form of electoral purchase. The system corrupted not only the elections but Parliament itself. If the sole function of a member who owed his seat to the Ministry or the Opposition was to give his support in crucial votes, why should he bother to attend except when his vote was needed? In 1770 as many as 400 members quite frequently crowded the House, but by 1780 the attendance rarely exceeded 150.[1]

Hence, though the victory of the North Ministry in 1780 seemed to confirm its policies and conduct, in fact it did neither. Such of the elections as had been reasonably free and uncorrupted—chiefly in the larger towns and counties—almost invariably favoured the Opposition. It was the urban centres that contained the middle-class elements of liberalism and progress, the commercial and industrial classes upon which much of Britain's economy and power to win a war depended. These citizens tended to sympathize with the American fight for parliamentary representation since they too wanted more of it.

It would be naïve to assume that the Ministry had a monopoly of electoral corruption. The Opposition leaders were not invariably motivated by higher principles, and many of them condemned corruption not because it was a sin but because it helped the Ministry. When they found that by inveighing against it they were winning public support, they made the Ministry's corruption a main topic of attack in Parliament. As a result, they have left the impression that the North Ministry was more corrupt than its predecessors, a charge which the facts might not substantiate. Nor was the British public of 1780 concerned about corruption until the Opposition speakers linked it with high taxes, high prices, and the losing war. Pitt and Fox, Burke and Sir George Savile could win applause by fulminating against 'the horrid, wicked and abominable American war',[2] but in 1780 many an Englishman inclined to support them for more personal reasons. The war was lowering their incomes and increasing their expenses. Inflation may be a new slogan in politics but it is not a new menace, and both city tradesmen and country squires were concerned about it in 1781.

The figures were simple enough. In 1775 the national debt,

[1] D. M. Clarke, p. 246.   [2] Christie, p. 123.

funded and unfunded, was £126,842,811. In 1783 it had become £231,843,631.[1] In the year 1780, in spite of Lord North's best efforts, it increased by £12,000,000,[2] yet on 20 December of that year England added another costly enemy by declaring war on the United Provinces of the Netherlands, still a potent antagonist on the seas and the world's financial centre.[3] Enlarged war meant even greater expenditure and more taxes and excises. Well before Yorktown Lord North warned the King and Ministry that he could not raise funds to support the wars for more than another year. Stocks were falling and government bonds were at a new low.

To the average man another aspect of the situation was even more immediate and painful. Prices as well as taxes were mounting. Even the poorest man in England wanted soap, candles, leather, and beer, and though Lord North had postponed as long as possible placing any excises on those essentials, they were costing 15 per cent. more in 1780 than in 1775. Men with property felt even harder hit. In 1778 the wine tax was increased and a new tax placed on inhabited houses. In 1776 and 1777 the stamp tax on deeds and documents (and in England nearly every document requires a stamp) had been doubled. In 1777 new taxes had been imposed on servants and on all property sold at auction.[4] Even those exalted prelates who had frowned on expressions of sympathy with the Americans were not so far above worldly things as to be undisturbed by diminishing church revenues. The Bishop of Peterborough bewailed in the House of Lords: '. . . the deplorable state of public credit, the enormous burthen of taxes, which is still increasing'.[5]

The objection was not only to the amount the Government was borrowing but to the way it was doing it. Lord North, forced to offer higher and higher interest rates for new loans, was thereby diminishing the value of earlier bonds and also increasing the annual interest charges on the national debt, and indirectly the interest rates on private loans. That was bad enough, but the Government seemed to be playing favourites by rigging its financing so as to bring profits to Ministry sup-

---

[1] Robertson, *England under the Hanoverians*, p. 533.
[2] *Annual Register for 1780*, p. 319.
[3] Lecky, iv. 162, 163.   [4] Robson, *Amer. Rev.*, pp. 147-9.
[5] Dr. John Hinchcliffe, 25 Nov. 1779; *Hansard*, xx. 1055.

porters at a cost to the rest. In 1780 there was a loud and widespread protest when the latest loan: '. . . was issued on such terms that the price at once rose from 9% to 11% above par, and the country was thus compelled to pay nearly a million pounds more for the bonds'.[1] Those friends of the Ministry who were allotted the bonds at the offering price thus made a quick profit of some 10 per cent., and it was assumed that the manœuvre had been deliberate. But it was above all the increase in taxes on land that shook a Ministry dependent on the support of 'the decisive balancing groups in the House of Commons',[2] and above all on the country gentlemen—those 'commoners possessed of armorial bearings and landed estates'.[3] As their taxes mounted by some 33 per cent., their enthusiasm for the Ministry and the war diminished. Early in April 1781 they put their handwriting on the wall of Westminster when some sixty of them voted for Dunning's famous motion that: '. . . the influence of the Crown has increased, is increasing and ought to be diminished'.[4] What was more, the pride of the country gentlemen in the superiority of British arms and British ships had been badly hurt by Saratoga, and 'the humiliating spectacle of a foreign fleet commanding the English channel had for the first time caused the country gentlemen to waver, and had convinced many of them of the necessity for abandoning America'.[5] Long before the news of Yorktown the country gentlemen: '. . . wearied by so many unsuccessful campaigns, exhibited symptoms of reluctance to continue their support'.[6]

These gentry were neither reformers nor idealists, and traditional corruptions like the purchase of votes did not greatly trouble them. But when it began to appear that corruption might account for lost battles and high taxes, they began to condemn corruption. Some of them even applauded Sir George Savile, a staunch Whig of unimpeachable character and 'unbending integrity though large fortune', when he spoke against the latest loan, '. . . which he branded with almost every opprobrious epithet in the English language; it was robbing and plundering the nation in order to bribe with the spoil the

[1] Lecky, iv. 184.
[2] Robson, 'Lord North', in *History Today*, ii. 8. 535, 536.
[3] Ibid.   [4] Robson, *Amer. Rev.*, pp. 147–9.
[5] Lecky, iv. 179.   [6] Wraxall, ii. 120.

members of that House. "If the names of those who were refused
and those who were accepted to share in the loan were all
revealed", he made no doubt but that such a scene of iniquity
and public robbery would have been detected as never before
disgraced the annals of any nation.'[1]

The Opposition spokesmen encouraged and guided the public
uneasiness over corruption, and talked as though no Whig had
ever bought or sold a vote or profited from a government contract. They claimed that the high taxes and new excises were
due to Ministry waste and graft, and they roused reformers and
business men into a strange partnership of protest. The country
rang with demands for higher ethics in government. 'The
agitation was conducted chiefly by the most weighty and respectable classes in the community . . . even great numbers of
the clergy took part in it, and in most counties it was supported
by the great preponderance of property . . . early in 1780 several
counties and cities passed petitions and resolutions on the corrupt
influence of the Crown.'[2] Even that staunch reactionary Admiral
Rodney, who was not above grabbing another Admiral's men
and stores, was moved to moral indignation by the unscrupulous-
ness of other men in the armed forces. In January 1780 he wrote
to Lord George that England was having her

. . . treasures squandered, her arms inactive, and her honour lost,
and by the very men entrusted with the most important and
honourable confidence of their Sovereign and his Ministers . . . to
make the fortunes of a long train of leeches, who seek the blood of
the State, and whose interest prompts them to promote the continuance of the war, such as quartermasters and their deputies *ad
infinitum*, barrack masters and their deputies *ad infinitum*, commissaries
and their deputies *ad infinitum*, all of whom make princely fortunes,
and laugh in their sleeves at the Generals who permit it.[3]

The resolution presented to the king from the City of Westminster was typical. It deplored: '. . . the large addition to the
national debt, a heavy accumulation of taxes, a rapid decline
of the trades, manufactures and land rates of the Kingdom . . .
much public money has been improvidently squandered . . .
many individuals enjoy sinecure places . . . with exorbitant

---

[1] *Hansard*, xxii. 469.   [2] Lecky, iv. 180, 181.
[3] Rodney to Germain, 22 Dec. 1780; *HMC, Stop. Sack.* ii. 191.

emoluments, and pensions unmerited by public services, to a large and increasing amount, whence the Crown has acquired a great and unconstitutional influence, which, if not checked, may soon prove fatal to the liberties of the country'.[1]

Many of the petitions urged the king to get rid of the Ministry, and Lord George was one of the principal targets of criticism, since he was believed to have added greatly to his personal fortune by the award of military contracts and appointments. It was known that Lord George was granted over £3,000 a year for his own secret service, and rumoured that he pocketed the greater part of it.[2] James Luttrell had said in Parliament in early 1779 that: 'He considered the post of secretary of state for the colonies at this time as no other than a contractor of emoluments and high honours, destructive of the independency of parliament: it could not be expected that those who fed on the continuance of the war would vote for its conclusion.'[3] Charles Fox was even more personal and '. . . told Lord George Germaine that he was a coward, as he always had been'.[4] Lord George did not let this insult goad him into a challenge to defend his honour; he was too old to fight all the men who insulted him, and whether from discretion or lack of argument seldom rose to reply to such attacks.

Political corruption was not enough to bring down a Ministry in the eighteenth century, but when combined with high prices, high taxes and a losing war, the administration thought responsible for it was doomed. Members of the Ministry knew it, and, like the undisciplined crew of a sinking ship, were quarreling among themselves. Even within the royal household there were a few men so at odds with the Crown policies that they felt they could no longer conscientiously hold their posts. On 27 January 1780 the young Marquis of Carmarthen, later Duke of Leeds, resigned his office as Chamberlain to the Queen, and told the king to his face (or so he said) that he did so in protest against the continuance of Lord North, Lord Sandwich, and Lord George Germain. 'The King seemed agitated and frequently made use of the expression "I am very sorry"; at the

[1] Wright, *Speeches of Fox*, i. 249.
[2] G. S. Brown, *Anglo-French Naval Crisis*; also see M. M. Spector, *The Amer. Dept. of the British Govt.*, p. 128.   [3] *Hansard*, xx. 128.
[4] Walpole to Mason, 1 Nov. 1780; Toynbee, xi, p. 309.

conclusion he said he was sure I acted from conviction, and therefore like a man of honour.'[1]

If Carmarthen thought that was the end of the matter he was soon disabused. George III counted any man who was not wholly with him as an enemy, and on 8 February the marquis received an official letter from the Secretary of State dismissing him from his Lord Lieutenancy of Yorkshire and other offices: 'My surprise could hardly have been greater had it been a warrant of commitment to the Tower. I went down to the House and . . . in the course of my speech I took care to give the real motives for my resignation, as well as to comment on my dismissions.'[2] The marquis minced no words before the Lords: 'He could no longer give his support to a ministry which had after a series of repeated trials proved themselves pusillanimous, incapable, and corrupt, who had brought the nation to the brink of destruction, and still persisted to plunge it deeper into calamity and danger.'

A week later Carmarthen was emulated by another man of principle. Lord Pembroke told the king:

. . . that the great personal civilities with which H.M. had been so good as to honour him, made the step he was taking extreamly painfull to him, but that he had no choice left . . . that he had for some time past suppressed his feelings, but they were such in respect to Ministers, and Measures, that he could not longer delay his opinion, particularly in respect to one Minister whom he could not, as a Man of Honour, & a Soldier, submit to be thought to countenance in the most remote degree, that he therefore was forced to throw his place of the Lord of the Bedchamber at H.M.'s feet.[3]

The Minister he referred to was Lord George Germain. Five days later Lord Pembroke was officially informed that: 'His Majesty has no further occasion for your services in the offices of Lord Lieutenant, & Custos Rotulorum in the County of Wilts.'[4]

Those two resignations had in themselves no great political importance, but they were significant, and the king's punitive

---

[1] Lecky, iv. 179; also *Polit. Memoirs of Francis, fifth Duke of Leeds*, Camden Socy., 1884, xxxv. 21; 27 Jan. 1780.
[2] Ibid.
[3] John Morris to Lord Herbert, 9 Feb. 1780; *Pembroke Diaries*, p. 404.
[4] Ibid., p. 406.

actions against Carmarthen and Pembroke exacerbated public feeling. Charles Fox made the most of them before the House of Commons: 'The Marquis of Carmarthen and the Earl of Pembroke had their lord lieutenancies taken from them, and for what? Why, because the noble marquis had written his sentiments on the York petition, and the other noble peer had presumed to vote agreeably to his conscience in parliament.'[1]

Viewed in retrospect, it seems impossible that the Ministry, and especially Lord George Germain, could have stayed in office so long against such constant attacks and with so few ardent defenders. Lord George's survival cannot be explained by his possession of extraordinary ability or industry, even in a Ministry notably lacking in both. Though he began his Cabinet career with a reputation for administrative capacity, he had clearly failed as an organizer of the military effort. Lord North had brought him into the Ministry primarily to act as its spokesman in the House of Commons, but in that service Lord George had been undependable in crises, and after Saratoga it was not Lord George who defended Lord North, but Lord North who had to defend Lord George. He had served the Ministry only a little better in Parliament than in America.

In so far as his personal talents account for his survival, it was not their quality but the way he used them that helped to keep him in his office. Some statesmen hold their supporters by winning admiration, confidence, or affection; others by less admirable appeals. Lord George was in the latter group. He was not a man of principle whom others followed by devotion to it and to him. He was not a leader but an astute manipulator of men: '. . . owing to the persistent English mistake', wrote an English historian, 'of confounding a certain dexterity in Parliamentary management with genuine administrative power, his capacity has been rated more highly than it deserves'.[2] Fear and self-interest were the motives that led men to acquiesce to his political power. He had long since demonstrated that those who opposed him were likely to suffer for it; that he could be unforgiving to men who stood in his way, and revengeful to those who openly opposed him. If he could not break a man, he could damage his reputation by the subtle arts of organized insinuation.

---

[1] Wright, *Speeches of Fox*, i. 245; 8 Mar. 1780.
[2] Fortescue, *HBA*, 2, iii. 174.

He was even believed to have maintained his private agents in strategic government and military posts, who reported to him covertly and who on his orders would defame any man, and certain passages in his letters seem to confirm that suspicion.

There were other and more creditable reasons for Lord George's political durability. One of them was the influence of his dominating personality on less forceful men. The letters of the Earl of Chesterfield show how high a value his time placed on a man's personal aura of birth, dignity, self-confidence, and 'address'. No statesman of his time possessed and used all of these more effectively than Lord George Germain. Colleagues who disliked him or his policies sometimes found themselves deferring, almost unconsciously, to the compulsions of his personality.

Quite apart from those assets of aristocratic origin and training, Lord George had the advantages of the dogmatist. In contrast to many of his associates he had strong opinions and expressed them vehemently. And though his casual assumption of superiority irritated, it also impressed politicians less sure of themselves and ready to accept him at his apparent valuation. Lord George sometimes used outrageous flattery, and flattery is all the more flattering when it comes from a man who thinks so well of himself. Though his pose of the simple soldier of open integrity fooled almost no one very long, it did provide an effective screen for the covert manipulation of the minds and machinery of Parliament.

All those considerations together could not have kept Lord George so long in office if the king had not thought he needed him. George III's first test of a good Minister was whether he ardently supported the royal prerogatives and the king's unyielding firmness toward the American rebels. Lord George met those tests as well as any man in Britain, and few others of comparable ability would do so. Lord George had been loyal to the king in the king's terms, and when he and the Earl of Sandwich were under the heaviest fire, the king remarked that he felt a stronger obligation to stand by them since no one else would.[1]

In the last months of the North Ministry, when Lord George was clearly a heavy liability to King and Ministry, the king had another reason for refusing to cashier him. Lord George had

---

[1] Walpole, *Last Journals*, ii. 395.

become the symbol of the king's determination not to grant independence to the American rebels. To have dismissed Lord George without visible honour or compensation would have implied that the king was weakening in that determination. Only when the king began to realize (though he would not admit it even to Lord North) that the American war was lost, would he consider dismissing Lord George, and even then not without 'honour'. But because the service had not been too great, neither must the honour be.

As the spring of 1781 moved toward summer, Lord George, in spite of the discontent that was fulminating throughout Britain, seemed more secure in office than in 1778. But rebellion against taxes, press-gangs, corruption, and military failure had been joined by a more shocking kind of rebellion—mutiny. On more than one occasion British troops had refused to embark on ships that were to take them to fight against the Americans. If these various signs of public unrest could be regarded as isolated phenomena they could perhaps be disregarded, but it would take only one more military defeat to weld them together and turn Opposition eloquence into Opposition votes. If that time should come, the Ministry would be doomed, and the most surely doomed of all would be Lord George Germain.

XXVII

CLIMAX OF STRATEGY

IN the spring of 1781 the achievements of Cornwallis began to seem less magnificent and his situation more dubious. He was still winning most of his engagements and advancing northward, but as reports from various sources trickled into London, they told between the lines that he had made no permanent conquest of the Carolinas or won their people's allegiance to the Crown. But few in England thought that Cornwallis might be marching to another Saratoga.

One of the exceptions was Admiral Rodney. What Washington had hoped in the spring of 1777 might happen to Burgoyne, Rodney feared in the spring of 1781 would happen to Cornwallis. As early as the previous November the downright Admiral had written from his ship off Sandy Hook to the Earl of Sandwich: '. . . the whole expedition appears to me to have been an ill-concerted measure, and, in my poor opinion, could tend only to weaken the army, and give the rebels opportunity of destroying his Majesty's troops by detail'.[1]

Another exception was General Clinton. Cornwallis sent back few reports, and those he sent were long in reaching New York. Clinton had never been happy over Cornwallis's brash advances into the Carolina hinterlands, and grew increasingly worried at the distance he was putting between himself and Charleston, the only secure base for supplies, communications, and, if necessary, escape. Clinton was even more concerned as each dispatch brought stronger hints that Cornwallis had set his sights on the conquest of Virginia.

As far back as the previous November, at the very time that Rodney was expressing his doubts about the strategy of the whole campaign, Cornwallis had apparently determined to move northward into Virginia. He did not then admit it to Clinton, but he hinted it to loyalists in Charleston, for one of them had written then that Cornwallis: '. . . waits the arrival of

---

[1] Rodney to Sandwich, 15 Nov. 1780; *Sandwich Papers,* ii. 261.

General Leslie in North Carolina to begin his Operations against
that Province and Virginia'.[1]

Though Clinton did not know the full plans of Cornwallis,
he was more than disturbed when Cornwallis wrote him that if
an army could only be sent from New York to Virginia to meet
him there, the rebellion could be broken in the entire South in
one campaign. Did not Cornwallis remember that New York
must be held? Did he not see what risks he was taking in moving
ever deeper into enemy territory and ever farther from supplies
and safety? His lifeline depended on the Navy, and so long as
bumbling Admiral Arbuthnot was in charge and the French
fleet intact, that lifeline was in jeopardy. On the Arbuthnot
issue Clinton was ready to risk his future career, as he had
intimated to General Phillips.[2]

Clinton, reluctantly and somewhat fearfully, nevertheless did
all he could to gratify the urgings of Cornwallis and Lord George
Germain. He had already sent 3,000 men to the Chesapeake
area under Benedict Arnold, but rebel troops had almost
trapped Arnold, and Clinton had been forced to send another
2,000 men under General Leslie to extricate him. General Leslie
and his men had then been told to join Cornwallis, and had
caught up with him by way of Cape Fear on 3 January.[3]

Cornwallis ignored Clinton's cautionary letters, partly because
he was receiving messages of quite another tenor directly from
Lord George. 'I make no doubt but your Lordship will, by this
time, have had the honour to recover the province of North
Carolina to his Majesty; and I am even sanguine enough to
hope, from your Lordship's distinguished abilities, and zeal for
the King's service, that the recovery of a part of Virginia, will
crown your successes before the season becomes too intemperate
for land operations.'[4]

Lord George, with the self-protective explanation that he
was only 'advising', pressed an equally aggressive strategy on
Clinton. 'I doubt not that you will avail yourself of his [Washing-
ton's] weakness, and your own great superiority, to send a considerable force to the head of the Chesapeak, as soon as the

---

[1] Alex Hewat to Germain, 9 Jan. 1781; Clements, *Germain Papers*, xiv. 2.
[2] Clinton to Phillips, 26 Apr. 1781; Clements, *Clinton Letter Book*.
[3] Ibid., pp. 249–54.
[4] Germain to Cornwallis, 7 Mar. 1781; Clements, *Germain Papers*, xiv.

season will permit operations to be carried on in that quarter. I flatter myself the southern provinces will be recovered to his Majesty's obedience before the long-promised succours (none of which are yet sailed) can arrive from France.' And he added of Cornwallis: 'I have no doubt his movements will be rapid and decisive.'[1] Clinton did not receive that dispatch until some fifteen weeks later, when his own reports regarding the French 'succours' were quite different.

Cornwallis was partly to blame for Lord George's excessive hopes, for like Burgoyne before Saratoga, he did not report how difficulties were multiplying around him. Unaware of them, Lord George continued his pressures on both generals to expand their operations. His letter of 2 May to Clinton urging him to send a large force into Virginia was in effect an order. '. . . it was a great mystification to me to find . . . your ideas of the importance of recovering that province to be so different from mine. . . . I am commanded by his Majesty to acquaint you that the recovery of the Southern Provinces and the prosecution of the war, by pushing our conquests from south to north, is to be considered the chief and principal object for the employment of all the forces under your command.'[2] This was a mandatory statement, but what precisely did it mean? Should Clinton abandon New York and take all his forces southward? The soundest part of British strategy had been the determination to hold New York. Clinton could imagine what would happen if he evacuated or lost it, and what Parliament and Lord George would say afterward. Clinton had already told Lord George that: '. . . all the forces that could be spared' were with Cornwallis.

Some weeks before those various letters reached their destinations, Clinton and Cornwallis had each taken steps unknown to the other. Toward the end of March Clinton had sent another force of 2,000 men by sea to the Chesapeake under the command of that admirable officer General Phillips, who had been made a prisoner of war at Saratoga and after long delays exchanged. General Phillips reached the Chesapeake on 20 March, but after

---

[1] Germain to Clinton, 7 Mar. 1781; Fortescue, *HBA*, 2, iii. 377. This was received by Clinton on 27 June 1781.

[2] Germain to Clinton, 2 May 1781; Clements, *Clinton Letter Book*, pp. 265–72; also Stevens, *Facsimiles*, i. 464–70.

some minor successes he sickened and died near Richmond on 13 May, and the little campaign flickered out. In view of Lord George's orders, Clinton instructed Phillips's men to join Cornwallis if possible.

Admiral Rodney and General Clinton envisaged from a distance the difficulties and hazards of Cornwallis's campaign several months before Cornwallis learned them from experience. He ignored or minimized various danger signals through the early spring of 1781, despite the fact that his defeat at Cowpens had cost him 600 men and encouraged the enemy, and his victory at Guilford on 15 March had been nearly as expensive.[1] But by April he was beginning to sing a different tune. The American troops that constantly harassed him simply would not stay beaten. Sickness and the beginning of devastating summer heat were taking a serious toll of his men's health and spirits. Loyalists were proving few and undependable. Cornwallis admitted discouragement in a letter to Clinton: 'My present undertaking sits heavy on my mind. I have experienced the danger, and distresses, of marching some hundreds of miles, without one active or useful friend, without intelligence, and without communication with any part of the country.'[2] But the very day after writing that letter, Cornwallis set out on a march of another 200 miles farther north.[3]

Cornwallis also confessed his troubles to General Phillips three weeks later: 'My situation here is very distressing . . . to form a junction with you is exceedingly hazardous', and he admitted 'the almost universal spirit of revolt which prevails'.[4] But Cornwallis adhered to his plan of marching through Virginia, though his motives for doing so may have been somewhat less happy ones than the original plan of confident conquest. He never made it very clear, even in his later tract defending his actions, whether he went into Virginia primarily with the expectation of conquering it effectively, or of forcing Clinton to meet and relieve him there, or in the hope of escaping the Carolina summer, though he later explained that: 'The amount of sickness among all ranks of the army was positively

---

[1] Lecky, iv. 187; 17 Jan. 1781 and 15 Mar. 1781.
[2] Cornwallis to Clinton, 3 Apr. 1781; Ross, *Cornwallis Letters*, i. 94.
[3] Fortescue, *HBA*, 2, iii. 378.
[4] Cornwallis to Phillips, 24 Apr. 1781; Clements, *Shelburne Papers, Amer. Dispatches*, p. 81.

alarming' and that he had hoped by moving north to improve their health.[1]

Meanwhile Lord George in London, as yet ignorant of the outcome of the expedition to the Chesapeake under General Phillips, wrote to Clinton that he expected the Chesapeake undertaking to be much more than a minor effort or a mere diversion, though he was well aware of the size of Clinton's army in America and the demands upon it. Early in July he sent to Clinton: '. . . positive commands . . . that not a man was to be withdrawn from the Chesapeake, but that a conquest should be pushed from south to north. This was nothing less than the rejection of the Commander-in-Chief's scheme in favour of his subordinate's.'[2] While Lord George was writing that letter Count D'Estaing arrived off the Atlantic coast with twelve ships of the line, four frigates, and about 4,000 French soldiers and blockaded New York harbour.[3]

Before Clinton received that order he had written to Lord George pointing out the reasons for his own limitations: 'I hope your Lordship will pardon me for again repeating, that had the reinforcement sailed as early as it was promised, and the three battalions not been detained in the West Indies, I should per- haps by this time have made such movements as would have obliged the enemy to be apprehensive for their own possessions, instead of meditating the attack they now threaten against this port.'[4]

Lord George paid no attention to such pusillanimous excuses and continued to drive toward his own objectives. As late as 12 October, when Cornwallis [though Lord George did not know it] was only three days from surrender, he wrote to Clinton: 'I trust therefore that Lord Cornwallis will retain the whole of the troops you so very properly spared for the service in the Chesapeake; or if he has sent you any part, you will return them to him.'[5]

Clinton's position in that summer of 1781 had become much like the situation of General Carleton four years earlier. Like Carleton then, Clinton had been compelled to turn over a great part of his force to a subordinate officer for a dubious campaign.

---

[1] Fortescue, *HBA*, 2, iii. 321.   [2] Fortescue, *HBA*, 2, iii. 390.
[3] Lecky, iv. 91.
[4] Clinton to Germain, 25 July 1781; *Narrative of Clinton*, 1783, p. 110.
[5] Germain to Clinton, 12 Oct. 1781; Clements, *Germain Papers*, xv.

He would not be praised if that subordinate succeeded but he would be blamed if he did not. The position was also painfully reminiscent of Clinton's dilemma just before Saratoga. With a force inadequate to both needs, he was expected to hold New York and also to redeem the mistakes of others at a distant spot. In both cases he had received highly optimistic reports from the general leading the distant campaign; then a long period of silence and then, at the eleventh hour, urgent pleas for immediate help. But in 1781 Clinton was even less his own master than in 1777, for he and Cornwallis were wholly dependent on the British Navy for transport, and a French army might at any time be landed near New York for an attack on Britain's only stronghold in America. And his effective army was smaller than most Englishmen thought or his manager in Whitehall would admit.[1]

All through the spring Cornwallis had kept Clinton in the dark regarding his plans until after he had embarked on them. In late April Clinton had written to General Phillips:

I cannot judge from Lord Cornwallis's Letter whether he proposes any further Operations in the Carolinas—what they may be—and how far you can operate in his favor. If I was to give a private opinion from reading his Letter, I would say, I cannot conceive from it, that he has any offensive Object in view. He says that North Carolina is a Country in which it is impossible for an Army to act or move without the Assistance of Friends—and he does not seem to think we have any there—nor do you.[2]

In mid-June Clinton had written to Cornwallis advising against a campaign in Virginia:

. . . for experience ought to convince us, that there is no possibility of restoring Order in any rebellious Province, on this Continent, without the hearty Assistance of numerous Friends. These, my Lord; I think are not to be found in Virginia, nor dare I under present circumstances positively assert that under our present Circumstances they are to be found in great numbers anywhere else, Or that their Exertions, when found, will answer our expectations . . . they are gone from us, and I fear, are not to be recovered.[3]

[1] See note L, p. 500.
[2] Clinton to Phillips, 30 Apr. 1781; Clements, *Shelburne Papers, Amer. Dispatches,* i. 68.
[3] Clinton to Cornwallis, 17 June 1781; Clements, *Shelburne Papers, Amer. Dispatches,* i. 75.

While Clinton wrote, Cornwallis and his men were already in Virginia and had been joined at Petersburg by Phillips's force.

Contact with their base at Charleston abandoned, Cornwallis's men plodded over hot dusty roads and through marshy pine-lands. They entered, and left again, nearly every important town in Virginia: Richmond, Charlottesville, Portsmouth, Petersburg, and Williamsburg. Nothing of value was accom-plished; the scrub and jackpines closed in again behind them, the dust settled on brown grass and silent hamlets as though the British had never passed. More men sickened and the Army kept on dwindling. It finally reached the sea near Williamsburg, eager for the assistance of the Navy, for Lafayette was marching from the northward with fresh French troops to join the American forces already at Cornwallis's heels. Cornwallis's dis-patches to Clinton sobered notably in tone, and implied that if he did not quickly have strong assistance by land he would have to dig in and await reinforcement or embarkation.

Clinton too faced new dangers. In his letter of 25 July to Lord George, he had reported that he expected an imminent attack on New York from a powerful combined Franco-American force. He expected it with good reason, for that was the precise plan of Washington and Rochambeau. Among Clinton's papers can be found a letter written in Washington's own hand, dated 31 May 1781, to Lafayette, informing the marquis that Wash-ington and Rochambeau had decided to co-operate in an attack on Clinton in New York. That letter never reached Lafayette for it was intercepted by Clinton's troops. 'On reading it one can understand why the British general decided to stay within his lines at New York waiting for the attack which never came.'[1]

The attack never came because Washington and Rochambeau changed their minds when they learned that a division of French troops they had been counting on to join that attack was still im-mured in transports in the harbour at Brest, blockaded by a British squadron.[2] Suddenly, too, it looked as though Cornwallis had made himself vulnerable at or near Williamsburg, espe-cially if the French squadron could get temporary control of the waters off the James River and the Chesapeake. Washington

---

[1] R. G. Adams, *Clinton Headquarters Papers*, p. 24.
[2] Fitzpatrick, *Washington, Works*, vii. 176; also Lecky, iv. 432.

quickly made a new plan; slipped with his army around Clinton in New York and hurried south to join the American and French forces crowding Cornwallis toward the sea.

Cornwallis's position seemed serious, but in September no one thought it hopeless. If the British navy could keep its mastery of the waters off the Atlantic coast, it could supply Cornwallis, bring him reinforcements, or embark him from any navigable point on reasonable notice. He had fortified himself at York-town, where his troops could be easily embarked, and his earlier letters to Clinton from that place gave assurance that he could hold out for many weeks. Clinton, freed of the menace of Washington's army near New York, was by that time ready to embark his own troops and go promptly to Cornwallis's aid. Cornwallis counted confidently on Clinton's arrival in plenty of time; Clinton counted with only a little less confidence on Admiral Graves's assurances that the squadron then in New York harbour could shortly transport his troops to Yorktown and if necessary bring all the British regiments back. There would be only a few days' delay to make repairs to two of his important ships.

Those repairs were needed as the result of an unsuccessful brush with a French squadron. Admiral De Grasse had crossed the Atlantic and in a brief running skirmish had damaged several British ships including the *Robust* and the *Prudent*. The repairs took longer than Admiral Graves had estimated. As September wore on, each of Cornwallis's letters to Clinton reduced the estimate of the time he could hold out, and each of Clinton's letters to Cornwallis extended the estimate of the time it would take him to get to Yorktown. Clinton and his men were ready but Admiral Graves kept postponing the date on which his ships could sail. They could not set out until in good condition, since De Grasse was presumably somewhere in the offing and might dare to fight again. It was a situation Clinton had long feared but Lord George Germain had not allowed for.

Meanwhile De Grasse, temporarily freed from the British squadron supposed to contain him, arrived at the mouth of the Chesapeake with twenty-eight ships of the line, several frigates, and the second and long-awaited division of French troops from Brest. He blockaded the York River below Yorktown and set

3,200 men ashore to augment the forces of Lafayette and the Americans, which already outnumbered Cornwallis—and Washington was on the way. A little later more French warships that had been off Rhode Island arrived with a large number of heavy guns and other materials for a siege.[1] The entire British force, numbering about 7,000 men and including the contingents from General Leslie and General Phillips, was being compressed into a smaller and smaller area. After Washington arrived, Cornwallis was encompassed on the land side by some 16,000 men. His only hope was escape by sea, and the French fleet that blockaded him was probably equal in fire power to any ships the British could bring to bear.[2]

Cornwallis and his men fought well, but one of their outer key fortifications was soon taken, and the enemy drew tighter bands around him. His position was similar to that of Burgoyne in the last days of Saratoga. His camp was raked by enemy guns and his ammunition and food were dangerously low. He made a daring and desperate attempt to break out by crossing the river, but was driven back. Realizing the futility of an attempt to relieve him at that late juncture, Cornwallis wrote to Clinton early in October advising him not to take the risk.[3] It was a gallant sacrificial gesture, but by the time Clinton received the message he had embarked with 7,000 men.

Those events were of course as yet unknown in London, but this time Lord George developed premonitions. He gave no hint of them to King and Parliament, but predicted privately to Knox that Cornwallis would be defeated, though he probably did not envisage Cornwallis's surrender.[4] He made that prediction on 4 November, which, ironically, was two weeks after Cornwallis's capitulation. For Clinton and his army arrived off the Cape on 24 October, five days after Cornwallis had surrendered his 7,157 men, 840 seamen, four frigates, and thirty transports.[5] There was nothing Clinton could do to retrieve the situation; in fact, had he arrived ten days earlier he might merely have augmented the Franco-American victory. Clinton and Graves wisely avoided an engagement and returned to New

---

[1] Lecky, iv. 199.   [2] Fortescue, *HBA*, 2, iii. 294.
[3] Hon. George Damer to Germain, 13 Oct. 1781; *HMC, Stop. Sack.* ii. 214.
[4] Germain to Knox, 4 Nov. 1781; *HMC, Var. Coll.* 6, *Knox*, p. 180.
[5] Greene, p. 275.

York. There was probably not a man aboard who did not know that the war with America was lost.

If the situation at Yorktown resembled that at Saratoga, so did the dissensions of the aftermath. Cornwallis blamed Clinton for not having sent more troops to Virginia many months before. He blamed Clinton for having sent him what he later claimed were firm orders to establish himself at Yorktown. That place, Cornwallis said, would not have been his own choice, though how the end could have been altered if Cornwallis had selected some other spot on those sandy peninsulas is not apparent. Clinton, in turn, blamed Cornwallis for rushing into Virginia, for moving so far from his base at Charleston, and for ignoring the cautions of his commanding officer. Clinton also denied that he had sent Cornwallis inflexible orders to entrench himself at Yorktown, and the record seems to bear him out. After both men were back in England they too indulged in a war of pamphlets, unfortunately against each other. It was a sad and futile effort, for few men blamed either general very much, or greatly cared which, if either, was to blame. The war was lost, and England was ready to change Ministries, make peace, and salvage whatever could be saved. Clinton and Cornwallis would have done better to make common cause against the men and policies that had contributed to their defeat.

The immediate cause of the surrender was the failure of the Navy. Clinton saw that clearly enough, and stated it in a dispatch to Lord George Germain: 'I have ever been of the opinion that operations should not be undertaken in the Chesapeake without having a naval superiority in these seas; and to the want of it, and perhaps to that alone, are we to impute our late misfortune in that quarter.'[1] In that dispatch Clinton suppressed his feelings about Lord George, but a few days before the surrender at Yorktown he had unburdened himself in a personal letter to his friend the Earl of Buckinghamshire, Lord Lieutenant of Ireland. He said the whole war had been badly directed, and continued: 'If I succeed in saving his Lordship I shall if possible bring W[ashington] to action, and then resign a command I have long determined to do the instant it could be done with propriety; the treatment I have of late met with, and the insinuations thrown out by his ministers, some of them

[1] Clinton to Germain, 6 Dec. 1781; Willcox, *Amer. Rebellion*, p. 590.

published in a rebel newspaper, are such as no man will submit to serve under.'[1] Shortly after Yorktown Clinton wrote again to the earl: 'This command, my dear Lord, is sufficiently arduous with all the support that a Minister can give me, and what must it be when I am neglected, and ill-treated, every opinion but mine taken, any plan but mine adopted. I am forced into operations planned by others, promised support, and unfortunate from that being wantonly withheld from me.'[2] And a month later: 'The Minister . . . often over-rates my numbers here altho' I send him the regular returns. . . . Your Lordship has no doubt seen a letter of Lord George Germain to me published in a Rebel paper, I should have quitted immediately on receipt of that letter.'[3]

This time Clinton took steps to make sure that his resignation would be accepted, by enlisting the help of his cousin the Duke of Newcastle. Newcastle took action, and it took Lord George only about six weeks to write to Clinton his Majesty's decision, though Clinton did not receive the dispatch until 27 April 1782: 'The Duke of Newcastle having applied to me in your name that I would obtain His Majesty's Permission for you to quit the Command in North America that you might return immediately to England, I have the pleasure to inform you that His Majesty has been graciously pleased to comply with your Request, and I am to signify to you His Majesty's pleasure that you embark for England the first convenient opportunity.'[4]

There was no word of appreciation for the past services of the only important general who had served throughout the war and who had been commanding officer for nearly four years. There was no expression of regret that Clinton was to leave the command. And Clinton, of course, noticed that although the standard form of reporting the king's wishes was to write that the king accepted the resignation with reluctance, Lord George wrote that he had the pleasure to say that the king (without reluctance) called Clinton home. It was the kind of subtle derogation that some angry men indulge.

With the American war virtually ended, every leading British

[1] Clinton to Buckinghamshire, 10 Oct. 1781; HMC, Lothian, p. 399.
[2] Idem, 29 Dec. 1781; ibid., p. 407.
[3] Idem, 25 Jan. 1782; ibid., p. 409.
[4] Germain to Clinton, 6 Feb. 1782; Clements, Clinton Letter Book.

general who had tried to implement the strategy formed in Whitehall had ended that service in anger if not in disgrace. Carleton, Burgoyne, Howe, Clinton, and Cornwallis all made their mistakes, but each was the victim of ineptitudes greater than his own. The chief formulator of that strategy had not yet met his own day of reckoning. As the year 1781 ended, Lord George Germain was still in office.

XXVIII

STRATEGY RECONSIDERED

HINDSIGHT is the unfair advantage time gives to later generations. We should not condemn our predecessors merely because they lacked our own omniscience. But the failure of British strategy in the American war cannot be excused so easily. Its formulators did not lack the necessary knowledge as much as the judgement to make good use of it. Lord George Germain and his Whitehall associates were led astray not only by bad maps, bad advice, and bad communications, but by their own myopia and shallow thinking. Their basic strategy was almost wholly wrong.

It was wrong, first of all, because men like Lord George, products of a self-assured society of narrow experience, were unable to project their imaginations into unfamiliar lands and the minds and emotions of unfamiliar people. They never understood America or Americans. The roads to Saratoga and Yorktown were in that respect not unlike Napoleon's later road to Moscow. A country of vast extent, primitive economy, and a determined population cannot be conquered merely by holding a city or two, and cutting narrow paths through its hinterlands. Clinton might hold New York, but nine-tenths of American settlers were too self-suffing to be dependent on New York any more than on London or even Rome. Howe might march and counter-march his army across New Jersey; Burgoyne might parade to Ticonderoga and then slog his way to Saratoga; Cornwallis might lead his sweltering troops across the marshy plains and sandy foot-hills of the South, but the paths their troops had cut would close in behind them like the vanishing wake of a passing ship. As Clinton wrote to Lord George in 1780: 'An inroad is no countenance, and to possess territory demands garrisons.'[1]

A false assumption oft repeated sometimes gains acceptance by later generations. Chroniclers have reiterated that the plan

[1] Clinton to Germain, 25 Aug. 1780; Fortescue, *HBA*, 2, iii. 331.

to cut off New England by blazing a line along its western boundary was a sound strategic concept. It has been the fashion to approve the plan of Saratoga and condemn its management. Mismanagement there was, but even without it the strategy could not have gained its end. To fence off New England effectively was beyond the powers of any army Lord George could have sent to America. Sir John Fortescue concluded that to isolate New England would require from 30,000 to 50,000 men, 'almost all of whom must be transported from the British Isles'.[1] He probably under-estimated the requirement.

Long thin lines of armed men, with occasional strong points, cannot be made impenetrable across rugged enemy country. Burgoyne and Howe could not have turned the Hudson Valley into a Maginot Line. To seal the Hudson below Albany against passage, it would have had to be constantly patrolled, day and night, by British gunboats, and its hundred miles of steep banks and flat shores controlled everywhere by British land forces in considerable strength and constantly on the alert. Above Albany the long stretch of rugged country to Canada would have had to be made into a barrier invulnerable at all points to sudden attacking concentrations of local militia and village volunteers, who knew intimately the local terrain. Lake Champlain comprises the last third of that distance, and only a British flotilla constantly patrolling its length could have sealed it against small boat crossings, especially at night. Burgoyne's experience revealed the problems of garrisons, supplies, communications, and reinforcements along that route. Burgoyne's experience also disclosed a fact that Lord George Germain never recognized. Lord George thought of American opposition in terms of organized armies, but Washington might never have needed to move nearer the Hudson barricade than New Jersey, and yet there have watched it penetrated again and again by self-raised and self-organized forces of local inhabitants, who would not enlist in the regular army but would endlessly harass an enemy near their own homes.

Below Albany, Clinton had been able to open the Hudson River with only 3,000 men, but he could not have kept it closed with three times as many. Even when the enemy was distracted by Burgoyne's army only some sixty miles away, Clinton could

[1] Fortescue, *HBA*, 2, iii. 166, 167.

not get his troops to Albany. Effective long-term occupation of the whole line from Rouses Point to Kingsbridge would have been dependent, too, on the long, slow, uncertain crossing of the Atlantic by scores of supply ships monthly, and then on the long, thin, tenuous supply lines by land and water from Montreal and New York. Burgoyne and Clinton did not have to cope in 1777 with a northern New York winter, with its constant snow and ice and frequent zero temperatures, in which tent encampments would be death-traps to inexperienced European soldiers with standard equipment. Discounting climate, guerrilla raids, and major enemy attacks, the effort would have required troops, ships, wagons, horses, sleighs, guns, ammunition, food, and other supplies far beyond Whitehall concepts and British capacity. What is more, much of the effort would have been wasted, since a great part of the barrier would have served no important end.

In 1961, as in 1777, nearly all the men and goods that enter and leave New England by land move through two narrow portals. One of these is the gap between the northern Catskill and the southern Adirondack foot-hills created by the Mohawk River. All major railway lines and highways north of the New York City area still follow that route, and the men and goods that cross the Hudson between Albany and the present George Washington Bridge, just above New York City, are a very small percentage of the whole. The other great artery of land traffic to and from New England passes now, as it passed in 1777, through or just north of New York City. Between Albany and Canada there is not and never has been east–west traffic of real importance, not only because of the dictates of terrain but because of the absence of heavy industry in areas which might want to use that route. In 1777 the populations and products of northern New England and northern New York state were tiny; in fact west of Albany they were almost non-existent.

Of those two arteries the route through Albany and the Mohawk Valley was in 1777 of trivial importance. It led only to the hamlets of up-state New York and a few small forts in what is now the middle, and was then the far, west. Beyond those—nothing. Unless British strategy hoped to prevent every American and every parcel from leaving or reaching New England, it could have ignored every mile of the western boundary of New England above Albany—the entire line along which Burgoyne so ardently and expensively fought his way.

South of Albany a British force could best have prevented large-scale crossings of the Hudson by heavily gunned small ships in perpetual patrol. But this too would have been largely wasted effort, since American goods and troops would have crossed the river above Newburgh (itself but a few miles above New York City) only when emergency required it. The important need was to cork the bottleneck of trade routes that ran through and a few miles north of New York City. It is ironic that at the very time Lord George was organizing the Great Design to isolate New England, Howe's army in and near New York City were already corking that bottleneck. Lord George's purpose could have been served almost as well (could it have been served at all) by the capture and possession of three small forts in the Hudson Highlands—forts Clinton was able to take in two days with only 3,000 men and the loss of forty.

But even if Howe and Burgoyne had been successful in cutting off all land communications between New England and the rest of the new states, they would not have effectively isolated New England or throttled the revolution. In 1777, even more than now, goods from New England to points south and west went by sea along the coast. Sea transport was the cheapest, easiest, and often the quickest way for men as well as goods from Boston or even from New Haven to Philadelphia and the southern ports. No land force could have prevented this sea traffic except by occupying all the ports, large and small, along the New England coast, or along the rest of the Atlantic seaboard. Only the British Navy could have bottled up New England, and though it did attempt to do so, and intercepted much shipping, it was never able to cut off New England merchants and soldiers from sea communications. There were too many places where only local shallow-draught boats could go, and too many little inlets where wily Yankee skippers could hide. The British Navy was trying to destroy a swarm of hornets with a blunderbuss. An intensified effort by small British armed ships—if Lord Sandwich had been able to supply and man them—would have been far more effective than Burgoyne's proposed march from Montreal to Albany. But success either way would have prevented Britain's land and sea forces from doing much else. Had Burgoyne won at

Saratoga, his victory might have proved as expensive to Britain as his defeat.

General Carleton's original plan for a 1777 campaign from Canada was more realistic, for he did not propose to isolate New England from the rest of the world. With the exception of General Gage, who was the most naïve general in America, and of General Burgoyne, who was the most optimistic, the idea of isolating New England by a land march was the drawing-board dream of men in London ignorant of America. Burgoyne is not to be excused for elaborating that Whitehall idea into one consistent with his own grandiose ambitions. But Burgoyne asked for authority to take alternate routes by sea as well as by land, and he did not stress the isolation of New England. What Burgoyne really wanted was an army under his command for some dramatic service. His 'Thoughts' were embraced and then emasculated by London strategists plotting paper conquests on inadequate maps while listening to self-interested loyalists and ignoring distant realities. The best that can be said for the plan is that had Burgoyne succeeded he would have greatly raised British morale and perhaps fatally discouraged the Americans— but any great British victory would have done that.

Except for Howe's unpardonable disregard of co-operation with Burgoyne, his plan to capture Philadelphia was a far sounder strategic move, though his circuitous approach to it cannot be justified. If Britain could have won the war by land operations alone, it could have done so only by taking and holding the large American seaports and as many smaller ones as necessary; throttling American trade and communications, and constantly raiding deeper and deeper inland from all of them. But this too would have required more men, and more service from the British Navy, than Britain could provide.

It is curious that Lord George Germain, who had once been thought a brilliant soldier, so ignored that strategy of interior lines. Nearly every plan he recommended was dispersive of Britain's power: the taking and holding of Rhode Island from New York; the raids on the New England coast; the sending of troops from New York to the West Indies, the Chesapeake, and Charleston; the Cornwallis venture in the South; the widely peripheral operations in Florida, Georgia, the Penobscot, the Mohawk Valley, and Canada. When Cornwallis, at the urging

and with the applause of Lord George, set out from Charleston
into the back country of the Carolinas, he was marching away
from everything worth military possession, into an area with
light population, no major cities, and no sources of supply for
his troops. When he turned northward into Virginia he compounded his earlier unwisdom by moving even farther from his
base of supply and escape, leaving along his way no permanent
traces except the graves of his stragglers. Yet Lord George urged
him onward, and would have had Clinton risk the loss of New
York to meet Cornwallis on that futile Anabasis.

Military strategy involves not only the movement of men but
their provisioning. In the American war the provision of supplies
was a problem of unprecedented dimensions. Given the state of
the British Navy and the supply organization of the Government, it was an almost insoluble one. Lord George must be
blamed not for his inability to overcome it but for his failure to
adjust his plans to it. Throughout the war he seemed to have
learned nothing from experience, and proceeded as blithely as
though the previous year's logistic inadequacies and delays had
nothing to teach. Reinforcements and supplies continued to
reach his generals too little and too late.

A minor illustration but a striking one is the record of cavalry
and work horses sent to the British forces in America. Howe,
planning in Boston for his attack on New York, sent his estimate
of the horses and wagons that would be needed. Lord George
declined to send them and told Howe he must secure them in
America.[1] Later in 1776 Howe again urgently requested 300
horses from England but Lord George replied that he could send
only 100, owing to lack of room in the ships, and the expense
and the hazards of the journey.[2] He took it for granted that
Howe could get plenty of horses, and hay, in America. But
Howe could not, and repeated his requests. In 1777 Howe
explained his delay in starting his Philadelphia campaign on
the grounds that since Lord George had not provided his mounts
with the hay and oats requested from England, he had to wait
until green forage was on the ground.[3] The excuse was partly

[1] Howe to Dartmouth, 2 Dec. 1775; PRO, CO/5, nos. 92, 93; Germain to
Howe, 5 Jan. 1776; Curtis, p. 144.

[2] Germain to Howe, 14 Jan. 1777; PRO, CO/5, no. 94.

[3] But Howe did not land his troops until August, and green grass grows tall in
Maryland and Virginia long before then.

specious, but on such excuses failure can be based.[1] 'The reason for Howe's delay in proceeding from Head of Elk to Brandywine ... was the need to replace horses lost during the long voyage for want of forage, and to secure waggons.'[2] Two years later, on his expedition to Charleston, Clinton lost every horse on the sea passage, from want of proper food and transport.[3]

Men as well as horses suffered from lack of provisions or food of poor quality. Anburey wrote that in the Saratoga campaign, for every hour that Burgoyne could give to planning how to fight the enemy he had to give twenty hours to contriving how to feed his men.[4] Clinton said that his inactivity in 1779 was partly due to a shortage of provisions from England.[5] Cornwallis wrote from the Carolinas to Lord George Germain: 'Your Lordship well knows how often this army has been on the Eve of being reduced to the greatest distress for Want of Provisions ... unless some Measures are speedily adopted to supply us more effectually then we have hitherto been, I have the greatest reason to apprehend that the most fatal Consequences will ensue. We have not yet received one ounce of this Year's supply.'[6] During his last two years in command Clinton had been seriously handicapped by receiving no money to pay his troops and contractors.[7]

The hazards and delays of ocean transport had been made painfully clear as early as the first winter of the war, when forty transports left England but only eight reached Boston with their goods intact. The rest were either taken by American privateers or blown all the way to the West Indies, and some of those which ultimately reached Boston or Halifax had their shipments of food spoiled.[8] After the intervention of France in 1778 supply became even more precarious, but at every stage of the war military operations were threatened or delayed by failure to receive necessities. On 6 August 1776 Howe reported to Lord George that he had sufficient men to begin operations but lacked essential camp equipment, particularly kettles and canteens.[9]

---

[1] Curtis, p. 102.   [2] Robson, *Amer. Rev.*, p. 106.

[3] Clinton to Germain, 14 Sept. 1780; PRO, CO/5, no. 100.

[4] Anburey, i. 384; also Robson, *Amer. Rev.*, p. 106.

[5] Curtis, p. 103.

[6] Cornwallis to Germain, 31 Oct. 1780; PRO, CO/5, no. 101; also Curtis, p. 103.

[7] Clinton to Robinson, 11 May 1779; PRO, 30/55, no. 1995.

[8] Robson, *Amer. Rev.*, p. 103.   [9] Ibid., p. 105.

In 1777 stores for the year's campaign that left England in March did not begin to reach New York until 14 May.[1] The delays were not due solely to adverse winds and enemy ships. Many of them were caused by inefficiency in planning transport, in loading ships, and in the delivery of goods from contractors. There was also a shortage of both transports and fighting ships, and that shortage was rarely admitted and never overcome by the Admiralty.[2]

The experience of 210 recruits embarked in Newfoundland for New York illustrates the hazards of transport. Their ship met adverse winds that forced it south, and the captain decided that his best course was to run for the West Indies. Before they reached the Caribbean they ran short of food and water and, the wind changing, turned and ran for England. Off the west coast of Ireland the ship was blown on the rocks, began to break up, and was burned to the water's edge and then pillaged by Irish natives. Fifty-six men were lost or died on the passage and there is no record that any of the survivors ever reached New York to fight, or even got back to Newfoundland.[3]

Morale as well as military operations was impaired by mismanagement and delay. One soldier in Howe's army wrote to London: 'Our army moulders away amazingly; many die by the sword, many by sickness, brought on by bad provisions we have had from Ireland. . . . I wish Government would look after the contractors, for without we are supplied with wholesome necessaries of life, it cannot be expected we will long fight their battles.'[4] The Government's insistence that its generals, admirals, and men attempt more than they could reasonably achieve without better support was a blunder in strategy.

In still another way Lord George Germain's strategy was based on illusion. It was not, at first, his illusion alone, but he cherished it longer than almost any other Englishman. In 1775 many men believed that the revolution could be suppressed mainly by loyalist American troops.[5] In the years that followed most Englishmen abandoned that conviction but Lord George, encouraged by the persistently optimistic statements of loyalists

[1] Ibid.
[2] *Annual Register for 1778*, p. 201.
[3] Capt. Robt. Rotton to Amherst, 12 Feb. 1780; PRO, CO/5, no. 123.
[4] Force, *Amer. Archives*, iii, p. 928; 20 Nov. 1776.
[5] Lecky, iv. 9.

like Galloway, Hutchinson, and Tryon, persisted in it to the
end.[1]

The pragmatic test of whether a man was a true loyalist was
whether he would join the British armed forces and fight for
the Crown. By that test there were relatively few ardent able-
bodied male loyalists in America. But many authorities insisted
to the contrary. Well after the rebellion had become a major
war, two members of His Majesty's Council in New York, for
example, reported through Governor Tryon that: '. . . they are
positive a majority of the inhabitants west of the Connecticut
River are firm friends to the Government'.[2] Governor Dunmore,
though driven from Virginia by the rebels, nevertheless pledged
himself to recover the province with a few hundred men.[3]

Every commander of a British army in America began his
American career accepting this optimism. Clinton was the single
exception. He had lived in New York as a boy and was dubious
of the number and ardour of the loyalists. Howe, Burgoyne, and
Cornwallis all had to learn by unhappy experience. Even before
Howe captured New York he informed Lord George that: 'We
must also have recruits from Europe, not finding the Americans
disposed to serve with arms, not withstanding the hopes held
out to me upon my arrival at this port.'[4] When Howe first
advanced into New Jersey, some months later, hundreds of
Americans responded to his proclamation and swore allegiance
to the king, but: 'In a very short time numbers of these people
were to be captured in arms against the British, with General
Howe's protections and certificates of loyalty in their pockets.'[5]
Two years later Howe found that Delaware and Pennsylvania
loyalists did not 'flock to his standard' as predicted by Lord
George.

In 1775 Carleton was confident that he could raise a regiment
or two in Canada to fight against the colonials in Boston, but
by the end of that year he reported that he could not do so, and

---

[1] 'The success that accompanied my endeavor to unite the inhabitants of this
city by an oath of allegiance and fidelity to his Majesty and his government has
met my warmest wishes: 2970 of the inhabitants having qualified thereto in my
presence' (Governor Tryon of New York to Germain, 11 Feb. 1777; *Documents
relating to the Colonial History of New York*, vii. 697; also Lecky, iv. 9).

[2] Lecky, iv. 22.   [3] Fortescue, *HBA*, 2, iii. 167.

[4] See p. 431, n. 1 above.

[5] Fortescue, *HBA*, 2, iii. 193.

that the loyalty of the Canadians was uncertain.[1] Burgoyne
began his campaign southward with the expectation that he
would find loyalists ready to enlist in up-state New York, but
after experience there he wrote to Lord George that he was
marching through territory in which every American hand was
against him. The British and German survivors of Bennington
ascribed their defeat as due in great part to natives who, protesting their loyalty to the Crown, joined the expedition and
then betrayed it.

Cornwallis was also optimistic about loyalist enlistments in
the Carolinas in 1780, though nine months earlier Clinton had
warned him and had also warned Lord George: 'I have as yet
received no assurances of any favourable temper in the province
of South Carolina to encourage me to an undertaking where we
must expect so much difficulty.'[2] Cornwallis too changed his
mind, and wrote from Wilmington, North Carolina, of the
loyalists: 'Our experience has shown that their numbers are not
so great as has been represented, and that their friendship was
only passive.'[3] At the high point of his success, Cornwallis once
called on local loyalists to join him, and failed to enlist a single
man. On other occasions 'loyalists' enlisted but proved undependable or worse. 'One whole corps which had been entrusted with the protection of sick soldiers, went over to the
enemy, giving up their officers and the sick soldiers as prisoners.'[4]
In another case: 'A rebel, who had sworn allegiance and obtained from Cornwallis not only a certificate of loyalty but a
commission in the royal militia, seduced his regiment from the
colonel and led it to join Sumter.'[5] Cornwallis found no alternative to shooting some American traitors from his ranks, which
naturally did not encourage further enlistments.

Lord George's deafness to such reports from his generals
became almost psychopathic. He preferred to believe the representations of men like Joseph Galloway, who as late as 1780

[1] '. . . the intrigues of the Canadians, who endeavored to persuade the Indians
to agree to a Neutrality with the Rebels, assuring them that such was their own
intention' (PRO, CO/5, v. 253, p. 16; Sept. 1775). '. . . the Canadians refusing to
serve against them, the greatest part of the Indians withdrew also' (PRO, CO/5,
v. 253, p. 6; 10 Sept. 1775).
[2] Clinton to Germain, 4 Apr. 1779; HMC, Stop. Sack. ii. 124, 125.
[3] Ross, Cornwallis Letters, 18 Apr. 1781.
[4] Lecky, iv. 213.   [5] Fortescue, HBA, 2, iii. 215.

wrote in *Plain Truth* that: '. . . a very great majority of the people in America are at this moment loyal to their sovereign, and wish to be perfectly united in polity with the British government and to become subjects of the British state'. A few months after Clinton's cautionary letter about loyalists in South Carolina, James Simpson assured Lord George that: '. . . whenever the King's troops move to Carolina, they will be assisted by very considerable numbers of the inhabitants'.[1] Governor Martin of South Carolina wrote to Lord George that the majority there were ardently loyalist.[2] But Cornwallis's aide Lord Rawdon reported in several letters directly to Lord George that even in South Carolina the loyalists had proved of little help, even in providing dependable information.[3] To the end Lord George preferred to base his strategy on reports such as those from his private agent Lieutenant-Colonel Balfour, who wrote that many of the chief citizens of North Carolina had sworn allegiance to the king and that many more would surely do so.[4]

It was probable that many Americans who would not risk fighting openly for the king privately preferred the British Government to the revolutionary one. There were other Americans who called a plague on both houses, and more who preferred to take no part and accept the winner. In the unfaltering belief that the majority of Americans did not wish independence, Lord George may, before Saratoga, have been correct. But when he drew from that belief the second one: that American loyalists would in great numbers enlist to fight the rebels, he was proved again and again to be wrong.

There is still wide disagreement as to the number of colonists whose real sympathies were steadily with the Crown. Were the Quakers of Pennsylvania to be counted as loyalist because, as pacifists, they would not take up arms on either side? Records of their meetings, and of the activities of many of them, indicate the contrary. In his examination before the House of Commons and in one of his pamphlets, Joseph Galloway insisted that nine-tenths, or at least four-fifths, of all the Americans were loyal to the king. General Grey, testifying on the same occasion, said

---

[1] Simpson to Germain, 28 Aug. 1779; *HMC, Stop. Sack.* ii. 137.
[2] Martin to Germain, 10 June 1780; *HMC, Stop. Sack.* ii. 168.
[3] Rawdon to Germain, Rawdon to Clinton, 24 and 28 Oct. 1780; *HMC, Stop. Sack.* ii. 185, 186.
[4] Balfour to Germain, 16 Jan. 1781; *HMC, Stop. Sack.* ii. 197.

that the American people were almost unanimously in favour of independence. General Robertson said that two-thirds of the Americans were loyal. Cornwallis, before his disastrous experience in the South, was cautious in his replies to Parliament, but appeared to agree more with Grey than with Robertson. Opinion in America was equally variant. In 1780 John Adams said that not more than one-twentieth of all Americans favoured the Crown, but in 1815, when he may have looked at the question with more detachment, he said that probably not more than one-third were opposed to full independence. Certainly the majority of America's influential leaders must have been on the side of the Continental Congress. Professor Crane Brinton reached in 1947 the conclusion that the group which engineered, actively supported, and largely fought the revolution comprised about 10 per cent. of the American population. But this does not mean that the rest opposed them, or opposed independence.

In proportion to the inducements offered in immediate pay and later rewards and standing if Britain won, the number of American loyalists who fought sincerely for the British cause is not impressive. It is far less impressive if one takes into account the loyalists who defected from the king's cause. At no time during the war were more than 7,000 Americans listed on the muster rolls of the British armies in the former thirteen colonies,[1] and the number did not increase as the war grated onward.

Whatever the number of latent loyalists, British strategy was bad in persistently over-estimating their potential military usefulness. 'At the bottom of the whole design lay the fundamental error of reliance on the help of the royalists.'[2] 'The mere fact that the British Ministry rested its hopes on the co-operation of American loyalists was sufficient to distract its councils and to vitiate its plans . . . of all foundations on which to build a

---

[1] Clinton's report of his total forces as of 21 May 1779 shows the maximum number of Provincials (American, Canadian, and West Indian) as 6,371, scattered from Newfoundland to the Leeward Islands (PRO, CO/5, v. 171, no. 35). On 5 July 1777 Howe wrote to Germain that his Provincials numbered about 3,000 (PRO, CO/5, v. 253).

On 29 Dec. 1779 Mr. Hopkins asked Germain in the House of Commons: '. . . what was the number of the provincial troops in America now, reminding the noble lord that he had formerly said we had a larger army of provincials fighting for us than Washington's whole army . . . Lord George Germain acknowledged he had last year stated the fact as the gentleman had alleged' (*Hansard*, xx. 1252, 1253).

[2] Fortescue, *HBA*, 2, iii. 206.

campaign this is the loosest, the most treacherous, the fullest of peril and delusion.'[1] 'Their purpose being vague and unconfined, the Ministers proceeded without any idea of what an army could or could not do, or of the force that was required for any given object.'[2]

That is hindsight, but there were a few men who, even in 1775, saw its truth. One of them was a military man of high authority. General Harvey, Adjutant-General of all the British armed forces, wrote in the middle of that year: 'Taking America as it at present stands, it is impossible to conquer it with our British army. . . . To attempt to conquer it internally by our land force is as wild an idea as ever controverted common sense.'[3] It is ironic that General Harvey's opinion was written to Lord George's friend General Sir John Irwin. Somewhat later, after Lord George had taken over the direction of the war and begun to reveal his strategy of charging in all directions, General Harvey wrote prophetically: 'Unless a settled plan of operations be agreed upon for next spring, our army will be destroyed by damned driblets.'[4] 'It was therefore the opinion of many, and among others of the Secretary at War, that the operations should be entirely naval.'[5]

Such opinions were disregarded, and the strategy substituted for them was first of all the strategy of Lord George Germain. One can hardly avoid agreeing with the conclusion of the most thorough student of British army operations that: '. . . when critically examined, the task of subduing the whole of the American colonies by force appeared to military men an impossibility.'[6]

---

[1] Fortescue, *HBA*, 2, iii. 168, 169.   [2] Fortescue, *HBA*, 2, iii. 169.
[3] Harvey to Irwin, 30 June 1775; Fortescue, *HBA*, 2, iii. 167.
[4] Fortescue, *HBA*, 2, iii. 169.   [5] Fortescue, *HBA*, 2, iii. 166, 167.
[6] Fortescue, *HBA*, 2, iii. 167.

XXIX

THE INEVITABLE HOUR

THE first certain news of Cornwallis's surrender reached London on 25 November 1781,[1] only two days before Parliament was to reconvene.[2] Lord George told Sir Nathaniel Wraxall that Lord North had received the news 'like a ball in the breast', and paced the floor exclaiming, 'Oh, God, it is all over!' The nation's apparent apathy changed overnight. After Saratoga the people had been mortified and angry; after Yorktown they accepted defeat and demanded a quick peace and a new government. Many supporters of the Ministry agreed that peace must be made, but disagreed with the Opposition as to who should make it, and whether it should be made at the price of complete independence of the former colonies.

Parliament opened as usual with an address from the Throne, and the country waited to hear what line that statement would take. But the speech had either been prepared before the news of Yorktown had arrived, or else it deliberately ignored it. It offered no realistic analysis of the situation, no new policies, no reforms, no changes, and revealed the mental bankruptcy of the Ministry. After another day or two of national dismay and stunned disorganization, the Opposition speakers took the floor with denunciations of the Government's failures at home and abroad, supported by petitions and remonstrances from all over England.[3] The Liveried Companies of London presented to the king a Remonstrance that minced no words: 'Your armies are captured; the wonted superiority of your navies is annihilated; your dominions are lost.'[4]

Burke, Barre, and Fox in the Lower House, Shelburne, Richmond, and Rockingham in the Lords, assailed the whole conduct of the war, and were joined by new voices like that of young William Pitt, second son of the Earl of Chatham. Fox as usual struck hard:

Gen. Burgoyne had been brave; gen. Burgoyne had failed; and

---

[1] Walpole, *Last Journals*, ii. 378.   [2] Lecky, iv. 201.
[3] Lecky, iv. 203.   [4] Walpole, *Last Journals*, ii. 386; 4 Dec. 1781.

gen. Burgoyne had been reviled, persecuted and proscribed; so had
general sir William Howe; so, perhaps in his turn, would be brave
and unfortunate earl Cornwallis: though he did not know where
those candid men [the Ministers] intended to fix the blame; whether
upon lord Cornwallis, or on sir Henry Clinton, or on both; or on
Admiral Graves, or on all. But it would soon be discovered; their
dirty literary engines would be set to work, and calumny would come
forth in all the insidious garbs that inventive malice could suggest.
They would place the blame anywhere but in the right place; but
on their own weakness, obstinacy, inhumanity, or treason.[1]

Lord North renewed his pleas to the king to be allowed to
resign, but the king, who still hoped to keep North in power and
America from independence, insisted that he needed him now
more than ever. The king's stubborn convictions gave him a
strength and stability in contrast with the discords and uncertainties in the Cabinet. George III declared privately that he
would lose his crown rather than the colonies, and even drew
up an announcement of his abdication. Lord North therefore
set himself once again, with reluctance, distaste, and foreboding,
to continue measures he did not approve, until he could persuade
the king to let them be altered. He tried to keep the country
gentlemen in line and to save at least a nucleus of the Ministry.
In those efforts he was faced with a quandary in tactics: should
he defend the Ministry by defending Lord Sandwich and Lord
George Germain, or should he let both be thrown to the Whig
wolves in the hope that the other Ministers would survive?
During December and January he vacillated between those
alternatives. He and the Ministry were given a chance to catch
their breaths and their balance by the Christmas recess of
Parliament from 20 December to 21 January 1782, but then the
Opposition renewed the attack.

What Lord George Germain really felt and thought cannot
be fathomed beneath his alternating outward defiance and
humility. On 12 December he ended his remarks before the
House of Commons with the rhetorical plea to: '. . . let ministers
be dismissed, be impeached, be punished, if they shall be found
to merit it'.[2] On other occasions he continued to insist that the
American loyalists were numerous and eager, and that with
their help the American war could yet be won. Previously he

---

[1] *Hansard*, xxii. 700.   [2] Ibid., xxii, 829.

had described the rank and file of the British Army in America as 'that fine body of soldiers', but in a new memorandum he made that 'fine body' a new scapegoat. 'The great mischief', he wrote, 'complained of in the prosecution of this war is that relaxation of discipline which disgraces the army and had alienated the affections of the inhabitants from the Royal cause. Plunder has been the object, and in the pursuit of it no distinction has been made between the well and the ill affected. This grievance cries aloud for redress.'[1] That magnificently inconsistent explanation threw light on Lord George's own military ethics, for he implied that plundering rebels was less reprehensible than plundering loyalists, if not highly satisfactory.

In that winter of national discontent Lord George occasionally gave voice to his old uncompromising defiance. He told the House of Commons, quite inaccurately, that: '. . . he had never solicited office; he had been called to it, and he was ready, without reluctance, to quit it; at the same time, he was not to be brow-beaten nor clamoured out of it . . . he yet believed we had many friends in the colonies, who would be happy at a reconciliation with this country, upon terms of dependence. He would never be the minister who gave up that dependence.'[2] Pownall, anticipating in late November the final act to come, and disregarding less noble motives, wrote: 'L. . . . G. G. goes out because he abides by his principles and will not give up the sovereignty.'[3]

Lord George's varying defence provided openings for his critics. Once when he used the word 'impeach', George Byng rose to comment: 'The noble Lord said "impeach me then; why do we not impeach him?". Let the noble Lord look round him, and he will see the reasons why he is not impeached. He will see a band of hired men ready to support him, or any minister who will pay them, against all the consequences of the American war. Give us an honest Parliament, and then let us see if the noble lord would desire to find his security in impeachment.'[4]

Two months later William Pitt returned to that charge:

[1] HMC, Stop. Sack. ii. 216 ff.　　　[2] Hansard, xxii. 726; 27 Nov. 1781.
[2] D. M. Clark, British Opinion, p. 251; also BM, Addit. MS. 20733.
[4] Hansard, xxii. 829; 12 Dec. 1781.

'. . . the noble lord and his colleagues, at the head of the American department, talked much at their ease of the effects of an impeachment; that they might well do so, backed by the present majority; but if the representative body was as pure and uninfluenced as it ought to be, he was very sure the noble lords would not feel so bold'.[1] He 'loudly called upon the House to extricate themselves from the disgrace of being subservient to the despicable views of a set of men who kept their places, and prosecuted the war from no other motive under Heaven than that of avarice'.[2]

However obscure were Lord George's innermost reactions, he was doomed and he knew it. But old habits remained, and he tried to make Admiral Graves the chief villain of Yorktown. He raised officially with the Earl of Sandwich, with whom he was bitterly at odds, the question of court-martialling Graves. He must have known that Sandwich would oppose it; perhaps he made the move only to irritate his colleague. Lord Sandwich replied with a straight face that he could find no evidence of any criminality in Admiral Graves's conduct: '. . . for want of success I can never allow to come under that description'. He told Lord George that if he wanted a court martial for Admiral Graves he would have to make charges and get the order directly from the king.[3] Lord George drew that red herring no further across the Yorktown trail.

He was ready enough to leave the Ministry, provided he could leave it with a peerage, and now, when most men thought he would be dismissed in disgrace, or fall with the Ministry, he had the rashness or persistence to hold to his price. On the very day that he defied the Opposition to impeach him he wrote to Irwin: 'You will have heard of nothing but changes &c in Administration. I was in hopes some arrangement would have taken place, and that I should have been released from the very unpleasant situation in which I find myself. I have said all that was possible to the King upon this subject, but hitherto it has produced no effect.'[4]

Lord George's desire for a peerage was understandable.

---

[1] *Hansard*, xxii. 846.
[2] Ibid., xxii. 845.
[3] Sandwich to Germain, 27 Jan. 1782; Clements, *Knox Papers*, vi. 34.
[4] Germain to Irwin, 12 Dec. 1781; *HMC, Stop. Sack*. i. 141.

Nothing less would give him an outwardly creditable exit from office, and also clothe the scar of Minden. His demand was not in itself unusual. Hanoverian monarchs bought Ministers out of service as naturally as they bought them in. A peerage was a high price to pay for the resignation of an unsatisfactory Minister, but it was not an unprecedented one. Under the curious *mores* of the court few men were openly dismissed outright: they were kicked or cajoled upstairs into innocuous posts or bought out with a title, ribbon, or income. The price depended on the greatness of the need of getting rid of the incumbent more than on the value of his past services. It also depended on the strength of his bargaining power. Under such heavy fire from all sides, Lord George's price seemed high only because his bargaining power seemed so small.

But it was greater than it looked. The king still had his reasons for not being willing to dismiss Lord George in apparent disgrace. It would be difficult to replace him with another Secretary who would support a continuance of the American war, and to dismiss Lord George without honour would be interpreted as a weakening of the king's determination not to grant Americans independence. Lord George must have his *pourboire*, but the king still stuck at making that *pourboire* a peerage. Lord George had not earned it, and that honour would anger many powerful men who had not forgotten Minden or the probable causes of the Saratoga and Yorktown disasters. As for Lord North, he was willing to see Lord George get a peerage to be rid of him, but he was not ready to fight out that issue with his sovereign. There were more important issues that would have to be fought out with the king. And as for Lord George himself, so strong was one of his personal enmities that even in this crisis he could not resist jeopardizing his strategic position in order to gratify it. He indulged once again in the detraction of Sir Guy Carleton.

When Clinton resigned after Yorktown Lord George asked the king who should succeed him. The king first replied that the appointment of a Commander-in-Chief was so connected with other uncertainties that he could not immediately suggest Clinton's successor, but a little later Lord George learned that Sir Guy Carleton had been summoned to the queen's house, and concluded that Carleton was under consideration as

Clinton's successor.[1] Then the king wrote to him regarding the replacement of Clinton:

Lord Cornwallis is now out of the case. . . . The Country will have more confidence in a new man, and I believe without partiality that the Man who would in general by the Army be looked on as the best officer is Sir Guy Carleton besides his place in the Commission of Public Accounts makes him well known in Parliament, his uncorruptness is universally acknowledged . . . whatever disagreements have been between you and him, I have no doubt if on consideration you should think him a proper person that both you and he will by some common friend so explain yourselves that . . . will make the public service be cheerfully carried on.[2]

Lord George replied promptly:

Sir Guy Carleton is looked upon by many people to be a good officer, and if your Majesty thinks him in that and every other respect qualified for so important a post, Lord George will be happy in hearing of his appointment. . . . The very extraordinary letters which Sir Guy Carleton chose to write Lord George still fill him with surprise and astonishment, as his motives for such conduct are still unknown, but the style and manner of them were improper to have passed between one gentleman and another, but Lord George would not presume to decide upon the propriety or impropriety used to your Majesty's servant when he was executing your command. . . . The little confidence which could ever subsist between Sir Guy Carleton and Lord George might, from your Majesty's great condescension and goodness, create some doubt in your mind whether the appointment proposed might not prejudice your Majesty's service, but in the present circumstances of affairs, there seems very little probability that your Majesty may find it convenient to continue the Seals much longer in Lord George's hands.[3]

Lord George had prepared most carefully that reply to the king, and had made at least two drafts of it before he sent the final one.[4]

This personal squabble was all the more foolish because Lord George was almost certain to lose it. The Cabinet was against

[1] HMC, Var. Coll. 6, Knox, pp. 272 ff.

[2] King to Germain, 15 Dec. 1781; Fortescue, Corresp. v. 313.

[3] Germain to King, 16 Dec. 1781; Fortescue, Corresp. v. 314. The document in the Clements Collection is dated 16 Oct. 1779, but neither its content nor Fortescue's assignment fits that date.

[4] Clements, Germain Papers, xvi.

him, and a week later resolved formally: '. . . that Lord George
Germain should take Your Majesty's pleasure upon the Appointment of a Commander-in-Chief in America to relieve Sir Henry
Clinton. It was thought improper to take any Minute upon the
subject until Your Majesty's sentiments were known. No officer
was named or so much as hinted at.'[1] This anonymous discretion
of the Cabinet was in contrast with the open directness of the
king, who replied to Lord Stormont three days later:

Sir Guy Carleton will certainly not accept the command if He is
to correspond with Ld. George Germain, the latter expects He should
unsay what stands in his correspondence, or the matter investigated
by the Cabinet that it may be seen whether the accusations are not
groundless: consequently if Sir Guy is appointed it decides that
Lord George Germain must, though with honour, give up the Seals
. . . if Sir Guy is fixed upon, Lord George Germain's successor must
be named at the same time. . . . On Friday I again pressed Lord
North for his opinion on the subject, and gained not the smallest
ground. He stated the advantages of the Measure and concluded
with desiring time to consider it. If Lord George is to go, a successor
must be immediately named to conduct the business . . . above all
I must be certain that a new Secretary is not of the yielding kind.[2]

Lord North's hesitation was justified. The issue of Lord
George and Carleton was part of a larger one. The withdrawal
of Lord George and the appointment of Carleton would not
save the Ministry if the king continued to insist on pursuing
the American war. That war must be promptly ended. But the
Carleton–Germain issue compelled Lord North to approach the
king on the larger one. He made his first attempt on 21 December, and the king's reaction was emphatic. Lord North's proposals for peace at any price would lead Britain, the king said,
to 'irrevocable destruction'.[3] Lord North characteristically postponed forcing the issue, hoping the king would soon see the
light. Of what use would it be to dismiss Lord George if the
king insisted that the new Secretary for America must be 'not
of the yielding kind'?

That impasse between George III and his First Minister
brought down upon Lord North stronger expressions of the

[1] Stormont to King, 22 Dec. 1781; Fortescue, *Corresp.* v. 318.
[2] King to Stormont, 23 Dec. 1781; Fortescue, *Corresp.* v. 319; also Almon,
Biog. Lit. Anec. ii. 137.
[3] King to Stormont, 21 Dec. 1781; Fortescue, *Corresp.* v. 317.

royal impatience than ever before. On 24 December the king wrote to him:

I shall therefore be very short on this occasion: undoubtedly if Sir Guy Carleton can be persuaded to go to America, he is in every way the best suited for the Service. He and Lord Germain are incompatible. Lord George is certainly not unwilling to retire if He gets his object, which is a Peerage; no one can then say he is disgraced and when his retreat is accompanied with the Appointment of Sir Guy Carleton the cause of it will naturally appear without its being possible to be laid with any reason to a change of my sentiments on the essential point, namely the getting a Peace at the expense of a Separation from America, which is a step to which no difficulties shall ever get me to be in the smallest degree an instrument. . . . If Lord North agrees with me that on the whole it is best to gratify the wishes of Lord G. Germain and let him retire, that no time may be lost, I desire he will immediately sound Mr. Jenkinson as to his succeeding him, for I must be ready with a successor before I move a single step.[1]

Lord North had at last won the king's conditional acquiescence to a peerage for Lord George, but that was cold comfort in view of the king's reiterated insistence on continuing the war if the alternative were 'separation'. He obediently approached Jenkinson, but that shrewd career man declined to accept the reversion of a post that Burke had moved to abolish and Washington had made anachronistic. Lord North remembered his classics; emulated Fabius Cuncator, and waited. The king restrained his impatience for nearly another month and then reported to his First Minister a conversation with Lord George:

Lord North not yet having come to any decision concerning Lord G. Germain put me this day in much difficulty. He having put the question to me whether he was or was not to look on himself as Secretary of State . . . to which I could only say that as yet no step had been taken to remove him, but that I thought I had a right to ask whether he was willing to remain, to which He spoke very candidly that if the War was carried on with vigour, if steps were taken to strike a blow in the West Indies, He was ready to stay, and that the separation with America was not adopted, but that He would never retract what he had said on that Head. He will be ready to talk with Lord North, but he will expect explicit and

[1] King to North, 24 Dec. 1781; Fortescue, *Corresp.* v. 326.

decisive language indeed I cannot blame him for that, for I think he cannot with honor continue unless he is supported by his Colleagues.[1]

By advocating vigorous war and no separation, Lord George had strengthened his position with the king.

Lord North was consequently forced to make another attempt to persuade the king to face the major issue:

I never suggested to your Majesty that the removal of Lord George Germain would prove of permanent benefit to your service, nor do I think it will, Because although many of my principal friends will become very lukewarm if he continues in office, I apprehend their objections are stronger against his System than his person. . . . If General Carleton were appointed Commr. in America, and Lord George Germain removed in an honourable and distinguished manner into the Upper House, and either Mr. Jenkinson or Lord Advocate[2] placed in a situation that would put it in their power to answer all American points, Your Majesty's affairs would certainly go with greater ease for a time. But I am afraid that the difficulties we are under will not be entirely removed by this measure. Peace with America seems necessary, even if it can be obtained on no better terms than some Federal Alliance, or perhaps even in less eligible mode.[3]

Still adamant on the peace issue and frustrated on the military front, the king made a final effort to bring about some agreement between Lord North and Lord George, who had been almost completely out of touch with one another. He urged that a private talk be arranged between them and it took place the following day. The king's faithful henchman Jenkinson must have listened at the keyhole or waited at the door to quiz the participants, for he reported immediately to his sovereign: 'The meeting . . . appears to have been very amicable, and as far as I can understand they differed less on American Politicks than might have been expected. They differed more on the person who was to have the Command in America, Lord George Germain objecting to General Carleton and proposing Lord Cornwallis, if he could be set at liberty, or General Vaughan.'[4]

---

[1] King to North, 17 Jan. 1782; Fortescue, *Corresp*. v. 331.
[2] Dundas, who was leading the fight to have Germain dismissed.
[3] North to King, 21 Jan 1782; Fortescue, *Corresp*. v. 336.
[4] Jenkinson to King, 22 Jan. 1782; Fortescue, *Corresp*. v. 340.

Other members of the Ministry cared less about the fate of
Lord George than their own. The astute Wedderburn, observing
the Ministry from his ringside seat, wrote to the equally shrewd
and observant Eden: 'My belief is that there is much jealousy
& uneasiness amongst the Ministers, that both Ld. G. and Lord
S[andwich] suspect designs agt. them and have much reason
for it. From the language of Persons about Lord N[orth] I form
a conviction that their removal would not be unpopular; at the
same time I am persuaded that Lord N. has no formed plan for
removing either.'[1]

Over Lord George's vehement opposition the Cabinet approved an immediate peace if it could be gained without conceding full independence. Knox reported:

. . . it was agreed that the troops now in America should remain
there and be kept up by recruits, but no new corps to be sent out.
Lord George Germain was called upon by the King to propose his
plan for employing those troops and bringing back the Colonies to
the sovereignty of this country. He put down his ideas on a paper
which I drew up in form and extended. A copy was sent to the King,
and another to each of the Cabinet ministers. In the meantime the
Bedford party were busy concerting a change in the Administration.
. . . Nothing was said about Lord George's paper for three weeks,
and by various accounts there was reason to believe a negociation
was going on for an alteration in the Ministry, and particularly for
the removal of Lord Sandwich and Lord George.[2]

Lord George's plan could not be expected to please the other
Ministers. He advocated holding New York, Charleston,
Georgia, and East Florida; maintaining an establishment of
14,000 troops in New York and another 14,000 effectives for the
other bases. He urged 'expeditions against the ports and towns
of the rebels along the coast' and spoke longingly of taking 'the
lower counties of the Delawarr, where the inhabitants in
general wish to return to their allegiance'. He also urged 'the re-
possessing of Rhode Island, should it be abandoned by the
French troops'.[3] The situation in America had changed since 1776
but not the strategy of Lord George. The plan may have pleased
the king, but the Cabinet virtually ignored it.

---

[1] Wedderburn to Eden, c. 13 Dec. 1781; Stevens, *Facsimiles*, x. 1045.
[2] *HMC, Var. Coll.* 6, *Knox*, pp. 272 ff.
[3] *HMC, Stop. Sack.* ii. 216 ff.

It is doubtful that any changes of policy could have saved
Lord George and the Ministry. Their ship of State was staggering and some of its paid hands were deserting. One of these was
Richard Rigby, a placeman of the Bedford junto, who had long
been Paymaster of the Forces and was believed to have made
a fortune from it.[1] Rigby had only once before shown independence, and that was when, as a friend of the Howes, he had
helped to bring about the last-minute continuance of the Howe
Inquiry. On 14 December 1781 he openly defected to the
Opposition.[2] James Hare described the event in a letter to the
Earl of Carlisle:

Changes in the Ministry are much talked of, and partial ones
generally believed. It is very clear that Rigby and some of his friends
are endeavoring to drive out Lord Sandwich and Lord George
Germaine; and when I have told you what he said in the House of
Commons, you will think he must have had this intention . . . Rigby
got up and said—'If there was any difference of opinion amongst
Ministers, and it did appear there was some difference, they ought
to speak out; the House had a right to expect it' etc. etc. Afterwards
in speaking of the necessity of keeping New York, he said—'What
can be expected in the present state of the Navy, God knows'.
. . . This was a direct attack on Lord Sandwich, as the former part
was understood to be on Lord George, who was suspected of still
intending to go on with the American War,—a notion that would
be extremely prejudicial to the Administration, as no measure of
Government would be more unpopular or odious than the prosecution of the War in America. Lord North, I am convinced, has
abandoned the idea, and wished to force Lord George to do so . . .
Lord George has lost only the good part of his speaking, his arrogance
and presumption, and is now all humility.[3]

Rigby may have been acting in secret collusion with Lord
North, and he certainly spoke with the approval of a more
dangerous opponent of Lord George within the Ministry. Henry
Dundas, later the first Viscount Melville, was Lord Advocate
for Scotland. 'Politically sagacious, blunt, indefatigably indus-
trious, convivial, utterly indifferent to money . . . for nearly
thirty years he was the most powerful man in Scotland.'[4] Dundas

---

[1] Jesse, *Selwyn*, i. 54. [2] Walpole, *Last Journals*, ii. 390.
[3] Hare to Carlisle, 1 Jan. 1782; *HMC, Var. Coll.* 5, 6, *Carlisle*, pp. 561, 562.
[4] *DNB*. Dundas (1742–1811), Solicitor-General for Scotland at the age of 24,
served as a member of Parliament from 1774 to 1790. He became Lord Advocate

did not think of himself as turning against the Ministry but as taking the only possible step to save it. He opposed independence to the Americans, but he had become convinced that Lord George Germain and the Earl of Sandwich must go if the Ministry was to survive and the war to be continued. The politically sagacious John Robinson—a party agent for the Ministry; steady, dull, shrewd, and humourless—advised him to concentrate his attack on one man or the other and recommended Lord George as the target—and Robinson was not likely to make any move that might offend the king.

Dundas at first attacked Lord George indirectly. He told the House of Lords that: '. . . if there was any disagreement amongst ministers, it was their bounden duty to declare it to the House', and with the weight of his authority implied that there was disagreement on basic policies.[1] Later he became more specific; deplored Lord North's having allowed himself to be overruled by Lord George, and openly demanded Lord George's dismissal. 'Fifty people', he wrote, 'came up to see me in private afterwards and thanked me for what I had done.'[2]

Dundas wrote to Lord North: '. . . that he could not serve any longer with Lord George Germain',[3] and held private talks on the topic with men in both parties. 'The ground they took was Lord George's declaration that he would never consent to any treaty with America by which the sovereignty of it was given up.'[4] When Parliament reconvened Dundas's forces gained new recruits, and not one member of the Ministry consistently defended Lord George. When he once again told the House of Commons that he would never concede American independence, Lord North made a very significant gesture. He rose from his place on the bench near Lord George and took a back seat. Everyone knew that the First Minister was pointedly dissociating himself from Lord George and his policies.

Lord George's disagreements with Sandwich had become so open and intolerable that Lord North was forced to make a

in May 1775 and though he supported the Ministry until 1782 he was always a man of his own mind. George III said in 1778: '. . . more favours have been heaped on the shoulders of that man than ever were bestowed on any Scotch lawyer, and he seems studiously to embrace every opportunity to create difficulties' (Fortescue, *Corresp.*, letter 454).   [1] *Hansard*, xxii. 852.
    [2] Christie, p. 289.   [3] Walpole, *Last Journals*, ii. 390.
    [4] Knox, in *HMC, Var. Coll.* 6, *Knox*, pp. 272 ff.

public choice between them. William Knox wrote flatly to his chief on 10 January that Sandwich had won: 'I have been told but not from high authority that Lord Sandwich is to remain & be supported and you are to be taken out of the House of Commons to prevent any disagreement on the conduct of the measure [the recall of Admiral Graves]. Jenkinson is intended to succeed you but not immediately.'[1]

Lord North's own position continued anomalous and unclear. He declared 'his wish for peace' but 'kept aloof about the terms'[2] and was losing some of his steadiest supporters. Just after Christmas Sir Walter Rawlinson, who had until then voted with the Ministry, gave notice that he would no longer support any continuance of the American war. Other Ministry dependables, one by one, began to make similar statements, and more might have done so if they had not yielded to the argument that the Ministry could negotiate a better peace if its hand seemed strong. The Opposition had an obvious reply to that: Since the Ministry and particularly Lord George were anathema to the rebellious Americans, they could not make a successful peace. 'I see plainly', Philip Yorke wrote to his uncle the Earl of Hardwick, 'that all Lord North's friends are desirous to reduce Lord George Germain to the necessity of going out.'[3]

Lord George continued to press for decisions. He asked the king flatly whether he was to continue, and who was to succeed Clinton. The king evaded both questions.

Lord George then told his Majesty that he thought it a proper time for him to go into the country, and wait till his situation was decided upon; that he had come into office in the hope of being of service, and that, if his Majesty found his going out would be of service, he was ready to take his leave. He requested his Majesty to be sure of his ground before he moved, and whatever he judged necessary to do for the strengthening of his government, not to defer it on personal consideration for his Ministers, for his case and theirs was very different, and affairs were now in such a situation that he must look to himself. After much conversation of this sort, the King agreeing that Lord George might properly go into the country, he took his leave and set off for Drayton.

---

[1] Knox to Germain, 10 Jan. 1782; Clements, *Germain Papers*, xv. 149; also *HMC, Stop. Sack.* ii. 295.   [2] Ibid.
[3] Christie, p. 291.

At least, that is the version Lord George reported to Knox, who wrote it down with his usual fidelity.[1]

Knox, left to deal with a Lord North so troubled that he had lost his genial equanimity, had a bad time of it. He was instructed to inform Lord George of the decision to appoint Carleton and reorganize the Ministry, and did so. Lord George replied with a message to Lord North, but as Knox delivered it, Lord North interrupted him: '. . . who had told Lord G. Germain that he [was] thinking of a plan for American affairs, or of making any alteration in Administration? It was an alteration of measures and not of men that was wanted, but perhaps Lord George thought the measures would be such as he should not approve. I made no answer, but pursued the delivery of my message, and when I had done, he said warmly, his own Department gave him full occupation, without attending to other matters.'

On 15 January Lord George returned to London. It was the fourth anniversary of his wife's death; his affairs were no happier now than they had been then. He tried to see the king but the king avoided him. He went to a meeting of the Privy Council and waylaid the king after that meeting. 'Here follows', wrote Knox, 'his report to me of what passed':

The King received him very kindly. Lord North had just come out from him. . . . At last, Lord George, finding an interval, ask'd him plainly, 'Am I Out'. 'Out', replies the King. 'What should make you suppose you were out?' He then assured him no proposition had been made to him for his going out. 'Why then, Sir, am I not told what are to be the measures? Why does not Lord North tell me what he intends?' 'Well', says the King, 'he will send to you'. Lord George then went into a repetition of the motives of his conduct . . . that his wish was to retire now, rather than be forced out some time hence, as he was sure must be the case if vigorous measures were not taken. The King answer'd, 'Conduct like your[s] occasion[s] a removal but to your satisfaction' . . . and so ended a conference of a full hour with that easy familiarity which meant to express satisfaction and to convey it.

The next day, a card came from Lord North, desiring Lord George to come to Downing Street the 19th at eleven o'clock. He went, and came away in a monstrous passion,

when he found that apparently Lord North had merely asked

<hr />

[1] Knox, in *HMC, Var. Coll.* 6, *Knox*, pp. 272 ff.

him to attend a general conference on Admiralty business. Lord George:

> ... had almost finished a letter to the King, telling him how he had been treated, and that it being evident Lord North meant he should go out, he desired his Majesty would acquaint him with his pleasure when he should bring the Seals, or to whom to give them. Robinson entreated him not to send the letter ... upon which he consented to keep back the letter till Monday. On Monday morning he received a very civil letter from Lord North declaring that he had no recollection of the King desiring him to converse with Lord George, and appointing Tuesday morning. ... The conference lasted an hour. ... Lord North said it was impossible to continue the war; that America was lost, and it was vain to think of recovering it. ... Nothing but Independence would do. ... Lord George said [that] would never be given by him, and, therefore, if such was his purpose, he must look out for another Secretary of State. ... Lord North: 'Your being out of the way won't mend matters, for the King is of the same opinion.' .. Nothing further having passed for some days, Lord George Germain spoke to the King upon the disagreeableness of his situation. ...[1]

That was Lord George's version of the interview and must be judged accordingly. It seems unlikely that he came as close to offering his resignation as his own account suggests.

Lord North might put off his advices to the king; the king might put off Lord George, but nothing could put off Dundas once he had made up his mind to rid the Ministry of Lord George Germain. Toward the end of January the Lord Advocate played his best trump. Accompanied by Rigby he stalked out of the House of Commons with the declaration that he would never return so long as Lord George was in office. Dundas was a valuable member of the Government, and the gesture was the more serious because he had many sympathizers who might decide to follow his example. Lord George read the handwriting on the wall. If he did not get his price for resigning soon, he might end by getting nothing at all. On 30 January he wrote to Lord North a letter that was all sweetness and self-sacrifice:

> I need not repeat to your lordship that I have no view in thus importuning you for decision than to promote as far as depends upon me the good of the King's service and the honour of your Administration.

[1] Ibid.

The uneasiness which is so universally expressed at the inactivity of government, the conjectures which are occasioned from those high in office and supposed to [be] high in your confidence absenting themselves from the House of Commons, call aloud for some declared plan of Government, and exertion in every department of business, and I should think myself inexcusable if I did not in the strongest terms again beseech your Lordship to dispose of me in that manner which may best answer your Lordship's views for his Majesty's service and the public good.[1]

Lord North knew what Lord George meant, and so did the king, who must at that point finally have committed himself to give Lord George a peerage if he would resign immediately.

Walpole was of course watching this drama and speculating on the motives of the several actors. Once again he anticipated events, for on 17 January he wrote to his friend Sir Horace Mann that: 'Lord George Germain has indubitably resigned, it is said, to be a peer, and that the office will not be filled up, its province being gone. His second tome has not been brilliant, but has made the first the more remembered—no advantage either.'[2] Lord George had not resigned and if his office became vacant there was no plan to let it stay so. Five days later Isaac Corry wrote to Eden the conviction that: 'Lord George is not yet formally disembarrassed of his office, but the thing is to happen: he seems to act not over graciously, & I believe it will appear that the King thinks so.'[3]

The politicians and gossips were watching and waiting like vultures. Eden, who must have regretted being on duty in Dublin and missing a front-row seat at the drama, was kept posted by Wedderburn: 'Ld. George I understand has expressed his wish to withdraw, but handsomely and submissively. He asks no Terms and does not press to be dismissed. His retreat whenever it happens is supposed to imply that our American pretensions are lowered.'[4]

Wedderburn should have known Lord George better. He might talk 'submissively' but he was still fighting hard for his terms. The odium of dismissal must be sweetened with a title. The king had also set his terms, and the two most stubborn men

[1] Germain to North, 30 Jan. 1782; HMC, Stop. Sack. i. 77.
[2] Walpole to Mason, 17 Jan. 1782; Toynbee, xii. 148.
[3] Corry to Eden, 22 Jan 1782; Stevens, Facsimiles, x. 1048.
[4] Wedderburn to Eden, 31 Jan. 1782; Stevens, Facsimiles, x. 1050.

in England stood with lowered heads and horns almost locked, while the one protested his devotion and the other his gratitude, and the nation slid further toward disaster. Walpole summed it up a week later. Lord George's exit, he wrote, was: '. . . not, I believe, an entirely voluntary act, much less a disgrace, but merely the effect of a disagreement with some of his colleagues'.[1] 'Don't imagine that *otium cum dignitate* was his own choice, still less his master's. . . . It is very diverting to hear how the courtiers now rail at Lord George, as if this was the moment of his greatest criminality.'[2]

Finally the king found a man who would accept the American Secretaryship. It was Welbore Ellis, '. . . a hack placeman', with 'the circumstantial minuteness of a church warden and the vigour of another Methusalem', 'who never minded what came into a day's work as long as it did not endanger a day's wages'.[3] But the king took no chances. He would not assure Lord George his peerage unless Lord George would first offer his resignation in the formal manner. The date for the interview was set and the king hastened to close the deal.

After . . . thanking Lord George for his services, his Majesty added, 'Is there anything I can do, to express my sense of them, which would be agreeable to you?' 'Sir', answered he, 'if your Majesty is pleased to raise me to the dignity of the Peerage, it will form at once the best reward to which I can aspire, and the best proof of Your approbation of my past exertions in Your affairs.' 'By all means', said the King. 'I think it very proper and shall do it with pleasure.' 'Then, sir', rejoined Lord George, 'if you agree to my first request, I hope you will not think it unbecoming, or unreasonable in me, to ask another favor. It is to create me a Viscount, as, should I be only raised to the dignity of a Baron, my own secretary, my lawyer, and my father's page, will all take rank of me.' The King expressing a wish to know the names of the persons to whom he alluded, 'The first', replied Lord George, 'is Lord Walsingham, who, as your Majesty knows, was long undersecretary in my office, when Mr. De Grey. The second is Lord Loughborough, who has always been my legal advisor, Lord Amherst is the third, who when page to my father, has often sat on the traces of the state-coach that conveyed

[1] Walpole to Mann, 7 Feb. 1782; Toynbee, xii. 154.
[2] Walpole to Mason, 7 Feb. 1782; Toynbee, xii. 158.
[3] Walpole to Mason, Walpole to Countess of Upper Ossory, 9 Feb. 1782; Toynbee, xii. 161.

him, as Lord Lieutenant of Ireland, to the Parliament House at Dublin'. The King smiled, adding, 'What you say, is very reasonable; it shall be so, and now let me know the title that you choose.'[1]

That is the version of the conversation that Nathaniel Wraxall claimed to have received from Lord George. Walpole did not report the king to have been quite so amenable, and said that Lord George 'insisted'.[2] It would have been interesting to have the king's own version, and the king's private comment on the explanation Lord George wrote to a friend: 'I am happily released from a most disagreeable situation, but I should not have quitted it, without the most avowed approbation of the King. He could not have shown it in a stronger light than by the honors he conferred on me, without any solicitation on my part.'[3] Walpole added colour but not accuracy to the episode by his comment: 'The universal belief is that the King approved entirely of his future plans respecting America, and was unwilling to dismiss him, but that the other Ministers were unanimous in desiring his removal.'[4]

The drama did not end there, but shifted to the House of Lords, where the last act was the most bitter of all. When the new peer was presented to the Lords as a *fait accompli*, and especially when his rank proved to be the exalted one of viscount, the Lords indulged in one of the largest,[5] most impassioned, and most vituperative sessions ever connected with the admission of a new member. Peer after peer rose to inveigh against the man of Minden and, by unspoken implication, against the king for honouring a man: '. . . whose disgrace was entered in the Orderly Book of every British regiment'.[6] Lord

---

[1] Wraxall, ii. 126, 127.

[2] 'It was intended that, as usual, he should be only a Baron, but he insisted on the higher step, as he said he would not take place after his aid-de-camp, his secretary, and his advocate, who all now were Barons' (Walpole, *Last Journals*, ii. 399).

[3] Germain to Edward Pery, 19 Feb. 1782; *HMC*, xiv. 9, *Emly MSS.*, p. 162. Pery was Speaker in the Irish House of Commons.

[4] Walpole, *Last Journals*, ii. 399.

[5] During the war years attendance at the House of Lords rarely exceeded 70. At the Howe Inquiry in 1778 the average attendance was just over 80. At the debate on the causes of Yorktown over 106 were present at one time. On the day when the admission of Viscount Sackville was scheduled, 128 peers were present (Turberville, *House of Lords*, p. 6).

[6] *Hansard*, xxii. 1003; also Fitzmaurice, *Shelburne*, iii. 125. The attack on Lord George began on 7 Feb., before the official announcement (*HMC, Var. Coll. 6, Knox*, p. 183).

Shelburne took advantage of the chance to condemn the whole
Ministry, since by '. . . intrusting him with the management of
the war, they in a manner began the war with the greatest
insult to America that could possibly have been devised'.[1] The
Earl of Southampton, who as Captain Fitzroy had carried the
orders from Prince Ferdinand to Lord George Sackville at
Minden, joined in the attack; rehearsed Lord George's conduct
there, and assured the Lords that his own testimony before the
court martial '. . . had not been animated by a factious spirit'.[2]
Other noblemen made even more emphatic their objection to
traitors, cowards, and blunderers, and the Earl of Abingdon
capped their remarks by pronouncing the new viscount '. . . the
greatest criminal his country had ever known', and 'the author
of all the calamities of the war'.[3] Through most of these tirades
Lord George was present, but he issued no challenges to a
morning exchange of aristocratic pistol-shots in Hyde Park.

The Marquis of Carmarthen, eldest son of the Duke of Leeds
and at the time only thirty years of age, tried to bring all the
talk to action. He protested admitting to their order a man
'. . . stamped by an indelible brand, and by a sentence that had
never been cancelled . . . a disgrace to the House of Lords that
any person labouring under so heavy a sentence of a court
martial, and the consequent public orders, should be recommended to the Crown as worthy the dignity of a peerage'. His
motion was supported by the Dukes or Earls of Chatham,
Devonshire, Pembroke, Craven, Derby, Egremont, Abingdon,
Rutland, Portland, and a few others.[4]

Fortunately for the new viscount this almost unprecedented
motion raised the constitutional question of the right of the king
to create any man a peer on the recommendation of the
Ministry in power, and the right of the Lords to reject such a
peer. That was a question neither party cared to make an issue
at the time. Lord George also had the good luck to be defended
by one of Britain's most heavy-weight debaters, the beetle-
browed and overwhelming Lord Chancellor Thurlow.[5] His
defence was pronounced: '. . . one of the most powerful speeches
. . . that perhaps ever fell . . . from the mouth of any member of

---

[1] *Hansard*, xxii. 1006.
[2] Ibid., xxii. 1013; also *HMC, Amer. MSS.*, ii. 2.　　　[3] *Hansard*, xxii. 1001.
[4] Ibid., xxii. 1001–21.　　　　　　　　　　[5] Walpole, *Last Journals*, ii. 143.

the House'.[1] When the vote on Carmarthen's motion was finally
taken it was lost by 75 to 28, but many who voted against it
were reluctant to welcome Viscount Sackville into the House of
Lords. Carmarthen and his supporters were successful in getting
recorded in the Journal of the House their opinion that Lord
George's elevation to the peerage was: '. . . a measure fatal to
the interests of the Crown, insulting to the memory of the late
Sovereign, and highly derogatory to the dignity of that House'.[2]

Selwyn, like Walpole, watched this exalted fracas with
mingled amusement and distaste, but his judgements were less
captious than those of the seigneur of Strawberry Hill. In suc-
cessive letters to Lord Carlisle, Selwyn commented:

I do not perceive that Lord Carmarthen has got any repu[ta]tion
from his violence against Lord George. . . . It was a Motion cruel
and illmannered, and not becoming one man of quality to another;
at the same time an unpardonable insult to the Crown.[3]

Public affairs are at a standstill till people are tired of arguing
about Lord Sackville. He came and played his whist last night at
Whites; Lord Car was not there. His Lordship, I mean Lord S,
preserves a steady countenance and *va son chemin*.[4]

I have no liking and esteem for Lord Sack, or ever had any more
than an acquaintance with him, but from the first to the last I have
believed that he has been sacrificed to the implacability of P.
F[erdinand], the late Duke of Cumb[erland], and the late King,
helped on by all the private malice and flattery in the world; and
all which I heard last night, of which I cannot have the least doubt,
confirms me in that opinion. I am clear in nothing concerning his
personal merit, or defects, excepting of his abilities, and when these
could be of any use to Party, they were extolled, and his imperfec-
tions forgot. He was invited to take a share in Government by the
people who think, or have pretended to think, him a disgrace to the
peerage.[5]

The new viscount, who had taken the peer's oath before the
worst of the attack, demonstrated once again that he was not
lacking in polemic courage. He listened quietly to the diatribes
against him, and after the motion to exclude him had been
defeated he rose to make a maiden speech that was not an
example of maiden modesty or the deference of a neophyte so

---

[1] Turberville, *Lords*, p. 24, footnote.   [2] *Hansard*, xxii. 1020, 1021.
[3] Selwyn to Carlisle, Feb. 1782; HMC, *Var. Coll.* 5, 6, *Carlisle*, p. 572.
[4] Ibid., p. 577.   [5] Ibid., pp. 579, 580.

reluctantly received. With a dignity that at times approached the old arrogance he offered no word of regret or apology for any word or action of his past. '. . . he knew not to whose advice he was indebted for his peerage, but as the sentence of the court martial did not amount to a disqualification, he was authorized to accept it.' The court martial 'amounted to no disqualification whatever . . . he was made the victim of the most unexampled persecution that ever a British officer had been pursued with. . . . Faction and clamour had condemned him, and punished him before his trial. He challenged his accusers; he had provoked inquiry and, in the pride of conscious innocence, he had persevered in demanding a trial. He would risk his honor and his life on the decision of the House, or even of the Marquess of Carmarthen as a man of honor.'[1]

It was an impressive performance though hardly a disarming one. According to one contemporary chronicler: 'His enemies confessed, that never was a more dignified or manly appeal within the walls of the House of Peers, than Lord Sackville pronounced on that occasion',[2] but for all his professed detachment Lord George did not disguise his resentment against the peers who had attacked him. He was reported so angry that the Duke of Gloucester had not supported him against Carmarthen: '. . . that he not only forebore going to Gloucester House but forbade his daughters going thither—thus excluding himself from the most creditable and honourable of those few houses where he was received, the number of which was not likely to increase now that he had lost all power'.[3] Later events would show how ardently he cherished resentment against Lord Carmarthen.

The removal of Lord George from the Ministry proved an inadequate sop to Opposition and people, especially since it was accompanied by so high a 'mark of the King's favour'. It postponed for only a few weeks the fall of Lord North. At the beginning of March most of the country gentlemen served formal notices that they would no longer support the war and consequently the Ministry,[4] and from that time both were doomed. Fighting back against personal attacks, Lord North for the first

<hr />

[1] *Hansard*, xxii. 1020–1.   [2] Wraxall, ii. 129.
[3] Walpole, *Last Journals*, ii. 401.
[4] Richard Pares, *Limited Monarchy*, Hist. Assn., 1957, pp. 22, 25.

time threw the chief blame for the loss of the American war on his recent Secretary for America, who, he said, had misled him regarding the numbers, devotion, and military value of the loyalists in America. But nothing could save a British Ministry that had both raised taxes and lost a war, and in March Lord North resigned and Lord Rockingham was reluctantly summoned by the king to form a new government. By that time Lord George had taken up his third and last incarnation as Viscount Sackville, retired statesman, of Bolebrook, Westminster, Drayton, Stoneland Park, and, on occasion, of the reassuring fastnesses of Knole.

XXX

PRIVATE LIVES

VISCOUNT SACKVILLE was free, as Lord George Germain had never cared to be, to cultivate friendships for their own sake. It was too late to plant new gardens; he could do little more than water the friendships he had begun in earlier years. Since he had cultivated few, the crop was meagre.

Lord George's ancestry had done much for him. Without the Sackville connexions and the Dorset influence he would not have risen so rapidly, and might have received a sterner sentence from the Minden court martial. But the family that helped him does not seem to have inspired him with much more than formal gratitude, and there is little to indicate that his affection for its members was very close or enduring. If there was an exception it was the first Duke of Dorset. Until Minden, father and son were on a basis of easy camaraderie. Lord George Sackville's letters to the duke show him at his most honest and attractive.

While all was going well, such a relationship was undemanding, and need not have gone very deep. Minden put it to the test. The old duke met that test; his loyalty to his disgraced son was steadfast, and went far beyond the conventional. He was so shattered by the verdict that he apparently never recovered his former spirits and pleasure in society. One can only conjecture what he really felt toward this son who had been branded by a court martial, but his loyalty and suffering deserved filial devotion of equal strength. There is no evidence that his last years were solaced by any special warmth or appreciation from his youngest son.

As for the duchess, if Lord George was ever more than dutifully deferential to her, there is no trace of it. Letters between them may have been lost or destroyed, but even so a close devotion between mother and son would have left some hints in the extensive family records. Reticence alone could hardly have left so clean a slate. The only clues are negative. Lord George's grandmother, the Dowager Duchess of Northampton,

was credited with much of his upbringing, and it was Lady Betty
Germain to whom his devotion in later years seemed greatest.
An unscrupulous romanticist might suggest that Lady Betty's
relationship with the gallant duke was more intimate than
friendship, and that the duke's son to whom Lady Betty left her
fortune was her son too. Such a story would be arrant speculation, and there is not a single fact to justify it.

In several long letters to his father from Germany in 1743
Lord George made but one reference to his mother. 'I hope the
Duchess is well', was all he wrote, though there were affectionate
messages to Lady Betty. Many years later, when the old duke
was dying, Lady Betty (and this is Lord George's own account)
was sent for. She came; she was stricken; she suggested to the
duchess that she ought not to remain; the duchess urged her to
stay, and she did stay. Lord George's letter to Irwin describes
in detail the deathbed scene but hardly mentions the duchess,
except to report: 'The Duchess is remarkably well and has
removed to town.'[1] The only later extant reference by Lord
George was three years later in another letter to Irwin: 'The
Duchess died on Sunday morning happily without pain or
struggling which I confess was beyond my expectation as her
Constitution naturally was so strong'—and the letter then
turned, without further comment, to political events in Westminster.[2]

Of Lord George's three sisters the eldest, Lady Anne, died
at the age of eleven in 1721. Lady Elizabeth, two years older
than Lord George, was married at the age of fourteen to Thomas
Thynne, second Viscount Weymouth, but they never lived
together. He died three years later while on the Grand Tour
with his sister and her husband Lord Bateman. Lord Bateman
supported Lord George after Minden, and they were on friendly
terms in 1775 when the Batemans visited Lord George,[3] but
there are no further references to Elizabeth. With his third
sister, Caroline, Lord George seems to have been on consistently
affectionate terms, and Lord George's own third daughter was
given her name. Lady Caroline became a person to be reckoned

---

[1] Sackville to Irwin, 25 Apr. 1765; Clements, *Germain Corresp.* iii. 40/88.
[2] Sackville to Irwin, 14 June 1768; Clements, *Germain Corresp.* iii. 66/140.
[3] Sackville to Irwin, 13 June 1775; Clements, *Germain Corresp.* iii. 88/182; and
DNB.

with in politics. She married Joseph Damer and became Lady
Milton and later the Countess of Dorchester. The Duchess
of Northumberland wrote that she '. . . governs the Duke of
Argyle and thro him Scotland'.[1] Lord George's Scottish connexions were among his chief political assets, and in the political
crisis after Saratoga Lord Milton defended Lord George vigorously in Parliament and expressed '. . . a violent animosity to
the Americans'.[2] The young Captain Damer who wrote privately
to Lord George from Cornwallis's army was his nephew, and
later became the Earl of Dorchester. But no matter what the
depth of Lord George's devotion to his sister Caroline may have
been, it held no possibilities for Viscount Sackville, for she died
in 1765.

Lord George's two brothers were not men to engender fraternal pride, and their conduct would have put to severe tests the
affection of the most devoted of brothers. Charles Lord Middlesex, heir to the dukedom and to Knole, added no lustre to the
Sackville name. He was not a son that the solid, conventional
Duke of Dorset could like or even understand, or that an
ambitious younger brother could admire. He was facile, irresponsible, unstable, and persistent only in his indiscretions. After
Westminster School and Christ Church, Oxford, and a year or
two on the Continent, he returned to disconcert and impoverish
his family. His radical politics and mounting debts were more
than the duke could endure, and for some years they were not
on speaking terms.[3] In 1734 Charles was given one of the family
seats in Parliament, but his politics so offended his father that
the duke insisted he vacate the seat. Charles did so, but with the
stubborn energy sometimes displayed by weak characters, he
won another seat outside the family bailiwick and held it until
1749. If he made any contributions to the wisdom of the House
of Commons they are not notable in its records.

In other activities, however, Lord Middlesex made his mark,
for he was a true Sackville in his propensity for pushing his
interests to extremes. The chief objects of his devotion were
London's operas and London's ladies of easy virtue, and the two
pursuits were not mutually exclusive. The family wealth he

---

[1] Greig, *Diaries of the Duchess of Northumberland*, p. 21.
[2] Walpole, *Last Journals*, ii. 125; 5 Nov. 1778.
[3] Fitzmaurice, *Shelburne*, p. 342.

squandered on them made him notorious even in a society tolerant of aristocratic debts and wild oats. The Dorset estates could not sustain these enthusiasms on such a magnificently all-embracing scale, and Horace Walpole wrote of the London opera in 1743: 'Lord Middlesex is the impresario, and must ruin the House of Sackville by a course of these follies. . . . The Duke of Dorset has desired the King not to subscribe.'[1] Lord Middlesex also wrote verses that were said to be frail imitations of Pope—an activity less expensive than divas and demi-mondes but not one especially consoling to the duke.

Lord Middlesex then temporarily improved his financial position by marrying a great heiress. Grace Boyle was the only daughter of the second Viscount Shannon, and Lord Middlesex must have fallen more in love with her pecuniary charms than with her beauty, for she was: '. . . very short, very plain, and very yellow',[2] 'low and ugly'.[3] Possibly Lord Middlesex married her for her mental attractions, as she was thought to be '. . . a vast scholar',[4] 'full of Greek and Latin, and music and painting, but neither mischievous nor political'.[5] Whatever the cause of his devotion it was short-lived, for he soon squandered her estate on mistresses as well as operas, until she was reduced to begging her husband's younger brother for financial help. Lord George replied: 'I am sorry that my Ld. Middlesex's behaviour toward me for a considerable time has been such as makes it impracticable for me to concern myself with his affairs.'[6] Other friends ultimately proved more helpful to Lady Middlesex, though not all perhaps from the purest motives. She must have had charms beyond her Greek and Latin to soothe the royal breast, for it was believed that she was on terms of great intimacy with the Prince of Wales,[7] 'to which her husband appears to have submitted very quietly'.[8] By 1752 both were members of the prince's inner circle and active in its political and social intrigues.

[1] Walpole to Mann, 4 May 1783; Toynbee, i. 344, 345.
[2] Greig, *Diaries*, p. 84.
[3] Walpole to Mann, 22 July 1744; Toynbee, ii. 40.
[4] Ibid.   [5] Greig, *Diaries*, p. 84.
[6] Marlowe, p. 74.
[7] Wyndham, *George Bubb Dodington, Lord Melcomb, Diary*, i. 150. I find nothing in these diaries to justify Shelburne's citation of them to support his suggestion that Lady Middlesex was actually the mistress of the prince.
[8] Fitzmaurice, *Shelburne*, i. 342, 343.

Lord George was also angling for the prince's favour, but that did not prevent him from displaying, even at Leicester House, his disapproval of his brother and his wife. The Princess of Wales told Bubb Dodington that: 'Lord George had been with Lady Middlesex twice, in the same house with her, and never once saw or asked after her.'[1] Dodington persistently worked to reconcile Lord Middlesex with the Duke of Dorset and was finally partly successful.[2] The duke paid off some of his son's debts, but between 1743 and 1763 Lord Middlesex was rarely if ever at Knole.[3] The break between the two brothers was enduring, and even after Lord Middlesex finally returned to Knole Lord George's comments to Irwin were lacking in fraternal warmth: 'Lord Middlesex intends going to Knole when he can settle his affairs with Stephenson, but his Lordship does not ride post in business.'[4] Two weeks later Lord George wrote again that: 'Lord Middlesex is arrived among us. He looks over the old place with a degree of curiosity and pleasure, but does not seem surprized at having been absent from it these twenty years.'[5] Another fortnight brought Lord George a little more sympathy with the returned prodigal: 'Lord Middlesex stayed ten days with us, and seemed really happy at being at liberty to please himself; and the air of Knole worked miracles in his favour, for he grew young and lively.'[6] Lord George's phrases imply that his brother had been suffering from some illness, possibly mental, that required supervision. His later career justifies that assumption, and so does a comment by Lord Shelburne that: 'his conduct savoured so strongly of madness'.[7] His return to Knole may also have been connected with the illness of the ageing duke.

Two years later, in 1765, the duke died and Lord Middlesex succeeded to Knole and the dukedom, though without his

---

[1] Wyndham, *Dodington*, p. 189.

[2] Ibid., pp. 155, 156; 2 Oct. 1752. Eight months later Dodington was still trying to effect a reconciliation, and told the duke that Middlesex's debts to tradesmen 'cannot much exceed £4000' (12 June 1753; Clements, *Germain Papers, Home Affairs*, photostats 12, 14).

[3] In 1763 Lord George wrote of Lord Middlesex as 'having been absent from it these twenty years' (Sackville to Irwin, 1 July 1763; *HMC, Stop. Sack.* i. 92).

[4] Sackville to Irwin, 15 June 1763; *HMC, Stop. Sack.* i. 92.

[5] Sackville to Irwin, end of June 1763; *HMC, Stop. Sack.* i. 92.

[6] Sackville to Irwin, 13 July 1763; *HMC, Stop. Sack.* i. 93.

[7] Fitzmaurice, *Shelburne*, i. 343.

Lady Grace, who had died two years before. He was immediately in disagreement with Lord George over the interpretation of their father's will. It was inevitable that the title and Knole should revert to the eldest son, but the duke had left his residuary estate to Lord George: '. . . as I understood it would be', Lord George wrote to Irwin. 'Lord Middlesex I still call him . . . was not pleased as you may imagine, tho' I often told him how it would prove.' The new duke questioned the will and made claims, but Lord George insisted that: 'I knew it was intended otherwise' and did not yield an inch or a pound, though he wrote to Irwin that he was: '. . . resolved above all things to avoid if possible any family discussion' and that he had suggested arbitration. Lord George received, he said: '. . . above half of what the Duke died possessed of'. Having had his way, Lord George wrote piously to Irwin: 'I sincerely hope that the present union in our family may continue; at least I am resolved to have nothing to reproach myself with if it should happen otherwise.'[1]

The family union thus achieved was neither close nor warm. Lord George's letter to his brother proposing the reconciliation was more like a diplomatic note to ease a cold war than a pledge of brotherly love: 'Lord George has nothing more at heart than to preserve that union in the family which he flatters himself now happily subsists, and he is sensible that any disagreement between Lord Middlesex and him will lessen the credit and consideration of them both. Lord George is resolved on his part to take every step that may prevent even the appearance of any misunderstanding and trusts he shall find the same friendly disposition in Lord Middlesex.'[2] Lord George had a special reason for goodwill; he wanted the control of the two parliamentary seats at East Grinstead. There is no sign that the duke embraced the advances thus made to him on the eve of his new prosperity and power, though Lord George continued to go occasionally to Knole.

By that time Charles had the appearance of: '. . . a proud, disgusted, melancholy, solitary man.'[3] He took almost no part in social or political life appropriate to his new station, and did

---

[1] Sackville to Irwin, 25 Oct. 1765; Clements, *Germain Corresp.* iii. 40/88.
[2] Sackville to Dorset (Middlesex), 10 Oct. 1765; HMC, *Stop. Sack.* i. 46.
[3] Fitzmaurice, *Shelburne*, i. 342, 343.

not improve a Knole that had suffered from his earlier extravagances. Indeed he embarked on still more shocking depredations.
To most Englishmen the duke's debts were more pardonable
than his wanton act of having the magnificent old trees of Knole
park cut down. 'He has not left a tree standing in the venerable
old Park', Walpole wrote in 1769,[1] and Lady Mary Coke was
even more vehement: '. . . happy had it been if he had died three
months ago, for since that time he has cut down all the wood in
the Parke at Knowle, even the trees of his father's planting'.[2]

By that time the duke was in his own final illness, as Lord
George reported without apparent great sadness to Irwin, adding that his brother was: '. . . surrounded by . . . a set of bad
people who are making him sign papers little to his credit and
less to his advantage', and that he, Lord George, was doing all
he could to prevent the mischief.[3] Lord George had more than
a sentimental interest in preserving the estate, since one of his
sons might in time succeed to it. Though he did not manage to
save the trees he did save most of the inheritance, for Walpole
reported of the dying duke: '. . . the family think themselves
very happy that he did not marry a girl he kept, as he had a
mind to, if the state of his understanding had not empowered
his relations to prevent it'.[4] In less unctuous words, the family
had secured legal opinion that Duke Charles was mentally
incompetent to make a will. He died 'in a fit' at the age of 58,
'having worn out his constitution and almost his estate'.[5]

Yet the unhappy Charles had some qualities that won him
defenders. In his efforts to mediate between Charles and the old
duke, Bubb Dodington had praised Charles's literary ability.
He wrote to the duke of an essay by Lord Middlesex: 'I believe
there is not One Man of his Rank, or near it, in this country,
that can write such another.'[6] The Duchess of Northumberland
recorded of Charles in her diary at the time of his death: '. . . he
was a great Patron of Musicians and by no means an inelegant
Poet himself he was reckined to have good Parts & to be an
admirable Scholar but he was shy & little known in the world'.[7]

---

[1] Walpole to Mann, 14 Jan. 1769; Toynbee, vii. 250.
[2] Lady Mary Coke, *Letters and Journal*, iii. 6, 7.
[3] Sackville to Irwin, 5 July 1768; *HMC, Stop. Sack.* i. 127.
[4] Walpole to Mann, 24 Jan. 1769; Toynbee, vii. 250.
[5] Ibid.   [6] Clements, *Germain Papers*.
[7] Greig, p. 84.

And no matter what people thought of the duke, the conduct of his younger brother shocked even sophisticated members of Hanoverian society. Lady Mary Coke threw light on one example of Lord George's brotherly affection: 'H.R.H. was surprised to hear of Lord George Sackville being at the Drawing-room on Tuesday. His brother the Duke of Dorset dyed only on Friday and could not then be buried. There is certainly very little Affection and still less Decency practiced in this Country'.[1]

Duke Charles left no legitimate children, but one of his by-blows, known as Charles Sackville, became a banker of some ability and standing. He made himself useful to the Sackville family by managing the financial affairs of his legitimate but less competent uncles and cousins and Lord George left him a legacy of £100 a year. He died in Venice in 1795.

The career of Lord George's second brother, Lord John, was equally brief and more sad. Though less given to devastating excesses than his elder brother, Lord John suffered earlier and more constantly from emotional imbalances and fits of melancholia that made impossible a normal life in Knole society.[2] He was conscious of his disorders, and his attempts to overcome them were pathetically recorded, and justify the term of 'fighting off madness'. Lord Shelburne called his malady: '. . . a disorder which there was much reason to suppose ran in the blood'.[3]

Hints from more than one source suggest that the title of Middlesex might have been more appropriate to John than to his brother Charles. Lord Shelburne wrote that: '. . . after marrying a daughter of Lord Gower under some very strange circumstances', Lord John 'behaved very strangely when he was embarking on some expedition', but does not explain.[4] Later he referred to an unhappy episode on the Continent. In 1744 Lieutenant-Colonel Russell, in camp near Lisle, wrote to his wife in London: 'Your account of Lord John Sackville surprises everyone here, we having a much more honourable way of

---

[1] Lady Mary Coke, *Letters and Journals*, iii. 6, 7.

[2] Lord John's melancholy was probably increased by a financial disappointment in 1743, when he failed to receive the estate of Lord Wilmington, as he had been given reason to expect. It went to Lord Northampton instead, possibly for reasons suggested in the next paragraph (Lord George to Dorset, 2 Sept. 1743; and Bishop of Kildare to Dorset, 14 July 1743; *HMC, Stop. Sack.* i. 37).

[3] Fitzmaurice, *Shelburne*, i. 343.   [4] Ibid.

thinking in this part of the world', but again no explanation is forthcoming. Six months later Colonel Russell reported from Plymouth: 'Lord John Sackville, I do suppose you know, has resigned, and Colonel Cesar is come down here and has his company.'[1] Lord Shelburne explained only that: '. . . his family thought it most prudent that he should resign his commission and undergo a sort of family exile near Lausanne'.[2]

Whatever the cause of these obscure allusions, Lord John was exiled to Vevey and spent the rest of his life there under supervision. In 1753 and 1754 he wrote pathetic letters to his younger brother George, constantly hoping: '. . . that I have a friend in you that will do me all the service he is able, and will listen to the voice of reason'; constantly reporting that his health: '. . . is much as it was';[3] acknowledging his faults without naming them; begging Lord George to intercede for him with the duke their father, and asking for 'a last trial' to let him show that he can be his own master, that he may 'have some comfort' in his life.[4] He complained often of his overseer-companion, and begged that he be replaced by 'a very worthy gentleman' who said he was a relation of Sir John Ligonier.[5]

Lord John's father and brothers never saw fit to leave him to his own management, to finance him comfortably, or to trouble to see him. 'I am very sorry', he wrote to Lord George, 'that you still advise me to reconcile myself to Mr. Villettes. Though he knows I am greatly in debt, he sends me but just enough to pay for my board and my servant's wages, so that I have to borrow money where I can get it, besides contracting debts with tradesmen for clothes, etc. . . . Could I be reinstated in my full income of 400 Pounds a year, I hope my future conduct would prove satisfactory to the Duke and Dutchess and all my friends.'[6] He reported that he had written to his wife, presumably in England: '. . . that she should come and live with me in this

---

[1] Russell to Mrs. Russell, 6 Aug. and 20 Sept. 1744; *HMC, Franklin, Russell, Astley* (1900), p. 333.

[2] Fitzmaurice, *Shelburne*, i. 343.

[3] 'I think if there be any difference the low fit does not last quite as long as it used to, the good spirits two or three days longer; but while it does last the low fit is more violent and the high fit less so' (Lord John to Lord George Sackville, 8 July 1753; *HMC, Stop. Sack.* i. 38).

[4] Lord John to Lord George Sackville, 23 Apr. 1754; *HMC, Stop. Sack.* i. 39.

[5] Ibid.

[6] Idem, 5 June 1754; *HMC, Stop. Sack.* i. 39.

country, and bring master and miss along with her . . . but I think I had better get settled and free from debt first'.[1]

It would be natural to assume that the Sackville family kept Lord John on a tight financial string because he was, like his brother, excessively extravagant, but three facts belie this. No reference to such extravagance exists; he appears to have been living at Vevey on an allowance of less than £400 a year, and Lord Shelburne saw him near Lausanne: '. . . in the winter of 1760 living upon a very poor allowance and but very meanly looked after. He was always dirtily clad, but it was easy to perceive something gentleman-like in his manners, and a look of birth about him under all his disadvantages. His conversation was a mixture of weakness and shrewdness as is common to most madmen.'[2]

Lord John's affairs are relevant only as they throw light upon Lord George. If Lord George answered most of those pathetic letters there is no record of it.[3] For twelve years there is no evidence of further correspondence, and during that period Lord George did not go to Switzerland. He made no reference to his brother until 1763, when he wrote to Irwin from Knole: 'I have bad accounts of Lord John from Switzerland. I shall not be surprised to hear of his death in a post or two', repressing stoically any signs of grief, and moving on to other topics. Two weeks later he reported with equal concealment of elation: 'I believe I sent you word how extremely ill Lord John had been. He is now out of danger.'[4] That, and no more. Lord John died in 1765, the same year as his father. He left one further written relic—a moving prayer in his own handwriting, apparently written in 1759, referring to his sufferings from melancholia.[5]

A man cannot choose his blood relations or make himself like them, and may perhaps be pardoned if he meets no more than the minimum obligations of uncongenial brotherhood. But most men choose their wives, or think they do, and feel an inclination to cherish them. Lord George did not marry Diana Sambrooke for her money or social position, and seems to have been genuinely devoted to her. Diana's early letters indicate a young

---

[1] Lord John to Lord George Sackville, 5 June 1754; *HMC, Stop. Sack.* i. 39.
[2] Fitzmaurice, *Shelburne*, i. 343.
[3] Lord John to Lord George Sackville, 4 Sept. 1754; *HMC, Stop. Sack.* i. 40.
[4] Sackville to Irwin, 15 June and 1 July 1763; *HMC, Stop. Sack.* i. 92.
[5] Marlowe, p. 75.

wife's adoration of her magnificent lord and master.[1] Lord
George's later references to her are chiefly in letters to Irwin,
and are in the tones of a contented and somewhat patronizing
husband. But the references are brief and casual. 'Di' has had
a child and is doing as well as can be expected. Or 'Lady George
has had no return of her Complaint', as a preface to a much
longer report to Irwin on his own ailments.[2]

Diana presented Lord George with two sons and three
daughters; she stood by him during the Minden ordeal and its
long, painful aftermath, and her popularity in the highest social
circles aided his rehabilitation. Her death during the crisis of
the January after Saratoga seems to have shattered, even if only
briefly, Lord George's ambitions and determination to hold his
Ministry post and have his way in the American war. Walpole
wrote of her just after her death: 'She was a good wife and
a sensible woman', which was high praise from that cynical
critic. Had there been more to tell, Walpole could not have
resisted telling it.

By the standards of his society, Lord George appears to have
been a faithful husband. Considering how detailed are the
records of the personal attacks upon him, any grounds of
criticism for unusual domestic frailty would certainly have been
cultivated by his enemies. In the absence of such charges it can
be assumed that he was not more than normally vulnerable as
a family man. Indeed it was recorded that: '. . . the number of
his mistresses were modestly few considering his period and his
station'. Only one of the mistresses can now be identified, but
she appeared in the records only after Lady George's death,
when Lord George was 62.[3]

---

[1] *HMC, Stop. Sack.* i.

[2] Sackville to Irwin, 1 Aug. 1774; Clements, *Germain Papers*, iii. 84/174.

[3] 'Derby is gone into camp near Winchester, and has built a kitchen and a
stable for twelve horses, while Lady Derby is living away at Brighthelmston. He
does not, however, think his establishment complete without a declared mistress,
and he is therefore to take Mrs. Armstead from Lord George' (James Hare to
George Selwyn, 27 June 1778; Drinkwater, *Charles James Fox*, pp. 276, 277).
Drinkwater assumes Lord George was Germain, and was almost certainly correct.
If so there is irony in Lord George's attachment to a mistress who had almost
certainly been the mistress of his nephew John Frederick Sackville, third Duke of
Dorset; that she was leaving Lord George to become the mistress of the best friend
of Burgoyne; that in 1782 she would be 'on terms of intimacy with the Prince of
Wales', and that in 1795 she would become the slightly shopworn wife of the man
who in 1778 was harassing Germain the hardest—Charles James Fox.

Such normal eighteenth-century diversions argue against Lord George having engaged in less normal ones. Few men are amorously attracted to both sexes, and Lord George was clearly susceptible to female charms. Though he may not have had, as Walpole reported, a seraglio in the Dublin days, he would hardly have inspired the remark if he had not shown more than a Platonic interest in Irish pulchritude. Nevertheless Lord George and his doings were sometimes referred to in phrases of that studied obscurity which imply inclinations toward sexual deviations of some sort. It is difficult to explain otherwise a letter from the Prince of Wales to the Marquis of Bute shortly before Minden, and another from Walpole to General Conway. But these can easily be discounted as fabrications based on crude humour, or the tendency of some men to hint perversion against other men they do not like. One scurrility, believed written by John Wilkes about the time of Minden, charged Lord George with sodomy. Lord George apparently ignored the charge; had he challenged Wilkes the fact would have been recorded. The charge was not openly repeated, and was probably mere political animosity. In the later years of Lord George's power, the Earl of Pembroke, inveighing against him with every expletive that came joyously to his uninhibited pen, made similar references, but only in one or two private letters to his son. The time-serving loyalist Thomas Hutchinson recorded in his diary reports that Lord George was perverted, but did not himself support them. Other rumours recorded by Hutchinson were so patently untrue that this one can be taken lightly.[1] That kind of gossip was almost inevitable against a man who aroused such strong emotions.

Those cautions and disclaimers are, however, an introduction to that brilliant adventurer Benjamin Thompson.[2] Thompson was born in New England and in 1775 became a spy for the British forces,[3] in which capacity he first appeared on the horizon of Lord George Germain.[4] Finding it dangerous to

[1] Hutchinson, *Diaries*, i. 289; 18 Oct. 1779.   [2] See note M, p. 501.
[3] Thompson sent to Germain, dated Boston, 4 Nov. 1775, his observations on the state of the rebel army, and they must have pleased Germain by their emphatic insistence that 'the doctrines of *independence* and *levellism*' would make impossible 'a proper degree of *subordination* in the Rebel army' (Clements, *Germain Papers*, iv. 1; also *HMC, Stop. Sack.* ii. 13 ff.).
[4] Thompson brought with him a letter from Howe, dated from Boston, 10 Mar.

remain in New England he took ship to London, bringing with him the first news of Howe's evacuation of Boston and flattering credentials from General Howe. Lord George immediately befriended him and soon appointed him Secretary (*in absentia*) of the Province of Georgia at £100 a year, and a secretary in his own office at a higher stipend.[1] Shortly thereafter he was living in Lord George's town house as an intimate of the entire family.[2]

Society found this relationship curious, and even so kindly and virtuous a woman as Lord North's daughter did not deny the scandal. 'Lady Glenbervie remembers him going about with Lady George and her daughters to balls as a humble dependant and dancing with the young ladies when they could get no other partners. At that time he was considered as the favourite, at once, of the father, mother and daughters, and the ill-fame of the father then, and the conduct of the daughters since, have served to keep the scandal alive with regard to them.'[3]

Thompson later took separate lodgings but continued to eat most of his meals in Lord George's home; to act on terms of great intimacy with the family, and to stay regularly with them at Stoneland Lodge. Meanwhile he advanced rapidly in Lord George's office, and in 1780 succeeded De Grey as Under-secretary: '. . . his income arising from these sources, I have been told, near seven thousand a year—a sum infinitely beyond his expectation'.[4] He somehow achieved a Lieutenant-Colonelcy

1776: 'I hereby certify that Benjamin Thompson Esq., having been forced to abandon a competent Estate in the Province of New Hampshire, from whence he was cruelly drove by persecution and severe Maltreatment, on account of his Loyalty and faithful Efforts to support the Laws and promote the services of Government, took refuge in Boston, Where as well as in the Country he has endeavor'd to be useful to His Majesty's service, and is therefore to be considered as deserving of Protection and Favour' (Clements, *Germain Papers*, iv).

[1] Thompson presented to the king, through Germain, a volume of letters written by Franklin and Governor Pownall before 1775, which were interpreted as casting reflections on revolutionary aims and the integrity of Franklin. The letters were written to Dr. Cooper, a loyalist Minister in Boston, who when forced to flee from Boston gave them for safe keeping to his friend David Jeffries, whose son brought them with him to England and showed them to Hutchinson. Thompson said Dr. Jeffries had made him a present of them (Clements, in MS. original; see also BM, King's MSS. 201, 202, 203).

[2] Though it seems curious that Walpole failed to comment.

[3] F. Bickley, *Diaries of Sylvester Douglas, Lord Glenbervie*, i. 248.

[4] Sparrow, p. 140. 'May 24, 1781. Went early, in order to be at Mr. Benjamin Thompsons in time and being a little before, heard he had not returned from Lord George Germaine's, where he always breakfasts, dines, and sups so great a favourite

of Horse Dragoons, and by the display of genuine talent in the sciences was made a Fellow of the Royal Society. But speculation and gossip did not die down.

Thompson was not as warmly cherished in other circles, and came under suspicion in other ways. He managed to get himself sent as a special scientific aide and observer to Admiral Hardy and Admiral Keppel when they resisted the Franco-Spanish armada, and wrote frequently to Lord George his far from modest criticisms of the naval management. Perhaps that offended the Admiralty; at any rate: 'On one occasion at least he had to transmit to Germain from the Lords of the Treasury a rebuke for dilatoriness.'[1] In October 1781 he quit his post as Undersecretary, not, apparently, from choice. He had been put in charge of equipment for the forces in America and was accused of being both inefficient and corrupt, and '. . . was supposed to have made some improper communication and Lord George found it necessary or advisable to remove him'.[2] Recent research suggests that Thompson was selling naval information to the French, and that the Earl of Sandwich would have brought him to trial had Lord George not circumvented it. Such an episode would provide another reason for the increasing animosity between Lord George and the earl.[3]

Thompson then returned to America, where the friendship and support of Lord George followed and aided him. He 'did good service and received the thanks of the Commander in Chief'.[4] At the end of the first year he was made a full Colonel and given half-pay for life, though the king was dubious about the justice of it.[5] During his service in America he did not neglect to repeat his gratitude to Lord George, and sent him by navy vessels impressive presents of deer and firewood.[6] He wrote long letters to Lord George, one of which ended: 'So good night. Bon soir mon tres cher Ami! Je m'en vais me coucher—Adieu.' Other letters called Lord George: 'My dearest, best of friends. . . . I shall not write a line to any body but yourself';[7] '*Je suis de*

---

is he' (G. A. Ward, *Journal and Letters of the Late Samuel Curwen*, London, 1849, p. 316).

[1] Sparrow, p. 140.　　　　　　　　　　[2] Bickley, *Glenbervie*, i. 244 ff.
[3] Ibid.　　　　　　　　　　　　　　　　　[4] *HMC, Stop. Sack*. ii. vi, and 249–56.
[5] Fortescue, *Corresp*. iii. 414, 415.　　[6] See letters cited in following note.
[7] Thompson to Sackville, 11 and 24 Jan. 1782; also 19 Jan 1782; Clements, *Germain Corresp*. xvi. 13/57; xv. 4, 17, 26.

votre ouvrage. Does it not afford you a very sensible pleasure to find your child has answered your Expectations. . . . I know you love me most affectionately. . . . What my dearest friend should I do without you? . . . I shall not have a moment's comfort till I hear from you again.'[1]

In 1783 Thompson went to the Continent on Lord George's advice, where he secured appointments, honours, and money as well as further repute as a man of science. When the Elector of Bavaria made him an Adjutant-General and Colonel of Cavalry, to 'constantly attend his person', Lord George took the occasion to secure him a British knighthood from George III. Thompson continued his long letters, full of devotion and gratitude, to his patron. One from Munich was characteristic: 'Rank, titles, decorations, literary distinctions . . . with some small degree of military fame I have acquired (through your availing protection) and the road is open to me for the rest. . . . How near would this approach to happiness could I but enjoy with all these, the society of my best, my only friend!'[2] The easiest explanation of this curious relationship is the discreditable one, but to the more fair-minded judge it is only another baffling aspect of Lord George's personal relationships.

Almost the only records that throw light on Lord George's relations with his children are those in the last half-dozen years of his life. Then, at least, he seems to have been on cordial paternal terms. There are a few brief glimpses: of family hegiras to country estates and spas; of the three daughters dancing with Benjamin Thompson while Lord George and his lady look on; of a son at Oxford being visited and generously financed by his father; of a proposed visit to a married daughter in the west of Ireland, and of three daughters cowering in their beds as rioters shattered their windows and invaded their house. From these, and a handful of letters to the older son at Oxford, little can be inferred and that little uncertainly.

Lord George's eldest daughter Diana married Viscount Croslie, who became the Earl of Glendore. In his last years she wrote him a few sprightly, gossipy and inconsequential letters— those of a daughter confident of her father's worldly tolerance

---

[1] From Munich, 16 Aug. 1785; Thompson to Sackville; Clements, *Germain Corresp.* xvi. 14/59; also partly in *HMC, Stop. Sack.* ii. 255, 256.
[2] Ibid.

if not of his deep affection. Diana is also mentioned in a letter by her sister Caroline as 'so popular in Kerry that when she goes to a play which is acted by strolling players at Tralee, the whole House rings with applause at her entrance, and she is obliged to curtsy her thanks like a Queen'.[1] She had three daughters; her father left her £3,000 a year, and she died in 1814 at 58.

Elizabeth, six years younger than Diana,[2] was more often mentioned in her father's correspondence and in the gossip of society. In the autumn of 1781 she married Henry Arthur Herbert of Muckross near Killarney,[3] and in the last year of his life Viscount Sackville planned to go to Ireland to visit her, commenting with the self-conscious jocularity of an elderly man: 'Such young frisky fellows as I am make nothing of a journey of that sort.'[4] It was Herbert whose political career Lord George attempted to advance in certain manœuvres with Pitt in 1783. Perhaps he did so in gratitude for Mr. Herbert's complacency as a husband,[5] for there were reports of Elizabeth's marital infidelity. It was, however, four years later that she deserted her husband and two young sons; came to London and led so promiscuous a life that the tongues of society wagged enthusiastically.[6] She never returned to wedlock and years later Herbert wrote to Lord George's son Charles: 'I had hoped long before this time to have met you and your brother in England, and to have consulted with you on several points relative to my unfortunate wife and my children now deserted by their mother.'[7] The Sackville family biographer did not record the date or circumstances of Elizabeth's death.

The third daughter Caroline was her father's constant companion in his last years. She was said to have been his favourite,

[1] Marlowe, p. 60; probably in late 1787.
[2] Marlowe, p. 60.
[3] HMC, Var. Coll. 6, Knox, p. 180.
[4] Sackville to Irwin, 12 June 1784; HMC, Stop. Sack. i. 146.
[5] Shelburne wrote that in 1785 Viscount Sackville was trying to obtain: '. . . some distinction for a son-in-law who consented to take back his daughter under very base and dishonourable circumstances' (Fitzmaurice, Shelburne, i. 361). If Shelburne was correct in his date, either his daughter Diana had indulged herself in a way reported nowhere else, or Elizabeth had had a notorious affair before her desertion of husband and children, which did not take place until after her father's death. Shelburne, writing from memory, probably confused the date of the latter episode.
[6] No specific mention of the lovers can be found; which suggests that their number was exaggerated.
[7] Herbert to Charles Sackville, HMC, Stop. Sack. i. 48.

but there are few clues to her personality. Nathaniel Wraxall,
who called at Drayton on New Year's Eve in 1784, found Lord
George: '. . . engaged at chess with his youngest daughter',[1] but
to this idyllic domestic glimpse there are no additions except
one letter—informal and high-spirited—from Caroline to the
wife of the steward at Drayton. When Viscount Sackville visited
his son at Oxford he took Caroline along, and when he died he
bequeathed her his property in Westminster and £1,000 plus
£300 a year if single. She never married and died in 1789.

Two years after Lord George retired he was writing occasional
letters to his older son Charles, born in 1767 and then an under-
graduate at Oxford. The letters are kindly, affectionate, and
communicative, though to modern youth they might seem
effortfully genial. They are no different from thousands of letters
from other fathers to their sons at college. But it was obviously
pleasant to Lord George to take a grown daughter to visit a
grown son at Oxford: 'I hope to dine with you at the Star on
15 July and stay there that night . . . I trust that you will entertain us well and that you will take Caroline and me under your
protection. . . . George seems happy at Westminster, he bears
the loss of you with great fortitude, and I daresay looks forward
with pleasure for the Holydays when he will be his own Master
in this place.'[2]

A year later, writing from his house in Pall Mall, the viscount
gave Charles the family news; urged him to come to Drayton
as soon as possible and added that: 'Caroline has a bad cold,
made worse by her going to Ranelagh. . . . Herbert is upon
a fishing party.'[3] And in June of that year, again from Pall Mall:
'I hope to get away from town in about ten days . . . the Herberts
had the happiness of catching and eating several pike. . . .
Tonbridge lost at cricket. . . . We have had a little rioting about
the taxing of shops and maid servants. . . . The Prince of Wales
has given a magnificent ball.'[4] Not all fathers have taken the
news of a son's college debts so easily: 'You do very right in
acquainting me when you want money, when I can spare it you
shall not be distressed for it: I send you a Bank note of twenty

[1] Wraxall, iii. 252.
[2] Sackville to Charles Sackville, June 1784; Marlowe, p. 76.
[3] Idem, 4 May 1785; HMC, Stop. Sack. i. 47.
[4] Idem, 17 June 1785; HMC, Stop. Sack. i. 48.

pounds, which I hope will do for the present.'[1] Two months
before his death, and in a somewhat shaky hand, Lord George
commented to Charles that William Pitt: '. . . must share the
fate of all ministers in this country, and submit for a time to be
unpopular'.[2]

In the available surviving correspondence there are no letters
to the younger son George, and the only references are to his
apparent happiness at Westminster School and a sincere concern when the boy was ill: 'My son George was so ill here that
I sent him up to town. I have today a very alarming letter from
Sir J. Elliot about him, but am thankful he is in such good
hands.'[3]

If Viscount Sackville had high aspirations for his two sons
they were not realized. Wraxall described them later as:
'. . . men by no means wanting talents [who] have nevertheless
hitherto remained in a sort of political obscurity, better known
at Newmarket or on Ascot Heath than at Westminster, on the
turf or at the cockpit than' in more worthy occupations.[4]
Wraxall may have overlooked the fact that the political career
of Lord George Sackville and Lord George Germain might not
have given his sons an inclination, or a warm welcome, to
politics. 'He was not content with obtaining for his sons rever-
sions of offices to a considerable amount, which ought to have
been executed by resident and capable persons and have since
become the subject of an express act of Parliament, but he made
the most of everything he had to give, particularly of the
Governments in the West Indies, and that in a moment when
it was of the utmost consequence to choose men of the highest
eminence and character for those important trusts.'[5] In want of
evidence to the contrary, however, the Earl of Shelburne may
have erected that mansion of misconduct on the single foundation of Lord George's attempt to secure a West Indies sinecure
for his six-year-old son in 1776.

The ageing Viscount Sackville would naturally have hoped
for higher posts than West Indian sinecures for his older son,
for only two lives stood between him and the dukedom of
Dorset. One was that of John Frederick, only son of the deceased

---

[1] Sackville to Charles Sackville; Marlowe, p. 77.   [2] Ibid.
[3] Sackville to Knox, 20 Sept. 1783; *HMC, Var. Coll.* 6, *Knox*, p. 192.
[4] Marlowe, p. 76.   [5] Fitzmaurice, *Shelburne*, i. 360.

exile of Vevey, and the other was John Frederick's son George John Frederick. John Frederick succeeded his uncle Charles to the title in 1769 and tried to wear it worthily, but he lacked the talents and energies of his more distinguished forebears. He served briefly as ambassador in Paris, where Walpole called him 'a proverb of insufficiency',[1] and where, according to Lord Shelburne, he could not conceal his ignorance and '. . . talks of the ceded islands as if he knew where they were'. He died in 1799 and was succeeded by his son, who in 1815 was killed by a fall while hunting, and Lord George's son Charles at long last became the fifth Duke of Dorset.

Charles did nothing that enhanced and little that impaired the Sackville name. A fashionable Regency figure and no more, he roused neither the admiration nor the ire his father had achieved. As a matter of course he accumulated some of the embellishments appropriate to a Duke of Dorset: Master of the King's Horse, Knight of the Garter, and the reputation for being a brisk hand with the ladies. On one occasion he paid Captain Powlett £3,000 as co-respondent in the Captain's divorce; on another he gave the celebrated Harriet Wilson £200 for her promise to omit from her memoirs 'any anecdotes personally offensive to your Grace'. By such episodes, by a devotion to the turf and a friendship with the prince regent, Charles maintained some of the lesser traditions of his family. But there the talents of this 'smart-looking little man' ended. He lacked the extremes of virtue or vice that had made his ancestors famous. A lifelong bachelor, he died in 1843 leaving no heir and little mark on men's memories. His younger brother George left still less. He was not mentioned in his father's will, though he was apparently living in 1787, for in that year his sister Diana named him in her own will for a legacy of £1,500. The viscount's title ended with Charles in 1843.

Beyond those meagre facts one can only guess at Lord George's character as a family man. He seems to have been a son at least dutiful, a husband at least conventionally satisfactory, a father at least outwardly affectionate, and a brother at best cordial and at worst coldly unsympathetic. Of many eminent men no more, if as much, could be said.

In friendships with other men Lord George's resources were

[1] Greig, *Diaries*, p. 84, note.

limited. During his salad days in Dublin, when every admiring young officer seemed a good chap, Lord George developed a camaraderie with several well-born young men attached to the Army and the State. Such friendships are usually based on little more than propinquity and a mutual devotion to sport, slipper, and bottle, and rarely endure beyond their common enjoyment. Lord George maintained for a few years a correspondence, based partly on mutual military advancement, with Waite and Cunningham, but if the relationships were ever close, they ceased to be in later life.

While Secretary of State, Lord George's most frequent correspondent was his Undersecretary, William Knox. To Knox he confided his personal opinions of many situations and many men, much as a busy executive today confides in his personal secretary or special assistant. These exchanges were intimate only in matters affecting office affairs and politics. The only evidence of personal regard is that in 1782 Lord George saw that Knox got a fat pension, and stood godfather to his son.[1] Knox seems to have been a loyal aide who kept his chief's confidence, but had private reservations about Lord George. After 1782 the intimacy and the letters between them dwindled to almost nothing, and after Lord George's death Knox wrote to Eden: 'I never had a political attachment but to George Grenville, nor do I feel obligations to any of them'.[2]

Only General Sir John Irwin can be called Lord George's personal confidant over the years and until the end. It was the closest and most enduring friendship of Lord George's life; indeed, so far as can be discovered, the only one. Lord George regarded Irwin and his wife as almost members of the Sackville family, and treated them rather more cordially than blood relations. He wrote to Irwin of intimate family affairs and went into great detail in planning occasional visits from the Irwins. 'If you intend riding while you are here I will order your old horse to be trimm'd and made handsome, for your reception.' Lord George analysed to Irwin at length, well in advance of one proposed visit to Knole, what other guests would be present and what rooms they would occupy, and the reasons for the various assignments. He offered his opinion as to whether or not

[1] Knox to Eden, 7 Jan. 1786; *HMC, Var. Coll.* 6, *Knox*, p. 195.
[2] *HMC, Var. Coll.* 6, *Knox*, p. 187.

Lady Irwin should take cold baths for her health and regretted the inability of Knole to provide her with a tub. All that was in 1764,[1] when friends were most rare and therefore perhaps most precious to Lord George, but three years later he wrote to Irwin: 'Unless you prefer the hurry of town to quiet and retirement, I hope you will come to see us. . . . You cannot go to those who love you better.'[2] In all the excitements of 1776, Lord George saved copies of many long letters to this one friend, then commanding at Gibraltar.[3] In another year he wrote to Irwin seven times between 13 October and 1 November.[4] And only to Irwin did Lord George plead his dependence on friendship: '. . . be so good as to write as often as you can'.[5]

Yet even in his letters to Irwin, Lord George sometimes indulged in posings and insincerities that must have been patent to one who had known him so long and well. At the very time when Lord George was doing his utmost to gain a post of political power, he wrote to this closest friend: 'I once imagined I could not have lived without Constant Business, I am now persuaded I am much happier without it.'[6] And even with Irwin, most of the content of Lord George's letters was concerned with politics and war. The two men were unquestionably on terms of great confidence, but there is little to show that their affection may have been deep. After the Ministry years had ended the exchanges grew fewer and more brief, though that may have been due merely to the declining energy of their mounting years. 'The loss of your society must ever be regretted by me', the viscount wrote to the general only two years before his death.[7] Most of Lord George's relationships dwindled or ended in rancour; that with Irwin survived strong and warm. But except for Irwin and a sycophant or two, Lord George, more than most men, walked alone.

[1] Sackville to Irwin, 1764; Clements, *Germain Papers*, ii. 31/64. The immediately previous quotations were from letters in the Clements Collection, mostly also printed in *HMC, Stop. Sack.* i.
[2] Sackville to Irwin, 24 Oct. 1767; *HMC, Stop. Sack.* i. 125.
[3] Sackville to Irwin; *HMC, Stop. Sack.* i. 88–91.
[4] Other letters were dated 17 Jan., 31 Jan., 10 Feb., 11 Mar., 27 Mar., 25 Apr., 12 June, 29 June, 27 July, &c. (Clements, *Germain Papers*, 42/91 to 50/108).
[5] Sackville to Irwin, 1 Nov. 1774.
[6] Idem, 13 June 1775; Clements, *Germain Papers*, iii. 88/182.
[7] Idem, 9 May 1783; *HMC, Stop. Sack.* i. 144.

XXXI

TWILIGHT OF WARRIORS

AFTER his drastic initiation into the House of Lords, Viscount Sackville took comfortably to his new incarnation. That final role, so controversially achieved, proved the calmest of his career. Age and retirement brought the semblance of mellowness, whether of ripeness or decay. His inheritance and tastes fitted him to play naturally the role of titled statesman in retirement. Though he could not assume the part of Cincinnatus, Drayton and rural ease might be made the backdrop for a minor Hadrian.

Inevitably the mellowness is a little suspect and the philosophic calm not quite Lucretian, for neither was consistent with the viscount's past performance. His power had always rested on fragile foundations and external props; his renunciation of it had not been exactly voluntary, and he entered his new Eden with not quite all passion spent. Old ambitions and resentments do not die easily, and without their company Lord George's new life might have seemed to him a little lonely and a touch tasteless. Occasionally he yielded to them, and belied the new idyll of the genial host and rural philanthropist.

Lord George's last act in office was calculated to avoid an unpleasant aftermath of his earlier ones. He removed from his Whitehall files whatever personal papers were there, and they might have thrown a clearer light on his character and his conduct in office. Other men prominent in controversy have done likewise; some of them for similar reasons, and not necessarily because the facts disclosed would have been discreditable. But as a result, and in comparison with the generous documentation of Lord George's public life, our light on the man behind the Minister is meagre. Possibly the meagreness was in the personal life as well.

The quality of Lord George's last years is confused by variant reports as to the sincerity of his new role. A few admirers pictured the new viscount in terms that remind us of a more exalted

Sir Roger de Coverley, but there is something slightly synthetic in their portrait of the former Lord George, now content to spend his days in a placid ritual of beneficent paternalism: riding the marches of Drayton, distributing largesse to servitors and sweets to village children, enhancing the natural beauties of Stonelands, concerning himself with the welfare of old soldiers once under his command, playing chess with a devoted daughter before the hearth-fire of a New Year's Eve, firmly herding his guests and servants to morning prayers, and interrupting with corrective interpolations the Sunday sermons of the local parson. One can accept those activities as facts, but still doubt that they constituted the whole portrait of the viscount.

In those admiring versions, Lord George: '. . . appears to have lived in a retired manner, occasionally at Drayton in Northamptonshire, or at Bolebrook, near Tunbridge Wells; but principally at his beautiful mansion, Stoneland Park. . . . Here, away from the bustle of public life, the cavils of party, and the rancourous spirit of his enemies, he passed the remainder of his days in retirement.'[1] Thus George Coventry, who neglected, however, to mention Viscount Sackville's dinner parties in his impressive town house in Pall Mall, his speeches in the House of Lords, his political animosities and negotiations, and his periods of morose distemper.

From the beginning, the viscount did not deny himself the sardonic pleasure of occupying his hard-won seat among the resentful Lords. Had he not faced an even colder welcome after Minden in the House of Commons, and won his place by sheer endurance and ability? He did not attend the Lords regularly, or speak often, but in his last year he made a significant address on a subject that had always held his special interest—the government of Ireland. He also maintained a steady watcher's brief on the course of politics, and more than once there were rumours that he would become more than an observer. He viewed the skirmishes between old friends and enemies (and many of the former had become, one by one, the latter) with a professional's relish. 'What a dressing Mr. Pitt gave Lord North', he wrote with gusto to his old aide William Knox some sixteen months after his retirement.[2]

[1] Coventry, *Memoirs of Viscount Sackville*, London, 1825.
[2] Sackville to Knox, 21 June 1783; HMC, *Var. Coll.* 6, *Knox*, p. 191.

Behind the placid front are glimpses of a man still subject to
the passions of the past. But years and failing health (for the
viscount was increasingly troubled by the stone) reduce the
fervour of a man's emotions; he may wish to be as angry as ever,
but lacks the energy to sustain hot hate. Viscount Sackville
could write, privately and just once, a half-compliment of Carleton, but even then it was only as an incidental preface to an old
belligerency: 'I am inclined to think he is too good an officer to
remain within his lines when the rebells divide their force for
the different attacks they may intend.'[1] Carleton was commanding in New York and Viscount Sackville was still Germain: he
wanted the Americans attacked when nearly everyone else in
England wanted them peacefully conciliated. Carleton's policy
and the peace negotiations soon angered him again: 'I am persuaded', he wrote to Knox, 'both Washington and Congress are
in the pay of France.'[2]

The viscount's retirement was not so complete that his political favour was not worth courting. In December 1783, when
Pitt was forming his first Ministry, he wrote to Lord George:
'In the arduous situation in which his majesty has condescended
to command my services at this important juncture, I am necessarily anxious to obtain the honour of a support and assistance
so important as your Lordship's.'[3] Incoming First Ministers
often wrote such letters to friends and foes alike, but Pitt's appeal
was more than perfunctory, and was pursued by several supporting letters from Pitt's adherents—among them Lord Sydney,
the critical Thomas Townshend of Lord George's halcyon days.[4]
His old Ministry colleague and America-hater, now Lord Thurlow, also wrote in Pitt's behalf, but Lord George was cool
toward a prospective ministry he had previously been judiciously
courting. The reason soon emerged. Lord Carmarthen was to
become one of its Secretaries of State.

There were some offences the viscount was not prepared to
forgive, and Carmarthen's attack in the House of Lords was one
of them. Thurlow begged Lord George not to weaken the standing of the new Ministry by condemning it solely because it

---

[1] Sackville to Knox, 13 July 1782; *HMC, Var. Coll.* 6, *Knox*, p. 186.
[2] Sackville to Knox, 1 Aug. 1782; *HMC, Var. Coll.* 6, *Knox*, p. 187.
[3] Pitt to Sackville, 24 Dec. 1783; *HMC, Stop. Sack.* i. 81.
[4] Sydney to Sackville, 24 Dec. 1783; *HMC, Stop. Sack.* i. 80.

included Carmarthen,[1] since the only hope of regaining political stability was to let the new Ministry 'swim out the storm', but Lord George replied the next day: 'I am sensible of the folly of taking objections to any individual for what might have passed while I was in office, but when I was no longer in that situation the attack made upon me by Lord Carmaerthen was so unprovoked and became of so personal a nature, that I can never act with or have the least connection with him, and whilst he bears so principal a part in the Administration I cannot ask or receive any mark of the King's favour.'[2]

Once again Lord George was sacrificing a greatly desired end to a personal resentment. He had been manœuvring with Pitt to obtain a good office in the new administration for his son-in-law Herbert of Muckross. In return for that favour he would have supported the Pitt Ministry. It had seemed certain that if Lord George had promised to do so, Herbert would have been given a good post in the Admiralty. He now wrote to Pitt that Carmarthen's appointment: '. . . made it impossible for me to ask Mr. Herbert to accept of the office which you were pleased to offer him. . . . I should have been happy had I been able to have added . . . any little assistance in support of the administration.'[3] Lord Shelburne, who rarely neglected to record a blemish in the Sackville family, commented later: 'Viscount Sackville . . . would if he had lived probably have secured the object he had immediately in view, of obtaining some distinction for a son-in-law, who consented to take back his daughter under some very base and dishonourable circumstances, and of forwarding lines of secret intrigue.'[4]

Lord George's political influence did not stop there. Six months later Thomas Orde wrote to the Earl of Rutland

---

[1] Thurlow to Sackville, 29 Dec. 1783; *HMC, Stop. Sack.* i. 80; also Clements, *Germain Papers*, xvi. 12/120, which date Thurlow's letter as 23 Dec.

[2] Sackville to Thurlow, 30 Dec. 1783; *HMC, Stop. Sack.* i. 80.

[3] Sackville to Pitt, 30 Dec. 1783; *HMC, Stop. Sack.* i. 81. Lord Sydney wrote Lord George that the post for Herbert 'still remains within his reach' (Sydney to Sackville, 29 Dec. 1783; Clements, *Germain Papers*, xvi. 53/122). Pitt also wrote again, urging acceptance for Herbert, for whom 'the opening may be made with the greatest ease at any moment', and Lord George's nephew, the Duke of Dorset, who was supporting Pitt's administration and being made Ambassador to Paris, wrote to Lord George: '. . . pray go along with me' (Clements, *Germain Papers*, 29 Dec. 1783 and 3 Jan. 1784; xvi. 54/124 and 58/128).

[4] Fitzmaurice, *Shelburne*, i. 361. See p. 476, note 5 above.

regarding the composition of the new Ministry: 'As for official
arrangements, I hear a variety of suggestions, but have no
authority for any. There seems, however, to be something in
agitation for Lord Sackville.'[1] Though the rumour bore no fruit,
Lord George became more active in the House of Lords, and
Lord Sydney did him the honour of believing his position on the
Irish question to be wholly disinterested.[2]

Apart from politics, Lord George maintained the Sackville
tradition of social entertaining on a generous scale. There were
many guests as he moved from home to home, and though none
of his estates was as lordly as Knole, there were plenty of the
well-born ready to forget Minden and later infelicities in a host
whose houses were so comfortable and whose fare was so good.
'There was not, probably, a nobleman in England who combined a more liberal economy with a hospitable and splendid
establishment', wrote Sir Nathaniel Wraxall, who enjoyed that
hospitality more than once, and paid amply for it by his compliments.

Richard Cumberland, minor playwright, former aide in Lord
George's office, satellite and beneficiary of his patronage, board
and lodging, did his best to repay his patron by describing
Viscount Sackville as a benign and benevolent precursor of
Irving's squire of Bracebridge Hall on a more splendid scale—
a man of 'placid temper, benevolent disposition, unostentatious
piety, cheerful resignation and constant and well-timed charities'. But other contemporaries, who owed no such dutiful
debt, presented variations to this description. They hinted that
as a host Viscount Sackville was more conventional than warm,
more measured than spontaneous. It was as though he recognized that hospitality and good works were the proper duty of
his station, but performed them without natural enjoyment. He
met the requirements of his role, but even one of his greatest
admirers admitted '. . . the measured, timed, economical and
punctilious quality of his friendships and generosities'. Moments
of geniality were followed by days of morose or irritable depression; the stern control of outward emotions broke on occasion
into sudden outbursts of petulance or wrath. Was he a lesser

[1] Orde to Rutland, 4 June 1784; *HMC*, xiv. i, *Rutland*, iii. 105.
[2] 'I believe Lord Sackville spoke and voted from opinion' (Sydney to Rutland,
20 July 1785; *HMC*, xiv. i, *Rutland*, iii. 229).

victim of the malady that impaired the lives of his brothers, or
did his low spirits come because he feared it? Were his bad days
due to no more than the more painful hours of his kidney ailment; were they fruits of his disappointed ambitions, or was the
ailment a deeper one derived from spiritual poverty?

Viscount Sackville was living by the book. But not literally.
He had never cultivated intellectual pleasures for their own
sake. He had once remarked, almost boastfully, that he seldom
opened a book. That was an exaggeration, but literature and
the arts were no more the solace of his later years than the
inspiration of his earlier ones. The style and content of his few
private letters was not distinguished; his dispatches and business
notes often fell into the jargon of officialdom; his studied witti-
cisms, few at best, were seldom relieved by originality or a feeling for the right word. But here again are contradictions, and
they give some support to Cumberland's high praises. Many
men of taste and judgement suspected that Lord George had
been the author of the Junius Letters, those sharp and saturnine
political essays whose polemic skill and masterly vituperation
have almost weathered the test of time.

The suspicion that Lord George was Junius is almost certainly
incorrect. Lord George himself denied it, and Wraxall added
his own opinion that: '. . . though in common with mankind at
large, I estimated very highly Lord George's talents, I considered
them as altogether unequal to such literary productions'.[1] Anyone who compares the style of Lord George's many letters with
that of Junius is likely to reach the same conclusion. Lord
Shelburne said he knew who had written the Junius Letters,
and eliminated Lord George when he insisted that: 'None of the
parties ever guessed at as Junius was the true Junius.'[2] The
enigma lies not in whether Lord George wrote the Junius Letters
but that he was thought capable of writing them. Yet there are
those who thought him a talented poetaster. In something akin
to an obituary tribute, the Gentleman's Magazine reported: 'The
late Lord Sackville, who was a man of extraordinary talents,
wrote a beautiful eulogy on the late Princess of Orange, but which
never graced the press. The genius, learning and exalted virtue of
the Princess were the themes of his Lordship's all-powerful pen.'[3]

[1] Wraxall, i. 338.   [2] Fitzmaurice, *Shelburne*, preface, pp. i, viii, ix.
[3] *Gentleman's Magazine*, Sept. 1785; quoted by Coventry, p. 47.

There are a few bits of evidence, too, to support Cumberland's account of Viscount Sackville's benevolence. There is the exchange of letters between the viscount and Alexander Lindsay, '. . . late Sergeant in the 20th Regiment'. Lindsay asked Lord George to help him get his name put on the list of charity patients of Chelsea Hospital. Lord George wrote in his behalf but later found that the hospital had not put down Lindsay's name. He wrote to the Sergeant: 'I cannot permit you to suffer by such an accident, and therefore enclose to you an order for ten guineas which I desire you to accept as a mark of my regard, and you may depend upon my sending you the like sum every year as long as I live.'[1] In his last years Lord George assigned one-tenth of the rental income from his Drayton properties to the welfare of the local church and community. Such tithes were a frequent practice among large landowners, but not a universal one. And on one occasion Lord George joined with Lord North, the Duke of Montague, and four other gentlemen in contributing £20 each to aid the Reverend Bennet Allen, apparently indigent from the loss of income on properties in the former colonies.[2] The surviving record of spontaneous generosity goes no further.

The heavy hand Lord George Germain had laid on the careers of his generals in America left its marks on the varying fortunes of their later years. Yorktown ended the serious fighting in America more abruptly than it ended discords in England, and it settled the fortunes of war more promptly than the misfortunes of warriors. Their fates had lost the interest of their contemporaries, and not yet gained the dignity of history or the accolade of research. Society no longer cared about Burgoyne's honour, Howe's self-justifications, Clinton's complaints, or Carleton's mistreatment. But old soldiers do not die simply because the public attention turns elsewhere, and some of them refuse to fade away. General John Burgoyne was one of these, and even found ways to foil with the pen the sword's law of diminishing returns. He had fought and lost at Saratoga; he had fought and only half won in Parliament; he had defied the Secretary of State for America, two Secretaries at War, and even his old friend the king, and though he had suffered

---

[1] Sackville to Lindsay, 29 June 1785; *HMC, Stop. Sack.* i. 47.
[2] Clements, *Shelburne Papers*, 87/270; 11 Oct. 1782.

serious losses he had never pulled down his colours or been contained.

Burgoyne's last years were in the literal sense more dramatic than his earlier ones. After his part in the Howe Inquiry of 1779 he continued active in parliamentary opposition to the Ministry and especially to Lord George Germain. In November 1781 he told the House of Commons '. . . he was now convinced the principle of the American war was wrong . . . reason and observation led him to the conclusion that the American war was only part of a system levelled against the constitution of this country, and the general rights of mankind'.[1] Under the complacent, inefficient, and inflexible management of the Ministry, he said, England was deteriorating in power, prestige, and character.

That was unquestionably a doctrine satisfactory to Lords Rockingham and Shelburne, and when their Ministry replaced Lord North's, it promptly named him Commander-in-Chief of his Majesty's forces in Ireland and restored his various military commissions. This was more than exoneration; it was full recognition, though painfully belated. When the Rockingham Ministry fell and Burgoyne's sword was thus finally sheathed, he turned to his pen, and attacked the North–Fox Ministry in the *Rolliad*, the *Probationary Odes*, and the somewhat scurrilous but witty *Westminster Gazette*. Men of all parties waited with more pleasure than resentment to see what Gentleman John, soldier turned wit, would write next. But political pamphleteering could not absorb all Burgoyne's energies and volubility, and he continued to take a robust part in Parliament. His last important speeches were to advocate the impeachment of Warren Hastings, as his earlier ones had been to attack Lord Clive. He played a significant part in the future of an India he never saw.

But Burgoyne was first of all a man of society with a flair for the dramatic, and he spent more and more time, seated at the desk in some friendly country house, as a late-blooming playwright. His comic opera *The Lord of the Manor* was praised almost as warmly by the critics as by friendly earls and dowagers. In 1785 he made use of his earlier studies of French literature to produce a translation of Sedaine's libretto for Grétry's popular opera *Richard Cœur de Lion*. It too was a success, and enhanced

[1] *Hansard*, xxii. 823.

his standing and friendships with leading literary figures of his time. That was a long way from the guns of the enemy in Portugal and the hell-bent charges of Benedict Arnold at Saratoga, but the following year Burgoyne moved still further. His comedy *The Heiress* became one of the great successes of the century on the London stage; it ran there for several months; went through ten English editions in a single year; was translated into French, German, Italian, and Spanish, and was included in Villeneuve's *Chefs-d'œuvre du théâtre étranger*. Horace Walpole, who had never been the most just or kindly of Burgoyne's critics, wrote of the play: 'Burgoyne's battles and speeches will be forgotten, but his delicious comedy of *The Heiress* still continues the delight of the stage and one of the most pleasing dramatic compositions.'[1]

The play is forgotten and the battle is not, but the play helped to cement Burgoyne's friendship with the current Earl of Derby, son of Burgoyne's school friend Lord Strange, and nephew of Burgoyne's lost Lady Charlotte. It was probably through Burgoyne that the current earl made the intimate acquaintance of the beautiful actress Miss Farren, an intimacy in due course sanctified by marriage. A friend of the new Countess of Derby was Miss Susan Caulfield, also of the stage, and with her Burgoyne the widower 'formed a connexion' as enduring as most marriages. The four children of that unhallowed but devoted union were brought up by Lord Derby with his own children. Lord Strange had not frowned on the elopement of his sister with his schoolmate the impecunious but gallant Burgoyne; the later earl did not frown upon an elderly soldier's less orthodox bliss with the friend of his own countess. Victorianism had not yet emphasized the distinction between sacred and profane love.

---

[1] Fonblanque, p. 401. The play first appeared anonymously, but when printed by popular demand it contained a preface dedicating it to Lord Derby. The play, Burgoyne wrote, owed: '. . . its existence to the leisure and tranquility I enjoyed during the last two summers at Knowsley', the earl's country seat. 'I long intended, as your Lordship can witness, to keep the name of the author concealed. After the success with which the play has been honoured, I must expect that the change in my design will be imputed to vanity: —I shall submit without murmuring to that belief, if I may obtain equal credit for the sincerity of another pride which this discovery gratifies—that of testifying in the most public manner the respect and affection with which I have the honour to be, Your most obedient and humble servant, John Burgoyne' (Burgoyne, *The Heiress*, London, 1786, preface).

Young Major Burgoyne had once told a fellow officer that he would like to meet death while leading his troops to some great victory. He had later come very close to his wish, and something of his bravado remained in the elderly dramatist. John Burgoyne the gentleman, without title or red ribbon, died appropriately to his new career—suddenly, after a gay night with friends at the Haymarket Theatre. After his long winter of discontent he had recaptured success and would sleep well. He had overcome his defeats not by dour endurance and covert connivings, but by being vociferously and boyishly himself. History, because it could not help liking the man, treated him kindly at the end. He never received the knighthood that Lord George Germain had, ironically as it developed, once offered him, but perhaps his more unique title of Gentleman suited him just as well. Sir Joshua Reynolds painted portraits of both men, but he painted Lord George for money and Gentleman John for love.

Sir William Howe's talents were less varied than Burgoyne's, and he played his last act less well, but he too did not vanish from the stage. In 1779 the Opposition had supported him, and in the years that followed he served them well. Whenever Lord George Germain came under fire, Howe could be counted upon to repeat his charges of over-direction and incompetence, and to tell Parliament that so long as Germain directed the war it could not be won. As the passions of that controversy subsided, the military authorities indicated that they would look favourably on further military service by Sir William Howe. In 1782 the Rockingham Ministry made him Lieutenant-General of Ordnance, a post held before Minden by that promising officer Lord George Sackville. In 1783 Howe was made full General and later put in charge of the northern, and then of the eastern, military district of England. Had Napoleon invaded England Howe would have been in a crucial post. But the French once again failed to invade, and in 1803, all chances for further military glory vanished, Howe retired from military service. As Viscount Howe he sometimes addressed his peers on military matters, but there his pretensions to statesmanship wisely ended.

Howe's last years paid their toll for his earlier strenuous life and pleasures. After a decade of illness with its uncongenial restraints he died in Plymouth in 1814. He left no legitimate children and had probably outlived most who would have mourned him. Time had pushed aside the man who made friends only at the mouth of a cannon. His qualities were those of his generation, and the next one valued his talents less and condemned his weaknesses more. But he had outlived Lord George Germain by nearly thirty years, and to Howe that may have seemed the ultimate victory.

As for Cornwallis, his successes and failures in America proved to be only the preface to a long and distinguished career in which he added the laurels of a statesman to the triumphs of a soldier. He replied to Clinton's post-war strictures with aloof dignity, but the tracts of neither man were as widely read as Burgoyne's had been. England was tired of crying over who spilt the milk, and events were moving too rapidly to pause and look back. Cornwallis went on to serve his country widely and well. In serious crises he put down revolts in Ireland and India with throughness and dispatch, and served as Lord Lieutenant in Dublin and twice as Viceroy in India, where he died on a tour of duty.

Burgoyne, Howe, and Cornwallis ended their careers with much to console them, but Clinton's was not a temperament to accept consolation easily or even to have been contented with contentment. His return to England in 1782 repeated the pattern established by other unsuccessful generals from America. He too found himself the victim of misrepresentations and apparently inspired detraction. He too demanded a hearing and was circumvented by the Ministry—or so he believed. He too wrote and published his defence, and though it was a far more thorough document than those of Burgoyne, Howe, and Cornwallis, it did not win him the full measure of exoneration and gratitude he demanded. He did not realize that no one really blamed him very much, and spent the rest of his life fighting for a cause that was lost because it was out-dated. Had Clinton been less sensitive he would have been less hurt. Most men would have been satisfied with the vote in the House of Commons on 27 November 1781 thanking him for 'eminent and very important service'. But not Clinton: the fact that the same vote had included the subordinate and captured Cornwallis and his *bête noire* Admiral Arbuthnot seemed to Clinton to be more insulting than consoling.

Frustrated and bitter, Clinton retired to unsociable self-pity; quarrelled with his powerful cousin the Duke of Newcastle and lost his seat in the House of Commons in 1784. In 1793, when old grudges had given way to new alarms, he was appointed Governor of Limerick, and in 1794 was made a full General. Whatever satisfaction he derived from those belated recognitions was brief, for he died at Gibraltar two days before Christmas in 1795. His ultimate defence, over which he had laboured for a decade, remained unpublished until the present century. It is one of the most valuable source-books of the Revolution, and does much to support the conclusion of an eminent military historian that: 'As to Clinton, who was made the escape goat for every misfortune that occurred during his command, it seems to me that no general was ever worse treated.'[1] But though Clinton could not live with resignation, he too had his final victories. Both his sons became generals in the British Army, and his laborious narratives of the war at last put him right with history.

Of all the generals on the American continent during the war, it was Carleton against whom Lord George Germain had shown the most implacable enmity and treated the most shabbily. Fate, in one of its undependable demonstrations of rough justice, decreed that Carleton should rise as Lord George fell. The man whose dismissal from Canada the North Cabinet had approved became the man that same Cabinet, despite Lord George, selected as the final commander of British forces in the former colonies. Appointed not so much to fight as to conciliate and withdraw, Carleton proved more patient as a statesman than he had sometimes been as a soldier. To maintain with dignity a defeated army in enemy territory for more than a year; to avoid inflammatory incidents; to arrange exchanges, compensations, and all the infinitely difficult business of withdrawal; to deal justly and in good temper with suppliant friends as well as overbearing foes: those were assignments that might have proved too much for even a Marlborough or a Wellington. Carleton saw the task through, and then in 1786 returned as Governor to Canada, where he was welcomed warmly, did his job well, and then survived shipwreck on his way, at long last, home to England. As a final touch of irony, the Carleton Lord George

[1] Fortescue, *HBA*, 2, iii. 397.

hated became Baron Dorchester, while the son of Lord George's
sister became Earl of Dorchester.[1]

If Lord George's career and letters have not revealed his
character no other pen can do so. Yet because he was the constant target of excessive praise, excessive blame, and excessive
resentments, justice owes him a more balanced summary. We
can judge our contemporaries only by what we know of them,
and in judging men of the past we are under an even greater
limitation. The biographer must advance his interpretations
with effortful humility. From the surviving records of Lord
George it seems clear that where events called upon him for
something deeper than dutiful obligations or the proper gesture;
where the head should have yielded to the heart, Lord George's
heart did not hear or did not answer. The ego ruled, and the
ego alone could not feel or understand the sensations of a proud
Irishman, a rebellious American, or a discouraged general. A
mind centred on military logic alone could see no reason why
Indians should not be enlisted to terrorize the wives and children
of rebels, or British troops should not be allowed to plunder
them, or why Washington and Franklin should not be treated
like ordinary traitors. A man who attributes the basest motives
to others reveals something of his own. The heart could not
expand beyond the bare call of fraternal duty to ease the
lonely melancholy of a brother living in shabby restraint in
a foreign land, or the financial problems of another brother
and sister-in-law whose ways he disapproved. In those in-
capacities of the spirit lay his failures as military leader and
statesman.

Not one contemporary who tried seriously to assess the character of Lord George failed to arrive at the question of heart. Even
his most unqualified admirer, Richard Cumberland, put his
finger on his hero's greatest limitation. 'Charity was in him, no
less the exercise of the judgment than of the heart.' The latter
phrase is perhaps more revealing than Cumberland intended,
for it was another way of saying that Lord George's charity was
controlled by the coolness of his judgement. Thomas Stockdale,
only a little less adulatory, went further: 'He had a want of
affection. . . . To attract the heart was not one of his abilities.'
Horace Walpole, a more detached critic, concluded that Lord

---

[1] R. G. Adams, *Germain Papers in Clements Coll.*, p. 37.

George '. . . lacked the art of conciliating friendship'. The Earl of Shelburne, adverse but perceptive, stated flatly of Lord George that he '. . . wanted heart on every occasion'.

But not all truth lies in documents and selected quotations. Paper records are often pallid distortions of the reality beneath. Lord George may be the victim of the scurrilous vituperations of his time, of too many contemporary but biased pens. When history cannot prove its case it behoves its servants to be cautious. There is always some truth in family traditions, even though they may be coloured by family loyalties. The critical estimates of Lord George's character in the preceding pages are at great variance with those held by his present descendants in so far as the latter have been ascertained. Family tradition regards Lord George as a loyal servant to the King, whose mistaken policy and that of the first minister he felt bound to implement. That tradition holds Lord George in esteem as a kind parent, an affectionate brother, a good landlord, and an extremely generous and loyal friend to all who stood by him during his misfortunes. One need not agree with all of that evaluation to respect its sincerity, admit the possibility of its truth, and honour the family loyalty that maintains it.

To those who accept the Whig verdict, Lord George had since Minden used his talents and energy chiefly to gratify his pride, his ambition, and his resentments. His life after Minden was spent in a private world made narrow and bitter by the distortions of egoism, enmity, and a deep sense of injustice. Yet even within that narrow and unhealthy world were a wife and children who doubtless gave, and received, affection and generosity.

Death came to Lord George on 26 August 1785, in his seventieth year. Richard Cumberland wrote that on his deathbed he repeated his innocence of any disobedience or cowardice at Minden, and ardently professed his faith in the Holy Catholic Church of England and embraced its consolations. No man can properly question the truth of Cumberland's account, or the sincerity of any man in those last assessments. But it is not unjust to suggest that other matters might well have lain more heavily on Lord George's final hours than the débâcle of Minden: matters in which he had committed, not suffered, injustice. He had not failed in loyalty to the king, but he had ignored loyalties still more exalted. He may not have disobeyed the orders of His Serene Highness Prince Ferdinand, but he had neglected the gentler instructions of a still Higher Serenity.

That is understandable, for the God to whom Lord George made his final devotions was that of the Old Testament, not the New. The God to whom he turned was one concerned with the righteousness of justice and vengeance. Lord George laid his case before that God alone; selecting his subjects, marshalling his defences, and perhaps withholding adverse evidence, as he might have done if summoned before a Celestial Parliamentary Committee of Inquiry.

The funeral of Viscount Sackville, sometime of Knole, Dublin, Minden, Pall Mall, Whitehall, Bolebrook, Stonelands, and Drayton, was doubtless attended by many peers of the realm. The real mourners present may have been very sincere, but I think they were not very numerous.

NOTES

Note A, p. 42. 'Lord Tyrawly demanded to be heard at the bar of the House in his own defense. A day was named. He drew up a memorial which he proposed to read to the House. It attacked Lord George roundly on having avoided all foreign command. Thus alarmed, Lord George got the day of hearing adjourned for near a fortnight, and having underhand procured the report of Skinner, who surveyed the works at Gibraltar, to be brought before the House, without mentioning what it was. Mr. Fox laid open the unhandsome darkness of this conduct, and Lord Tyrawly himself appeared at the bar, and made good by his behaviour all that had been taken for vapour before he appeared there; for, leaning on the bar, he browbeat Skinner, who stood on his left hand, with such arrogant humour, that the very lawyers thought themselves outdone in their style of worrying a culprit. He read his memorial, which was well drawn, with great art and frankness, and assumed more merit to himself than he had been charged with blame. Such tough game tempted few hunters; Lord George was glad to wave the sport; and the House dismissed the affair' (Walpole, *Last Ten Years*, ii. 293).

Note B, p. 54. 'I have the honour of a letter from your Lordship, with a copy of one from you to Lord Holdernesse, requesting a public opportunity of justifying your conduct by a court martial; wherein I wish your Lordship all success. You are pleased to make very undeserved acknowledgements for such offices only of a common candour and humanity, as I judged consistent with my duty to the King and zeal for the service to employ; but those offices went no further than using my endeavors that your Lordship might return from your command by his Majesty's *permission*, not by *order*.

'I hope you will think it is the same temper of mind which at present compels me to deal frankly on this very unhappy and delicate occasion, when delusion might prove dangerous. Give me leave then, to say, that I find myself (from the turn of your Lordship's letter) under the painful necessity of declaring my infinite concern at not having been able to find, either from Captain Smith's conversation, or from your own state of facts, room, as I wished, for me to offer my support, with regard to a conduct which, perhaps, my incompetence to judge of military questions, leaves me at a loss to account for.

'I cannot enough lament the subject of a correspondence unlike every thing I had wished for a person to whose advantageous situation my poor endeavors had not been wanting' (Pitt's draft of a letter to Sackville, 9 Sept. 1759; Taylor and Pringle, *Pitt Corresp.* i. 423, 424). The same letter, with slight variations, is in *HMC, Stop. Sack.* i. 315. Pitt's draft is given here because it presumably represents his actual feelings more accurately.

Note C, p. 79. 'If I am to continue unrelieved till every part of the administration should wish to see me restored to favour and employment, I may pass the remainder of my life in vain expectation. . . .

'As to the latter part of the letter, it must have been in answer to something you wrote of your own ideas of what I may be reduced to do, as I do not recollect that I desired you to mention anything relative to my future conduct. . . . Nothing but the utmost necessity shall oblige me to give any degree of opposition to such ministers as the King shall employ, but if I am sensible that those about his Majesty shall persist in preventing me from receiving those marks of the King's justice which his own benign and amiable disposition would incline him to show to the meanest of his subjects, surely I may be allowed to declare in Parliament my disapprobation of the measures of such men, as the only constitutional resentment which can be shown by individuals to the servants of the Crown' (Sackville to Erskine, 10 Apr. 1763; *HMC, Stop. Sack.* i. 59; Clements, *Germain Papers*, ii. 60).

NOTE D, p. 104. Thomas Thynne, third Viscount Weymouth and later first Marquis of Bath, was unusual in that widely variant opinions of his character and ability seem to have been based less on political partisanships than on moral judgements—yet there is little evidence that his morals were worse than those of many of his respected contemporaries. In his youth he was certainly a blade. George II said of him in 1757 that: 'he could not be a good kind of man, as he never kept company with any woman, & loved nothing but play and strong beer' (R. Rigby to the Duke of Bedford, 3 Feb. 1757; *DNB*). In 1765 his private affairs were in such bad shape that he was on the point of fleeing to France to escape his creditors (*DNB*), but at the last moment he was saved by the influence of friends at court, who got him appointed Lieutenant Governor of Ireland. During his brief term in that capacity he never once set foot in Ireland (Lecky, iv. 371, note). Thurlow became his protégé and adviser, and he gained in stability and political stature. In the first years of the American war he supported the king's policy, but by 1778 he became, according to Walpole (quoted in *DNB*), an advocate of 'peace at any rate'. On Suffolk's death in Mar. 1779 Weymouth took charge of the Northern Department of State as well as his own Southern Department, but in late 1779 he resigned from the Ministry. He was tall, handsome, elegant, and quick-minded, but his ambitions were qualified by laziness.

NOTE E, p. 104. William Knox was born in Ireland in 1732; became Provost Marshal of Georgia in 1756 at 24; was appointed in 1762 by the Georgia legislature to serve as its agent in London. Arrived there, he was sponsored by Shelburne, Charles Townshend, and Grenville, and in 1770 appointed joint Undersecretary for the Colonies with Pownall and served under Hillsborough, Dartmouth, and Germain. While in Georgia he had acquired property there which would prove a total loss if independence were established and he strongly opposed it. Lord North valued his opinions and sometimes consulted him privately. When the American Secretaryship was abolished in 1782 he lost his position but (thanks partly to special efforts by Germain) secured an unusually large pension. He then bought a small estate in Wales and claimed the king had promised him a baronetcy, but after repeated efforts failed to secure it. In 1784 he was appointed agent of the Province of New Brunswick in London at a very small stipend, but never regained either the prosperity or the employment to which his abilities and services entitled him. His accounts of events appear substantially accurate and sometimes throw light in otherwise very dark corners.

NOTE F, p. 110. Robson, 'Lord North', in *History Today*, ii. 8. 533. Lord North drew a distinction between his lack of responsibility for the actions of other ministers in matters within their departmental duties, and his recognized share (but no more than a share) of responsibility for decisions formally made in Cabinet meetings. On 14 Dec. 1778 he defended Germain on the latter grounds: 'As to the personal attacks made on the noble lord near him, relative to the measures respecting the war, there, if censure were due, he laid his claim for part; they were measures of state, originating in the King's councils, and were of course no more the noble lord's measures than they were of any other member of the cabinet' (*Hansard*, xx. 89). In practice North's distinction was a difficult one, since Cabinet meetings were casual and sketchy, minutes not always officially kept and votes not always taken. Replying to North, Charles Fox expressed amazement that Lord North could agree 'to share the guilt with the secretary of the colonies' but 'disown having any share in that of the first lord of the admiralty' (*Hansard*, xx. 90).

NOTE G, p. 112. No meetings of the Cabinet could have been more crucial than those in early 1778 during the political and military aftermath of Saratoga and the French declaration of war. The Cabinet meeting of 18 Mar. 1778 was attended only by the Lord President, Lord Privy Seal, Lords Sandwich, North, Germain, Weymouth, and Amherst (PRO, CO/5, v. 263, no. 12). The Cabinet meeting of 29 Apr. 1778 had the same attendance without the Lord President (PRO, CO/5, v. 263, no. 30).

'The eighteenth century system of government in Great Britain was in any case ill-suited for the conduct of war. Even when ministers had agreed upon definite measures, the ordinary routine of administration encumbered action; there was a lack of co-ordination between departments, and in the supervision of preparations. . . . The practice of each department of government being separate and self-contained, and the minister in charge responsible directly only to the King' (Robson, *Amer. Rev.*, p. 103).

NOTE H, p. 150. Carleton was born in County Down in 1724 of a good but not rich or powerful family. He had been with Amherst at Louisburg; at Belle Isle, Port Andros, and the taking of Havana in 1762. He had served as Colonel and deputy Quartermaster-General under Wolfe at Quebec in 1765 (Mahon, *Life of Murray*, p. 93), and 'had long been a close friend of Wolfe' who had left him £1,000 in his will (Tracy, *History of Canada*, ii. 578 ff.). Carleton had served as acting Governor of the Province of Quebec in 1766 and as Governor and commanding officer after 1770 (*DNB*, under Carleton). He was a professional soldier who had won advancement by ability and had been wounded three times in action. In Canada he had proved not only a 'good soldier' but 'a firm, if arbitrary ruler' (Mahon,

History of Canada, p. 369). Compelled to govern a population largely of French origin and loyalties, Carleton was beginning to weld them into a loyal society by moderation, conservative beginnings of self-government and the passage of the Quebec Act in 1774 (Tracy, ii. 578 ff.). In 1772 he married Maria, daughter of the Earl of Effingham.

NOTE I, p. 155. 'I doubt very much whether the Red Ribbon will be the mark of royal favour which would be most agreeable to you. I confess I took the liberty of expressing my thoughts upon it to his Majesty, and could have wished there had been any other method of shewing the high sense the King has of your merit and services, especially as the giving that distinction to General Carleton, before he had any claim to it by his Operations in Canada, made it appear to me of less value. The King, however, was pleased to say that as he gave it to you *unasked*, and at this time, it would carry with it a strong mark of his approbation. . . . Without . . . that additional assurance I should have been unhappy to have seen your services and those of General Carleton put on the same footing' (Germain to Howe, 18 Oct. 1776; *HMC*, *Stop. Sack.* ii. 43). Howe's knowledge of Germain's spite towards Carleton may have been a factor in Howe's later decision to take no part in the Saratoga campaign which, at the time, he thought would be led by Carleton.

NOTE K, p. 356. From testimony before the Parliamentary Committee, 20 May 1779:

QUESTION: 'Do you know any circumstances of General Burgoyne's military conduct, while under your command, that you disapproved?'

CARLETON: 'I had no reason to disapprove any part of his conduct while under my command.'

QUESTION: After he had received the letter from General Howe informing him that Howe's aid to Burgoyne would be at most very limited, 'whether on that information you considered that you had any discretionary power to detain General Burgoyne after that information?'

CARLETON: 'I could not change General Burgoyne's orders one tittle, that was my opinion.'

QUESTION: 'Should you, if you had been in General Burgoyne's situation, and acting under the orders which you know he received, have thought yourself bound to pursue them implicitly, or at liberty to depart from them?'

CARLETON: 'I should have certainly thought myself bound to have observed them to the utmost of my power. . . . What I would have done I really don't know.'

QUESTION: 'Did not the order from the secretary of state go to the detail of the smallest posts within the province?'

CARLETON: 'The letter is before the Committee.'

(Burgoyne's *Narrative*, Almon, 1780.)

NOTE L, p. 419. 'State & Distribution of his Majesty's Forces under General Sir Henry Clinton, by returns from New York, dated 1st September, 1781, as reported "Present fit for duty".'

In New York and area: 4,156 British, 6,451 German, 1,287 Provincial. Total 11,894.

In Virginia: 3,337 British, 1,565 German, 502 Provincial (with Arnold and Phillips). Total 5 404.

In South Carolina (presumably including some 2,500 from Leslie's Chesapeake expedition): 3,553 British, 1,196 German, 2,021 Provincial. Total 6,770.

Other troops: In Georgia 626; in Nova Scotia 2,723; in East Florida 400; in Bermuda 313; in Providence 47; in West Florida 180.

By Clinton's own report his army fit for duty numbered 28,401, of which 10,012 were German and 5,415 were Provincial. But Germain's listing of 'Effectives' brought that number on paper up to 37,876. (Clements, *Germain Papers*, xv.)

NOTE M, p. 472. Benjamin Thompson (Count Rumford) (1753–1814). Born at Woburn, Mass.; early orphaned; good local schooling; precocious, especially in mathematics and 'science'. Went to Boston and studied French and mathematics; married a wealthy young widow; one daughter, Sarah. Ingratiated himself with loyalist Governor Wentworth of New Hampshire but professed to neighbours that he was a revolutionary like themselves. In 1775 he tried to get a commission in Washington's army but was refused because suspected of Tory sympathies. He then worked secretly for the British forces as a spy. On being suspected he fled to Providence, deserting his wife and baby daughter, and took ship for England.

After the revolution he became an important officer of the Elector of Bavaria and in 1788 Major-General and head of the war department of the Bavarian Government. Member of various scientific academies; made Count Rumford by the Bavarian Government in 1791. Returned briefly to England in 1795 and there published the first volume of his *Essays: Political, Economical and Philosophical* and gave £1,000 to the Royal Society for a medal for researches in heat and light. Also gave 5,000 dollars to the American Academy of Arts and Sciences for a similar award. In that year he sent for his daughter Sarah from America, who lived with him in Europe for several years.

Head of the Council of Regency in Munich in 1796. Minister to Britain. Offered superintendency of West Point Military Academy but declined. In 1805 he married the widow of the chemist Lavoisier but they soon separated. Died 1814 leaving, in addition to Sarah, an illegitimate son and daughter. Left a bequest to Harvard for a professorship in the physical sciences. Was said to have had 'few friends' even among scientists.

APPENDIX I

Germain's Orders to Carleton and Burgoyne

(Germain to Carleton, 26 March 1777)

'. . . It has become highly necessary that the most speedy junction of the two armies should be effected . . . and therefore as the security and good government of Canada absolute[ly] require your presence there, it is the King's determination to leave about 3000 men under your command for the defense and duties of that province, and to employ the remainder of your army upon two expeditions—the one under the command of Lieut.-General Burgoyne, who is to force his way to Albany, and the other under the command of Lieutenant-Colonel St. Leger, who is to make a diversion upon the Mohawk River.

'As the plan cannot advantageously be executed without the assistance of Canadians and Indians, his Majesty strongly recommends it to your care to furnish both expeditions with good and sufficient bodies of these men. . . .

'In order that no time may be lost in entering upon these important undertakings, General Burgoyne ha[s] received orders to consult with you upon the subject, and to form and adjust the plan, as you shall both think most conducive to his Majesty's service.'

[The letter then instructed General Carleton in mandatory detail that virtually removed any freedom to 'adjust the plan', specifying the precise regiments and companies Carleton is to turn over to Burgoyne, to a total of 7,173 regulars and Germans,] 'together with as many Canadians and Indians as may be thought necessary for this service. . . . You are to give him orders to pass down Lake Champlain, and from thence, by the most vigorous use of the force at his command, to proceed with all expedition to Albany and put himself under the command of Sir William Howe.

'I shall write to Sir William Howe from hence by the first packet. But you will nevertheless endeavor to give him the earliest intelligence of this measure and also to direct Lieut.-General Burgoyne and Lieut.-Colonel St. Leger to neglect no opportunity of doing the same, that they may receive instructions from Sir William Howe. You will at the same time inform them that until they have received orders from Sir William Howe, it is his Majesty's pleasure that they shall act as exigencies may require and in such a manner as they shall judge most proper for making an impression on the rebels, but that in doing so they must never lose view of their intended junctions with Sir William Howe as their principal objects.'

[The letter was endorsed: 'No. 6, A copy of this letter was sent to Sir William Howe in a letter from Mr. D'Oyley, by the Somerset man-of-war, which arrived at New York the 24th May. Sir Wm. Howe acknowledged the receipt of it in his letter of the 5th July, No. 9.]

The Character of Lord George

The baffling qualities in Lord George's character and personality are reflected in the variant estimates by his contemporaries. Five men with different motivations and points of view recorded their judgements of him. The Earl of Shelburne was his political enemy, but was well acquainted with his family and was a man of considerable perception and judgement. Horace Walpole opposed Lord George's American policy but often praised his abilities. Sir Nathaniel Wraxall was a chronicler of reputation, though inclined to be sympathetic with men possessed of titles and comfortable estates. Thomas Stockdale, who soldiered in his youth under Colonel Lord George Sackville, developed then an admiration which he later transferred, with some qualifications, to Lord George Germain. Stockdale was not inconsiderate of the personal advantages of praising the rich and powerful: he dedicated an essay on Pope to Lord George and then commented: 'He afterwards set his interest in motion to befriend me.'

Richard Cumberland's untempered praises are not to be taken without salt. Lord George found him a clerk in the office of the Board of Trade; promoted him to a secretaryship in his own office (Germain to Dartmouth, 23 Jan. 1776; *HMC, Dartmouth*, ii (1896), 412) and after 1777 used him in covert negotiations and espionage on the Continent, sending him to Lisbon in May 1880 and on to Madrid to join Hussey in undercover negotiations for peace (*HMC, Stop. Sack.* i. 323 ff.). In later years Lord George continued to employ, patronize, and often to house and feed Cumberland, who gained a considerable reputation as a minor playwright. The highly laudatory pamphlet Cumberland published after the death of his patron led Robert Hobart to write to the Duke of Rutland: 'I send you Cumberland's pamphlet, designed, I suppose, to rescue Lord Sackville's character from oblivion. It seems to me calculated to provoke discussion, which the friends of the late Lord will repent of' (Hobart to Rutland, 24 Dec. 1785; *HMC*, xiv, I, *Rutland*, iii. 271).

Since his career and relationship to Lord George are unknown, the obituary tribute of John Fisher, written to William Knox immediately after Lord George's death, falls into a different category, and there is no basis for its evaluation.

To contrast the contradictions in the various estimates, I have placed selections from these statements in juxtaposition. For the full estimates, see (1) Le Marchant, *Walpole Memoirs*, iii. 231–3; (2) Fitzmaurice, *Shelburne*, i. 362, 363 (1912 edition, pp. 250, 251); (3) Wheatley, *Wraxall Memoirs, 1772–1784*, i. 385–8; (4) Stockdale, *Memoirs*, i. 436; (5) Cumberland, *Memoirs*, 1806, pp. 288, 289; (6) Cumberland's Memorial Pamphlet, Stockdale, London, 1785, 24 pp.; (7) Fisher to Knox, *HMC, Var. Coll.* 6, *Knox*, pp. 193, 194.

'In perspicacity he has never been excelled.' Cumberland.
'He knew neither mankind nor did he know himself.' Shelburne.

. . . to sift out the truth by discussion seemed his only object.' Cumberland.
'He had no desire of searching out truth, he had no scruples.' Shelburne.

'In . . . integrity he was not to be surpassed.' Cumberland.
'. . . . his intolerable love of corruption'. Shelburne.

'He was very conversant with books.' Stockdale.
'He possessed little education derived from books . . . rarely opened an author.' Wraxall.

His afflictions: '. . . neither hardened his heart, depressed his spirit, nor soured his temper. . . . Charity was in him no less the exercise of the judgment than of the heart.' Cumberland.
He: '. . . had a want of affection. . . . To attract the heart was not one of his abilities.' Stockdale.
'He lacked the art of conciliating friendship.' Walpole.
'He . . . wanted heart on every occasion.' Shelburne.

His opponents: '. . . did not attack him on the score of capacity; his abilities were too well established . . . they could not deny he was a capable man.' Cumberland.
'. . . his former parts so entirely forsook him, that younger men, who had not seen his outset, would not believe what was attested to them of his precedent abilities.' Walpole.

'He was an adept at that art which tends to put others in humour with themselves.' Cumberland.
'. . . there was, likewise, a reserve and haughtiness in his manner, which depressed and darkened all that was agreeable, and engaging, in him.' Stockdale.

BIBLIOGRAPHY

ADAMS, C. F. *Studies Military and Diplomatic 1775–1865*. Macmillan, New York, 1911.

— 'Contemporary Opinion on the Howes', *Proc. Mass. Hist. Socy.* xliv (Nov. 1910), 94 ff.

— *Family Letters of John Adams and his wife Abigail*. Boston, 1875.

ADAMS, R. G. *Papers of Lord George Germain in the Stopford-Sackville Papers in the Clements Library*, secured from Mr. Nigel Sackville in 1927. Ann Arbor, 1928.

— *The Headquarters Papers of the British Army in North America—a Brief Description of Sir Henry Clinton's Papers in the William L. Clements Library*. Ann Arbor, 1926.

ADOLPHUS, JOHN. *History of England from the Accession of King George III to . . . 1783*. 7 vols., Cadell, London, 1802.

ALBEMARLE, *see* KEPPEL.

ALMON, JOHN. *The Parliamentary Register: History of the Proceedings and Debates of the House of Commons 1774–1780*. 17 vols., Almon, London, 1775–80.

— *Correspondence of the late John Wilkes*. 5 vols., Almon, London, 1805.

— *Biographical, Literary and Political Anecdotes, Anonymous*. 3 vols., Almon, London, 1797.

— *An Epistle to Lord George Germain on the American War*, pp. 13. Almon, London, 1778.

ANBUREY, LT. THOMAS. *Travels through the Interior Parts of America, in a series of Letters*. 2 vols., Houghton Mifflin, Boston, 1789.

ANDERSON, T. S. *The Command of the Howe Brothers during the American Revolution*. Oxford, 1936. Also in the form of a typed thesis in the Rhodes House Library, Oxford.

ANDREWS, C. M. *Guide to the Materials for American History to 1783 in the Public Records Office, London*. 2 vols., Washington, 1912.

— and DAVENPORT, F. G. *Guide to MSS. Materials in the British Museum, Oxford and Cambridge*. Carnegie Inst., Washington, 1908.

Annual Register, or a View of History, Politics and Literature for the Year. 3rd edition, Dodsley, London, 1796.

ANSON, W. R. *Autobiography and Political Correspondence of Augustus Henry, Third Duke of Grafton*. Murray, London, 1898.

BAKELESS, JOHN. *Turncoats, Traitors and Heroes*. Lippincott, Phila., 1959.

BALCH, T., *see* GALLOWAY.

BALL, F. E. *Correspondence of Jonathan Swift, D.D.* 6 vols., Bell, London, 1910–14.

BANCROFT, GEORGE. *A History of the United States*. 10 vols., New York, 1848.

BARKER, G. F. R., *see* LE MARCHANT.

BARNES, G. R., and OWEN, J. H. *The Private Papers of John Montague, Fourth Earl of Sandwich, First Lord of the Admiralty 1771–1782*, vols. lxix, lxxi, lxxv, lxxviii, 1932–8.

BARROW, SIR JOHN. *Life of Richard, Earl Howe.* London, 1838.

BASYE, A. H. 'The Secretary of State for the Colonies, 1768–1782', in *Amer. Hist. Review*, xxviii (1922), 13–23.

BAXTER, J. P. *The British Invasion from the North . . . with the Journal of Lieut. W. Digby of the 53rd or Shropshire Regiment of Foot.* Munsell, Albany, 1887.

BELCHER, HENRY. *The First American Civil War, First Period, 1775–1778.* 2 vols., Macmillan, London, 1911.

BELSHAM, WILLIAM. *Memoirs of the Reign of George III . . . to 1793.* 4 vols., Robinson, London, 1795.

BEW, J. *Historical Anecdotes in a Series of Letters written from America, 1777–1778.* London, 1779.

BICKLEY, F. *Diaries of Sylvester Douglas, Lord Glenbervie.* Constable, London, 1795.

BLADON, F. McK. *Diaries of Colonel the Hon. Robert Fulke Greville, Equerry to his Majesty King George III.* John Lane, London, 1930.

BRINTON, C. C. *The Anatomy of Revolution.* New York, 1947.

British Museum (BM): relevant papers including:
  Add. MSS. 35349–36278. Hardwick Papers, Joseph Yorke, Robert Murray Keith.
  Add. MSS. 28060–8. Francis Godolphin Osborne.
  Add. MS. 20733, fols. 106–11. Almon Corresp. and Pownall.
  Add. MS. 24322, Misc. letters relating to American affairs, 1718–96.
  Add. MS. 29237. Johnson family letters, 1774–83.
  Add. MSS. 34412–71. Auckland Papers (William Eden), 1772–8.

BROOKE, JOHN. *The Chatham Administration, 1756–1768.* Macmillan, London, 1956.

BROUGHAM, H. P. (First Baron Brougham and Vaux). *Historical Sketches of Statesmen who Flourished in the Time of George III.* 3 vols., London, 1839–43.

BROWNING, OSCAR. *The Political Memoranda of Francis, fifth Duke of Leeds, now first printed from the originals in the British Museum.* Camden Society, vol. xxxv. London, 1884.

BURGOYNE, JOHN. *The Substance of General Burgoyne's Speeches on Mr. Vyner's Motion in the House of Commons on March 26, 1778.* Exshaw, Dublin, 1778.

— *A Letter from Lieutenant General John Burgoyne to his Constituents upon his late Resignation, with the Correspondences between the Secretaries of War and him relative to his return to America.* J. Almon, London, 1779; also Marchbank, Dublin, 1779.

— *Burgoyne's Narrative before Parliament, as published in A State of the Expedition from Canada as laid before the House of Commons, written by himself.* 2nd ed., Almon, London, 1780.

— *The Heiress, A Comedy in Five Acts by J. B., as performed at the Theatre Royal.* London, 1786.

— *The Maid of the Oaks, as performed at the Drury Lane Theatre.* Dublin, 1786.

Cambridge Modern History, 13 vols. Vol. vii, Cambridge, 1903.

CHRISTIE, J. R. *The End of Lord North's Ministry.* Macmillan, London, 1958.

CLARK, DORA M. *British Opinion and the American Revolution.* New Haven, 1930.

CLARK, JANE. 'Responsibility for the Failure of the Burgoyne Campaign', *Amer. Hist. Review*, xxxv (April 1930), 542 ff.

CLEMENTS. The William L. Clements Library of the University of Michigan, Ann Arbor, Michigan.

CLINTON, SIR HENRY. *The American Rebellion: Sir Henry Clinton's Narrative of his Campaigns*, ed. by W. B. Willcox. Yale, New Haven, 1954.

— *Historical Detail of Seven Years' Campaigns in North America*, with other unpublished papers in the William L. Clements Library of the University of Michigan, Ann Arbor, Michigan.

— *Narrative Relative to the Conduct of the War*. London, 1783.

COBBETT, WILLIAM. *Parliamentary History of England 1066–1803*. 36 vols. (1806–20). Taken over by *Hansard* in 1812 with vol. xiii, and continued. Longman Hurst, London.

COKE, LADY MARY. *Letters and Journals*, ed. J. A. Home. 4 vols., Douglas, Edinburgh, 1889–96.

COLERIDGE, E. H. *Life of Thomas Coutts, Banker*. 2 vols., John Law, London, 1920.

Colonial Office, *see* Public Records Office (PRO/CO).

CORNWALLIS, *see* ROSS, also Braybrook MSS. at Audley End, Saffron Walden, Essex, and MSS. of J. B. Fortescue at Dropmore, in Hist. MSS. Comm. vols. H.M. Stationery Office, London, 1881 and 1905.

COVENTRY, GEORGE. *A Critical Enquiry regarding the real Author of The Letters of Junius, proving them to have been written by Lord Viscount Sackville*. Phillips, London, 1825.

CRESSWELL, NICHOLAS. *The Journal of Nicholas Cresswell 1774–1777*. Cape, London, 1925.

CROKER, J. W. *Letters from Henrietta, Countess of Suffolk*. 2 vols., London, 1824.

CUMBERLAND, RICHARD. *Memoirs*. 2 vols., London, 1807.

— *Character of the late Lord Sackville*, a pamphlet, pp. 24, printed for John Stockdale, London, 1785; C. Dilly, London; copy in the Bodleian Library.

CURTIS, E. E. *The Organization of the British Army in the American Revolution*. Yale, New Haven, 1926.

CURTIS, L. P. *Letters of Laurence Sterne*. Oxford, 1935.

DE BRETT, JOHN. *The History, Debates and Proceedings of both Houses of Parliament*. 7 vols., London, 1792.

DE FONBLANQUE, E. B. *Political and Military Episodes in the Latter Half of the 18th Century, derived from the Life and Correspondence of the Right Honourable John Burgoyne*. London, 1876.

— *Administration and Organization of the British Army*. Longmans, London, 1858.

Dictionary of American Biography. New York.

Dictionary of National Biography. London (Oxford).

DOBRÉE, BONAMY. *Letters of Philip Dormer Stanhope, Fourth Earl of Chesterfield*. 6 vols., London, 1932.

DONNE, W. B. *Correspondence of George III with Lord North*. 2 vols., London, 1867.

DRINKWATER, JOHN. *Charles James Fox*. Benn, London, 1928.

EDEN, WILLIAM (Lord Auckland). *The Journal and Correspondence of*, with a Preface and Introduction by the Bishop of Bath and Wells. 4 vols., London, 1861–2.

EDGERTON, H. E. 'Lord George Germain and Sir William Howe', *Eng. Hist. Review*, xxv (1910), 315, 316.

ELLIOT-MURRAY, E. E. (Countess of Minto). *Memoirs of Hugh Elliot*. Edinburgh, 1868.

FEILING, K. G. *The Second Tory Party, 1714–1832*. London, 1938.

FISHER, S. G. *The True History of the American Revolution*. Lippincott, Philadelphia, 1902.

FITZMAURICE, LORD EDWARD. *Life of William, Earl of Shelburne, afterwards first Marquess of Lansdowne*. 3 vols., Macmillan, 1875–6.

— *Charles William Ferdinand*. Longmans, London, 1901.

FITZPATRICK, J. C. *The Writings of Washington*, complete edition, 1745–99. 39 vols., U.S. Govt. Printing Office, Washington, 1933.

— *Diaries of Washington*. 4 vols., New York, 1925.

FITZWILLIAM, EARL CHARLES WILLIAM, and BOURKE, SIR RICHARD. *Correspondence of the right honourable Edmund Burke between the year 1774 and . . . 1797*. 4 vols., London, 1894.

FONBLANQUE, *see* DE FONBLANQUE.

FORCE, PETER. *American Archives, A Documentary History of the United States*, Fifth Series. 9 vols., Washington, 1853 (chiefly vol. iii).

FORD, W. C. 'Parliament and the Howes', *Proceedings of the Mass. Hist. Socy.*, vol. xliv.

— *Writings of George Washington*. 14 vols., New York, 1889–93.

FORTESCUE, SIR JOHN. *The Correspondence of King George III from 1760 to December 1783*. 6 vols., Macmillan, London, 1927.

— *A History of the British Army*. 13 vols. and 6 atlases, 1899–1930; Part II, vols. ii, iii, iv. Macmillan, London, 1902.

FOSTER. *Peerage*. London, various dates, under individual names such as Sackville, Howe, &c.

FOX, HENRY (Lord Holland). *Memoirs of the Last Ten Years of the Reign of George the Second*. 2 vols., Murray, London, 1822.

FOX-STRANGEWAYS, G. S. H. *Henry Fox, First Lord Holland*. London, 1920.

FREEMAN, D. S. *Life of Washington*. Several volumes, uncompleted, New York, 1951 ff.

French Archives: Angleterre, vol. 528, fol. 5; see selections also in Stevens, *Facsimiles*, cited below.

FROTHINGHAM, T. G. *Washington, Commander in Chief*. Houghton Mifflin, Boston, 1930.

FROUDE, J. A. *The English in Ireland in the 18th Century*. 3 vols., Longmans, London, 1886.

GALLOWAY, JOSEPH. *Historical and Political Reflections on the . . . American Rebellion by the Author of Letters to a Nobleman*. Wilkie, London, 1780.

— *Letters to a Nobleman on the Conduct of the War*. Wilkie, London, 1779.

— *The Examination of, by a Committee of the House of Commons beginning June 16, 1779*, edited by T. Balch. Collins, Phila., 1885; also Wilkie, London, 1779.

GEE, CLIVE. 'The British War Office in the later years of the American War of Independence', *Journal Modern Hist.* xxvi (June 1954), 11.

Gentleman's Magazine, Monthly, 1731–1907, for the relevant years.

GERMAIN, LORD GEORGE, *see* SACKVILLE.

GOLDSMITH, OLIVER. *The History of England . . . to the death of George II.* 4 vols., 1771; 11th edition corrected, with a continuation to . . . 1815, ed. by Charles Coote, 4 vols., 1819.

GORE-BROWN, ROBERT. *Chancellor Thurlow, The Life and Times of an XVIIIth Century Lawyer.* Hamilton, London, 1953.

GRAHAM, G. S. 'Considerations on the War of American Independence', a paper read at the Anglo-American Conference 10 July 1948 and printed in *Bulletin of the Institute of Historical Research*, xxii (1949), 22–34, Longmans, London.

GREENE, MAJOR-GENERAL FRANCIS V. *The Revolutionary War and the Military Policy of the United States.* Murray, London, 1911.

GREIG, JAMES. *The Diaries of a Duchess; Extracts from the Diaries of the first Duchess of Northumberland (1716–1776).* Hodder and Stoughton, London, 1926.

GRENVILLE, R. P. (Second Duke of Buckingham and Chandos). *Memoirs of the court and cabinets of George the third, from original family documents, 1782–1810.* 4 vols., London, 1853–5.

GUTTRIDGE, G. H. 'Lord George Germain in Office', *Amer. Hist. Review*, xxxiii, no. 1 (Oct. 1927), 23 ff.

HADDEN, LT. J. M. *Journal and Orderly Books . . . kept in Canada and upon Burgoyne's Campaign*, with notes by Horatio Rogers. Munsell, Albany, 1884.

Hansard: The Parliamentary History of England, published by Longman Hurst and others, London, 1810 ff. (began as Cobbett, *Parl. History*).

HARCOURT, E. W. *The Harcourt Papers.* 13 vols., privately printed, Parker, Oxford, 1876–1903.

HEADLAM, CUTHBERT. *Letters of Lady Harriet Eliot, 1766–1786.* Constable, Edinburgh, 1914.

HEATH, MAJOR-GEN. WILLIAM. *Memoirs of the American War, Part II. Collections of the Mass. Hist. Socy.*, 7th series, vol. iv, Boston, 1904.

Historical Manuscripts Commission—in notes as *HMC*—being reports of the Royal Comm. on Hist. MSS., H.M. Stationery Office, London, various dates. Relevant volumes as indicated in individual notes.

HERBERT, LORD. *Henry, Elizabeth and George, 1734–1780; Letters and Diaries of Henry, Tenth Earl of Pembroke, and his Circle.* Cape, London, 1939.

HEWINS, W. A. S. *The Whitefoord Papers, 1739 to 1810.* Oxford, 1898.

HOLDEN, FURBER. *Henry Dundas, first Viscount Melville, 1742–1811.* Oxford, 1931.

HOME, J. A., editor, *see* COKE.

HOWE, GEN. SIR WILLIAM. *Narrative of Lieut. General Sir William Howe in a Committee of the House of Commons on the 29th April, 1779, relative to his conduct, etc.* London, 1780.

— *View of Evidence Relative to the Conduct of the War.* London, 1779.

HUDLESTON, F. J. *Gentleman Johnny Burgoyne.* Cape, London, 1928.

HUDLESTON, F. J. *Warriors in Undress*. Castle, London, 1925.

HUNT, WILLIAM. *The History of England from the accession of George III to the close of Pitt's first administration (1760–1801)*. London, 1905.

HUTCHINSON. *Diary and Letters of Thomas Hutchinson*, original MS. in William L. Clements Library of the University of Michigan, Ann Arbor.

HUTCHINSON, P. O. *Diary and Letters of Thomas Hutchinson*. 2 vols., Sampson and Lowe, London, 1883–6.

ILCHESTER, COUNTESS OF, and LORD STAVORDALE. *Life and Letters of Lady Sarah Lennox 1745–1826*. 2 vols., Murray, London, 1901–2.

JACKSON, R. *A View of the Formation, Discipline and Economy of Armies*. 3rd edition, London, 1845.

JESSE, J. H. *George Selwyn and his Contemporaries*. 4 vols., Bentley, London, 1843–4.

— *Memoirs of the Life and Reign of King George III*. 2nd edition, 3 vols., Tinsley, London, 1867.

KEPPEL, GEORGE THOMAS (Earl of Albemarle). *Memoirs of the Marquis of Rockingham and his Contemporaries*. 2 vols., London, 1852.

KINGSFORD, WILLIAM. *The History of Canada*. 10 vols., Kegan Paul, London, 1893 (especially vol. vi).

KNOX, WILLIAM, *see* Clements Library, University of Michigan, Knox Papers, and in *Hist. MSS. Comm. (HMC)*, especially *Var. Coll. 6, Knox*.

LAMB, SERGEANT ROGER. *An Original and Authentic Journal of Occurrences during the Late American War, from its commencement to the year 1783*. Wilkinson and Courtney, Dublin, 1809; also London, 1809.

LECKY, W. E. H. *A History of England in the Eighteenth Century*. 8 vols., Longmans Green, London, 1882 (especially vol. iv).

LE MARCHANT, DENIS. *Horace Walpole's Memoirs of the Reign of King George the Third*, re-edited by G. F. R. Barker. 4 vols., London, 1894.

LEWIS, WILMARTH S. (General Editor). Yale edition of the *Correspondence of Horace Walpole*. 14 vols. and forthcoming, Yale University Press, New Haven, and Oxford University Press, London, 1934– .

LLANOVER, LADY. *The Autobiography and Correspondence of Mary Granville, Mrs. Delany*. 6 vols., London, 1861–2.

LONG, J. C. *Lord Jeffery Amherst*. Macmillan, New York, 1933.

LUCAS, SIR C. P. *A History of Canada, 1763–1812*. Oxford, 1909.

LUCAS, REGINALD. *Lord North, second Earl of Guilford . . . 1732–1792*. 2 vols., London, 1913.

MAHON, MAJOR-GEN. R. H. *Life of General the Hon. James Murray*. Murray, London, 1921.

MANNERS, W. E. *John Manners, Marquis of Granby*. Macmillan, London, 1899.

MARLOWE, LOUIS (pen-name for Lewis Wilkinson). *Sackville of Drayton*. Horne and Van Thal, London, 1948.

MASSEY, W. N. *A History of England during the reign of George the Third*. 4 vols., London, 1855–63.

MAXWELL, CONSTANTIA. *Dublin under the Georges, 1714–1830*. Faber, London, 1936.

MINTO, COUNTESS OF. *Life and Letters of Sir Gilbert Elliot, First Earl of Minto, from 1751 to 1806*. 3 vols., Longmans, London, 1874.

MUMBY, F. A. *George III and the American Revolution*. London, 1924.

NAMIER, SIR LEWIS. 'The Country Gentleman in Parliament', in *History Today*, iv. 10 (1954), 676–88.

— *England in the Age of the American Revolution*. Macmillan, London, 1930.

— *The Structure of Politics at the Accession of George III*. Macmillan, London, 2 vols., 1929.

— *Personalities and Powers*. Macmillan, London, 1955.

NICKERSON, HOFFMAN. *The Turning Point of the Revolution*. New York, 1928.

NORTH, LORD. *Private Papers of Frederick, Lord North and his family*, an unpublished MS. collection in the Bodleian Library, Oxford.

NUGENT, CLAUDE. *Robert, Earl Nugent*. London, 1898.

ORRERY, COUNTESS OF CORK AND. *The Orrery Papers*. 2 vols., Duckworth, London, 1903.

PARES, RICHARD. *Limited Monarchy in Great Britain in the 18th Century*. A pamphlet, published for the Historical Association by Routledge and Kegan Paul, 1957.

— and TAYLOR, A. J. P., eds. *Essays Presented to Sir Lewis Namier*. Macmillan, London, 1956.

PARGELLIS, STANLEY, and MEDLEY, D. J. *Bibliography of British History; The Eighteenth Century*, issued under the direction of the Amer. Hist. Assn. and the Royal Hist. Socy., Oxford, 1951.

PARKES, S. J., and MERIVALE, H. *Memoirs of Sir Philip Francis*. 2 vols., Longmans, London, 1867.

PARKMAN, GEORGE. *Montcalm and Wolfe*. 2 vols., London, 1884 (especially vol. ii, chap. xxvii).

PAUSCH, F. G. *Journal of Captain Pausch of the Hanau Artillery During the Burgoyne Campaign*. London, 1886.

PEMBERTON, W. B. *Lord North*. Longmans Green, London, 1938.

PHILLIMORE, R. J. *Memoirs and Correspondence of George, Lord Lyttelton, from 1734 to 1773*. 2 vols., London, 1845.

PHILLIPS, C. J. *A History of the Sackville Family*. 2 vols., Cassell, London, 1930.

Public Records Office, Chancery Lane, London—in notes as PRO—including War Office Correspondence (WO), Colonial Office Correspondence (CO), Home Office Correspondence (HO), and Carleton Papers (30/55). Relevant volumes as indicated in individual notes.

RIEDESEL, MAJOR-GENERAL BARON. *Memoirs, Letters and Journals . . . during his Residence in America*, translation by Von Elking. Munsell, Albany, 1868.

RIEDESEL, BARONESS F. C. L. *Letters and Journals relating to the American War of the Revolution*, translation by W. L. Stone, Albany, 1867.

ROBERTS, WILLIAM. *Memoirs of the Life of Mrs. Hannah More*. 2 vols., Seeley, London, 1836.

ROBERTSON, SIR C. G. *England under the Hanoverians*. Methuen, London, 1911.

ROBSON, ERIC. *The American Revolution in its Political and Military Aspects 1763–1783*. Batchworth Press, 1955.

— *Letters from America of Sir James Murray, 1773–1780*. Manchester University Press, 1951.

ROBSON, ERIC. 'Lord North', in *History Today*, ii, no. 8 (Aug. 1952), 532–9.
— 'Purchase and Promotion in the British Army in the Eighteenth Century', in *History*, xxxvi (Feb.–June 1951), 57–72.
ROSCOE, E. S., and CLERGUE, HELEN. *George Selwyn, His Letters and Life*. London, 1899.
ROSS, CHARLES. *Correspondence of Charles, First Marquis Cornwallis*. 3 vols., Murray, London, 1859.
RUSSELL, LORD JOHN. *Correspondence of John, fourth Duke of Bedford*. 3 vols., Longmans Green, London, 1842–6.
— *Memorials and Correspondence of Charles James Fox*. 4 vols., Bentley, London, 1853.
SACKVILLE, LORD GEORGE. *His Lordship's Apology*. London, 1759.
— *His Vindication of Himself*. R. Stevens, London, 1759.
— *A Short Address to the Public*. London, 1759.
— *Proceedings of a General Court Martial, held at the Horse Guards on Friday the 7th of March etc.* A. Millar, London, 1760; and Ewing, Dublin, 1760.
SACKVILLE (GERMAIN), LORD GEORGE. *A Letter to, on the American War*, pp. 84. London, 1778, Bodleian Collection.
— *The Papers of Lord George Germain*: a brief description of the Stopford-Sackville Papers, now in the William L. Clements Library of the University of Michigan, edited by R. G. Adams, Ann Arbor, 1928. The collection itself is unequalled.
SACKVILLE-WEST, VICTORIA. *Knole and the Sackvilles*. London, 1922.
SEDGWICK, R. *Letters from George III to Lord Bute 1756–1766*. Macmillan, London, 1940.
SMITH, W. J. *The Grenville Papers*, being the correspondence of Richard Grenville, Earl Temple, K.G., and the Right Hon. George Grenville, their friends and contemporaries. 4 vols., London, 1852–3.
SMOLLETT, TOBIAS GEORGE (continued by T. S. Hughes). *The History of England from the Accession of George III, 1760, to the Accession of Queen Victoria, 1837*. 5 vols., London, 1834–6.
SMYTHE, G. *Memoirs and Correspondence of Sir Robert Murray Keith, 1769–1792*. 2 vols., London, 1849.
SPARROW, W. J. 'Benjamin Thompson and Lord George Germain', in *Historical Journal of the University of Birmingham*, v, no. ii (1956), 138 ff.
SPECTOR, M. M. *The American Department of the British Government, 1768–1782*. New York, 1940.
STANHOPE, PHILIP HENRY, VISCOUNT MAHAN (later fifth Earl Stanhope). *History of England from the Peace of Utrecht to the Peace of Versailles, 1713–1783*. 7 vols., London, 1836–54.
STEDMAN, CHARLES. *History of the Origin, Progress and Termination of the American War*, by C. Stedman, who served under Sir W. Howe, Sir H. Clinton and the Marquis Cornwallis. 2 vols., London, 1794.
STEUART, A. F. *The Last Journals of Horace Walpole, 1771–1783*. 2 vols., John Lane, London, 1910.
STEVENS, B. F. *Facsimiles of MSS. in European Archives, relating to America 1773–1783*. 25 vols., London, 1889–98.

STEVENS, B. F. *The Clinton–Cornwallis Controversy*, a collection of contemporary pamphlets. London, 1888.

STOCKDALE, PERCIVAL. *Memoirs, written by himself.* 2 vols., Longmans, 1809.

STONE, W. L. *The Campaign of Lieut. Gen. John Burgoyne and the Expedition of Lieut. Col. Barry St. Leger.* Joel Munsell, Albany, 1877.

SULLIVAN, A. M. *Two Centuries of Irish History, 1681–1870.* Kegan Paul, London, 1888.

TAYLOR, W. S., and PRINGLE, J. H. *Correspondence of William Pitt, Earl of Chatham.* 4 vols., Murray, London, 1838–40.

THEMISTOCLES (pseudonym). *A Reply to Sir Henry Clinton's narrative*, 'including the whole of the public and secret correspondence'. J. De Brett of Piccadilly, London, 1783.

THOMAS, W. MOY. *Letters of Lady Mary Wortley Montague.* London, 1887.

THOMSON, M. A. *Secretaries of State 1681–1782.* Oxford, 1932.

TOWER, CHARLEMAGNE. *Essays Historical and Political.* London, 1911.

TOYNBEE, MRS. PAGET. *Letters of Horace Walpole.* 16 vols., Oxford, 1902–5.

TOYNBEE, PAGET, and WHIBLEY, LEONARD. *Correspondence of Thomas Gray.* 3 vols., Oxford, 1935.

TRACY, F. T. *Tercentenary History of Canada.* 3 vols., Macmillan, New York, 1908.

Trade, Board of. *Journal of the Commissioners for Trade and Plantations, 1704–1782, in the Public Record Office.* 14 vols., 1920–38.

TREVELYAN, SIR G. O. *The American Revolution.* 4 vols., Longmans Green, London, 1905.

TURBERVILLE, H. S. *The House of Lords in the Eighteenth Century.* Oxford, 1927.

TURNER, E. R. *The Cabinet Council of England in the 17th and 18th centuries, 1622–1784.* 2 vols., Baltimore, 1930–2.

VAN DOREN, CARL. *Secret History of the American Revolution.* Viking, New York, 1941.

VAN TYNE, C. H. *Loyalists in the American Revolution.* 3 vols., New York, 1902–3.

—— *The War of Independence.* Boston and New York, 1929.

VON ELKING, M. *German Allied Troops in the North American War of Independence, 1776–1783*, trans. by J. G. Rosengarten. Albany, 1893.

VON RUVILLE, ALBERT. *William Pitt, Earl of Chatham*, trans. by H. J. CHAYTOR. 3 vols., Heinemann, London, 1907.

WALPOLE, HORACE. *Letters on the American War of Independence.* London, 1908.

WHEATLEY, H. B. *The Historical and Posthumous Memoirs of Sir Nathaniel Wraxall, 1772–1784.* 5 vols., London, 1884.

WHITTON, F. E. *History of the Prince of Wales Leinster Regiment.* Murray, London, 1931.

WHITWORTH, REX. *Field Marshal Lord Ligonier.* Oxford, 1958.

WILKIE, J. (publisher). *A Reply to Lt. Gen. Burgoyne's Letter to his Constituents.* London, 1779.

WILKINSON, LEWIS, *see* MARLOWE.

WILLCOX, WILLIAM B. (*see* CLINTON, *Narrative*). *The American Rebellion.* Yale, New Haven, 1954.

WILLIAMS, BASIL. *The Whig Supremacy, 1714–1760.* Oxford, 1939.

WORTLEY, J. A. S. *Letters of Lady Mary Wortley Montague*. 3 vols., Wharncliffe, London, 1887.

WORTLEY, E. STUART. *A Prime Minister to His Son*. London, 1925.

WRIGHT, J. *Speeches of the Right Honourable Charles James Fox*. 6 vols., Longmans Hurst, London, 1815 (especially vol. i).

WRONG, G. M. *Canada and the American Revolution*. New York, 1935.

WYNDHAM, H. P. *Diary of George Bubb Dodington, Baron of Melcomb Regis*. Wilkie, London, 1784; also London, 1828.

YORKE, P. C. *Life and Correspondence of Philip Yorke, Earl of Hardwick*. 3 vols., Cambridge, 1913.

INDEX OF PERSONS AND PLACES

Abingdon, Willoughby Bertie (1740–99), 4th Earl of: opposed peerage, 457.

Abercromby, James (1706–81), 34.

Acland, John Dyke, 249.

Adams, Henry Brooks (1838–1918), 8.

Adams, John (1735–1826), 221, 437.

Adirondack Mountains: difficulty of terrain, 14; military equipment required, 199; foot-hills, 231; strategic considerations, 428 ff.

Adolphus, John (1768–1845), 98.

Albany, New York: military significance, 161, 162; proposals for meeting there, 163–81, 196, 200, 203, 206–12, 217–22, 228; reinforced by Washington, 236; attempts, 230, 238–41, 245–7, 250; Vaughan's attempt, 251; Schuyler host to Burgoyne, 252, 254; later discussions, 257, 259, 262, 263, 274, 277, 285, 295; strategy reviewed, 347–57.

Albemarle, George Keppel (1724–72), 3rd Earl of, 60, 68, 76.

Allen, Ethan (1737–89), 204, 337 n. 2.

Allen, Rev. Bennet, 488.

Almon, John (1737–1805), 66, 132.

Amherst, Jeffery (1717–97), 1st Lord: at Louisburg, 42; in Canada, 74; commander-in-chief, 118; American terrain, 120; the *Lady Townshend*, 130, 135; command declined, 140, 164; unsigned memorandum, 169; on Lord George's policy, 299; on command against colonists, 305, 331; cabinet decision, 332; appointment of a captain, 336; Lord George displeased with, 384, 385; as Dorset's 'page', 455.

Anburey, Thomas: letters on Carleton, 185, 201; on Ticonderoga, 195; on military leaks and Canadians, 197; on use of bayonets, 200; on General Phillips, 205; on war in America, 228, 229; on Saratoga, 243, 244; on Howe–Burgoyne meeting, 253; on Burgoyne, 432.

Antigua, West Indies, 128.

Arbuthnot, Marriot (1711?–94): his incompetence, 127; troops to Clinton, 338; character, 365, 366; Clinton's protests, 368–74, 415; vote of thanks to, 492.

Archenholz, Johann Wilhelm von (1743–1812), 49.

Argyll, John Campbell (1693–1770), 4th Duke of, 463.

Armagh, Archbishop of, *see* Stone.

Arnold, Benedict (1741–1801): at Lake Champlain, 150; at Quebec, 151, 161; at Lake Champlain again, 187; at Fort Stanwix, 222, 234, 242; at Saratoga, 248 ff.; at the Chesapeake, 415; comparison, 490.

Aubrey, John (1626–97), 2.

Auckland, Lord, *see* Eden.

Azores, The, 396.

Balcarres, Alexander Lindsay (1752–1825), 6th Earl of, 195, 249.

Balfour, Nisbet (1743–1823): at New York, 148, 177, 179, 236; his reports, 371, 436.

Balfour, General, 60, 61.

Baltimore, Maryland: retreat of Congress to, 216.

Barre, Isaac (1726–1802): on Lord George, 94, 159; on war with France, 159; on hiring Indians, 193; on Saratoga, 265–7; denunciations, 274; opposition to independence, 401; final attacks on ministry, 439.

Barrington, William (1717–93), 2nd Viscount: after Minden, 58; suggested dismissal, 95; as Secretary at War, 112, 113, 116, 118, 143, 152; to Buckinghamshire, 262; to Burgoyne, 300; appointment of a captain, 336; his comments, 360, 383.

Bateman, Lady, 462.

Bateman, Lord: support of Lord George after Minden, 462.

Bathurst, Henry (1714–94), 2nd Earl: resignation, 360, 383, 390.

Batten Kill, New York, 240.

Baume, Colonel: his German troops, 231; to Bennington and death, 232; blamed by Skene, 233.

Beauclercs: as heirs of Lady Betty Germain, 97, 98.

Beaumarchais, Pierre Augustin Caron de (1732–99): on war policies, 118; on Parliament, 290–1, 312.

Beckford, William (1709–70), 30.

Bedford, Gertrude Leveson-Gower (d. 1794), Duchess of, 104.

Bedford, John Russell (1710–71), 4th Duke of, 36, 104, 448, 449.

Bee, Thomas, 303.

Bennington, Vermont: raid by Burgoyne, 224, 231, 232; Lord George on the defeat, 239; effect on Americans, 242; reasons for defeat, 435.

Berkeley, Lady Elizabeth, see Lady Betty Germain.

Berkshire Valley, New England, 231.

Bermuda: frigate assigned to, 130; Arbuthnot's fleet at, 374.

Bertie, Peregrine: resignation in protest, 306.

Bertie, Willoughby, see Abingdon.

Blenheim, Battle of, 49, 119.

Bligh, Thomas (1685–1775): resented by Lord George, 44.

Bloomfield, Captain: at the Inquiry, 355.

Bolebrook, Kent: as home of Lord George, 460, 483, 496.

Boston, Massachusetts: Lord George on, 92, 94; communications, 121; effect of defeat, 137; Howe's evacuation, 122, 139–41, 473; its burning advocated, 146, 311; instructions to Gage, 155; Clinton's arrival, 156; as objective of 1777 campaign, 216; defence troops, 218; Burgoyne's inexperience, 242; arrival of transports, 252; centre of disaffection, 271; Burgoyne's orders, 300; strategic considerations, 429 ff.; Canadian attitude, 434.

Boucher, Jonathan (1737–1804): on North Carolina, 366.

Boyle, Grace (d. 1763), Lady Middlesex, 464.

Boyle, Henry (1682–1764), Earl of Shannon: and Lord George, 24–29; made Earl, 28.

Braddock, Edward (1695–1755): Lord George as replacement of, 34; and American warfare, 120; expedition and death, 217, 229.

Brand, Joseph (Thayendanega), 200.

Brandywine Creek, Pennsylvania: battle, 145; Howe's force, 339; Howe's management, 347; strategy reconsidered, 432.

Brest, France: harbour blockaded, 420.

Breyman, Colonel: near Bennington, 232; killed at Saratoga, 248.

Brinton, Crane, 437.

Bruce, Colonel, 373.

Brunswick, Duke or Prince of, see Ferdinand.

Buckingham, Marquis of, see George Grenville.

Buckinghamshire, John Hobart (1723–93), 2nd Earl of: letters from Irwin, 240, 254; letters from Barrington, 262, 360; on politics, 401; letter from Clinton, 423.

Bucks County, Pennsylvania, 221.

Bunker Hill (Breed's Hill), Boston, Massachusetts, battle of: Lord George on, 93; his position after the battle, 100; Harvey to Irwin comment, 118; Howe's conduct, 139, 140, 145, 146; Clinton's conduct, 156; opposition reactions, 306.

Burgoyne, John (1722–92): and the king, 101; lost opportunity, 121; his pay, 124; size of his command, 125; rank in America, 138; his praise of Howe, 140; his arrival from England, 150; his report on Christie, 152; on Crown Point, 155; Carleton's proposals, 161; in London, 163–7; command of northern army, 167; death of wife, 166; plans and obstacles, 168–74; initial organization, 175–85; Carleton's assistance, 190–2; comment on his appointment, 193; his return to America, 195; letter to Harvey, 196; problems in Montreal, 197–200; his address to his troops, 201; Crown Point, 202; Ticonderoga, 203–6; approbation of his success, 208–9; Howe's abandonment of, 211–14; progress to Skenesborough, 224–6; letters to Lord George, 227, 228; and Howe, 231; Fort Edward, 230; Bennington, 232; before Saratoga, 233–43; Freeman's Farm, 244–8; withdrawal to Schuylerville, 249; surrender, 251, 252; results of Saratoga, 253–67; captivity, 259, 268; blame for defeat, 274–6; attitude of the king, 278; post mortems, 279–89; popularity, 290, 291; plans to silence him, 292; military inquiry, &c., 293–8; ordered to America, 300–2; recalled by Congress, 303; exchanged, 304; in the Howe Inquiry, 352–61; strategy reconsidered, 422, 423, 430–9; literary successes and death, 488–92.

Burke, Edmund (1727–97): on Lord George's appointment, 99; on Weymouth, 104; on a third Secretary of State, 107; on Burgoyne's address to his troops, 202; on the country gentlemen, 272; on the clergy, 273; on papers for Parliament, 274; on Lord George's conduct, 275; letter to Franklin, 303; on the weakness of the state, 313; on Carlisle, 316; on the American war, 325; on Carleton, 329; at the Inquiry, 357; on Lord North, 378, 379; on attempts to stifle inquiry, 300; on the riots, 400; on American independence, 401; as minister, 401; final attacks on North ministry, 439 ff.

Bute, John Stuart (1713–92), Marquis of: and George III, 31, 42; and Lord George, 37, 38; and Pitt, 33; letters from Lord George to, 44–55; on the court martial, 67, 77, 79; letter from Prince of Wales to, 73; on Lord George, 76, 77, 79; Erskine's efforts, 78; Clinton's comment, 158; on Lord George, 80; on need for Chatham, 385; patron of Jenkinson, 383; on Lord George's conduct, from the prince, 472.

Byng, George, 441.

Byng, John (1704–59), 59.

Byron, Admiral, 130.

Cambridge, Massachusetts: Baroness Riedesel interned at, 199; Anburey's letters from, 253–8; Burgoyne at, 268.

Camden, South Carolina, 370.

Campbell, Colin (1754–1814), account of Burgoyne, 245, 247, 257.

Campbell, John, see Loudon; see Argyll.

Canada: taken from France, 117; Carleton's army in, 125, 138; Christie urged on Carleton, 142; the British task, 149; Carleton's defence, 150;

unsuccessful recruiting, 160; plans for 1777 campaign, 161–72; 183–200; ordnance and horses, 230; communications, 245, 250; Lord George on strategy, 287; defence, 333; terrain, 427.

Canterbury, Archbishops of, 3, 273, 361.

Cape Fear, North Carolina, 415.

Cape May, New Jersey, 220.

Carleton, Sir Guy (1724–1808), Baron Dorchester after 1786: in Canada, 101, 121, 125, 138, 142, 143; character and disputes, 144, 149–56; Knight of the Bath, 155; and Gage, 160; campaign plans, 161, 168–71; orders from Lord George, 163–5; Burgoyne's criticisms, 167; orders and dispatches, 168, 169, 176, 177–82; character and activities, 183–8; reply to Lord George, 189; use of Indians, 184–8; recriminations and offer to resign, 190–4; his conduct, 197, 198; Anburey's opinion, 201; no garrison for Ticonderoga, 224; communications with Burgoyne, 234, 236, 260, 261, 264; his dismissal and the consequences, 327–30; at the Inquiry, 352–7; new appointments, 383; comparisons, 418; on the original plan, 430, 434; as commander-in-chief, 443 ff.; disputes with Lord George, 444–7; 452; 484, 493, 494; as Lord Dorchester, 494; and see Appendix.

Carleton, Major, brother of Sir Guy, 152.

Carlisle, Frederick Howard (1748–1825), 5th Earl of: at cards, 72; Walpole on Lord George, 136; head of peace commission, 315–18; disillusionment and complaints, 322–4, 393, 394; duel with Lafayette, 322; Commissioner of Trade, 323; from Hare on Rigby, 449; from Selwyn on Carmarthen and Lord George, 458.

Carmarthen, Francis Osborne (1751–99), Earl of, and 6th Duke of Leeds after 1789: resignation from court, 409–11; on Lord George as a peer 457–60; 484, 485.

Carolinas (North and South): difficult military conditions, 119, 120; Clinton urged to recover them, 334, 339; loyalists there, 336–69; Cornwallis in, 370–4, 414; Clinton on Cornwallis's operations, 419, 431; shortage of supplies, 432; loyalist enlistments, 435-7.

Carter, Dr., 25.

Cartwright, Capt., 58.

Castleton, New York, 227.

Catherine, Empress of Russia, 125.

Catskill Mountains, New York: strategic considerations, 428 ff.

Caulfield, James, see Charlemont.

Caulfield, Susan, 490.

Cavendish, John (1732-96), 79.

Cavendish, William, see Devonshire.

Cavendish, William Henry, see Portland.

Champlain, Lake, New York: Arnold and Carleton, 150; Carleton's attack, 161; Burgoyne's campaign, 167; American forces there, 182-7; Burgoyne's progress, 201, 206, 218, 226, 233; communications, 234; strategic considerations, 427 ff.

Charlemont, Ireland: Carleton appointed Governor, 328, 385.

Charlemont, James Caulfield (1728-99), 4th Viscount and 1st Earl of, 396.

Charleston, South Carolina: Parker-Clinton attack on, 134, 156, 157, 164; possible attack on, 218, 330; trade, 236; and Lord George, 311, 337, 338; Clinton's hesitancy, 367; Cornwallis's abandonment of, 414, 420, 423; Lord George's reactions, 431; Clinton's losses at, 432; strategy, 448.

Charlottesville, Virginia, 420.

Chatham, Kent: military camp, 32.

Chatham, William Pitt (1708-78), 1st Earl of: and Lord George, 32-46; after Minden, 53, 59, 69, 77, 82-85; on taxing the colonies, 92; on Lord George as a minister, 99; his plans, 138; his attack on the ministry, 261, 263, 272; on Burgoyne's campaign, 275; approached by the ministry, and consequences, 385-7.

Chesapeake River and Bay: sinking of the Terrible, 127; Howe's plan and progress, 176-9, 210, 213, 221, 265, 285; Lord George orders raids on, 337; White, on military action there, 347; Phillips's expedition, 374, 415-18; Lord George and Cornwallis, 418, 420, 423.

Chesterfield, Philip Dormer Stanhope (1694-1773), 4th Earl of: letters, 8; on Irish education, 11; to Irwin on Lord George, 21; on Lord George in Ireland, 26; on a Secretary for the Colonies, 102; on profiteering in the army, 123; on fighting Americans, 306; on aristocratic birth, 412.

Cholmondley, James, 60, 68.

Christie, Colonel: sponsored by Lord George, 142, 152, 153, 184, 330.

Cinque Ports: Dorset as Warden, 14; Lord George's bid for, 338, 392.

Clarke, Sir Francis, 249.

Clinton, Sir Henry (1738?-95): delayed dispatches, 121; his pay, 124; his troops, 125; proposed resignation, 127; Charleston failure, 134; rank in America, 138, 156, 157; London and knighthood, 157, 164-6; plans, 162-6; Canada command, 167; forces in New York, 175-80; use of Indians, 188; relations with Lord George, 140, 194; Howe's orders and Burgoyne, 204, 209-14; Washington's moves, 223; the problem of Burgoyne, 230-64; offered resignation, 268; Howe's orders again, 277, 278; retreat to New York, 321; disputes with Lord George, 330-42, 363-75; concern over Cornwallis, 414-35; efforts to quit, 443-5, 451; return to England, 492, 493; last years, 493, 494.

Clinton, see Newcastle.

Clive, Robert (1725-74), Lord: Burgoyne's attack on, 489.

Coke, Daniel P. (1745-1825): electoral attitude, 403.

Coke, Lady Mary 87, 467, 468.

Collier, Sir George (1738-95), 341.

Colyear, Walter Philip (d. 1730), 6, 11.

Concord, Massachusetts, 119.

Connecticut: as alternative campaign, 161, 168, 196, 197; Howe on plans for, 241.

Contades, Louis-George-Érasme de (1704-93): at Minden, 49.

Conway, Henry Seymour (1721-95): rivalry with Lord George, 14, 33; from Walpole on Lord George, 40, 46; his letter dismissing Lord George, 85; on Boston, 137; condemned by Fox, 274; on the American war, 305.

Conway, *see* Hertford.

Cope, Sir John (d. 1760), 404.

Cornwallis, Charles (1738–1805), 1st Marquis and 2nd Earl: surrender, 127, 135, 422–5; favoured by Lord George, 144, 146; on Howe's strategy, 211; Gates's service under him, 217; ordered back to America, 291; urged on by Lord George, 327; difficulties as second in command, 335, 336; to Charleston, 338; his testimony opposed, 349; testimony on war, 355–7; to America and the Carolinas, 363, 364, 367–75, 414–22; strategic analysis, 430–7; news reaches London, 439; on a command in America, 447; return to England, and later career, 492.

Corry, Isaac (1755–1813), 454.

Coutts, Thomas (1735–1822), 313, 314.

Coventry, George, 483.

Cowpens, Carolina: Cornwallis's defeat at, 417.

Coxe, Rev. William (1747–1828), 350, 351.

Craven, William (1738–91), Earl of: opposed Viscount Sackville, 457.

Cresswell, Nicholas: on Howe, 218, 346.

Crosbie, William (d. 1781), Viscount and Earl of Glandore, 475.

Crown Point, New York: taken and left by Carleton, 151; Burgoyne's plan, 167; base for supplies, 168; taken by Burgoyne, 183, 202; troops left there, 224.

Culloden, battle of, 13.

Cumberland Bay, Lake Champlain, 201.

Cumberland, William Augustus (1721–65), Duke of: with Lord George in Scotland, 13; and on the Continent, 14, 15; enmity with him, 21, 38, 43, 458; on the court martial, 60; Lord George and the Irish appointment, 84.

Cunningham, James, 18, 27, 480.

Damer, Captain, *see* Dorchester.

Damer, Joseph, *see* Milton *and* Dorchester.

Dartmouth, William Legge (1731–1801), 2nd Earl of: on change of office, 95–97; and Lord George, 100; as Secretary of State, 103; with-drawal, 118; Hutchinson on successor to, 137; on Boston, 140; appoints Peter Livius, 154; on cutting off New England, 160; change of opinion, 270; letters from Skene, 227, 233; disagreements on policy, 346, 360.

De Fonblanque, E. B., 283.

De Grasse, Comte François Joseph Paul (1723–88), 421.

De Grey, Thomas: ignorant of Philadelphia evacuation order, 320; coaching of witnesses, 358; succeeded by Thompson, 473; as Lord George's aide, 455.

De Kalb, Johann (1721–80), 370.

Delany, Mary (Mrs. Patrick) (1700–88), 10, 16.

Delaware River, Bay, and State: embarkation of troops, 176; difficulties of passage, 177, 210, 213–16; Washington's march, 220, 221; loyalists there, 214, 215, 434, 448.

Derby, Edward Smith-Stanley (1752–1834), Earl of: on Burgoyne's knighthood on, 208; on Burgoyne's reports, 254, 255, 291; motion for papers, 299; opposed peerage for Lord George, 457; and Burgoyne's family, 490.

D'Estaing, Charles Hector (1729–94), Comte: blockade of New York, &c., 418.

Detroit, Michigan, 186.

Dettingen, Germany, battle, 12, 32.

Devonshire, Georgiana (1757–1806), Duchess of, 72.

Devonshire, William Cavendish (1720–64), 4th Duke of: on Lord George in Dublin, 11; head of Treasury, 37; and Duke of Rutland, 81 (5th Duke, 457).

Diamond Island, Lake George, New York, 224.

Digby, Henry, 32, 184, 185.

Dodington, George Bubb (1691–1762), Lord Melcomb: diary, 37; Lord George's court martial, 66; seats controlled by, 402; mediation between Dorset and Middlesex, 465; on Middlesex, 467.

Dogger Bank, state of ships there, 127.

Dorchester, Lord, *see* Carleton.

Dorchester, George Damer (1746–1808), 2nd Earl of, 463, 494.

Dorchester, Joseph Damer (1717–98), 1st Earl of, 31.

Dorchester Heights, Boston, Massachusetts, 141.

Dorset, Earls and Dukes of, see Sackville.

Dorset, Elizabeth Colyear (d. 1768), 1st Duchess of, 462.

Dover: Lord George at camp at, 74.

D'Oyley, Christian: activities, 238; resignation, 282; explanations, 284–6.

Drayton House, Northants.: Walpole's description, 97; as home of Lord George, 451, 460, 477, 482, 483; charitable use of income, 488.

Dublin, 10, 11, 16, 17.

Dundas, Henry (1742–1811), 1st Viscount Melville: character, 449; and Lord George, 450–3.

Dunmore, John Murray (1732–1809), 4th Earl of: his optimism, 434.

Dunning, John (1731–83), 1st Baron Ashburton: his motion on the Crown's influence, 407 ff.

East Grinstead, Kent: Sackville control of seats, 14, 403, 466.

Eden, William (1744–1814), 1st Lord Auckland: and Lord George, 94, 95; on Secretary for Colonies, 105, 106; in America, 111; Lord George and D'Oyley, 282; peace commission, 307, 308, 315–24; on Lord George's resignation, 328; Lord George's plans, 332; from Smith on Lord George, 348; and Clinton, 372, 373; on Pitt's joining the ministry, 386; his dismay, 390; on jealousies in the ministry, 448; letters from Corry and Wedderburn, 454.

Effingham, Thomas Howard (1746–91), 3rd Earl of, 305.

Egremont, George Wyndham (1751–1837), 3rd Earl of, opposed peerage, 457.

Eliot, Lady Harriet (Pitt) (1758–86), 369.

Elk River, Maryland: Howe's landing, 213–15; Washington's reaction, 223; Lord George's reaction, 352; delayed dispatch, 354; strategic considerations, 432 ff.

Elliott, George Augustus (1717–90), 1st Baron Heathfield, 65.

Ellis, Henry (1721–1806): to Knox, on Howe, 209, 212; on peace commission, 308.

Ellis, Welbore (1713–1802), 1st Baron Mendip: as Secretary of State, 455.

Erskine, Henry (d. 1765), 5th Baron Alva: on Hugo, 74; as agent for Lord George, 78 ff., sent to Howe, 142.

Falkland Islands, 91.

Farren, Elizabeth, Countess of Derby (1759?–1829), 490.

Fay, Edward, 195.

Ferdinand (1721–92), Prince of Brunswick: his British troops, 42; experience, 44; and Lord George, 46–63; and Newcastle's message, 69; Lord George's later comments, 75, 81, 85, 94; his technique imitated, 330; Selwyn's comment, 458; comparison, 496.

Fiske, John (1842–1901): on Howe, 213.

Fitzmaurice, Edward, Lord, 49.

Fitzpatrick, Richard (1747–1813), 288.

Fitzroy, Charles (1737–97), Earl of Southampton: and Minden, 50–60; at the court martial, 60–64; aide to the king, 69; with Burgoyne in America, 195; as Earl of Southampton, 457.

Fitzroy, see Grafton.

Florida: campaign plans, 333, 336, 338, 430, 438.

Fonblanque, see De Fonblanque.

Fontenoy, Battle of, 12, 32, 40.

Forbes, Major: at Inquiry, 355.

Fort Anne, New York, 225.

Fort Clinton, New York, 247.

Fort Edward, New York: under Schuyler, 219; strategic location, 224, 225, 229; taken by Burgoyne, 230–3; transport difficulties, 238; Howe dispatch received, 241; Burgoyne's delay, 256; his defence, 296.

Fort George, New York, 225.

Fort Montgomery, New York, 235, 247.

Fort Stanwix, New York: St. Leger and Burgoyne at, 222, 234.

Fort William, Scotland: administration of, 301, 302.

Fortescue, Sir John (1859–1933): on Minden, 49; on Sandwich, 126; on the campaign, 181; on Howe, 181, 213; on Lord George, 411 n. 2; on force needed in America, 427.

Fox, Charles James (1749–1806): on Lord George's appointment, 99; North's comments, 110; on the ministry, 132, 133; on Clinton, 157; on Americans, 207; on war blunders, 261, 263; on Indian barbarities, &c., 264–7, 272; attacks on ministry, 274, 288, 289, 291, 294; friend of Carlisle, 316; on evacuation of Philadelphia, 324; on Carleton, 329; on avoiding an inquiry, 349; on hiding behind the king, 356; disgust in the House, 400; possible part in new government, 401, 405, 411; on Lord George's cowardice, 409; on Carmarthen, 411; final attacks on ministry, 439 ff.

Fox, Henry (1705–74), 1st Lord Holland: and Conway, 33; and Lord George, 37, 83.

France: at war, 12; loss of Canada, 117; intentions of war, 124–6, 130; support to the Americans, 159; invasion plans, 268, 281, 399; in American waters, 364, 367, 368; help for Washington, 416; blockade of New York, 418, 422; Yorktown, 422–5.

Francis, Sir Philip (1740–1818), 286, and see Junius.

Franklin, Benjamin (1706–90): in Paris, 281; on exchange of Burgoyne, 303; not an ordinary traitor, 310, 494.

Frazer, Simon (d. 1777): letters from Burgoyne, 170; at Hubbardtown, 225; on Burgoyne's withdrawal, 247; death at Saratoga, 248.

Freeman's Farm, New York: H.Q. in battle of Saratoga, 244–9.

Gage, Thomas (1721–87): delayed orders, 121; his pay, 124; replaced by Howe, 138–40; his command at Boston, 155, 156; offer from Carleton, 160; Burgoyne on his treatment, 296; his military naïveté, 430.

Galloway, Joseph (1730–1803): on ex-

tent of loyalist support, 215, 357, 366, 434–6; attacked by Burke, 358.

Gansevoort, Colonel: at Fort Stanwix, 234.

Gates, Horatio (1728?–1806): his canard against Schuyler, 217, 222; from Washington, on strategy, 221, 223; reinforcements, 233; Saratoga, 235–52; agreement on captured troops, 268, 299; Cornwallis at Camden, 370; strategy, 258.

George I (1660–1727), 5, 379.

George II (1683–1760): Lord George as aide, 12; Kildare's protest, 26; family disputes, 31, 73; disputes with Lord George, 43, 68, 69, 79; death, 76.

George III (1738–1820): political position and intentions, 31, 37; and Lord George, 42, 54, 73, 89; king, 76; courted by Lord George, 94; no concessions, 107; attitude toward ministers, 112, 116, 118, 119, 131, 132; knighthood to Carleton and attitude, 155, 156, 189, 191, 193; on Ticonderoga, 206; dispatches sent to him, 236, 237, 267; and Burgoyne, 278, 279, 290, 291, 300; attitude toward Lord George, 328, 383, 386, 391–5, 397; toward the Howes, 343, 344, 347, 348–53; on Gower's resignation, 360, 361; on responsibility of ministers, 376; on Hillsborough, 378; character, 379; on cabinet changes, 386–95; support of candidates, 403; dismissal of Carmarthen and Pembroke, 409–11; usefulness of Lord George to, 412, 443–7, 451; peerage to Lord George, 455.

George, Lake, New York: as an alternate route, 168; occupation by Americans, 195; and by Burgoyne, 224, 225, 230; communications, 234.

Georgia: as winter objective for Howe, 162; proposed recovery, 334, 338; loyalists there, 366; plans, 368; strategy, 448; Benjamin Thompson, 473.

Germain, Lady Betty (Berkeley) (1680–1769): at Knole, 5; income, 7; letter to Swift, 10; heirs, 97; bequests to Lord George, 98; Lord George's devotion to, 462.

Germain, Lord George, *see* Sackville.

Germantown, Pennsylvania: battle, 145.

Gibbon, Edward (1737–94), 263.

Gibraltar: Lord George's letters to Irwin at, 80, 481; French alarms, 124; in the war, 327; Clinton's death, 493; French fleet, 396.

Glandore, Earl of, *see* Crosbie.

Glenbervie, Lady (Catherine North, d. 1817), 473.

Gloucester, William Henry (1743–1805), Duke of, 459.

Goldsmith, Oliver (1728–74), 10.

Golver, General: at Stillwater, 222.

Gould, Sir Charles (1726–1806), 60.

Gower, Granville Leveson-Gower (1721–1803), 2nd Earl (Marquis of Stafford after 1786): on the American war, 270; resignation, 360, 383; on Carlisle, 393.

Grafton, Augustus Henry Fitzroy (1735–1811), 3rd Duke of: 36, 50, 61, 79, 84, 85, 274.

Granby, John Manners (1721–70), Marquis of: in Germany, 43; relations with Lord George, 46; Minden, 50–59; testimony, 63, 65–75; in Grenville ministry, 80.

Grant, James (1720–1806): in West Indies, 338.

Grant, Major: at Hubbardtown, 225.

Grantley, Lord, *see* Norton.

Graves, Thomas (1725–1802): at Leeward Isles, 374; at Yorktown, 421, 422; attacked by Lord George, 440; defended by Sandwich, 442; Knox on his recall, 451.

Gray, Thomas (1716–71): on the Minden trial, 62, 68, 71, 72; Carlisle's ode, 316.

Green Mountains, Vermont, 231.

Grenville, George (1753–1813), 1st Marquis of Buckingham and 2nd Earl Temple: on the war, 361; on Chatham, 385.

Grenville, Richard (1711–79), 1st Earl Temple: and Lord George, 35, 82, 89; his party, 36; the ministry, 80; from Lord Vere, 98; Knox's attachment to, 480.

Grey, Charles 'Flintlock' (1729–1807): on reinforcements, 340; his testi-

mony at the Inquiry, 355, 356, 357, 436, 437.

Guilford, Francis North (1704–90), 1st Earl of, 96, 273.

Guilford, North Carolina: Cornwallis's victory, 417.

Gwynn, Nell (1650–87), 3.

Haldimand, Sir Frederick (1718–91), 122, 192.

Halifax, George Montagu (Dunk) (1716–71), Earl of, 77.

Halifax, Nova Scotia: defences, 125, 333, 334; hospital and gaol arrangements, 129; as Howe's base, 141–5; his report, 160; Massey in command there, 350; arrival of spoilt shipments, 432.

Hamilton, Alexander (1757–1804), 221.

Hamilton, Lt.-Gov. of Detroit: enlistment of Indians, 186.

Hancock, John (1736–93), 310.

Hannard, Sir Andrew, 355.

Harcourt, Simon (1714–77), 1st Earl, 381.

Hardwicke, *see* Yorke.

Hardy, Sir Charles (1716?–80), 474.

Hare, James (1749–1804): on misinformation, 298; on Howe, 348; on Rigby, 449.

Harrington, Charles Stanhope (1753–1829), 3rd Earl of, 195, 355.

Harvey, General: on the army, 118; from Burgoyne, on Carleton, 190; on Burgoyne's advance, 196, 197; comments on British forces, 305, 438.

Hastings, Warren (1732–1818), 489.

Heath, William (1737–1814), 218, 219.

Heathfield, *see* Elliott.

Heatley, David, 267.

Herbert, George Augustus (1759–1827), 11th Earl of Pembroke, 299, 325, 357, 359, 395.

Herbert, Henry Arthur, of Muckross, Ireland, 476, 477, 485.

Herkimer, Nicholas (1728–77), 222, 234.

Hertford, Francis Seymour Conway (1719–94), Marquis of, 239.

Highlands, of the Hudson Valley, New York, 233, 235, 241; strategic considerations, 429 ff.

Hill, Lt.-Col.: at Fort Anne, 225.

Hillsborough, Wills Hill (1718–93), 1st Viscount: Secretary of State, 102, 378, 383; replaced by Dartmouth, 103; on George III, 108.

Hobart, John, *see* Buckinghamshire.

Holdernesse, Robert D'Arcy (1718–78), 4th Earl of: on Lord George in Ireland, 17; Lord George's explanations to, 26, 47; warning to Lord George, 48; congratulations to him, 52; Lord George's resignation, 53; the court martial, 55, 56; last days, 388–91.

Holland, Lord, *see* Henry Fox.

Hopkinson, Francis (1737–91), 202.

Howard, Frederick, *see* Carlisle.

Howe, Richard (1726–99), 4th Viscount: at St. Malo, and Lord George, 43, 134, 139, 350, 361; 95, 139, 236; and Sandwich, 127; first peace commission, 145; on his brother's capacities, 146; on trade with Charleston, 236; American sympathies, 305; second peace commission, 307–10; wanted in ministry, 343 ff., 390, 391; on Lord George, 354.

Howe, William (1729–1814), 5th Viscount: at St. Malo, 39, 46; reinforcements in New York, 116 n. 3; toward Philadelphia, 121; his pay, 124; army, on paper, 125, 129; commanding officer, 138; relations with Lord George, 95, 139, 146, 148; Boston and Halifax, 121, 138–43; first victories, 144, 145, 146; reinforcements, 147, 148, 160, 162; proposed junction at Albany, 161, 163–70; new plan for Philadelphia, 171, 172, 181; Lord George on reinforcements, 173, 174; on Burgoyne junction, 175, 176; reinforcements again, 177–81; on use of Indians, 188; on the Albany meeting, 195–210; strategy dispatch to Lord George, 210; the Philadelphia campaign, 211–15; on the Albany meeting again, 237–41, 253–65, 274, 277; replaced by Clinton, 278; delayed dispatch, 285; peace commission, 307–11; American sympathies, 305; estimate of forces, 339; Lord George's manœuvres, 343–62; reconsideration of his conduct, 429–34; final years, 491–2.

Howes, Chancellor of Ireland, 66.

Hubbardtown, New York: skirmish, 225, 228.

Hudson River, New York: British plans, 160, 162, 168, 171, 177, 178, 203, 207, 209, 218; Clinton's advice, 210; Putnam, 219; Clinton's move, 244–56; Burgoyne's crossings, 140, 249; Howe's defence of his strategy, 354; White's comment, 347; strategy reconsidered, 427–9.

Hugo, 'a Hanoverian', 74.

Hutchinson, Thomas (1711–80): Crown Governor, 93; on America, 108–11; on postal services, 122; on Lord George, 136, 137; on withdrawal from Boston, 140, 141; on Burgoyne, 167, 201, 298; on the Howes, 238, 265, 291; on D'Oyley, 282; on Jenkinson, 301; on voting corruption, 404; on loyalists, 434; on Lord George's morals, 472.

India: in the war, 327; Cornwallis as Viceroy, 492.

Ingraham, Mrs. Charles, 79.

Ireland, 9, 22–29, 483.

Irvine, Sir John: variant spelling of Irwin.

Irwin, Sir John (1728–88): Chesterfield on Lord George, 21; with Walpole, 71; Lord George on Ferdinand, 75; on negotiations with France and Spain, 79; at Gibraltar, 80; letters from Lord George on a daughter, 81; on his appointment, 83; on newspaper abuse, 84; on politics, 91–95; on taking office, 100; General Harvey on America, 118, 438; Lord George on his installation, 136; on Burgoyne, 209, 236, 254, 264; to Buckinghamshire on Howe, 240; comments on papers before the House, 287; on Amherst, 385; on Irwin's seat for East Grinstead, 403; from Harvey, 438; Lord George on release from office, 442; and on death of the duchess, 462; and on Lord Middlesex, 465; and on family union, 466; and on his brother Charles, 467; and on his brother John, 470; their friendship, 480–1.

Jackson, Richard (d. 1787): the peace commission, 315, 317.

Jamaica: Arbuthnot's command, 373; a vacancy, 380; Parker's activities, 396.

James River, Virginia, 420.

Jefferson, Thomas (1743–1826), 310.

Jenkinson, Charles (1727–1808), 1st Earl of Liverpool: confidences with the king, 88 ff.; Secretary at War, 112–15, 131; exchanges with Burgoyne, 300–3; on Lord George, 352; his character, 383, 395; as successor to Lord George, 446, 447, 461; on the command in America, 447.

Johnson, Guy (1740?–88), 186.

Johnstone, George (1730–87): the duel, 88; peace commissioner, 315; attempted bribery by, 322.

Jones, John Paul (1747–92), 389.

Junius: his letters, 487; *and see* Francis.

Kentucky: raids, 184.

Keppel, Augustus (1725–86), Viscount: against the French, 127; not against the Americans, 305; controversy with Palliser, 399; and Benjamin Thompson, 474.

Keppel, Lady Eliza, 72.

Keppel, George, *see* Albemarle.

Kildare, James Fitzgerald (1722–73), Lord: memorial against Dorset, 26, 27.

Kingsbridge, New York: strategic considerations, 428 ff.

Kingston, Lt.-Col.: witness for Burgoyne, 355.

Knole, Kent, 2–7, 71, 81, 286, 460, 465–7, 470, 480, 481, 486, 496.

Knox, William (1732–1810): on Lord George's position, 104, 132; ship sailings, 123; regarding Carleton, 190; on use of Indians, 167; on Howe and Burgoyne, 207, 208, 209, 212, 238, 242; on misinformation about America, 270; on the ministry's defence, 280; and poor communications, 283, 284; on papers for Parliament, 287; on Lord George and peace, 307; on negotiations with Congress, 316, 320, 325; on complaints of Clinton, 335, 371; on Howe, 343, 348; on Carleton, 329; on naval affairs, 372; on Cornwallis, 422; on troops in America,

448; on Lord George's decline, 451; on interview with the king, 452–4; his pension, 480; his career, 498; other letters from Lord George, 375, 397, 483; his session with Lord North, 452.

Lafayette, Marie Joseph du Motier (1757–1834), Marquis de: duel offered to Carlisle, 322; against Cornwallis, 420, 422.

Lamb, Sergeant, 229.

Lamb, William, *see* Melbourne.

Laurens, Henry (1724–92), in Tower of London, 303.

Lausanne, Switzerland: John Sackville at, 469, 470.

Lecky, W. E. H., on age of Pitt, 387.

Lee, Charles (1731–82), 362.

Leeds, *see* Carmarthen.

Leeward Islands, West Indies, 374.

Leicester House, 34, 37, 72, 73, 465.

Leith, Sir Alexander (1758–1838): on use of Indians, 274; on Burgoyne, 296.

Leland, Colonel, 264.

Lennox, Charles, *see* Richmond.

Lennox, Lady Sarah, 72, 349.

Leslie, General, 251, 415, 422.

Lexington, Massachusetts: skirmish at, 160, 305.

Ligonier, Edward (1729?–82): Minden, 50–60; on court martial, 61, 63, 69; with Burgoyne, 195.

Ligonier, John (1680–1770), Viscount: 34, 35, 45; on court martial, 56, 57, 61; on the sentence, 69, 153, 195, 469.

Lincoln, Benjamin (1733–1810): at Stillwater, 222; severed Burgoyne's communications, 250.

Lindsay, Alexander, *see* Balcarres.

Lindsay, a sergeant, 488.

Little Elk River, Maryland, 213.

Liverpool, Lord, *see* Jenkinson.

Livingstone (1746–1813), 220.

Livius, Peter: and Carleton, 154, 184, 329, 330.

Lizard, the, 396.

Locke, John (1632–1704), 8.

Long Island, New York: Howe's victories, 144, 145; Clinton's comments, 260; Arbuthnot's naval parades, 374.

Loudon, John Campbell (1705–82), 4th Earl of, 34.

Loughborough, Lord, *see* Wedderburn.

Louisburg, Canada: Amherst's capture of, 42, 153.

Luttrell, James (1751?–88): and Lord George, 137, 296, 297, 409.

Lyttleton, George (1709–73), 1st Lord, 96.

Maine: Arnold's expedition, 150; Penobscot Bay expedition, 430.

Malone, Edmond (1741–1812), 396.

Mann, Sir Horace (1701–86), 39, 88, 454, and other letters from Walpole.

Manners, Charles, *see* Rutland.

Manners, John, *see* Granby.

Mansfield, William Murray (1705–93), 1st Earl of: and Lord George, 41, 43, 56, 89, 93; on need for Chatham, 385.

Marlborough, Charles Spencer (1706–58), 3rd Duke of, 38–47.

Martin, Josiah (1737–86): on Carolina loyalists, 436.

Maryland: Howe's campaign, 239.

Maseres, Francis (1731–1824), 169.

Mason, William (1724–97), 297.

Massachusetts: disorders, 92; as a base for operations, 161; in campaign plans, 168, 175, 311.

Massey, Sir Eyre (1719–1804), 1st Lord Clarina: at Halifax, 350.

Maudit, Israel (1708–87): attacks on the Howes, 311, 345.

Mauvillon, Colonel: at the court martial, 62.

Mawbery, Sir Joseph (1730–98), 107.

McKean, Thomas (1734–1817), 303.

Melbourne, William Lamb (1779–1848), 2nd Viscount, 362.

Melcombe, Lord, *see* Dodington.

Melville, Viscount, *see* Henry Dundas.

Mendip, Lord, *see* Welbore Ellis.

Middlesex, County of: taxes and representation, 403.

Middlesex, Lord, *see* Charles Sackville.

Milton, Lady, Countess of Dorchester, *see* Lady Caroline Sackville.

Milton, Lord, *see* Dorchester.

Minden, battle of, 49–70, and references: 75, 77, 86, 88, 94, 101, 119, 137, 142, 195, 199, 205, 274, 292, 299, 306, 330, 395, 398, 443, 457, 461, 472, 486, 491, 495.

Minorca, 32, 238.

Mohawk River and Valley, New York: Carleton's proposal, 161, 167; St. Leger's expedition, 200; Gates near by, 233; St. Leger at Fort Stanwix, 234; his withdrawal, 240; strategic considerations, 428 ff.

Money, John (1752–1817), Captain (later General): witness for Burgoyne, 355.

Montagu, George (1737–88), 68.

Montagu, George (Dunk), *see* Halifax.

Montagu, John, *see* Sandwich.

Montgomery, Richard (1738–75): at Quebec, 150, 151, 161.

Montreal, Canada: Carleton's defence, 150, 151, 167; Burgoyne's first service there, 180; Burgoyne's logistic problems there, 197; St. Leger's return, 234; communications, 257; supply lines, 428 ff.

Mordaunt, Sir John (1679–1780), at Rochefort, 38, 40.

Morgan, Daniel (1736–1802), at Saratoga, 242, 248.

Morristown, New Jersey: Washington's base, 236.

Mostyn, 'Jack' (1710–79), 41.

Muir, Lord: death at Jamaica, 380.

Munster, Germany, 44, 47.

Murray, James (1719?–94): and Lord George, 21; on Minden, 74; on Americans, 159; on conquest from Canada, 161; on strategy, from Minorca, 238.

Murray, John, *see* Dunmore.

Murray, William, *see* Mansfield.

Napier, Francis (1758–1823), 7th Lord: with Burgoyne, 195.

Neinburgh, Germany: magazines, 47.

Netherlands: war declared, 406.

New England: raids on the coast, 148, 160, 168, 180, 209, 337; dread of Indians, 187; attitudes of settlers, 217, 225; as alternative for Burgoyne, 226, 227; Lord George on, 287, 311, 333; Fortescue on strategy, 427; population and products, 428; strategic considerations, 427 ff.

New Hampshire, 175, 222, 311.

New Haven, Connecticut: strategic considerations, 429 ff.

New Jersey: Howe and Cornwallis in, 114, 162, 177, 216; Washington's moves, 218, 219; Clinton's retreat, 321; loyalists, 434; strategic considerations, 424 ff.

New York: strength of forces there, 121; Howe's occupancy, 121, 144–8; Clinton, 180; Howe's embarkation, 211, 212; attitudes of citizens, 217, 225; reinforcements, 245; British withdrawal to it, 317–21, 333, 336, 337, 367; French blockade and plans, 418–20; Lord George's plans, 448, 449; strategy reviewed, 428 ff.

Newburgh, New York: strategic considerations, 429 ff.

Newcastle, Delaware: Howe's attempt, 213.

Newcastle, Henry Clinton (1720–94), 2nd Duke of: electoral influence, 402; on resignation of Clinton, 424; quarrel with Clinton, 493.

Newcastle, Thomas Holles (1693–1768), 1st Duke of Newcastle: and the Dorsets, 30, 31, 34, **37**, 43; reconciliation with Pitt, 33; to Lord George, 45, 47; Granby on Minden, 52; court-martial aftermath, 69; tells 'confidence' to the king, 73; on resigning, 81.

Newfoundland: squadron, 130; troops, 338; transport hazards, 433.

Noailles, Marquis de, 382.

North, Brownlow (1741–1820): as Bishop of Worcester, 96, 273.

North, Francis, see Guilford.

North, Frederick (1732–92), Lord, and 2nd Earl of Guilford after 1790: his ministry, 36; and Lord George, 77–96, 101, 103; his weaknesses, 107–10; his personality, 111; and East India Company, 125; lack of leadership, 131; friendliness with the Howes, 140, 143; letters, 164, 167; on Clinton, 166; defence of Lord George, 264–70, 297; strength in Parliament, 271–6, 279; papers withheld, 287; peace commission, 306–24; Board of Trade, 323 ff.; on Carleton, 328, 329; on Admiral Howe, 343–8, 391 ff.; the Inquiry, 350–60; on the war, 360; on finances, 366; and Lord George, 377–83, 392–4, 411; attempts to resign, 386–8, 392, 397, 398; his difficult

position, 389; Cinque Ports, 388–91; and Sandwich, 396; cabinet changes, 401–3; his talents, 404; cost of war, 406; news of Yorktown, 439; his last defences, 440 ff.; on Carleton, 443–8; dismissal of Lord George, 443–56; final weeks and fall, 450–60; his philanthropy, 488; his responsibilities as first minister, 499.

North Carolina: Indian barbarities, 188; Boucher's description, 366; Cornwallis, 368; loyalists, 371, 436; Leslie expected, 415; Clinton's comments, 419.

North River (Hudson River), New York, 211, 220, 330.

Northampton, Elizabeth (1682–1749), Dowager Countess of, 461, 462.

Northumberland, Duchess of, 59, 463, 467.

Northumberland, Duke of, see Percy.

Norton, Sir Fletcher (1716–89) (later 1st Lord Grantley), 397.

Nova Scotia: Gates under Cornwallis in, 217.

O'Brien, Lady Susan, 349.

Ohio: raids proposed, 184.

Ontario, Lake, New York: diversionary force, 161, 167, 200.

Orde, Thomas (1746–1807) (later 1st Baron Bolton), 485.

Oriskany, New York: defeat of Herkimer, 234.

Osborne, Francis, see Carmarthen.

Osborne, Sir George: witness for Howe, 355.

Oswego, New York: and St. Leger, 200, 234.

Oxford University, 9, 11, 477.

Palliser, Sir Hugh (1723–96): orders, 121, 129; controversy with Keppel, 399.

Parker, Sir Peter (1721–1811): at Charleston, 134, 156; relieved by Arbuthnot, 373; to Sandwich from Jamaica, 396.

Patterson, John: on Ticonderoga, 204.

Peekskill-on-Hudson, New York, 221.

Pelham, Henry (1696–1754), 22–5.

Pembroke, Henry Herbert (1734–94), 10th Earl of: on Burgoyne, 299; on

Lord George, 325, 395, 357, 351, 472; on Howe inquiry, 350, 357, 359; his resignation, 410, 411.

Pembroke, 11th Earl of, *see* Herbert.

Pennsylvania: Howe on attacking it, 177, 178, 184, 214, 241; Braddock, 217, 229; Morgan, 248; loyalists, 434.

Penobscot Bay, Maine: operations, 430.

Pensacola, Florida: operations, 88.

Percy, Hugh (Smithson) (1742–1817), 3rd Duke of Northumberland: on the war, 159, 306.

Perth, Scotland, 13.

Peterborough, Bishop of: on public credit, 406.

Petersburg, Virginia: Cornwallis, 420.

Petersham, Charles Stanhope, *see* Harrington.

Philadelphia, Pennsylvania: Howe's plans and operations, 121, 171–81, 207–22, 250–60; Lord George comments, 278; peace commission, 317; evacuation orders, 323; Fox's questions, 324; Clinton's evacuation, 334; on Howe's management, 347, the Inquiry, 354–60; strategy reconsidered, 429 ff.

Phillips, William (1731?–81): under Burgoyne, 195; at Ticonderoga, 205; on transport, 228; at war council, 247; attitude toward war, 306; at Delaware and death, 416–22; from Clinton on Arbuthnot, 374.

Phillipson, Colonel: Burgoyne's reports, 255, 291.

Pitt, John (1756–1835), 2nd Earl of Chatham: resignation, 305; opposed peerage, 457.

Pitt, William (1759–1806): on the war, 325; and its conduct, 439, 441; trials of a first minister, 478; and Lord North, 483; his ministry, 484, 485.

Pitt, William, 1st Earl of Chatham, *see* Chatham.

Portland, William Henry Cavendish (1738–1809), 3rd Duke of: opposed peerage, 451.

Portsmouth, Virginia, 420.

Powlett, Thomas Orde, *see* Orde.

Pownall, John (1722–1805): on Lord George's dismissal, 441.

Pratt, Charles (1714–94), 1st Earl of Camden, 56.

Prescott, Robert (1725–1816): on Indians, 186.

Princeton, New Jersey: Howe's defeats, 215, 216.

Providence, Rhode Island, 216.

Putnam, Israel (1718–90): on Howe–Burgoyne meeting, 219; brigades to Gates, 233; in the Hudson Highlands, 241.

Quebec, Canada: climate, 120, 122; Carleton's defence, 121, 130, 150, 161; Burgoyne, 168, 170, 195; as a British province, 198; communications, 234; the king on Carleton's defence of, 385.

Ramsden, Mrs. Arabella, 79.

Ranelagh Gardens, 477.

Rawdon, Francis Rawdon-Hastings (1754–1826), 2nd Earl of Moira: on loyalists in the Carolinas, 370, 436.

Rawlinson, Sir Walter: on war with America, 451.

Red Bank, New Jersey, 347.

Reynolds, Sir Joshua (1723–92), 491.

Rhode Island: Howe to occupy, 141; occupation by Clinton and Parker, 157; Lord George's hopes, 161, 162, 177, 311, 333, 334, 335, 430, 448; Clinton's withdrawal, 367; French threat, 422; strategy considered, 448 ff.

Richmond, Charles Lennox (1735–1816), 3rd Duke of: messenger from Minden, 50; friendship with Carleton, 51; on Lord North, 99; on America, 240, 265, 271, 275, 401, 438 ff.; on Chatham's collapse, 387.

Richmond, Virginia: Phillips's death at, 417; Cornwallis at, 420.

Riedesel, Baron: in command of German troops, 185, 195; pursuit of St. Clair, 225; need to horses, 231, on withdrawal to Ticonderoga, 247; at Saratoga, 248.

Riedesel, Baroness: in Burgoyne campaign and captivity, 199, 229, 249.

Rigby, Richard (1722–88): on Burgoyne inquiry, 294; as friend of Howe, 351, 352; on the ministry, 449; actions against Lord George, 453.

Robertson, James (1720?–88): in New York, 250, 254; at the Inquiry, 357; on American loyalists, 437.

Robinson, John (1727–1802): on the cabinet, 111; election management, 403; on Dundas and Lord George, 450, 453.

Rochambeau, Jean Baptiste Donatien (1725–1807), Comte de, 420.

Rochefort, France: Mordaunt's raid, 38.

Rochford, William Henry Zuylestein (1717–81), 4th Earl of, 96, 101, 103, 385.

Rockingham, Charles Watson-Wentworth (1730–82), 2nd Marquis of: his party, 36; on Lord George, 83, 84, 89; on American war, 240, 325; on parliamentary difficulties, 400–2, 439; final attacks on ministry, 439 ff.; his ministry, 460; Burgoyne appointed, 489; Howe promoted, 491.

Rodney, Sir George Brydges (1719–92), 1st Lord: not a Whig, 126; orders from Lord George, 130; on Lord George as minister, 136; on Clinton, 365; Arbuthnot's resentment, 366; on corruption in the armed forces, 408; fears for Cornwallis, 414, 417.

Rouse's Point, New York: strategic considerations, 428 ff.

Rush, Benjamin (1745–1813), 362.

Russell, Lady Caroline, 72.

Russell, John, see Bedford.

Russell, Lt.-Col.: on Lord John Sackville, 468, 469.

Rutland, Charles Manners (1754–87), 4th Duke of, 43, 81, 457, 485.

Sackville, Anne (1709–21), 462.

Sackville, Caroline (d. 1789), 476, 477.

Sackville, Caroline (1718–75), 1st Countess of Dorchester (Mrs. Joseph Damer, Lady Milton), 462, 463.

Sackville, Charles (1638–1706), 6th Earl of Dorset, 2.

Sackville, Charles (d. 1795), 468.

Sackville, Charles (1710–65), Lord Middlesex and 2nd Duke of Dorset, 5, 463–7.

Sackville, Charles (1767–1843), 5th and last Duke of Dorset, 476–9.

Sackville, Diana (1756–1814), Lady

Crosbie and Countess of Glandore, 475, 479.

Sackville, Edward (1591–1652), 4th Earl of Dorset, 2.

Sackville, Elizabeth (1712–29), 2nd Viscountess Weymouth, 462.

Sackville, Elizabeth (1762–?) (Mrs. Henry Arthur Herbert), 476.

Sackville, George (1770–1836), 380, 477–9.

Sackville, George (1716–85), Lord George Germain, Viscount Sackville: birth and youth, 3–11; military career, 11–15; character, 17, 18, 21, 75, 504; marriage, 19, 20; in Ireland, 22–29; Major-General, 29; House of Commons, 30–33; Lt.-Gen. of Ordnance, 34; Parliament, 36–41; Germany, 43–53; Minden, 49–60; court martial, 57–70; Vice-Treasurer, 84; dismissal, 85; name changed to Germain, 98; Secretary of State, 99–113; direction of war, 127–35; opinions on the war, 136–9; and Howe, 144–8; war plans and orders, 159–75, 181; to Clinton, 182–4; on use of Indians, 185–8; and Carleton, 189–94; Howe–Burgoyne operations, 207–11, 214, 227, 235–40, 254–62; defences in Parliament, 262–302; peace commission, 306–26; unpopularity, 327–49; the Inquiry, 350–62; Clinton and Cornwallis, 363–72; character revealed, 376–85; Cinque Ports, 388–90; Pitt's demands, 386, 387; and Sandwich, 389–97; control of seats, 403; Carmarthen and Pembroke, 409–11; character, 398, 411–13; aggressive policies, 415, 418, 426–38; defence in Commons, 440–56; dismissal and peerage, 456, 457; Benjamin Thompson, 471–5; friendships, 480, 481; last days and death, 482–95.

Sackville, George John Frederick (?–1815), 4th Duke of Dorset, 479.

Sackville, Herbrand de, 2.

Sackville, John Frederick (1745–99), 3rd Duke of Dorset, 478, 479.

Sackville, John Philip (1713–65), 5, 70, 468–70.

Sackville, Lionel Cranfield (1688–1765), 1st Duke of Dorset, 3, 6, 7, 9, 13; in Ireland, 21–29; the Minden disgrace, 59, 71; and Lord George, 461–4; and Lord Middlesex, 464–7; death, 465; and Amherst, 384.

Sackville, Thomas (1527–1608), 1st Earl of Dorset, 1, 2.

St. Clair, Arthur (1736–1818), at Ticonderoga, 204, 205, 217, 218; pursuit, 225, 238.

St. Lawrence River, Canada, 150, 182, 215.

St. Leger, Barry: to Mohawk Valley, 200; at Fort Stanwix, 222, 233, 234.

St. Lucia, West Indies: orders to attack, 333.

St. Malo, France: the raid, 39–43, 139.

Sambrooke, Diana (1731–78), Lady George Germain: character and position, 19, 20; and the Duchess of Devonshire, 72; and Lady Mary Coke, 87; her death, 286; and Lord George, 470, 471.

Sambrooke, Sir Jeremy, 19.

Sambrooke, John, 19.

Sandwich, John Montagu (1718–92), 4th Earl of: on court martial, 68; and Lord George, 115, 116, 126, 129, 130; and Keppel, 127; on army control of navy men, 143; dispute with Howe, 147; administrative procedure, 108, 109, 112; on Clinton, 342; on Arbuthnot, 365; on Ticonderoga, 206; criticism, 270; on Lord George, 327, 372–7, 384, 395; support by the king, 389; attacked, 401, 409, 412, 448, 449, 450; from Rodney, 414; and Thompson, 474; his confidence, 261.

Saratoga, New York: logistics of defeat, 119; effect on Lord George's power, 135; causes of disaster, 149; battles, 242–52; post mortems by generals, &c., 253–60, and in London, 261–8, 290, 293 ff., 331 ff., 426 ff.

Savile, Sir George (1726–84), 405, 407.

Saxe, Frédéric-Auguste de (1696–1763), 14.

Schmidt, General, 251.

Schuyler, Philip John (1733–1804): his forces, 216–22; Ticonderoga garrison, 224–6; road-blocking, 229; host to Burgoyne, 249, 252–4.

Schuylerville, New York, 249.

Selwyn, George (1718–91): on Lady Betty Germain, 6; on Lord George,

136, 137; from Storer, 265; from Hare, 348; on Carmarthen, 458.

Shannon, Earl of, see Henry Boyle.

Shelburne, William Petty (Fitzmaurice) (1737–1805), 2nd Earl and 1st Marquis of: on the Duke of Dorset, 9; on Lord George, 11, 21, 22, 29; on dismissal of Dorset, 28, 29; his party, 36; on Lord George and Marlborough, 44; on Lord George and Ferdinand, 47; on the court martial, 67; on Lord George as first minister, 70; on Lord George in obscurity, 71, and as Vice-Treasurer, 84, and on his efforts with the ministry, 95; on Lady Betty Germain, 97; on Lord George's manners, 99, military talents, 133, orders to Burgoyne, 169; attacks on the ministry, 260–5, 275; on Pitt's joining the ministry, 386; peace negotiations, 326; attack on Lord George, 439 ff., 457, 489; as first minister, 400, 401; on Lord Middlesex, 465; on Lord John Sackville, 468, 470, 478; on Viscount Sackville, 485; on the Junius letters, 487; on Lord George's lack of heart, 495.

Sidney, Earl of, see Thomas Townshend.

Simpson, James, 366, 436.

Sismondi, Sismonde de (1773–1842), 49.

Skene, Philip: with Burgoyne, 226–32; on Baume, 233; at Cambridge, 259.

Skenesborough, New York (Whitehall): Burgoyne's operations, 168, 223–6, 229, 296.

Sloper, Robert: testimony at court martial, 61–68; promotion, 69.

Smith, Lt.-Col.: Minden, 51–60; absence of ministers, 111; on North's desire for peace, 312; on colonial affairs, 320; on Lord George, 348; on Suffolk, 377.

Smith-Stanley, see Derby.

Smollett, Tobias George (1721–71), 58.

South Carolina: as Howe's objective, 162; Lord George's plans, 337; temper of settlers, 367, 368, 371, 435, 436.

South River, New York: and Burgoyne, 225.

Southampton, Earl of, see Fitzroy.

Spain, 124, 126, 159, 268, 327, 361, 400.

Spencer, see Marlborough.

Spithead, 127.

Stanhope, Charles, *see* Harrington.

Stanhope, Philip Dormer, *see* Chesterfield.

Stanhope, Spencer, 314.

Stark, John (1728–1822), 232.

Staten Island, New York, 213, 218.

Sterling, William Alexander (1736–93), claimed 8th Earl of Sterling, 221.

Sterne, Laurence (1713–68), 72.

Stillwater, New York: Schuyler's headquarters, 219; Gates in charge, 222, 230.

Stockdale, Thomas Percival (1736–1811), 18, 494.

Stone, George (1708?–64), Archbishop of Armagh: his politics with Lord George, 16–28; the court martial, 66.

Stoneland Park: and Lord George, 460, 473, 483, 496.

Stony Point, New York: and Clinton, 247.

Storer, Anthony Morris (1746–99), 265.

Stormont, David Murray (1727–96), Viscount, and 2nd Earl of Mansfield, 281, 445.

Strange, Lord, *see* Derby.

Stuart, Charles (1753–1801), 158.

Stuart, John, *see* Bute.

Suffolk, Henry Edward (1739–79), 12th Earl of: no compromise with Americans, 93; Secretary of State, 102; as sponsor of Lord George, 103–6; on recall of Carleton, 156; on Lord George's resignation, 286; on Clinton, 316; his death, 360, 383; alliance with Lord George, 377.

Sullivan, John (1740–95), 216, 221.

Sullivan's Island, South Carolina, 166.

Sumter, Thomas (1734–1832), 371, 435.

Swift, Jonathan (1667–1745), 5, 10, 12, 81.

Temple, Lord, *see* Grenville.

Temple, Henry (1739–1802), 2nd Viscount Palmerston, 35, 98.

Thompson, Benjamin (1753–1814), Count Rumford: friendship with Lord George, 472–6; 501, note M.

Thurlow, Edward (1731–1806), 1st Lord: at the court martial, 67; ability, 111; his study of the orders, 280, 281; defence of Lord George, 290, 298; as

Lord Chancellor, 383, 390; and Carmarthen, 457; and Pitt, 484.

Thynne, Thomas, 2nd Viscount Weymouth, 462.

Thynne, Thomas, 3rd Viscount Weymouth, *see* Weymouth.

Ticonderoga, New York: Carleton's decision, 150–4; Burgoyne's plans, 161, 167, 177; American garrison, 168, 195; criticisms of Carleton, 183, 184, 189; Burgoyne's advance, 200–5, 224; news in London, 206, 208, 211; Gates and St. Clair, 217; Washington's concern, 219, 220, 224, 225; Phillips's guns, 306; Lincoln's attack, 250–2; strategy, 231, 239, 257; communications, 234; strategy reconsidered, 424 ff.

Torpichen, James Sandilands (1759–1815), Lord, 195.

Townshend, Charles (1725–67), 83, 85.

Townshend, George (1724–1807), 4th Viscount, 76, 240, 291.

Townshend, Thomas (1733–1800), 1st Viscount Sidney: on propaganda against the Howes, 345; on Galloway, 358; on Pitt, 484, 486.

Trenton, New Jersey: Washington's operations, 214–16, 347.

Trumbull, Jonathan (1740–1809), 219.

Tryon, William (1725–88): his corps, 245; his optimism, 434.

Tyrawly, James O'Hara (1690–1773), 2nd Lord, 41, 497 note A.

Vaughan, Sir John (1748?–95): in West Indies, 130; on the Hudson, 251, 264; as possible commander, 447.

Vere of Hanworth, Lord, and the Beauclercs, 97, 98.

Vergennes, Charles Gravier (1717–87), Comte de, 118, 290, 291, 312, 382.

Vermont, 168, 337.

Verplanck's Landing, New York, 245.

Vevey-Lausanne, Switzerland, 469, 470.

Virginia: proposed raids, 184; Indians, 188; Morgan's men, 248.

Waite, Thomas, 19, 27, 480.

Waldegrave, John (d. 1784), 3rd Earl of, 38.

Walpole, Sir Edward (d. 1784), 376.

Walpole, Horace (1717–87), 4th Earl of Orford: on Lord George before Minden, 15, 17, 18, 20, 23, 28, 29, 30, 33, 35, 38; on the Howes and Lord George, 39, 40, 46, 52; on Holdernesse, 52; on Minden and the court martial, 58–61, 65–73; on Lord George's future, 72, 83–88, 94; on Drayton, 97; on not trusting Lord George, 100; on Weymouth, 104; on North, 109; on Sandwich, 126; on Lord George's management of the war, 133, 137; on Carleton, 152–4; on Clinton's knighthood, 166; on Burgoyne's speech, 201, 202, and his Ticonderoga dispatch, 207, and his knighthood, 208, and rumours of his defeat, 260, and his defence, 288, 294–7, 352; on the Howes, 238, 239, 288, 355; on alienation of the Americans, 263; on Fox's attack on Lord George, 264, 267; on Thurlow, 280; on D'Oyley, 282; on Cornwallis, 291; on Wedderburn, 298; on Jenkinson, 301; on Carlisle, 316; on Clinton–Cornwallis disagreements, 375; on Sandwich and Lord George, 381, 396; on new barons, 397; on resignation by Lord George, 454–7; on Lord Middlesex, 464, 467; on Lady George Germain, 471; on John Frederick Sackville, 479, on Burgoyne's comedy, 490; on Lord George's character, 495.

Walpole, Sir Robert (1676–1745), 1st Earl of Orford, 402.

Washington, George (1732–99): strategic value of the Atlantic, 120; Dorchester Heights, 141; outnumbered, 142; battles avoided, 146; skill, 172, 180, 183, 195, 204; in New Jersey, 209–13; concern over Howe's plans, 215–39; and Burgoyne, 252, 258–61, 268, 276, 295, 303; and Clinton, 321, 325, 336, 339, 354; not an ordinary traitor, 310; and Rodney, 365, 367; weakness of his army, 367; his prescience, 414; co-operation with the French, 420, 421–7; in pay of France?, 484.

Wedderburn, Alexander (1733–1805), 1st Lord Loughborough, 1st Earl of Rosslyn: rapport with Lord George, 79, 83, 89, 94, 105, 106; defence of Lord George, 289; support of Rigby, 294; on Burgoyne, 298; on restrictions on Howe, 309; Eden's complaints, 319; his manœuvres, 323, 324; Eden's comments on the decline of Britain, 390; comments on the ministry, 448; on Lord George's withdrawal, 454; as Lord George's solicitor, 455.

Weir, Daniel, 113.

West Indies: their vulnerability, 124, 126; troops there, 130; widening of the war, 327, 336; Grant's operations, 338; troops detained there, 418; ships blown off course, 432, 433; Lord George's plans, 446.

West Virginia: Indian barbarities, 188.

Westphalia, Germany: Lord George's military views, 38, 47, 120, 227.

Weymouth, Thomas Thynne (1734–96), 3rd Viscount and 1st Marquis of Bath: character, 104; as Privy Seal, 96; as Secretary of State, 102; on no concessions to America, 311; his resignation, 360; biography, 498 n. D.

White, Henry, 347.

White Plains, New York: Howe's victory, 144, 145, 347.

Whitefoord, Charles (d. 1753), 21.

Whitehall, New York, 225.

Wilkes, John (1727–97): on Lord George, 73, 274, 472; his case, 91 ff.; denounced by Sandwich, 126; exclusion from Commons, 298; riots, 399.

William III (1650–1702), 6.

Williamsburg, Virginia: and Cornwallis, 420.

Wilmington, Delaware: Washington's march, 222.

Wilmington, North Carolina: and Cornwallis, 435.

Wilson, Harriet, 479.

Wintzegerode, Captain: at the court martial, 61–70.

Wolfe, James (1727–59): in France, 14; letters to Lord George, 42; death at Quebec, 76; praise of Carleton, 153.

Worcester, Bishop of, see Brownlow North.

Wraxall, Sir Nathaniel William (1751–1831): on Lord George, 99, 133, 455, 456; on North after Saratoga, 439;

on life at Drayton, 477; on Lord George's sons, 478; on the Junius letters, 487.

Wyndham, *see* Egremont.

Yarmouth, Amalie Sophie Wallmoden (1704–65), Countess of, 73.

York River, Virginia: French blockade, 421.

Yorke, Joseph (1724–92), Lord Dover, 54, 66.

Yorke, Philip (1690–1764), 1st Earl of Hardwicke, 37, 54.

Yorke, Philip (1720–90), 2nd Earl of Hardwicke, 56.

Yorke, Philip: nephew of above, 451.

Yorktown, Virginia: military position, 119, 135; Cornwallis's situation, 303; the battle, 421–6; news in London, 439; post mortem, 443; comparisons, 488.

Younge, Thomas, 13.

PRINTED IN GREAT BRITAIN
AT THE UNIVERSITY PRESS, OXFORD
BY VIVIAN RIDLER
PRINTER TO THE UNIVERSITY

Date Due